Black Liberation/
Red Scare

Black Liberation/ Red Scare

Ben Davis and the Communist Party

Gerald Horne

INTERNATIONAL PUBLISHERS, NEW YORK

© 1994 by Associated University Presses

© 2020 by International Publishers

All rights reserved.

PRINTED IN THE UNITED STATES OF AMERICA

ISBN10: 0-7178-0862-9   ISBN13: 978-0-7178-0862-5

Contents

Acknowledgments	7
Introduction	9
1. Origins of a Black Revolutionary	17
2. The Making of a Black Revolutionary	27
3. The Road to the Communist Party	35
4. To Be a Professional Revolutionary	53
5. Squeeze Play, 1940–1942	83
6. A Turning Point in U.S. History, 1943	97
7. "Browderism," 1944	119
8. Unity and Struggle, 1945	137
9. Victory, 1945	154
10. Cold War Coming, 1946–1947	167
11. Red Scare Coming, 1948	192
12. "The Trial of the Century", 1949	210
13. Purged from the Council, 1949	227
14. Fighting Back, 1950–1951	244
15. Jailed for Ideas, 1951–1955	254
16. Party Wars, 1956–1959	271
17. When Black and White Unite, 1958–1959	285
18. Black Communist in the 1960s	305
Notes	326
Selected Bibliography	406
Index	425

The illustrations appear as a group following page 226.

Acknowledgments

This study was aided immeasurably by the cooperation of the family of Ben Davis, particularly his widow, Nina Goodman, his niece Jean Carey Bond and his sister, Johnnie Carey. It was aided in a different way by the largesse of the Schomburg Center of the New York Public Library (which provided a generous grant and access to their numerous collections, which formed the backbone of this work) and the librarians of Sarah Lawrence College and the University of California at Santa Barbara. They all merit my most sincere thanks.

My editor and various readers have been helpful as well, along with the staff of the Black Studies Department at the University of California-Santa Barbara.

The endnotes provide a guide as to how and where this research was conducted, yet I want to thank the libraries of Columbia University, New York University, Yale University, Howard University, Providence College, Harvard Law School, Boston University, Emory University, University of California-Los Angeles, Stanford University, the Federal Bureau of Investigation, and the University of Wisconsin; the State Historical Society of Wisconsin, the New York Police Department, the New York Public Library, the Municipal Archives of New York City, and the Communist party were also helpful. I also thank those who consented to allow me to conduct an interview. This type of history will be continuing for some time to come since archives are just opening and collections are now becoming accessible; I particularly look forward to the complete opening of the archives of the Comintern in Moscow, which should allow us to answer many questions.

Introduction

This is a study of an African-American Communist leader. Though it examines the numerous grassroots campaigns that he was involved in, it is first and foremost a study of Ben Davis and secondarily a study of the Communist party from the 1930s to the 1960s. Though lengthy, this study does not purport to study every dramatic event of party history during this time. As time has passed, several studies of the Communist party have been published. The earlier interpretations tended to see the party as a vehicle of Moscow and the Communist International (the umbrella grouping of worldwide Communist parties based in Moscow) and Communists as virtual robots carrying out orders from afar. More recent studies have drifted away from this approach but have substituted another in its place: the stress has been on local party branches explaining how they were able to overcome or subvert orders from Moscow and/or their minions, the party "bureaucrats" from party headquarters in New York City. By looking at a party leader or "bureaucrat" I suggest in this study that both approaches fail to understand why the party rose—and fell.

Moreover, these newer studies rarely go beyond 1945. The Depression decade and the period shortly thereafter is a fine field of study; however, for the full flavor of what happened to the Left and the Communist party one should venture into the minefield of the Red Scare and the Cold War. Now that the Cold War has apparently ended, one can hope that more scholars will feel freer and more courageous in tackling this prickly subject. I continue to find it mind-boggling that few scholars have noticed that in the 1950s civil liberties were being restricted while civil rights were being expanded and that Washington was prating about "human rights violations" in Eastern Europe while tolerating the same at home. How and why this happened is a subject of my past work as well as this book.

This work will concentrate on the public life of Ben Davis, Jr. This is not to say that Davis did not have meaningful personal relationships. As noted below, he was quite close to Paul Robeson, William Patterson, and others who have come to symbolize black resistance to the Cold War and the Red Scare. He married at age fifty-one and, if one chooses to believe the Federal Bureau of Investigation, there were tensions between his personal and political lives. Moreover, as I suggest in the first chapter, an understanding of Ben Davis, Sr., is necessary for understanding Ben Davis, Jr. However, the documentary record barely addresses this aspect of his life and the interviews I conducted to fill this gap were at some points so contradictory and sparse that from a methodological point of view—if nothing else—I have chosen not to follow the current fashion and elevate this aspect of Davis's life.

Still, there are references to his personal life in the endnotes that are noteworthy and can be followed up. I do follow the popular trend of conducting interior arguments and fleshing out putatively arcane points. This is even more necesssary, I think, in a study of this kind since at a number of points I break with conventional wisdom, requiring detailed substantiation.

Inevitably this is not just a study of Davis but of the Communist party as well. It is important to understand that a number of Davis's controversial viewpoints were not just personal opinions but party policy. Hence, to understand Davis, some knowledge of the party is necessary.

Like many Communist parties, the United States party was inspired by the Bolshevik Revolution of 1917. This international instigation caused many to see the party as an agent of Moscow. However, the competitors to the left and right of the Communist party were similarly inspired internationally, albeit differently. For example, a major split in the international socialist movement occurred at the time of World War I, when a number of Marxist-oriented parties chose not to oppose this global conflict; many of these parties formed the basis for the political tendency known as social democracy and entities known as socialist parties. Similarly, there was a "Trotskyite" political tendency in the U.S. that was inspired by the life and ideas of Leon Trotsky, a Bolshevik who came into conflict with the Soviet party and Joseph Stalin, was exiled, and later murdered. Davis had numerous conflicts during his life with these latter two political formations, and he tended to reflect the policies of the Communist party.

This study reflects the language of the Left. I refer often to the ruling elite, by which I mean those who have controlled the means of production in this country such as Henry Ford, John D. Rockefeller, and those at the highest levels in Washington, D.C. Intermittently I use the terms *black* and *African-American* and *Negro*, depending on the context. At times I call the party's policies "sectarian," by which I mean narrow and not sufficiently forthcoming to centrist forces like the NAACP. At times I refer to the "united front" and "popular front", policies enunciated formally in the Communist movement in 1935 and focused on building alliances between Communist and non-Communist forces for a common goal. Naturally, when I refer to *Reds* I am using the shorthand for Communists.

This study is critical of Davis and the party from time to time, though preliminary readings suggest it that is too critical for the tastes of some and not critical enough for others. So be it. Like many authors, I do have a point of view that is reflected in my work. However, unlike many who publish in the field of political history, I do not purport to not have a point of view;

moreover, my own political life is no doubt reflected in my writings. As I grow older and eager graduate students begin to interview me about my role as an attorney with the trade union movement in New York City or my anti-apartheid activism over the decades or my role as an international lawyer with both the National Conference of Black Lawyers and the National Lawyers Guild, I have become quite conscious of the role of 20-20 hindsight that seems to be a particular approach of scholars of the Left.

What I mean, in part, is that many of these scholars fail to "contextualize" political questions, to use a term made popular by the literati. For example, in most writings on the Communist party the German-Soviet Non-Aggression Pact of 1939 is presented as a turning point leading to the devolution of the party's fortunes and the end of the party's heyday. Yet, as noted in this book, this approach fails to take account of the electoral successes of the party—for example, Ben Davis's election to the New York City Council in 1943—which came precisely after the pact. Nor does this approach note that many on the Left and in the civil rights movement were highly suspicious of the war—until 1941. Many saw it as a replay of World War I, which promised so much but provided so little. Others were taken in by Tokyo's idea that it was the savior of the "colored races" and was just seeking its proper place in the sun. Still others hesitated to rush to the aid of London because they were familiar with British oppression in Africa and the West Indies; Harlem particularly was influenced by this attitude. Hence, to understand Davis's and the party's view of this matter, one has to place it within this context.

To understand Davis's and the party's approach to both "white chauvinism" and the "Negro Question," it is important to recall the context in which they operated—lynchings, Jim Crow, severe and racist economic deprivation. Similarly, until the 1950s Davis and the party saw African-Americans in the Black Belt South—or most of the Old Confederacy—as a nation worthy of self-determination. My own view is that this thesis should have been revised well before the 1950s and it was a mistake not to do so. Often it is presented as yet another example of an idea imported from Moscow. Yet it is difficult to understand the Black Belt thesis without understanding the popularity of Marcus Garvey—especially in Harlem—the South African question, the attachment of African-Americans to the *land* of the South, and so on.

In addition I criticize the approach taken by Davis and the party—particularly before the formal articulation of the policy of the "united front" or "popular front"—to alliances with the NAACP and other centrist forces. However, one must understand the context, the jockeying for position of the party and the association within the African-American community. Unlike today, during the 1930s there was no centrist hegemony in the African-American community, nor could many both inside and outside the Left envision it for the future. This context should be kept in mind.

I criticize the political tendency known as Browderism, which led, for example, to the Communist party not fighting the internment of Japanese-Americans. Of course, there are those who see Browderism, a policy of conciliation between labor and capital, as the appropriate path for the party. I also criticize the soft line taken by Davis and the party toward the White House during the war. Whatever the case, the context of what was happening that led to this turn must be explained to understand the full import.

To understand the concept of party discipline one needs to comprehend the context of persecution that bedeviled much of the party's life during the period discussed. This era featured wiretapping, infiltrators, political jailings, long periods underground, and other harassments not designed to facilitate the emergence of a democratic culture. Moreover, there was a tendency of the U.S. party to emulate their Soviet counterpart, which during the period in question was confronted with an international harassment—including a number of murderous invasions—that along with internal factors similarly hampered the emergence of a democratic culture.

What I perceive as errors by Davis and the party also must be seen in context. For example, in the early post–World War II period, Davis was a proponent of the idea that fascism was on the horizon in the U.S. In this study I point out—with perfect 20-20 hindsight—that this was mistaken and, furthermore, if fascism was on the horizon, then their approach to potential allies was misguided in any case. However, a peculiarity of the United States is that fascist like measures are often dispensed against African-Americans—as in the Columbia, Tennessee pogrom, the explosion of police brutality in New York—and not accorded to the same degree to others. I think that this imperfectly understood tendency was reflected in party viewpoints.

A part of comprehending this context is knowledge of the kind of support garnered by Davis, especially during his runs for public office. I list his support from figures as diverse as Lena Horne, Joe Louis, Duke Ellington, and Teddy Wilson, not only to provide context for understanding his public backing, but also to signal that the question of black celebrities and the Communist party in the pre-Red Scare era merits fuller study.

In short, what I am suggesting is that to understand the Communist party—or any other political organization for that matter—we need to know the context in which it was operating before we judge, condemn, or praise.

An essential part of the context of this work is New York City and Harlem. As scholars of the "Harlem Renaissance" have noted, it is not accidental that this phenomenon occurred in this community. New York was unique in its diversity, having large and progressive black and Jewish communities and a strong trade union tradition. Such features allowed Davis to be elected to the City Council in 1943 and reelected in 1945. Though his elections may have been a New York peculiarity, my contention is that, like the "Renaissance," the potential and actuality existed for this tendency to spread from Manhattan. At least until 1947 in New York City, the citadel of capital, there was a significant electoral "threat" by the Communists, the American Labor Party, and their allies. Moreover, it was recognized in the party and among elites that a strong Communist movement ineluctably meant a strong trade union movement and a strong progressive movement. Hence, measures directed ostensibly at the party were aimed as well at progressives, not to mention democratic practice. After the Red Scare started and Davis began to lose elections—in 1949 and spectacularly in 1958—and the party's role began to shrink, political repression was not reduced correspondingly. Even after the threat was significantly lessened, repression was not reduced; indeed, the 1956 initiation of COINTELPRO, intense FBI surveillance and dirty tricks, when the party was going through crisis, suggests that repression may have been increased as the threat was reduced.

I believe that not only was this repression the significant factor in reducing Davis's post-1947 electoral totals and the party's role but that understanding this phenomenon is crucial to the thesis of this work and, in fact, its title.

In the pre-World War II era, the devastating racism visited upon African-Americans—economic, political, and social—created favorable conditions for Communist advance in the Harlems of this land. This is the import of Davis's electoral victories, which were steps in the direction of the Black Liberation movement, or the liberating of blacks from the most egregious aspects of Jim Crow. However, after the war the rulers decided to ease the horror of Jim Crow, partly because of the need to be able to charge Moscow with human rights violations. Yet this civil rights victory had to be carried out while ousting black Communists like Davis from previously held positions of influence among African-Americans. This opening of democratic space for blacks carried the possibility of creating more room for Communists, trade unions, and so on. The trick was to open democratic space for blacks while closing it down for their traditional allies—in other words, *black liberation/red scare*. This would guarantee that the civil rights movement could only advance so far. Thus, *Brown v. Board of Education* and its progeny came in 1954 in the midst of the Cold War and the Red Scare. The USSR responded belatedly, and ultimately inadequately, on the human rights front with the devaluation of Stalin and the reforms of 1956.

Hence, the support enjoyed by Davis and the party after the Red Scare was only a shadow of what it had been before that time. Yet fresh in the minds of J. Edgar Hoover and his ilk was the knowledge that Davis and the party only recently had enjoyed no small amount of support among blacks. They also knew that people like Davis had relationships of various sorts with figures like Adam Powell, Martin Luther King, and Jack O'Dell and that blacks were not as favorable toward the Red Scare as were others. The FBI feared that as democratic space was being opened, a comeback by Communists would be triggered. This helps to explain why repressive anti-

Communist measures did not necessarily decrease as the party was shrinking. Moreover, such measures were convenient handcuffs for the civil rights movement as well. Thus, in assessing Communist party influence in the post-World War II era, one must not only count votes, but one must also make a political assessment that takes into account pre-Red Scare events, the nature of the Cold War and the confrontation with the Soviet Union, and the fear that a leftist- or Communist-influenced civil rights movement would detour from the approved track.

Creating an opening for Black Liberation while launching the Red Scare was akin to riding two horses going in different directions at the same time. Yet apparently this maneuver was "successful." Certainly Davis's vote totals dropped sharply, even in 1949, just as this operation was taking off. One can see in retrospect that a combination of concessions and repression helped to significantly reduce Communist influence among blacks. Though Davis continued to have some support after 1949, there is little doubt that by then his popularity, and that of the party, was over.

On the other hand, the reduction of leftist and Communist influence among African-Americans, like the situation in Eastern Europe, helped to pave the way for the rise of various forms of narrow nationalism. This trend was one of the many factors in the Watts area of Los Angeles in August 1965 when a major urban uprising took place that was characterized in part by an "antiwhite" flavor.

The post-1949 history of Davis and the party is suffused with political persecution, internecine internal conflict, and, in a sense, political eclipse. Yet, COINTELPRO, the civil rights movement, the Cuban Revolution, decolonization of Africa, and the beginnings of a campus movement—significant developments all—figure directly in this history. Along with W. E. B. Du Bois, Claudia Jones, Paul Robeson, William Patterson, and Lorraine Hansberry, Ben Davis was a central figure in the rise and fall of the organized Left in the African-American community.

Black Liberation/
Red Scare

1
Origins of a Black Revolutionary

How does the scion of one of the elite African-American families of the Deep South become the top-ranking Communist in the United States? A thorough understanding of the background of Ben Davis helps us to understand this phenomenon. The evolution from the top Republican Ben Davis, Sr., to the top Communist Ben Davis, Jr., is not especially difficult. As in many elite families, the impact of this father on his son was paramount; it will be the central focus of this chapter.

Katherine Davis, Ben's grandmother, was born in 1835 in Wilkes County, Georgia. She was a slave of the Reverend Jefferson Davis, who emigrated from Wilkes County to Lee County then on to Decatur County. She in turn was the daughter of the Reverend Ben Davis, a slave preacher for whom Ben and his father were named; the middle name of both—Jefferson—came from the slavemaster. The Reverend Mr. Davis had three sons—Ben, George, and Aaron—and three daughters—Katherine, Sylvia, and Elizabeth. Katherine became the wife of Mike Haynes and they produced four sons and two daughters, three of whom—including Davis's father—were not born in slavery. Just before the Civil War Ben senior's mother was separated from her husband by her master moving to Decatur County, and they were not united again until 1868 or 1869, after the war. The husband took the name of Davis, which was the name of his wife's old master. His father, too, had belonged to a Davis in slavery. Ben Davis's father was born in Georgia in May 1870.[1]

Ben Davis, Jr., was born on 8 September 1903 in Dawson, Georgia, a tiny hamlet of less than five thousand people. His mother, "Willa" Porter, who was educated at Hampton and Tuskeegee, was also born in Dawson. She married Ben senior in 1898. In his prison memoir, Davis reminisced about his roots:

> My maternal grandmother was extremely fair, with coarse gray hair that hung below her waist when she let it down . . . . Mother was light brown with soft rounded features, big eyes and a splendid straight carriage . . . [grandmother] was a domestic for a rich white family [for 25 years].

His "mother's family line was always shadowy," he wrote, and lacked the kind of detail that was available on his paternal side.[2]

According to Clarence Bacote, Ben senior was a teacher in Terrell County, Georgia, and then was employed by Tom W. Loyless, a Euro-American publisher and printer in Dawson, from whom he learned the trade. He then moved to Athens but was indicted by a federal grand jury for stealing liquor and selling it to white men. The charge was dropped without a conviction, Davis later claiming that it was all a frameup emerging from political squabbles. This did not stop him from owning a fifteen-room home in Dawson, a modern mansion situated upon a hill.[3] In any event, he moved to Atlanta, started his newspaper, and quickly became not just one of the more affluent blacks in the nation but also, in his capacity as a leading Republican party official, one of the most powerful.[4]

NAACP leader Walter White, who also grew up in Atlanta, recalled that Ben senior "owned one of the first automobiles for either whites or Negroes in Atlanta." But he may have been better known for his ability to stir controversy than his net worth. White recalled a "kind of ruthlessness" on Davis's part.[5] Bacote observes that "he did not have a single prominent friend who at one time or another did not feel the stinging blows from his pen." That is not all: "lacking in character . . . treacherous, selfish" were Bacote's kindest words about Davis. According to him, Davis wrote "some of the most devastating editorials ever to be written by a Negro about Negroes."[6] John Dittmer echoes and expands this theme:

> The champion mulatto baiter was Ben Davis. Not himself of pure African descent, neither was he part of upper class black society. In his editorial columns he railed against what he perceived as a light-skinned aristocracy.[7]

Strikingly, this negative view of Davis senior is reflected in some of the views expressed about his son later in life.

Davis senior's reputation as a "stormy petrel" was generated in part by words flowing from his newspaper, the *Atlanta Independent*. One student has called it "the strongest of the early Georgia papers . . . as late as 1932 reported a circulation of 27,000 copies weekly . . . discontinued after the Democratic landslide in 1932."[8] By contemporary standards it is difficult to see why this paper was so popular, given its layout and style of writing. Another scholar of the Negro press agrees:

> In 1909 the *Independent* was still an eight-page, six-column weekly devoted largely to club news, social notes, church notices, and other religious news. It plugged away at developing Negro businesses and gave new Negro insurance companies and other firms large amounts of publicity. Much of the writing was crude. . . . The best writing and thinking in the paper was to be found on the editorial pages where Editor Davis wielded a forceful pen in a very capable [manner] . . . [he] was one of the Negro editors invited to a wartime conference with the President.[9]

Still, he notes: "The *Atlanta Independent* did not stoop to the tricks of many Negro journals who patterned themselves after yellow journalism at its worst. To the end the *Independent* devoted itself to news that was largely wholesome and constructive." The paper was influential " . . . practically every financial institution of any importance in the city of Atlanta advertised in it."[10] This fact was extraordinary considering the era's high tide of racism but only underscored Davis's power in the Republican party. The support of banks was also helpful economically, for as Emma Lou Thornbrough's careful study notes, "the results suggest that Negro newspapers were not successful business enterprises."[11] Since they were pressed to defend the interests of poor blacks whose interests often conflicted with wealthy advertisers, Davis junior received an early education in the intersection of race and class. Ben junior joined the paper's staff of twelve at an early age, and the paper's content seemed to improve when Ben senior played a smaller role in reportage.[12]

In his prison memoir Davis wistfully recalled the days when his father "was the idol of the backwoods poor Negro farmers. . . . The *Independent* became famous all over Negro America for the fearlessness of its editorial policy . . . [it was the] most influential Negro weekly in the South. . . . In many towns in Georgia it was not allowed."[13] When he was about sixteen, his father showed him a bundle of papers returned from Covington, Georgia, with a bloody warning attached. So the family patriarch decided to go there and hand them out personally, taking his wide-eyed son with him. As fifty whites and one hundred and fifty blacks—virtually all armed—watched, he handed out the papers. This kind of clout could allow Davis senior to confront racism more directly than most blacks could; these lessons were absorbed and applied by his son.[14]

Davis used his paper to bolster his other enterprises, particularly his role in the Grand United Order of Odd Fellows. Indeed, his paper's offices were located in the Odd Fellows building.[15] Michael Leroy Porter has noted the "Negroid shaped terra cotta on the Odd Fellows Building . . . an aesthetic expression of Atlanta's Black experience." Davis was the major force in this "largest secret order among Blacks in the world," which in turn was the foundation for the famous "Sweet Auburn" district that produced, among others, Martin Luther King, Jr., and his Ebenezer Baptist Church. Moreover, it was the first commercial building in the city "to be free of Jim Crow regulations."[16]

Davis joined the Odd Fellows in 1889. Frederick Detweiler gives him primary credit for their membership rise of "10,000 to 50,000."[17] The Odd Fellows had eleven hundred lodges and thirty-three thousand members with assets close to a million dollars and a fund of $300,000 to finance loans for purchasing businesses, farms and homes. But, as John Dittmer observed, "several times Davis found himself in court on the wrong end of a lawsuit" involving the Odd Fellows.[18]

Though Ben Davis, Jr., did not evoke as much personal enmity as did his father, what they did have in common was versatility. Just as Junior was a lawyer, violinist, and near tennis pro, Senior—after leaving Atlanta University in the late 1880s—was alternately a bricklayer, teacher, and journalist. Both were joiners and leaders. Davis senior was a Mason, an Elk, a member of the Knights of Pythias, and served as president of the Baptist Laymen's League of Georgia; above all he was an entrepreneur. The *Atlanta Independent* did not exaggerate when it referred to the "palatial home" of the patriarch at 286 Martin Street in Atlanta, where parties and music by "a select orchestra" often reigned.[19]

Most African-Americans in early-twentieth-century Atlanta were not as lucky as Davis. In his useful dissertation Porter avers, "In virtually every aspect of city life, the Black citizenry of Atlanta were haunted and taunted by white Atlanta's social segregationist practices." Ku Klux Klan pogroms and lynchings were common. This tense and charged atmosphere could help to account for some of the negative reactions to Davis senior insofar as he was a black leader at the point of protest and saw himself as a tribune. Thus, when he blasted black doctors in Atlanta in 1914 for using only white orchestras at their balls, they fired back heatedly: "When you get sick again, if we get a chance at you, we will fix you."[20] Rayford Logan and Michael Winston are not far from the mark when they characterize the *Independent* as "the most militant Negro newspaper in the Deep South."[21]

An examination of some of the issues of 1904 finds articles and editorials denouncing the racists for suggesting that blacks should not be educated and condemnations of lynching, convict labor, and disfranchisement. This militant tone lasted for years and helps to explain why Davis senior would join W. E. B. Du Bois, Emmett J. Scott, and other black leaders in a June 1918 meeting to discuss black grievances and the war and why the *Independent* would be noted in congressional investigations of the time exploring the perceived radicalization of the black press.[22]

The contradictory viewpoints expressed by scholars like Logan and Winston, Dittmer, and Bacote on Davis senior partially bespeak the diversity of his career. One could argue that his militance was inconsistent because of his close alliance over the years with Booker T. Washington. Davis was president of the Atlanta Board of Trade, a symbol of Washington's black business orientation, and an intimate friend of the Tuskeegee wizard. Without equivocation Davis told his ally in a letter dated 30 March 1910, "You know that there is not a journal in America that have [sic] stood by Tuskeegee with the enthusiasm that the Independent has without the hope of personal gain."[23]

Still, quarrels at times erupted between them. Washington placed numerous ads in Davis's paper but was not always timely in paying the bill. Fortunately all of their contact did not concern jealousies and capital squabbles. When Atlanta passed an urban residential segregation ordinance, Washington demanded of Davis, "What are you all going to do about it? I advise that you hire the best lawyer you can get. . . . Let me know if you need outside help."[24]

The ties between the two giants were no chimera. The pages of the *Independent* were used to praise Washington. Washington wrote for the paper, and along with Theodore Roosevelt, was on the front page frequently. When the Odd Fellows building was dedicated in 1914 the Alabama leader not only spoke but "appeared . . . upon the arm" of Davis. A historical irony is that the leading black Communist, Ben Davis, Jr., was sired by a man in alliance with someone perceived to be the leading black conservative, Washington.[25]

Davis senior often assailed antagonists of Washington. Du Bois and the Niagara Movement were frequent targets. There were moralistic condemnations of the controversial Bishop Henry Turner after his messy divorce. Despite the lineal ties between Tuskeegee and Marcus Garvey, the Jamaican immigrant was often scored. In turn, according to Theodore Kornweibel, "the politicians most frequently disparaged by the *Messenger*" were Davis senior and his allies. In carrying on bitter polemics with presumed ideological foes, Davis junior was following in the footsteps of his father.[26]

Despite his past criticism, W. E. B. Du Bois in 1953 did not hesitate to praise Davis senior, whom he "knew . . . while I was teaching there in the university. He was a fearless and forceful man." J. Pius Barbour, who influenced Martin Luther King, Jr., and was a leader in Baptist circles, also recalled Davis senior affectionately in the early 1950s: "One of the most fond recollections of my school days is the memory of sitting in the office of [Davis senior], who with Henry Lincoln Johnson, the great lawyer and political leader of Georgia, dominated the thinking of the young college men of Atlanta. My ambition was to be like Link Johnson in law and Ben Davis, Sr., in leadership."[27]

This leadership was expressed in the Republican party, for Davis was a living embodiment of the close alliance between blacks and the GOP.[28] Davis junior was not the only staunch party member; both father and son recognized the value of political parties in pressing for gains for their people. From 1908 to his death in 1945 the father attended all of the Republican conventions. In 1916 he was on the platform committee that tried to force a plank on lynching and advocated that southern representation in Congress be decreased in proportion as black citizens were disfranchised.[29] He served six years as GOP committeeman, was secretary of the the GOP State Executive Committee for eighteen years, and served as president of the Young Men's Republican Club of Georgia as late as 1943. As head of the party in Georgia he had a substantial role in handing out patronage during the intermittent GOP administrations in Washington. This power gave his son a perspective and experience unlike those of his African-American contemporaries, since whites seeking favor would come hat in hand to their door seeking federal judgeships, positions as postmaster, and other posts. But his position also had a negative side that was indeed part of the experience of other African-Americans, for the Klan and racists did not look benignly on this abject violation of racial etiquette. Later Davis junior recalled "a campaign of terror and violence against his father . . . [and] our house. Twice on different occasions the Ku Klux Klan burned crosses on our front yard or boulevard . . . for a month, the windows in our home were stoned and broken. At night the tires on my father's automobiles were cut to ribbons. . . . It was a virtual reign of terror."[30] Police protection was required and the health of his mother worsened. In the long run the experience of his father with the Republican party helped to sour Davis junior on the two-party system, facilitating his move to the Left.

But as tormenting as this experience with the KKK may have been, it paled in comparison with what Davis senior was to endure subsequently. He was at the epicenter of a political temblor, the mass exodus of blacks from the GOP, an event that had substantial impact on Davis junior. As his father was being assailed by erstwhile GOP allies, the political options of Davis junior were narrowing. In this time of impending economic depression he could no longer turn to the GOP and he knew too much about the racist character of the Democrats to look in that direction. He was ripe for recruitment by the Communists. John Hope Franklin is correct in suggesting that the "real disaffection" of blacks with the Republicans began in 1928 when the lily-white policy of the party was entrenched and "prominent Negro Republican leaders" such as "Benjamin Davis of Georgia . . . lost influence in their states as the Republican high command began to recognize white leaders in those states and to seat white delegates." This was the turning point in Davis junior's ideological evolution.[31]

Davis junior recalled this time poignantly in his memoir, indicating the enormous impact it had on him. He noted that Herbert Hoover and Senator Walter George of Georgia launched an investigation of patronage that kept his father "on the stand a week." The press carried "lurid stories of . . . a Negro 'humiliating' white men and women who had to come to him for jobs. . . . The terror and violence began again. . . . Hoover had told my father to resign . . . ." Davis junior attended some of these sessions where his father was grilled and all of it " . . . left a lasting impression upon me." Because these events were so central in the son's ideological evolution, it is worthwhile to examine Davis senior's role carefully.[32]

This specter of scandal haunted the Davis family name. In a book written in 1936, well after the headlines had disappeared, an author referred to Davis junior as " . . . son of a Georgia Negro Republican leader whose venture into politics was not without scandal and investigation. . . . "[33] *New York Amsterdam News* columnist Earl Brown, who was later to dislodge Davis from his City Council seat, in 1944 turned the knife by referring to Davis senior and his colleague Perry Howard as those who "have made political collaboration a lifetime career and [all] they desire is somebody with whom to collaborate—somebody to sell out to. . . . " The fact that Davis senior continued to support the GOP despite their orchestrated attacks on him gave credence to Brown's attacks.[34]

Lawrence Hogan in his history of the Associated Negro Press refers to the "Big Six" of black GOP politics; first among equals was Davis. Davis joined in the partisan attacks in 1928 on Democratic candidate Al Smith, referring to his being "evasive" on the "liquor question." The months leading up to the 1928 election found Davis in partisan battle. He stumped the country for Hoover, speaking to "thousands" in Ohio alone.[35] But the GOP had a classic and, seemingly, eternal problem. As the *Independent* put it, if they ousted Davis "the adverse reaction would be felt in the large Negro Republican vote in New York, Massachusetts, Philadelphia. . . . " But if they did not remove him, then the GOP would lose the sizable racist vote. Being politicians, the GOP moved aggressively to eject him right after the election.[36]

Quoted by Donald Lisio, Mabel Walker Willebrandt, assistant attorney general, conceded that she was "a little harsh" on Davis when she paid him a curious compliment: "the reputation of Ben Davis is that he stands by his word—at least he 'stays bought' instead of selling out to the next bidder who comes along with a higher price." This personal friend of Hoover also observed that "Davis favored Coolidge's renomination," a fact that might have turned the administration against him. There were other problems, as Lisio points out: "Because Atlanta blacks could vote in municipal elections, Davis had always enjoyed a greater degree of power and independence than most other black politicians in the South. His successful registration drives rallied the black vote and earned him the political respect of his Democratic opponents." And apparently it earned him their enmity as well. Citing the *New York Times*, Lisio suggests that Davis "made [a] very unfavorable impression" on the Senate committee investigating funds expended in campaigns. He seemed "awestruck" by the senators and "became nervous and confused by the barrage of questions." The fact that this leading newspaper stated that he "still looks and talks like an old time Southern darky" puts their portrait in the proper perspective. Davis, they reported, "could not specifically recall how he had spent" campaign funds and "had kept no records and had no receipts." At one point the senators burst into open laughter at his testimony. Lacking apparent skill at this type of cross-examination, Davis created the incriminating impression that he had been bribed in return for patronage jobs. His position was not helped when patronage appointee Postmaster L. F. Peterson of Douglas, Georgia, shot a clerk and committed suicide; rumors were floating that graft to Davis was a key element motivating this crime. Then charges arose concerning graft to another member of the "Big Six," Robert Church. The Senate committee traveled to Georgia "to interrogate Davis . . . [they] tried repeatedly to trap [Davis] into admitting that he had used [GOP] money ... for personal rather than party purposes and that he had accepted bribes from white appointees who wished to obtain or keep patronage jobs. Davis represented himself better than he had before.... He made few errors, admitted nothing." But the *New York Times*, which covered this matter assiduously, was not buying. Said the journal of record, if Davis is to be believed, "the twenty-six letters of the alphabet were tossed into the air on Peachtree Street and the heap in which they [fell] pointed out as the works of Uncle Remus."[38]

Lisio suggests that the "two Democratic Senators from Georgia" were the chief enemies of Davis. Davis would let none forget that the Klan backed the Democrats, that black "spectators [were] ... penned ... behind a chicken wire fence at their convention in Houston ...." Moreover, Davis's "humiliation greatly angered northern blacks, who believed that he had been driven from his position of leadership primarily because he was black." Lisio concedes that the evidence of corruption was "weak." Yet the fact that a black county GOP leader in Georgia was murdered by "lily-white" Republicans dressed as Klan members indicated operative trends. Davis continued defending Hoover; however, his son and the African-American community generally were being pushed to the Left by these maneuvers.[39]

The tensions of those days are reflected in both the correspondence of Herbert Hoover and the pages of the *New York Times*, which took the lead in urging the ouster of Davis.[40] However, Kelly Miller of Howard University was one of the many blacks who complained about the ill treatment of Davis: "You will have to be a very skillful housekeeper, Mr. Secretary, if you are to manipulate a political household which shall contain as inmates both the Negro and the Ku Klux Klan."[41] But a racist Republican from Folkston, Georgia, took an opposing view in a letter to Hoover: "We who supported you here did so in the face of the scorn and taunts of our friends and neighbors, who taunted us with the criticism that we were working for the Negro Ben Davis.... I do ask that you and the Republican party do not slap we Georgians in the face by reappointing Negroes to control the party in this state."[42]

The ouster of Davis from his top GOP post in 1928 did not altogether remove his influence from the party; the plan was to complete his removal as midterm congressional elections approached in 1930. Josiah Rose of Georgia was the source for much of the intelligence fed to top Hoover aide Walter Newton.

> ... the activity of the white people is Ben's basis for the statement in his paper that the white people are going to steal the county conventions away from the colored people.... [Davis] is writing some editorials in his paper which on the face of them do not look good but Ben knows better how to get a following among his people and get them tied to him than we do. He says the best way to do this is to make his group believe that something is about to be taken from them, and he must be in the attitude of fighting for their protection.[43]

Frank Darden of the Republican Club of Savannah promised trouble when he told Newton of plans of "taking steps toward suppressing these firebrands in the county meetings to be called in a few weeks."[44]

Trouble arrived. Charles Adamson of "Quaker origin" and president of the Cedartown Cotton and Export Company in Georgia confessed to Newton, " . . . I have no hostilities to the colored man." But he called Davis a "grafter" and went on to describe fierce clashes at the county meetings. Davis was accused of attempting to "bar out at least 32 white delegates. . . . The colored delegates placed on the temporary roll by Davis held rump conventions in the Negro homes or Negro churches . . . the riot was led as usual by Ben Davis and his colored supporters . . . the impudence of Ben Davis . . . is astonishing . . . he should be under indictment."[45]

But ousting Davis was not easy. Yet another informant, Walter Akerman, chair of the Bartow County GOP committee, outlined the problem to Newton: "There are Ben Davises [sic] organization Negro county chairmen in over 100 counties out of 165 counties in the state." He added: "There are about 15,000 Negro registered voters in this state and not half of these ever vote in a national election, yet Mr. Hoover received 100,000 votes for President. There are thousands of voters in Georgia who would like to vote the Republican ticket, but who will not do so in those counties where they have Negro county chairmen as the head of the party."[46] In a "personal and confidential" letter to Newton, Davis revealed how the racists approached this problem: " . . . the assassination of S. S. Mincey of Ailey, Georgia, County Chairman of Montgomery County and a member of the Republican State Central Committee of Georgia, July 29th, 1930, is directly chargeable to the political propaganda and race hatred stirred up as the result of the demand from Washington for a 100 per cent white organization in Georgia. . . . This man was killed because he would not give up the Chairmanship after having defeated the lily-whites in his county."[47]

The following year, 1931, Josiah Rose reported the results of the routing of African-Americans from the GOP: "It is known that Ben Davis is very hard up. His income now is nothing like what it used to be. . . . His newspaper is run at a loss and he now owes his printer several thousand dollars."[48] Davis's fortune shrank along with his political role. By early 1932 the *Oklahoma City Black Dispatch* was reporting the ouster of Davis from his post as secretary of the Georgia GOP and his replacement by a "white man . . . a third class postmaster." This was a "bum's rush," according to the paper. "The passing of Mr. Davis from a position of influence in the state [GOP] ranks would seem to indicate that for a time at least the Negro will have lost the principal symbols of power in the Republican party which he once possessed."[49] The massive shift of blacks to the Democrats and away from the GOP marked an important moment in history, and Ben Davis was at the heart of this process. Picking up the baton, his son ran further to the Left. But the father remained true. Late in 1939 he was engaged in debates where he attacked the New Deal. Rose reported gleefully: "I am glad to say that our friend Ben stood his ground and got more applause from the audience. . . . I was the only white man present."[50] But around the same time Ralph Bunche was reporting that the party in Georgia generally and among blacks in particular was as "dead as a doornail."[51]

Understandably all these events left a deep imprint on the mind of Ben Davis, Jr. Referring to the difficulties of his father and other blacks in the GOP, he wrote in August 1928, "The time has long since arrived when the Negro must think for himself, when he must make his own political place. . . . The Negro cannot afford to vote the Republican ticket [just because of abolition]. . . . Blind party fealty is a dangerous political platform for the Negro. . . . The Negro's place in politics is not forever and anon with one political party."[52]

Father and son were steadfast in their commitments; both were stubborn, proud, courageous, and both were party stalwarts. The two were considered personally "difficult" by some and gregarious fellows by others. The father, seemingly self-interested and inconsistent at times, had taught his son well. Though he represented a party that came to epitomize private ownership of the economy and his son was associated with a party that symbolized public ownership, the two men were quite similar.

Ben Davis, Sr., died in 1945 at age seventy-five. Supporting his Communist son during his campaigns, his name recognition and contacts within the African-American community were no small factor in Ben junior's success. As Ben junior admitted more than once, the experiences of the father shaped the consciousness of the son; indeed, Davis senior's experience with the two-party system virtually left Ben Davis, Jr., with few political alternatives but to veer sharply left. The evolution from black elite to black Left, black Republican to black Communist, was not a profound anomaly, particularly when considered within the context of this father-son relationship.[53]

2
The Making of a Black Revolutionary

Benjamin Jefferson Davis, Jr., was born in Georgia in 1903 and died in New York City in 1964. For half of his life he was a leader of the Communist party. This task was so all-consuming that he only found the time to get married when he was fifty-one, and like many of the Left kept his inner and personal life shrouded. To some onlookers this tie with the Left was inconsistent with the trajectory of his father but certainly a kind of militance and concern for black folk was characteristic of both. The context suggests why Davis's evolution was not an aberration. Paul Robeson, William Patterson, W. E. B. Du Bois, Shirley Graham—the foremost black intellectuals—were oriented to the Left. Making African-American revolutionaries was not that difficult in Jim Crow USA.

Even Davis junior's name was a result of the cranky and rebellious nature of his father. As the *Afro-American* explained in 1960, he was "christened 'Morton.' He was named for a colored postmaster of Athens, Ga. . . . But when Ben Sr. and Morton fell out over Odd Fellows business, Davis Sr. renamed his son Benjamin."[1]

At the age of four Davis went to an all-black school in Dawson, Georgia. As he recollected, "It was a ramshackle, wooden frame house with one room, a hazard to life and limb." His father's concern for his children's education was "one of the principal reasons why the family migrated north to Atlanta." He spent first through sixth grade's at Summer Hill School there; his recollection was of "no sidewalks. . . . I can remember wading through seas of mud whenever it rained." This was the other side of being born into an affluent Negro family. Education was no crystal stair for African-Americans, irrespective of class. In his 1911 study W. E. B. Du Bois noted that Atlanta had long waiting lists to get into Negro schools: "Hundreds do not apply at all because of the crowded condition . . . [schools] are in bad condition." In his memoir Walter White recalled bitterly how blacks in Atlanta were taxed but "no high school of any description for colored" existed. In this detailed exposition of black Atlanta, White mentions that Davis senior led the fight against this abomination, which led to the construction of David T. Howard High School.[2]

Mary Church Terrell, daughter of Robert Church of the "Big Six," recalls in her autobiography how life could be sweet for elite African-Americans despite the frequent encounters with racism.[3] This too was true for Davis. He had access to an automobile and had the opportunity to drive black leader John Hope around. His father owned three cars and had a four-car garage. It was not uncommon for a visiting dignitary like the president of Liberia to pay a courtesy call at the Davis household. Davis junior's niece, Jean Carey Bond, recalls that the Davises hired whites to purchase clothes for them from white stores so that they could avoid the more odious affronts of Jim Crow; the irony of this "benefit" suggests why Davis—who had reached the highest level of the black elite—could be quite critical of U.S. society.[4]

Young Ben was not able to escape certain impressions of the other major population group of Georgia: "I lived in the Negro American world . . . white people were a strange lot to me. The only contact I ever had with them was hateful. . . . I regarded them as colorless—especially physically—somewhat inferior, wicked and authoritarian."[5]

Davis senior was a patriarchal type of man. Although he sent Ben junior's sister, Johnnie, to Radcliffe, it was clear that he was preparing his son for even bigger things, which may explain why sister and brother were not particularly close. He would take him to many of the meetings he attended. Ben junior was featured in his father's newspaper at an early age. He became a part-owner of the paper and worked there after school and on vacations. While his mother encouraged his talent with the violin (which he began at age eight), his father encouraged his political interests.[6]

Ben junior boarded for seven years at Morehouse, going home only once or twice a month. At that time the future alma mater of Martin Luther King, Jr., was not only a college, it was also a secondary school. Davis junior remembers Morehouse being for the "sons of the slave field hands" and Atlanta University as being the "school of the Negro elite." This characterization can be questioned. Still, although only the Herndon family "exceeded my father in individual wealth," Davis senior—who had certain antielite tendencies of his own—chose to steer his son to Morehouse. Davis junior was also struck by the connection between class and color in his community: "None of these aristocratic families were ever dark in complexion—to say nothing of black."[7]

Davis's days at Morehouse were tumultuous. He rebelled against singing spirituals to get funds from white philanthropists, then became friendly with the atheist students on campus: "we subsequently passed many idle hours in radical and orthodox discussions." Since many of these students were older, his intellectual development accelerated: "some juniors and seniors were 30 and over . . . so that at an early age, my ideas and approach to life was prematurely serious and severe." At fourteen he led a petition drive against a mandatory postdinner faculty-supervised study hall. Mass meetings erupted, then a four-day strike. He was suspended, then expelled, then reinstated.[8]

As reported years later by Abner Berry in *New Masses*, "In his father's newspaper . . . he defended the student strikers at Fisk University. In an adjoining column his father opposed the strikers and chided the opinions of his son. The same positions were taken when the Boston police went on strike. Young Ben held to his convictions and his father allowed him to express them in the news column." His rebelliousness was also shown by his style of driving. His sister recalls that he drove as close to whites as possible without hitting them. But since the family had a chauffeur, white pedestrians were for the most part spared this indignity. Although part of an elite, Davis was rebelling; like many youthful black rebellions, his actions had an antiwhite character from time to time.[9]

Davis's tenure at Morehouse was not entirely filled with din and tumult. Days before his election in 1943 to the New York City Council, the *New York Amsterdam News* published a striking recollection by Kay Burris of Spelman College about these halcyon days:

> I first knew Ben Davis, when as a mere strip of a girl I heard him play a concerto beautifully and expertly . . . on the occasion of a Morehouse Annual Glee Club and Orchestra concert . . . the music critics on the Atlanta daily papers wrote glowing comments. . . . I must have had a sort of congenital weakness for six-foot Morehouse men who played the violin beautifully or sang divinely. . . . [Davis was] not unlike Lenin, who once while listening to a playing of Beethoven's Sonata Appassionata remarked, almost tearfully, on the genius of man to create beauty in the arts, and turned suddenly to leave, with the comment, "beauty must wait for the few until we can win creative comforts for the many. . . . " Paderewski is not the only musician in history who made a great statesman.[10]

Davis's love for the violin and music was so abiding that the *Morehouse Maroon Tiger* subsequently reported that "a disagreement between Davis and the director of the orchestra contributed to the former's transfer to Amherst." Yet another informant suggests that he left Atlanta for Massachusetts because "he was very anxious to play football, but his mother—for fear someone would spoil the part in his hair or step on his corn—strictly refused." Whatever the case, Davis left the Jim Crow South for the allegedly different climate of the North.[11]

Davis was at Amherst from September 1922–June 1925; he was admitted as a sophomore. His transcript reveals good but not excellent grades: C in History of Religions, A in Music, C in Philosophy, B in Public Speaking. In his application, in addition to noting his "special attention" to debating and his attendance at Friendship Baptist Church in Atlanta, he writes that he is "interested in journalism and writing in general—my intention is to study law. . . . A very good friend of mine, Charles Houston, finished college here."[12]

Davis's militance was exhibited during his Amherst career as well. During one vacation in Atlanta he apparently forgot where he was: "I was arrested and manhandled by the brutal police because I sat in the 'white section' of the trolley car in order to give a pregnant Negro woman my seat. . . . I was wearing a black sweater with a purple 'A' on it." His father accompanied him to court, where Ben junior was not allowed to speak and Ben senior did all the talking. Davis was "furious" as the fine was paid: "If this could happen to me—the son of a so-called well-to-do Negro—what, indeed, would have been the fate of some Negro who had failed to get himself born into a 'well-to-do' family." Such experiences were indispensable in converting a member of one of Afro-America's elite families to a leader of a party that professed to speak for the downtrodden.[13]

But Davis found time for other pursuits in college. The six-foot, 230-pound Davis played left tackle, though he confessed, "[I] was not a great player." Even so he was named to the All-East football squad in 1925. Next to him at left end was Charles Drew, who Davis said helped him improve his skills. But so did Paul Robeson: "I first met Robeson during my summer vacation in 1923. . . . I sat at the feet of Paul and he used to take me out to a lot to teach me how to protect myself in a game. At that time it was pretty tough for a Negro to play football and if you didn't know how to take care of yourself you'd be messed up something awful." There was the infamous game with Princeton in 1924 where a rumor was floated that the Tigers were going to crucify Amherst's black players. At Palmer Stadium they were told, "We don't allow Negroes in here." But Amherst captain Jack Hill replied, "This man is one of our stars and if he doesn't play, we don't play." That was the end of that—but it was not the end of Davis's increasing anger at the scourge of racism.[14]

Despite the plaudits, Davis was not impressed with his own gridiron skills: "In my own case, for example, at Morehouse College . . . I couldn't even make the 4th scrub football team. Yet when I journeyed to Amherst College, the very next year . . . I suddenly became an 'ace' tackle—a 'towering pillar of strength' on the line. Now I never was much of a football player." This overly self-deprecating attitude may have allowed Davis to make his point that "reactionary 'race superiority' theories" should be thrown "into a cocked hat." The fact is that Davis was an extraordinary athlete, like his friend Robeson. He won the Georgia State Championship singles and doubles in tennis. In Harlem he belonged to the Cosmopolitan Tennis Club and officiated at the National Negro Tennis Championships, awarding prizes to winners. Abner Berry was not far from the mark when he commented, "Old tennis players still speak of his dazzling speed which terrified his court opponents." Davis's tennis skills were sharpened at Amherst. In short, his days there were so memorable that even in 1955, when his financial state was shaky, Davis still contributed to the alumni fund.[15]

Davis's days at Harvard Law School were not so idyllic: "I was never too keen on the law . . . I was much more enamored by the arts—music in particular. . . . My father, however, succeeded in persuading me to try the law." This ambivalence was reflected in his grades. During his 1925–28 tenure his highest grade was 72 in Civil Procedure; appropriately, his lowest was 55 in Property.¹⁶ Returning there thirty years later, he recalled Harvard's "revolutionary traditions" and observed: "Actually my first brush with the labor and radical movement came here . . . when I sat in on the lectures of the late William F. Thompson, who was defense counsel for the martyred Sacco and Vanzetti." Still, it was the prevailing racism in this bastion of legal conservatism that seemed to influence him deeply. Students were assigned to "law clubs" to get brief and trial work, but all seven Afro-American students were put together in one club while the others—Jew and Gentile, Catholic and Protestant, even Asians and Europeans—were mixed. Davis sought to raise this point with the eminent scholar Roscoe Pound:

> I walked into his dishevelled office. . . . He said he was sorry, that nothing could be done about it. . . . Pound spoke as if he was off in the clouds probably toying with some legalistic abstraction, too celestial to permit a momentary descension to a little thing like segregation. . . . This incident stood out in my mind throughout my 3 years at Harvard, and for a long time afterward. . . . The law school taught one thing and practiced another . . . all of us took a pledge not to enter a segregated law club.¹⁷

Years later when he was on the City Council, a *New York Amsterdam News* reporter detected that Davis was "somewhat moody as he discussed his experience at Harvard Law School."¹⁸

As often told, Davis's radicalism commenced in 1932 with his involvement in the Angelo Herndon case. While this is not false, the record shows that he was moving steadily to the Left even before his encounter with Herndon. Months after leaving law school, he was writing scorching articles in his father's paper on the two-party system; no doubt his father's difficulties with the GOP helped to deepen his disaffection. Yet his words seemed to presage his joining the Communist party. Just before his articles appeared the *Independent* had reprinted an article from the *Daily Worker*—perhaps due to the influence of the increasingly radicalized Davis scion.¹⁹

Although he is renowned as a political activist, Davis could just as well be known as a journalist for the hundreds of articles he wrote for the press during his career. After leaving Harvard Law he did not join a law firm or hang out his shingle—he continued working in the newspaper business. Just after graduation he set out his credo in an article published in the *Independent* entitled "The Folly of the Negro Press":

> Perhaps no group in the entire country has less esteem and respect for its own press than the Negro group. . . . in practically every competitive test in which he has not been victor, it has proclaimed in gay red headlines that the color of his skin defeated him . . . the average so-called editorial policy of the colored newspaper is petty and almost exclusively concerned with the topic of race prejudice. In modern times the Negro's problems are so interwoven with those of other groups that any attempt to deal with these problems solely from a Negro point of view is wholly inadequate and often misleading.

He went on to complain that "lynching and segregation" were virtually the exclusive concerns of the black press. What is arresting about this is what Davis himself might have subsequently termed the liquidation of the National Question or the denigration of the black press's prominent concern with racism. Still it does reveal Davis's groping toward a class perspective that was to characterize his tenure with the Communist party.[20]

After leaving law school Davis toiled "in the headquarters of the *Baltimore Afro-American*" and then for W. B. Ziff in Chicago. Ziff, who was not black, "grew wealthy through the Negro press"—or so said the *New York Age*.[21] His advertising agency charged a high commission but still helped the black press to boost income, a dire necessity since this institution depended on circulation for 80 percent of its income. Ziff was an admirer of Marcus Garvey and something of a military historian; "back to Africa" was one of his proposed remedies for African-Americans. Davis worked for a magazine insert that appeared in a number of black papers. But then another turning point in Davis's life arrived: "The firm proposed that I should be the front for the scheme" to start a black version of the Associated Press. "I wanted no part of it . . . I didn't relish seeing myself used to undermine the independence of the Negro press—for a mess of pottage. . . . I did not possess any deep political feeling or consciousness . . . I might as well, I reasoned, begin the practice of law. So I did in January of 1932."[22]

Yet this experience with Ziff was useful, if only for the star-crossed relationship Davis initiated with George Schuyler, the influential writer and godfather of black conservatives. Schuyler, who served as NAACP business manager at one time, joined the John Birch Society in the 1960s and became a staunch critic of Martin Luther King, Jr. He also backed Senator Joseph McCarthy. He edited the magazine insert that Davis worked on; it included book reviews, short stories, music reviews, and was a worthy addition to the papers it appeared in.[23] In a 1962 interview he recalled that Davis "succeeded me as the editor, although he knew nothing about editing, but he was a smart man, a very intelligent man . . . so he picked it up very fast. . . . it was one of the most enjoyable months I've spent because when Ben was not discussing Communism, he was a very jovial fellow." If his recollection is accurate, it too shows a pre-Herndon interest in socialism. Through the years Davis and Schuyler maintained a remarkable relationship—implacable Red and unyielding conservative. Neither minced words in public denunciation yet maintained a personal relationship. As Schuyler put it, "He's one of the few Communists I know that has a sense of humor. . . . Once in a while, we meet, and we'll have a couple of drams, a glass of something—I know where he stands and he knows where I stand, so no need of battling." Davis's engaging personal nature partially explains his enormous political success and the high esteem in which he was generally held in his community; on the other hand, Schuyler's view contrasts sharply with those who clashed with Davis in party battles.[24]

This kind of relationship was not limited just to Schuyler. Davis had the remarkable ability to maintain relationships with other ideological adversaries—particularly if they were African-American (many of those he clashed with in the party were not). Davis had known Walter White of the NAACP since his youth but later they were at swords' points. Yet even during the height of the Red Scare when a passing favorable reference to Davis could bring persecution, White in one of his last writings did not hesitate to praise his fellow Atlantan.[25] The fact is that Davis was difficult to isolate, despite his political affiliations, not just because of his personality but also due to his ramified network of associates. He graduated from Amherst, for example, with Dr. Montague Cobb (president of the National Medical Association), William Hastie, Mercer Cook (former U.S. Ambassador to Senegal), and other luminaries in the "largest number ever [of blacks] graduated at one time from Amherst."[26] Jack O'Dell, former top aide to Dr. King and aide to Jesse Jackson since the early 1980s, has termed Davis "impressive, charismatic."[27] At a memorial for Davis held five years after his death, Nation of Islam journal *Muhammad Speaks* called Davis "a man among men, a champion of the underdog, a leader who could follow and a follower who could lead." These favorable views of Davis contrast sharply with other opinions that have painted him as self-centered and egotistical. Possibly these latter appraisals can be explained by the fact that they come disproportionately from Communists and ex-Communists, many of whom were white in a racist society; certainly in the midst of party battles he could be particularly unyielding and difficult. In these struggles, however, Davis was reflecting the mood of the Communist party at that time.[28]

Part of the admiration and fascination for Davis was sparked by the knowledge that he had the skills and background that could have taken him down a less onerous path. This viewpoint was mirrored in the words of J. Pius Barbour: "Raised in luxury with Packards, servants, brick homes. . . . Every seduction has been offered him to 'Take it Easy' . . . Ben Davis is a burning and shining light in the day of 'Cadillac leadership.' He takes his place with the saints of old who went to jail for their opinions . . . a quiet studious boy who turned a deaf ear to the call of luxurious living: who took serious what he heard his pastor . . . preach."[29] Davis did not become wealthy from being a professional revolutionary; in reality, toward the end of his life he was quite poor. This was quite a switch from his early days when he wore a derby, wielded a cane, and was draped in tailor-made clothes.

Paul Robeson, Jr., has described Davis's late-1940s Harlem apartment on 126th Street as "small . . . adequate for one person."[30] This respect for Davis's chosen asceticism, which tended to transcend politics, was reflected during his 1963 visit to Atlanta after an absence of seventeen years; his effort to avoid friends and keep them from being tainted by the red brush was noticeable: "[he] went out of his way to avoid having his friends feel embarassed in being seen talking to him, and says he understands their feelings or positions."³¹

It is unquestionable that Davis's experiences with Jim Crow in Georgia were a formative experience for Davis. Even after moving north, he maintained an abiding interest in his home state and Jim Crow generally. To ascertain how a member of the black elite could become a black revolutionary, one need look no further than Jim Crow Georgia.

3

The Road to the Communist Party

Returning to Atlanta from the comparatively comfortable racial climes of Chicago and Massachusetts took courage. In 1932 Atlanta was not too busy to hate. It was a mean town with a racist edge made sharper by a spreading economic depression. Communist journalist Joseph North was stunned by what he observed: "Atlanta, Georgia, is the only city where I ever saw cats and human beings roam the main streets searching for food. . . . I saw white farmers . . . begging for a nickel for something to eat. . . . I saw a chain-gang."[1] John Hammond Moore has written effectively about how these conditions were a breeding ground for "American Fascists and Order of Black Shirts."[2] Clarence Bacote saw yet another angle when he described this era as the "'Dark Ages' as far as Negro political participation in Atlanta is concerned. Registration reached an all-time low. Denied the right to vote in the primaries, the Negro voter was more or less a political outcast."[3]

This oppression weighed keenly on Ben Davis. When he left to go away to school, his father was a kingmaker; when he returned his father was by comparison a political pauper. The African-American community was in limbo—rejected by the GOP and not yet entwined with the Democrats. Objective forces were pushing Ben Davis, Jr., to the Left. The case of Angelo Herndon was an almost perfectly suited vehicle for the further radicalizing of Ben Davis.

One contemporary observer distilled the importance of this case: "There probably isn't a Negro in the United States who is not familiar with the case of Angelo Herndon."[4] Like Scottsboro, this case not only struck massive blows against southern racism but popularized the role of the Communist party as well. This was probably not the intention of Ben Davis when he took an office in the Odd Fellows building in Atlanta. At the time there were few black attorneys in Georgia. One of Davis's sponsors for the bar was A. T. Walden, an associate of his father and an inspiration for Vernon Jordan and a later generation of civil rights lawyers. Davis met his law partner—John Geer—when they opposed each other in court: "I admired in Geer his determination, his free and independent thinking . . . I [handled] matters of civil rights and corporation law and he negligence and insurance cases." Their practice proceeded fairly well—until Herndon entered their lives, which was a setback that soared beyond them: "after I had participated in the Herndon case . . . no Negro passed the Georgia bar for several years."[5]

Herndon, a young Communist organizer, ran afoul of the authorities when he organized a militant demonstration demanding relief for the poor. He was convicted under a slave insurrection statute and received a sentence of twenty years on a chain gang. An aggressive struggle took the case to the U.S. Supreme Court and won his freedom. The free speech implications of the case were enormous; involved was not just the demonstration but the allegedly seditious literature utilized by the defendant. Dorothy Healey, a one-time Red leader, in an interview fifty years later still grasped the issue: "The selling of these pamphlets, the selling of literature generally, was one of the high points of the thirties, the recognition of the importance of material that went beyond what the speaker, the agitator could do."[6]

Before he accepted this case, Davis was perceived as an up and coming member of the "black Bourgeoisie." Puffing on a pipe from time to time, nattily dressed, not unappealing to women, he seemed to be on a swift track to prosperity. Just before Herndon entered his life "the Republican party offered me a highly lucrative campaign tour in the Mid-West and East in behalf of the Herbert Hoover presidential ticket. . . . I would be either politically seduced with carrots or beaten." But Davis's conscience had moved beyond the realm of the GOP.[7]

It was the fiery African-American attorney William Patterson, leader of the International Labor Defense—the New York-based organization fighting racist and political repression—who brought Davis into the case. Typically the ILD tried to employ black lawyers. After Herndon was arrested, Patterson gave a white lawyer eight hundred dollars to take the case but the latter objected to Davis serving as cocounsel. He was dismissed and Davis, an inexperienced trial lawyer, took over.[8]

In a sense Davis accepted this awesome responsibility by default. There were few other lawyers who would take the case or would argue it in the political manner both Herndon and Patterson desired. Roger Baldwin of the American Civil Liberties Union told George Haynes of the Federal Council of Churches that even the usually reliable A. T. Walden backed down: " . . . they all refused to raise the issue of the exclusion of Negroes from the jury."[9] The key parties—Herndon, Davis, and Patterson—saw this case as not just an opportunity to free one defendant, though that was the top priority; they also saw it as an opportunity to both expose and educate the people about racism. Exposing Jim Crow juries, an injustice that irked and vexed a generation of blacks, would educate, but winning on this issue would deeply influence the politics of the Deep South and thereby the nation by eroding the bone and sinews of racism.[10]

The diminutive, light-skinned Herndon outlined the drama of the trial in his popular memoir of the 1930s. He "rotted" for three months in jail before the trial, then Davis and Geer got a habeas writ challenging the validity of the indictment on the grounds of vagueness, barring blacks, and so on. It was denied. Finally on 16 January 1933, a scant year after Davis's return to Georgia, the trial began.[11]

The Georgia authorities were not accustomed to the kind of militance that Herndon and his colleagues had displayed. In June 1932 the Fulton County courthouse was surrounded by hundreds of demonstrators. Blacks and whites were demanding relief from the economic depression. Ultimately Herndon was arrested at the courthouse, though this was not his first encounter with the authorities over relief. As soon as he heard of Herndon's arrest, Davis visited him in jail. His jailers would not accept bail money from ILD, so Davis used his "influence and high standing among the leading people of his race" to solve this question, getting two black pharmacists to put up the money. His father's contacts had proved helpful once more.[12]

Davis was acerbic about presiding judge Lee Wyatt. He was "ignorant and crude, breathed fire and brimstone from his nostrils, steeped in Klan hatred for Negroes, coarse and vicious. He used the law with respect to Negroes like a butcher wielded a knife to kill a lamb." As for prosecutor John Hudson, he "was like a character out of a caricature. . . . His face had the florid appearance of an alcoholic . . . small pig-shaped eyes . . . a thin metallic voice."[13]

When the trial began, Davis moved immediately to have the case dismissed: "But like the fellow with a royal flush against the chap with the gun—the latter won."[14] As Herndon put it, "The judge glowered at the Negro attorney who dared challenge white justice. But young Mr. Davis could not be put out of face by any display of white superiority. Unafraid and with the dignity of a man who knows his worth, he fought both judge and prosecutor with great energy." When Davis was overruled after objecting to the use of racist epithets, "he was besides himself with rage." Herndon continued:

> This is not only a trial of Angelo Herndon [said the prosecution] but of Lenin, Stalin, Trotsky, and Kerensky and every white person who believes that black and white should unite for the purpose of setting up a nigger Soviet Republic in the black Belt. . . . My defense attorney, Mr. Davis, knew that he was fighting a losing battle. But he nevertheless jumped to the attack. [He] moved for a prima facie case in my favor because the state had admitted that there were no names of Negroes in the Grand Jury box from which the Grand Jury that indicted me was drawn, and because the state did not think it necessary to offer any evidence that Negroes were not excluded from the jury. . . . [Davis was] under a great mental and emotional strain. . . . He was tense and his voice shook.[15]

The *New York Times* did not ignore this drama. They quoted Davis, "himself a Negro," as saying that a book used to convict his client "should have been written in the blood of Negroes who were burned at the stake by mobs. I say lynching is insurrection. The only offense Herndon committed

was that he asked for bread for children—his only crime is his color
. . . . You can't kill a man because of the books he reads."[16]

But the prosecution got away with asking questions like, "Would you want a nigger to marry your daughter?" There was a ferocious battle going on between Davis and the prosecution as journalists and a fascinated audience watched. The young lawyer's closing "provoked a hostile reaction from whites in the packed courtroom. Several members of the jury became visibly angry. Three of them turned their backs on him as he paced near the jury box . . . a spectator fainted."[17] His argument, however, did not impress *Time* magazine. Davis, they said, "made no things easier for his client" by talking about the subversiveness of lynching; but the death sentence staring his client in the face for decidedly nonviolent acts no doubt stiffened Davis's resolve.[18]

The ripples from this case were ever-widening. But the most important result for Davis was that he was recruited to the Communist party during the course of the trial, though it is apparent that his experience with racism and the experience of his father with the two-party system had facilitated his recruitment. Patterson felt that Herndon "was an effective political mentor to Ben."[19] In his memoir Davis observed, "It was arranged that I should attend a few sessions of a Communist branch meeting . . . headed by a sixty year old Negro iron worker . . . at an Atlanta foundry. . . . 10 members were present—3 white and seven Negro. . . . I liked these experiences so well that I never permitted a week to pass that I did not attend a meeting. . . . I entered the trial as his lawyer, but ended it as his Communist comrade."[20]

Ben Davis was already a celebrity in his community because of his father. After the trial he stood even larger because of the significance of the Herndon case. Charles Martin has suggested that due to the case "many Black Atlantans . . . became more outspoken and increasingly challenged racial discrimination in the city."[21] Perhaps one can draw a straight line from this case to Atlanta's role as the capital of the civil rights movement. The case was lost at trial and won on appeal, which effectively destroyed, at least temporarily, the insurrection laws as a tool of state repression. Davis's tactic of calling qualified blacks in the voir dire process and asking if they ever served on a jury presaged the crucial 1935 Supreme Court opinion in the Scottsboro Nine case, *Norris v. Alabama*.[22]

Naturally, the *Daily Worker*—the official organ of the Communist party—was both prescient and enthusiastic about the case and their new recruit. Weeks before the trial they told their readers that for the "first time . . . the question of exclusion of Negroes from juries is being raised in Georgia."[23] Days before the trial they announced that Davis's tactic had already produced fruit, for in a larceny case "for the first time since 1872, two Negroes were called to serve on a trial jury."[24] This premature integration flowed into the movement. In May 1933, after the trial, the *Daily Worker* reported: "for the first time in the history of the city a gathering of Negro and white workers took place with absolutely no segregation."²⁵ Leading Communist Otto Hall agreed about the significance of the case, "one of the most important . . . in the history of our movement." Davis and Geer "astounded every one by the way they bearded the bourbon lion in his den. . . . Never in the memory of any Negro in that courtroom had any lawyer attempted to stop white policemen and prosecutors from referring to their clients as 'niggers' and 'darkies.' [During the trial] the courtroom was crowded. . . . Jim Crow laws were broken for the first time when Negro and white workers occupied the same benches. The court room became a political forum."²⁶ Political and economic goals were important for blacks but the social goal of simple dignity—not being addressed as "boy," not being called by one's first name by unfamiliar white strangers and even youths—was also important.

The *New York Amsterdam News* echoed this line on 25 January 1933: "All of these years white juries in the South have been convicting colored people on the most flimsy evidence imaginable . . . yet it remained for the Communists to be the first to raise this." The victory of the Reds in the Euel Lee case in Maryland was compared with Davis's heroism: "The spotlight Communists have turned upon the South's crimes is a service to humanity in general and the Negro in particular." On 4 March 1933 the *St. Louis Argus* added, "[Davis] enjoys a splendid reputation, both because of his family connections and of his own acquisition." George Schuyler was pointed in his praise. His employer, the *Pittsburgh Courier*, saluted the "masterly plea" of Davis on behalf of his client.²⁷ Davis and the Communist party attained a more positive image among blacks as defenders of the race as a result of the Herndon case.²⁷

This case represented more than publicity for Davis. A movement arose whose impact continued to influence Atlanta for years to come. For example, after the conviction, a conference of one thousand people was held in the Odd Fellows auditorium: Davis wrote, "It was perhaps the first conference of its type ever held in Atlanta. . . . from the conference there arose a movement. All over the city among the Negro people in particular various types of action took place. Churches passed resolutions; ministers preached sermons. . . . Business people joined in . . . the defense campaign snowballed . . . above all the organized labor movement took up the case . . . the campaign was taking on a very significant, deep going and prophetic character." ²⁸

Right away, on 20 January 1933, the *Daily Worker* noticed that "in Atlanta many Negro liberals and intellectuals already have come forward with promises of support and a pledge to raise any amount of bail necessary to get Herndon out of jail pending the appeal." The *Atlanta World*, on 31 January, noticed a movement also, pointing out that the "27 club . . . composed of the most representative and successful Negro leaders in Atlanta," blasted the frame-up of Herndon at length. Davis, said the *Daily Worker*, "addressed the members on the significance of the case and the necessity for all Negroes to join the fight of the white and Negro workers to smash the sentence." Further, "hundreds of protests are pouring in." Later, when "100 prominent Atlantans" assembled for a "testimonial dinner in honor of W. A. Scott," owner of the *World*, the presence of a "brilliant young attorney" was noted—Ben Davis. When Thurgood Marshall, Charles Houston, Arthur Garfield Hays, Morris Ernst, Lester Granger, and others joined the defense committee, any suspicion of the "redness" of the committee could be assuaged by the presence of the well-connected Davis.[29]

Roger Baldwin of the ACLU contacted Georgia power-broker Will Alexander to check out the bona fides of Davis before committing his support to Herndon. Alexander supplied incorrect facts: "according to my information he did not finish" at Harvard, said the Atlantan. Baldwin made the mistake of sending Alexander's dismissive note to Patterson and received a decided rebuff to his questioning of Davis's skill. Suitably chastened, Baldwin proved helpful to Herndon.[30]

The breadth of the movement defending Herndon was significant. The participation of Socialist party activists, who had been known for avoidance of projects led by Communists, was remarkable. Norman Thomas was involved in this case. One ILD press release in 1935 recorded the participation in a meeting on Herndon of Sidney Hook, Ashley Totten of the Brotherhood of Sleeping Car Porters, and Lester Granger of the Urban League. This was a living example of a "united front" or "popular front," a principal though often urealized objective of Communists in the 1930s. This effort to bring together Communists and non-Communists in a "front" for a common goal became formal policy among U.S. Communists in 1935.[31]

After Herndon was convicted in early 1933 and Davis joined the Communist party, a whirlwind of activity arose on behalf of Herndon. Davis's efforts—leading a crowd of thousands in singing the "Internationale" in Harlem's Rockland Palace in August 1934, leading a torchlight parade of fifteen thousand through the Bronx—aided the party's image in New York. Soon Communist leader James Ford was reporting proudly, "Every movement in Harlem has Communists in it or has Communist Negroes as leaders. . . . Comrade Ben Davis has taken a leading part in this movement and he is becoming a helpful leader among the people of Harlem."[32]

Not only did the Herndon case give a boost to the united front, but it aided in building the ranks of the Communist-led ILD and the party itself. Not coincidentally, ILD opened an Atlanta office in January 1933. When "for the first time in the history of [Atlanta] a gathering of Negro and white workers took place with absolutely no segregation," it was sponsored by ILD at the Royal Theater.[33] By September 1933 their office in Atlanta was being raided by the authorities. Davis nemesis and Atlanta's rabidly anti-Communist prosecutor, John Hudson, threatened to indict all ILD members in the state on charges of "inciting for insurrection."[34]

But by mid-1934 the *Daily Worker* was confident: "During the last year the Communist party has been growing stronger and more powerful in Georgia. . . . [ILD has] also grown. . . . This scared the bosses and the so-called old guard of the state." A. W. Morrison, a white attorney, was accused of turning over party and ILD names to the police, who then raided, beating and slugging as they went.35 But the comrades trudged on. Early in 1936 their correspondent was reporting on a party meeting in Atlanta. Afterwards both black and white members entered a "street car. . . . We make, of course, no sign of recognition. I take my seat with spirits dampened. Only a short time ago we had sat side by side as equals. Now they sit in the rear of the car." The perceived "Communist threat" in Atlanta sparked surreptitious activity and forced Davis to leave his home state.36

The increase in party membership also sparked a surge of hostility against Davis and other progressive forces. Veteran black Communist Harry Haywood captured the tension of the times in his memoir:

> [Davis] had [an] office on the fifth floor of the Odd Fellows building. He spoke about the threats against him by the authorities and the Ku Klux Klan. . . . He showed me a hole in the door between his office and an adjoining room . . . [he had] noticed a kind of tube sticking out of the hole in the door . . . it was the barrel of an empty revolver which was set up against the door. He pulled a paper out of the barrel and read the message: "The Ku Klux Klan rides again. Georgia is no place for bad niggers and red communists. Next time we'll shoot." [Later] a whole gang was waiting for him. . . . He was backed up against the wall, into a corner. No one touched him, but they shouted at him calling him a nigger son-of-a bitch, threatening to get him or run him out of town. . . . I was worried about Ben Davis, about his safety. . . . I had sized him up as an up-and-coming young communist, with great leadership potential.37

Hosea Hudson, a black Communist who knew Davis, had similar memories: "a big pastor named Reverend Martin . . . took some of his deacons [to court]. . . . They was afraid that someone was going to try to lynch Ben . . . he and two-three of his deacons, they put on they overalls and they pistols in they pockets, and they went in and sit in the courthouse. Ben didn't know it. Nobody didn't know it. . . . When Ben would leave the courthouse, they'd leave, follow him, stay some distance, see that nothing happen to him."35

This atmosphere was captured by Erskine Caldwell. In *New Masses* he referred to "a reign of mob rule" in Georgia and the fact that "no arrests have been made" despite lynchings and various mutilations: "the daily papers of the state have failed to report the actions of the mob. . . . No local correspondent for the dailies can be found who have made reports, perhaps because of a rule in the book of instructions sent to local correspondents by the daily newspapers of Georgia: 'If a white man is murdered, telegraph it in; if a Negro is murdered, mail it in.'"39

Davis also commented on the unfriendly environment. One day as he left the courtroom he was told, "'Watch yourself, or we'll string you up.' ... Another had an open knife in his hand. ... There were seven or eight of these ruffians."[40] A typical day at court, these events exposed the naive NAACP-inspired notion of reliance on the courts to vindicate rights. A cross was burned at the home of a key organizer for the Herndon case. Later there was an attempt to frame Davis and charge him with attempting to smuggle letters from Herndon past the prison censors. The racist authorities seemed to take particular umbrage at this educated black lawyer whose very existence wiped out simpleminded notions of white supremacy and black inferiority. As one jailer was reputed to have told Herndon, "As long as that nigger lawyer keeps coming down here swelling your head you're going to stay in solitary."[41]

Certainly this was the import of Davis's noted meeting with Governor Eugene Talmadge, who told him: "Ben you've been sent up 'Nawth' [sic] to school. I know all about it. You got too much education to love your own state."[42] Black militants with higher education were perceived as particularly dangerous. The ever-sober *New York Times* even managed to note this phenomenon. They lamented that in present-day Georgia even Thomas Jefferson might be under arrest for his beliefs. They regretted the "tendency of prosecuting officers to lose sight of the inherent rights of persons charged with or suspected of communistic beliefs." Thus in November 1934 under arrest were union leaders, attorneys, and Nathan Yagol, "a graduate student ... [and] Jew ... the student body as well as all professors, under whom Yagol have studied [at Emory] came to his aid."[43] C. Vann Woodward, a noted writer, got caught up in this turmoil and eventually felt compelled to leave the state.[44] The *Chicago Defender* noticed that even moderates were touched, thus underlining the notion of the indivisibility of civil liberties: "flying squadrons of special police in Atlanta raided the Southern offices of the Urban League in a vain hunt for 'Communist literature.'"[45] A Red Scare was being used to squash any aspect of Black Liberation in a dramatic precursor of what was to come. During raids in June 1934 police asked those swept up "if they knew Ben Davis ... one of 'them Reds.'"[46] The crackdown continued, with the *Atlanta Constitution* on 24 November 1935 urging that "every effort should be exercised to round up this group of radicals."

Davis sensed the historical moment. He observed that after the trial, "the fat was in the fire. The whole situation changed for me. Where formerly, I had received the benign cooperation and tolerance of the city's ruling circles, I now was regarded with suspicion at best, and as a 'Rooshan'-inspired Bolshevik at worst."[47] He was right. In any event, as the leftist writer Don West put it, "A Negro lawyer in Atlanta has about as much chances for success as the proverbial snowball in hell."[48] The burden of being black was one thing, but the red coloration tended to magnify the pain. Yet the Communists had tapped into something in Atlanta, for this city continued for some time to be the heart of Communist operations in the Deep South; later—not coincidentally—it was the center of the civil rights movement. But Davis, already a public figure, took on a notorious reputation after Herndon's conviction, which numbered his days in Atlanta.

Davis's prominent role in the Atlanta Six case, in 1933–34, which involved a group of black and nonblack activists who were framed on charges akin to Herndon's, also was viewed with a jaundiced eye: as he tells it, "When I spoke up as representing the white women, one could have heard a mouse walking on cotton. The court gulped and all eyes were agog. . . . The judge, thrown into utter confusion by this 'daring challenge' to white supremacy sought to ignore me altogether and talk to the women." The sixth Amendment guarantee of right to counsel apparently was revocable. "A few days later, I received a call from an attorney advising me that disbarment proceedings were being considered against me. . . . I could not serve in this capacity without running afoul of the laws restricting Negroes and whites to segregated relationships."[49]

Davis's experience with Jim Crow Georgia was becoming more difficult, as it was for the black community as a whole. Police brutality was nothing new in Atlanta but even the jaded were moved when Glover Davis, a blind black man, was killed by the police. His funeral in September 1933 turned into a mass antiracism demonstration. The church in which it was held only could seat a thousand but the crowd estimate ranged as high as eight thousand. Davis spoke at the rally and later recalled the gripping scene: "Along the streets in the block surrounding the church, police were stationed in battle formation. Guns and tear gas as equipment were prominently displayed . . . mounted guns manned by cops. . . . The corpse lay in front of the pulpit and sobs mingled with indignant protest. Police had roped off the streets. . . . Inside the church the atmosphere was redolent with expectancy. Police threatened to break up the meeting at the first sign of a speech." So the pastor dove right in and said, "God, give us Negro and white men who are not afraid to fight police brutality. Bind the black and white people of this South . . . give us the courage to fight back." Davis termed this the "first revolutionary prayer."[50] The *Daily Worker* was blunt: "The tremendous demonstration at this funeral . . . has shaken the officials and white ruling class of Atlanta."[51]

When Davis joined the CP in early 1933, his collective had to decide if he would be more effective in New York than in Georgia. They worried that it was risky to keep such a valuable comrade—who unlike many Communists in Georgia had visible and open Communist affiliations—so close to cutthroats. Davis agreed with them. So when at the early 1934 National Executive Board meeting of the League of Struggle for Negro Rights—an organization within the Communist party's orbit—Maude White left as editor of their allied journal, *The Harlem Liberator*, Davis replaced her. At that time contributing editors included such Red stalwarts as James Ford, Louise Patterson, Ted Bassett, Cyril Briggs, James Allen, and Henri Barbusse.[52]

Davis did not waste any time utilizing his contacts for the Left. At a June 1934 banquet for Davis at the Lido Hall, Countee Cullen, his old Harvard classmate, was the honored guest. Davis's rise in the Left was meteoric, which was not difficult for a talented black in a movement that had not reached the outer limit of its potential. Soon he was being seen in the company of Ford, Earl Browder, Robert Minor, Israel Amter, and other Communist leaders.[53]

According to Davis, the *Liberator* had a "devoted staff of 1/2 dozen—Negro and white. . . . We were at it day and night, often from 7 in the morning until 1 or 2 a.m." Wages were at best ten dollars per week, a meager sum even then, and sometimes nothing. Such was to be Davis's economic fate until he died in 1964—his city council years nothwithstanding. Commenting on the prevalent notion that the Soviet Union globally controlled Communists and leftist forces, he added, "I remember once that I had to borrow a pair of pants to attend a benefit affair to make a collection speech for the *Liberator*. If there was any 'Moscow gold' around, none of it came our way." But there was another trend manifested as Paul Robeson "would send a few pounds to keep us going."[54]

The party knew they had won a prize by recruiting Davis and they moved quickly to take advantage of this simple fact, although Davis's new working conditions were no prize. The *Daily Worker* described the conditions under which he toiled: "You walk up two flights of rickety narrow wooden steps, traverse a large room that once served as a table loft, enter a smaller office at the rear and there you will find [Davis] editor, business manager, advertising chief and general factotum of the *Negro Liberator*. For ten and twelve hours a day . . . he works like a Trojan." They were aware of his ability to attract others to the party's banner, noting in passing that he "has boosted the circulation from four to six thousand and has managed to keep it fairly regular as a semi-monthly." Davis had plans to make it a daily with a fundraiser at the Savoy: "The popularity of Ben Davis throughout the city as well as in Harlem proper is [attested] by the number of theatre stars who have volunteered to give him a hand." But just in case some might think that Davis and the party were overly impressed by those of a certain class background, the *Daily Worker* reporter added quickly that Davis had had a "complete split with his reformist father and childhood associations"; his father had recently written a "four-column story" that Davis "demolished with acumen and great glee."[55]

Davis's arrival at the *Liberator* was deemed by the party as an event of political importance. He was treated not like some new raw recruit but was quickly granted access to higher party circles. Simultaneously an effort was made to bolster the *Liberator*. A plan was launched to expand the paper from eight to twelve pages with a circulation of twenty-five thousand and two thousand paid subscriptions. Allied organizations like the International Workers Order urged that its branches raise funds. Davis himself was proud of his journal despite the difficulties of production. By June 1934 the *Harlem Liberator* became the *Negro Liberator*. Since the journal was designed to win support for the program of the League of Struggle for Negro Rights, becoming a weekly or daily was an essential way to achieve this goal.[56]

This journal's future was to be uncertain, perhaps because of the positions they took. Even before Davis's arrival his father was being referred to in their pages as "leader of the treacherous Negro petty bourgeoisie" and attacked for his "treacherous sellout to lily whites."[57] After Davis came it seemed that the party wanted to be sure that the younger Davis was far different than his father. After one particularly harsh attack by Davis junior the *Harlem Liberator* on 3 February 1934 noted, "Mr. Davis refused to retract his statement even after it was verified that the resolution in question had been introduced by his father. . . ." This approach was not without consequence. The International Workers' Order found that "only a few branches . . . responded" to their appeal for the journal.[58] On 11 August 1935 the *Negro Liberator* reported, "results show that the drive for new readers of the 'Liberator' is seriously lagging." Soon thereafter the journal was moribund, due in part to sectarian attacks on figures like Ben Davis, Sr.—a practice shared, ironically, by Ben Davis, Jr.[59]

The *Liberator* and the *Daily Worker* were not the only Leftist media organs that Davis toiled for after moving north. In the mid-1930s he became assistant editor, then later headed the Crusader News Agency. This unheralded entity was founded in 1919 by Cyril Briggs after he resigned from the *New York Amsterdam News*. It was run successively by Richard B. Moore, Elizabeth Lawson, Maude White, and Davis. Richard Wright, Langston Hughes, and Jacques Roumain were just a few of the talented writers who wrote for the agency. They provided copy for more than 250 black newspapers in the United States, which had a combined circulation of 3.5 million. The CNA helped to shape the leftist tilt of the black press and at the same time reflected the fact that Jim Crow had in effect pushed blacks to the Left. That is to say, particularly before the onset of the Red Scare and McCarthyism, atrocious racist attitudes, combined with horrible economic conditions, facilitated Communist inroads within the African-American community. This situation was particularly true in Harlem, and, as the CNA demonstrated, its influence spread to the rest of the nation. Certainly the party was well aware of CNA's importance; on 28 October 1938 the *Daily Worker* reported, "If today it can be said . . . that the Negro Press is vigorously anti-fascist . . . it is owing in large measure to the work of a Negro news service of which very little is known in white labor or progressive circles . . . the oldest Negro News Service in the country and one of the three leading news agencies in its field today. . . ."[60] The CNA had worldwide circulation and was particularly popular in India, Jamaica, and Trinidad.

This Harlem-based service provided free copy and was often without funds as a result. But penury was becoming common for Davis and he worked with the service until its demise during World War II.

Still, it was at the *Daily Worker* that Davis made his mark over time. Looking back in 1943 he observed that this was where he received his basic training in the theory and practice of the party.[61] A black journalist working at a nonblack-owned paper was unusual during the 1930s (not to mention nowadays), leaving an impression on African-Americans. In 1940 only one of the many New York dailies had a black on staff, according to CNA, and this was Ted Poston, a stringer for the *New York Post*.[62] On the other hand, a quite talented group was with the *Daily Worker* when Davis came on board. Erskine Caldwell, Harold Clurman, Malcolm Cowley, James Farrell, Waldo Frank, Josephine Herbst, Langston Hughes, Matthew Josephson, Corliss Lamont, Albert Maltz, Clifford Odets, Loren Miller, William Gropper, Hugo Gellert, Margaret Bourke-White, Granville Hicks, Harvey O'Connor, Romain Rolland, Lincoln Steffens, and Meridel Le Seuer were among the contributors to this self-proclaimed "newspaper for the entire family."[63] But of all of the literary lights at the paper then, Davis had the added advantage of direct contacts with an overwhelmingly working-class black community.

Davis's earliest responsibility with the paper was heading the Harlem bureau in 1936. By 1939 he was vice-president of the company that controlled the paper and held one of the three major shares. Ultimately he served as secretary-treasurer and president. By 1938 he was associate editor of the paper itself. His political responsibilities with the National Negro Congress and allied groups provided him with the contacts to build the paper's constituency in Harlem. When the budding novelist Richard Wright joined him in Harlem in 1937, he could concentrate more on organizing and less on writing. It also freed him to launch a regular column, initially titled "Lift Every Voice." Shortly before this, Davis's prominence in the party was underscored when the paper featured him, along with William Z. Foster (party chairman) and Clarence Hathaway (*Daily Worker* editor-in-chief), as a leading columnist. Conditions at the paper were not as unruffled as the accompanying posed photograph indicates, however. It was being harassed by officious interlopers, hit with libel suits, and their sister paper, the *Southern Worker*, was being published in underground conditions. But Davis was becoming accustomed to these problems as part of the lot of a Communist attempting to make the revolution.[64]

The onerous conditions of the Great Depression of the 1930s and the growing pains that afflicted the Communist party no doubt helped to make Davis's relations with his family and his class more troubled, as was reflected in his writings in the *Daily Worker* and the various versions of the *Liberator*. Strain developed in his relationship with his father, who felt that he was throwing away his life and wasting his education by working as a full-time

Communist operative. Indeed, it was striking that a self-proclaimed party of the working class would promote so vigorously a refugee from the black elite; it was similarly striking that Davis would make such a vigorous effort to distance himself from his origins, going so far as to criticize his father stridently.[65]

It is easy to speculate that the then-prevailing Communist practice of intermittent sharp attacks on the kind of leadership represented by the NAACP felt comfortable for a budding radical emerging from the middle class himself. Unquestionably Davis took easily to this line of attack. In a commentary on James Weldon Johnson in late 1934 he blasted the "doctrine of Negro reformism . . . [which] contains no solution . . . the old claptrap. . . . ." Johnson, said Davis, "is a 'cultured' spokesman of the Negro upper class, as well as the ambassador of the white ruling class of America to the Negro masses . . . replete with confusion. . . . "[66] This was only the beginning. Later he gave the "Order of the Bandanna" to the "most prominent Negro misleaders. . . . The insignia of the new order will be a large bandanna handkerchief which the members may on occasion use to wipe away their crocodile tears over the suffering and oppression of the Negro masses. The pass-word by which fellow members may immediately recognize one another is 'Me too, boss' . . . The list we have compiled is, we admit at the outset, far from complete, of uncle Toms there seems to be no limit. . . . "[67] In this so-called hall of shame were R. R. Moton, Thurgood Marshall, William Pickens, Johnson, Schuyler, Frank Crosswaith, even Charles Houston.

The *Liberator* juxtaposed this approach with what they termed the "New Type of Negro Intellectual"—that is, Davis. He is "afraid of nothing. . . . He weighs over 250 pounds; he is a powerful Titan of a man. . . . Ten years ago he might have joined the NAACP."[68] Davis was diverting consciously from the path of his father by his own admission.

There were inherent contradictions in Davis's and the party's view at that time: it could be seen as sectarian and ultra Leftist, to use Marxist jargon. In other words, it would not bring potential allies into an alliance but would drive them into the arms of a common foe. Some of those being condemned—like Houston—were part of the alliance defending Herndon and Scottsboro.

Though the rhetoric in the *Liberator* flowed against Houston, the effort to build an alliance in practice was advancing. Davis was in frequent contact with Roger Baldwin. He appeared at rallies about Herndon with Walter White and Stephen Wise, which showed that Houston and others could work with the forces who were attacking them.[69]

This practical trend during the 1930s was motivated in part by the fact that Herndon still had to be rescued and allies were needed. Mid-1933 found Davis at the Georgia Supreme Court. His memoir was blunt: "I lectured the court speaking with an attitude that they were very undeveloped and confused students. They watched me in utter contempt." The court reporter at the trial "had expunged from the record . . . prejudicial remarks. . . . I called these shocking omissions and tampering to the attention of the prosecution and the court." After his argument, Chief Justice Richard Russell (father of the senator) warned him to stay away from such cases: "It was another aspect of the 'gentle' pressure which had been gratuitously applied to me since I had been in this case."[70] Even the *New York Times* on 2 May 1937 had to concede that there were some curious aspects to this case: "most Atlanta lawyers . . . felt too that there was something ironic in that Herndon was sentenced to prison for possessing communistic propaganda, and that in that same year the state of Georgia printed on its official ballot the names of [CP] candidates. . . . They could not see Herndon as thereby more subversive than the state itself."[72]

Charles Houston, Davis's old friend from Amherst and Harvard Law School, presented the case of Herndon before the Supreme Court. Davis contended that his friend's brilliant legal argument, no matter how compelling, was not the decisive element. It was this approach that helped to separate Davis from Houston and other friends in the NAACP. Herndon was able to escape his conviction under a slave insurrection statute and a twenty-year chain gang sentence, with Davis maintaining stoutly that a mass struggle was responsible. His inability to convince his friends in the NAACP of this opinion accounts in part for his attacks on them.[71]

But it was not just the NAACP that Davis and the party sharply criticized. After he was freed, Herndon's ties with the party and Davis were not very good. In 1944 the party denied that Herndon was part of their ranks. In 1948 he was called to testify against black Communist leader Claudia Jones but he refused to cooperate. On 8 May 1954 the *Pittsburgh Courier* reported that Herndon, "alias Gene Braxton [was] nabbed in Chicago for allegedly accepting $25,000 from five prospective buyers of the same six-flat building."[72]

But the importance of the Herndon case extended beyond the defendant. With the Scottsboro Nine case it launched the Communists into a new relationship with African-Americans. Emblematic of this new relationship was Ben Davis. Because of the atrocious racism visited upon African-Americans, U.S. rulers had virtually conceded this group to the Left. This was to be the case until the post–World War II effort by elites to reclaim this community by diminishing Jim Crow—a concession that ironically reflected their need of new allies. An essential aspect of this entire development was the effort by all sides—Communists and anti-communists alike—to influence the NAACP. Though Davis knew well Walter White, Charles Houston, William Hastie, Thurgood Marshall, and other association leaders, his periodic assaults on them were not helpful when political conditions began to change in the 1950s. Yet it was not easy for Davis to contemplate the vagaries of the future when he was in the midst of trying to first save Angelo Herndon, then the Scottsboro Nine.

"They Shall Not Die"

The Scottsboro Nine has been the subject of numerous written accounts and films. The story of nine African-American males accused of raping a white woman easily captured the public imagination. The ire roused by the Communist party's conflict with the NAACP and certain other liberal forces continues to this day to raise sparks; some have suggested that the Reds used the defendants for their own narrow purposes, misappropriated funds, and improperly ousted the association from the defense effort. This belief shaped and reinforced a negative line then pursued by the party concerning the NAACP. Davis was not peripheral in this matter. With his famous name, legal training, and Marxist outlook he was a walking advertisement for the party; his reputation gave credence to the party and its espousal of socialism.

The Scottsboro case has been given more than a cursory look. A recent, more objective, and less hostile approach to the party's role is shown by Carroll Van West: "Although constantly harassed, the communists were the first to combat the hostile atmosphere of Alabama in order to save the nine."[73] George Schuyler, however, reflects a more common view: "[The] NAACP lost control of the case through the machinations of [Davis] who had scurried around the South and secured the signatures of the parents."[74] The interpretation of Red deviousness and client naiveté has been the usual approach to this case. But as in many cases involving the Civil Rights Congress (a Communist-led organization focusing on "Scottsboro"-like cases in the 1950s)—with William Patterson again playing the lead role—the clients themselves proved to be less anti-Communist than the critics. They were appreciative, recognizing that the cases of numerous black defendants did not receive such publicity, resulting in jail sentences or executions.

The only other agency that may have been more concerned with the Reds and Scottsboro was U.S. Military Intelligence. Davis's central role was noted, of course. They were worried about the case's impact on Afro-Americans but observed shrewdly that the KKK in Birmingham had cooled black ardor for Communists. Military intelligence spied incessantly on blacks, using fear of Communism as a main reason. This would have been no surprise to Davis: "Whenever I visited the boys, I had to be armed with a sheaf of credentials, identifications and documents a foot high, before I was allowed to see them. I almost had to secure a dispensation from the holy ghost—who, of course, was white."[75]

While Davis was in the middle of fighting on the Herndon battlefront, the Scottsboro case erupted in Alabama. Over his protests Joseph Brodsky brought Davis into the case. Defendant Haywood Patterson has recalled Davis's role vividly and gratefully in his memoir. It is interesting to note that the pastor of the church that served as the headquarters of the nascent civil rights movement in the 1950s—Dexter Avenue Baptist in Montgomery—was also involved in the case.[76]

Weeks after the Herndon trial Davis was in Birmingham, hearing the anguish of the defendants. As in Atlanta, the authorities did not accept this black-Red alliance with equanimity. The police and the American Legion wrecked the ILD offices in Birmingham; there were dynamite bombings. The jailers were often discourteous and spouted racist epithets. Davis himself witnessed jailers jabbing Haywood Patterson in the stomach with a police club. Davis's eyewitness accounts drew attention to the Scottsboro case and attracted blacks to the party. Davis met with Governor Bibb Graves in 1934, arguing for a commutation of the death penalty at the same time that he was spending considerable time teaching classes to other budding Communists on voting, history, and the like.[77]

Because he was present ultimately as both a legal counsel and reporter, Davis could bring his *Daily Worker* readers a singular perspective. This case, which catapulted the Reds into the forefront of the Black Liberation struggle, was interpreted frequently through the lens of Ben Davis. Consider his reportage for the 16 February 1935 issue of the *Daily Worker*: "We are in the court chambers of the United States Supreme Court [for the Scottsboro appeals].... The entire Court was plainly attentive. The justices asked questions frequently.... A dramatic moment occurred when [he] exhibited the book containing the alleged forged jury rolls. The entire bench and audience became quiet.... Justice [Harlan] Stone ... examines the book spectacularly with large magnifying glass...."[78] The court was "attentive" because the whole world was watching. This is what Davis kept trying to tell the NAACP but its funders wanted the organization to have no dealings with the Reds—even if one of them had gone to Harvard Law. The failure of black leftists and nonleftists to collaborate consistently was not beneficial for the community they professed to represent.

Like a number of the Civil Rights Congress cases years later, the Scottsboro case had the drama of alleged rape, blacks versus whites, and males versus females. Here the international ties of the Communist party proved useful as the Communist International and their allies were able to rally worldwide support for the Nine and condemnation of racism. The overriding atmosphere of terror meant that it was difficult not to stumble. This is the context in which the much-ballyhooed conflicts between the Communists, the NAACP, and attorney Samuel Liebowitz should be considered. Once more, Davis was not an outsider. Even in July 1949 the House Committee on Un-American Activities had not forgotten. Professional stoolpigeon Manning Johnson told them that the Communists "had trouble with Samuel Liebowitz, counsel for the defense. He opposed the Communist line in the defense of the boys. We discussed that and decided to get rid of him. Benjamin Davis was appointed to go talk to the mothers of the boys and get them to decide to drop Liebowitz as counsel. Ben Davis went down there ... and [the CP] praised him highly for that."[79]

There were complications that Johnson neglected to mention. Communist theoretician James Allen maintained that when Davis visited the Nine in jail, he learned that John Terry, "former gangster and Liebowitz's right-hand man," was making threats on the black lawyer's life. The *Negro Liberator* claimed on 27 October 1934 that he also made a "threatening gesture" by drawing a pistol on Davis, an event that the *Daily Worker* made into a front-page story.[80]

A similar conflict, though not as murderous, was brewing within the NAACP. As with the Civil Rights Congress cases of the 1950s, elite forces were uncomfortable with the notion of the ILD leading blacks; strenuous infighting led to a tussle between the ILD and the association over the right to defend the Nine. When Davis visited the Nine in jail, the defendants would score the NAACP. The "boys" told him that beatings were used to get them to disavow the ILD; they were even promised release, he was told. This contretemps was not helpful to a CP-NAACP alliance. It colored Davis's views on the National Question—his Marxist theoretical view of the position of blacks in the United States—and helps to explain the ultra-Left attack on the black middle class that characterized his early association with the party.[81]

The tension between the NAACP and the ILD occurred in the early days of the Roosevelt administration, a spreading depression, and a concomitant growth of the Left. Thus, in early 1933, after the Herndon trial, Davis was in Harlem with Louise Thompson of the Scottsboro Action Committee questioning an alleged unauthorized collection of funds by groups other than the ILD. Davis also took the lead in assailing Samuel Liebowitz. He appeared on platforms with Walter White and the owner of the *New York Amsterdam News* in Harlem rallies for the Nine, which suggests the contradictory nature of the ties between party and nonparty allies.[82]

Nevertheless, it was difficult to be indifferent to the crowds and excitement that Davis and the Scottsboro Nine were receiving in Harlem. In April 1933 twenty-five hundred people jammed St. Mark's Church at 138th and St. Nicholas: headlines read, "hundreds turned away . . . a tremendous ovation was given" as Davis and Geer were introduced. "Thunderous cheering" was the response when Davis proclaimed, "The Herndon and Scottsboro cases are inseparable."[83] Days later, "over a thousand Harlem workers, jammed every foot of space in the St. Luke's Hall." It was the CP's "largest mass meeting" ever held "indoors in Harlem" on the Scottsboro case. Davis spoke of a "new type of militant leadership in the leadership of the Communist party."[84]

It is possible to excuse Communists for thinking in April 1933 that the Revolution was nigh; fifteen hundred people marched in Harlem for the Scottsboro case: "Never before was so much revolutionary literature sold on the streets of Harlem," said the *Daily Worker* on 24 April 1933. A few months later the League of Struggle for Negro Rights, an alleged "Communist front" that had difficulty achieving a mass base, was receiving a respectful hearing for its Bill of Rights for Negroes from a Scottsboro-Herndon conference in Harlem attended by representatives of 210 organizations representing 133,000 persons. Davis had a role to play in these events because of his name. His education—a commodity highly valued in an African-American community that had been systematically denied it—also was important. He also enjoyed the confidence of the mothers of the defendants, especially Ada Wright and Ida Norris.[85]

After his 1934 move to Harlem, Davis was not as active on the Scottsboro case as he had been earlier. He did appear at important times, such as the hearings at the U.S. Supreme Court. In his voluminous articles for the press he returned frequently to their plight. As he wrote in 1936, the Scottsboro Defense Committee was a united front including the NAACP, ACLU, and other groups. But this unity may have had a weakness: it may have diluted the party's emphasis on mass action and demonstrations.[86]

The Scottsboro and Herndon cases catapulted the ILD and the Communists into prominence among African-Americans; it also underscored Davis's growing role as a leading Communist intellectual-activist and journalist. This high profile helps to explain why an opponent of Davis in his 1945 reelection campaign rehashed a Scottsboro story about a half-million dollars raised for the Nine that was allegedly purloined by Davis and his comrades.[87] But like Willie McGee and other Civil Rights Congress defendants, the Nine continued to speak highly of the young attorney who had ridden to their rescue. In 1951, at a birthday celebration for William Patterson, Olin Montgomery repaid the historical debt when he demanded Davis's release from prison. The crowd at Small's Paradise in Harlem cheered.[88] But it was left to Davis to point out the importance of the Scottsboro case for posterity: "It was the first time in modern years that labor took up the battle cry for Negro rights. . . . The fight laid the basis for the growth of the labor and progressive movement in the South."[89] The case set legal precedents on such key issues as the right to a fair trial, adequate counsel, and exclusion from juries. Still, the conflict with the NAACP did not augur well for Davis's hope for a united front.

4

To Be a Professional Revolutionary

Comrades and Friends

The Harlem that Davis now lived in was becoming one of the country's most depressed yet most vibrant communities. The presence of the NAACP leadership (Walter White and Roy Wilkins), the Urban League's Lester Granger, union leader A. Philip Randolph, the militant cleric Adam Clayton Powell, artists, and celebrities all gave it a unique character. A contradiction of Jim Crow was that residential segregation forced the left and center elements of the African-American community to live cheek by jowl, thus facilitating their relationship. Many black leaders lived in northern Manhattan, several of them at 409 Edgecombe Avenue. Racism, combined with the Great Depression, made it easy for African-Americans to accept some of the Communists' precepts. At the same time it was difficult to be impressed with the beneficence of U.S. elites. Until the complications of World War II, left and center—the party and the association—were able to maintain a kind of unity. Harlem was fertile ground in all classes, for as the *Daily Worker* pointed out, "Negro professionals . . . have been harder hit by the depression than any other similar group in New York City. . . . "[1] It is necessary to explore four major areas to gain insight into Davis's unique role: the people he worked with inside and outside the party, the state of the Harlem party in the thirties, the Marxist theory that motivated his actions (in other words, the "National Question"), and the practical applications of this theory in a depressed Harlem and elsewhere.

Ben Davis entered a Harlem Communist party that already was establishing a reputation as the flagship organization of the movement. Though he may have been engaging in a bit of puffery, Harlem Communist leader Howard "Stretch" Johnson was not too far from the point: "Party members in other parts of the country didn't have the kind of time we had in Harlem. They didn't know how to party out there in the boondocks . . . being a communist in Harlem was like being the swinging present and the swinging future simultaneously . . . you were enjoying all the boogying and boozing and everything in the present, while you had your socialist perspective to give you inspiration to continue."[2] This statement may better reflect Johnson's life than the party's role, but it does suggest that stereotyped views of robot Reds programmed from Moscow should be reconsidered. His comment also reveals the uniqueness of Harlem, for it was true that New York City—then as now—was the center of leftist and progressive political activity in the United States.

The entire mosaic of the Communists' relations with African-Americans will be discussed below, but suffice it to say for now that the party—despite its weaknesses—was far in advance of other U.S. organizations on this crucial question of race. Even Nathan Glazer, certainly no Communist dupe, has seen this; according to him it was "the only institution in American life in which Negroes commonly worked with whites on a level of equality, which was truly color-blind, which was really indifferent to issues of race."[3] For example, party leader Eugene Dennis was posted to South Africa's C.P. by the Communist International—a Moscow-based agency that provided counsel for Communist parties globally—in the 1930s and he played a useful role in turning it from an all-white party to one that was mostly African. He brought to the table experiences beyond the realm of most of his fellow Euro-Americans. The International had played a key role in establishing the International Trade Union Committee of Negro Workers, which published journals, held conferences, and gave many a sleepless night to colonial bureaucrats in Africa.[4]

In his study of Philadelphia Communists Paul Lyons has commented on what he perceived as a high turnover of black recruits to the CP.[5] A look at the overall record shows a mixed picture. In August 1933, just before Davis's permanent arrival in New York, James Ford said that as of 1928 "less than fifty" blacks were Reds: "Today there are several thousand Negro members, of whom over two hundred are leading functionaries."[6] A number of developments had occurred in the interval such as Scottsboro and Herndon. Indicative of the fact that Ford may not have been distorting the figures is a contemporary account on 28 February 1934 from a supposedly more objective source, the *New York Times*; there a source was quoted who saw the "possibility of a Communist election victory [in 1934] in the Southern section of Chicago, populated chiefly by Negro workers in the slaughter houses . . . the 'danger' of the election of the Communist candidate for Congress is being seriously considered." As for New York, Robert Minor filed a report showing that 1,039 blacks were members of the state party as of May 1936 (along with 14,775 whites), while there were 1,841 of the former by May 1938 (and 24,542 of the latter). This suggests that black membership was growing at a rapid rate. Ben Davis in July 1936 averred that the Harlem party had a membership of fifty or less in 1934 but "more than 850" as of the time of his writing.[7]

What Lyons suggested about party turnover in Philadelphia may also have been true for New York. George Blake in 1938 also pointed to a "question of fluctuation . . . especially among Negro comrades" in Harlem.[8] This vacillation was due in part to a more vigorous repression visited upon those so bold as to be both black and Red and to unresolved questions of internal chauvinism. Early in 1936, in reviewing a pamphlet by Gil Green, Davis was a bit scolding: "The fly leaf contains a picture of six national [Young Communist League] leaders but it unfortunately omits the picture of any Negro leader."[9] But the party was growing nonetheless. In 1938 it moved from 415 Lenox Avenue to larger quarters at 101 West 132 Street, though it had two entire floors at the former address. In 1939 the party launched a postcard campaign for antilynching legislation that involved seventy-four branches of the Harlem party.[10]

Such was the milieu that Davis entered. Even Irving Howe and Lewis Coser in their partisan tome on the party acknowledge Davis as "a talented lawyer with a following in the Negro world."[11] But those who still wonder why Davis may have chosen his path need look no further than Daniel Aaron's words in *Writers on the Left*: "Not the 'aberration of individuals' drew men into Communism in the 1930's but the 'aberration of society.'" A significant part of this "aberration" was a Great Depression that disproportionately hit African-Americans.[12]

A consideration of various contemporary accounts of Davis and his impact on the party and movement provide an idea of the temper of the times. In late 1936 his old paper, the *Afro-American*, commented at length:

> . . . he enjoys a whole-hearted contempt for everything associated with the capitalistic world and expresses his contempt in no uncertain terms from the tops of soapboxes and step-ladders in Harlem. In short, the Hon. Mr. Davis is the race's Public Communist, No. 1. . . . To me, he represents a horrible example of what radical changes a political dogma can bring about in a man. I knew Ben Davis when he was a fashion plate of New York and the South. Ben isn't a fashion plate any more. I knew Ben Davis as a dapper young law graduate, mustache trimmed to a Parisian nicety, his finger nails manicured to an inspiring gloster [sic], his hair slicked down and parted at just the right angle. This was the Ben Davis of Auburn Avenue, Atlanta . . . Sugar Hill, New York, [who] . . . wore smartly tailored clothes, many varieties, cuts and shades, but always according to the dictates of Vanity Fair, Esquire and the Country Gentleman. The Ben I knew wore studs in his shirtfront, a gold clasp under his collar points, a wrist watch on his arm and fawn-colored spats over his patent leather shoes. . . . carried a gold headed cane which he twirled at a rakish suaveness as he perambulated down the avenue of a morning en route to work, making a delightful spectacle for the servant girls who missed their street cars to get a fetching glimpse of him in all his magnificent splendor. Envious men . . . thought Benjamin an exhibitionist but he wasn't at all. Ben was merely a gentleman to the manner born [sic] and an ardent practitioner of the art of being sartorially correct. . . . [He] used to smell very sweet . . . annointed with oil of a dainty odor. I have seen the clerks of our office pause in their chores to inhale the fragrance of him as he passed their desks.

But according to the author, veteran journalist Ralph Matthews, that was then and this is now:

> But Ben the Communist doesn't smell sweet any more. . . . How did this strange transformation come about? Communism did it, I presume. When Ben took on the religion of Moscow, he shook all the sins of the money world from his sandals. . . . No longer do servant girls turn when he passes. . . . Benjamin is not a matinee idol but a tragic character. He is almost as fat, but not quite as defiantly sloppy as Heywood Broun. . . . He is a champion of the downtrodden, the overworked, the underpaid. Just why he couldn't champion these causes in a stiffly starched shirt as well as he can in a collar with dog ears is one of the mysteries that confound me. Why he did not try to lift the laborer up to his own exalted elegance instead of himself dropping down to the dissheveled state of the working man, I do not know. . . . Ben is a sorry spectacle. But maybe today Ben is of lots more value to humanity than he was as a Beau Brummel. Maybe Ben prefers to be serviceable instead of ornamental. If such is his reasoning, I forgive him.[13]

Despite the final bouquet tossed by Matthews, some of his words are misleading if taken as literal and absolute truth. Even during the dog days of the 1960s when his income had fallen precipitously, Davis was always known to be turned out well—though not with a cane and derby. In fact, his assimilation of this key characteristic of African-American and U.S. culture—appearance—was partly why he was able to maintain a mass base.

George Charney, a former Red leader, sought to capture the Davis persona in his memoir of the times:

> Ben was one of the new personalities in the leadership of the party. He had emerged as the dominant Negro figure in the movement. Ford had not managed to survive the downfall of Browder . . . [and was] on the fringe, isolated, lonely, embittered. . . . Ben by contrast was a luminous personality. He was a striking figure of a man, gifted with an exceptional intelligence. . . . He was one of the finest orators I had ever heard and could speak as well on a street corner as in Madison Square Garden. His street gatherings in Harlem were extraordinary experiences. He was to Upper Harlem what Marcantonio was to East Harlem and when both shared the platform, with Paul Robeson to fill in, the walls of the ghetto came tumbling down. Ben was not just an agitator of the old school. He had a keen interest in all the political activities of the party and took part in its deliberations. He had little patience with involved matters of doctrine, but with his quick mind could follow the twists and turns of ideological controversy and on occasions add his own twist. He cared least of all for the humdrum, daily life of the party. . . . He was the most popular mass figure in the party. On a more intimate basis he attracted people by his warm and engaging personality. And yet he was ambitious and self-centered and invariably expressed irritation with people slow to do his bidding. . . .[14]

These words of Charney, an apostate, may be suspect because of his running afoul of Davis during some of the sharper party battles, and, as noted, Davis could be particularly difficult during these conflicts, especially with Euro-Americans. But other parts of his description—particularly those concerning the reasons for Davis's mass base—are corroborated by other sources. In any event, when considered in the context of other black party leaders—the lawyer William Patterson and college graduates like James Jackson—Davis's defection to the Left is better understood.

For example, black party leader James Ford was a graduate of Fisk University and a stellar athlete, like Davis and Robeson. He was born James W. Forsch but on his father's pay envelope the name was changed to "Ford." "Keep the name," advised the foreman, adding, "It don't make no difference about a nigger's name no how." The future Communist was born in 1893 in Pratt City, Alabama; his grandfather was lynched after "getting fresh with a white woman." He joined the party in 1926 and rose quickly through the ranks.[15]

Also rising with him was Ben Davis. They quickly developed a mutually beneficial relationship. Like Davis, Ford was a star football player; he was on an undefeated team and was the fastest one hundred-yard-dash sprinter in the school, in addition to being on the mile relay team. His fleet-footedness won him the nickname of "Rabbit" Ford. He also played baseball and was a member of the popular black fraternity, Omega Psi Phi. Like Davis, he had a modestly furnished apartment in Harlem and had attended an elite institution, the University of Chicago, where he studied history and finance. Early on he attracted attention as leader of the postal workers' union—a frequent redoubt for black college graduates (along with operating an elevator, then known as "indoor aviation"), which underscores the fact that since opportunities to excel and rise were few and far between for black intellectuals, the party offered a form of social mobility.[16]

The relationship between the two party leaders congealed during the presidential campaign of 1940, when Davis managed Ford's vice-presidential bid. Towering over him by at least four inches, Davis accompanied him on his West Coast tour, appeared with him in Harlem rallies, escorted him to North Carolina's predominantly black Shaw University, and went with him to Baltimore. The reactions of the assembled masses were telling. A Ford rally with 350 present (including a handful of white citizens) in Richmond, Virginia, was held in the church of moderate black leader Gordon Hancock. Such a rally shows that moderates like Hancock could align with the Communists in the pre-Cold-War era and that Jim Crow generally forced blacks to the Left. In words that are reminiscent now of Jesse Jackson, Hancock declared that he was glad to see a black with the courage to run, for it would inspire the youth. The vicious Jim Crow of the prewar era was even driving what Davis called an extremely conservative minister into the arms of the Left.[17]

There was a similar reaction when Ford, Patterson, and Davis were campaigning near the Schomburg Library on 135th Street in Harlem. Reported Davis, "'Look at Ford, Mama,' a tiny Negro lad said to his mother. . . . 'Look at Ford, dear,' she told her child. 'We're all looking at him.'"[18]

Voters, especially black ones, were not uncomfortable with the prospect of Reds having the reins of power in their hands; certainly they could do no worse than the usual assortment of Jim Crow advocates that too often held elective office in the United States. This insight was to be applied fruitfully by Davis himself when he ran for the City Council from Harlem.

Davis's move to Harlem also brought him into contact with a talented array of black women Communists such as Maude White, the only black woman member of the Central Committee. Then there was Marvel Cooke, whom Davis recruited to the party during the 1935 *Amsterdam News* strike. She was related by marriage to Roy Wilkins and was a neighbor of his and Thurgood Marshall's, living at 409 Edgecombe Avenue in Harlem. Davis and Cooke were in the same party cell together, which at one time included Richard Wright. She and Davis "were very good friends—when I saw him, I kissed him . . . I was his baby, he recruited me."[19] There was also Claudia Jones, a party leader whom Davis became quite fond of.

Davis became quite close to other top black leaders of the party besides Ford and Jones. There was the talented journalist Abner Berry. Born in Beaumont, Texas, in 1902, Berry toiled as a factory worker in Chicago and as a journalist in Houston before arriving in Harlem. The party's influence was manifested in the fact that 50 percent of leading journalists of the *New York Amsterdam News* were Reds, according to his account. The house of Louise Thompson, future wife of William Patterson, was a crossroads for many black intellectuals, including Langston Hughes.[20]

Howard "Stretch" Johnson was also part of the Harlem party coterie. He came to New York in 1933 in pursuit of theater opportunities, and he too was an athlete, a basketball player. Along with his sister he danced at the Cotton Club. He became acquainted with the party as a result of the play *Waiting for Lefty*. He joined in 1938 and thereafter used his theater contacts to promote Communist activity. For example, he was able to get Lena Horne to do benefits for Left-led organizations. From time to time he was able to get Jackie Robinson, Joe Louis, Billie Holiday, and other celebrities to perform similar tasks. In 1939 he went to "party school" to learn the fundamentals of Marxism-Leninism and organizing. The Harlem Young Communist League had 250 members then, he recalled, but was able to extend its tentacles widely in Harlem. The party realized the ideal of black-white equality, he recalled, though white Reds were "subject to pressure of outside society [and] white chauvinist pressures."[21]

Party leader John Pittman had a similar background to Davis's; he was born in Atlanta in 1906 into a family of school teachers and dentists. He recalled in 1970 that Davis "was a friend of mine—we grew up in Atlanta together. . . . [In 1934] I talked with Ben quite a bit. He explained quite a number of things I hadn't thought about before." At that point Pittman joined the party. Like Davis, he went on to become editor of the party newspaper. Thus Davis was not alone in being attracted to the Left.[22]

Even blacks who did not take out a membership card were often found in the party's orbit. Thus during the election campaign of 1940, an impressive group of African-Americans protested attacks on Communist candidates. This list included Arthur Huff Fauset, Aaron Douglas, Paul Robeson, Hope Stevens, and Dr. Richard Carey (Davis's brother-in-law).[23] As one careful student has pointed out, "Most blacks in many southern states could not believe that the threat of communism was as much a menace to their freedom as the actual and present danger of mob violence."[24]

Davis closely interacted with a number of not well known but nonetheless important African-American activists. There was John Goode, brother-in-law of Robeson, who spent a good deal of time in the 1930s in the USSR. There was O. J. Golden, a transplanted southern black living in Tashkent in the Soviet Union, who when interviewed by Davis proclaimed, "I feel free. . . . "[25] There was Doug Roach, who had attended the state college at Amherst, Massachusetts, when Davis was there. Like other Davis friends and associates such as Dr. Arnold Donawa, Oliver Law, Salaria Kee, and Oscar Hunter, Roach was part of the African-American contingent who went to Spain to fight fascism. There was John Sutton, brother of Percy Sutton, the future borough president of Manhattan and advisor to Jesse Jackson. Sutton had spent four years at Tuskeegee with George Washington Carver before fleeing racism for socialism in the USSR. On one of his infrequent trips to the United States, he visited with Davis, who reported that "he made the original discovery of producing a strong fibre from rice-straw, which was suitable for tough condor rope."[26] Many others, too numerous to mention, were similar to Sutton, Roach, Golden, and Goode, which shows how the Depression decade helped to turn many blacks, and not just Davis, to the Left.

A bridge between Davis and the Reds on the one hand and the progressives and artists on the other was Paul Robeson. By their own accounts and the accounts of others, Davis and Robeson were quite close. In an undated letter Davis told Robeson directly that "A guy like you is born once every century. . . . Every ounce of you is pure gold."[27] Robeson had similar feelings, though they were more detailed: "Ben and I first met here in Harlem some 35 years ago . . . often passers-by on the Avenue would be startled and amused as Ben and I worked out some football tactics on the sidewalk. Again, we would discuss our hopes as future lawyers, and where and how we would work." Robeson also said that his friend "had influenced [my] ideological development."[28]

Lloyd Brown, the African-American novelist and activist, knew both men well. He recalls their relationship as being "very, very important" to both. Robeson had "great admiration [and] respect" for Davis.[29] Paul Robeson, Jr., concurs with Brown's evaluation. Davis and Robeson were "really good friends", he says. Davis would frequently visit Robeson's Connecticut home for weeks at a time. At those times he and Paul junior would play tennis.

He was considered "part of the Robeson family." Davis would play chess with his friend, a passion they shared with two of their mutual friends—Harlem businessman cum "racketeer" Ellsworth "Bumpy" Johnson and the Reverend John Johnson. More often than not Robeson triumphed; Davis was only an "average" player.[30]

Despite their friendship and the "puff" pieces that Davis the journalist would write for the *Daily Worker* from time to time about his friend, Davis could be harsh about Robeson's cultural undertakings. For example, in a 1936 interview Davis pointed to the boycott of Robeson's film *Sanders of the River* and would not accept the excuse that editing had made it a distorted, negative film: " . . . that explanation may be acceptable, but good faith alone is not enough. The picture was an out and out betrayal of the African colonials, whatever may be said of your good intentions and the imperialist twist came about in more than the cutting of the film. You became the tool of British imperialism and must be attacked and exposed whenever you act in such pictures or plays." Said Robeson weakly, "you're right. . . . " This was a friendship that apparently could withstand criticism.[31]

"Stretch" Johnson maintains that " . . . 75 percent of black cultural figures had Party membership or maintained regular meaningful contact" during the thirties.[32] To the extent that this assertion is accurate, it reflects a strong tie between artists and the party. This was due in part to the Depression's impact on the arts, the leading role of figures like Robeson and Langston Hughes (who were known to be close to the party), and the fact that the party paid musicians union scale.

Such strong ties were not replicated to the same extent in other sectors, yet there was significant influence. Certainly the party's ties with the civil rights establishment were substantial. Lester Granger of the Urban League, in reviewing a book by James Ford in 1939, termed him the "best-known Negro in the world today with the possible exception of Paul Robeson . . . this reviewer entertains a deep friendship and respect for the man." He even rationalized the party's apparent tactical shift from attacking the Urban League to making "offers of cooperation" by referring to changed conditions presented by the fascist threat.[33] Dorothy Height, then and now a prominent leader, worked closely with Communist leader Henry Winston in the Depression decade and later: "I learned so much from the Communists. Those were some of the best minds that I ever came upon."[34] Benjamin Mays, dean of the Atlanta black leadership and a deep influence on Martin Luther King, Jr., also has acknowledged the influence of the Left on his own thinking and practice.[35]

Civil rights leaders were not the only sector influenced by the Left in the 1930s. As noted by "Stretch" Johnson, writers like Langston Hughes, Richard Wright, and Ralph Ellison—or the cream of that era's crop—were similarly influenced. Hughes served as president of the League of Struggle for Negro Rights, with Davis and Patterson as vice-presidents. Paul Peters, writer of the popular work *Stevedore*, and leading actors like Leigh Whipper and Rex Ingram, were also connected with the party.[36]

Ralph Ellison has recalled the period when he and Richard Wright began "to hang around the Harlem Bureau" of the *Daily Worker*, which was Davis's headquarters. Whichever story of Wright's relationship with the Left is believed, there is little question that Davis was at the very nucleus of the matter. Wright initially was a journalist with the party paper. He was in a party club with Davis, Marvel Cooke, and Ollie Harrington, among others. Cooke recalls a time when Davis said he knew of a "young man from Chicago" who had just arrived in town. It was Wright.[37]

The beginning of the rupture between Davis and Wright came with the publication of *Native Son*. Cooke believes that even though party protocol should have allowed Davis to read the manuscript before publication, the reaction of Davis and others to the book may have been too sharp. Actually Davis was not one-sided in his approach. He observed, "reactions to the book have differed even among Communists. . . . It is an achievement in the world of letters and, despite its shortcomings is a document of positive racial significance. . . . The book is a terrific indictment of capitalist America. . . . [but] would have been immeasurably strengthened with a Communist character more typical of the Communist party."[38] Davis was particularly incensed with the portrayal of the Left's defense of Bigger Thomas. His restraint did not assuage Wright, who shortly thereafter bolted from the party's ranks.

It was apparent that there were sharp problems before Wright left. Mark Naison asserts that James Ford "hated and mistrusted Wright" while Davis and V. J. Jerome, so-called party cultural commissar, "protected him from political attack."[39] One *Daily Worker* correspondent prematurely declared victory: "Knowing that the party had not yet officially expressed itself on 'Native Son' there have been some Trotskyites and other enemies of the people who have hoped desperately that we should blast Richard Wright. They hoped that we should drive [him] away from us."[40] But the wind direction was signaled by a May 1940 forum entitled "Native Son: A Challenge," with Davis as the main speaker. In a longer review Davis compared Wright with Maxim Gorky in his stress on "reality" but he again attacked his comrade's "serious inadequacies in the picture presented of the party." Not long after that Wright was no longer a comrade and had moved away from the organized Left.[41]

The party's appeal was not limited to the oppressed minority. Leading literary lights like Nelson Algren, Josephine Herbst, and Upton Sinclair were associated with Communists. Nevertheless, among artists, African-American musicians may have had the broadest contacts with the party. A largely untold story is jazz's early association with the Left. The party and its allies, unlike other organizations did not shun blacks and welcomed their cultural contributions. Thus Duke Ellington and his orchestra played in Harlem for the *Liberator* and the Trade Union Unity League in a well-attended 1930 affair. It was not unusual to find Erskine Hawkins, Asadata Dafora Horton, and similar entertainers appearing at Harlem CP events of the mid-1930s. Similarly, the party tended to criticize artists who veered from the party's political outlook. For example, Davis denounced Noble Sissle after he had praised the Duke and Duchess of Windsor, despite the erstwhile king's ties to fascists, and Davis was quick to praise Marian Anderson after she had unstintingly praised the artist's role in the Soviet Union. The party was able to align with many of these artists, who were not necessarily cultural heroes outside of the black community. Chick Webb and Ella Fitzgerald were among those who performed at events organized by Davis's *Daily Worker* Harlem bureau. The role of leftists like John Hammond and Barney Josephson in spreading the popularity of black music—which ultimately became the basis for U.S. and even worldwide popular music—needs to be underscored.[42]

The relationship of Joe Louis to the Left became apparent during Davis's successful run for office. During the early career of Joe Louis, Davis—as a former athlete—sensed Louis's growing symbolic role in Harlem and wrote at length about his exploits. In 1937 he waxed enthusiastic about Louis's victory over James Braddock, noting an "Ethiopian flag at the head of a victory parade of 5,000 people.... There was not bitterness against Braddock. There were no angry or hostile anti-racial demonstration," as many whites joined in and "numerous miniature snake dances" ensued.[43] During the Tommy Farr fight, the Harlem bureau held a "Joe Louis Radio party at 415 Lenox Avenue, at 9:15 p.m." The Nazis saw the victory over Max Schmeling in 1938 as a setback to their racist theories. Both Davis and Richard Wright wrote at length in the *Daily Worker* about Harlem's reaction to this triumph. Davis was estatic. "Indescribable joy and unprecedented exuberance" swept Harlem: "There was never a Harlem like the Harlem of Wednesday night. Take a dozen Harlem Christmases, a score of New Year's eves, a bushel of July 4ths and maybe—yes, maybe—you get a faint glimpse of the idea ... parades, meetings, demonstrations, snake dances, speeches ... Negroes ... Jews, Spanish, Puerto Rican ... traffic on Seventh Avenue was cut off from 116th St. to 145th St.... militantly anti-fascist enthusiasm..." The Communist party was flexible enough to ally itself with this sentiment. "Thousands crowded around two meetings under the auspices of the Harlem Communist party at 415 Lenox Avenue and at 702 St. Nicholas Avenue."[44]

A rival to Joe Louis in building ties with the party was Henry Armstrong, a boxer who held the record for holding most championships in various weight divisions. In 1937, after blasting a high court decision on Scottsboro, Armstrong praised the *Daily Worker* for its position on blacks. He signed Young Communist League petitions on desegregating baseball and called for an end to discrimination in all sports.[45]

Davis's interest in popular culture paid dividends when he ran for office, but this interest did not just extend to the stars. The Harlem *Daily Worker* organized a basketball team, for example. Nevertheless, the party's high-level connections were too obvious to ignore. During this period a photograph of black baseball star Josh Gibson signing a petition held by James Ford that demanded baseball's desegregation appeared in the *Daily Worker*. New York Yankee third baseman Red Rolfe went beyond Gibson by writing a regular column for the party paper, as did Chicago Cub star Rip Collins.[46]

Davis's most controversial dalliance with popular culture was with film. Davis received substantial publicity nationally because of his attack on *Gone with the Wind*. The so-called mainstream press typically cast the dispute in racial terms. The *New York Times* told how a mere "Negro member of the editorial board" of the *Daily Worker* attacked in-house critic Howard Rushmore allegedly because of his favorable view of the film: "the Negro member . . . in particular, had instructed him to write a 100 per cent attack and to call on readers to boycott" it.[47] The *New York Post* cited Davis as saying to Rushmore, "You can't say anything that would indicate that the picture showed there were nice people in the South."[48] The *New York Journal American* quoted Rushmore: "As a compromise I asked Mr. Davis if I could at least praise the producing and acting. His reply was that we praise nothing about this picture and the most I could say was that Vivian Leigh and other stars were forced to appear in such a reactionary picture." Some in the press saw the attack on Rushmore and his alleged deep U.S. roots as an apparent contradiction of the party's "Americanism" policy in the wake of the commencement of World War II.[49]

Davis was not deterred by this spate of publicity. His opinion was that this film was a "newspaper made sensation . . . unquestionably one of the most vicious assaults . . . slander against the Negro people . . . particularly dangerous now . . . does such violence to American history that it practically lynches it . . . not just another picture . . . they want to show how the Civil War unjustifiably dislocated the feudalistic economy of the slave-owners . . . basest and trashiest sex stuff." He considered the burning of Atlanta "the arsonous doings of the retreating Confederate forces," not a Yankee misdeed.[50] Davis's hostile reaction to this wildly popular film is a partial reason for why he is often depicted as unyielding and rigid. Yet the differing reactions to this film also help to explain in part why some commentators saw two nations inhabiting these shores. The *New York Age* termed the film "not only libelous to the Negro but also pictures Sherman's army and Union soldiers [as] thieves and hoodlums. . . . glories the civilization of the slave-owners."[51] Blacks in Britain picketed, as did Howard University professors and students and black trade union leaders. But most white opinion avidly cheered this film. Davis, however, was not courting stand-pat white opinion but a surging black opinion, and his views and ties in the arts and sports community were helpful in heightening his popularity.

The Harlem Party in the Thirties

Davis's opinion "As Harlem goes, so goes Negro America" was not far from the mark. Similarly, his view that the Harlem Communist party was "the largest and most influential Communist party in any Negro community in the country" was equally accurate.[52] Although unique, Harlem influenced all of Afro-America. Not having the steel mills of Chicago and the auto plants of Detroit did little to retard its ideological development. But if Harlem was advanced ideologically, it was not advanced socioeconomically. In 1935 Loren Miller found 80 percent unemployment: "The housing situation is remarkably bad. . . . police brutality. . . . health and sanitation are bad."[53] Larry Greene has painted a worse picture: "the average Afro-American family's income was not sufficient for the maintenance of a healthful and decent standard of living." The tuberculosis mortality rate was twice as high as that of New York City. "Some parents trembled uncontrollably from weeks of semi-starvation to assure their children enough food."[54] When the subway system finally decided to hire blacks, they were placed in menial posts. A typical company was Metropolitan Life, discussed in more depth in later chapters, which had one hundred thousand black policyholders in Harlem but employed no blacks in a work force of twenty thousand. These were the conditions that led to the popularity of a Communist like Davis.

Ben Davis quickly gained a reputation as an expert street-corner speaker, investigative journalist, and political organizer. The fact that such a talented person would throw his lot in with the Reds helped to bring many more to the Harlem party. Obviously the authorities did not greet this development casually. New York City Police Commissioner Grover Whalen was candid although rather alarmist in calling the party "one of the greatest problems I had to face as Commissioner." Because of his concerns he sent fifty agents to infiltrate the party; daily reports were received, with some of his agents "even rising to positions of trust and importance." But Whalen may not have been receiving credible information, as his own words demonstrate: " . . . The girls in these Communist groups were urged to wear long hatpins . . . and use them effectively against horses . . . [and] taught to yell hysterically in rasping, fiendish voices in order to create panic."[55]

The apotheosis of Whalen's complaint came in 1935 with the so-called Harlem Riot, which was sparked by an attack on a black youth by a white. The authorities quickly accused the party of fomenting this uprising, an accusation that at once accorded the party too much credit and not enough sense; Larry Greene agrees but adds that their leaflets may have influenced the crowd to attack property rather than people. Although there were few interracial clashes, the focus was on what was perceived to be the most visible source of economic exploitation: the white-owned stores in Harlem. The party did play a role in the official inquiry and launched their own "mass trial" of the authorities, in which Davis acted as prosecutor. Their activism paid off. Greene's figures indicate that from January to August 1935 the party in Harlem grew from three hundred to seven hundred.[56]

Davis, on the scene during this entire contretemps, was angry: "Club-wielding, quick-trigger policemen were fought to a standstill; plate glass windows of the large department stores, which refused to employ Negroes, were smashed. . . . A people living in a near-concentration camp oppression had been driven to desperation."[57] In answering the essential question for a Communist—what is to be done?—Davis provided an outline of what would later become the text of his successful campaign for the City Council. A "broad People's Labor party" was needed; African-Americans should be "pooling their votes to elect representatives in city and state offices to fight for the needs and demands of Harlem. Too long have Harlem's representatives jumped at the crack of Tammany's and Wall Street's whip."[58]

The spirited organizing in the wake of the Harlem uprising was carried on after 1935. In the spring of 1936, after some blacks were beaten by police in Harlem, a united front developed that included Charles Houston, the ACLU, and Davis. A "Provisional Committee for the Defense of Civil Rights in Harlem" was cobbled together. The members met with leading police officials and held "open-air meetings." They led what was considered the first campaign resulting in the holding of a Harlem policeman for brutality. The issue of police brutality was recurrent during Davis's years in Harlem and his resolute, uncompromising stand on this issue brought him wide support among blacks.[59]

According to some, the party had no policy toward the Harlem religious community. Davis, however, was friendly with Father Divine, a leading black religious figure in Harlem. His opinion of their January 1936 gathering at the St. Nicholas Arena,—progressive despite confusion on the question of trade unions—was typical of his view of religion in Harlem. It was well that he should take such an approach. Over five thousand of the cleric's flock came to the 1935 May Day rally. Davis encouraged a united approach, even in the face of Father Divine's anti-union approach.[60] This kind of open-mindedness paid dividends when followers of Divine contributed to the "Browder Radio Fund," which subsidized the broadcasts of the general secretary of the party. Though the party's and even Davis's attitude toward Father Divine fluctuated, Davis's willingness to attend Divine's rallies and hold dialogues with him paid off when he ran for the City Council in 1943.

Health, religion, politics—these issues were the core of Davis's beat in Harlem. But a fundamental feature of all of his work in the community was education. He played a central role in the Harlem Peoples School for Negro Liberation, Democracy, and Peace at 415 Lenox Avenue. The curriculum included not only anti-imperialism but also "social hygiene," dental hygiene, and sex problems, along with trade unionism, English, and political economy. Ted Bassett was the director and W. E. B. Du Bois was a teacher. Nearby at 115 West 135 Street was the Harlem People's Book Shop, where among the best-sellers were a number of pamphlets by Davis. Indicative of the party's ideological hegemony was the fact that this was one of the few book shops in Harlem.

Davis and his party also intervened in the public school system. Davis and Bassett formed a "Permanent Committee for Better Schools" that eventually ousted a 250-pound Harlem principal who attacked and beat a ninety-pound black youth.[61]

While Davis brought Harlem issues to a national audience through the pages of the *Daily Worker*, he also brought national issues to a Harlem audience. Here too he played an educational role, especially apparent during battles of the New Deal era concerning "court packing," the nomination of Hugo Black to the high court, and the overall question of law and society. His prominence was suggested when he joined twenty-six other Harlem leaders—including Powell and Granger—who attended a Senate Judiciary Committee hearing supporting Roosevelt's "court-packing" proposal. He was the moving force behind the "Harlem Non-Partisan Committee for Supreme Court Reform," with his law background adding to his influence. Though the American Bar Association opposed this measure, the Harlem Lawyers Association did not, thus implying the progressive nature of the proposal. Again, it must be underscored that the black view on "court packing" differed from the resultant scorning of this proposal by the mainstream press. Blacks saw the need to expand the court to dilute the conservative influence and were less concerned about trampling traditions.[62]

Davis was sufficiently perspicacious to back the ascension of Hugo Black to the Supreme Court despite his past ties to the Ku Klux Klan. Law was a key issue of this era and Davis was a key interpreter of complex legal questions. He believed that laws are a reflection of class struggle, whether these laws be good or bad. In a militant echo of the NAACP, he urged that blacks seize upon the law and use it as a weapon in the class struggle for full black Liberation. However, he objected to the tendency to deify the law, rather than seeing it as an instrument of class and race rule. The high court's slogan of "Equal Justice Under Law," he wrote ruefully, had "about as much value as a peace treaty signed by Hitler."[63]

The National Question

The efforts of the Communist party and Davis to forge political alliances was based on a theory that encompassed more than the notion of a united front. The theory embraced what Marxists liked to call "The National Question," or in the U.S. context, the approach to the African-American community and remedies for racism. This was and is viewed by many Marxists as one of the most complex questions of social science. All this was seen dimly by the party's adversaries. Herbert Philbrick, who worked with the FBI against the party, encapsulated the view of many anti-Communists: "The importance of the race question to the Communist party and its purposes is indicated by the fact that it has [devoted] more printed matter to the American Negro [than] any other segment of the American population."[64]

Unfortunately, in analyzing this complicated phenomenon, many historians have resorted to cliche by suggesting that the party view of "self-determination" for the Black Belt South—which could include secession—was developed by the ubiquitous "hand of Moscow." In fact, this "hand of Moscow" thesis has been not only a major factor slowing the spread of Marxist ideas but a retardant to social progress as well. Moreover, since this supposition is the reason why Davis himself has been viewed as a dupe, traitor, and worse, it is worthy of examination. The relation of the CPUSA to Moscow is an issue that seemingly refuses to die—even today. Bernard and Jewel Bellush tell us, "What was good for Mother Russia was good for American Communists. . . . At no time during the New Deal was the response of the CPUSA determined by factors indigenous to this nation . . . the Communists contributed significantly to the demise of the Left." This still tends to be the consensus view, despite certain historiographical advances. Eric Foner has pointed to the benefit of comparative study for the post-emancipation South. In an area where it is assumed that one nation has had so much influence on the policies of so many other nations—in fact virtually every nation—one would imagine that someone would have compared Marxist-Leninist parties historically. How did the National Question manifest itself in Brazil, as compared to the United States? How did the approach to Quebec by the Canadian party compare with the approach to the South of the U.S. party? Was Moscow sending similar messages to both? Why or why not? The philosophical rigidity of too many analysts has not only meant that they failed to answer these questions, but that they neglected to ask them.[65]

The U.S. party did see itself as the advanced detachment of the Communist International, the global headquarters of Marxist-Leninist parties, based in Moscow. The tendency is to only give credence to the opinions about the inner workings of both groups to those who have left the party. Thus it is useful to examine the viewpoint of Sam Darcy, one of the highest ranking party leaders until his departure in 1945. He was posted by the U.S. party to Moscow and worked directly with Joseph Stalin, Nikolai Bukharin, and other Soviet leaders. He alleges that it is "completely wrong" to portray the CI as "monolithic" or "homogeneous" since there was "constant inner struggle," often "with the most violent language used [by] contending factions." The CI "had no method of enforcing its decisions, " just "moral influence. " In fact, Darcy views Gerhart Eisler, CI representative in the U.S., as a conciliator of the various U.S. factions grouped variously around party leaders Jay Lovestone, Earl Browder, and William Z. Foster.[66] In another interview he goes further: "From all I have said . . . about the international influence on the Communist party I hope no one gets the idea that these class struggles were initiated by the Comintern or other outside forces . . . they were born of conditions that exist in this country."[67] This was particularly true of North America though I believe a different pattern could be detected in Europe, where Moscow's influence could be exercised more directly in the era before secure telephone transmission and fax machines.

So when Ben Davis came to the Harlem party he was entering a maelstrom. At the 1928 CI meeting it was decided collectively that the party should reorient its policies toward blacks. The CI operated on the principle of democratic centralism, as did the CPUSA; theoretically this meant democratic discussion, then a decision that must be carried out by all participating political parties. The "Black Belt thesis" that emerged from this gathering was centered on the notion that blacks in the Black Belt South—black majority areas of the Old Confederacy—constituted a nation with the right to self-determination—which could include secession. This simple idea was to cause a good deal of trouble for both the party and its chief black spokesperson, Benjamin J. Davis. The idea of secession in particular was interpreted by party foes to suggest that Davis and his comrades were in league with the racists to separate blacks from whites.

At the sixth congress of the CI in 1928 the U.S. delegation included five African-Americans but, according to Philip Foner and James Allen, Harry Haywood was the only American black to back the thesis: James Ford and Otto Hall opposed it. Only one Soviet citizen was on the subcommittee that formulated the thesis. U.S. debate may have been influenced by the fact that the policy that the South African party should adopt was being debated at the same time. Yet at the end of the day one often forgets that the Black Belt thesis was intended only for propaganda purposes and that the keynote for the struggle was to be equal rights. Separatist themes continue to find their way into African-American discourse, which illustrates that this approach was not foisted on the United States by Stalin.[68]

Margaret Wilhemina Jackson, in a 1938 thesis written at Howard University, has written one of the few works that reflects a less dogmatic approach to the CI. If there is to be a valid criticism of the Black Belt thesis it would be that the hand, but of the world, not Moscow, was too intrusive. Otto Kusinen and Georgi Dimitrov were influential within the CI; both were eastern Europeans. The legendary Sen Katayama from Japan had as much influence on the U.S. party as any foreigner; he helped found the parties in the United States, Mexico, and Japan.[69]

Davis's comrade James Ford has been accused of refracting the Soviet view in his pamphlet *The Negroes in a Soviet America*, published in 1935.

According to Ford, a United Soviet States of America would mean "complete independence of the Black Belt region"; Blacks could choose "federation with or separation from" the United States. The party would "urge and fight for federation" but "would respect" sovereignty. In the North, Blacks could "remain in Harlem" or move; moving would be encouraged as it would "hasten the destruction of all forms of separation." In the Black Belt Republic, Blacks would play the "principal" but not the exclusive role; there would not be a "dictatorship of the Negroes" but the "workers" since the "Soviet Negro Republic" would not necessarily be all-Black. Though many whites might find such a program totally objectionable, many African-Americans still find it worth considering.[70]

To divine why the Black Belt thesis was adopted, one need look no further than the four corners of the United States. Cyril Briggs of the African Blood Brotherhood enunciated a Black Belt thesis in the early 1920s. In 1918 many Texas Blacks wanted to make a part of this largest state the 49th state—for Blacks; this movement may have been sparked in part by the then-current talk about Woodrow Wilson's "Fourteen Points," which included self-determination. The experience of Oklahoma as the land of the Indians was still familiar. And how could any self-respecting Marxist ignore the success of Marcus Garvey in organizing U.S. Blacks? Those who gathered in Moscow in 1928 did not have to construct the Black Belt thesis from whole cloth.[71]

Though a number of commentators have castigated the Black Belt thesis as being out of touch with African-American reality, evidence suggests that this view is misleading. Abner Berry, who left the party in the 1950s but who worked in the South for some time before then, felt that this opinion was received more favorably in the South than in the North. Below the Mason-Dixon line, Berry averred that people still remember how land had been taken from Blacks. Moreover, in the South Blacks understood the need for a conspiratorial organization. Like Darcy, he saw Eisler's role as CI representative in the United States as not intruding on the Black Belt thesis and related issues. Davis agreed: "If one goes into the Black Belt today and asks a Negro farmer if he wants 'self-determination' he may not understand at once just what is meant. But if you explain, if you ask him if he wants the land, he will answer 'yes.'"[72]

Generally speaking, the party was true to its original plan to use the Black Belt thesis for propaganda but to focus on the struggle for equal rights in terms of praxis. The Foster-Ford presidential ticket of 1932 reflected this trend.[73] Robert Minor, the party's specialist on the Negro Question in the pre–World War II era, in his 1938 "Report on Negro Work" declared, "The main link to be seized is that link around employment discrimination or limitation in employment opportunities." He also urged that comrades join Black churches.[74] The 1938 "Election Platform Demands of the CP" were similar to those of 1936 in neglecting the Black Belt thesis. Yet despite this, on balance the Black Belt thesis probably was not an asset for the party, particularly in the postwar period when Blacks moved en masse North and West. It was particularly unhelpful during key moments when Ben Davis was running for office.

This position is understandable, however, in light of the relative success of the movement led and symbolized by Marcus Garvey. Communists had direct experience with this movement. Claude Lightfoot, longtime party leader in Illinois, was a member of the Universal Negro Improvement Association as a child. In an interview he was asked what he learned: "Black pride, for one thing," he responded.[75] Party leader Israel Amter was not Black but he had a similar experience. In Cleveland he worked closely with the UNIA.[76] The Communists and Garveyites did clash intellectually but often they were able to find unity in action.

The party had to treat Garvey gingerly since he was such a complex and mercurial figure. After the government started investigating his movement and began issuing indictments, Garvey's radicalism—as symbolized by his pro-Bolshevik comments—tended to ebb. He allied with Tammany Hall and even backed white Democrats against Black Republicans. But there were other nationalist trends that the party viewed less benignly. During the "don't buy where you can't work" campaign in Harlem in the 1930s a Communist spokesperson captured these tensions: "We denounce the present methods of barring those sympathetic whites—workers, intellectuals and professionals—who have manifested a desire to sincerely fight for the rights of the Negro people by picketing stores where whites are only employed at the present time. These 'leaders' are taking advantage of the nationalist feelings of the much oppressed Negro people in order to gain security for themselves."[77] Just as the First Amendment carries an inherent tension between the free-exercise clause and the no-establishment-of-religion clause, the party's position on the Negro Question carried a similar tension between the notion of self-determination, which could conceivably mean all-Black segregation, and the idea of equal rights, which could mean integration. Unfortunately, neither Davis nor most party leaders plumbed this tension deftly.

Ben Davis was at times caustic in his analysis of certain nationalists. He denounced "Sufi Abdul Hamid, Harlem self-styled 'Black Hitler'" and his comrades, who stabbed an ILD leader in Harlem as he was speaking against low wages paid to black butchers.[78] These black nationalists had been hired by Julius Malin, owner of the market. One writer for *New Masses* claimed that "nationalist speakers who nightly attack" Harlem progressives "are said to be sponsored by Tammany."[79] When Marcus Garvey died in mid-1940, Davis again was acerbic in suggesting that his "Back to Africa" theories had "feet of clay":

> He organized perhaps the biggest movement of Negroes in the history of the country. . . . The Negro people were sound and progressive in their feelings for a government of their own and for independent existence as a nation . . . fantastic dream of a trek to Africa . . . ridiculously impossible. . . . He neither saw nor understood the class struggle, but instead, saw as the solution, the building of a parasitic Negro imperialism . . . petty bourgeois nationalism. . . . Garvey's methodology was a sort of inverted segregation . . . the real blow to Garveyism was given by the Communist party. . . .[80]

After charging Garvey with supporting Mussolini during the conflict with Ethiopia and accusing him of breaking strikes in Jamaica, Davis reiterated the Black Belt thesis. In this article he did not see any connection between the party's view of self-determination and the early success of Garveyism.

Former Communist leader Dorothy Healey has observed, ". . . when we [the party] make mistakes, it's considered part of a terrible conspiracy; and when others do, it's just a momentary lapse of judgment."[81] This reaction could be applied to perceptions of the Black Belt thesis, for despite its flaws, the party was probably unparalleled in not just fighting racism in society but within the ranks as well.

James Prickett's comments on Red trade unionists should be considered in that light: "As unionists, they were far superior to their anti-Communist counterparts, but they were poor Communists."[82] Could this statement also apply to the work of Reds in the Black Liberation movement? Were they, too, poor Communists? Insofar as they held to the Black Belt thesis after the facts on the ground had changed, Prickett's observation would hold. Were they "far superior" to many of their "anti-Communist counterparts?" They undoubtedly were.

These considerations help to explain the party's relative success among African-Americans. Abner Berry believes that the dislocation arising from the GOP attempt to oust blacks from their ranks in the early 1930s led this community to thrash around and look for leadership, causing the party to step forward. Ironically, he feels, this led blacks back to being "American" and away from feeling alienated. The Red slogan about Communism being "20th-century Americanism" may have been more accurate than all sides realized.[83]

Over the years Davis was one of the staunchest advocates of the Black Belt thesis, although if he objected to Browder's ditching of the thesis during the war, the evidence does not survive. He was also one of the first Communists who attempted to interpret black history in a manner that would uphold revolutionary traditions. At times his positions could be seen as reflections of "Browderism," or conciliation with U.S. elites. Davis wrote an article in 1938, for example, entitled "Thomas Jefferson—the First Abolitionist" and observed that "although Jefferson owned slaves . . . ." Yet his more dominant theme was expressed in another article that same year that outlined "the revolutionary traditions of the Negro people" as he praised Abraham Lincoln, Frederick Douglass, and John Brown.[84]

Applying Theory

Davis's and the party's theories of history and the National Question were put to the test after his move to Harlem. Mark Tushnet has noted inferentially that W. E. B. Du Bois's controversial positions, which led to his departure from the NAACP in 1934, were remarkably similar to the Black Belt thesis. This intellectual convergence did not prevent Davis from terming him a "liberal but confused scholar" and ridiculing his "dictatorship of the proletariat" description of Reconstruction. Davis's detraction was part of a CP tendency to attack black leaders not deemed sufficiently radical—a tendency harshly criticized in the 1950s but particularly evident in the period before the formal promulgation of the "popular front" in 1935. A. Philip Randolph, Arnold Hill, and especially Walter White were also assaulted.[85]

Davis was a regular visitor to NAACP conventions. Just as his hallowed family name was an admittance ticket, so too were his Red credentials helpful. At the 1939 association meeting in Richmond, Ed Strong of the Southern Negro Youth Congress was on the youth panel with Thurgood Marshall. When Davis asked the "young NAACP special counsel" if the NAACP was "radical," he replied, "We find it necessary to work with other organizations because often times one organization is not strong enough to put its program through."[86] The idea of a united front was not solely a party concoction.

The NAACP was a major but not the sole focus of Davis and his comrades as they sought to put the National Question into practice. The party helped to initiate like-minded organizations such as the Southern Negro Youth Congress during this period. However, their premier effort in this regard was the National Negro Congress, which involved a direct application of the principles of both the united front and the National Question. Davis's elevated status from the beginning of his stay in Harlem is evident in the fact that he served as secretary of the New York City Sponsoring Committee for a NNC; veteran labor leader Frank Crosswaith served as chair with Benjamin McLaurin of the Brotherhood of Sleeping Car Porters and Lester Granger of the Urban League as vice-chairs. It was noted that "at present communications should be addressed to [Davis]."[87]

From the beginning the NNC was a prime area of political work and commentary for Davis. He reminded his *Daily Worker* readers that the NNC was heir to the Negro Convention Movement of the nineteenth century. This enthusiasm was not unique to Davis or the party. There was "unanimous consensus" in the "Negro Work Committee" of the Socialist party to work with the NNC.[88] The NAACP was initially hesitant but Davis's

Amherst and Harvard Law classmate William Hastie suggested to Walter White and Charles Houston that they should act otherwise: "I feel that the [NAACP] is making a mistake in keeping out of the National Negro Congress . . . it is quite possible that the Congress will prove the greatest opportunity in a generation for the orientation and direction of Negroes in a national program for their betterment." The leftward tilt Hastie and his community shows in his comment, was also reflected. "By the way, if Roy can get Max Yergan's speech before the Philadelphia conference on Imperialism and the Negro Peoples, I think the Crisis will have one of the best articles of the year."[89]

The opening session of the NNC convened in Chicago in mid-February 1936. Davis was on the presiding committee and served as chairman of the Committee on Education and Culture; he also served on the National Executive Council. The 817 delegates represented over five hundred organizations with membership of over 3 million, but thousands showed up for the rally they held. Davis was ecstatic. In these happier days, Davis referred to A. Philip Randolph as "an outstanding Negro Socialist."[90] Forty years later Dorothy Height recalled fondly that era when "a Republican, and a Communist and a Socialist and a Democrat, and whoever else, could all sit down together."[91]

The initiation of the NNC certainly led to sharpened ideological discussion. Davis took the lead for the party on this important matter by asserting that the NNC represented "self-determination for the Black Belt" and denying that the NNC meant that the party "has abandoned its independent position on the struggle for Negro liberation." An "emphatic 'NO!'" was Davis's unvarnished reply to this question.[92] He assailed those who questioned the need for the congress, such as Kelly Miller and black Republican Perry Howard. He attacked *The Nation*, which had questioned the NNC's focus on the black church, though he did acknowledge that the glaring weakness of the NNC was the absence of sufficient representation from the South.[93]

Organizing the NNC in Harlem had the added benefit of deepening Davis's nascent relationship with the Reverend Adam Clayton Powell. The report on the Chicago meeting took place at Powell's church: "The meeting ended with 'Give Me that Old Congress Spirit' which was sung to the tune of 'Give Me that Old Time Religion.' . . . Verses went: 'If it's good enough for Adam Powell,'—'for Ben Davis'—and 'for Fred Douglass'—'it's good enough for me.'"[94]

Davis had expressed concern about the relative lack of labor participation in the NNC and the NAACP, which was consistent with his growing belief after joining the party that labor organization was needed. He felt that oppression of blacks dragged down the wages and living standards of white workers and sharecroppers, just as the low wages and living standards of the South depressed the rest of the nation. In this he saw a link for black-white unity against Jim Crow.[95]

These beliefs were put to the test during another practical application of the united front concept—the massive Congress of Industrial Organization drives of the 1930s. In July 1937 at the Harlem YMCA, amid stirring applause, he called on blacks to join these drives and ripped into the American Federation of Labor.[96]

These were not just empty exhortations however; they were a commitment to action. Just before the NNC convened in 1936 he joined Norman Thomas, Randolph, and the labor leader Frank Crosswaith at a "mass meeting in support of the National Shoe strike at the Harlem Labor Center."[97] These salesmen had been on strike for three months and there had been over one hundred arrests. Months later he joined with Crosswaith, Powell, Granger, and McLaurin in seeking to prevent the recruiting of black scabs to break a seamen's strike. Throughout there were close relations with Socialists and centrist forces in further demonstration of a united front.[98]

Yet most of Davis's attention during this period was on labor in New York. He was a prime mover in the Coordinating Committee for Employment, a united front that included the CP, NNC, NAACP, the Porters, Powell, and Randolph, among others. Primary targets were Consolidated Edison and "its notorious anti-Negro employment policy" and AT&T. They forced Con Ed to hire four blacks as cashiers and service clerks in its Harlem branch; they demanded "jobs for Negroes without displacement of white workers" and wanted these employers to "take into consideration the race" before hiring. This 1938 victory was complemented by another a few years later that called for the hiring of blacks as bus drivers. Davis, who was pivotal in the process, claimed that this was the "first time . . . that a major trade union has ever entered into a contractual relation with an employer in which the union becomes a co-party with the Negro people." The agreement included quotas. But it was "meetings, demonstrations, delegations, picket lines" that brought the result. The United Negro Bus Strike Committee included both the NNC and the CP. But fissures were now appearing in the united front as Davis asked plaintively, "Where were the great leaders?", referring to Crosswaith and Randolph. By then disagreements about international affairs loomed large, as Davis's caustic comment suggests: "If they are so opposed to fascism, why weren't they on the scene against the fascist job discrimination against Negro workers?"[99]

Davis adopted other controversial viewpoints. In 1936 the *Pittsburgh Courier* endorsed the use of the Sherman Anti-Trust Act against unions for antiracist purposes, suggesting that racism was an illegal restraint of trade and competition. Davis dissented vigorously. His was the type of position that was later pointed to as an example of what came to be called "Browderism," which involved, among other things, a more conciliatory approach on racial matters.[100]

Defending of labor united Davis with Crosswaith, Randolph, and other Socialists. But from its zenith in 1936, the united front, as represented by the NCC, soon disintegrated, and bitter recriminations emerged. Crosswaith in particular was a key participant in this scenario. He worked closely with Randolph in the Brotherhood and David Dubinsky—deemed by Davis and the party as an ideological adversary—in the International Ladies Garment Workers Union. Crosswaith, a Virgin Islander, liked to be called the Eugene Debs of Harlem. But as one analyst has observed, "He hated Communists. . . . He would not give them any attention, even unfavorable." Although exaggerated, the comment nonetheless conveys the flavor of the discord, and the analyst also notes that Crosswaith's "uneasy relationship" with Davis and the Reds broke down in 1938, ending their quasi-alliance. It is also useful to note that this fissure occurred before the 1939 Soviet-German Non-aggression Pact, which is usually spoken of as the beginning of the end of CP-SP unity.[101]

The Socialists attracted some blacks with profiles akin to Davis's. For example, there was Julian D. Steele of Boston, a Harvard graduate who was married to the granddaughter of former Vice President William Dawes and a relation of one of Paul Revere's close associates. Steele was friendly with Randolph and Crosswaith and knew Davis through Harvard. Such connections facilitated working alliances as the NNC dawned in 1936. So when a banquet was given late that year honoring Thyra Edwards upon her return from the USSR, Randolph, Crosswaith, and McLaurin joined Davis, Ford, and James Egert Allen of the NAACP in heaping praise on her. Lester Granger continued the alliance by singing the praises of the *Daily Worker*. As late as mid-1937 Davis was returning the compliment by averring that "the great majority of the [Socialist] party is composed of honest socialists," though Trotskyite elements were present and Norman Thomas, their premier leader, was questionable in his opinions.[102]

On 29 January 1937 at Crosswaith's New York office at 312 West 125 Street a meeting of Socialists and Communists took place with the purpose of furthering their cooperation. This meeting was a turning point in the evolution of the united front generally and CP-SP relations specifically. Naturally Davis was there, but Abner Berry, Manning Johnson, and George Blake also attended. The meeting was held under the auspices of the Negro Labor Committee, which had 130 affiliate unions. The Communists wanted to bring their union contacts to the NLC so that, said Davis, they could plan jointly and intelligently. Days later Davis and his comrades put it bluntly to Crosswaith: "We are now writing to suggest that we hold an unofficial joint Socialist and Communist party conference of trade union activities in Harlem . . . for our part we are prepared to bring to the conference a group of trade union members active in Harlem who are in a position to aid in the realization of these objectives." Crosswaith was not forthcoming, so Blake addressed him as "Dear Comrade." Still no response. Finally an exasperated Davis in late March pleaded that he was "very anxious to have you send regular news releases and statements." Since even this low-level proposal for cooperation failed to budge the Socialist leader, it was not surprising that Richard Wright's effort to initiate political cooperation by requesting Crosswaith's opinion on "recent invasion of China by Japan" was met with granite silence. Eventually, but without the good offices of Crosswaith, there was some Red participation in NLC ranks, but the cooperation was so flimsy that the slightest breeze could destroy it.[103]

In 1935 the Communist International had called for a united front against fascism; the U.S. and particularly the French parties had been moving in that direction even before this call. But the experience with this concept in Harlem showed that it was no easy task to accomplish; the slightest misunderstandings could prove fatal. The Socialist Alfred Baker Lewis, close to many NAACP leaders, complained frequently about NNC attacks on the Socialist party's Negro Resolution. John Davis, the conciliatory NNC leader, reproached Lewis and called for a conference of NNC and SP activists involved in Negro work to clear up these problems. Lewis was adamant, however, which caused Davis to wonder if there was an alternative explanation: "Is it not possible that you have confused me with Mr. Benjamin Davis, Jr.?"[104]

There was no confusion in the minds of top black Communists James Ford and Ben Davis. They were convinced that the Socialists were not living up to their lofty name with their activity on the Negro Question. Ford put it succinctly: "we find serious shortcomings . . . not a single Negro is a member of the party's National Executive Committee—its leading body."[105] Typically, Davis was even harsher in a mid-1937 philippic. Their "Resolution on Negro Work" was a "concession to the anti-Negro policies of the most reactionary capitalists and a flagrant insult to the Negro people." He denounced the alleged Trotskyite influence on this party and their implication that Negros were a "race of strikebreakers." Their resolution had artlessly given rise to this implication; a livid Davis pointed out that there were "far more white scabs and strikebreakers" than black; he also highlighted the black role in the CIO drive and the racism of the American Federation of Labor. The united front was unraveling.[106]

Davis found this issue so compelling that despite the peril it presented to the united front and NNC, he returned to it a few days later in a more general way. First he quoted from the Socialist Resolution ("It is important that where there is capability, Negro comrades should be quietly and unobtrusively placed in positions of responsibility. As much precaution against the danger of 'black chauvinism' as white chauvinism should be kept in mind.") Why, growled Davis, should there be a "'capability' requirement for Negro party members but not . . . for white. . . . There can be no such thing as 'black chauvinism' since obviously the Negro people are an oppressed minority group and are victims of white chauvinism." He went on to make discerning comments about the two trends in black nationalism—reactionary and revolutionary. What this showed at bottom was that Davis and the Reds generally were more advanced on the question of race than their Socialist counterparts, which helps explain why the CP had more black leaders and rank-and-filers. The result, however, was complication for the united front and the Negro Question.[107]

Perceptive friends of the Socialists like Lester Granger were not unaware of this party's "Negro problem." The Urban League leader confided in Alfred Baker Lewis in mid-1936, "One reason for the failure of the Socialist Party to reach any considerable number of Negroes, lies in the tendency of Socialist writers and speakers to use invective instead of reasoned argument."[108] This difficulty and related problems finally caused Julian Steele to resign from the party, and the SP lost one of its few black leaders.[109] The missed opportunity for Socialist-Communist unity was manifested in labor and other areas, but it is fair to say that the sharpest consequence of this issue was evident in the Harlems of the United States as the Negro Question became the major challenge for the united front.

Another black leader of note was A. Philip Randolph. His association with the NNC in 1936 was a coup and symbolized a black united front. His defection in 1940 showed that a new stage had been reached. Davis cooperated with Randolph's union, as did the Communists generally. But more than once Davis was disturbed by Randolph's actions, such as denying Red dominance of the NNC in 1936 and then alleging it in 1940.[110]

Randolph's union was useful in constructing the black united front. In an era before advanced mass communications, the porters who traveled from coast to coast were veritable towncriers, conveying messages far and wide. E. D. Nixon of Montgomery helped the Communist-initiated Southern Negro Youth Congress and went on to work with Martin Luther King, Jr. But this promising beginning came crashing down at the April 1940 convention of the NNC in Washington, D.C. This meeting was far from being a disaster, however. When CIO leader John Lewis spoke, his remarks were punctuated so frequently with applause that he had to rush through the latter part of his prepared text to comply with his half-hour broadcasting time over the NBC network. But this meeting was not necessarily to be remembered for Lewis's stormy peroration. The NNC split on the issues of support for the Soviet Union and the Communists' view of blacks; the speeches of John Davis and Randolph conflicted as the latter blasted the USSR as a "dictatorship"; he added that African-Americans could not afford to add to the handicap of being "black" the handicap of being "red." The *Daily Worker* begged to differ. Its opinion was that Randolph left the NNC "after his splitting red-baiting tactics had been decisively rejected by the delegates again and again . . . [he] refused to join in unequivocal opposition to the war-mongering policies" of Roosevelt "and instead concentrated his fire on" the Soviets.[111]

Randolph fired back. He focused on the party's alleged treatment of its black leaders. Ford had been "submerged," he claimed. Davis "is having his honeymoon now. But it won't last . . . though prominent now, [he] will, too, be ruthlessly consigned to the limbo of political oblivion."[112] The NNC moved on. It endorsed the Randolph-initiated march on Washington in 1941 while continuing to chide him, but the Randolph controversy inflicted a severe wound from which the congress was not to recover. Not long after the war had ended the NNC was folded into the Civil Rights Congress and a fascinating experiment in the united front disappeared.

It is often suggested that the Soviet-German nonaggression pact of 1939 and the Communists' defense of it spelled the U.S. party's doom; similarly, analysts also believe that its slowness to align with those European nations, principally Britain, that were fighting Germany also undercut its support. While there may be some truth to this assertion, it overstates the case. Throughout this controversy, which was to shape the public perception of Communists for decades to come, Ben Davis was speaking, commenting, and acting—trying to stave off a devastating blow to the united front and advance clarity on the National Question.

Black Communist leader Claude Lightfoot has conceded, properly, that the party erred in criticizing both Britain and Germany after the 1939 pact: "[this] was the Soviet position but did not necessarily have to be ours."[113] The party's view was similar to that of the Communist party of Germany; after some initial disorientation, sharper attacks on Britain because of London's tardy approach to concluding a collective security pact with Moscow combined with relentless assaults on the Nazis. Then, with the German invasion of the USSR in June 1941, the U.S. party pulled back on its attacks on the U.K. and on the United States for aiding London. This chain of events caused a torrent of complaint to be rained down on the Reds.[114]

Critics often forget that this was an extremely complicated period and that the Communists were not alone in backing and filling. The NAACP convention in mid-1940 saw a Youth Council resolution opposing conscription as "undemocratic" pass unanimously after a stirring speech by a delegate who declared that African-Americans were not "interested in defending the colonial possessions and markets of either imperialist side in Europe or of Wall Street."[115] Seeing this war as a replica of World War I, which was viewed as a feast for the merchants of death, was common. The resolution was defeated after it left the Youth Council, 66–44. In the *Daily Worker* respected black lawyer and businessman Earl Dickerson of Chicago in that same year echoed the opinion of many: " . . . the frontier of democracy is here at home. Our boys do not need to die in European trenches. . . . Every right won by the Negro people is endangered by the present drive toward war." "Strict neutrality" was his call. "Isolationism" has been an intermittent trend in this country that has affected African-Americans, who in turn have influenced Communists.[116]

Though Randolph is perceived as a defiant symbol of opposition to the party's positions on this question, he too reacted to the shifting political winds. In 1938 he was vice-chair of the Greater New York Committee to Keep America Out of War. This group began to fall apart only after May 1940, when Hitler surged. At that same NAACP convention in 1940 fellow labor leader John Lewis proclaimed that involvement in war was repugnant and claimed that his allies in labor and liberal circles agreed. He received a prolonged standing ovation. On 24 November 1939 the party held a rally at Madison Square Garden that expressed opposition to Britain's and France's policies. But it is often forgotten that these positions were echoed in the *Afro-American*, the *Pittsburgh Courier*, and other black newspapers; they too were hard-pressed to see these colonial powers, with their boots on the neck of Africa and the West Indies, as guardians of liberty. In March 1941 the "Negroes Against War Committee," chaired by George Schuyler, held a forum in Harlem that was addressed by Adam Clayton Powell, J. A. Rogers, and Senator Gerald Nye, the last of whom had exposed the profiteering of munitions manufacturers—the "merchants of death"—as a cause of World War I. That same year "Defend Democracy at Home" was the theme of the NAACP convention. West Indians, organized in the Caribbean Union in Harlem and whose homelands were colonized by Britain, also urged the United States to stay out of the war—and did so after the nonaggression pact of September 1939.[117]

Consequently, if the party and Davis could be accused of moral blindness in their approach to World War II alliances, they were not alone. In this complicated political period not everyone could see a difference between the colonizers of London and the butchers of Berlin. Part of being a Communist was support of existing though imperfect socialism in the USSR, and Davis was a party man through and through. He joined his friend William Patterson in reprimanding the *Afro-American* in 1936 after they had criticized Soviet foreign policy. He wrote glowingly of Soviet policy toward national minorities and compared them favorably to the United States. In 1938 he raged at the "Trotskyist-Bukharin Clique who Fought Lenin on the National Question." The problem for Davis and the party was the rationalization put forward by A. A. Berle in June 1941 after the German invasion of the USSR. Democrats and the GOP could flip-flop but the Reds were held to a different standard: "A party line which could change from one of hostility to one of collaboration overnight could change back with equal speed." Continued FBI surveillance of the party was advised.[118]

Neither the position of Davis nor the party wavered after the Stalin-Hitler pact and the opening of the war; a few days after the pact was signed the seriousness of the ideological challenge was reflected in Davis's address to an open membership meeting of the Upper Harlem Section of the Communist party entitled "What the Soviet-German Pact Means for the Negro People." The *Daily Worker* did publish an editorial at this time criticizing U.S. "neutrality" and seeking help for Poland "without delay," but this position was not pursued consistently. Thereafter, "Keep America Out of the

Imperialist War" became the familiar slogan. Davis reinforced this attitude in an interview with his friend Paul Robeson. The actor-activist argued that the conflict was an imperialist war in which the blacks had nothing to gain no matter which side won . . . Davis tended to agree with his friend that support for the war—before June 1941—meant support for British and French colonialism.[119]

In the cold light of history, the party and Davis are subject to criticism. For example, their view did not seem to dovetail with the theory of the united front, which distinguished between "bourgeois democracy" and fascism. In addressing the war, the *Daily Worker* seemed to be neutral between Britain and Germany. Oakley Johnson, writing in the *Daily Worker*, at one point referred to the chief South African racist as "anti-war General J. B. M. Hertzog"; he was so eager to assail London that he glossed over the fact that the general's "anti-war" sentiments were motivated by a sympathy for racism. A subsequent editorial suggested that "South Africa's anti-war outburst" was sparked by "resentment against the rule of British imperialism."[120]

Davis's approach to the war was sound on many counts. The posturing of Japan as "protecter of the colored races" did influence some members of the African-American community. One student has pointed out that "Lester Granger could say that the war would probably never have broken out had Japan been a white nation."[121] George Schuyler was invited to visit Japan in the late 1930s and wrote a number of pro-Japan articles upon his return. Davis noticed this tendency at work at the 1939 NAACP convention in Richmond, where an agent of Tokyo was permitted to solicit delegates in support of Japanese aggression in China. Kaju Nakamura of Japan's Parliament made a lecture tour of the United States in 1938, paying special attention to blacks. Davis was incredulous: "What does the Hon. Mr. Nakamura think the Negro people are, fools and idiots? . . . he should be shunned as poison ivy."[122]

Davis was equally perceptive about the challenge presented by the Spanish Civil War, appealing for aid to the Republican cause. He lauded the Negro People's Committee to Aid Spanish Democracy, which sent an ambulance to Spain and sixty-year-old African-American C. Gibbs Carter, who after returning from fighting in Spain in 1939 went immediately to fight in China. Davis was part of a united front in 1939 that included Benjamin McLaurin and William Pickens that sought to gather food, medical supplies, and cash for the Republican cause. He engaged in similar efforts after the Italian invasion of Ethiopia.[123] And though he may have equated Britain with Germany, Davis did not flinch in denouncing Nazi atrocities. During that period the *Daily Worker* was raising the slogan "Keep America Out of War by Keeping War Out of the World."[124]

What clouded the vision of Davis and the party was the brutal lash of colonialism visited on Africa and the West Indies by London and Paris. Before the reality of Auschwitz became clear, it was difficult for many people to distinguish between Berlin's actions in Europe and London's actions in Africa; the failure of bourgeois analysts to condemn the latter helped to impel Davis and the party to equate the two antagonists. The presence in Harlem of an alert and militant West Indian community was another salient factor. In 1937 Davis was quick to denounce London's "bloody reign of terror" in the Caribbean; he wrote at length on Trinidad in particular—home of his close friend Claudia Jones—and its color bar, prostitution, repression of strikes, and civil liberties. He affiliated with the Harlem West Indian Defense Conference. He was also upset with London's support for the racist regime in Pretoria, as well as its vacillation on Italy's invasion of Ethiopia.[125]

Davis did not hesitate to take these concerns to larger arenas such as the NAACP. At its 1940 Philadelphia convention he argued that there was little substantive difference between Germany and Britain. "Negroes are in little mood for forgetting discrimination in favor of [FDR's] fake 'defense' program" was his reply to William Pickens, who argued otherwise. Davis wrote, "Yells and cheers met every attack upon the position of Pickens." "Mocking laughter" greeted Pickens's charge of "outside influence" on delegates.[126]

Davis's broadsides were not limited to the NAACP convention. After this gathering he repeatedly attacked Walter White's "war-mongering attack" upon the Soviets. He was with James Ford in Birmingham when the Communist vice-presidential candidate screamed, "stay out of the imperialist war." This was their major focus as they campaigned across the country. This was an "imperialist war," Davis charged, in response to an article by Thomas Lamont of the House of Morgan in the *Harvard Alumni Bulletin*; "[French and British] empires . . . keep in subjection a half billion oppressed colonial peoples—empires whose imperialist aims in this war are just as reprehensible as those of German imperialism." Later Davis was even angrier. The call for "national defense . . . means in actuality intensified national oppression." African-Americans were "supposed to forget" racism "for the benefit of plucking Churchill's chestnuts, or of making Wall Street" richer. Blacks were to be "cannon fodder" to "smash Hitlerism" while "Hitlerism is enforced against him at home."[129]

The authorities were not sitting quietly as Davis hurled his thunderbolts. From 1939 to 1941 the party seemed to be coming under fiercer attack than usual, probably because of its position on the war. Ben Gold, Earl Browder, Clarence Hathaway, and other leaders were dragged into court on various charges. Party offices in various cities were bombed. Legislation was introduced to outlaw the party. And Harlem, where black enthusiasm for another war may have been at its lowest, was a particular target according to the *New York Amsterdam News*: "A Red hunt conducted by the [FBI] has been going on quietly in Harlem . . . fearful lest Negroes become innoculated with Red virus in larger numbers." Apparently these detectives had not been briefed thoroughly, for "[Davis] stumped G-Men investigating Reds in Harlem when they learned of his Republican party background."[128]

This increased repression did not seem to deter Davis. One of his foci was the military. He abruptly dismissed then-prevalent notions that blacks could see better at night or stand heat better and thus be better suited for tank duty. Not only could Britain be equated with Germany, but so could the United States: "How does U.S. naval 'discipline' differ from the Nuremberg laws which Hitler enforces upon the Jewish people in Germany and Central Europe?" This difficulty in distinguishing bourgeois democracy from fascism was understandable since this form of democracy was virtually denied to blacks of any class in the United States, thereby creating at least a quasi-fascist plight, but it proved damaging when the party formulated political tactics in the 1939–41 period and was a major reason why Davis and his party could not consistently develop a united front and, ultimately, advance black rights.[129]

The perception of Franklin Roosevelt by Davis and his party fluctuated during his administration. But during this period there was a consistent line of hostility, particularly toward FDR's foreign policy. Davis was notably vitriolic. This mixed view of Roosevelt was later reflected in the black press, as well, just as Davis's attack on other black leaders was prompted in part by their devotion to Roosevelt.[130]

Certainly Davis, the party, and others who resisted U.S. entry into the war were captivated by the history of World War I as an interimperialist conflict. Davis admitted as much. But some of his toughest talk was reserved for fellow black leaders like Randolph and White. Davis put words in their mouth: "Lynch us, oppress us, discriminate against us, you great and wise gentlemen of American imperialism. We know it pains you to do it. But we will be ever faithful to your jim crow system—we will die for you and like it!"[131]

Such harsh words did not help Davis and the party reach out to the NAACP after the Nazis invaded the USSR in June 1941. Yet since the party had its own strengths, it could not be ignored. The party was the country's most implacable and outspoken foe of Jim Crow, which brought them support in the nation's Harlems. The alienation of the African-American community became evident when the Japanese began to make inroads with their phony policy of championing the colored races. By virtue of its racism, the U.S. ruling class had handed blacks to the Left on a silver platter. Leaders like Ben Davis assured that this gift would not be fumbled, though the sectarian spasms of the party were not helpful. Ultimately these divisions were to prove damaging to Black Liberation when the Red Scare arose. Still, the votes Davis received during his numerous races for public office were quantitative evidence of African-American support for himself and his party.

5
Squeeze Play, 1940–1942

Many observers see the 1930s as the heyday or zenith of Communist party activism. This perception may be true, particularly when one considers membership figures and mass impact. But if so, the 1940s cannot be far behind. There is a tendency to see the German-USSR nonaggression pact as a watershed that revealed the party as some sort of foreign agent, causing all decent and sane people to depart the ranks forthwith. But this analysis does not explain the success of the party during this decade, an achievement that included the electoral victory of Davis. However, it is true that there were a number of ideological and other pitfalls that befell Davis and his party. More specifically, conflicts with the NAACP and the Brotherhood of Sleeping Car Porters complicated the effort to construct a united front.

Evidence of Davis's and the party's heightened profile during this decade was his appearance before a congressional committee in March 1940. This incident augmented his growing reputation as an uncompromising fighter against Jim Crow, which served to distinguish him and the Communists from other companions in these trenches. It could be termed a turning point in the perception of Davis as a leading public figure.

It all began innocently enough when Davis and Red leader Pat Toohey wrote to all members of the Senate Judiciary Cammittee, asking to testify on antilynching legislation. Snapping up the bait, the Senate accepted. Before this august body they assailed "Democratic reactionaries and Republican hypocrites . . . despite heckling, insults and frequent interruptions . . . [they] refused to be sidetracked or brow-beaten. . . . " At one point there was a threat to "eject" Davis. The senators seemed to take particular umbrage at his taking the lead in the denunciation. They expunged from the record his portrayal of Vice President John Garner as an "evil old laborbaiter." Davis was irate: "When statements have been made in the Senate derogatory to the Negro people, I have not seen any Senators getting up and showing the same indignation which they are showing here today." He specifically challenged Senators Tom Connolly and Warren Austin. Though scheduled for fifteen minutes, the session stretched on five times as long.[1]

The reaction to Davis's pillorying of the racists was electric. Recall that this was a time when African-Americans were not just shuffling on the silver screen; it was seen as part of normal social etiquette. Then comes here a black who does what many blacks yearned to do: lambast the Dixiecrats face to face. The *Daily Worker* described the reaction to their star reporter: "Negro organizations approved . . . very heartily. They crowded around . . . shook hands with them and congratulated them."[2] The party's public persona of black-white unity in action (Toohey was Euro-American) in the fight against Jim Crow was exemplified here; again, this happened during an era when most organizations and virtually all political parties saw such integration as being far beyond the pale. The reaction of the *New York Age* on 16 March 1940 was typical of the black press: "[Davis] is being hailed a hero in Harlem . . . he proved that he has physical and moral courage of a high order. . . . If more of our leaders showed the courage that Davis displayed they would get more respect for themselves and the race."

The *Pittsburgh Courier*, home of George Schuyler, was not always friendly to Davis or the party, but on 16 March they sang a different tune about this incident.

> We are glad that young Benjamin Davis went to Washington, D.C., and baited the lynch apologists in their den . . . when he referred to Garner and his Southern congressional colleagues as "stooges for the landlords and mill-owners who degrade white womanhood by refusing to pay them a living wage," he was saying what everybody familiar with the South knows to be true. . . . It was high time that some Negro of prominence went to Washington and "got them told" instead of pussyfooting and bootlicking as has been the custom. . . . Most of these black politicians are much too polite . . . would that Congressman Mitchell had the courage to . . . say what his people are thinking, in forthright, understandable language such as that used by the young Communist editor.

These hearings, as much as the Herndon case, helped to make Davis a nationally recognized militant figure among African-Americans and progressives. It even touched E. Frederic Morrow, future aide to President Dwight Eisenhower and leading black commentator:

> . . . a masterful exhibition of intestinal fortitude . . . [he] held his ground . . . left even the most daring liberal gasping with admiration. . . . Communists can tell the truth and what [Davis] said is truth. . . . Almost anyone can present with aplomb to even the most hostile body a statement prepared well in advance. . . . The acid test comes when the high executioners start firing questions . . . if one has the right answers then, he is a genius. Davis had the right answers . . . when your correspondent wants to be sure of what Mr. Average Man is thinking about events, he manages to spend an hour in a barber shop listening to mature men with C.S. degrees (Common Sense). Their opinion is that Davis did the thing that every honest and red-blooded Negro wishes he had the opportunity to do. [Racists] fight jungle-style and the only defense for that kind of fighting is the same style with a little more effort. I am not a Communist or a fellow traveler. I try to be an exponent of the truth.[3]

Morrow's newspaper, the *New Jersey Herald News*, editorialized in a similar vein: " . . . he gladdened our hearts. Ben Secundus reminded us of Ben Primus, a fighting crusader if ever there was one. . . . 'Old Ben' they called him—was a contagion of courage, personal dignity and manhood. If Ben, the father, was a Republican, and Ben the son is a Communist, perhaps it is because the fighting instincts of the family have from father to son, found the best means available for carrying on the fight for human rights. . . . like the way Ben Secundus told them off. And if his manner of telling is used as an excuse for blocking the bill, he is not to be blamed; rather is the American mind to be pitied and the Congress to be rebuked."[4]

This ecstatic reaction among blacks mirrored and reinforced the reaction among Reds. Davis's rise in this working-class party had been spectacular; he had entered the party as a leader, which was not typical. So their faith in him was fortified by this incident. His comrade William Patterson was in high spirits: "Say they tell me that when young Ben Davis got through with that lyncher from Texas named Connally the breasts of the Negro people who heard him swelled so they couldn't button their coats, they were that proud . . . that buzzard closed up like a clam in a hot stew."[5]

Not only blacks and Reds took note of Davis's accelerated celebrity. James Webster of the American Federation of Labor was horrified about the attempt to "gag" the young Communist. "Everyone would have expected such a thing to happen in Germany. But I always thought this was the 'land of the free and home of the brave.'"[6] Others were of a different view, calling Davis tactless and worse, but the *Daily Worker* rose to the defense of their man, knocking the "nonsensical contention that Communist support 'hurts' the bill is the same thing the Ku Klux state officials said [in Scottsboro]"; critics, they concluded, are "following [FDR's] 'national unity' policy of uniting with the reactionaries for the scrapping of civil liberties and for war."[7]

Davis himself was not a potted plant in the aftermath of this cause célèbre. He ridiculed those Dixiecrats whom he "caught with their political pants down . . . the gentlemen threatened many times to call several conveniently stationed policemen to their rescue."[8] All this, he averred, showed the "complete perfidy of the Roosevelt Administration." His invitations to speak increased sharply after this incident, and Davis continued assaulting the Dixiecrats at every opportunity. But this firestorm created more than just headlines, according to the *Daily Worker*: "Just one week after the Communist representatives testified, the subcommittee decided to stop stalling and by a vote of five to one reported the measure to the full Judiciary Committee." Davis and Toohey "succeeded in putting new life and vigor into the whole movement to pass the anti-lynching bill."[9]

These attacks on FDR, Dixiecrats, and Republicans were no accidents, for 1940 was turning out to be a pivotal election year. With FDR about to reach an unprecedented third term, with the winds of war blowing ever more insistently, and with party strength being put to the test as a result, the Washington incident came as manna from heaven. Ironically, just before the incident Toohey had lamented Red fortunes: "Comrade Browder was compelled to register a certain decline, a sagging in Communist work among the Negro masses . . . our National Committee is disturbed and dissatisfied with this situation . . . weaknesses indicated are undoubtedly due to the fact that party branches in some places have not yet fully adapted themselves to the new situation . . . [accelerate the] policy of boldly bringing forward the Negro comrades into the leading work of the party in all spheres."[10] It is not unfair to suggest that from March 1940—when Davis challenged the U.S. Senate—until the launching of the Cold War, the party's fortunes in the African-American community were rising, albeit with some backing and filling caused in part by "Browderism."

The important election year of 1940 included Davis's run for election to Congress from the 21st congressional district in New York. James Ford may not have gone too far by suggesting that "I am not exaggerating when I say that Ben Davis and William Patterson can be elected to Congress."[11] This was not just Communist propaganda. The *New York Age* on 30 October crowed, "One of the surprises of the campaign is the strong showing of [Davis]." Simultaneously Davis was playing a leading role in Ford's vice presidential campaign. As such he toured the Deep South and was greeted warmly at Durham's North Carolina Mutual Insurance Company, one of the largest black-owned businesses of its kind.

All the while Davis was continuing to play a major role in the party administrative apparatus and at the *Daily Worker*. As of 1940 he was listed as secretary-treasurer of the corporation that controlled the paper and a member of the Executive Board. In that capacity he traveled to the NAACP convention in Houston just after the June 1941 Nazi invasion of the USSR, where three hundred delegates from thirty-five states were present. Though he was not altogether pleased with the composition—"The Negro workers and sharecroppers are not here to any large extent"—he was not altogether displeased with the political line espoused; the gathering was "singularly without red-baiting . . . progressive . . . [no] lumping communism and fascism together," as had happened at the previous convention in Philadelphia in 1940.[12] That former *Daily Worker* staffer Richard Wright received the Spingarn Award, the NAACP's highest award, was also symptomatic of prevailing trends. But two major ideological trends were in evidence that was to occupy his attention for some time to come. Davis lambasted A. Philip Randolph for calling off the March on Washington and he assessed the new international situation created by the Nazi invasion of the Soviet Union.

Though it is understandable why Davis and the party switched from opposition to the war to support for it after the USSR was invaded, it is also understandable why some of those less nimble may have been left sprawling in the dust. In March 1940 he was hissing Walter White for urging U.S. entry into war, and then he carried this same view to the NAACP convention in Philadelphia weeks later.[13]

Then Davis's line changed. In July 1941 he cited approvingly Du Bois' view that the Nazi invasion of the Soviet Union required all to "reorientate all our thinking." This, said Davis, "shows the quick response of the Negro people to sharp turns in history. . . . [Blacks] feel they have a stake in this war now [since] the Soviet Union is the embodiment of racial equality, opportunity and freedom." The formerly scorned William Pickens was now being cited approvingly for his call for U.S. intervention in the war. But—and this is an exceedingly crucial point in light of the charge that Davis dropped the fight against Jim Crow during the war—Davis, like Frederick Douglass, lamented the "continued discrimination" against blacks, charging that it "is depriving the entire country of its 'proverbial black arm' [for war]."[14] Davis played a pivotal role in an all-day conference in New York in September 1941 that urged an "anti-Hitler front."[15] The line adopted there, however, did not call for the abolition of Jim Crow as a prerequisite for support of the war effort. It is the distinction between this and the above-mentioned view that often leads to the mistaken allegation that Davis abandoned the antiracist fight during the war.

Davis, like many U.S. progressives, was confounded by the question of how to fight Jim Crow while maintaining anti-Axis unity. Davis averred perspicaciously that the fight against Hitler created an atmosphere for black and white unity in the South and for obtaining common action. Black progress during the 1941–45 era proved Davis to be prescient. But two events in late 1941 point up the difficulty Davis and the CP faced. He was forced to assail the usually liberal journal *PM* after it charged the party with being the local hand of Moscow after their line on the war changed. Then, to bolster the view of party critics, in the days after Pearl Harbor the script of the play *Native Son* was altered, supposedly in the interests of national defense. The effort to soften the sharp antiracist tone of this work was applauded by a number of people in the party, thus adding to the impression that the fight against Jim Crow would be sacrificed during the war.[16]

Pearl Harbor raised other racial issues not noted by many, such as the attempt by Tokyo to gain adherents among blacks. Davis laughed at the idea that Tokyo was the friend of the "darker races" and castigated their "bloody exploitation of Korea and Formosa . . . [and] China. . . . The real identity of interest lies between the oppressed people of East and West . . . "[17] Of necessity he accelerated this line after the Nazi invasion of the USSR in 1941, given an increasingly prevalent opinion that appeared in the *Afro-American*: "The cólored races as a whole would benefit [from war]. . . . This would be the first step in the darker races coming back into their own."[18] As the war progressed, so did the government's concern about this development. That this was no small matter is evidenced by the fact that African-Americans were the only ethnic group continuously surveilled, according to Kenneth O'Reilly, during the war; others were watched due to occupation or political affiliation.

As the opinion in the *Afro-American* suggests, the black press was a particular carrier of these dissident opinions. Patrick Washburn has discussed the immense concern of Washington about these developments. The FBI labeled a number of leading black journalists, including three at the *Pittsburgh Courier*, as "either Communists, communist sympathizers or radicals."[19] Early in the war William Hastie, Davis's old classmate, then serving as aide to the secretary of the war, met with African-American leaders in New York to discuss their support; a significant percentage agreed that blacks "were not totally behind it." From another shore, the black press also saw fit to heap massive praise on Moscow, which did not please Washington, despite the wartime alliance. The war years brought civil rights gains to blacks, prompted by the need to motivate this oppressed minority to fight for rights that they did not enjoy. The gains also came about because of the perception that U.S. national security would be in continual peril as long as blacks could be swayed by Washington's adversaries.[20]

While the government tried to explore this issue covertly, others saw fit to publicize their concern. Repeatedly during the war right-wing columnist Westbrook Pegler attacked the black press for its alleged leftist ties. He charged that the *Courier* and *Defender* "resemble such one-sided publications as the Communist party's *Daily Worker*." Later he alleged that "Negro Communists and fellow-travellers always receive recognition as racial leaders" in these organs.[21] Davis struck back swiftly; raising the ire of the right wing more was the fact that leading black editors like Louis Martin of the *Michigan Chronicle* (later an aide to President Jimmy Carter), William Harrison of the *Boston Chronicle*, Fred Moore of the *New York Age*, P. L. Prattis of the *Courier*, and Roscoe Dunjee of the *Oklahoma Black Dispatch* agreed with the Communist leader's venomous response to Pegler.[22]

This was no small matter. The black press was an important forum and barometer of opinion. World War II and the alliance with the USSR were creating favorable conditions for deepening of the black-Left alliance insofar as it undermined the notion that the party's admiration of Moscow was "un-American." The prospect of such a development was long seen by Davis as the fruition of the united front, so he paid significant attention to it. Davis was no stranger to the black press or these editors, given his family's interest in the *Atlanta Independent*.[23]

Davis's relationship with the black press was heightened during the war. He was in touch with Claude Barnett, chief of the black press's version of the Associated Press. He attended the annual meetings of the Negro Newspaper Publisher Associations, where his reception was friendly and familiar; in 1942, fifty editors from twenty states were present. This spurred even further favorable comment in the black press about the Communists.[24]

These ties between the black press and the Left were revealed during Davis's race for Congress in 1942, a dry run before his successful race for the New York City Council in 1943. Initially he was slated to run for attorney general of the state but then it was decided a few days later that a race for Congress would provide a more effective vehicle. According to the *New York Age*, this campaign was "not without enthusiastic support. This seems to be especially true among working elements . . . where Ben the younger has become a popular and forceful figure." Already they were bruiting that "it'll be pretty awkward trying to keep Ben out of Congress just because he's a Communist now." Their reporter, Peter Dana, decided to take a "canvas. . . . During the better part of three days, I broached the subject wherever I went. In no case did I find that the voter was not pulling for Davis. . . . To questions about his communism not a one but didn't dismiss the suggestion with impatience. . . . One man said, 'Ben won me when he was down at Washington that time at the hearing on the anti-lynching bill. He told 'em off for my money and he gave them poll-taxing senators hell; oh, but good' . . . an old timer who had known Ben's dad . . . [said] 'the boy is just naturally a fighter, his old man before him was. . . . He's a smart boy too; they say he studied law at Harvard—just like the President.'" This reporter perceptively drew out some of the elements key to Davis's electoral success: his Washington appearance, his family ties, his education, and his militance; all this superseded any qualms about his Red ties; such apprehension would be attentuated in any case during the relatively pro-Soviet 1941–45 period. The *Age*—a staunchly GOP paper—backed Davis as being "well qualified by training and experience for the post." Strikingly, they called on blacks to vote for black candidates, even on minority party tickets, as "a protest to the major political parties to name a Negro candidate."[25]

This race was not just a quixotic tilt. In 1938 Israel Amter of the party received 106,000 votes while Herbert Lehman beat Thomas Dewey by 65,000 for governor. As the *Worker* put it, "The Communists ran no candidate for governor and the bulk of their vote went to Governor Lehman, thereby providing more than the margin of victory." Davis's platform was explicit: "second front now, all-out support to the President, establishment of a centralized war economy and mobilization of manpower." This second point may have been necessary, given the exigencies of war, but it is not hard to see how it set the stage for the opportunism that often characterized Browderism.[26]

Still, Davis was energetic in bringing black issues into the debate in a way that linked them with the demands of the war: "Harlem is a reserve of power for opening up a second front. This power can be tapped by remedying conditions which hog-tie the black arm of America. The opening of a second front in Europe would loose a democratic flood which would sweep away all barriers to the integration of Negroes in America life." Davis's own campaign experiences made it difficult for him, as a black leader, to go as far as others in downplaying black issues for the sake of unity for war:

> While I was attending an open air scrap rally in the Bronx last week, a Negro fellow, dressed in his working clothes, very earnestly insisted on making a speech at the same time someone else was speaking from the platform . . . our Negro guest consented to listen a while, although later on he burst out and by comparison reduced our loudspeaker almost to a whisper. What lungs! The Negro fellow kept repeating: "What about us? They're lynching us, discriminating against us, and then want us to fight. What about that?" This continued increasingly loud. When I began to talk I offered him the microphone and urged him to speak. He declined by ignoring the invitation. I then discussed how the rights of the Negro people . . . are even more vital to our country today because jim-crowism and anti-Semitism are weapons which do Hitler's work . . . [but his] question is not being answered sufficiently either in speed or in deeds. . . . [He] is a reflection of the failure to satisfy the just grievances of the Negro people. . . . It is a expression of the slowness of the great labor movement itself . . . to speak and act boldly. . . . [Racist barriers] are a disgraceful and stupid policy which must be wiped out as a war necessity. . . . Under President Roosevelt's leadership . . . racial discrimination is being broken down. . . .[27]

This experience encapsulated Davis's dilemma during the war. Yes, he was vigilant about not neglecting black rights, but he was too generous toward the Roosevelt administration, which after all, was fighting the war with a sable arm tied behind its back, a Jim Crow army. In his mind, attacking the president could run the risk of eroding the antifascist unity so necessary for prosecuting the war.

It was not as if he had deep illusions about the president. At this same time he was demanding that "as Commander-in-Chief" he employ his " . . . emergency executive action to see that lynchers are put to death." This was much too ambitious for the president and Davis knew it. Yet his support for the president may have reflected the increased acceptance of the party and its relatively new access to previously forbidden areas. Davis was becoming a virtual regular on WQXR radio in New York, for example.[28]

Davis's electoral campaign was gathering support. The NAACP, the Negro Labor Victory Committee, the Powell-influenced Coordinating Committee on Employment, and the National Negro Congress were some of the groups giving full or unofficial support. The Congress of Fraternal and Benevolent Organizations, representing thirty-five groups, also endorsed him. They and others were flocking en masse to his rallies. In October 1942 he addressed the Holy Trinity Baptist Church in Brooklyn, which was "preceded by a giant community parade." As reported in the *Daily Worker*, "One of the dramatic moments of the meeting came when [Davis] was introduced to the audience [by Rev. Thomas Harten] as 'one Communist I'm going to vote for.' . . . As Davis came to speak the entire audience gave him a standing ovation." Swaying with the mood, Rev. Harten proclaimed, "I say that any Negro who does not vote for Davis is a traitor to the cause of Jesus, the Negro people and the country."[29]

Davis's popularity was accelerating. Four hundred people at Powell's Abyssinian Church "left no doubt where Harlem stands. . . . Placing his hands on Mr. Davis' shoulder Reverend Powell continued, 'Here is a candidate who affords the Negro people their first real opportunity to vote for a Negro win-the-war candidate for a state-wide office.'" Replied Davis, "I'm not going to be elected. . . . But that's all the more reason why you should vote for us." Harold Burton, GOP candidate for the assembly, chimed in, "I am a Republican but I'm going to vote for Ben Davis, Jr."[30]

Even the staid *New York Times* decided it could not ignore the campaign. On 2 November they flashed a picture of Davis, Elizabeth Gurley Flynn, Earl Browder, and Amter with a headline noting the attendance of seventeen thousand at a Madison Square Garden Communist rally. The *Times* reported that the Red leaders asked those assembled to vote for Democrats for most state-wide offices. But the reporter could not resist observing, "The Communists for the first time in years, failed to fill [MSG] completely but they did have an enthusiastic cheering crowd of 17,000 who paid from 25 cents to $1.10 for admission, apart from the usual collection taken up between speeches."

Davis's campaign ranged across the district. He appeared on the radio in Elmira, where many black churches supported him. According to Rev. Henry Brantley, pastor of Bethel AME and chair of the Davis election committee, "One of the finest things for the colored people to link up with is the Communist party. Remember that the letters 'c' and 'p' stand for community and purity. Now we have been buying steaks for the other fellow's wife long enough—its time we bought some for our own. . . . Don't let them frighten you about Communists, just be sure that in the end righteousness will win out. And it's winning out now for I can remember when they put Communists in jail for speaking. But they're too strong for that now." The U.S. alliance with the Soviets was creating openings for the party that Davis was able to take advantage of; finally his platform was no longer being sideswiped by the "Hand of Moscow" issue.[31]

The right wing was not taking kindly to these developments. The party charged that the American Legion conducted a campaign of "terror and harassment" against their petition-signers, joined in some cities by local police. They attempted to knock the party off the ballot as well; apparently the prevailing pro-Soviet sentiments had not reached their eyes or ears. Dusting off his legal skills, Davis joined Emmanuel Bloch, Arthur Garfield Hays, Abraham Isserman, and Arthur Madison of the Harlem Lawyers Association in a suit to halt them. They won.[32]

The right wing of the U.S. government was also not indifferent to the party's apparent gains during the war. J. Edgar Hoover in his 1942 "General Intelligence Survey" was explicit:

> ... the Party is still loudly championing the cause of civil rights at the slightest provocation. It is still campaigning among the Negroes in the South and in densely populated metropolitan areas on the theory of race discrimination in national defense plants and the Armed Forces ... in many of the larger cities the Party has created Fair Employment Practice [Councils] or organizations of similar name through which it impresses the Negro, Mexican and other minority groups with the alleged discrimination that is being perpetrated against them in national defense industries, the armed forces, et cetera.[33]

This worry could have been based on Davis's words alone, for during his campaign and this pivotal war year, he continually discussed Jim Crow and how it hampered the war effort. After a black was arrested for sedition in New York for working for Tokyo, he asked why not arrest the lynchers and "diehard industrialists who still refuse to abide by" FDR's executive order on discrimination. Continually he drew an analogy between the world war and the Civil War, when the Emancipation Proclamation allowed the North to seize the high moral ground and gain a military advantage as well; similar bold moves could produce a similar result, he suggested. Constantly he implored, "The Negro people are rightfully demanding that the Four Freedoms for which we are fighting and for which they are willing to die be applied here and now in the United States and Harlem."[34]

Davis repeated this theme so many times in so many ways that it makes even more curious the postwar claims of his more trenchant critics that he abandoned Negro rights during this period. He was particularly outraged and outspoken about the polltax and lynchings: the record is replete with evidence. But his major weakness came out here; he did not criticize sufficiently Roosevelt, who did not give antipoll tax legislation his full backing, who did not speak out forcefully on lynching, and who remained dependent on the Dixiecrat vote in Congress.[35]

Davis emphasized continually the abominable housing conditions in Harlem and pressed for improvements. That this might be seen by some as fomenting "disunity" did not matter to the leading Harlem Communist. With his close comrade Audley Moore he pressed the city's housing department to do something about 302, 304, and 306 128th Street, called a "house of horrors" by Davis, perhaps because of the rotting floors, "mounds of garbage," rats, and broken windows. He counseled other tenants, who successfully balked at a 10 percent rent hike after a five-month struggle. He demanded that rents be rolled back to the 1 January 1941 level and deplored the fact that blacks often paid more for inferior housing. Moreover, he worked closely with Harlem Communist Ted Bassett in the Permanent Committee for Better Schools, which protested segregation, overcrowded classrooms, and budget cuts.[36]

The war and other international questions remained at the forefront of Davis's activity during his electoral campaign and 1942 generally. Inevitably this card-carrying Communist praised the role of the USSR, which was then carrying the main brunt of the war against Hitler. More than once he scored Norman Thomas, John L. Lewis, Westbrook Pegler, and the *New York Daily News* for their perceived insufficient support of the Soviet war effort and their lack of support for the second front.[37]

Similarly, Davis sought to emphasize the special role of the colonial nations and their needs. He cited Singapore, where the British effort to mobilize the people was stymied because of resentment over colonialism, thus leading to Tokyo's takeover. His view on freedom for colonial peoples was linked to his view on African-American freedom; later he was to suggest that freedom for the former accelerated freedom for the latter, and vice versa.[38]

Despite—or perhaps because of—these positions, Davis lost the election; however, his respectable showing laid the basis for his successful 1943 race for the New York City Council. Still, there were worrisome problems. James Egert Allen, president of the New York State Conference of NAACP branches and a usually reliable Davis ally, supported one of his opponents, Layle Lane of the Workers Defense League. But this negative event was outweighed by far by the positive happenings. On election day, despite "rainy weather . . . from 5 A.M. when 90 campaign workers swarmed into the [CP] headquarters . . . material ran out four times . . . additional pieces had to be printed . . . Harlem Communist leaders estimate the campaign as the 'best in the Party's history.'"[39]

Without a doubt his fighting campaign and high profile helped to propel Davis upward in the party hierarchy. Just before the campaign started he became executive secretary of the Upper Harlem Section and chairman of the New York County Communist Party. The party proudly declared that he was "the only Negro to head a county political organization in New York . . . [and was a] unanimous choice"; at the same time he remained secretary-treasurer of the *Daily Worker*. At the state convention days later he was head of the all-important Nominations Committee. Though he was not part of the Political Committee, the top level, he was a step below on the National Committee: after eight years in the party this status was extraordinary. More and more he was seen in the company of Robert Minor, Gurley Flynn, Browder, Amter, and other top Reds. But unlike most of these leaders, he was also well known outside of the party.[40]

Because of his increased notoriety and high profile, Davis was drawing more fire as well. This was coming especially from his old ally *cum* antagonist, A. Philip Randolph, and other social democratic leaders. The labor leader was sophisticated enough to be sensitive to the often-noxious nature of anti-Communism. When the artist Gwen Bennett was suspended in 1941 as director of the Harlem Community Art Centre because of her alleged ties to the Reds, Randolph rose to her support, though he did it by denying "Communist influence" at the Center, as if that would be harmful. Lester Granger agreed.[41]

But any residual positive feelings about Reds were dropped in mid-1942 after Davis questioned the bona fides of a rally spearheaded by Randolph. In an unusual editorial in the 12 June 1942 *Worker* printed under his name, Davis sharply questioned the rationale of the rally to be held in Madison Square Garden on "Negro rights." He was worried that the traditional anti-Sovieteers organizing it would transform the rally into a "forum for the defeatists," channeling legitimate grievances in a direction that would prove harmful to unity for the war. Even more troubling to Davis was the appearance at the rally of his ally the Reverend Adam Clayton Powell and Mary McLeod Bethune.

Randolph was angry. He requested that Davis and the party organ provide publicity for the rally but he was met with a stiff refusal. To Davis the rally was designed to "fish in the troubled waters of the Negro's just grievances." Optimistically he added that "the opportunities are greater than ever for securing the equality of the Negro people through the very prosecution of the war." Davis objected to their slogan that blacks should show "white people" that their demands were just. He was troubled by the absence of class content and the fact that Randolph had sought to bar whites from his March on Washington Movement, as much for anti-Red reasons (whites who allied with blacks during this era were often assumed to be Red or at least susceptible to their entreaties) as pro-black ones. The *Daily Worker*, he concluded, "cannot unreservedly" support the rally. He was upset about the role in the rally of the *Socialist Call*, that party's organ. Randolph was charged with being a "political bed-fellow of the disgraceful appeaser Norman Thomas"; plaintively he asked why they omitted all mention of winning the war in their program. Indeed, the Socialists were asking why blacks "should fight" at all in the war. Davis huffed, "This is a direct incitation to disloyalty." In case Randolph did not read the *Daily Worker*, Davis directly sent him the substance of this open letter.[42]

This rally and political orientation placed Davis and the party in a ticklish situation. Obviously if the war were lost, existing black rights would be destroyed, and if blacks did not give their all to end fascism, the antifascist effort could be harmed. But certain blacks could not understand why Davis and the party would object so sharply to a "Negro rights" rally, even if it did not mention winning the war.

This reality and the fact that eighteen thousand people showed up for the rally influenced Davis's subsequent reaction. This gathering was "a new high point in the militancy and aggressiveness of the Negro people," he now said. This was "perhaps the largest number of Negro citizens ever to attend a Garden rally." This suggested that the "all out mobilization and enthusiasm" for the war was "distorted" by Jim Crow, which "resulted in widespread unclarity." He remained critical of Norman Thomas and his ilk but acknowledged there were "honest" elements in the March on Washington Movement. Yet he remained disturbed by a skit that suggested that "the main enemy of the Negro people is not Hitler . . . but the national government" and unions and that "no resolution in support of the war" was introduced.[43]

Davis had reason to be concerned, though he may not have been aware of all the reasons why. Weeks before the rally, in May, Benjamin McLaurin of the Brotherhood of Sleeping Car Porters wrote confidentially to his colleague Randolph, "We are having quite a number of conferences with secret agents of the Federal Government on our program. Thus far we have had nothing to fear but my guess is that the Communists are doing everything possible to sabotage our program. I have never been more concerned about them before."[44] And on 25 April Frank Crosswaith had told the readers of the *New York Amsterdam News* that despite the Socialists' rhetoric about pressing Negro rights, "It would not be tactful at this time to organize another march on Washington, for such a move would play directly into the hands of Hitler and the other enemies of our country." Also not to be forgotten are the words of the historian Bernard Nalty: "Even Secretary Stimson, confident of the superiority of the white race, felt that concessions had to be made, not out of any sense of justice but because he had come to believe that Randolph and the other leaders were trying to head off a communist takeover of the civil rights movement."[45]

This was all rather curious. The Reds, who were not just pro-FDR but were throwing every ounce of energy into the war effort, were being surveilled and subjected to government harassment. Randolph and Co., who—in the eyes of many—were sowing discontent about the nature of the war and were producing skits pointing to the government, not Hitler, as the foe, were apparently meeting with that same government; both Randolph and the government seemed to be overly concerned about the Communists. The government seemed to be more concerned with Red influence among blacks than the question of maintaining black enthusiasm for the war. In any case, Davis and the party were caught in a squeeze play between civil rights forces charging that they were soft on Washington and that same government—which the Reds were trying to support—that sought to erode their support among African-Americans.

Soon thereafter the Communists were charged with being derelict about Negro rights. Though the NAACP failed to support Winfred Lynn when he refused induction into the military due to segregated units (indeed, they called him "unpatriotic"), Roy Wilkins did not hesitate to charge that the party's view on the war was leading to subordination of black rights. Though Randolph's March on Washington Movement had an eight-point program similar to that of the party, he did not hesitate to sharply criticize the Communist program. Though the Socialists for many years, according to Davis, had "not a single Negro [as] a member of the party's National Executive Committee, its leading body," they were posing as the staunch defender of black rights. Hence, Davis and the Reds had to spend considerable time defending their record, which planted a seed among many that their growing reputation as a defender of blacks was questionable. Further, Randolph and his allies were constantly attacking groups in the black community that were formed to fight for civil rights—and this included the Reds—such as the Negro Labor Victory Committee. Randolph seemed to be somewhat paranoid about Communist influence when he accused the conservative publisher of the *New York Amsterdam News*, C. B. Powell, of being under Communist influence when his ally Crosswaith was forced from his post as a columnist. Meanwhile, a not-disinterested spectator—the U.S. government—worried in a report drafted by the FBI that in "[Germany's] opinion the only way to defeat America is through internal disruption—[the] Negro situation is a likely menace to the United States." Overall, from Randolph on the Left to Washington on the Right, there was utmost concern about the apparent popularity of Communists among Blacks, not to mention their most notorious speaker, Ben Davis.[46]

The early war years marked the rise in Davis's prestige among blacks. He was a symbol of a united front that was moving toward black Liberation. The recognition was dawning that Jim Crow was a national security question, a belief that the Cold War would solidify. Moreover, the presence of Jim Crow in the economic, political, and social arenas facilitated Communist recruitment in the Harlems of this nation, a problem that would be tackled on two fronts: undermine both Jim Crow and Communists. Anti-Communism and the Red Scare handicapped the Black Liberation movement, but this was not evident in 1943, when Davis stunned the nation by winning election to the New York City Council.

6
A Turning Point in U.S. History, 1943

The U.S. alliance with the Soviet Union during the war meant that the party's pro-Sovietism was not the impediment it once was. The need for national unity also curbed antiprogressive sentiment generally. The party's emphasis on black-white unity began to make more sense; in fact it now appeared to be more farsighted than most in "prematurely" proclaiming this increasingly accepted dictum. Moreover, the exigencies of war meant that concessions to blacks were on the agenda, akin to the Civil War pattern. These conditions, combined with the uniqueness of Davis's own strength and the peculiarities of New York, allowed him to become the first black Communist elected to political office in this country, one of the key events of 1943. Yet this victory carried negative seeds, for an illusion was growing in the party that a country that could elect a black Communist might be on the verge of eliminating all manner of illiberal shibboleths and beginning a new era where monopolies and workers would lay down together like the lion and the lamb. This is the meaning of "Browderism," a phenomenon that extended far beyond the real and imagined weaknesses of Earl Browder. As the nation entered a new epoch, Davis stood as a resolute symbol.

The year of Davis's election was also the year the party began to disengage from the Communist International. The party was not and could not be oblivious to other trends in fraternal parties. Moreover, they could not be oblivious to past CI policy on electoral politics. For even in a period when CI policies could be interpreted as sectarian and hostile to the united front, there was a need expressed to participate in electoral politics. Reds in municipal bodies, it was said in 1930, should "do everything in their power to be of service to the poorest sections of the population . . . the work of the communists . . . must form part of their work for the disintegration of the capitalist state. . . . The Communists must use the municipal, as they do the parliamentary bodies as a platform for mobilizing the masses for the revolutionary struggle." These words marked the spirit if not the letter of Davis's tenure in the New York City Council.[1]

From the beginning the U.S. party had not been indifferent to electoral campaigns. Pete Cacchione, the first Communist elected to office (to the New York City Council in 1941), noted, " . . . Communists had been running for various offices in many parts of the country since 1924. While they were rarely successful, some had been elected, and one had even become mayor of a small midwestern town."[2] Reds had been prominent in organizing the highly successful Democratic Farmer Labor Party in Minnesota and the American Labor Party in New York, and before the end of the war they had been involved in electoral politics in thirty-five states. Despite this clear historical record, Joseph Starobin reflects a certain consensus by stating, "The Party did not concentrate on electoral activity because its chief intention was to influence the existing two-party system."[3]

This electoral emphasis was particularly striking in New York City, then (as now) the party's largest district. With one of the largest concentrations of African-Americans in the nation and their attendant penchant toward progressive politics, a similarly oriented Jewish population, and a long tradition of trade-union struggle, this city was uniquely configured to tolerate Red political advances. Although New York was unique, its influence was national. Party political maven Si Gerson called New York "without question the pivotal political state in the Union [in terms of] the Electoral College . . . largest labor movement . . . headquarters of American finance capital."[4]

Thus Robert Minor of the party received 26,654 votes for mayor of New York City in 1933 while Communist leader William Weinstone had gotten 5,622 in 1929. This was a prelude to the elections of 1937, where four candidates ran for City Council; Israel Amter obtained 7,147 votes in Manhattan and Cacchione missed winning by 245 votes. The recently organized American Labor Party emerged as the city's second largest party, sending six to the assembly, and electing one judge and two borough presidents; all this was with decided Communist aid. At the state convention of the Communist party in 1938 Charles Krumbein noted a "100 per cent increase" in votes for the Communists in 1937 "over the previous year. . . . A decisive factor . . . was the unity of the AF of L and the CIO unions behind the same candidates. . . . This was contrasted to Seattle, Detroit and other parts where unity had not been achieved."[5]

This spadework allowed Cacchione to be elected in 1941, despite the fact that he was sick for most of the campaign. However, his supporters visited four hundred thousand homes and held 250 rallies; indeed, during his successful campaigns of 1943 and 1945 the often-ill politician campaigned very little. But Cacchione and his handlers were shrewd politicos—they printed literature in Polish, Spanish, Hebrew, Italian, and English and were more than up to the task. New York was also unique in that top officials like Fiorello La Guardia, Stanley Isaacs, and Vito Marcantonio did not shrink from working with those of pink or red hue. Still, there were other peculiarities that even Cacchione had to acknowledge: "The New York City Council receives little publicity in the press, and very few of the citizens of New York are aware of what goes on in the Council."[6] This did not prevent Tammany and other forces from repeatedly seeking to knock the Communists off the ballot because of their proven success in garnering votes. Hence, although he was not on the ballot, Cacchione still managed to get twenty-five thousand votes in 1939.

Harlem was not lagging behind these advanced trends. In the 1928 elections the party ran a number of African-American candidates, including Richard Moore for Congress, Lovett Fort-Whiteman for state comptroller, and Edward Welsh for state assembly. This political independence culminated in 1936, when delegates from 115 organizations representing more than one hundred thousand people formed an "All Peoples Party" in Harlem; thirty-one unions endorsed the effort. As ever, political independence caused the two major parties to become more tractable toward black concerns. Davis charged in 1936 that recent gestures by La Guardia were "an election gesture to forestall independent political action by the people of Harlem."[7] Circumstantial evidence substantiated Davis's jaundiced view. J. Raymond Jones, the "Harlem Fox," has pointed out that not until 1937–41—when political independence was accelerating—were there substantial numbers of black district leaders in Harlem.[8]

Naturally this went hand in glove with a growing party apparatus. Carl Brodsky, state campaign manager in 1936, marveled that "organization for the election campaign is more advanced in Harlem than in any other district of the state."[9] The next year the *Daily Worker* exulted that "Harlem leads City in *Daily Worker* drive" to raise funds.[10] J. Ray Jones connects this Red record with restrictive election laws; "in this way socialists, Communists . . . and others were kept out of the political process in New York City prior to 1938."[11] But the dam broke at that point; in fact, in 1937 three blacks ran for City Council. In 1939, after James Ford had suggested it, a Trade Union Non-Partisan Committee for the Selection of a Negro to the New York City Council was organized that included Max Yergan, Lester Granger, Dorothy Height, and the ultimate beneficiary—Adam Clayton Powell. This political ferment also aided La Guardia. In 1941, as the Communists pointed out, "the Negro people registered the largest plurality for La Guardia." They added portentously that these "elections confirm once more that red-baiting has grown too stale for public consumption."[12]

When Davis ran for congressman-at-large in 1942 he received 47,488 votes; compare this to the 40,389 votes that Robert Minor received in running for governor in 1936. The similarly charismatic Elizabeth Gurley Flynn received a few thousand fewer votes than Davis when she ran for Congress in 1942. So obviously he had more going for him than the hammer and sickle on his ticket. Paul Robeson, Jr., has suggested that "more than any party leader" Davis understood and related to the masses.[13] That Davis is still not forgotten is evidenced by the lengthy article extolling his electoral accomplishments that appeared in the 14 February 1989 edition of the New York-based *Carib News*.

Davis was in the thick of the 1936 events that heightened political independence. His conclusion was typically caustic. The GOP was singled out as "the Negro's main enemy" for their "purge" of blacks "in order to make [Republicans] palatable to the most reactionary Southern lynch class." At this moment FDR was not a Davis favorite either; he "has vacillated and retreated" and, yes, he appointed blacks but as a "buffer between the demands of the Negro people and the responsibility of the federal government." The Reds were "alone the 'party of the Negro people' . . . the twentieth-century party of abolition," he concluded.[14]

It was easy to see what motivated Davis. Harlem particularly was suffering during the Great Depression, causing Davis to work assiduously on the 1936 Communist electoral campaigns. The next year, along with other Reds, he was nominated for the City Court but was withdrawn in favor of a American Labor Party candidate. But that did not stop him from using his stentorian voice on statewide radio hookups for ALP candidates. He felt that the ALP "leaves something to be desired but . . . has on the whole been progressive."[15]

As time passed, Davis's influence increased commensurately. In 1938 the state assembly was considering a measure to bar Reds from public-sector jobs; it was clearly aimed at Si Gerson, Davis's comrade and an aide to leading New York politician Stanley Isaacs. Davis scored this "Red-baiting measure" but went further and brought a delegation to Assemblyman Robert Justice, a black Democrat, who reversed field and repudiated the bill. Davis was suggested by many for attorney general that same year, but like others he was entertaining the notion of a black being elected to the City Council.[16]

Nevertheless, a salient factor in propelling Davis into office was the existence of the electoral system known as proportional representation. As explained by Dennis Anderson,

> In elections conducted under the method of [PR] the voter indicates his/her order of preference among the candidates by placing Arabic numerals instead of x's next to the candidates being voted for. While only a specified number of candidates are to be elected, the voter may mark numbered rank order preferences for as many of the candidates as he or she wishes. The first step in determining the winners is to count the first choice votes. Once the total number of valid ballots cast is known, a quota, which is the number of votes required for election to council, is computed. The quota is determined by dividing the total number of ballots by the number of candidates to be elected plus one and then adding one. . . . Any candidate receiving the quota on the count of first choice votes is declared elected. Any "left-over" ballots in excess of the quota that would normally have been counted for the victorious candidate are counted for the candidate indicated on the ballot as that voter's next highest preference. Candidates who fail to reach a minimum vote threshhold on the count of first choice ballots . . . are eliminated. The second choice votes on the ballots whose first choice candidate has been eliminated are then counted or "transferred." After each count the candidate with the fewest votes is declared a loser and ballots originally counted for the eliminated candidate are transferred to the next choice indicated on each of these ballots.

This method brought Toledo its first black city councilman in 1945 and first labor representative in 1947.[17]

Proportional representation enabled the Communists to overcome the historic obstacle faced by third parties in U.S. politics, the compulsion to vote for the "lesser evil." Under PR, a voter could make the Communist his or her first choice and the liberal a second choice without the fear of "throwing away" a vote; if the Communist were eliminated, a vote still would go to the liberal, thus blocking the right wing. In New York City each borough held boroughwide elections, thus a citywide majority was not needed to be elected; this blocked the strength of more conservative boroughs like Queens and Staten Island.

Political theorist Frederick Shaw has commented at length on the impact of PR: "Borough-wide constituencies under PR eliminated 'safe' districts in which party regularity was the prime qualification for nomination. There was even competition among candidates of the same party within boroughs. With no assurance of automatic elections, candidates found it more profitable to 'sell' themselves to the public than work for the district machines. Party managers viewed these developments sourly . . . airtight control of the municipal legislature could be restored only by abolishing PR . . . after ten years the magic formula was discovered—the 'Red Menace.'" So PR, which became popular in the nineteenth century, bit the dust in 1947 in a fury of Red-baiting. Democracy, however, was the ultimate victim.[18]

Even after Davis was ousted from office in 1949, his election continued to have repercussions. In 1953 a litigant passed the test to become a New York City police officer but was removed from the civil service eligible list because he had signed a nominating petition for Davis and sent a telegram supporting his candidacy. Similarly one could argue that the political lynching of the Reds during the McCarthy era was designed to remove a growing political force on the Left impelled by mechanisms like PR. As late as 1952, Charles Nusser, running on the Communist ticket for Freeholder in increasingly black Essex County, New Jersey, received 5,459 votes; in 1953, when he got 4,057 votes for the state assembly on the party ticket, it "touched off Red-baiting articles under big headlines in the Newark press." Nevertheless, one must realize that although the elimination of PR was aimed ostensibly at Communists, the effect was felt by progressive forces generally.[19]

It was clear that Davis—despite his personal popularity—would not have an easy time getting elected in 1943. In his memoir, Davis recalled that even his own father was dubious. But Davis senior was not a social scientist, and apparently he had misjudged the direction of the political winds.[20]

Yet the direction of the political winds was not the only factor working in Davis's favor. He did have an organization behind him. Just before the election Cacchione, doubtful about his own reelection, laid out electoral plans for the Reds. He proposed tasks for "e.d.," or electoral district "captains." This included obtaining "subs for the *Worker* . . . to engage in activities of civilian defense insofar as informing the people and enlisting them for this work." They were to push war bond sales and canvass families, "spending a minimum of 20 minutes in each home.... On the second week the e.d. captain takes three new families and goes back [to] the three families of the first six he canvassed.... At the end of 20 weeks, the e.d. captain will have canvassed 83 families.... At the end of the 20 weeks the e.d. captain finds that fifteen families are being serviced by the party for war stamps and 10 are getting the *Sunday Worker*."[21] The goal was fifteen thousand subs by election day. The party was trying to build itself up, support the war, and mobilize for the election simultaneously.

The party also held "speakers class . . . to train a minimum of 40 women comrades to take to the platform starting April 1, 1943.... By April 1st, we will guarantee a minimum of 40 open air rallies . . . [including] puppet shows, elocutionists, singers, musicians, etc. and . . . a hill-billy band." There was to be a "special appeal to Italians" in Cacchione's case, just as Davis did for African-Americans. A popular song book was to be printed. Small meetings, for example with housewives in the afternoon, were suggested.[22]

Since the United States entered the war Davis had been protesting vigorously the self-defeating nature of the Jim Crow army; his protest continued, if not accelerated, in 1943. Before an audience of 1,200 at Renaissance Casino at 138th Street and Seventh Avenue in Harlem, he repeated this favorite theme. But those on the platform with him stole the day: Hulan Jack (future borough president of Manhattan), Channing Tobias, Duke Ellington (who donated a complete set of his records to Davis), Langston Hughes (who turned over a set of his books), and Josh White (who sang). This theme of the Jim Crow army, along with the second front and the "stupid and insulting system of blood segregation" of the Red Cross were the focus of Davis's action and discussion on the war.[23]

But this same year saw the publication of one of his more popular pamphlets, *The Negro People and the Communist party*. To the naysayers he stressed that the party "must [not] give up the fight for Negro rights for the sake of national unity in the war," nor should blacks "oppose our country's victory . . . victory will help smash Jim Crow"; if Hitler wins, "we're destroyed." Thus he said, as if speaking to Randolph, "civil disobedience" at this juncture was a "danger" as it "places the fight for Negro rights as though the interests of the Negro people was opposed to the interest of the nation." Yet it was this counsel that fueled the misinformation that the Reds were ditching Negro rights.[24]

Nonetheless Davis was forthright in pointing to the real causes of the "riots" that marked the urban landscape in 1943. His words did not condemn those in the riots, as might be expected from one accused of abandoning Negro rights for the sake of the war. Instead, he pointed to "perfectly legitimate grievances" as the motive for these disturbances.[25]

These urban uprisings were a reflection of what appeared to be an ironic increase of police brutality during the middle of an antifascist war. But, as ever, the authorities presented this to the public as a response to the latest Negro "crime wave." In fact, Davis's concern had mushroomed in the summer of 1942, when he sought to activate Powell and Assemblyman William Andrews on this question. He criticized Roy Wilkins's remedy to "let heads be cracked" since it "leads to frame-ups and wanton police brutality." He also scored "current hate-the-Negro campaign in the commercial daily press." Striking a still-current issue, he questioned why they "never fail to mention the racial identity of Negroes in 'crime' news." Little wonder that at many mass meetings during his campaign, blacks were less than enthusiastic about prosecuting the war. This "crime wave" line not only fueled police brutality, but it led to the closing of the Savoy Ballroom, a mecca for the new music. There were other reasons: "They object to the fact that Negroes and whites have been attending the ballroom as free and equal citizens." Further, Charles Buchanan, manager of the ballroom, was one of the owners of the Left-leaning *People's Voice* and a strike at the Savoy was seen as "an underhand attack" on the paper. And there were other ramifications. Davis and a delegation forced Macy's to halt the selling of a "mugging night stick . . . advertised for white women" to use against black male muggers; this was inciting to violence and racism, he charged. But such developments indicated the delicacy of Davis's position in trying to rally support for a government at war that discriminated against its black citizenry. They also illustrated that a major reason for Communist popuarity among African-Americans was the Reds' resolute attack on racism at a time when this was not a widely accepted approach.[26]

Other than the "crime wave" question, Davis's other major issue that brought him added recognition was his focus on the price gouging of monopolies and landlords during the war. His repeated attention to this question makes the Browderist claim all the more surprising, for even during the war the economic royalists did not seem eager to compromise with their class adversaries. He led protest delegations to meet with the Office of Price Administration. He helped to organize party-led conferences on the question. As usual, he wrote voluminously in the *Daily Worker*. But his position still carried a tone that he later criticized as suffused with Browderism: "The fight for rent control is a fight to uphold President Roosevelt's anti-inflation program and, thereby, to back up the home front."[27]

Davis's increasingly high profile on issues of the moment was paving the way for ultimate electoral success. He was becoming a regular on local radio broadcasts. He worked closely with local assemblymen, Canada Lee, Langston Hughes, and others in trying to organize a "People's Institute for Harlem." Yet with all these hosannas, there were troubling signals. Early in 1943 he was back at the Brooklyn church of Rev. Thomas Harten, addressing one thousand and two hundred people on the war and Jim Crow. Then a few weeks later there was talk of pressure on the reverend to cease his favorable comments about Communists and cut his ties to the Left generally. Finally in April Davis had to wire his sorrow as a fire gutted the church.[28]

These were disturbing and sobering events but they did not dim the overall optimism that gripped the Communists in 1943. At this point they were not only talking about a socialist future but getting elected to office and having the opportunity to implement some of their ideas. Nevertheless, it was not preordained that Davis would be nominated, much less elected. After the Reverend Adam Clayton Powell made it clear that he would be leaving the City Council, it appeared that there would be no African-American representation. According to the *New York Age*, "The last hope of Negroes of electing a representative in the City Council" was lost when Channing Tobias declined to run. Tobias felt that the GOP would not back him seriously. At that juncture the Communists had put forward Carl Brodsky, a lifelong New Yorker and an insurance executive. But when Tobias declined the party decided that Davis should substitute for Brodsky. This gave added impetus to Davis's candidacy, according to the *Daily Worker*: "Marking the first example of its kind on record, a white candidate for City Council last night withdrew from the Councilmanic race in order to give place to a Negro nominee." Brodsky was even more dramatic: "As a member of the Jewish people I can appreciate what it means not to have the great Negro minority represented."[29]

It was not inevitable that Tobias would withdraw; some encouraged him to do otherwise. In the late spring of 1943 Davis had a long conversation with Powell about his departure from the council; then he met with Tobias. Said Davis, Tobias "was not well known among the masses . . . he was spread as thin as tissue paper among the ruling circles of the country and to many he was just as transparent." Davis backed him still, though he was "as clever and foxy an opportunist as ever double-talked." There was a similar concern about the Reds' electoral choices too after Brodsky was selected.[30] The *New York Amsterdam News* for 3 July 1943 was curious: " . . . Communists noted their candidates for City Council Sunday. No Negroes were included. . . . Political observers considered it rather unusual that no Negro was nominated here in Manhattan, since some of the party's most prominent members reside in Harlem." This was a pointed reference to Davis that the party decided not to ignore. Their flexibility won them praise. William Harrison, associate editor of the *Boston Chronicle*, called Brodsky's withdrawal "without a precedent in American politics."[31]

Davis enjoyed great support from his predecessor, Adam Clayton Powell. They had known about each other since not many blacks attended the virtually lily-white schools of the East such as Amherst and Powell's alma mater, Colgate. Marvel Cooke recalls them as being "quite friendly" then, though Powell was "not well liked" by a number of blacks since they thought he "was trying to pass for white." But in the 1930s and 1940s she saw them together on the "streets of Harlem quite often."[32] Yet even in the 1930s they had public disagreements, such as Powell's opposition to La Guardia in the 1937 elections. At this point Powell worked closely with Davis and a party apparatus that included skilled organizers. The party, on the other hand, benefited from association with the charismatic Powell.

By the time Davis ran for office in 1942, all was forgiven and Powell was effusive " . . . one reason I have always given credit to the Communist party [is] because they have had the courage to run Negro people in national, state and county elections. Ben Davis, Jr. deserves the vote of every Negro. . . . My vote goes to Ben Davis, Jr."[33] Again in 1943 he was similarly enthusiastic. In his prison memoir Davis saw Powell as an opportunist, one who sensed the party's strength and decided to take advantage of it: "He might be compared to a big howitzer gun that could be fired by the class enemy into the ranks of the people, or fired by the people into the citadels of reaction . . . a shrewd and cunning politician."[34] Powell's own subsequent view does not contradict this assertion: "My critics have often cited the names of many Communist-front organizations with which my name was associated. . . . I used everyone that had any strength whatsoever, including the Communists."[35] Claude Lewis's account of Powell agrees: "The party had Powell pegged correctly. He would bear left only while left was a fashionable—and useful—direction."[36] But Powell's flexibility did not prevent the FBI from placing him on their list for "custodial detention" in the case of a national emergency.[37]

Davis's support from the leading black clergyman of Harlem was evidence of his support from the black church generally. As a man of the Deep South, he was not unaware of the importance of this institution. During his trips to this region after he joined the party, he was often found addressing parishioners. So it was no surprise that during his 1943 campaign there was a highly active Ministers' Committee led by Rev. James Robinson. The *Daily Worker* reported happily, "Father Divine followers are clapping hands for him. Some Democratic captains in Harlem are throwing entire districts behind the candidate."[38] Rev. Moran Weston advised support for Davis in his *Amsterdam News* column. Rev. Ben Richardson was more melodramatic, alleging that the party "approximates what Jesus stands for [more] than any other group." Rev. Ethelred Brown was similarly biblical: "Miracles are happening all over the world so it won't be a miracle if Mr. Davis is elected."[39]

The conditions of war and alliance with the USSR allowed Davis's message to be heard by less-prejudiced ears; the party as the local "hand of Moscow" was not then a dominant theme, as it was to be during the Red Scare. After one woman heard him speak, she volunteered to do something—anything—for the campaign. His campaign manager Audley Moore commented, "People are doing that all the time. Enthusiasm for Davis is mounting steadily. People we never saw before are coming here to help."[40] Five movie houses in Harlem had trailers sponsored by the Davis committee calling on voters to register; bus lines carried his posters.

Labor was a major participant in the Davis campaign. The Negro Labor Victory Committee, headed by Davis ally Charles Collins, "opened what is perhaps the most intensive campaign ever launched to get out the Negro vote," according to the 21 September 1943 *Daily Worker*. They distributed one hundred thousand circulars and put out posters. The CIO of New York and Painters District Council 19 were among the labor groups backing him.[41]

Davis's appeal helped to generate innovative effort on his behalf. Lewis Allen composed a popular ditty that was on the lips of many Harlemites: "Ben, Ben we're voting for you, when you get into the Council, Here's what you do, let the whole world know, New York City's gonna end Jim Crow, Yes, yes, end Jim Crow, Yes, yes, end Jim Crow, Democracy has got to grow, New York City's gonna end Jim Crow." This was the first of four stanzas, accompanied by a snappy tune.[42] This was not the only artistic contribution to the campaign. In his memoir Davis recalled, "Many of the people of Harlem wanted various campaign pieces as ornaments for their walls, so beautifully decorative was the artists' work that they could even tolerate my photo plastered over the covers."[43]

Part of Davis's appeal was his familial connection. Ben Davis senior still had helpful ties, which became apparent as the candidate campaigned. "They'd slap me on the back and say: 'Davis, your father was a Lincoln Republican. You must be a Lincoln Communist. I'm going to vote for you.'"[44] But there were other forces that remained adamantly opposed to Davis. Herbert Bruce, a power in Harlem, Tammany, and nationally, not only opposed Powell and Davis but termed J. Ray Jones, leading Harlem political leader, "houseboy," among other names, for his support of progressives like Davis. Jones was not cowed. This consummate politician, who eventually became the first black to head Tammany, termed Davis "charismatic . . . very intelligent . . . brilliant . . . tremendously gifted in the arts and politics."[45]

As for the candidate, he continued to wage a fiery campaign, hammering home his favorite themes. Yet this was a practical campaign in that Davis would use his electoral effort to try to effect concrete change while making political points. In response to the Atlantic Charter he was instrumental in drawing up the "Harlem Charter," which focused on improved housing and health care. In the middle of the campaign he visited a "gloomy, ill smelling tenement flat at 118 W. 135th St. . . . while rain showered through the ceiling." Davis asked, "Does he regularly collect his rent? . . . Does he? 'Sure he does' . . . Then don't pay him another cent until he's done something about these awful conditions. . . . And if he wants to make trouble you come or send somebody to us."[46] Subsequently the landlord agreed to repairs after being told he would be taken to court otherwise.

The nerve center of this campaign was imbedded in the Citizens Non-Partisan Committee to Elect Benjamin J. Davis. Dr. George Cannon, most recently president of the Manhattan Medical Association, headed this effort. Ben Gold, Countee Cullen, Ferdinand Smith, and Richard Wright were among the officers. Audley Moore and George Murphy, member of the family that controlled the *Afro-American* newspaper chain, were two of the key functionaries. This luminous list helped to attract others like Julian Steele, former socialist leader and head of the Boston NAACP and William Harrison of the *Boston Chronicle*, both of whom "proudly announced that they were fellow students with [Davis] when he attended the Harvard Law School." J. W. Lancaster, Jr., president of the Colored Citizens Organization of Fairfield County in Connecticut spoke similarly: "I would be less than a man if I didn't find out what I could do for Davis, the most wonderful man who God let live, who did so much for the people of Bridgeport . . . The time has come when colored Americans are breaking away from unquestioning allegiance either to the Democratic or Republican Parties and forming a new alliance which will mean much to colored people in the days to come."[47]

Such comment was symptomatic of growing support. A Davis "'Worker' Brigade" was formed that engaged in "door to door canvassing in addition to nightly street sales"; interestingly, most of these brigadistas were non-black. "Every registered voter in Harlem" received a picture story on Davis. The *New York Age* chose not to ignore this groundswell and endorsed him, but they hedged by urging a third-choice vote for him, after John Ross and Layle Lane.[48] Marvel Cooke recalls Thurgood Marshall being "very friendly" with Davis. During the height of the campaign he posed for a picture with him after Davis raised a substantial sum for his campaign against school segregation in Hillburn, New York; this association also proved helpful to Davis's campaign and image. One black interviewed by the *Daily Worker* confessed, "Every time I hear of a colored man running for office I'm going to vote, because that's making things better for us." A certain nationalism and the party's antiracism were key factors in Davis's electoral success.[49]

One could not deny that, as election day approached, the Davis campaign had an air of victory about it. Crowds flocked to his rallies. Cacchione asked Davis to bring his magic to Brooklyn, though one would have thought that the incumbent would have been called on more to come to Harlem. The apex of this campaign—and perhaps of Communist strength in the United States in this century to this point—came in late October. Over seven thousand supporters cheered Davis at two rallies. He recalled subsequently, "The Golden Gate was sold out 10 days before the rally. On the day of the event, the Fire Department closed the hall 2 hours before the hour of performance when I, the guest of honor, appeared on the scene, it was all I could do to get in . . . another 5,000 people had gathered outside the Golden Gate."[50] They had to rent a second hall on the spot. The recollection of the *Daily Worker* was similar. "[The hall was] jammed to its 4,500 person capacity. By 3:15 the Renaissance . . . 121 W. 138th St. was crowded with an additional 2,300 and the fire department was turning away thousands of Negro and white citizens. When the Communist candidate walked down the aisle . . . to the platform the entire audience leaped to its feet and rocked the hall with applause." Powell spoke. Robeson sang "Purest Kind of Guy." Mother Bloor, Gurley Flynn, and James Ford graced the platform. Hazel Scott gave a sizable contribution.[51] Years later a participant recalled her little boy being carried to the platform and emptying "his piggy-bank into your hands to assure your election to the City Council."[52]

What was remarkable about this rally was the incredible number of African-American celebrities who saw fit to align with a card-carrying Communist. Then as now, celebrity was a significant factor in U.S. political life. Celebrities have always been known to be reluctant to jeopardize their often-tenuous careers by taking forthright political stands, much less campaigning for a Red. But the candidate was so compelling and the times so different that the unusual became the commonplace. This form of support was an example of the breadth of Davis's support; it truly signaled, in the phrase of the day, that a "new world is coming." The pianist Teddy Wilson, who was chair of Davis's Artists' Committee, played a key role in getting Lena Horne, Duke Ellington, Count Basie, Mary Lou Williams, Coleman Hawkins, Billie Holiday, Jimmie Lunceford, Art Tatum, Ella Fitzgerald, Lucky Roberts, Josh White, Pearl Primus, and Fredi Washington to express public support for Davis. The cast of *Oklahoma!* pledged one hundred dollars each. When Powell called Davis, "my logical successor," he was attempting as much to grab Davis's coattails as he was trying to share his own. The *People's Voice* was correct in suggesting that this affair "brought out more top-flight stars than have ever honored any political candidate in the history of Harlem."[53]

This development was so extraordinary that it merits closer examination. The British musicologist Ian Hall has observed that many whites who admire black music in Britain see it as a form of rebellion against the established order. Although the "established order" of the 1930s and 1940s did not embrace the kind of music made by those listed above, the Reds did—the later flap over "bebop" notwithstanding. Their love of black music allowed a striking political alliance between Communists and black celebrities to develop that has generally managed to escape notice. Yet what is even more striking is the resilience of this phenomenon. As late as 1952, Charles "Yardbird" Parker was still performing benefits for Davis. And in 1956 W. C. Handy was still referring to Davis as "my dear friend." In 1959 Ted Curson was still doing benefits for Davis. Billie Holiday was a regular at May Day during the 1940s. Cab Calloway and Lionel Hampton—the latter subsequently a leading Republican—were major Davis supporters for some time.[54]

This tendency of celebrities to lean in the party's direction was becoming apparent, even before 1943. When the CP's right to exist was challenged in 1941, Countee Cullen and Charles Houston—two old classmates of Davis—objected stridently. Raymond Pace Alexander, E. Franklin Frazier, and even Ben Davis, Sr., affiliated with the Citizens Committee to Free Earl Browder in 1942. When Edwin Barclay, the president of Liberia, came to New York in 1943, Davis joined Mayor La Guardia and other notables in a dinner at the Hotel Roosevelt.[55]

Perhaps the most well-known celebrity in the party's orbit was the star-crossed Richard Wright, a former member of Davis's party cell who still supported him in 1943. Margaret Walker calls Davis the "most important of the black reviewers" of *Native Son*. Yes, Davis was critical, but Lloyd Brown recalls that "I was much more critical . . . than [Davis]." Indeed, Addison Gayle agrees that Davis protected Wright from even harsher censure from party leaders like Ford. Davis was mild toward Wright's *Twelve Million Black Voices*, calling it "the first realistic, class-conscious narrative of the Negro people in the United States," though he cautioned, "one could wish, however, that the picture would have been a bit more balanced." Davis also objected sharply to the forced closing of *Native Son*, the Broadway play.[56]

But Wright's backing of Davis in the 1943 election was to be his swan song with the party for some time to come. Months later he publicly attacked the party. Gayle declares that a FBI tap picked up Davis expressing reluctance to respond. But Davis did respond—sharply and publicly—to Wright for his "wholly unjustifiable attack upon the Communists—the very organization whose outlooks had helped him create his masterpiece. . . . The Communist organization took no official position [on his work] but rather invited and stimulated broad, free discussion and comment upon it. . . . However, Wright sulked and chafed at all criticism; and rejected it all. Who was intolerant in this case?" Wright says he left the party in 1940, but "why did he wait until now" to announce this, Davis wondered: " . . . whether Wright wants to or not, he is qualifying for very green, open, and prosperous pastures. Time will tell."[57]

Wright's association with C. L. R. James during this period might have influenced him to attack the party at this moment, in that the intellectual from Trinidad was influenced by Leon Trotsky and his lack of sympathy for Stalin's USSR. In any event, when his *Black Boy* was published, Davis pulled no punches in denouncing it. Other critics have found fault with much of Wright's work after his Communist period. Nonetheless, one of his stronger critics, Margaret Walker, is probably correct when she notes that "Wright seemed in 1956 to be revising both his feelings about black nationalism and his attitudes toward red internationalism." Abner Berry in the *Daily Worker*, at this moment of much Communist rethinking, also revised somewhat the view of Wright held by some comrades. For example, Wright refused during this time to contribute to the anti-Communist screed *The God That Failed* and then led a committee in Paris to free Henry Winston.[58]

But this experience with Wright did not keep other writers from flocking to the party banner before, after, and during the 1943 election campaign. Langston Hughes was the most prominent. Just as musicians during this era were fascinated with the Left, so were the scribes. Walter Lowenfels, Harold Cruse, José Yglesias, and Doris Lessing were a few in this category.[59]

Davis's support from the artistic community was an extension of his own interest in this area; he was an accomplished violinist and something of an arts critic. He consulted closely with the Negro Playwrights Company, which included his close friend George Murphy, along with Hughes and Locke. That Paul Robeson was one of his closest friends was no accident. In turn, Robeson's ties with this community—particularly with Lena Horne and José Ferrer—redounded to Davis's benefit during the campaign. Repeatedly Horne was quoted as saying, "It is my duty as an American to endorse [Davis]." The prominent black actor of the 1940s, Rex Ingram, also endorsed Davis.[60]

It was logical that sports figures like Joe Louis would be involved in the Davis campaign. In turn, Davis, a former top athlete, was intimately involved in the effort to advance blacks in sports. The Communists in 1943 had gathered thousands of signatures to present to Branch Rickey of the Dodgers concerning the "need for adding star Negro players to the Dodgers." Later Davis, Max Yergan, Cacchione, Robeson, Robert Murphy of the *Afro-American*, and Ira Lewis of the *Pittsburgh Courier* met with baseball moguls at New York's Hotel Roosevelt to further discuss desegregation. In a sports-hungry black community, this move was bound to win votes and support.[61]

The ruling class did not forget this support from celebrities. One can speculate that the Red Scare was inspired in part by fear of the growth of the Left, as evidenced by the broad support Davis generated; the point was not that the Left was on the verge of seizing state power but that the specter of this possibility arose. In any case, the backlash against many of these celebrities was daunting. Merle Miller, by his own admission "one of the most successful radio-television producers," was blacklisted partly because of his backing of Davis.[62] So was Hazel Scott and Lena Horne. Canada Lee pleaded that "I am as much a Communist as an Eskimo" but did not persuade anyone. Professional stool-pigeon Louis Budenz sought to discredit José Ferrer by linking him to Davis. And in the 1960s the FBI tried to discredit Sidney Poitier by claiming he was acquainted with Davis.[63] The news reported by the *Daily Worker*, as the Red Scare was launched, was baleful: " . . . such big agents as Moe Gale, Joe Glaser, the William Morris Agency and other managers had refused to okay the contracting of such stars as Erskine Hawkins, Louis Armstrong, Bennie Goodman . . . Count Basie and Billie Holiday . . . [and] threatened the cancellation of contracts for recordings, television, dances and other engagements" unless they cut all ties with the Left.[64]

But celebrities alone could not win an election; they had to be organized, mobilized, and fused with the masses. The engine of the Davis campaign was the Communist party, particularly the branch in Harlem. This was something of a change. In 1934, when two hundred blacks were recorded in the Harlem section, the *Party Organizer* complained of persistent problems: " . . . Harlem for a long time was one of the sorest points in the work of our Party. . . . The weakest point in our work has been the inability of the Section Committee to enforce the most elementary discipline on its members. Petty personal questions have been on the order of business at the great majority of our section Committee meetings."[65] But coincidentally with Davis's arrival, the Harlem party's fortunes improved. By 1936 Davis noted this, adding proudly that there were now seven blacks on the Central Committee (compared to none on the Socialist party's top body). By 1938 the Harlem party reported a membership of 2,800.[66]

During the war generally and 1943 specifically, the membership of the Harlem party and the ranks of black communists increased dramatically. This growth belies the notion that the Communists lagged profoundly on the civil rights front, for if this had been the case, one would not have expected such a development. On 10 April 1943 the *New York Amsterdam News*, certainly no friend of the Reds, touched on the underlying reason: "Many sincere non-Communist Americans find it impossible to reconcile our unabated national game of Red-baiting in the face of the incalculable aid the Red Army has been to the cause of democracy." The party's development was also a type of social science experiment, for it demonstrated the potency of the party's appeal when anti-Communist prejudices were not on the upswing. The *Daily Worker* reported on 19 February 1943 that blacks were joining the party in "growing numbers"—forty-four out of ninety-four recruits in Michigan, fourteen of thirty-four in Maryland, eight of fifty-two in Wisconsin, eight of sixty-four in New England.

At that juncture Davis announced a recruiting competition between the Upper Harlem and Chicago Southside sections of the party. With the eager assistance of the leading black women Communists Audley Moore, Rose Gaulden, and Elizabeth Baker, by April three hundred had been recruited in Harlem; that spring five hundred were recruited in Upper Harlem altogether. Excitedly the *Party Organizer* reported, "The winning of entire families . . . the in-laws and cousins, has been a feature of a new kind in our drive."[67] Doxey Wilkerson claimed that "nearly 5,000 Negroes joined the Party [nationally] during the 1943 spring recruiting drive alone."[68] Davis exclaimed to Essie Robeson, "the Harlem Section of the Communist party is beginning to break records. We have doubled our membership (securing 400 new members in three months) since I've been here. We've just begun."[69]

So when Davis decided to throw his hat in the ring, he was doing so during a Red resurgence. Si Gerson, a skilled Communist who had worked with Cacchione, points out that Davis "had patterned his own campaign after

Pete's."⁷⁰ What he had noticed particularly was the value of an energetic Communist cadre. The campaign literature of Davis and Cacchione was very effective because it was done by two party clubs of talented advertising and public relations workers. In Manhattan County alone there were 6,200 Communists at the time of the election, all of whom were active to some degree in Davis's behalf. They worked out of four offices in Harlem alone. The *Daily Worker* also called on members to work for the candidate; by late October there were "25 sandwich men—day and night . . . 5 wagons, trucks with signs touring city continuously . . . 3 sound trucks on streets." There were "close to one thousand canvassers" combing the neighborhoods regularly for Davis. As extraordinary as it may sound, it was not unusual for Davis to address thirty open-air meetings in one evening; he was in churches more often than pious sinners.⁷¹ The *Party Organizer* happily wrote of the "first year high-school boy who came in day after day from his civics class to help us explain P.R. [Proportional Representation] to the voters and marched back triumphantly the day after the final count to prove to a skeptical civics teacher that Ben could be elected."⁷²

A striking aspect of this Communist effort was the leading role played by African-American women. Paramount among them was Audley Moore, a nationalist leader in her nineties living in Harlem at the time this book was written. Her father was a deputy sheriff in Louisiana, the son of a white man who raped his mother. Her mother died when Moore was five; afterwards she spent several years in a convent. She came to New York for the launching of the Black Star Line, got involved in GOP politics, and became a businesswoman. Scottsboro brought her to the party but she says that she never left the Garvey movement throughout, which bespeaks a certain nonsectarian attitude by the party. Moore was a peerless recruiter for the party, topping the Harlem drive by recruiting thirty-seven people, twenty-seven of whom were women, all but one black; in contrast, Davis managed only sixteen. Another eager campaigner was Dorothy Jenkins, born in Panama, a hotel chambermaid who joined the party in 1940. Yet a third was Rose Gaulden, a nurse at Harlem Hospital who was born in Thomasville, Georgia, and graduated from Vorhees Institute in South Carolina in 1923.⁷³

Another woman who was helpful in the campaign was Elizabeth Gurley Flynn, the top woman leader among Communists. Davis's campaign stretched across gender and nationality lines, for as Israel Amter put it, Davis "cannot be elected by the people of Harlem alone. This is the task of all Manhattan and particularly the white citizens of Manhattan." Appropriately, the *Daily Worker* made the election of Davis a top priority, not just for the city and state but the nation as a whole. This was reflected most clearly on election day itself, as Amter remembered how vote-stealing efforts were squashed by a brigade of alert Communists:

Charlie Loman, young Negro, the chief watcher of the Davis votes as they were being tallied . . . stood by the Davis table . . . at the 69th Regiment Armory . . during the six long, tense days it took to compile the PR vote . . . Theft of Davis ballots could have been accomplished only over Loman's dead body . . . . Then there's Ed Bender, the Davis campaign manager. . . . He led it. He organized it down to the finest detail. Short, stocky, dark-haired . . . he reminded me of a speedy bantamweight fighter . . . and that's something when friends of Frank Costello are hanging around. . . . Davis might have lost the election if Si [Gerson] hadn't rushed over on Monday to Manhattan from the Brooklyn Armory . . . and compelled directors of the count to produce nearly a thousand votes for [Davis] which had mysteriously gone astray.[74]

The Davis victory was a success for the entire party and especially for party leaders like Flynn, Amter, and Gil Green.

It would be one-sided to portray the Davis campaign as an unalloyed success, for there were certainly objections to him and his party. Right after the election Randolph and Walter White warned ominously that the party was making serious inroads among blacks; one can question the accuracy of this assertion but not the impact of this perception. This news was deemed sufficiently important for the *New York Times* to print it on 22 December 1943: "To counter this trend, [they] suggested that the other political parties assume a realistic approach to the Negro problem and make a sincere effort to combat existing prejudices." In this sentence one glimpses the role the Reds played in hastening black liberation from Jim Crow. The perception of a black drift to the Left was seen as suitably threatening for the ruling circles to make antiracist concessions, but the Left had to be repressed as a condition precedent and as a quid pro quo: concessions to Black Liberation had to be accompanied by a Red Scare. Simultaneously, a *Daily Worker* headline summarized the party's conclusion after the election: "Davis' Election Shows Negroes Reject Randolph's Red-Baiting."[75]

Retaliating, White and Randolph took up the attack on the George Washington Carver School, which for some time had been accused of being a Communist front. The attack was a reversal for Randolph, who earlier had defended school leader Gwen Bennett in the face of these charges. Sensing that they had larger fish to fry, Doxey Wilkerson responded suspiciously that "it was not until after the election of Benjamin Davis to the City Council that the false issue of 'Communist control' was raised."[76] But the school was not able to survive such broadsides, and Harlem was the ultimate loser in the wake of this precursor of the Red Scare.

Despite the success of his 1942 rally at Madison Square Garden, it appeared that the popularity of Randolph and his March on Washington Movement were waning in 1943. Harvard Sitkoff has asked, "Why . . . did all the major civil rights spokesmen and Negro newspapers shun and denounce Randolph's call for civil disobedience to protest Jim Crow schools and railroads?" Why did their convention in Chicago in 1943 "attract virtually no blacks other than a handful of Sleeping Car Porters?"[77] The *New York Age* on 4 September 1943 wondered how Randolph and the MOWM could reconcile blasting local Reds while praising Reds in Moscow; they puzzled over how they could praise integration yet bar whites and Reds: " [they're] acting like the well-known ostrich which sticks its head in the sand to hide from its enemies . . . what of the Negro Communists who are already in the organization but who, because they can do more effective work, prefer not to be known as Communists?" The conservative *New York Amsterdam News* raised similar questions on 31 July 1943 and added, "Contradiction seems to be the keynote of MOWM." First they'll march, then they won't, averred the Harlem weekly. First they exclude whites, "yet on the other hand the best programs sponsored by the group to date have been through interracial cooperation."

Now it seemed that Randolph was having the worse end of this longstanding ideological battle with Davis. His "dangerous path of civil disobedience," Davis warned, "plays into the hands of Hitler." Randolph was taunted after the failure of his Chicago meeting although Davis did finally concede, "It is true that the Administration has not been sufficiently consistent in fighting Jim Crow."[78] At the same time the line of Davis and the party seemed to be gaining popularity. That was the import of their Negro Freedom Rally at Madison Square Garden in June 1943, a direct response to the success of Randolph's previous effort. Jim Crow and the Second Front were the focus as twenty thousand gathered inside and ten thousand huddled outside. Hughes, Robeson, Canada Lee, and others supplied the art; Lester Granger, Tobias, Powell, and Davis supplied the words. This rally served to ratify Davis's stature and popularity, making his election months later seem less surprising.[79]

The party was quick to recognize Davis's election victory was a landmark and a watershed. Davis had gotten about forty-four thousand votes, but as Israel Amter pointed out, "19,300 valid first choice ballots [that is, ballots properly marked and not spoiled] out of 34,000 to 35,000 first choice votes cast, were cast for Davis in greater Harlem. This represents between 55 and 60 per cent of the first choice ballots by the Negroes in that area. Fifteen thousand additional first choice votes in the white districts went to Davis . . . . In the final choice, 23,000 votes in the white districts outside of Harlem, out of a total of 44,000 were cast for Davis."[80] But he was not the only big winner, for Cacchione had received the "largest first choice vote of any candidate in the city." It was left to party leader Gil Green to put matters in context in a speech to party workers at the Manhattan Center on 15 November.

> In the Councilmanic elections our party scored a great advance of far-reaching consequence. If correctly appraised and followed up, it may well mark the turning point in the relationship of our party to the main forces in American political life—the beginning of full integration of our party in the camp of national unity

... while we have left the bush league, we are not yet in the major league ... [our candidates] came out of their corners swinging both fists, landing upper-cuts to the jaw of their opponent instead of gentle slaps on the wrist. ... They fought against every form of discrimination.[81]

He proudly recalled their willingness to support Tobias before Davis ran and their penny-wise campaign on election day: "not $10 was spent on that day because our watchers gave of their time for a noble cause and not for a few paltry dollars."[82]

Green was proven wrong. This was a turning point, but not in the direction he surmised. Despite Davis's smashing reelection in 1945, 1943 was to be the high-water mark for the party in U.S. life since the ruling class was so frightened by Communist electoral success and progressive advance in general that it could barely wait until the war ended before launching the Red Scare. The Red Scare was a disaster for civil liberties and democracy, not just for the Communists. Yet it is ironic that although 1943 did not mark the "integration" of Communists into U.S. life, it did indicate the beginning of the "integration" of blacks; it appeared that the price for a form of Black Liberation was a Red Scare. It was becoming clear that Jim Crow was not just hampering the war effort but was serving as a catapult for a domestic force whose major goal was the expropriation of the property of the economic royalists, the ruling elite. When black and white vote Red, massive shifting of the tectonic plates of politics is in order.

As it turned out, Davis barely beat Samuel DiFalco, a Democratic incumbent, for the fourth seat from Manhattan, though "the count in Manhattan was marked in its earlier stages by considerable confusion" and hints of fraud. The party moved swiftly to capitalize on this gain, moving to add five thousand *Daily Worker* readers in New York by February 1944. One commentator marveled, "the sentiment for the Communist party is strong in Harlem today. That's because the party is trusted as an unyielding fighter for the rights of [blacks]." One black campaign worker, Charles Rose, was able to get 442 votes for Davis in one Harlem electoral district; he joined the party on election day.[83]

The response to Davis's win in the black press was almost as ecstatic as the *Daily Worker* reportage. One reason was advanced by Dominic Capeci, who has written that the Davis "election proved to one black editor that whites would vote 'for qualified Negroes.'"[84] If whites would vote for a black with the added "handicap" of being Red, then racism was perceived as receding. The black progressive Eugene Gordon concluded, "The fact that Davis is a Communist is taken in two ways: either it is regarded as totally unimportant or is taken to be especially important in view of the Communists' known position on the Negro question."[85] *The New York Age* of 20 November 1943 concurred: "Negroes no longer look at a man's party label as the sole standard ... voters in New York generally are becoming more liberal." The *New York Amsterdam News*, after recounting how "over 1,000 Davis votes 'disappeared' but were later 'found elsewhere,'" then remarked that his victory confounded the pundits.[86]

Despite Walter White's cavil, other voices in the NAACP hailed the Davis win. Theodore Spaulding, president of the Philadelphia chapter, called it "wonderful news."[87] In Boston there was a joint celebration of CP and NAACP leaders. Roy Wilkins, in the 20 November 1943 *New York Amsterdam News*, was effusive:

> ... the town is in a dither.... What to do? What to do? A Negro in the council is bad enough but a Negro communist.... The *World Telegram* has been throwing little fits with every editorial and the Hearst press is purple with apoplexy. And yet we have the *World-Telegram* wringing its hands because jolly Ben Davis shook hands with the Duke and rested next to Lena Horne.... More seriously, the *World-Telegram* forgets the vicious racial and religious campaign carried on by the Republicans during the Lehman-Dewey race for governor. It is a great crime for the Communists to use racial appeals, but for the Republicans to do so only means a "hard fight" or a "bitter battle." Moreover the Communist appeals were not vicious or based on hatred, whereas the governership battle was the slimiest waged here in many a decade.... If our system of government is so weak that two Communists out of a Council of 17 members constitute a danger then we had better be looking to our foundations.

Wilkins was glowing about his intermittent political foe: "He is young and able. It is to be doubted whether there is a single council member of any higher calibre.... He is probably as good a politician as any man in the council.... [he] is affable and personable. He does not knock you down with a Communist argument if you should happen to mention that it is a fine day."

As Wilkins's comments suggested, the bourgeois press was not happy about the Davis win. The *World-Telegram* asserted that Davis won by "exploiting national, racial and religious feeling." In other words, blacks were more prone to vote for a party that did not compromise with Jim Crow, unlike the GOP and Democrats.[88] The *New York Herald Tribune* on 11 November 1943 was quizzical: "Emergence of the Communist party was a strong factor ... had many of the political experts baffled ... but almost everyone agreed that the Communists conducted the best organized, hardest hitting and, perhaps, the smartest campaign." These same "experts" were trying to "figure out" how Davis and Cacchione got 113,483 votes when, they alleged, there were no more than 15,000 Communists in the two boroughs; even with "more liberal tendencies at work these days," they couldn't understand. Immediately the *New York Times* featured prominently "a new drive to eliminate the proportional representation system of voting."[89] Robert Moses, the preeminent powerbroker of New York, privately contacted the president of the Bronx Chamber of Commerce, sending him a pamphlet suggesting that PR leads to fascism and adding darkly, "I can't take the lead [against PR] because I am too busy, but I can help."[90]

One correspondent asked Governor Thomas Dewey, "What is our wonderful and beloved country coming to . . . you are the Governor . . . How is it possible to allow Communists to hold office of any sort when they cannot [unless they falsely] swear by the American flag . . . [I am] very furiously outraged."[91]

As for Davis himself, he was predictably ecstatic about the victory. As election day began, the "worst downpour of the season" began, which did not augur well. But after the votes were counted and he won, Davis also instantly recognized the epoch-making significance. He affirmed that it was laughable that the bourgeoisie was irritated that a black Red had focused on their dastardly treatment of African-Americans as part of a successful election strategy. Yet he vigorously denied the allegation that appeals to racialism explained his triumph. He even went as far as saying he was not "elected by Harlem alone or by the Communist party alone," suggesting he got twenty thousand votes from blacks and twenty-three thousand from whites. In his memoir, he waxed fondly about his support from Jewish people:

> The tremendous vote that I received from the Jewish working class community was one of the highlights of my election . . . . I was told by experienced election campaigners that my name had become as familiar in Jewish workers' families as one of their own and that never before had a Negro candidate received such a high percentage of votes in a white neighborhood. . . . There were many Jewish candidates among the white aspirants for the Council posts but in certain Jewish districts I topped them all. . . . On each of the occasions that I spoke in the Jewish community at the other end of the Manhattan islands, I received ovations and huge crowds that rivalled those in Harlem.[92]

Davis was quick to hit back against his critics. His press conference at the Hotel Theresa in Harlem was jammed and unusual: "there [were] as many newspapermen who want to tell [Davis] what they thought about his election as there were that wanted to ask him about it."[93] Since his 1940 attack on Congress on antilynching legislation, he had attained a hero's status. Now he had advanced to another level, quite unlike that enjoyed by any Communist in the United States. When he entered one meeting in Harlem after his victory, "bedlam broke loose. The men, women and children laughed, screamed, wept, shouted, sang, hugged the winner and became breathlessly quiet to hear him talk." Then like a Pied Piper he traveled over to Small's Paradise, entourage in tow: "New rounds of applause, cheers, demonstrations occurred at street corners and in the club. . . . Paul Robeson came shortly after the closing of Othello. Max Yergan was there. So was James Ford."[94]

So a black Communist had won. And anti-Communists were stunned. It did seem to many that Gil Green was right and a turning point had been reached. This was truer than Green or Davis recognized. The turning point was the beginning of the integration of blacks into U.S. life and the devolution of their "skunk-at-the-party" status, a development assisted by Red electoral success and the exigencies of the war. It was not lost on elites that Davis's condemnation of racism had convinced many voters to cast their ballots for the Communist party; the mid-1950s' retreat from Jim Crow in the United States had become inevitable. The turning point was the glimmering of a Red Scare that would almost destroy the party; this development, according to Davis, was assisted by the ideological trend known as Browderism.

7
"Browderism," 1944

The electrifying election of Davis was a "shot heard 'round the world." In faraway Algeria there were reports of "enthusiasm" among workers after his election. The impact of detente or the easing of tensions between socialism and capitalism was an international phenomenon. There were even two Communists elected to the Capetown City Council. In Cleveland Communist Arnold Johnson, running for the Board of Education, got forty-seven thousand votes. Even in usually staid Hollywood, after Davis was elected "near bedlam broke loose." But after the shouting ended, Davis had to turn to the difficult task of being a Communist legislator in the citadel of capital; even the favorable objective conditions did not make this a simple task. And the development of "Browderism" (or a policy of conciliation with the ruling class in Washington and on Wall Street) did not make the job any easier. When the leftist journal *New Masses* backed the Japanese-American internment as "necessary" though "harsh and undoubtedly unjust to many," it was an indication of the abdication of responsibility of the Left—particularly on the important issue of "race"—that was sparked by Browderism at a critical moment, 1944. Davis too was influenced by this atmosphere.[1]

This abandonment was especially unfortunate, for despite this reborn "era of good feeling," the class enemy was busily seeking to undermine Davis and the party from the moment he was elected. Right after the election, cronies of Robert Moses began plotting the downfall of proportional representation, the electoral procedure that had helped to bring the Davis triumph; this was done "after consultation with our principal newspaper supporters." But they had to move slowly for the time being due to "the fact that united nonpartisan support cannot be presently obtained." Tammany Hall was also part of this cabal. PR had been adopted in 1936 by an overwhelming margin and a constitutional amendment to bar it had been rejected in 1938. Weeks after the 1943 election Democrats in the State Assembly called again for PR's repeal.[2]

Davis and the party had not taken leave of their senses. There were signs that did indicate that the much-heralded "new world coming" had arrived. Who could ignore or downplay the flocking to the banner of noted artists, which continued unabated in 1944? When Davis made his first report to

Harlem on the City Council at the Golden Gate Ballroom, the entertainment included Count Basie, Canada Lee, Pearl Primus, Mary Lou Williams, Billie Holiday, Teddy Wilson, Wlll Geer, and Josh White. "Thousands" were "turned away" for Davis's birthday party at 135th and 7th Avenue, possibly because Teddy Wilson was playing. The party's office at that location included a bookstore with Marxist literature, thus allowing the art to bolster the politics.[3]

Perhaps Davis and the party could be excused for the initiation of Browderism in 1944, for masses were drifting into the party as if a new day truly had arrived. The Left generally was affected. Powell's *People's Voice* of 20 November 1943 was wide-eyed about the "astounding vote for the progressive candidates—[Mike] Quill, Cacchione and Davis—we note that together they pooled 165,000 votes. This is almost four times the total membership of the Communist Party in New York City." At an "End Jim Crow" rally in Harlem held by the party in May 1944, it was announced that Harlem Communists had recruited over one thousand members recently, topping their quota by four hundred; fifty-five more were recruited on the spot. After Davis had spoken to the members of the New Redeemer Church on 128th Street, "the pastor, the assistant pastor, and all members of the congregation who were not members of the Communist Party, immediately joined the organization in a body." Katie Thompson, a thirty-three-year-old mother of two from Harlem, recruited 120 alone but gave all the credit to the attractiveness of Davis as a symbol.[4]

Little wonder that Powell hurried to call his paper the "Lenox Avenue edition of the *Daily Worker*." Like successful revolutionaries in the past, Davis and the party rushed to export their example. Dispatched to Cleveland, Davis recruited fifty to the party in one meeting: "every prominent and influential Negro leader in Cleveland was there." Similar results occurred in Detroit. Heady with the wine of success, Cacchione challenged Davis, pledging that Brooklyn would surpass Manhattan in new recruits. But it was Davis who was the symbol of this new success; in fact, the party named a Communist club after him and opened an office for it in the heart of Harlem.[5]

Nineteen forty-four was a year of travel for Davis since the party was eager to display this powerful recruiter, spokesperson, and symbol. In May he was in Mexico City representing the party at the convention of the Mexican Communist party. There he was cheered by thirty-five hundred and conferred with leading Marxists of the hemisphere. In Rochester he spoke at Mount Olivet Baptist Church, where his stentorian preaching style was as popular as always with the predominantly African-American audience. He was in Chicago twice, speaking before thousands. Simultaneously the party was seeking to export their electoral example to Philadelphia.[6]

Davis's political views, his education, and the times guaranteed that he would rise to the apex of black leadership. Those who came en masse to see him from coast to coast substantiated his popularity.[7] At the same time Davis's power insured that his contradictory relationship with both the NAACP and Randolph—neither of whom was adverse to jealousy—would continue. Randolph seemed to be his favorite target, as when Davis accused him of "hovering between defeatism and confusion . . . when this writer along with many others, ask for his assistance in numerous matters in the City Council to end Jim Crow, one is drowned with silence from Mr. Randolph's direction."[8] Walter White was charged with "Red-baiting" for his remarks on the party. But the detente with Wilkins continued in a "Dear Roy" missive, as Davis congratulated him on his "wonderful work" on the white primary and offered his skill as a lawyer. In an intimate "Dear Ben" letter, Wilkins gushed appreciation.[9]

Davis had exhibited his status as one of Harlem's leaders even before he was elected. He pressured both the Democrats and the American Labor Party to assist Judge Francis Rivers at the expiration of his term. He had assisted Rivers at a reception at the Golden Gate by having the bands that usually played for Davis—Ellington, Basie, Hampton—perform there. Thus it was not surprising that the Schomburg Library put Davis on their "Honor Roll of Race Relations," comprised of twelve blacks and six whites. The *Defender* of Chicago accorded him the same honor.[10]

Davis's increased prominence also meant that Adam Powell, ever one to sense a political opportunity, tightened his grip on the Communist councilman. The lineup for a spring 1944 "City Wide Action Conference" at his Abyssinian Church indicates the political winds then blowing. Powell was to speak on "Issues Facing the New Negro," Wilkins on "National Issues," and Davis on "Local Issues." Davis was an avid supporter of Powell's race for Congress and repeatedly attacked his GOP opponent, black attorney Sara Pelham Speaks. The Republicans, he intoned, were "trying to cover their reactionary tracks behind the skirts of an intelligent woman." Davis accepted Powell's suggestion that he join him on sound trucks campaigning in Harlem. Powell's victory in the primaries in August 1944 was hailed by Davis as suggestive of the "political maturity" of Harlem. And when Powell won the election Davis was a central speaker at a seven-thousand-strong rally at the Golden Gate.[11]

Yet there were difficulties in the Powell-Davis relationship. Eyebrows were raised when Davis ally Dr. George Cannon endorsed Sara Speaks, though he was a registered Democrat; his explanation that he was rebelling against Tammany's plantation politics did not convince everyone. When the conservative *New York Amsterdam News* then hinted that Davis would run against Powell for Congress and termed the Red "capable, rational and a hard worker," some sensed an anti-Powell conspiracy; the *Amsterdam News*, an enemy of both Powell and Davis, was no doubt pleased with this result. So Powell's failure to show at a Communist rally in May 1944—after he recanted his "Negro first" campaign theme—was played up even more.[12]

Powell and Davis were too sophisticated to be oblivious to their mutual antagonist's tactics. In a letter to Powell the councilman praised the *People's Voice* and added tellingly, "I am genuinely sorry that I cannot say the same of certain other major Negro newspapers, which for partisan or other considerations, deserted their readers."[13] The *Amsterdam News* was the intended target of this broadside. The progressive *PV* was in a constant sniping war with their Harlem competitor, which railed against the growing leftist tide. The dichotomy between the two newspapers was emblematic of a larger fissure among blacks that was to deepen as the Red Scare was initiated. Rev. Powell's paper assailed the "below-the-belt blow . . . aimed at the *People's Voice* with the remark that the *PV* is 'edited by a regular contributor to the *Daily Worker* . . . .'"[14] But when William Harrison, associate editor of the *Boston Chronicle*, took out his membership with the Communists the direction of the trend was clear—at least for the time being.

Though he may have had problems with the local Harlem press, Davis, like the party, tossed high praise at the president. He called for the reelection of President Roosevelt and praised his platform as a blow to the polltaxers. This point highlighted the quandary of Davis and the party, for the political situation did cause FDR in particular to make progressive statements that most Democrats since that time have been reluctant to make. Yet Davis and the party could be accused of going too far in the interests of prowar unity. When Eleanor Roosevelt denied that she had ever advocated social equality for blacks, Davis still praised her and assailed her usually Right-leaning critics—such as the *New York World-Telegram* and *New York Daily News*—that had attacked her from the left. He hailed the huge black vote for FDR as proof of the "spectacular political maturity" of this community and said the president "has been the architect of historic and fundamental gains in the status of Negroes."[15]

At the same time Davis was repeatedly giving hell to the GOP. Thomas Dewey was treated like a punching bag. He even gave credit to FDR for Dewey's black appointee and warned of "danger" if "this man becomes President." When black tennis champion Edgar Brown endorsed Dewey, Davis was unsparing in his criticism.[16]

After Davis was elected to the City Council in November 1943 his work schedule had to shift. Some felt that a Communist would be a force of obstruction and hollow rhetoric in the Council's hallowed chambers. However, Davis and his comrade Cacchione proved to be highly effective and provided a model for how Communists in capitalist legislatures should conduct themselves. They did not win all battles but they used the bully pulpit provided to educate and sensitize, particularly on questions relevant to African-Americans.

The scholar Edwin Lewinson has concluded that Davis "acquired a reputation for availability to his constituents and a willingness to listen to their problems."[17] Though regarded as the councilman from Harlem, after the banning of proportional representation Davis's district ran from 97th Street to 160th Street on the West Side and was only 40 percent black. In 1944 the council itself consisted of eleven Democrats, three Republicans, two Communists, and two Laborites. The *Daily Worker* on 31 December 1944 concluded that "there is perhaps a greater unity of action on war-time home front needs in the New York City Council than in any other legislative body in the country." Undoubtedly there were few legislative bodies more representative and hence more democratic than this one.

The veteran Communist Si Gerson, who worked closely with Cacchione and Davis, has presented a useful portrait of their days in the council:

> Pete and Ben were a superb team in the City Council and the Democratic majority, if it would not pass their bills, was still respectful and a bit fearful . . . [they] pooled the work of their talented assistants, discussed legislation, in advance and generally were more deeply grounded in the problems of the city than were most of their colleagues.[18]

They also sought to provide a model of antiracist unity for their colleagues to follow. This came to the fore dramatically after Councilman Ed Rager attacked a Davis resolution on Negro History Week; normally such a resolution was unanimously adopted, but said Rager: "We should stop petting the Negroes and playing up to them by passing such a resolution." Davis and Cacchione "were arguing about who should answer Rager. [Cacchione] pointed out that a Marxist understands that it is the duty of the white worker to rise to the defense of the Negro people . . . it was a political question . . . For years afterward the incident burned bright in Davis' memory. . . . Never again was there such an argument between the two Communist councilmen either publicly or privately."[19]

Pete and Ben were too formidable a pair to ignore. One was an articulate, fiery, nationally respected leader of blacks; the other had received the largest vote of any candidate for City council in the previous election. They were industrious not only in introducing bills but also resolutions that would express the sense of the council on all manner of issues. Cacchione had political vision but his actual eyesight was failing so Davis recalled, "On the Council floor, I was Pete's eyes. I read to him the legislative calendar, the bills up for consideration, and prepared my own remarks in memoranda form so that they could be relayed to him." They collaborated with other council members such as Stanley Isaacs and Mike Quill in a minority caucus; they pooled funds for everything from research to postage. Thus the two Reds were not isolated, for to do so would have meant isolating tens of thousands of voters along with them.[20]

Before the onset of the Red Scare, Davis was in no danger of becoming quarantined within the council, particularly when communists in Europe were keeping the Nazi hordes away from the gates.[21] Davis had a particularly positive working relationship with the liberal Republican Stanley Isaacs. Born in Manhattan and a resident of the borough all of his life, Isaacs was a lawyer and Columbia graduate prominent in Jewish affairs; he was elected borough president in 1937 but ignited controversy for being reluctant to dismiss his aide, Si Gerson, who happened to be a Communist; he was elected to the City Council in 1941 and stayed there for twenty years. Isaacs was also something of a patrician whose family had enjoyed close ties with that of Theodore Roosevelt. He and Davis got on quite well, and he went as far as helping Davis with his winning campaign of 1943. Inevitably the right wing took umbrage at this and often viewed him with disdain.[22]

Davis's activities in the council show that his role was constructive. This was particularly so in the area of education. Alice Citron later recalled "vividly the many conferences Mr. Davis had with parents and teachers on this subject [of purging] racial slurs [from textbooks]. . . . He not only met with us but he called a large and important conference which delegated him to speak on the subject before the Board of Education . . . he attempted to have a bill passed in the City Council of New York which would bar all books that slander minority groups."[23] As a result, Dr. S. F. Bayne, head of the curriculum department of the board, pledged to Davis to correct these racist textbooks (Davis was especially upset with their portrayal of Reconstruction). Davis moved to bolster this position by pushing for more aid for Harlem libraries.[24]

Another major concern was race and racism. Davis served as vice-chair of the Committee on the Improvement of Race Relations, which was comprised of Harlem business and labor leaders and was sponsored by the Uptown Chamber of Commerce. Even Randolph was involved with this broad aggregation. The committee was charged with arbitrating disputes between groups such as landlords and tenants and shopkeepers and shoppers when race was involved. The committee had a program to eliminate racial friction; they educated employers on the value of hiring blacks, appealed to the press to accurately portray Harlem, and encouraged developers to invest in Harlem housing. In the council one of Davis's first measures was to introduce a law making it a misdemeanor to slander citizens on the basis of race and creed. Continually he argued in the council for a permanent Fair Employment Practices Commission (FEPC). He put forward a seven-point program for racial harmony and intervened often to combat racist manifestations. Showing that he was not a typical politician, Davis frequently attacked the press—particularly the *New York World-Telegram* and *Daily News*—for their racist pecadillos. Finally, we should not forget that Davis' antiracist pressure, applied even in the face of collegial belittling, played the pivotal role in the integration of the fire department.[25]

The still-raging war was also never far from Davis's attention when he was in the council. Ineluctably a big issue for him was the black side of this conflict. Wielding his influence within the council, he played a large role in the opening of the still-existing playground at Lenox and 143rd street—a huge 6.5 acres in crowded Manhattan—which was named after black military hero Colonel Charles Young. Thousands attended this impressive ceremony, including Robert Moses and Walter White. Further, the interests of black veterans were often brought before the council in the face of arguments that this was not in their jurisdiction. Nevertheless this was part of Davis's approach to use this forum for significant issues, whether or not direct legislation could ensue.[26]

One cannot ignore the subway fare in this litany of Davis's council activities. Here he and Cacchione enjoyed much support, especially from the unions. Part of the struggle concerned their opposition to the creation of a transit authority that they felt would not be responsive to citizen needs. Another battle involved their effort "providing for a referendum before [transit] fare is increased." "No tampering with the five-cent subway fare" was Davis's battle cry.[27]

This was not the only economic issue that loomed large in the council in 1944. One of Davis's first acts, in January, was to call for higher taxes on cigarettes and utilities, to be used principally for higher education. He was an adamant foe of budget cuts that affected his favorite projects. Unlike legislators who would be mobilized by their constituency, with Davis and Cacchione it often worked the other way as they galvanized support for their budget proposals. The issue was joined in June 1944 when Davis, Cacchione, and Quill refused to cast a vote for a 1 percent sales tax. City Council President Newbold Morris called this a "Communist demonstration." Davis dissented. But, in a decision difficult to separate from Browderism, Davis and Cacchione changed their minds. (Quill refused to budge.) Davis explained that he and his colleague did not seek to "create a difficult situation for the city . . . [it was] under compulsion . . . in order that the needs of the city should be met."[28] The *New York Times* candidly explained that the Democratic majority "maneuvered to force the two Communist members . . . to vote for the tax" and that they would be held responsible for resultant payless paydays and loss of funds for the needy and blind if they did not. Later Davis explained, "We don't want men to walk the streets and sell apples after this war. They won't do it and they shouldn't do it." Later still Davis and Cacchione viewed this vote as a flagrant error. It was an early warning signal that the new political line adopted by the party, soon to be known derisively as Browderism, was not an insignificant change; a non-Browderist line would have meant higher taxes on elites and lower taxes on all others.[29]

Yet even a socialist-oriented party that stubs its toe can surpass in performance most bourgeois parties. At the same time Davis and his party were ensuring their lasting fame with their remarkable position on the controversy surrounding Stuyvesant Town and the epic struggle to integrate this massive housing complex in Manhattan. Stuyvesant Town was sponsored by the Metropolitan Life Insurance Company, which in the words of Dominic Capeci, "was notorious for seeking black customers at the same time neglecting to employ black people." In fact this brazen giant had 2 million black policyholders carrying $77 million in insurance while employing no blacks and trying to bar them from this housing project. Every step of the way they were assisted by Robert Moses, who "countenanced racial discrimination in state and municipal parks and withheld public works from Harlem." Yet, as Capeci has noted, "it was, however, the controversy over Stuyvesant Town that prevented discriminatory tenant selection in similar projects of the future.... The ... project set the precedent for quasi-public housing and the controversy which it created set the precedent for nondiscriminatory tenant selection."[30]

It is well to remember that Davis's premier role in this struggle was not as heralded as one might think; many elites were not pleased with the fact that a black Red was leading a just struggle against racism. Both the *New York Times* and the *New York Herald Tribune* argued passionately for the right of Met Life to bar blacks from the complex. Council members like Stanley Isaacs were deluged with letters from voters arguing the same point; one voter, for example, called integration "the tragedy of democracy.... Would you my dear councilman like to live with a Negro next door to you. ... Or, would you like to see your daughter marry a Negro?"[31] In a confidential letter from Robert Moses to F. H. Ecker, head of Met Life, the power broker assailed "agitation on the part of certain politicians, demagogues and agitators to compel the company to submit regulation of management including selection of tenants on civil service principles.... This is the real issue ... there is no escaping it." He worried nervously that "colored tenants will ... adversely affect the success of the enterprise." He craftily advised Ecker how to avoid integration.[32]

Naturally this kind of maneuvering left Davis fused with anger. Speaking to the city's powerful Board of Estimate he charged that Met Life's "policies of Jim Crowism—which are the policies of Adolf Hitler as expressed through the Nuremberg laws," would be given official sanction unless the city moved legislatively. He made this project a major campaign issue during his race for the council in 1943, and the party itself launched a petition campaign on the issue. Thousands of signatures were eventually turned over to Mayor La Guardia, and the *Daily Worker* proclaimed proudly that the party was the first political organization in the city to protest the unfair practices. In the waning days of the campaign Davis began to charge that discrimination at Met Life also encompassed the Jewish people; he printed twenty-five thousand copies of a special election handbill in "Jewish" [sic] and English.[33]

Davis backed up his campaign rhetoric by focusing on this project from the "opening day" of the council in January 1944. He and Isaacs introduced a law that would bar the granting of exemption of taxation to any corporation that refused to accept tenants due to race, color, and creed. This was a follow-up to a bill introduced by Powell and Isaacs. As an indication of how activity of the Left spurred other sectors is the fact that the Democrats sought to steal the thunder by introducing a similar bill. Davis's bill was the most stringent, calling for a fine of one thousand dollars for any corporation guilty of discrimination and a hundred dollars fine and ten days in jail for any officer of such a corporation. Moses's crony, Fred Ecker of Met Life, was the obvious target here. One could only wonder how the party could engage in the cognitive dissonance of fighting captains of industry while holding to the theoretical tenet of Browderism that said that a new era had begun in which it would be possible to cooperate with them.[34]

Davis did not just introduce his bill and wait for its passage; he mobilized his constituents throughout the city to pressure the council. This tactic proved successful since the Davis-Isaacs bill received unanimous support in the Finance Committee; however, the bill was amended so that it would not apply to Stuyvesant Town. Davis was not deterred by the fact that some critics alleged that his original bill had constitutional infirmities; he argued that these problems would be better put to the courts.[35]

This compromise bill presented a cruel dilemma for Davis: the prime target—Metropolitan Life—was let off the hook. His words were brave, promising a continued fight, but were unconvincing to some people. Should Davis have opposed the compromise bill? A number of Communists subsequently took that view. But at the time some of the more retrograde right-wingers nonetheless termed this watered-down version "Communist propaganda." Such comments outraged Davis and his supporters. Later he warned, "I intend to make the fight on hospitals and other tax-exempt institutions in New York and I consider this bill a major victory."[36]

Davis's exertions were not without impact, for Met Life pledged to build housing in Harlem. But this concession was a mixed blessing, for was heightening residential segregation in Harlem a remedy for maintaining Jim Crow on the East Side? Davis sensed this latest dilemma. He said, "No doubt the fight which we conducted influenced to some degree" the decision to build the Riverton in Harlem, but obviously it was no "substitute" for integrating Stuyvesant Town. Moses and Ecker agreed with the first part of this statement, for they felt the Davis generated heat. Moses suggested calling it the "Harlem project," though politically he felt "Carver town" would be the most appropriate name since George Washington Carver "was in no sense a revolutionary and belonged rather to the Booker Washington school of thought." There was some debate in Harlem as to whether this further application of the "separate but equal" principle should be accepted; as time passed, the struggle for Black Liberation was becoming more complicated. But virtually all blacks in Harlem and nationally praised Davis's role. Gwendolyn Minerbrook, comptroller for Chicago's Rosenwald Housing project, visited Harlem, seeking to learn from their struggle, and added that "she wished they had a duplicate Councilman Ben Davis in Chicago."[37]

Throughout his six-year tenure in the City Council Davis continued to focus on Metropolitan Life and Stuyvesant Town. This and his threat to extend his gaze to other powerful New York institutions did not win friends among this city's elite. Late in his term the party sponsored a rally at Met Life's offices at 23d Street and Madison; when Davis and his comrades (Gaulden, "Stretch" Johnson, and others) sought to meet with Ecker, a "cordon of company guards" blocked their path. But by then the political winds were chilling and this bill was scuttled.[38] Even his old ally Stanley Isaacs backed down.[39] But Davis plunged on. He helped to organize a citywide pressure group that involved unions, the NAACP, Powell, and others. He increased his attack on Ecker, calling him "the white supremacy architect of Stuyvesant Town [and] head of the biggest Jim Crow oligarchy in the world." Even after being ousted from the council he continued to speak out on one of his "pet" issues.[40]

Some might consider it remarkable that Davis could take such a strong antiracist line against Met Life during the same year—1944—that the Communist party was transformed into a Communist Political Association and proclaimed a new approach to class struggle that stressed conciliation. The notion was that since the United States and USSR could unite at Teheran in 1943 despite their class antagonisms and contradictions, the coming new world also meant that there was no longer a need for a class struggle. The Marxist-Leninist party could wither away and what happened at Teheran could happen domestically; that is, labor and capital were not inherently antagonistic but could join forces instead. This was the essence of what was called Browderism, a philosophy named after party leader Earl Browder, though as used here I do not mean to suggest—as some have—that every party flaw could be ascribed to this leader. Conventional wisdom suggests that this line, which was enunciated in February 1944, was reversed in mid-1945 because of the impending end of the war and the intervention of Stalin. But once again conventional wisdom does not dovetail altogether with the historical record.

The Communist parties have tended to be connected. The first revision of the conventional wisdom would be that the CPSU did tend to have significant influence on the parties in nations bordering the USSR but that the further a nation was in miles from Moscow, the lesser amount of intervention from Moscow could be expected; this latter tenet also applied to the CPUSA. Yet similarly the Cuban party could be negatively influenced by the U.S. party, though it would be unfair to suggest that the latter controlled the former. What was involved in the Communist parties' relationship with Moscow was more emulation than dictation. Moreover, if the USSR initiated Browderism, why would their U.S. acolytes advocate universal military training during this period, which would inevitably be aimed at Moscow? Even after the war there were some U.S. Communists still pushing this program. Still, it is not overly difficult to see how the illusions that led to the Teheran line (or Browderism) were formed. There was evidence that a new world was coming, and it was possible to see how the rapidity of events could lead to confusion. This was not just a U.S. trend but was present worldwide. In 1943 Communists were named to the cabinet in Cuba; earlier Reds won election as aldermen in Toronto. South Africa suspended its pass laws in 1942–43. Similarly the Cuban party was influenced by the Teheran line, as was the U.S. party. In Jamaica the nascent party was liquidated in 1944, as it was in Puerto Rico and Greece. All of these developments were later criticized in each country. Why would Moscow want to introduce such turmoil into these parties? Given that the U.S. party, for example, was watched incessantly by the authorities, where are the telephone transcripts or purloined telegrams that would add credence to the "hand of Moscow" thesis? Perhaps archives now being opened in Moscow will provide answers.[41]

At home it was not hard to see why Marxists may have felt that a new world had arrived. In July 1942 Davis announced happily that "for the first time in Arkansas' history, a number of Negro citizens voted in federal elections." Again in 1943 he proclaimed "for the first time—perhaps since the Civil War—a trial is taking place in the poll tax state of Mississippi growing out of the lynching of a Negro citizen"; the sheriff of Hattiesburg was being tried under federal civil rights laws. Then there was the fall of the "white primary." In 1945, before the Teheran line was reversed, Davis expressed similar glee about the introduction of racially mixed armed forces units in Europe: "A revolution is in process with respect to Negro rights. . . . Is there any doubt that a new and better world is in the making?" Unlike some, Davis recognized instinctively that these changes were motivated largely by the need of the ruling class to assuage and keep in fighting fit an increasingly disaffected African-American community. But others saw this wartime spirit carrying over to the postwar era and felt that progressive change would come of itself and certainly without the aid of a Marxist-Leninist party.[42]

Even before the formal proclamation of the Teheran line there were troubling and telltale signs suggesting misguided policies of the party. On 29 December 1938 the *Daily Worker* featured a highly offensive ad for a "Red Indian Dance . . . Red Hot Bands . . . We furnish the feathers" with a stereotyped picture of a Native American. More substantively, at the 1939 NAACP convention in Richmond Davis attacked a resolution calling for "amendment of the Wagner Labor Act to deny its benefits to unions where discrimination exists." That same year the *Daily Worker* featured a generally favorable article on the arch-racist Andrew Jackson. The acquiescence to the internment of Japanese-Americans has been noted already. Earlier the execrable Stephen Foster was called a "musical genius."[43]

It would be reductionist to suggest that all of this could be laid solely at the feet of party general secretary Earl Browder; though he may have been first among equals, his policies had to be validated by others. It is too easy to reduce the 1944–45 policies to Browder, which means that once he was axed, then the underlying problems that led to Browderism would be purged along with him. Still, his subsequent post-1945 deviations imply that the harsh attacks on him by the party may have merit. As early as 1933 he was acknowledging criticisms from "Negro comrades" because of his "lack of sufficient emphasis upon the importance of Negro work. I accept that criticism." By the time the Teheran line was inaugurated he was harsher on "liberals" than the GOP and was thanking those who were comparing him to leaders of the National Association of Manufacturers.[44]

Davis was as complimentary of Browder in the pre-1945 period as any; some might even say more so. When Browder was facing prison in 1941, his black comrade was one of his staunchest defenders, complaining about the "brutality of the . . . unprecedentedly harsh . . . sentence. . . . White House's calculated revenge"; he invidiously compared the lesser sentences of others convicted of passport violations. He took to the stump to speak out on his behalf, particularly in black communities. His columns in the *Daily Worker* were increasingly devoted to Browder, and he used his influence to get his father and other black leaders to sign ads calling for Browder's freedom.[45]

After the war began, Davis's defense of his leader seemed to heighten. He was rather effusive about the general secretary's writings. He was not alone in this opinion, however; Rev. James Robinson spoke similarly at a Harlem meeting focusing on Browder's political analysis of the prevailing historical era.[46]

Arguably Davis's election was a material factor in helping Browder form the Teheran line, for if Communists were being elected to office in the citadel of the capital, then a new world *was* coming. According to the general secretary, the Davis election "is going to influence the political life of America in 1944." In China, France, and Yugoslavia there was an "all inclusive unity that transcends all party lines, a unity of non-Communists with Communists." The Davis election would be a "sign" of this trend hitting American shores. In turn Davis believed that he "couldn't have been elected without your leadership."[47]

Davis and Browder communicated about sensitive matters during this time. In 1944 Davis again was downright effusive: "[The] correctness of your report on Teheran to the National Committee receives fresh confirmation every day. . . . The regrouping of forces in this country is taking place with breathless speed." Like the party, Davis was apparently assuming that wartime exigencies were not the prime reason for the "regrouping of forces" and certain antiracist decisions by the Supreme Court.[48]

Since Davis's election was brought forward as prime evidence justifying the Teheran line, it was not surprising that his relationship with Browder seemed to deepen in 1944. Salutations in his letters became "My dear Earl." When Browder was announced as editor-in-chief of the *Daily Worker*, Davis again was unreserved in comment: "Browder, who has made so many original and vital contributions to our nation's cause . . . will . . . bring greater clarity and authority to the editorial policy of our papers."[49]

Davis's unrestrained praise of Browder and Teheran was mirrored in the party at large. The Young Communist League began to take on the same aroma. No doubt there was unease, as evidenced by the fact that one writer in *The Communist* felt compelled to repudiate the idea that Teheran meant easing up domestically so that Wall Street would not drop out of the antifascist alliance; this was "betrayal," he intoned. *The Communist* itself was going through changes, from the "magazine of the theory and practice of Marxism-Leninism" in June 1944 to the "Marxist magazine devoted to advancement of Democratic thought and Action" in July 1944 to being renamed *Political Affairs* by January 1945.[50] As early as March 1944 David Goldway was conceding that in the party "a few even think we are being forced to step backward, to accept a bitter pill . . . that we are postponing or abandoning socialism . . . falling victim to revisionism or vulgarization. . . . The cold fact is that the bulk of existing classical Marxist literature seems on the surface to condemn, not to support, our present approach."[51]

The signs of disquiet about Browderism were proliferating publicly, which was even more unusual given the tight rein on questions of dissent usually evidenced in party publications. Their *perestroika* was not accompanied by *glasnost*. But Doxey Wilkerson reported "real concern" by "a branch of white collar and professional Negro comrades" over the idea of the Communists "'giving up'" socialism. "Their anxiety grew out of the fact that they had come correctly to associate the achievement of socialism with the complete liberation of the Negro people, the primary basis upon which many of them entered the party."[52] This latter sentence encapsulates why black comrades tended to be less compromising about liquidationist sentiment and thus in the next party crisis twelve years later tended to side with the so-called hard-liners. Hence party leader John Williamson worriedly recounted in January 1945 that "while the Communists proportionately have a greater influence and support among the Negro people than in any other strata of the population, nevertheless we must face the fact that during the July roll call into the CPA fluctuation was greatest in the ranks of our Negro members."[53]

There was another trend evident among black comrades too, and that was unease about the cry in the black community over a double victory against fascism abroad and racism at home. As Claudia Jones put it, "Some among the Negro people say we need a 'Double V'—a victory at home and abroad. . . . But are there really two 'V's' here? We have already shown that everything depends upon defeating Hitler. . . . Clearly there is only one 'V'—single and indivisible."[54] Eugene Braddock of the YCL concurred: "the slogan tends to separate the problems of the Negro people from the problems of the oppressed masses in other parts of the world; thus, through this separation the fight for Negro unity and for Negro rights is weakened."[55] Eugene Gordon in the *Daily Worker* for 28 March 1942 said that Hitler and Tojo should be seen as the primary enemy of blacks and U.S. racists as secondary; in the face of dissent from Ludlow Werner of the *New York Age* and St. Claire Bourne of the *People's Voice*, he scored the Double V campaign. Yet it should not be ignored that the party may not have been alone in this. Patrick Washburn points out that in 1942 in the *Pittsburgh Courier* "space devoted to the Double V campaign declined by half between April and August and by the end of the year the campaign was virtually dead. . . . A more positive tone also began creeping into articles and picture cutlines."[56]

Though others may have looked askance at the Double V, it was the party that took lumps about its rhetorical position, despite the fact that Davis's usual line was that Jim Crow had to be defeated for fascism to be defeated. The *New York Age* in particular confronted the party directly on this. They called Davis "and others of kindred thought . . . political bedfellows with the white South . . . who insist that now's the time to keep silent. . . . The Negro can less afford to keep silent at this time than at any time in his history." His attack on Randolph's rally was recalled. Davis replied at length but the *Age* would not relent: "The masses of Negroes cannot understand why if the war was 'imperialistic' at the start, it should suddenly become a holy crusade upon the entrance of Russia."[57] As late as 1948 the *Age* was still chiding the Reds: " . . . who ran for cover on the question of the rights of Negroes during the war? The *Daily Worker* and the local comrades then were not so red as they were yellow on the issue of freedom for blacks. Listen, *Daily Worker*, don't fool with us."[58] Though Davis and the party continued to struggle in practice on this front, the words of Claudia Jones and others haunted them all for years to come.

Though some critics were charging the Reds with retreating on black rights, others were making the opposite allegation, that they were behind Negro unrest. The FBI went on at length about this: " . . . it is said that the '*People's Voice*' . . . has completely given itself over to the Communist Party . . . law enforcement agencies are hampered in their work by Communist groups who characterize the actions of the Police Department in enforcing law as attacks on the Negro people. . . . the Party no longer thinks in terms of individual Party members here and there but rather in terms of hundreds and thousands . . . subversive forces at work among the American Negroes causing unrest and dissatisfaction . . . the most outstanding . . . is the Communist Party . . . in several Party districts throughout the country the number of Negro recruits in the recent recruiting campaign total well over 50 per cent of all recruits in the particular districts." This was just before the inauguration of the Teheran line, so one must also take into account the FBI's tendency to inflate the Red threat for their own purposes; yet it does provide an interesting perception of party strength by the authorities.[69]

From defending the party against charges of inaction, Davis now had to take the opposite tack. He focused on the party's role in calming Harlem during the uprising of 1943; they "worked jointly with others to curb window smashing and looting . . . bringing the disorders under control." They issued one hundred thousand leaflets under his name calling the looting "utterly wrong." But the authorities would have none of it. The U.S. Army joined the FBI in charging that the black press in particular was being influenced by Communists like Davis to inflame the African-American community.[60]

What helped to confuse the overall situation and lead to Browderism generally was the looming figure of Franklin Roosevelt. His support among African-Americans, his backing of the Wagner Act, and his historic and extremely progressive inaugural speech of 1944 in particular created a climate for confusion. But again, the party was not alone in being disoriented by FDR. Christopher Johnson suggests that labor was in the same boat and says that the party was not alone in backing the "no-strike" pledge urged by FDR. But even here there were conflicting signals. Cyril Phillip, known to be close to the party, was explicit in opposing a fourth term for FDR in 1944 because "the Negro needs a President who is not dependent upon the South." P. C. Joshi, general secretary of the Communist party of India, was allowed to urge his U.S. comrades to pressure FDR in the pages of the *Daily Worker*. The threat from the Right, FDR's popularity, and the exigencies of the war led to a surprisingly uncritical party attitude toward the White House.[61]

Davis's attitude toward FDR reflected these shifting currents, especially in 1944. In July he reprimanded Walter White after he criticized the Democratic party platform, although this important document failed to mention FEPC or integration of the armed forces. In September, however, he was calling this same platform "inadequate." Then in October he declared that FDR "is a statesman and has placed issues above party label." In personally calling for FEPC, Roosevelt, according to Davis, merited high praise.[62]

But after the election there was another shift in emphasis. In December he counseled that it would be a "fatal mistake" if "we rested on our oars and expected the mandate given to Roosevelt automatically to fulfill itself."[63] Days later, after hitting the underutilization of Negro nurses in the military, he declared, "It is true that certain important democratic principles have been won through President Roosevelt. . . . But not enough have been won."[64] The reluctance to criticize FDR from the Left helped to tip the political spectrum to the Right, although the latter did not suffer a similar inhibition in their attack on the White House.

Davis was not reluctant to take on the economic royalists; they would rather lose the war then yield on black rights, he warned. He recognized that "powerful industrialists" were trying to "scrap the FEPC." He recognized that "powerful real estate interests" were blocking support for rent and price controls. His opposition to subway fare hikes had a similar tone. He never wavered on antimonopoly measures like FEPC.[65]

Nonetheless, Davis was swept up in the Teheran euphoria. He even tried to peddle this line to African-Americans, urging the "development in Negro communities of non-partisan people's political action, joining together Negro Republicans, Democrats and Communists with labor and all the other anti-fascist sections of the population, irrespective of class, race or creed." This was a laudable sentiment, even in pre-Teheran days, but in 1944 he began to speak of "those dominant ruling circles . . . which place the fate of the nation above greed and class prejudice." Understandably, he was not specific on who these "circles" were. At a conference at Abyssinian Church he opined that blacks did not feel that the seniority system would need adjustment to accommodate black workers.[66] Davis was not alone. James Ford hailed the new line as an "outstanding example of maturing political relations between the Negro people and broad progressive political forces."[67] Gus Hall, a Communist leader from the Midwest, called Browder's work a "great document." Bob Minor was similarly enthusiastic.[68]

The Teheran line was ratified at a top party meeting on 8 February 1944. James Ford was unequivocal, calling the line a "turning point in world history [and] a turning point in the history of our country." He cited China's experience with Chiang Kai-Shek as a model. The recent liquidation of the Comintern itself was also seen as providing a useful model. The doubting William Z. Foster, top party leader, was hushed: "In Moscow, some of us, including Comrade Foster, were talked to by some of the leading most influential comrades there, and they said to us that factionalism in America would be a very dangerous thing." Citing conversations with miners and autoworkers, Pat Toohey too rejected Foster. William Schneiderman, Morris Childs, Irving Potash, and Gil Green agreed. Ben Gold compared the new line to Lenin's New Economic Policy and Stalin's pact with Hitler of 1939 while noting shockingly, "I haven't talked matters over with Comrade Lenin personally for about ten or twelve years, since 1931 (that is, I haven't had much time to read)."[69]

Earlier Browder had written that as a result of the summit at Teheran, the United States and Britain "have closed the books finally and forever upon their old expectation that the Soviet Union as a socialist country is going to disappear some day . . . the policy of destruction of the Soviet Union . . . is finally ended." Even if this were true, did it justify taking a softer line on monopoly capital at home? Here one begins to understand the origin of the idea that the U.S. party was unduly influenced by their Soviet counterpart. While in the United States, progressives "must help to remove from the

American ruling class the fear of a socialist revolution," argued Browder; this, in the understatement of the millennium, requires "readjustment," Browder suggested.[70]

Before this February 1944 meeting Browder had come to the National Committee of the party in December 1943 with a proposed change in the party line. According to Foster, this "at once met with opposition in the Party." On 20 January 1944 Foster wrote a long letter opposing his demarche but by that time opinions had been changed by Browder's lobbying: "I had to agree to confine my opposition within the ranks of the National Committee," said Foster.[71]

Sam Darcy, the other dissenter, was not as tactful as Foster. He recalls coming to the February meeting; usually twenty-eight numbers were present but the room was packed with five hundred on a Saturday morning. He and Foster were isolated but Darcy would not yield. Darcy was ultimately expelled from the party, though he recalls that other Communist parties and internationally recognized comrades like Walter Ulbricht and Harry Pollitt wrote in his support. But even the bitter Darcy connects this rigid discipline to the kind of repression visited upon the party, such as the constant surveillance and pressure from on high that tended to elicit a reliance on military-style discipline—including a lack of glasnost—in the party. This fact is often forgotten.[72]

As these events unfolded Davis was no passive bystander. His election was being pointed to as Exhibit A in explicating the change in party line. When the party was dissolved, he was on the Committee on Constitution and secretary at the convention that moved this decision. Afterward he was named one of eleven vice-presidents (along with Foster, Ford, Flynn, and others) of the new Communist Political Association; Browder was president. He was one of thirteen members of the National Board. Along with his City Council election it did seem that a turning point had been reached and a new world was coming. But as it turned out, 1944 was the high-water mark for Davis and the party; with the repudiation of the Teheran line and the ending of the war in 1945, Davis was about to face some of the more trying times of his career in the party.[73]

At the vital 8 February 1944 meeting of the National Committee, Davis stated that Foster was "completely wrong":

> Comrade Gil and others . . . have gone into this very thoroughly and very deeply . . . much more deeply than I could . . . [the Darcy-Foster] statement [is] of complete hopelessness and despair . . . means-taking a step backward and carrying through a policy that unquestionably would lead to the most bitter class conflict, racial strife. . . . This is a statement that certainly I could not take to the Negro people. . . . [It] does not conform to the very elementary rudiments of Marxism; it does not conform to the facts. . . . [Foster] says nothing whatever about the Negroes. . . . [Jim Crow is] being battered down today in an unprecedented manner . . . it is obvious that this is due to the fact that there is a different relationship

of forces and that it is possible to work with all these forces, irrespective of class . . . policy of national unity [is responsible] and the only way we are able to carry this further and have the perspective is by a closer alliance with the dominant sectors of the capitalist class. . . . [FEPC] could not be possible with a perspective of class conflict and bitterness and regarding monopoly capital as one solid mass . . . .

Blacks have chosen integration, not self-determination, was his conclusion, à la Browder. In the "99th Air Squadron. . . . In the marines for the first time time since 1860 Negroes are being trained equally in the South in officers' training school." The Foster-Darcy approach called for a party, not an association, focused on class struggle, as in the traditional Leninist approach. The Foster line should be "crushed," was Davis's conclusion; instead, in a related maneuver, there was an attempt by the state to crush Davis.[74]

Browderism disrupted the party at a crucial moment. With the war concluding, the process of granting concessions on the black liberation front while launching a Red Scare was commenced. Davis's election to the City Council was a signal that black voters in particular would be searching for radical solutions unless Jim Crow were eased. The Red Scare insured that one option for black voters would be removed and that what has come to be called the Civil Rights Movement could proceed without the fear of its being diverted into more radical channels, such as fundamentally challenging property and control of the means of production.

8
Unity and Struggle, 1945

For many reasons, 1945 was yet another turning point in history. The end of the war and the world's experience with fascism was a severe setback to the theory and practice of chauvinism and racism; Hitler's Germany exemplified what could happen if this tendency were left unchecked. It was the beginning of the end for Jim Crow in the United States, not least because concessions had to be made to African-Americans to enlist their support in that war and in future conflicts. The proclamation of the Atlantic Charter and the Four Freedoms was difficult to keep from the ears and eyes of Africans as a whole and marked the beginning of the end of colonialism. The failure to overthrow Soviet power and the increase in strength of Communist parties not just east of the Elbe but west as well would subject the Teheran line to new strain, just as atomic diplomacy was commenced. Ben Davis was up for reelection and in addition to manifestations of the above events, he had to contend with the turmoil caused by Browder's ouster, a new controversy ignited by the existence of the Black Belt thesis, and a tumultuous City Council campaign. His hectic pace was signaled to Essie Robeson when he complained of how "my own book project seems hopeless unless and until I get time off. The pace is killing and irresistibly demanding, what with an election year nearing its heated stage." Ollie Harrington suggests that blacks came back from the war with the knowledge of how to defend themselves with weapons, which created fear, along with a "tremendous effect" on racist "attitudes." Whatever the case, this was also the onset of Black Liberation confronting the Red Scare.[1]

A letter from Jacques Duclos, the well-respected French Communist leader, was a critical factor accelerating Browder's ouster. Duclos's intervention was not totally accidental. Fluent in German and considered an expert on Hitler and fascism, he had pioneered in the theory and practice of the Popular Front; he and his party were emerging from the war in a relatively strong position, given their heroic fight against the Nazis. He was no stranger to U.S. Communists, having written an influential series entitled "Communist Attitude Toward Writers" in the *Daily Worker*.[2]

Years later William Z. Foster confided that the Duclos letter attacking the Teheran line "was caused by Browder's dabbling in the French and many other Communist Parties." As I noted earlier, some parties seemed quite receptive to these overtures, though they were not necessarily "puppets" of the CPUSA; apparently, Duclos's article was intended for internal French consumption: "So little did the French comrades think of it as an international article, that they did not send our Party a copy . . . we had to dig it up from a subscriber in New York weeks later, having heard about it by chance."[3] Foster's 1944 objection to the Teheran line was no secret and Duclos drew heavily from it in his 1945 demarche.

The reasons for Duclos's concern were obvious. Before the liquidation of the party and its conversion into an "association," there were ninety thousand Reds, but as of 16 July 1944 only forty-five thousand had reregistered in the newly named Communist Political Association. The Cuban and Colombian parties emulated their U.S. comrades while the parties in South Africa and Australia came out openly against Browder's position. One view was that the party may have been correct in backing FDR, but why did it have to dissolve to do that? Worth noting are the 25 May 1945 critique of President Harry Truman's United Nations plan and the 26 May 1945 critique of Henry A. Wallace attacking inciters of World War III; both were prominently featured in the *Daily Worker*.[4]

Davis was "shocked and astonished" at first by the Duclos letter but quickly viewed it as correct. Like other Communists, he shifted with the political winds. Initially he tried to praise both Duclos and Browder but the latter's intransigence made that an untenable position; Teheran may have been acceptable for war but not for the postwar period, he concluded. At a crucial National Committee meeting in late May 1945, days after victory in Europe, Davis plaintively asked Browder, in mantralike fashion, "[What is your] view with regard to monopoly capital?"[5]

At another critically important meeting of the National Committee in June, William Patterson, one of Davis's closest comrades, was not so gentle. He attacked sharply Browder's "arrogance" and Browderism generally, particularly its impact on African-Americans. As for the National Negro Department, "Nothing came out of there, not even articles. . . . For years we [had] no serious attempt to enrich our theoretical understanding of the Negro question." He assailed the line on "integration" and the ditching of the Black Belt thesis. What was signaled here? Browder's plausibly appropriate 1944 idea that the Black Belt thesis should be abandoned and recognition that the transition from "nation" to "national minority" of the Negro people at minimum had been accelerated were caught up in the detonation of Browderism; in other words, the baby was thrown out with the bathwater. But real issues were raised, as, for example, the fact that International Publishers, in "vital research on the South . . . has never seen fit to utilize a Negro." With typical understatement James Ford admitted, " I share a large responsibility"; he later recalled ruefully, "we had to whisper about discrimination in the blood bank, around the corridors."[6]

Elizabeth Gurley Flynn regretted never talking with her "Old Wobbly" friend, William Z. Foster, "because I was afraid he was going to convince me and that if I was convinced I would be out of step with the organization as a whole. I wanted unity and was willing to conform to achieve it." She recalled her past "inferiority complex" as a theoretician. At this meeting the monolithic unity of the party, traditionally a strength, may have manifested a dialectical downside.[7]

Alexander Bittleman of the party leadership was similarly sorry: "I will tell you frankly, as I recall now from experience of the last 18 months I ask—damn fool, why didn't you listen to your wife? She was questioning and doubting every single day." The usually perceptive Nemmy Sparks was equally puzzled. He read volume 4 of Lenin on "liquidationism. For several days, I spent my spare time reading and trying to figure out how to square this with the change from the CP to the CPA. Finally, I couldn't figure it out, so I divorced theory from practice." Like Doxey Wilkerson, he lamented the general lack of discussion in the party that proved so fatal in this instance.[8]

Others were more unkind. One questioned a perceived coolness of Browder toward Henry Wallace and alleged that the soon-to-be-defrocked general secretary spoke "as [a] member of the bourgeoisie": Browder had claimed that his own personal work led to Davis's election, about the only remaining shred of evidence that could be invoked to justify Teheran. This was deemed "complete arrogance."[9]

Davis was bitter, recalling that many leading comrades did not even think he could win. Worse, the "danger of [Browder's] line was noticeable in Negro work, and were it not for our past achievements in this field, this would have been followed by catastrophe and disaster. I am extremely dissatisfied that this question has not been discussed sufficiently by the speakers here today." But his criticism was accompanied by self-criticism: "However . . . I must take special responsibility with regard to our line on the Negro people." Bella Dodd was not moved by this *mea culpa*: "Ben has been on the National Board and . . . the State Committee . . . and I want to know where he was all the time and why he has not been more militant in the past." True, Davis concurred, "I did what should not have been done, I thought for a while solely of questions of the Negro people and not at all on the basic line . . . I lacked Marxist maturity." Of course, his "especially high regard" for Browder had to be a factor.[10]

Davis continued to praise Browder on the National Question: " . . . I can remember shortly after the war changed its character that there was [a] tendency to soft-peddle the Negro question and we have been constantly polemicizing against the tendency ever since . . . and one thing I am confident of, was that mistake was never corrected until Earl returned from prison." He pleaded with Browder to reverse field, plead guilty, and agree with the newly evolving line, but Browder was adamant. He maintained his position of days before, when on a unanimous draft resolution reversing the line, he had at first voted yes, then switched to no. Browder, the probable notetaker of these minutes, wrote, "Foster, Dennis, Thompson most militant" on these matters, along with Gil Green.[11]

Recriminations were swift and bitter. This was a fine time for the party to be undergoing turmoil; the end of the war facilitated the gathering counterattack by the monopolies on labor and its allies; ruling circles were in the process of changing their line on Jim Crow. Inevitably feelings were intense. Since the conflict began, Audley Moore had had a "bad stomach" and "nightmares." Like Gurley Flynn (and note that these were two of the leading women cadre), she spoke of her "inferiority complex." Similarly Meridel Le Seuer felt a "sense of inferiority," along with a "deep personal and social anguish and pain . . . confusion, dismay." Perhaps these startling words expressed by three leading women comrades needed investigation then, along with the devolution of the National Question. Moore said that the New York party had had a "very sharp . . . struggle" about liquidation; although this was the biggest district, such a rush of feelings necessitated a deep inquiry.[12]

Doxey Wilkerson, the intellectual black scholar and journalist, was angry: "I remember the quieting of our struggle on the blood bank issue." Browder gave "official public sanction to the idea of not struggling against discrimination in the armed forces. . . . I raised this in discussion in a small group and was slapped down for it . . . we have virtually liquidated the National Negro Congress." Wilkerson was to leave the party during the mid-1950's crisis, when some of the purged forces were analogized to him; ironically, he had been one of the more articulate opponents of the Black Belt thesis.[13]

Davis expressed his opinion about Teheran at the National Committee meetings: "I remember when it came up in the Board, and I was new on the Board and did not know how to participate in the discussion—the thing was pretty vague to me and it never became clear—and suddenly we did not have a party in the deep South." He sadly recounted events at the *Daily Worker* about fund drives: "Every time the comrades express themselves on this question, they are shouted down and made to feel that all [they] have to do is raise the money and not be concerned with the policy." According to him, this lack of democracy helped to explain the "extremely small circulation of the paper." The Flynn-Moore-Le Seuer inferiority syndrome may have influenced Davis; at this CP meeting he said, "even for me that has had lots of public speaking exercises I feel ill at ease."[14] If nothing else, this debate over Browder's fate raised profound questions about the nature of the party; its monolithic unity and tendency to march in lockstep—a strength in many instances—could also be a profound weakness. This characteristic was exacerbated by state repression, an underdeveloped U.S. political culture, and the party's emulation of the beleaguered Soviet party, all of which helped to induce a paramilitary discipline that may have eroded democracy and heightened centralism.

An FBI bug apparently picked up a Davis-Robeson conversation in which Davis said, " . . . I feel terrible." Robeson saw the liquidation as "tactical . . . that at some later time it will be necessary for us to regroup ourselves in the old party . . . he says that is obvious that we went too far." Robeson recounted a West Coast meeting with leading capitalists who planned to lay off "40,000 Negroes." Robeson: "its obvious that Foster is right." Davis conceded "modesty, a feeling of humility," in challenging Browder. A negative side of such turmoil was the reinforcement of pessimism, as Davis inferentially suggested: " . . . any group as we are made such a basic error so that there must be plenty of imperfections in everything we do, must be" [sic]. Because Browder "thinks a lot of [you]" Davis suggested that Robeson talk with him. On that day it was not necessary to treat Browder as an "enemy," but Davis was frightfully worried about him.[15]

It is instructive to examine the evolution of Davis's thought before the Duclos letter. As Doxey Wilkerson's example suggested, one would expect the black comrades to be particularly sensitive to any radical change in line; the abandonment of black issues was apparently part of the bargain for Browderism. Yet during this period Davis actively supported Mrs. Recy Taylor, an African-American woman who was raped and kidnapped by whites in Alabama. He was also particularly vocal, as usual, on the FEPC question. This was an obvious response to certain Browderites, but then he went on to criticize four black WACs who went on strike to protest discrimination. "To condone the strike of these young women is as bad, if not worse, than condoning the action of trade unionists who let [our] boys down by violating their no-strike pledge . . . unexcusable misguided method of the WACs complicated the solution. . . . Such undisciplined methods play into the hand of provocateurs. . . . The armed forces are in the main current of the democratic resurgence."[16]

Was this harsh indictment of black WACs correct? Was their action similar to violation of a no-strike pledge? Does the fact that this was written a few weeks before victory over Hitler make any difference? A look at another controversial position may tip the balance against him. Analyzing the NAACP legislative program, Davis endorsed it "on the whole," but disagreed with the NAACP on universal military training in peacetime, which he called "necessary." He also disagreed with their opposition to "national service legislation." What was his view? "A coalition cannot be one-sided," he said. This is why trying to analyze the party as a simple tool of Moscow is so misguided. Did Stalin endorse military training in peacetime for the United States or was this the view of a wing of the U.S. bourgeoisie? The Teheran line has to be seen first as class conciliation and second as an emulation of Moscow.[17]

Other issues were also germane to the NAACP. In reviewing Walter White's *A Rising Wind*, Davis criticized his fellow Atlantan for not drawing the appropriate "profound" conclusions of Teheran. Davis believed that "one of the surest signs that Jim Crow is on its way out in America is the terrific battering this un-American principle has received in the armed forces.... Mr. White does not emphasize the positive aspects of the world that is to be." It may have been that the optimism that is historically part of any Communist had a downside. But by July in reviewing Du Bois' *Color and Democracy* Davis had reversed field and by implication repudiated his earlier words. The point is that even when Davis's words were misguided, he still remained an active anti-racist.[18]

An action involving a NAACP ally also helped to awaken Davis and the party. In early March 1945 the CPA donated five thousand dollars to Freedom House, an anti-Communist group. Though the CPA may have taken leave of their class senses, Freedom House had not; they returned the contribution huffily, saying that it distinguished between the USSR—assuring them that it was pro-Soviet—and the CPA. The CPA never seemed to recognize that this at best was the import of Teheran: the USSR could be accepted but not the CPA. Freedom House, like other non-Communists, did not accept the full import of the "hand of Moscow" thesis; the CPSU could be praised, but not the CPA. Davis, who was one of the founders of the Wilkie Memorial Fund, for which the money was designated, was equally irate: "What is needed in Freedom House is some freedom!" But he never questioned why the CPA was giving such a large sum to these forces in the first place.[19]

It was obvious that Davis and his comrades had a lot of explaining to do once Browder was ousted. In late July 1945 Davis struck back at the "revisionist errors" and called for "uncompromising struggle" against them:

> As a member of the National Board, I bear a heavy responsibility for the error.... I applied it [Teheran] in all my work ... with resulting serious weakness in that work. I had ample opportunity to see the incorrectness of the position.... I did not detect the errors because I was not sufficiently mature and equipped as a Marxist.... Specializing in a particular field of work, I did not give sufficient consideration to questions of over-all CPA policy.... I was heavily influenced by the fact that the Negro people made perhaps greater wartime gains than any other underprivileged section of the population, many of these gains being directly contributed to by the Communists.... I drew from partial electoral and other successes in our Harlem work and from certain limited legislative successes in the City Council, wrong and illusory conclusions. It became comfortably easy to regard these as much more than wartime gains, but rather as evidence of the "long term class peace" in which monopoly capitalism had changed its reactionary spots and would extend these gains into the post-war period as a part of its "own good sense and class interests."[20]

There was much to agree with in this analysis; the overestimation of the ruling class; the impact of the City Council victory, which assumed that wartime gains were signifying new trends; and the victories of African-Americans all had helped to point Davis in Browder's direction. He did accelerate his study of Marxism-Leninism after Browder was ousted but he remained passionately concerned with Black Liberation in the first place.

This was not necessarily a problem, as his comment might suggest; concern about the most degraded sector of the working class is hardly cause for indictment. On the other hand, his remarks on the liquidation of the Black Belt thesis were not as prescient, since he regretted his agreement with the idea that blacks had become a national minority seeking integration rather than a nation. Allowing Browder to steal the march on this question, so close to his heart, may have influenced another controversial view, that the campaign against "white chauvinism" within the ranks of the Communists needed renewal.

These Davis errors did not cost him his party position, unlike James Ford and Robert Minor, who were considered most closely identified with the line and who also, coincidentally, were the major theoreticians on the Negro Question. This meant that Davis was now considered the preeminent black party leader and, given his City Council post, the leader with the most significant mass base. In any case, after rejecting Teheran, he led the way—along with Foster—in the critique of Browder, at one time calling him "Wall Street's 'official Communist expert' . . . political faker . . . intellectual crook . . . white chauvinist. . . . He has no more in common with Marxism-Leninism than a pig with a full dress suit." And these were some of his kinder words.[21]

After a three-day national convention of the CPA in July 1945, Browder's ouster was confirmed and Davis was named to the National Board. The post mortem of this group mirrored Davis's. Browder merited the "main responsibility" for the errors but "the former National Board and National Committee must assume a heavy responsibility for the bureaucratic system of work which prevailed in all Party organizations. The former National Board . . . set a bureaucratic example and did not carry on a struggle to establish genuine democracy in the organization. This was also reflected by the former Board's inadequate self-criticism during the preconvention period." Despite Browder, the CPA "fought hard and effectively against Jim Crow practices. . . . However, the struggle for the national liberation of the Negro people . . . was often lost sight of." And there was an effort "at times . . . to soft-pedal the struggle to eliminate Negro discrimination in the armed forces."[22]

It was not sufficient for the Communist party to rectify past errors; individual comrades had to explain as well. Foster, who had opposed the Teheran line from the start, expressed views that echoed the sentiments of many. "Super-centralization" was a major cause of the debacle. Most regrettable was the backing of FDR without "serious self-criticism." "Mistakes are serious matters," he warned; "they involve the welfare . . . even the lives of large masses of people." What was to be done? The party must "radically improve the social composition of its membership and of its leadership" by bringing in more workers. This was a knock at Browder the clerk, but also recognition that the party belonged to the working class.[23]

Claudia Jones, Davis's closest woman comrade, went on in a similar vein: "It cannot be denied, of course, that Browder's thesis was supported and accepted on such apparent evidences in our national life as . . . the first election of Benjamin J. Davis, Jr." Like Foster, she stressed that the party "failed to criticize sharply the liberal-bourgeois policies of the Roosevelt Administration [vis-á-vis] Jim Crow practices in the armed forces" and put a "wet blanket" on those who tried; "leading comrades" Ford, Davis, and Patterson reflected, although to an insufficient degree, the deep postwar concern of the Negro people for victory over Jim Crow. She wrote, "That Negro comrades accepted Browder's opportunist thesis makes the error all the more grave, because in effect we accepted the false and bankrupt logic of reformism as a solution to the problems of the Negro people."[24]

Also like Foster, A. B. Magil warned of the "danger of committing new errors of over-correction," such as "writing and speaking as if our movement had achieved nothing at all; the fact is that even in the recent period our practical work, despite the harmful effects of our revisionist theory, adds up to a plus." Although this was true, "over-correction" was not avoided then and was even more prevalent in the wake of the Stalin devaluation of 1956; indeed, one can see aspects of this over-correction in the post-1985 (former) Soviet Union. The U.S. party, he cautioned, was "relatively weak functioning in the most powerful imperialist country in the world and within a labor movement dominated by capitalist ideology"; this magnified the "lazy thinking" and "bourgeois and petty bourgeois pressures" that dogged the party.[25]

Other opinions were similar. The *Daily Worker* opened its pages to a burst of opinion on this issue—a practice that should have been begun earlier and lasted longer. Many of these letters to the editor endorsed the ouster of Browder and change of line on the basis that at minimum the ruling class had not upheld their end of the bargain. Jacob Mindel, one of the top educators in the party school, pointed to "complacency" and "trust" in Browder as key errors. Years later Davis, on more sober reflection, acknowledged, "One of the main reasons why modern day revisionism got such a strong grip on the left and Communist forces was the low educational level of many miliant workers and progressives."[26]

Davis could put up a brave front but there was no mistaking the party's disarray. "Let the poisonous press rave and lie!" said Davis. "They are frightened!"[27] His typically aggressive response could not mask this crisis. Puerto Rican Communists began to rebel: "Until now the policy of the American Communists with respect to Puerto Rico has been defective, when not altogether negative."[28] Sam Darcy, like Foster a premature anti-Browderite, began to raise a ruckus and eventually left the party in a rancorous mood.[29]

Though Darcy and Foster may have broken their alliance, the downfall of Browder ignited a deepening relationship between Davis and party chairman

Foster that was to prove critical in the post-1956 period. In his official history of the party Foster graciously observed that Davis "warned of the evil effects the present policies were having in Negro work."³⁰ Davis in turn quickly resumed the old-time religion once again, attacking the bourgeoisie with gusto. After the United Negro College Fund placed Henry Luce and other "reactionary and aggressive American imperialists" on their National Advisory Committee, Davis flew into a rage. This was 10 June, days after the reversal of the line, but Davis was writing as if he had not skipped a beat. The blacks' best friend "in the first place [is] organized labor." "Reactionary financial tycoons" were the enemy. Davis was back with a vengeance.³¹

In retrospect it is not unfair to say that though the political line, and even the practice, may have faltered at times, the party played a positive role overall in advancing Black Liberation during the time of Teheran. Also, other conflicts that helped bring the party to its senses was the attack on Henry Wallace by the White House and the brewing Polish crisis. Yet this was not a happy time for the party, despite the joyous victory over fascism. Davis's patience was strained further when the revived Black Belt thesis became an issue as he sought the endorsement of Tammany Hall for reelection.

In the January 1944 edition of the party's theoretical journal, *The Communist*, Browder had enunciated a change in the party line on the Negro National Question; his remarks were first stated at a 19 November 1943 seminar on the Negro people and the war at the Workers' School. His thrust was that blacks had made their choice "once and for all . . . for their complete integration into the American nation as a whole, and not for separation." What was the evidence of this? The New Deal, CIO, the antipoll tax fight, he replied, and "recent elections, when Benjamin J. Davis, Jr., was elected to the New York City Council by a combined vote of Negroes, trade unionists and progressive white people." African-Americans were "not demanding separate military units" but "joint participation" in the war. Thus blacks "exercised their historical right" of self-determination. This was not an altogether unsound approach. Browder had grasped the problem and resolved the possibility that the Black Belt thesis could be interpreted as an endorsement of segregation by pushing the line of integration—which was to be the major thrust in the black movement after the war. If he had made a mistake, it was in not acknowledging that integration should not preclude forms national in character—for example, all black forms. The recent complaint that integration has decimated a number of African-American institutions, from sports teams to schools to businesses, has relevance in this case. But Browder opened himself to massive attack by adding that in the United States there was the "approximation" of having "no problem of national minorities anymore," akin to the assumed pattern in the Soviet Union; this "is within our reach today under the existing American system." Since he was desperately trying to reassure the ruling class, Browder had to concede that it would not require socialism to attain this goal.[32]

It may have been possible for the party to have thrown Browder out while keeping the new line on integration. But at that time, in mid-1945, the bourgeois press began to pick at this issue as another way to raise questions about Tammany's endorsement of Davis. It may not have been coincidental that this attack was made despite (or perhaps because of) the fact that the popular African-American journalist Roi Ottley declared that the party "did more than any other agency in American life toward breaking down the rigid color barriers that once existed between the races. . . . One factor at least made a deep impression on Negroes—the ruthless manner in which the party fought in any form within its own ranks 'white chauvinism' or race prejudice."[33] The leading black writers St. Clair Drake and Horace Cayton later agreed with him,[34] yet the press was charging that the party sought to segregate blacks even further.

The notorious self-proclaimed "Red-hunter," Fred Woltman of the *New York World-Telegram*, led off; an editorial on 23 July 1945 claimed that Davis "advocates a Negro Soviet Union in the United States . . . fantastic program." According to the *New York Times* the next day, the ouster of Browder meant that the "the Communist dream of an independent Negro Soviet Republic to be carved out of the American South" was being revived. Did Tammany endorse this too, they wondered. The Association of Trade and Commerce in Harlem chimed in, hitting his "sinister propaganda" and accusing "Davis [of] following the Soviet pattern personally and professionally of craven, subversive foreign ideology of the Soviet."[35] Black Liberation was confronting the Red Scare.

To some extent Davis and the party could blame themselves for not taking account of demographic and political changes; the war meant more blacks moved, for example from Louisiana and Texas to California; the concentrated Negro nation in the Deep South was fragmenting. When the issue was joined and Davis was attacked, it provided an opportunity for black leaders like Lester Granger, Walter White, Lloyd Dickens, even his ally Guy Brewer to blast the idea of a separate state. Apparently Davis himself was hedging a bit. According to the *New York Amsterdam News* on 28 July 1945, "Mr. Davis in his statement to the *Amsterdam News* did not say he does not favor a 'separate state' nor did he seek to clarify the stories that appeared in the daily press." This gave an opening to this longtime foe of Davis. In an editorial entitled "Adieu to Davis" and published on 4 August, they scolded him gently but firmly: "While he has not sought the advice of leaders representing all of Harlem, we believe his acts of commission were praiseworthy-. . . . But now Mr. Davis has changed fronts . . . as an intelligent, fearless and aggressive representative of the whole community [he] is a man whom many respect . . . we doubt that the Negro in America is ready for a major war with the United States government. . . . We are sorry to see Mr. Davis go. He had promise."

This was one of the worst possible lines of attack on Davis and the party. By raising the issue of a Negro Soviet, their adversaries could at once link them with a foreign power that was about to become quite unpopular and with the increasingly discredited idea of segregation. It could allow the same press that counseled segregation at Stuyvesant Town while the party advised otherwise to pin the discredited notion of segregation on Communists, who so far had been the most resolute opponents of Jim Crow. A tipoff to the party should have been the fact that the usually sensible J. A. Rogers called the Black Belt thesis "goofy and impractical to the last degree" and an "imitation" of Woodrow Wilson's idea. He noted the decline of the black population in the South and its increase in the North and how this was undermining the Dixiecrats. But he refused to join the lynch mob, calling Davis "an able lawyer [who] by all accounts has been doing good work" and adding, "were I the editor of a journal even for the insane, that story about self-determination in the 'black belt' would have gone straight into the waste basket."[36]

Rogers's paper, the *Pittsburgh Courier*, was not as kind.[37] Their columnist Horace Cayton was somewhat more diplomatic and only suggested, correctly, that the thesis smacked of Garveyism. Then piling on began. Julius Adams of the *New York Amsterdam News* reached out to Walter White, demanding that he take a position on Davis and the Black Belt thesis; similar demands were being made at both the city and national levels.[38]

Davis's old antagonist George Schuyler smelled blood and zoomed in for the kill: "[Davis the] notorious Negro Stalinist cries 'witch hunt.' Well, it is a witch hunt long overdue. These foreign agents and disrupters should be muzzled or jugged." Davis, he cried, was "one of the chief Negro Communist stooges in the United States."[39] Davis was angry, denouncing this "villification . . . scurrilous pro-fascist remarks . . . hogwash." Schuyler was unruffled: "there is a question in my mind whether such people are any better than the man Bilbo." This became an issue in the City Council reelection campaign since Davis's chief opponent, Benjamin McLaurin, issued a leaflet making similar allegations. Davis was getting an early introduction to the coming Red Scare.[40]

At the same time this difficult issue was becoming a major issue in the controversy over Davis's reelection. There was a remarkable sea change from the beginning to the end of 1945, leading to a confusing set of twists and turns by political leaders and opinion-molders. In February Moran Weston, then field secretary of the Negro Labor Victory Committee, abjectly refused to run against Davis after being asked to do so by Harlem political leader J. Ray Jones. Yes, Jones said, "Davis has made a very good record," but his Red ties meant that he was "responsible to other persons than to the community." But Weston, soon to be one of the most influential Harlem leaders, objected: "It is unfortunate that the issue of his Communist affiliation has been raised."[41] Then Jones suggested that Lt. Col. Vernon Riddick run against him, which also fell through; this time the *New York Age* took exception, on 17 February 1945.

By this time Jones thought he had figured out which way the weathervane had turned. At a Davis ball in early May, he announced that the Democrats would back Davis. The seven thousand present were incredulous, and according to the *New York Age*, "a hilarious uproar ensued."[42] Adam Powell captured their wonder: "The new world we hear about as coming is already here, when Tammany Hall nominates a Communist. . . . We told Tammany that if it wanted the Negro people, it would have to take Ben Davis along with them." He disparaged the Red-baiting that already was gripping the campaign and announced he would be co-chair of Davis's campaign. Davis also made a concession, announcing "I am proud to be associated with the party of Roosevelt and Truman."[43] Since there was no Communist party as such at this point, it was fortunate that he did have the Tammany backing.

A number of Harlem leaders called for all four parties—Democrats, Republicans, American Labor, and Liberals—to give Davis their nomination. Even the incorrigible Red-baiter, Democratic leader Herbert Bruce, backed Davis.[44] But that was all before the Browder ouster. After that public relations debacle, many doubted Davis's chances of getting reelected. Trench warfare in the press had begun. The traditionally Republican *New York Age* editorialized on 23 June 1945 that the GOP should nominate Davis but doubted it would occur.

At the same time Harlem Democratic leaders were expressing surprise at the fact that Davis was not on the list of council candidates, though Jones had pledged otherwise. Then the wily Jones reversed field again and "sponsored" Davis. At that point all hell broke loose. The *New York Herald Tribune* called Jones's last maneuver a "surprise move" that was "attributed to the influence of the Harlem left-wing leader" Adam Clayton Powell. Naturally Cacchione disagreed, calling the Tammany tiger's demarche a "smart move. . . . If they wanted to hold the Negroes in the Democratic line, they had to nominate him."[45]

The *New York Times* placed the story on page one of its 21 July issue: "For the first time in its history Tammany endorsed a Communist as a candidate for public office." Jones, Powell, Joseph Pinckney, Joseph Ford, and Guy Brewer were seen as the moving force, although their "recommendations were reinforced by a petition for the designation of Mr. Davis signed by clergymen, social workers and representatives of many labor unions." Tammany boss Edward Loughlin praised Davis. The nomination was moved "in response to overwhelming popular demand for his re-election." Ominously the *Times* noted that Davis was aligned with Foster "for a more militant Communist policy." But this was no love feast. Edward Barry, another Democratic leader, hit Loughlin's "shameful conduct" in backing Davis; it "merits condemnation by all decent and God-respecting citizens of this city." No Davis petitions "shall be circulated in my district," he asserted.

In the *Times* the next day Democratic boss Thomas Cohalan blasted the Tammany "cynical endorsement . . . clinching evidence that Tammany and its Communist allies are working hand in hand to take over this city government." This was linked to the "Communist-dominated ALP," which engineered "[William] O'Dwyer's mayoralty nomination." Said one Democratic leader: "The boys of our city did not go to the battlefields to offer their lives as a sacrifice to the ideologies of Communist Davis and his followers." Although this was spoken even before the war had ended, the point was that the ouster of Browder had provided a pretext for the anti-Davis attack.

Then the *New York Herald Tribune* on 23 July denounced the Davis designation. Yet they could not ignore that Davis's popularity meant that if Tammany wanted the black vote, they had to swallow the Red council member, or so progressives thought. But within hours Tammany had dropped Davis and the fear arose that this would lead to loss of the black seat. Immediately Herbert Bruce and Fred Dickens of Harlem assailed the original designation. Bruce explained that the Tiger was "frightened" by the ALP vote in Harlem so "they decided they would have to do something to hold the Negro vote . . . they did such a good job of keeping down the Negro Democrats that they now find themselves at the mercy of the radicals." It was Reconstruction once more.[46]

What had happened in the interim between Tammany's designation of Davis and their reversal? The *Times* reported that the Davis nod was bringing Edward J. Flynn, Bronx leader and Democratic National Committee member, into the fray and the resulting turmoil was affecting federal patronage. With Eleanor Roosevelt's involvement, Loughlin was under siege. Loughlin and O'Dwyer had met at length on the Davis question, so it was argued that he capitulated to heavy outside pressure and O'Dwyer's behest. Besides the expected anti-Communism, Davis was caught in the crossfire between two Democratic bosses struggling over patronage and judgeships.[47]

Black leadership was not capitulating. The elusive and pressured Jones spoke directly to the *Daily Worker* on 25 July, praising the Communist councilmember. Channing Tobias was equally forthright. Edward Lewis of the Urban League agreed, as did James Egert Allen of the NAACP. These figures reflected an emerging consensus in Harlem. It was easier to stampede labor away from the Reds; civil rights concessions had to be granted in order to stampede blacks.[48]

When Davis was dropped by Tammany, pressure was then mounted for Eugene Connolly of the ALP to be ousted from the Democratic list. A textbook case of Red-baiting was unfolding. First the Reds, then all other progressives were ousted. In the *Daily Worker* of 26 July Davis assailed the "reactionary forces" that "hope to destroy the democratic coalition . . . under the smokescreen of Red-baiting. . . . To capitulate in this instance leads to capitulation on other principal issues and questions until reaction emerges victorious." The dropping of Davis can be seen as a key step toward the Red Scare and McCarthyism; Davis's words proved to be prophetic. But the *Times* on 26 July stated that his ouster was worth it, though the Democrats "may lose some votes" as a result in Harlem. However, concessions to blacks could assuage their anger. The pattern for the Red Scare was set: to blunt Communist and leftist popularity among blacks, an effort would be made to bludgeon the progressives, then provide concessions to some African-Americans so that their complaints would not grow too loud. At this juncture Davis and the party were in a quandary. He had to deny that he backed a separate Negro state, though this was disingenuous at best; the concept of self-determination was complicated and easily subjected to demagogic assault. This complication and the turmoil surrounding Browder's removal allowed the Right to mobilize very effectively at this crucial turning point. This was taking place in a rapidly changing political situation in New York, as the Popular-Front approach of LaGuardia was being replaced and as the labor movement was being driven to the Right.

The *New York Amsterdam News* filled in more blanks. Apparently mayoral candidate William O'Dwyer was refusing to run on the same ticket with Davis. Simultaneously, Brewer, Ford, Jones, and James Pemberton—who were backing Davis in Harlem—squared off against Bruce and Lloyd Dickens, who claimed that the designation was made without their consent, although they were duly elected members of the Democratic County Executive Committee. Bruce and Dickens lost out to Jones and his group in internal Harlem Democratic elections. Loughlin was running scared, going as far as to claim that he did not know Davis was a Communist. Despite this naive view, his opponents in primary elections lost—suggesting that Davis may not have been as unpopular or as large a liability as some thought. After that, Bruce was defeated after ten years of leading Harlem's twelfth Assembly District. It was beginning to seem that the tide was shifting. The *Herald Tribune* suggested that O'Dwyer lost more adherents with his insistence that it reverse its endorsement of Davis.[49]

Earl Brown, who was to be the vehicle for dumping Davis from the council in 1949, provided another angle of vision. Apparently in the spring Jones had broached the issue of Tammany designating Davis in return for the Communists backing their mayoral ticket. Davis and Loughlin consented to it, but Davis would have to register as a Democrat. "This Mr. Davis at first failed to do," since he was reluctant to ally with the "party of Bilbo and Rankin," but "after a bout with his conscience" he agreed. Jones's view was that he could build a "powerful political organization in Harlem" with the aid of the Left: "The left-wingers particularly the Communists are the best campaigners in Harlem [thus] . . . the Hall wants to enlist their support in the oncoming mayoralty election. Tammany recalls, meantime, that it has been defeated in Harlem in every local election since 1933, when Mayor La Guardia was elected the first time." The black vote could "decide" a close election. According to this scenario, Vito Marcantonio—the "real head of the left-wingers in New York"—had "done business together" with many of the Harlem District leaders "for years." All had "profited by their sub rosa alliance." Strikingly, Brown added, "Except for a handful of Socialists and a few professional race leaders, Red-baiting leaves Harlemites cold. . . . They do, however, listen to the Communists' sales talk because it is always about the facts of life, such as jobs and housing. . . . In Harlem, the Communists are close to the masses and the masses are close to the Communists." Like Marcantonio, Jones and Davis should have proceeded on a sub rosa basis, he concluded—but they did not. After all, Davis's opponent four years hence concluded, the Communist had a "good record. . . . Maybe this is a point worthy of consideration."[50]

Perhaps. In any case, after Tammany picked Ruth Whaley and the Liberals Benjamin McLaurin as Davis opponents, there was worry in the *New York Age* on 11 August that "there will be little likelihood of any Negro being elected in Manhattan this time." But Davis was still showing strength. The *People's Voice* reported triumphantly on 11 August that "every Harlem and Washington Heights Democratic leader who had supported Davis in the past and refused to turn against him in the Tammany split were victorious in the primaries." At that point the Red Scare had not yet gathered sufficient strength. Weeks later, on 6 October, the *Amsterdam News* was giving further hope to the Davis forces: "Reports are that [Jones] will knife the party's councilmanic candidate, Mrs. Ruth Whitehead Whaley in favor of Ben Davis." But the trend that was to dominate the next decade was stated by Davis's old foe Frank Crosswaith, who acerbically declared that Davis "has his feet in the City Council but that his head is in Europe." Presumably the writer intended the eastern section of this continent. This was also an attempt to erode Davis's antiracist credentials by linking him with whites.

As if this battle royal with the Democrats and the flap over the Black Belt thesis were not enough, Davis had to contend with more internecine struggle: the reluctance of the American Labor party to give him a designation. The issue boiled over at the 18 June 1945 CP National Committee meeting, which was considering the party line and Browder's fate. Davis remarked bitterly how Tammany was offering him a line because of his strength among blacks and progressives but because of "red-baiting in reverse . . . the ALP does not endorse me." Worse yet, the comrades in that party were going along with it; the situation was "shameful and disgraceful . . . entirely inexcusable." The ALP's nonendorsement came in the wake of press speculation that the CP was becoming hostile to Sidney Hillman, the labor leader, who played a large role in ALP and national Democratic politics; it was felt that if Davis received the ALP nod, then Hillman forces would be alienated. The next day at the continuation of the National Committee meeting, one party leader suggested that Davis the Red had to be sacrificed so that ties to labor and the ALP could be maintained.[51]

The party disagreed on the role of the ALP; it was undergoing wrenching self-criticism in the aftermath of Browderism and the repudiation of the Black belt thesis. Sacrificing Davis to keep labor leader and New Deal Democrat Sidney Hillman was seen as a reflection of continued Browderism. Firmly against Davis's view were Gil Green and Israel Amter. Davis remained insistent; he was "100% in favor of keeping" good ties with Hillman but "this is a public question. It has already been raised in one of the newspapers in Harlem [and] by the Independent Citizens' Committee who have asked: How can you be a unanimous candidate of the Negro people of the Harlem community, a candidate of the Democratic party and not be the candidate of the ALP? The answer Gil gives us today will not be accepted by the people. In my opinion, it is a question of the Negro people. It is a question of the Harlem community uniting around a candidate who is recognized by a bourgeois party but not by a party representing labor."[52]

Pettis Perry, the black party leader who was to spearhead the party's internal campaign against white chauvinism, was irate: "Comrade Davis was too mild with himself." No one should "doubt [Davis's] motives," he argued, wondering why it is that blacks have to be sacrificed in the name of "unity." Teheran was hard to sell but they had done it, if a black had not, he would be called "nationalist." So why was there reluctance to sell Davis to Hillman, labor, and white progressives? This was all "white chauvinism," he concluded bitterly.[53]

These were difficult questions. Labor was being pressured to distance itself from Communists, even black ones with mass support. On 11 June the *Daily Worker* had published an editorial on the failure "to designate Davis," which "has shocked and puzzled. . . . The reasons advanced for this failure appear utterly inadequate." The ALP had argued that backing both Davis and Eugene Connolly, given the machinations of proportional representation, meant that the latter might lose, a point that was contested in the 17 June *Daily Worker*. The *People's Voice* was even more angry, threatening a rupture in its labor ties because of Davis's treatment.[54] Then the *New York World-Telegram* got hold of the issue in an effort to drive a wedge between the CP and ALP. Gil Green spoke out on the ALP's "responsibility" to Davis, even if Connolly were to be defeated; with that the ALP yielded and backed Davis.[55]

PM, the newspaper of choice of many New York progressives, pointed the finger at Marcantonio, who felt that "nominating anyone else would only split the approximately 30,000 ALP votes in Manhattan. It is not a matter of red-baiting; we want to protect our position."[56] In the election both Davis and Connolly won, but it is unclear if Marcantonio's position was also Eugene Dennis's later point: "Such leftist views crept into the practical work of our Party's municipal election campaign in certain cities, such as New York, and were responsible for limiting the vote of the ALP and for weakening our ties with certain democratic elements."[57] The designation of Davis was a difficult question, but the sad part was that it had to arise when the party was in the midst of turmoil and dealing at once with so many difficult questions.

Admittedly, a good deal of this pain and turmoil was self-inflicted, as for example the removal of Browder and the reluctance to revise the Black Belt thesis. These errors created an opening that aided in galvanizing the Red Scare. The Red Scare was motivated in part by the kind of electoral success that Davis, the CP, and the ALP had enjoyed. This success was particularly buoyed by the ballots of blacks; weaning them away from the Left had involved anti-Jim Crow concessions that later proved to be a condition precedent for the Red Scare itself.

9
Victory, 1945

The victory over fascism, the controversy over Browderism, and an incipient Red Scare all made this an extremely complicated time for Davis. With all that, he still had to seek reelection; certainly the brouhaha with Tammany did not markedly increase his chances. Yet the times had not changed altogether and he still maintained a reservoir of goodwill among his Manhattan constituents.

Not least among his most avid supporters was the heavyweight champion, Joe Louis. Popular artists and athletes were barometers of public opinion; their support for him suggested broader currents in Harlem. This support not only reflected the breadth of Davis's appeal but the backing from the "Brown Bomber" also led others into the Davis camp. He served as honorary chair of the Veterans Committee for Davis. The *Afro-American* was not wrong in speculating that Louis's support "is scheduled to swing a lot of votes his way from the sporting element [along with] the musical and theatrical crowd."[1]

This support from sports heavyweights was reciprocated; the astute Davis recognized that this was one area where it was difficult to bar qualified blacks and that its high profile could lead to a positive effect in the fight against Jim Crow. So all through 1945 desegregating baseball was a top priority for Davis. Even before the Browder expulsion he was avidly backing Vito Marcantonio's effort to institute a congressional probe of the nation's pasttime. On his own he called on the City Council to investigate. The *Times*, now calling him a "Manhattan Communist" and not a "Negro leader," reported that his measure "would seem to have an excellent chance of adoption"; under the Ives-Quinn state law, basing employment on race could lead to fines and prison for the lords of baseball.[2] Quickly Davis accepted an invitation from baseball commissioner Albert "Happy" Chandler to confer with the moguls.[3]

The lords of baseball were perceptive, for the council backed Davis's resolution unanimously, although it was amended. Eleanor Roosevelt, Paul Robeson, even William O'Dwyer endorsed his effort. But Larry McPhail, speaking for the baseball owners, disagreed with Davis's approach; Davis in turn termed this a "ridiculous travesty. . . . It exposes this committee as being worse than useless." The record shows that until Jackie Robinson entered the big leagues, Davis used his council seat to press for desegregation.[4]

The Davis alliance with Paul Robeson on this issue marked a continuation of one of Davis's most important political and personal relationships. The great singer-actor chaired the Committee of Artists for Davis's reelection that included José Ferrer, Lena Horne, Leonard Bernstein, Frederick O'Neal, Count Basie, Jerome Robbins, Langston Hughes, and a number of other well-known artists. Robeson performed at a number of fund-raisers for his friend. Again, Robeson's prestige was such that it could convince some voters to cast their ballot for a Communist.[5]

Just before the November election another fund-raiser featured Duke Ellington, Roy Eldridge, Pearl Primus, Katherine Dunham, Billie Holiday, and others. This alliance between the arts and the Left in the black community was a prime aspect of the pre–Red Scare era; arguably it influenced the content of art. Similarly, it could be argued that this alliance was rather shallow in that it could not withstand pressure. Certainly the Red Scare wounded this tendency of African-American artist to align with the Left.[6]

With this kind of support, it was little wonder that Davis was able to construct a broad united front. Even the NAACP moved closer to him.[7] Dave Watkins in the *People's Voice* for 24 March 1945 observed that they "plastered the town with his election posters . . . and they are a very neat job, with Ben looking like one of those collar ads." Again, party clubs specializing in this field were responsible for these posters. The *Afro-American* on 27 October 1945 noticed another fashion statement:

> Women and girls, who one would suspect would have little knowledge of things political, are making a fad of wearing Davis buttons for earrings. Strange, too, are the leaders who refuse to be frightened off by the Communist bugaboo and are coming out strong for the former Georgia boy with the Moscow tinge. Rabbis, priests, physicians, businessmen, teachers, all of whom would be expected to run and hide under their beds at the mere mention of Davis' name, are crawling boldly on the big red bandwagon and figuratively tell the Committee on Un-American Activities to go plumb to Hades. . . . Davis . . . is soothing his nerves by playing the higher grade concertos on his violin and trying to keep his boyish figure down to a nimble 250 pounds by daily jaunts on the tennis court.

His Republican father was backing him, "even if he can never look another honest Republican in the face again."

Davis did not compromise on his fierce opposition to racism in order to get this broad support; indeed, this facet of his campaign probably brought him adherents in the wake of the Holocaust and from the public's revulsion to racialism.

The progressive journalist Earl Conrad echoed the sentiments of many when he wrote in the *New York Age* on 13 October 1945, "You can be assured that every time a Negro community sends a Communist into public office this will liberalize the Republicans and Democrats." This fact struck him when he visited Davis's office: "As you enter the small, modern office of [Davis] the first item that greets your eyes is, appropriately enough, a fine etching of the late Frederick Douglass which hangs on one of the walls." Close by were bookshelves groaning with volumes by Engels, Stalin, Lenin, and the like.[8] Davis, Conrad concluded, "is Douglass' true son in our time." Some might have considered this hyperbole but Davis's herculean labor in the council at the same time he was fulfilling major party responsibilities in other areas was impressive.[9]

Some felt that one of Davis's most significant efforts in the council was his effort to make Negro History Week a regular part of New York City life. Others felt that this was surpassed by his push to get the city to establish a local version of FEPC, what was eventually called the Commission on Human Rights. Whatever the case, Davis's activism was even more daunting given that he was up for reelection, embroiled in party struggles, and under attack daily in the press. He was energetic in pushing for heavier penalties against black marketeers. He assailed the Office of Price Administration and sponsored a hearing that was jammed with "housewives and consumer group leaders.".This event was coupled with a militant march of hundreds through Harlem; the line of march began at 145th Street and St. Nicholas and wound its way to 125th and 8th Avenue: "The food situation has long been a deep problem in Harlem. Eggs are offered only with cheese and other tie-in sales. . . . All over Harlem the people are offered bones for sale . . . fish that sells at 25 cents a pound in other areas sells for 40 cents in Harlem."[10]

Davis kept up a drumbeat of criticism aimed at the Office of Price Administration, meeting with their regional director about "blackmarket prices for inferior goods." This broad delegation included Powell, the church, and the PTA; their action led to a temporary but not a permanent halt in this kind of price gouging. Other economic issues focused on by Davis included a perennial problem: the housing emergency. Veterans were sleeping in parks. With homelessness proliferating, Davis had to intervene repeatedly to halt evictions. Utilizing preventive medicine, he organized free rent clinics to educate tenants about their rights. He called for commandeering of vacant housing, at times held off the market by profit-hungry landlords. He did not ignore the racial angle either, blasting Dewey's allegation about no discrimination in housing allocation.[11]

Davis was furious about the profiteering of the titans of capital, while the poor got poorer. At a budget hearing he recalled how his father had died in early 1945 and how ashamed he was as a councilmember to see cracked ceilings and other evidences of neglect in that city hospital. These conditions were exacerbated by the low pay for hospital workers. His concern for Harlem workers also extended to those toiling at the branch of Manufacturers Hanover; as vicechair of the Uptown Chamber of Commerce, Davis led a delegation to protest their plight. This all-round concern with the needs of his constituents would mean that despite an incipient Red Scare, Davis would be hard to beat in 1945.[12]

This was one reason why Powell, writing in 1945, could strongly praise the party, noting that racism naturally inclined blacks toward radicalism. Because of Davis's potency, Red membership in Harlem "tripled during the past year." The flamboyant Powell concluded, "Today there is no group in America including the Christian church that practices racial brotherhood one tenth as much as the Communist party."[13]

When Walter Hoving, president of the Lord & Taylor Department Store, ran into Powell at a United Negro College Fund function, he charged that the Reds were "merely using the Negro." The congressman disagreed: "The Negro doesn't worry about the Communist label or any other label. Harlem didn't have more than 500 enrolled Communists last fall [in 1943] but it gave Ben Davis, Jr. 25,000 votes. We voted for the man and not the party. . . . The truth of it is the Negro has been used for centuries before Karl Marx was born."[14]

These bold remarks to Hoving indicated Powell's increasing collaboration with Davis—and vice versa. When the *New York Amsterdam News* on 29 September 1945 asked Davis about electoral matters, he was "reluctant to discuss the campaign developments and his chances for success in the re-election campaign before taking the whole matter up with 'Adam.'" Their enemies recognized the power of their alliance and sought to destabilize it. The *Amsterdam News* headlined, "Ben Davis May Seek Powell's Seat in Congress," adding "odds are even that Davis will be a candidate." Davis was outraged by these "vicious lies. . . . First, they tried to discredit Powell by dragging his family affairs into his campaign for Congress, though they knew it was none of their business. Defeated there, they are raising petty objections to every move he makes in Congress."[15] Davis went on at length, for he knew that an essential goal for proponents of the Red Scare was to break the alliance between the Reds and progressives like Powell; this would allow the political spectrum to tilt toward the Right.

Other forces were at work as well. The esoteric African-American nationalist James Lawson, of the self-styled "United African Nationalist Movement," Red-baited the Powell-Davis tie: "We can say that Communism must go because we have concrete proof that the Communists through the Jefferson School and other agencies of Moscow are using men like Powell, without whose aid Ben Davis could never have been elected." Citing John Huber, "FBI undercover informer," Lawson insisted that Powell was a card-carrying Communist, which was horrible since "every Communist [is] a potential spy." Earlier Lawson's colleague Herbert Bruce had wanted to challenge Powell's seat on the basis of this Davis-Powell relationship. The FBI agreed with Lawson, arguing that the *People's Voice* "reflects Communist activities and propaganda. Known Communists hold positions in this paper." Though one would think that certain black nationalists could look favorably on the CP because of their Negro Nation thesis—other philosophical disagreements notwithstanding—the actuality was that these forces often viewed the Reds as competition for the hearts and minds of Harlemites and responded accordingly.[16]

The specter of angry opposition did not halt the Davis-Powell collaboration. Powell personally backed his reelection. Right after his reelection, their collaboration reached a new level when they again marched to Washington for a FEPC. Powell stood by his man, though others were drifting toward Davis's chief opponent, the labor leader Benjamin McLaurin.[17]

McLaurin, a colleague of Randolph in the Brotherhood of Sleeping Car Porters, had a younger life as difficult as Davis's was charmed. According to his campaign literature, he was "homeless at nine, worked successively as Western Union messenger, tobacco picker, elevator operator, Pullman porter." He was born in Jacksonville in 1906; his father, a "grocery merchant and pioneer Negro businessman," was "murdered" by racists jealous of his success; they also "burned his home . . . [his] head was cut off" and intended to murder the whole family. He graduated from Edward Waters College and later became a vice president and national secretary of Randolph's union.[18]

McLaurin ran a hard-hitting campaign. After obtaining the Liberal and GOP designations, he assailed Davis's "fantastic scheme of a Soviet Negro Republic"; blacks wanted "complete integration," he argued persuasively. Unmoved, Charles Collins of the Negro Labor Victory Committee (comprising 107 CIO, AFL, and other unions) curtly asked him to withdraw in the name of unity. He refused. At his early August press conference at the Hotel Theresa, the session was "marked by searching and embarrassing questions by the press," according to the *People's Voice*.[19]

Rising to the challenge, the *Daily Worker* announced on 24 August that the campaign would need two thousand workers since the GOP-Liberal bloc was "ganging up" on Davis: "The Liberal Party in particular is determined to defeat Davis, even if it means there will be no Negro spokesman in the City Council." Other blacks in the race—McLaurin, Ruth Whaley, Louise Simpson—would drain votes from Davis, they insisted.

Campaigning was spirited in the streets of Harlem, with the Women's Committee to Re-elect Davis being particularly active. But as time wore on, the campaign got nastier. Davis's friendly enemy, George Schuyler, wrote a piece of campaign literature that termed Davis a "prominent agent of the international communist conspiracy." On Scottsboro he argued, "Davis and his associates got the money; the boys got prison." He turned against Davis the allegation that Browderism had meant the weakening of the fight against racism. Davis's bid for Tammany support meant that he was a "bedfellow of . . . Bilbo, Eastland . . . and their ilk."[20]

McLaurin did not stop there. On 20 October he issued an acerbic press release: "Here in Harlem and other neglected sections, a new kind of political machine with a foreign trademark is making lavish campaign expenditures to elect a candidate who takes his orders from a foreign boss. . . . It still tries to exploit our grievances for their own sordid aims. . . . I never tried to make a deal with the corrupt Tammany Tiger. My opponent did and he still has the secret backing of every Tammany racketeer. I have never deserted the fight for equality because of orders from above. My opponent did just that when he condoned Army Jim Crow and discrimination in war industries."[21] Since McLaurin was a top Harlem labor leader, his words would have impact.

Davis showed him no respect in kind, consistently forgetting his name. This only served to anger McLaurin more: "I have concluded by your continued usage of that incorrect title that you intend to mislead the citizens of New York by creating the impression that I am an Irishman rather than a Negro . . . it is a sound indication of the corruptness of your philosophy of life and the depths to which you will sink while working to destroy America; to set race against race." He dredged up Scottsboro again. "This is only one instance of your misuse of the people's faith in you. This is just one instance which illustrates why you are not fit . . . you have hoodwinked [the people] for over 15 years. . . . You have risen to fame and fortune while the Scottsboro boys rotted in a diseased Southern jail."[22]

But when McLaurin's hot words did not melt the rock-solid support of Davis in Manhattan, the Randolph associate became even more pointed:

> Mr. Davis has the ability to hold public office, but so did Hitler. So has Bilbo. Ability alone is not enough. Being a Negro and having the education that he has, he certainly knew that this was a notorious Quisling trick, but he had to do the Charlie McCarthy stunt and obey his Communist master's voice. And let me tell you the Communist party maintains a real Gestapo over its members. Whenever a Communist or fellow-traveller fails to hit the ball by following the line, his neck is due for the noose. He will be purged. He will be liquidated. This means gangster language, rubbed out politically. Davis knows this. That's why he sacrificed the Negro during the war . . . Because of the shifting political climate of Soviet Russia, Davis doesn't really know what he can think from one day to the other.

Part of the growing Red Scare meant that Davis's previously uncontroversial defense of Moscow would be turned against him. Such attacks, combined with the Red Scare that was being whipped up in the newspapers and on radio, gave added validity to McLaurin's harsh words.[23]

These statements were all on the record and above board. Curiously, in the files of McLaurin's union are letters to William O'Dwyer and Newbold Morris stating, "we feel that you are doing us a great injustice by accepting the support of Mr. Davis. . . . If [Davis] is re-elected it would be you who has given him the legitimacy . . . to push the Communist party program of a 'Black Republic.' . . . This is the same policy advocated by Bilbo, the anti-

Catholic Rankin, Eastland and the late Cotton Ed Smith." Davis's theses on Black Liberation were now being used to generate the Red Scare. As election day approached, half a million copies of Schuyler's attack were distributed. McLaurin seemed to be on the move.[24]

Again and again, McLaurin returned to the Black Belt thesis. "Under this plan the Negro alone would stand to lose one million homes, 18,864 stores doing $57,036,307 worth of business plus unaccounted millions in insurance companies, banks, newspapers."[25] But McLaurin may have been too shrill, too strident. On 3 November the *People's Voice* dismissed him: "We have seldom seen a campaign so void of real issues and so filled with lies and slanders and distortions." Numbers did not lie. Only six hundred came to one of McLaurin's recent rallies while six thousand came to Davis's. Near the *Voice* anti-McLaurin article was a cartoon with a cemetery featuring a deathly looking soldier holding a sign stating: "Make it worthwhile . . . Vote for Ben Davis." Apparently this graphic did not persuade McLaurin supporters like John Dewey, James Farmer, Reinhold Niebuhr, Morris Ernst, Arthur Garfield Hays, and Lester Granger. Part of the liberal establishment had joined with civil rights leaders in an anti-Communist alliance —a precursor of events to come. This powerful liaison ultimately spelled doom for the Communists. But Davis had a virtual monopoly on black celebrities and his opponent was able to attract relatively unknown artists such as Carol Brice, Avon Long, Una Mae Carlyle, Elwood Smith, and Eddie South.

McLaurin's friend Randolph weighed in heavily against Davis. Davis, he said in the 3 November *New York Amsterdam News*, "stabbed the Negro in the back" during the war. "Suppose there is a war. Mr. Davis would have to oppose the United States, the interests of his own country and fight on the side of Soviet Russia, since he is a Communist; for if he didn't he would be promptly kicked out and smeared as a traitor to communism." Davis should "withdraw" from the race, he believed. "Do the citizens of Harlem want to send a man to the council who must wait on instructions and orders from Soviet Russia before he can speak out? . . . . Davis is a member of a party which takes its orders from an alien government." Davis's plaint that he was not "sufficiently mature" to oppose Browderism meant "he had not grown up. . . . Negroes haven't time to hold their leaders on leading strings, like nipple-sucking babies. . . . Davis has exhibited the yellow streak. . . . But the record, like Banquo's ghost, will not down. It must be faced." The Black Belt thesis meant that Davis "would have Communists pull up root and branch Negroes, homes, farms, stores and all their belongings where they now live all over America and huddle them into a restricted, segregated black belt of slums in the south. Even were it desirable . . . and of course it stinks to high heaven, it would require a civil war of fire and blood, nameless death and destruction of Negro life to oust the present southern white Negro-phobists."

Frank Crosswaith also had an opinion on the campaign. "Ben Davis and his crowd are worshippers and profound believers of the Barbarism God of confusion." He defended Truman, whom he called "genuinely progressive," against Davis's thrusts.[26] But this anti-Davis broadside could not mask deep differences between Crosswaith and McLaurin, whom he later denounced as "unethical . . . not the [man] in whose hands I would entrust an enemy with such potential powers."[27] Davis could afford to ignore this attack but he could not pass up the opportunity to term Crosswaith "bankrupt . . . paid hireling of David Dubinsky."[28] He reminded the Social Democrat of his post on the City Housing Authority and his shilly-shallying when Davis was in the midst of trying to desegregate Stuyvesant Town.

Although McLaurin was a man of and from labor, black trade union leaders and their rank and file mostly backed Davis. They came to his rallies in the thousands, though Davis acknowledged at one point, "one of the vacuum spots in my background was always the absence of substantial and individual trade union experience." No matter; Davis had labor, particularly the progressive sector.[29]

In 1943 the National Maritime Union had covered 110 polling places in Harlem for him; they had bigger plans for 1945 and gave him more money. They set up a Harlem office at 110th and Lenox Avenue; even a sizeable number from McLaurin's own union backed the incumbent. It was black labor that was the locomotive behind the support for Davis.[30]

Blacks were extremely concerned with escalating police brutality. McLaurin spent so much time fighting Davis that he lost sight of such bread-and-butter issues; indeed, at this stage of the Red Scare, traditionally contrary black voters were predisposed to look askance at his line, which mirrored that of the same press that accused blacks of being responsible for a "crime wave." But not Davis. He felt that a "crime wave" manufactured by the yellow press of New York was partially responsible for fueling police misconduct. Dismissing First Amendment claims, he introduced a resolution in the council calling on the papers to cease this kind of reporting. He cited an instance of police arresting light-skinned blacks in Harlem after midnight on the premise that they were white and did not belong there. Davis was furious: "We can see from this that soon they will be trying to keep the Negro people away from downtown New York after midnight."[31]

Then the police beat Guy Brewer, Democratic leader of the Twelfth Assembly District, at 156th Street and St. Nicholas, after a minor incident. Brewer held a press conference at Davis's office. Davis, speaking for himself, Assemblyman William T. Andrews, Congressman Adam Clayton Powell, and Councilman William Carroll, denounced this brutality against a fellow black politician who grew up with the Communist leader in Atlanta.[32] Publicity was generated but the brutality continued.

In response, Davis and Cacchione called a "Conference to Protest Police Brutality" at the Harlem YMCA. Davis reiterated, "There seems to be an unwritten law among the police that no white person has a right in Harlem after a certain hour . . . they're striking at the very basis of the cooperation we have been able to achieve between Negroes and progressive whites." Brewer agreed, pointing out that "Negroes not only aren't found in white sections after sundown; if any person is found in white sections after a certain hour . . . he can be arrested, beaten up or shot." If the Democratic party would not act, "there's another councilman who can be counted on. Some people call him the Communist councilman. I call him the Harlem councilman." James E. Allen of the NAACP warned of taking too many soldiers into the force, "men who have been shooting first and asking no questions," and mused as to why these cops could not be as aggressive in confronting taxi drivers who refused to drive uptown. These attacks on interracialism can be viewed as an attack on Davis and the Left, for Euro-American leftists were a bulwark of his campaign. Thus, the Red Scare can be seen as indirectly—or perhaps directly—heightening racial tensions, undermining whatever concessions may have been gained on the Black Liberation front.[33]

While McLaurin was attacking Davis, Davis was usually attacking the issues. Helping him was a smooth-running reelection machine cochaired by Powell, Fred Field, and Dr. George Cannon. There were nine divisions (women, doctors and dentists, artists and writers, bankers and businessleaders, labor, fraternal, religious, first-time voters, nightclub and cafe owners) and a speakers' bureau.[34] Meetings were held every Thursday at the Harlem Y of each division and committee. The affiliate of the National Council of Negro Women was usually well represented. Funds were received from all over the nation, including California, Texas, and Georgia. Support was broad.[35] Literature was distributed in many languages, including Italian, Yiddish, and Spanish. Issues stressed in every language were jobs, equality, veterans' rights, and peace. Davis was not running like a man who dismissed his opposition, but he did not think highly of his opponents in whatever language that was used.[36]

Ruth Whaley had as a "sole qualification . . . that she won some elocution prizes umpteen years before and could get up from a deep sleep at 3 o'clock in the morning quoting Wendell Phillips without batting an eye." McLaurin was the "protégée candidate of the pompous turncoat and Dubinsky lackey, A. Philip Randolph . . . like his mentor whom he religiously aped he had the most stilted manner of saying nothing—and doing less." Schuyler, that "gangster of the pen," wrote the literature that "brought me hundreds of new campaign workers out of sheer revulsion." Their Scottsboro charges were "beneath human contempt."[37]

This molten lava of rhetoric did not bar the black press from endorsing Davis, virtually unanimously.[38] Newspapers in Los Angeles, Chicago, Norfolk, Pittsburgh, and other cities endorsed him. The *Chicago Defender* called on its readers in New York to "rally around Ben Davis as a man best qualified for the councilmanic post"; "red-baiting," they charged, was akin to "Negro-baiting" and an abject "red-herring."[39] Ludlow Werner of the *New York Age* was one of Davis's staunchest backers, using his paper to praise him repeatedly on the premise, "I am a firm believer in giving people flowers while they can smell them." The paper urged readers to give Davis their first-choice vote, then McLaurin and Whaley.[40]

The *People's Voice* was pro-Davis all the way. Their religious columnist concluded, "the role of the churches in Harlem was a considerable factor in the success of the campaign." A considerable number of black ministers in late October not only endorsed Davis but urged his opponents to withdraw.[41]

A group of black doctors led by Dr. Richard Carey raised substantial funds for the Davis campaign. Veteran Harlem journalist Dave Watkins suggested that Davis would "receive wide support from every veterans group in town . . . they are all hep to the outstanding efforts Ben has given to make their lot less difficult." Increasingly influential Harlem minister Moran Weston agreed, though after the Red Scare unwound he was forced to repudiate this view.[42]

Harlem beauticians mobilized for Davis, as did nurses. Many blacks mentioned Roy Wilkins's endorsement as a plus. All this symbolized a depth of support among African-Americans that McLaurin's Red-baiting could not budge. Nationalists, Marxists, Democrats, Republicans, professionals, trade unionists, athletes, celebrities—all backed Ben Davis.[43]

Moderate whites during this period voting for an articulate, intelligent Davis could feel that they were part of an antiracist movement, an increasingly important part of the consciousness of whites in the postwar era. Blacks too were impressed with the white support for Davis. On 5 May the *New York Amsterdam News*, no friend of the incumbent, felt it "noteworthy as a symbol of growing inter-racial unity and cooperation . . . the large number of white musicians and actors who will appear on the musical program" at a Davis fund-raiser. The International Workers Order raised money and provided troops. Howard Fast wrote campaign literature. While the Citizens Union did not endorse Davis, they praised him. His only barriers came from the top elite, such as Robert Moses.[44]

The party saw the Davis campaign, among other things, as an opportunity for recruitment. Tessie Abramowitz, who had recruited ten black members, acknowledged that Davis's appeal was the main reason. During the campaign, Manhattan clubs single-mindedly focused on his victory. Communists were in the forefront of petitioning for Davis, where they were met with an overwhelming response. The state party saw their number-one short term job as reelecting Davis; 2,000 signatures were needed and 18,000 were collected. This compared favorably to Cacchione's 13,600 and Mike Quill's 25,000.[45]

The *Pittsburgh Courier*, ever watchful of Davis and the Reds, warned its readers on 29 September about a "secret" Communist plot to reelect Davis.

This was no secret but the lurid reporting reflected their concern about his impending reelection. Meanwhile party clubs were busily campaigning, handing out literature, and making calls.

The authorities were not oblivious to the giant strides of the Davis campaign. In the middle of the reelection effort he was handed a subpoena and ordered to Washington to be questioned by the House Un-American Activities Committee (HUAC). The *Daily Worker* responded by pointing out that Davis actually got eight times more votes than Congressman John Rankin, Dixiecrat leader of the inquisition chamber.[46]

HUAC intended to keep Davis in Washington all week in a not-too-subtle effort to derail the campaign. HUAC wanted to ask about the alleged hidden relationship between the traditional political parties and the reconstituted Communist party. Davis was angry about this interruption of this campaign and denounced the hearing as a witch hunt. But just like in 1940, his militant and uncompromising denunciation of the Dixiecrats—which was broadcast widely—won him even more supporters.[47]

Saul Mills of the NY-CIO Council also condemned HUAC's interference in the election, and even the *New York Amsterdam News* conceded that in the confrontation with Rankin, Davis had come off the better of the two. The *Defender* observed that Davis's action escalated his prestige higher than ever in the metropolis, and even the *Times* pointed out that Davis stood defiantly before HUAC. The *Oklahoma Black Dispatch* wrote that "there is not a black man on the outside of an insane asylum who should pay one iota of attention" to the Red-baiting attack on Davis: "Since Stalin and the Russians whipped Adolf Hitler, the term 'communism' has a different significance than it had before." Their viewpoint is a reminder to avoid unnecessarily "modern" analyses of Stalinism, such as the notion that Stalinism was viewed then as it is now.[48] Davis was typically contemptuous of Rankin: "This creature was in an apoleptic rage. He was doing everything but foaming at the mouth. . . . Rankin looked like a bleached mummy-like fugitive from an undertaker. All his malignant hatred for Negroes was on his face."[49]

It would take more than HUAC to keep Davis from winning this election. After the election, the *Times* sadly carried a page-one headline, "Communists lead in PR First Count," though they tried to rationalize this development by alleging that it was "attributable to 'bullet' voting. . . . They have a single choice, and all their supporters vote for that choice as their first choice."[50] They should not have been surprised by the vote. When Davis won in 1943, he ran in a field of thirteen (including two other blacks) and got 56 percent of first-choice votes in Harlem: 15,000 first-choice votes in the rest of Manhattan and a total first-choice vote of over 34,000 and a final count of over 44,000. By 11 November 1945 the *Times* was reporting Stanley Isaacs topping the Manhattan vote with 59,830 and Davis second with 56,540; Quill led the Bronx with 71,191. As it turned out, Quill, Cacchione, and Isaacs led the vote with about 75,000 votes each. Davis and Cacchione got 123,000 votes in Brooklyn and Manhattan, a 40 percent increase over 1943. They received as many votes as the Liberal Party in the entire city. Across the country, the Communist Arnold Johnson obtained 56,330 votes in Cleveland and Otis Hood received 26,693 votes in Boston; both were running for the school board.[51]

Davis's total represented a 65 percent rise over his 1943 total in the face of McLaurin's vicious attacks (McLaurin received 10,234 votes and Whaley edged him by getting 11,013). The Left—the ALP and CP—got 326,550 votes, or 19 percent of the entire vote; this was not only more than the Liberals but they beat the GOP as well. Davis's final vote total was 63,498, though he lost an approximate ten thousand votes, which were declared invalid because of improper marking.

Davis benefited from a wave of Red support, but other black candidates throughout the nation fared badly with but few exceptions, a possible reflection of an upsurge of racism that greeted militant black veterans returning home to claim their due. The stark lesson for blacks was that moving to the Left not only did not spell defeat but failing to do so could spell defeat. Harlem was the center of Afro-America and the vote there for Davis was startling to some; he got over 75 percent of first-choice votes. The Reds ran cost-effective campaigns also, with about sixteen thousand dollars being spent on Cacchione's campaign in Brooklyn and a like amount in Manhattan for Davis. Max Gordon in *Political Affairs* recognized that the "vote received by Davis is of special significance nationally . . . he was the target of attack not only by local reactionary elements but by such national spokesmen" as Rankin. More remarkable was the fact that this huge vote came "after [the party] had passed through a severe crisis. . . . It must be admitted, however, that largely as a result of the past mistakes of the party, the number of active Communists in this campaign was not so great as in past elections."[52]

Gordon was not the only analyst sifting through the political tea leaves. Norman Vincent Peale immediately denounced proportional representation and urged "clearer thinking" about the so-called communist threat. The *Times* was decidedly upset, condemning the "complications and absurdities of PR . . . took nearly two weeks of ballot counting to establish the final result . . . Manhattan alone . . . had 250 tabulators steadily at work." They expressed "disillusionment" and "shock . . . that on the very first count the Communist candidates in Brooklyn and Manhattan, respectively, led all the rest."[53] All of these expressions of fear and anger were to be aggressively acted on in the near future. The same held true for the reverse trepidation of Matthew Cronin, who sent a telegram to Mayor LaGuardia demanding a "full and complete investigation" of the Board of Elections due to "acts of incompetence, gross and wilful irregularities," or vote fraud.[54] The ten thousand spoiled votes that Davis lost and Gerson's heroic initiative that prevented Davis from going down to defeat in 1943 were harbingers of extralegal tactics that were to flower in subsequent city elections.

Thus, those who have not been able to understand why the Red Scare arose when it did have not pondered the dramatic impact of the Left's strength in the citadel of capital. It was not just the party but the influence they wielded in the unions and among African-Americans in particular that was of concern to the authorities. Concessions to unions were out of the question at this time; the bludgeon was to be reserved for them. But blacks were not just a domestic issue but increasingly an international one as the United States chided other countries about human rights violations in eastern Europe while being embarrassed about similar violations aimed at people of color within its own borders. As black brethren across the sea were rising to independence, courtship of them was complicated by anti-black racism in the United States. Concessions had to be granted in the United States; moreover, the ruling class could no longer afford to concede this powerful constituency to the Left. The Red Scare was one way to confront Black Liberation, and the forming of an anti-Communist alliance between liberals and African-Americans while isolating the Left was the response. Davis was at the center of these events. The voters of Harlem in particular had seen to that.

10
Cold War Coming, 1946–1947

The euphoria of the electoral victory of 1945 was short-lived. It was clear that a new world was coming by 1946 but it was not exactly what the comrades had in mind. Winston Churchill's "Iron Curtain" speech at Fulton, Missouri, was an early signal that fighting Reds could be done just as well at home as abroad. But the election of a black Red in the City Council of the premier city of the "free world" was a living contradiction of the White House's new line. Blacks were being denied rights in the United States, so what gave the country the right to clamor about alleged similar developments abroad? Although Communists were supposed to be antidemocratic and unpopular, they had just rolled up impressive vote totals. Something had to give . . . and it did.

This pivotal year started brightly for Davis. He was elected as "minority member" to the key council committees, Rules and Finance; this was a reflection of his vote totals and the respect for his competence, despite his political outlook. His office remained at 200 West 135th Street in Harlem and he continued to set aside extensive time to meet with his constituents. Indeed, his schedule continued to be filled with party meetings, council meetings, ribbon-cuttings, and the other kinds of activities that elected officials must endure.[1]

Economic questions that weighed heavily in postwar New York were reflected in the council. From his post on the Finance Committee, Davis proposed an "alternative tax plan" to raise $65 million; the plan involved higher taxes on big business, horse racing, and the like. Other forces sought to double the sales tax, which Davis and Cacchione considered quite regressive. They helped to mobilize antisales tax groups, who brought 52,900 postcards to City Hall and hundreds to testify in opposition. But the tax passed 17–6, despite their staunch opposition. This fissure in the council was deepened when the council voted a budget of over $200 million; two Democrats joined with the Communists, ALP, and GOP bloc in opposition. These economic questions, along·with transit fares and rent control, found the Communists not in isolation; aligning with them was later seen as a stigma.[2]

The issue was joined on ground that was unfavorable, a religious one. Though the Reds' charter did not admit discrimination against religious believers, Communists had a reputation as militant, atheistic anticlerics. In March 1946 Davis and Cacchione opposed a resolution to greet Francis Cardinal Spellman, who had just arrived in town from a trip to fascist Spain. They were outvoted 20-2; even Quill joined the attack against them. There was an "open threat of personal violence," according to the *Daily Worker*. Seated with Cacchione, Davis listened to the barrage without flinching. His cool, quiet demeanor was in sharp contrast with the oratorical venom surpassing anything veteran City Hall reporters had ever witnessed in those chambers. Ben Richardson in the *People's Voice* praised Davis, but already his was becoming a distinctly minority view.[3]

It was not altogether coincidental that this incident erupted just as the "Iron Curtain" speech was being splashed on the front page. Retaliation was quick. John J. Sheahan, chair of the Committee on Arrangements of St. Patrick's Day Parade, demanded that Davis and Cacchione not march in the parade—which had been a tradition in city politics. The two issues were connected further when Davis introduced a resolution denouncing the Fulton speech as an invitation to World War III. Although this brought forth a fusillade of invective, Davis was unmoved.[4]

It got worse. Councilman James Phillips called Davis a "menace to civilization" after a heated debate on taxes. Then the right wing went after Mike Quill, transit leader, Irish nationalist, and ALP ally of Davis. Davis questioned the "way the word 'communist' is used to hide the fundamental issues before the people." This was too much for Queens Republican Alfred J. Phillips; he roared that he was not "going to sit by and be insulted by a communist." Davis did not flinch: "Sit down, you'll have an apoplexy." Phillips demanded that Davis be denied the privilege of the floor but he was defeated by 16-7; GOP members split on this, as did Democrats and Liberals. The unruffled Davis "lambasted Phillips with a zeal and vigor seldom heard in the Council," but even the split vote could not obscure the rapidly changing political climate.[5]

One of the fascinating aspects of the Red Scare was the fact that civil liberties could be curtailed as civil rights for blacks were expanded. The coming to independence of African nations made Jim Crow an Achilles' heel in the execution of U.S. foreign policy. Moreover, the recent experience with Hitler's racism discredited the more blatant aspects of Jim Crow. Elites had to simultaneously snatch blacks away from the Reds while bludgeoning the latter. The Red Scare was used to derail a leftist-influenced Black Liberation movement, of which Davis was the most prominent symbol. Blacks in Harlem and elsewhere received some concessions; the question was whether this was worth the long-term cost of routing some of the movement's most militant, intelligent, and resourceful members.[6]

Thus, despite the battering he took on so many other issues in the council, Davis had a much easier time of it on questions of race. Early on Cacchione "reported that he would not be willing to continue the 'Gentlemen's Agreement' which involved the introduction of no legislation pertaining to racial discrimination, without first obtaining the sanction of the Majority Leader."[7] Hence, a Davis resolution on Negro History Week, which called on the mayor to urge schools and libraries to put up displays, and so forth sailed through unanimously. The Rules Committee also unanimously adopted his resolution aimed at his old antagonist, Congressman Rankin, because of his racism and anti-Semitism; there was "sharp debate" but Davis "stood up and ripped their argument to shred. . . . Davis fought this pussy footing and got in some sharp blows." The Left-led antilynching crusade was endorsed unanimously. But signaling what was to come, Isaacs had to introduce the Davis bill that called for a city analogue to FEPC, since the Union for Democratic Action did not want to back a Communist-formulated bill.[8]

Davis continued to attract a host of celebrities and public figures to his banner; although the Red Scare can be said to have commenced officially by March 1946, it took some time for the new line to percolate down. Thus in January Davis was a recipient of an award from *New Masses* at a black tie ball at the Hotel Commodore. On the dais with him were his old friend Charles Drew, Mary McLeod Bethune, Alain Locke, Jacob Lawrence, Charles White, Sterling Brown, Pearl Primus, and Dean Dixon—a veritable all-star team of the black arts community. U.S. Minister to Liberia, Dr. R. O'Hara Lanier, Ilya Ehrenberg, Albert Gomes (deputy mayor of Port-au-Spain, Trinidad), and Canada Lee were among those sharing platforms with Davis in the following weeks. It was not unusual to have the future leading black Republican Lionel Hampton playing at Davis's birthday ball or Leadbelly performing at a party sponsored by the Harlem and Waterfront CP cells.[9]

Davis's own celebrity continued unabated, particularly before March. The party attempted to take advantage of this by sending him on a cross-country tour. In Seattle in February he spoke before fifteen hundred people at a Lenin Memorial meeting, flanked on the platform by labor and black leaders from across a broad spectrum. This was part of a ten-day trip that took him to all of the major cities on the West Coast. Davis was greeted like a conquering potentate; he was seen as a militant and intelligent symbol of resistance against Jim Crow.[10] Robert Minor sensed this: "I was in Montgomery, Alabama, a few weeks ago . . . and [spoke] to a Negro woman leader. . . . I found that the 'Open Sesame' to the attention of people was Ben Davis' election. . . . When you mention Comrade Davis' election, eyes open and faces glow, although they really know pathetically little about it. It is as though Ben Davis was elected a sort of 'Moses' for the South."[11] Thus, when Davis arrived in Jim Crow St. Louis, four thousand five hundred supporters packed Municipal Auditorium and "over one thousand were turned away. . . . Many white trade unionists attended."[12] The other contender for the title of the most well-known Communist at that time was Gurley Flynn, but when she went to Phoenix to speak she was advertised as "co-worker and friend of Ben Davis, Jr."[13]

Davis's image was enhanced by his visible role in attempting to save FEPC from a garroting in Washington. He was acerbic in castigating Truman's "masterpiece of double-dealing" and lamented that he "has deserted Roosevelt's main line of policy." With Powell he sparked the organization of a CIO-led delegation to Washington to save FEPC. Theodore Ward, the well-known black playwright who was part of the delegation, recalled that their train cars were cold, unlike the others, and surmised that the authorities did not approve of their integrated delegation. Davis was the main speaker, however, and they met with Truman aide David Niles in the White House after the president refused to meet with them; they also met with the majority and minority leaders of the House and Senate (with the exception of Congressman Joe Martin, who also refused to meet with them). One thousand people from twenty states were present (including Democrats, Republicans, NAACP members and so forth). In a surprise move the bill, which was a precursor of the Equal Employment Opportunity Commission, was brought to the Senate floor as a direct result of the presence of these delegates; yet it would be a long time before a similarly broad but Communist-led delegation could come to Washington.[14]

But the apparent success of the delegation may have been a "false positive," for Dixiecrats hit the bill with a stinging filibuster. At a jam-packed Manhattan Center rally Davis termed the filibuster "legislative fascism" and boldly threw down the gauntlet, but times were changing and his words were beginning to pack less power.[15]

Davis requested an appointment with President Truman again, but it was becoming clear that the climate had been altered and no meeting would be forthcoming. Part of the problem was an eruption that periodically characterized this era. Davis and A. Philip Randolph were at each other's throats again. The deep-voiced labor leader was a formidable foe, having ties to socialist forces that Davis did not respect; moreover, Davis held firmly to the party line of hostility to the doctrines of Leon Trotsky. This and the fact that despite Davis's protestations Randolph had no small influence in Harlem added to the fervor of their frequent confrontations. The Red council member berated Randolph's ties with "despicable Trotskyites" in the National Council for FEPC, as well as those "poisonous Norman Thomas 'Socialists.'" According to Davis, the Socialists were trying to "turn his March on Washington Movement into a March on the Communists Movement." Turning the tables on a traditional anti-Communist charge, he wondered, "what does it do with the money it collects?" and denounced them for suggesting that the Davis-led delegation to Washington be boycotted. Claudia Jones charged that Randolph and Company were behind the strategy that led to the bill being brought to the floor of the Senate, where it faced an inevitable filibuster, whereas the Davis forces wanted to see it go to the House. Davis, however, blamed the Dixiecrats for the debacle. The point was that this disunity was not helpful to Davis and his party just as the Red Scare was developing.[16]

This setback did not deter Davis from moving on other antiracist fronts. This disunity among progressives must have been sensed by the reactionaries, for at that moment a reign of terror was unleashed against blacks across the nation. The worst example of this trend was in Columbia, Tennessee, where a horrible pogrom was launched. Davis praised the role of the NAACP during this hate-filled episode but was leery of their legalistic approach. This mob violence illustrated the difficulty of Red joining black to fight back. When Thurgood Marshall went to Columbia to investigate, he was arrested and some feared he would be lynched. Riding in the front seat of Marshall's car was *Daily Worker* reporter Harry Raymond; not only was the NAACP reluctant to broadcast this fact, but they felt that the revelation might even justify a lynching or at least detract from the sympathetic response.[17]

But for Davis, words were not enough, no matter how militant they might be. He was instantly on the scene in Freeport, New York, after the slayings there and immediately blamed the two major parties for the outrages. In late July a rally attended by five thousand people was held at 125th Street and 7th Avenue in New York at which Davis called this spate of slayings "the beginning of an all-out war against the Negroes." He joined Canada Lee at another Harlem rally and lashed the GOP and Democrats who are "sitting idly by while we die." He demanded that federal troops be sent south: "lynchers and pogromists should be lined up against the wall and shot like the fiendish dogs they are." Some of his white liberal friends might have deemed this "Stalinist," but it was raw meat for his predominantly black constituency.[18]

It is easy to speculate that the turn to the right signaled by Fulton emboldened the racists, who were not only disturbed by black advances but leftist-led black advances as well. Certainly as the White House was blasting Red "perfidy" across the water, it must have seemed incongruous that they had to accept the indignity of negotiating with a domestic Communist. When the "Crusade Against Lynching" mobilized twelve hundred people to go to Washington, Davis recalled in his memoir that he "was spokesman of the delegation to the State Department. We spoke to Acheson, then Under-Secretary of State," indicating the foreign policy implications. And certainly the Dixiecrats were not enthralled with Davis's characterization of their own Senator Bilbo as "a stench in the nostrils of every decent American" and his warning about a "serious fascist danger."[19]

The Dixiecrats struck back. When Davis's old friend William Hastie was nominated governor of the Virgin Islands, their association became an issue: "In response to questions by Senator Ellender, Judge Hastie said he had known Benjamin Davis, Jr., for about 25 years . . . Judge Hastie said he and Mr. Davis had been close friends."[20]

Their ire over Davis was understandable, given his increasingly effective tweaking of a major U.S. flaw—clamoring about human rights abroad while denying them at home. After the Fulton speech, Davis's voice became even more insistent on this point, and he was not alone. Raymond Pace Alexander called the historic words of Winston Churchill " . . . a warmongering speech and an affront to the American people which could only mean that he wanted the U.S. and Great Britain to align themselves against Russia." Charles Houston called it " . . . an appeal by Churchill for the U.S. to bail out the British Empire and preserve the old imperialism." But it was Davis who was striking out most vigorously. He wondered sarcastically how Secretary of State Jimmy Byrnes could demand democracy in Iran when he backed the poll tax in South Carolina. Repeatedly he hailed the human rights petition of the National Negro Congress, which tried to bring this contradiction before an international audience.[21]

This line was accompanied by a fervent defense of Moscow. At a sixteen-thousand-strong Madison Square Garden rally sponsored by the Council on African Affairs and featuring Powell, Robeson, Du Bois, and Bethune, Davis told the audience, "Only the socialist Soviet Union has spoken out for the freedom of Africa." When the *New York Times* raised the issue of political trials in eastern Europe, he contrasted the trial of the "traitor Mikhailovitch" in Yugoslavia and the "copious tears" shed, to the newspaper's milder response to the Columbia, Tennessee, pogrom and the "biggest frameup in the last quarter of a century" in Freeport: "As for me," Davis said, "I would rather entrust the lives of the 25 innocent Negroes in Columbia to the antifascist Yugoslavian judiciary than to all the justice that the lynch-minded poll-taxers in Tennessee could muster." For good measure, he wondered why the *Times* was not as concerned about Puerto Rico and Indonesia. Subsequently he contrasted elections in Mississippi with the the alleged "fraudulent" elections in Poland; and when Bilbo incited lynching he said, "The President of the United States did not see fit to do one thing—not even say a word."[22]

Davis also extended his criticism and action to labor relations. When Western Union workers went on strike, joining them on the picket line were Marcantonio, Quill, Cacchione, and Davis. The *New York Times* worriedly reported on 11 January 1946, "All phases of the city's commercial life, from florists to financial houses, felt the impact of the strike. Dun & Bradstreet announced that its weekly bank clearings would be delayed." In part Davis blamed the Truman administration for the spate of strikes that greeted 1946; he sounded the alarm that "trade unions face the danger of extinction" and detected a "rising tide toward fascism." The American Federation of Labor chief came in for attack too, as Davis assailed his Red-baiting and compared him to Goebbels. But again, this harsh approach to potential allies was not useful in aiding the mobilization against the Red Scare.[23]

Even so, Davis's militance in the face of a gathering Red Scare was not hindering party growth. The Communist party was both active and visible on the same issues—FEPC, racist violence, strikes—that Davis was speaking about. He was still serving as chair of the Harlem party and worked closely with Bob Campbell, Rose Gaulden, Maude White, Cyril Phillip, Ted Bassett, and other African-American Communists. The party was active in the National Negro Congress and its emerging successor, the Civil Rights Congress. From 15 March–7 June 1946 the party recruited 250 new members; 55 percent of their new members were veterans and by July their membership had doubled. This both fortified and accelerated their activism, for example, they forced landlords to clean up garbage in their slum tenements, resulting in the biggest court fines so far leveled against landlords for such violations.[24]

This growth in party ranks gave Davis renewed confidence. The numerical growth was accompanied by the promotion of Henry Winston to third-ranking Party leader, behind Foster and Dennis; Davis reminded readers in the *Daily Worker* that "hundreds of Negroes hold extremely minor posts within the two major parties." He repeated the wounding experience of his father with the GOP, when in 1944 he went to the Credentials Committee at the national convention to protest the seating of a white group instead of his integrated delegation. The elder Davis had replied, "My son . . . was elected on the Communist ticket. If this convention doesn't seat our delegation, we Negroes know where we can go and get seated." They were seated. In contrast, according to the council member, "although a small fraction of the membership of the [CP] are Negroes," there were three African-Americans on a National Board of twelve, and ten on the National Committee of this party of radicals.[25]

Though there were problems of white chauvinism within the party, they paled in comparison to the problems encountered in other parties, both specifically and in society generally. This unity helps to account for black participation in this party, even in the midst of a burgeoning Red Scare. For example, at a time when a significant percentage of whites not only sent their children to segregated schools but actively opposed integration, Gerald Goodman of Brooklyn was telling "Dear Comrade Pete" Cacchione, "I, and the other friends are very anxious to have our children play and learn with Negro children . . . [a] committee was appointed to raise funds for a scholarship program so that we could accept working class children."[26] Cacchione quickly responded so that this nursery at 134 Sterling Street, in an increasingly black Brooklyn, could better reflect the racial composition of the neighborhood.

This premature antiracism held the party in good stead during the crucial elections of 1946. In an effort to take advantage of his growing popularity the party nominated Davis for U.S. senator. Then he was withdrawn as a candidate so that a "common electoral front" with the American Labor Party and the Democrats could be built to beat the GOP, the Reds making it clear that the electoral front was a "temporary limited move." Davis was now to run for attorney general.[27]

Premature antiracism was a major theme of his barnstorming through upstate New York. The party's opponents retaliated by seeking to bar the Reds from the ballot—a clear signal of the growing Red Scare; Davis flashed his legal credentials and joined the defense team. He did not check his political approach at the door, however, as Judge William Murray chastised him for allegedly "grimacing" at witnesses.[28] The *People's Voice*, on 5 October 1946, was not alone in being "aghast" at the effort to oust the party. Finally Judge Murray agreed to allow Communists on the ballot, but adumbrating what was to come, the party had to spend time in court that could have been better spent spreading a political message to the masses.

It was clear why there was concern about the Left. The *People's Voice* headline on 5 October said it all: "Put These Harlem Men in Office," it proclaimed, accompanied by a picture of Powell and Marcantonio for Congress, Charles Collins for state senate, and Davis for attorney general. These candidates—representing the Democrats, the ALP, the "People's Rights," and Communist parties—signified the growing strength of the Left among African-Americans and their allies. Upstate, Davis was attracting maximum attention on the radio, in churches, and in union halls. The failure to knock the party off the ballot did not deter their enemies, so there was an effort to bar Davis from speaking at a black church in Albany, the Israel AME.[29]

Davis pressed on. Arriving in Buffalo, he was guest of honor at a luncheon hosted by William Evens of the Urban League and James Miller of the CIO. He spoke at the Elks Hall before an audience that was 60 percent black. Though it was evident that Davis would not win the election, the race provided him and the party with a platform from which to project their message, which was also carried to his home base in New York City. After he addressed wholesale and retail workers, twenty people stepped forward to join the party on the spot.[30]

The party recognized that this election was critical; Fulton had signaled the political direction. The *Daily Worker* announced that all thirty thousand party members in New York were mobilizing; two million pieces of literature were distributed in the ten days preceding election day. Davis's campaign took out a quarter-page ad in the *New York Age* urging a vote for the CP and ALP against "Dewey's Hooey!" As the *Daily Worker* suggested, he literally took his challenge to the streets: "More people listen to street speakers in Harlem than in any other urban community in the land. . . . It is on the Harlem 'soap box' that [Davis] . . . can be found almost any time now during the pleasant fall evenings."[31] Like Martin Luther King, Jr., and Malcolm after him, Davis's ability as an orator was part of his appeal.

The harvest of this sowing was reaped on election day. There was a record vote for the ALP as they elected their first state senator. Davis obtained 95,787 votes; his comrade Robert Thompson, running for comptroller, got 85,088, which was probably a testament to Davis's unique popularity. Davis rolled up 8,652 votes upstate, "the largest ever received by a Communist candidate up-state," according to the *Times*.[32] The votes were scored even though his name was removed from the voting machines in a number of districts. Israel Amter, running in 1938, secured 105,681 votes running for congressman at large, a figure Davis did not reach, but in Nassau County he captured 95 percent more votes than Amter; 50 percent more in populous Erie County; and 50 percent more in Westchester.[33]

But even as the votes were being counted, clouds were gathering to blur the rainbow of forces arrayed around the party; these forces, which probably had much in common, were quickly fragmenting under the hammer of the Red Scare. Naturally Davis was in the thick of this development. He scalded Channing Tobias for his support of Thomas Dewey. He lambasted Walter White for his foreign policy views and his characterization of "Russian imperialism." Then the "drivers and route men of the Great Eastern News Corporation" launched a boycott of the *People's Voice* on the ground that it was "not for labor." This development, coming weeks after Fulton, rang the death knell for this Red ally.[34]

Soon it seemed as if the progressives were coming to resemble crabs in a barrel. The *New York Amsterdam News*, still no friend of the Left, reported their frequently cited rumor that "had been whispered about for some time that there was a rift between the Congressman and the Councilman and that Davis would take Powell on in the primary." Davis's repeated denials only fueled their repetition of this story. Still, Davis's review of Powell's book *Marching Blacks* did not quell these rumors. Though providing positive evaluation of Powell and the book, Davis termed this work "quite spotty and erratic . . . hastily put together. . . . basic misconceptions on many aspects of Marxism." He termed his idea of mass migration from the South as "unsound and divisive . . . obviously impracticable . . . defeatist." His coda, that "one must admire Rep. Powell's fearless, crusading spirit," may have assuaged the thin-skinned Powell, but overall his words were not helpful in cementing an important alliance during difficult days.[35]

Davis was not alone in his opinion of Powell's book. Ben Richardson, writing in Powell's own newspaper, sharply disagreed with his boss's idea that blacks would work with the Communists but not join. There were alleged rifts between Davis and Marcantonio and Marc and Powell; whatever the truth of these allegations, it was clear that with tension rising with the Red Scare, personal relations were inevitably complicated.[36]

Other antagonisms appeared veritably eternal. Davis was attacking Randolph for his plan to engage in civil disobedience over military segregation; it "leaves unanswered the whole question of war." NAACP board member Alfred Baker Lewis and his colleague Frank Crosswaith were busily conspiring against the Reds. Lewis was trying to sabotage a political candidacy: "If I can get a clipping from the *Daily Worker* endorsing his candidacy, I will try to use that as a sort of kiss of death." Ruefully he told his friend, "you are about the only person whom I know who reads the *Daily Worker* regularly." Contradictions between black Communists and black Socialists—who, though few, were influential—continued unabated, which helped to propel the Red Scare.[37]

Nevertheless, it would be a distortion to see such attacks—on actual foes or putative allies—as the main note sounded by Davis in 1946.[38] As ever, he was working overtime to build alliances, be they with unions in Chicago or the CIO or Father Divine or progressive veterans or Joe Louis. But what complicated matters was the Red Scare attack. Marcantonio maintained a file on "campaign violence" that was jammed with incidents. These attacks were part of an overall Red Scare that was coming to dominate the political scene.[39]

George Lipsitz has suggested that the postwar attack on the Communist party was an excuse to smash rank-and-file militancy in the labor movement and create support for a foreign policy that would open up foreign markets for the United States. His rationale could also be applied to the Black Liberation movement—that is, the gathering strength of the Left within these ranks, as symbolized by Ben Davis, demanded smashing for similar reasons. Davis and Company seized upon the complaints about human rights in eastern Europe to ask why these protections did not apply to African-Americans. With Du Bois's guidance, the NAACP in 1947 filed a petition with the United Nations. Limning this point, Davis called this petition of "national and world significance." In Geneva Moscow was simultaneously proposing to outlaw racism and national and religious discrimination. Fearing investigations in the United Nations, U.S. delegates Jonathan Daniels and Eleanor Roosevelt were unsympathetic; Davis termed their reaction "shameful." Increasingly in his newspaper columns and public addresses Davis focused sharply on this contradiction of protesting about human rights abroad while denying them at home.[40]

This same contradiction helped Truman to see that new initiatives on the question of blacks were needed. This compelled him to issue his *To Secure these Rights: The Report of the President's Committee on Civil Rights*, a landmark publication in presidential politics. Though deeming it "of considerable importance," Davis was otherwise unmoved. Still, he issued a caution, anticipating how this initiative would peel off center forces from his coalition. His private and public sentiments dovetailed; in a letter to Essie Robeson he expressed further concern. Davis saw at an early stage this contradiction of expanding civil rights for blacks while civil liberties were being restricted, but his tactics toward centrist forces like the NAACP and Randolph were not designed to take advantage of this situation; in fact, they seemed designed to drive these groups further into the embrace of the White House and other ruling forces.[41]

This year 1947 saw a continued effort by Davis to combat the racist terror that was escalating against blacks. He increased his activism with the Civil Rights Congress. With his friend Paul Robeson, along with Clark Foreman, the Reverend Charles Hill of Detroit, and Max Yergan, he led a delegation of a group called the American Crusade to End Lynching to Washington in January 1947 to pressure the Senate to oust Bilbo. Along with Millard Lampell, he served as co-chair of the Committee to Aid the Fighting South, which was raising ten thousand dollars to aid striking tobacco workers, helping the writer Don West fight a libel suit, and assisting the Southern Negro Youth Congress.[42]

Sensing the growing danger, Davis accelerated his already busy activity against racism. He spoke at street rallies in Harlem to protest the acquittal of lynchers in Jesse Jackson's hometown of Greenville, South Carolina, introducing a resolution in the City Council to protest this development. He organized picketing of the two major parties in light of their inability to "stop lynch terror." He hailed Henry Wallace's speaking tour of the Deep South.

This buzzing activity reached a crescendo when Davis and two friends were stopped by police at Sixteenth Street and Seventh Avenue in Manhattan: "Both of them searched my car. They removed all the seats, looked in the trunk . . . lifted up the hood, etc." The police claimed that they "'[looked] suspicious down in this part of the City this time of morning.'" Davis was cool: "Purposely, I did not identify myself as a City Councilman." But afterwards he blasted this parallel to the South African pass system and the inherent racism that would cast suspicion on any blacks found below Ninety-sixth Street. Yet being consumed with this fight did not prevent Davis from pursuing more mundane pleasures; at this juncture he was eager to visit Robeson in Connecticut "so that we could talk over many things, not to mention a few games of uninterrupted and concentrated chess."[43]

It is highly possible that one of the "many things" that Davis wanted to discuss with Robeson was the evolving theory and practice of the Black Liberation movement. Any such discussion would not just cover the escalating racist violence and what this meant for the black Left. Also involved was the party's approach to this question, their theoretical view of the "National Question." Davis's election suggested that the perception of party backsliding in this area during the war was not shared by African-Americans. In his autobiography Malcolm X vividly recalled his impression of the Communists: "Negro and white canvassers sidled up alongside you, talking fast as they tried to get you to buy a copy of the *Daily Worker*: 'This paper's trying to keep your rent controlled. . . . Make that greedy landlord kill them rats in your apartment. . . . This paper represents the only political party that ever ran a black man for the Vice Presidency of the United States. . . . Just want you to read, won't take but a little of your time. . . . Who do you think fought the hordes to help free those Scottsboro boys?'"[47] On 31 August 1946 the *New York Age*, a barometer of opinion in the black press, did not dispute Malcolm: "Some of the people who constantly cry about the dangers and pitfalls of communism in the United States would do well to look around and find out what makes people discontented with their own form of government." They echoed compliments of Moscow. However, such votes of confidence did not mean that the party was adverse to reexamining their approach to this question. Davis's own view was also evolving but was always within the bounds of party discourse. Truman's initiative would mean that more blacks would be appointed to high office in an effort to break the hold of the Left on this community, a tactic that Davis saw coming during the war. But this maneuver placed the Left in a quandary; after all, absence of blacks from all levels of U.S. society was a complaint, so how could people be angry when it was corrected? The issue was joined further when Truman sought to appoint Davis's Amherst classmate William Hastie as the first black governor general of the U.S. Virgin Islands. Davis was torn about this appointment, pleased about the chipping away of segregation but concerned about making "imperialism" appear more attractive. Still he ironically endorsed his friend: "Considering some of the punks it has confirmed, surely the Senate must confirm [him]." The tendency of Davis and other comrades to appear confounded by the integration of blacks into elite circles continued over the next decade.[45]

Davis was not alone in pondering the irony of advocating the integration of blacks into an imperialist system. Of course, it could be seen as illustrating Lenin's dictum about the road to revolution being paved by the struggle for democracy and that blacks and their allies would come to see that the problem was that capitalism could not satisfy their democratic demands. Robert Minor, one of the party's main thinkers on this question, said in response to an increase in black elected officials, "The election of isolated Negro Congressmen in the 1930's on the basis of permanent 'ghettos' changed nothing in the lives of the people."[46] But Minor's critics argued that the Black Belt thesis meant precisely that—"permanent ghettos"—and certainly the concentration of blacks in Harlem facilitated Davis's election.

Davis was grappling continually with such issues. After an African-American, Francis Turner, was named to a high-level city school post, Davis praised the appointment. This view was fueled by his conception of blacks as "essentially anti-imperialist, pro-labor, anti-Jim Crow and politically progressive" and that their presence would help in liberalizing the system generally.[47]

The multiclass support Davis received from blacks during his campaigns suggests that they agreed with him on this question. Davis was a frequent guest at gatherings like that of the National Dental Association, an all-black group; he thanked them for their "major role" in his reelection. Barring this kind of complimentary language from reaching blacks was part of the ruling class's two-pronged strategy of clubbing the Left and coopting the center. But before the Red Scare had become established, Davis was still being greeted warmly among all strata. Wherever he appeared, however, the questions he was asked did not concern the USSR or Fulton but rather Jim Crow and the poll tax. This was the grim reality of the United States. African-Americans were more concerned with racism than Stalinism.[48]

Yet at the same time it was clear that the trajectory of racism was shifting inexorably, as Truman's report indicated. It was seen in the career path of J. Waties Waring, who went from racism to antiracism in the postwar period as he perceived that racism was assisting the growth of the Left.[49] The party's mistake was not its failure to perceive this trend but in failing to grasp the significance of what James Ford pointed out in 1943, the "present migratory tendencies of Negroes from the South to Northern industrial centers."[50] Migration had served putatively to undermine the Black Belt. Moreover, part of Browder's legacy was to suggest that blacks had made a choice and that they had chosen not self-determination but integration.

Robert Minor was one of the party's closest students of the National Question. His files contain many clippings, some from as early as 1925, that note the south-to-north population shift; these files reflect a sharp scrutiny of black reality as well. After the war, with Robert Thompson, he was one of the first to call for adjustments in seniority to preserve a certain percentage of black workers in case of layoffs. In a report on Negro Work presented to the CP National Committee in 1946, he acknowledged the influence of Garveyism on the party's view of the National Question. In an undated article that probably was written during this era he said, "The trend of all progress is toward racial assimilation, and this takes place inevitably."[51] However, he carried the taint of Browderism and his star, along with many of his ideas, did not continue to rise in the postwar period.

Thus, in reaction to Browderism and Truman's civil rights initiative after the war, a debate erupted in the party on the National Question. In early 1946, at an enlarged meeting of the National Negro Commission, varying views were expressed. Davis's comrade Claudia Jones was resolute in observing that "integration cannot be considered a substitute for the right of self-determination, national liberation is not synonymous with integration, [and] neither are the two concepts mutually exclusive." She conceded that "the problems of the Negro people in the North are akin to those of an oppressed national minority." Still she did not flinch in asserting that the Black Belt thesis remained valid since it "does not exclude the struggle for partial demands." Davis's election surely showed that. She dismissed the notion that "migrations" had changed the question.[52]

Party patriarch William Z. Foster also spoke out at the meeting. He acknowledged as "fact" that blacks "have not responded favorably to the slogan of self-determination." This did not mean that the slogan needing adjusting, however. Blacks were a young nation and had "not yet matured politically." He did add some tantalizing tidbits, suggesting that the party move away from the "Negro republic" idea and adding that "we must study more carefully the whole question of bi-national and multi-national states." The northern neighbor, Canada, was high on this list. He also added that "we must not brush aside the question of race . . . [and] racial prejudice." Since the Communists viewed race as an unscientific notion, they had tended to dismiss the concept altogether.[53]

There were other viewpoints expressed by individuals that reflected various views within the party itself. Francis Franklin, who eventually left the party, took a middling view; yes, blacks are a nation but not a national minority, though now they can go "toward further separate development or toward complete voluntary amalgamation." The past error, he suggested, was posing self-determination as just secession or autonomy: "Many Negroes friendly to our party . . . have pointed out that, while in our practical activity we fight constantly for the fullest unity between Negro and white, our perspective of either secession or separate statehood for the Black Belt constitutes a perspective of disunity." Franklin felt that these "many Negroes" were right. He also touched on another sensitive issue when he noted that "some comrades" say that since Browder pushed "democratic integration . . . it is Browderism if we continue to say the same thing now." No, said Franklin, the party should not "reject . . . the one true statement he made on the Negro question." Needless to say, this did not win overwhelming plaudits for Franklin.[54]

Doxey Wilkerson was even more forthright; reviving the "slogan of 'self-determination in the Black Belt' . . . would be theoretically incorrect and therefore, tactically disastrous." Even more striking is the fact that Wilkerson held this view throughout his tenure in the party and was still highly regarded, which serves to puncture the prevailing notion of how democratic practice and centralism worked among Communists. He pointed out that none of the comrades had the "necessary factual information," meaning statistics, trends, information on mechanization of agriculture: "we should discard the slogan and develop an entirely new approach." He disputed the idea that the only solution could be either "separatist or autonomous" and was even more livid about the "more or less mechanical application of Soviet policy" to African-Americans. Blacks, he felt, "have already reached their maximum stage of development as a nation" and the "future growth curve of this Black Belt nation is downward." The trend of blacks was "toward further development as a distinct national minority."[55] History has proven that on virtually every point, Wilkerson—who left the party after 1956—was probably correct, but at this juncture he was subjected to a withering polemic by James Allen and other party stalwarts.[56]

But Wilkerson was virtually disregarded when the draft resolution on this issue was put forward in mid-1946. The boundaries of this Negro Nation would have to be adjusted—according to the resolution—akin to the creation of West Virginia, assuming that blacks opted for separatism; self-determination was a "bourgeois democratic" demand that did not require socialism. In the North, blacks were deemed an "oppressed national minority." The resolution targeted Browder for the "glossing over of the Negro question during the war, especially the question of Jim Crowism in the armed forces. Even on these issues on which we did conduct a fight, we placed far too much emphasis on equality for the Negro people solely as a war measure." It called for "seniority adjustment" against "the false slogan: 'Everyone must be treated alike.'" In what was to reverberate in the postwar years, the resolution called for a crusade against "white chauvinism . . . if necessary, demonstration trials must be held . . . such manifestations . . . will be burnt out with a red-hot iron." This red-hot rhetoric warmed the cockles of many hearts, especially those of black comrades, but it was an action that served to alienate some people, especially white Communists.[57]

The draft was finalized and publicized in 1947. It added that the party does not raise "prematurely . . . self-determination as an immediate slogan of action . . . does not attempt to impose any specific solution in advance of the form in which self-determination will be exercised."[58] Davis, who was a prime mover in this matter, praised the resolution for avoiding sectarianism.[59] It was apparent that in the midst of a Jim Crow nation, the party was reluctant to state that blacks were no longer a nation deserving the right to self-determination since this might suggest that even the Reds were engaging in a veiled attack on African-Americans, depriving them of a "right" that none were so brave as to acknowledge.

Davis went further in averring that the original 1928 view "suffered" from "left sectarianism." The "Negro question . . . is different from that of all other minority groups and peoples" in the United States. The party's main "failure [was] to emphasize sufficiently the stake of the white workers and poor farmers in the South in supporting the right of self-determination." Why were blacks so loath to flock around the self-determination banner? Due to the "myth of racial inferiority and the segregationism that accompanies it . . . [African-Americans are] highly suspicious" of any proposal, "even those of self-determination, that would set them apart from the white population." He later added, as he had said in the past, that equality, not self-determination, was the immediate issue. Fortunately equality was the keynote for Red activity in the postwar period, but unfortunately at this important historical moment and shift in line, the party was not entirely up to the theoretical challenge.[60]

In the meantime the party's ongoing squabbles with Walter White and other mainstream leaders seemed to be deepening as Truman increased his contact with them. Being known as a friend of the party was the surest way to be surveilled by the FBI, as Joe Louis discovered. The National Negro Congress and its successor, the Civil Rights Congress, were receiving maximum scrutiny. Davis was still attacking Randolph, now calling him "Dubinsky's boy." Some of the juxtapositions were startling. As Lester Granger was praising Davis ("likable figure worthy of public respect"), Davis was censuring this Urban League leader. Similarly Socialist Layle Lane could praise the Reds ("the Communists have found fertile ground in Negro discontent and everywhere have done much well-organized work among them") and study their literature, despite Davis's frequent assaults on his party. Such attacks made a left-center united front difficult at a time when it was needed more than ever.[61]

Davis's advice to White and others who were being pressured to denounce their former Red allies was strikingly pointed and public. Davis jumped on George Weaver, director of the CIO antidiscrimination committee, and Willard Townsend for using the Race Relations Institute in Nashville as a "platform for [a] vicious red-baiting campaign." He also clashed again with Frank Crosswaith in his capacity with the City Housing Authority.[62]

The ruling class as symbolized by Robert Moses was moving to isolate Davis and the party, while the latter was busily attacking erstwhile allies. Complicating the matter was the pressure these ersatz associates were receiving from elites and other quarters. In May 1947 James Lawson of the African Nationalist Movement was picketing Abyssinian Church and Congressman Powell because they were selling tickets to the leftist-led Negro Freedom Rally at Madison Square Garden; among other things they were protesting the inclusion of whites. Lawson worked overtime to expose and condemn Powell's ties to the Reds, and he attacked his support of labor leader Harry Bridges. At this point Powell was in seclusion due to a heart attack but Lawson was unmoved: "You cannot ride spiritual and political horses at the same time."[63]

All of this bickering was the backdrop to the split between Powell and the Reds and the demise of the *People's Voice*; both were major setbacks for the Left and accelerated the rise of the national reaction. The ruling class was not unaware of the party's influence within the black press; during the war military intelligence had placed undercover agents with certain black newspapers such as the *Michigan Chronicle*. Robert Minor particularly analyzed these organs carefully and, of course, Davis's personal familiarity with a number of black publishers was a factor in assuring the Communists favorable press notices. It also helped when he collaborated with Robeson and Wendell Smith of the *Pittsburgh Courier* on the integration of major-league baseball. It was left to George Schuyler to sound the alarm: "The Communists have made severe inroads among newspaper writers and editors of the Negro press."[64]

Naturally Davis was quite close to the *Voice*, as was the Left generally. Esther Cooper, later a founder of *Freedomways* and wife of leading Communist James Jackson, was their southern correspondent. The board included Powell, Hope Stevens, Ferdinand Smith, and Max Yergan; Doxey Wilkerson became executive editor in 1944 and Marvel Cooke also worked on the paper. A harbinger occurred in early 1946 when Powell took a leave from the paper and announced pointedly, "during this period I shall not be responsible for the editorial policy and news presentation of the paper." Weeks later the newspaper was in court with a one hundred thousand dollars lawsuit for slander after charges that they switched to a "white distributor who won't hire Negroes"; the paper was "forcibly removed . . . from newsstands" and received threats "to overturn the stands of dealers selling" the paper. Red-baiting was never as popular in the black community as elsewhere, but "white-baiting" was a different matter; in response to this broadside the paper printed a picture of all involved in the operation—but it was too late and the vaunted First Amendment was in shreds.[65]

By November 1947 Wilkerson had been ousted with the wan excuse that the move was "non-partisan. . . . [The paper is] neither controlled by nor allied to any political party." The editorial line changed; now readers were counseled not to picket merchants on 125th Street over high prices. By January the columns of Robeson and Lena Horne were gone, though Du Bois' was still being published. By April there were editorials about "communist dirty work," written under the ideological tutelage of new "president" Max Yergan.[66]

Wilkerson disputes the notion that he was receiving "directives" from the party to turn the paper a certain way (an allegation that reflects the basic misunderstanding of how the party worked) though there were many discussions about the orientation of the paper. He terms Powell "opportunist" for his role in the conflict ("very bright . . . not taken in by anybody . . . seldom came around the paper") and speaks more favorably about his co-owner, the nightclub owner Charles Buchanan. Marvel Cooke insists that the party bent over backwards to avoid undue influence on the paper. But in the end the paper folded, done in by "white-baiting," Red-baiting, and difficulty in distribution.[67]

Davis was distraught at this turn of events and pointed the finger directly at Max Yergan. They had known each other for some time; his close friend Diane Sommers served as Yergan's secretary. But that did not spare the future apologist for imperialism a tongue-lashing from Davis. In this attack Davis stepped back and waxed philosophical: "As the struggle gets sharper for Negro rights, for peace instead of war . . . many self-seeking careerists will reveal themselves. It's unfortunate but often so are the facts of life . . . the saying goes: 'I am with you through thick and thin, but when it gets too thick, I thin out,' And so it is with the summer soldiers." Certainly these words are true, but one wonders why Davis and the party did not pursue a less harsh posture toward these vacillating forces in an effort to keep them within the fold. The Yergan episode also sheds light on the party's difficulty in addressing the problem of integrating of previously white elite circles and the concomitant development of elites reclaiming black comrades from the Left; quite candidly, U.S. elites had more to offer figures like Yergan who previously were attracted to the left because the Left offered a form of mobility otherwise denied to them. Davis's and the party's unease about integration may have reflected this fact.[68]

Davis was also not pleased at Powell's disappearing act, although at first he did not state this publicly. He openly defended his colleague, as when Truman sent an invitation to every member of Congress to attend a White House reception except the Harlem congressman. But Powell did not want to be isolated with the Reds and began a steady march away from them. This did not save him from attacks and even Red-baiting, however. By 1950 Davis was not so diplomatic and lamented Powell's "making concessions to the warmongers," urging that he "stand up and fight more consistently and militantly." By 1951 Davis dropped all pretense of diplomacy and swung at his former ally with ferocity. A fruitful alliance had collapsed.[69]

The Red Scare meant that any association with the Communists was becoming a distinct liability. If ever there was a time to get off this moving train, it was now. But Davis did not follow Powell; if anything, he heightened his party association. In early 1947 he appeared with the other "fighting Ben," Ben Gold, in a parley of club and section leaders; recruiting for the party, Davis intoned, was a race against time and reaction.[70] Even the *New York Times* for 2 May 1947 and their aptly named reporter Warren Moscow conceded that May Day that year "drew heavy crowds of onlookers"; they claimed that thirty thousand came, the party claimed sixty thousand. The Red contingent chanted, "Join the Communist Party and fight for peace." Davis was a principal speaker.

Nowadays Davis had to become an even more convincing speaker. This fact was recognized by the *Worker*, which noted that after Davis had spoken at meetings in Harlem, the East Side, and the Bronx, scores stepped forward to join the party. What was Davis's method? "I personalize myself and the Party. I often tell how I joined the Party," he wrote. He discussed the "vision" of socialism, the "mood of the people," what is to be done, Truman, and other topics. Whatever the case, as the party's isolation increased, Davis became more important as symbol, recruiter, and speaker.[71]

Davis's talents were recognized in the ranks of the party. "This Ben Davis recruiting is becoming a phenomenon" was the message from the *Worker* after he spoke to the Freedom Road Club in Harlem and "all fourteen [guests] are now present and accounted for in the ranks of the Party." In June his eloquence convinced "more than 100 people to join." Of course, this was not an unalloyed plus, for after recruitment, the party had to hold on to the new members in a tense atmosphere. Nonetheless, as a morale booster alone, the Davis recruiting magic was a healthy tonic.[72]

Davis seemed to be more than one person, given the diversity and volume of his activity. While he was fighting the Red Scare, writing columns, and recruiting, he was also one of the most active members of the City Council. As in 1946, his pace there was feverish. He was named to the Finance, Rules, Parks, and State Legislation committees and was an active participant in each one.[73]

The onset of the Cold War meant economic devastation for a significant percentage of the working class, particularly African-Americans, so financial questions occupied a significant part of Davis's time. In early 1947 he called for salary increases for teachers, more state aid for education, and more money for childcare. Davis and Cacchione were vocal in demanding that O'Dwyer hold the line on the transit fare. He was vitriolic in criticizing the effort to raise certain Board of Estimate salaries to fifteen thousand dollars per year. In the debate on the city's $255 million dollar capital budget Davis hit the refusal of the Corporation Counsel to give an opinion on the use of housing funds outside debt limit for schools, lamented the lack of funds to Harlem Hospital, and questioned an allocation of $485,000 for a stage at Lewisohn Stadium: "I like music but I prefer people," was his comment. But his budget proposal was defeated soundly, 15–4.[74]

Race questions were a prime staple for Davis during this term. Not only did he hurl invective at a $25 million dollar boondoggle for the construction of yet another new Madison Square Garden building, but added that their barring of black basketball teams should totally disqualify them from quaffing at the public trough.[75] His technique in mobilizing against racist and anti-Semitic stereotypes indicates his approach as a legislator; in a letter to Davis, Cacchione summarized the method: "I am suggesting the following, and if I receive the o.k. from your office, I shall proceed . . . a folder of 1/2 million copies should be distributed by the progressive organizations of New York City in a house to house canvas. . . . On the day we have the appointment with the Mayor, we should call for a mass demonstration at City Hall and a picket line. If no results are obtained from that appointment, we should follow it through with a mass demonstration and picket line at one of the meetings of the Board of Education. We also can discuss the question of calling a mass conference. I think that the best defense is a real offensive." These Communist legislators were *activists* as well as solons.[76]

Their activism was fueled by Davis's mass contacts and his ability to make social appeals that contradicted the stereotype of the rigid, unsmiling Red. In September 1947 he hosted two block parties for one thousand eight hundred, then two thousand Harlem children to mark his forty-fourth birthday; there was "music, magic and assorted goodies . . . Fredi Washington, screen actress and journalist, participated as song leader."[77] As his gift to the children, he announced a program of a city-financed vacation for disadvantaged youngsters.

This approach assisted Davis in retaining popularity, even in the face of growing repression. When the Reverend Kenneth Williams, newly elected to the Winston-Salem City Council (the first black since Reconstruction) visited New York to galvanize support for striking tobacco workers, he made a beeline for Davis's office. So it was not overly surprising when Conrad Clark, eastern director of publicity of the United Negro Allied Veterans of America, struck back at attacks on Davis: "Benjamin Davis, a councilman in the City of New York, who is an acknowledged member of the Communist Party, does not make the government of the city Communistic any more than a Communist who fought in World War II and joins UNAVA does." But it was quickly becoming clear that this unassailable logic would not prevail in the early postwar years.[78]

Already the clouds of Cold War were forming. The Negro Freedom rallies had become regular events at Madison Square Garden since 1942 and had involved a number of AFL and CIO unions. But at the June 1947 event, according to Davis, there was "no program of action . . . unrepresentative . . . platform for red-baiters." There was an attempt to "commercialize" the struggle, as 60 percent of the funds collected went to the promoter, Neil Scott. Only four thousand supporters came, compared to the usual fifteen to twenty thousand of past years, and many of those stalked out in disgust. It was definitely a flop. But particularly striking was the fact that it was picketed by black narrow nationalists—a maneuver seen by some as akin to Lawson's attacks on Powell and the attacks on the *People's Voice*; if Red-baiting didn't work, apparently the Left's enemies felt that "white-baiting" would.[79]

Then controversial domestic and international issues began exploding in the City Council. When the Marshall Plan was raised, there was a "bitter 2-hour debate . . . involving interchanges of personal remarks," according to the *New York Times* on 29 October 1947. This debate came after Davis had blocked consideration of a resolution in support of the plan. But it passed 16–3, with Davis, Connolly, and Quill dissenting. Davis labeled the Marshall Plan and the Truman Doctrine "the doctrine of Hitler." Councilman Walter Hart made sarcastic and angry references to "agents of Moscow" and "fifth columnists." But that was not the end of the battle, according to the *Daily Worker*: "Quill tore into the red-baiters with a fury seldom seen in the Council. 'I don't give two hoots in hell for those swashbuckling, goosestepping fascists who shout "red." You can't bulldoze me or the people with that sort of thing'." Davis demanded an apology: "I have been called a fifth columnist, an agent of Moscow. I have been asked if I love my country. I regard this as a personal insult. . . . I respect every member of this council. I love my country but I do not love its discrimination; I do not love the Negro-haters and the anti-Semites."[80]

When Taft-Hartley and other antilabor bills were introduced in Congress, this debate was reflected in the council. As usual, Davis sought to rally his labor allies to pressure the more recalcitrant council members. The "debate was bitter," according to the *Daily Worker*, when the issue reached the council. Then this issue snarled the party's access to the radio, which had been a virtual constant at least since the war; WOR-AM refused to broadcast an anti–Taft-Hartley talk by William Z. Foster, though time had been bought by the party. Davis protested this "arbitrary exercise of censorship in a discriminatory manner" in an impassioned letter to the Federal Communications Commission, but to no avail; again, the heralded First Amendment was victimized.[81]

That was not the end. Queens Democrat Gary Clemente sought to amend the city charter to oust "subversive civil service officials and employees," by which he meant Davis, Cacchione, Quill, and Connolly. Davis warned of a rancorous fight in such an event, but Clemente also sought to bar organizations on the attorney general's subversives list from recruiting on street corners, at parks, and so forth. When Davis attempted to introduce a counter bill banning the curbing of minority parties' rights, the council refused to allow Si Gerson and an American Labor Party official to testify. Simultaneously, the *New York Times* began a searching scrutiny of the party, which at once was testament to the CP's effectiveness and a warning to hunker down.[82]

As the battle was heating up, Cacchione died; this was a grievous blow to Davis and the party. With his death, this division of labor, which had brought so much to the Left and working class generally, was also dealt a mortal blow.[83]

Consonant with his interpretation of relevant law, Davis moved to have Si Gerson inserted as Cacchione's substitute. His opponents were not impressed; they countered that the Communist party was not a political party within the meaning of the election law and city charter. Davis pleaded his case in the *New York Times*, noting that section 24 of the city charter and "tradition" called for "election by the Council of a candidate of the same political faith and borough as the deceased." In a rare occurrence during this political age, the august *Times* agreed. But Louis Goldberg of the Liberal party ardently argued otherwise. Davis beseeched his colleagues to avoid "outright political discrimination" which "weakens the whole fabric of representative democracy."[84] But with Cacchione's death and the abrupt change in the political climate, Davis was hard pressed to find allies. There was only Quill, Connolly, and Stanley Isaacs from time to time. The council turned a deaf ear to Davis's plea.[85]

Cacchione's untimely death made simpler a prime task of the anti-Communists—removing Reds from the City Council. How could the argument about antidemocratic and antielectoral tactics of Communists globally carry weight when a Communist—a black one no less—sat in the highest electoral body of the largest U.S. city? The *Daily Worker* got it right when they editorialized on 24 October 1947 that the current maneuver to repeal proportional representation had as the "main motive" a "desire to defeat Benjamin J. Davis." Apparently the city fathers did not agree with the considered opinion of the historian Charles Garrett, who has stated that "always the PR elections apparently produced Councils whose make-up reflected with relative accuracy the wishes of the electorate; certainly there was always a close correspondence between the percentage of seats a political group won and the percentage of votes it received on the final count."[86] For example, in 1945 the party received 9 percent of the votes and 9 percent of the seats. Garrett is also correct in perceiving that "the 1947 campaign to repeal PR was one of the most dramatic and emotionally charged campaigns ever waged in New York City over an issue that did not involve the election of candidates to public office." As usual, the immediate target was the party, but others were wounded since eliminating PR effectively shoved women from the council as well; unusual for this era was the fact that liberals—Americans for Democratic Action, NAACP, ILGWU, even some Republicans—stood with Davis in supporting PR.

The scholars Belle Zeller and Hugh A. Bone agree with Garrett in averring that "there is no doubt that the one issue above all others responsible for the repeal of PR in 1947 was Communism." PR helped "nonorganization" Democrats like Isaacs and Genevieve Earle: "one of the most important reasons why the [major] party organizations repeatedly fought PR was that it deprived them of control over nominations." Moreover, "there is general agreement that the average ability of PR councilmen was higher than that of the board of aldermen during its last years." This was why this campaign was "one of the most dramatic ever waged," involving "scores of debates and forums . . . the radio carried carried many debates . . . neighborhood rallies . . . ringing of doorbells." PR means "People's Rule" or "Preposterous Representation" were two of the key slogans, along with the anti-Tammany "Hold that Tiger." This drama led the *New York Herald Tribune, New York Post, PM,* and the *Daily Worker* to endorse PR. But harming PR was the fact that some centrist forces backing PR opposed the vets' bonus on the ballot, which complicated coalition building.[87]

These fusillades hurled at PR were not new. Days after Davis was first elected in 1943, the *Times* attacked it. After printing letters from readers, the Times displayed its anxiety by referring to the "doubtful blessings" of PR, which "by its very nature, makes possible the election of extremists." The CP was disciplined, "whereas the rest of the electorate who took the trouble to vote put their numbered choices down in a half-blind fashion and in a state of bewilderment. . . . The voting showed a significant relationship between [CP] votes and [ALP] votes. . . . There was obviously a good deal of racial voting." Fascism in Europe was blamed on PR in a final flourish. This could not mask the newspaper's real worry—that the growth of the Left was being facilitated by PR.[88]

The *Times* was not finished. After Davis's smashing reelection in 1945 they took up the cudgels again; heatedly, their editorial denounced the "complications and absurdities" of PR, lamenting the two weeks it took to count ballots for Manhattan and the 250 tabulators required, the "high percentage of invalid ballots," and so on. But "further disillusionment" was engendered by the reelection of Reds: "it must have caused a shock to at least some of the voters to see that on the very first count the Communist candidates in Brooklyn and Manhattan respectively, led all the rest . . . Its fundamental purpose is to do a doctrinaire mathematical justice to minorities."[89]

The *Times* was not the only elite that became very worried about PR and the electoral successes of Reds. Robert Moses, in a frequently repeated canard, confided, "My German visit has more than ever convinced me of the unwisdom of proportional representation. It is the device by which the Nazis came into power and it is now being used by the Communists to elect an undue proportion of their members. . . . It has encouraged irresponsible splinter representation. I think we should have an end of it just as soon as possible." But the elites were not united. Thomas Jefferson Miley, secretary of the Commerce and Industry Association of New York, adamantly disagreed with Moses " . . . the real force behind the movement to repeal [PR] is the longing of the Democratic Party machine to regain the totalitarian position of one-party rule it enjoyed in the days of Hylan and Walker. The 'grass roots' civic organizations which fronted the movement for repeal last summer were just a false face . . . they condemn PR as an importation from the Kremlin in order to reestablish something which is far dearer to the Kremlin than PR—one-party rule." Miley was perceptive; the tragedy of the Red Scare was the use of anti-Communism to destroy democratic forms. The difficulty was that he felt compelled to express this in the constrained anti-Red discourse of the day, thus undermining his central point.[90]

The split in elite opinion and the presence of Communists guaranteed a campaign with a desperate and urgent tone. The influential Judge Samuel Seabury passionately defended PR, which brought a vicious Red-baiting reply from Moses. Mayor O'Dwyer, perplexed, denied he was anti-PR but there was some doubt about this. The *New York World-Telegram* flip-flopped, attacking PR although they "supported" it originally. The *Times*, the quarterback of anti-PR forces, sought to link the debate in the council on the Marshall Plan with PR. The *Daily Worker* charged that the thousands of signatures placing the anti-PR referendum on the ballot were studded with forgeries. Given the tone, one would have thought that the fate of the nation was at stake—and in a sense it was.[91]

Which was the bigger danger—Tammany or the Communists? The answer to this determined the vote on PR for many people; Red supporters backed PR, while those opposed to it looked forward to the domination of the council by Tammany. The *People's Voice* of 19 April 1947 was explicit; repealing PR was designed "to keep Negroes out of City Council." After all, how did Davis get there? Others felt that district elections would mean the election of more blacks. One black GOP leader agreed with the *PV*. The *New York Amsterdam News* told its readers, "Left of center influence in

Harlem, for instance, is far stronger than the Tammany and Republican leaders have been telling their county chairmen and . . . it is safe to say that no candidate for public office can attract the cynical voters of this community without the active support of such well known political extremists as [Davis]." The elusive J. Ray Jones opposed PR, while the NAACP backed it.[92] This kind of division did not augur well for PR or Davis's future in the council.

Davis and the Reds fought this campaign as if it might be their last; in that respect they had the gift of prophecy. Davis dug deep into his rhetorical bag in charging that gutting PR would bring to the council "hacks and stumblebums subservient to the real estate interests, the bankers, the labor haters, the race baiters and the 10-cent fare profiteers." Anti-PR petitions "are shot through with . . . fraud and chicanery . . . no trick is too low for these unscrupulous manipulators . . . like a dog returning to his vomit the diehards keep manufacturing new but unoriginal campaigns against PR."[93]

Davis took to the airwaves with this message, appearing on WMCA-AM. The Harlem CP held more than forty meetings during the campaign on this one issue, under the leadership of Davis and Rose Gaulden. A testimonial for Davis at Irving Plaza turned into a PR rally. The kind words spoken about him apparently revved up Davis. He denounced the proliferating posters in the city with the slogan "Throw the Communists Out," calling them "a Nazi whoop for violence." Evidently the American Legion said they would go to "every poll to compel people to vote 'yes' on PR . . . hoodlums have attempted to provoke riots and break up pro-PR street meetings." He charged that their real targets were not just himself but Isaacs and Earle as well and that certain elites wanted to oust him because of his opposition on the Stuyvesant Town question. He engineered the production of literature that proclaimed, "Save PR to Keep Rent Control to Keep the [$.05] fare Keep Negro Representation in the City Council." Yet, with all that, PR was destroyed.[94]

Proportional representation lost 936,464 to 586,743 and in every county. Right after this loss, the Democrats made Davis a prophet by seeking to devastate welfare by limiting it to those living in the city for two or more years before 1 November 1947; Davis called this a "starvation move against the underprivileged and unemployed whose ranks are growing daily and especially against the Puerto Rican people."[95] A sign of the changing times was the joy a *New York Age* editorial showed at PR's passing " . . . we as Negroes must stop being so Negro and become a little more American." Those who see the Red Scare as unnecessary because of the small size of the Communist party overstate the case. The fact is that the Red Scare was aimed not just at Reds but at democracy and social progress generally. The fact is that the Left was growing in the country's financial capital and had to be stopped. The alliance between centrist and leftist blacks—a black united front yet to be rebuilt—was torn asunder. Davis told Essie Robeson after the referendum, "We got a terrific shellacking on PR, but there are other rounds coming." How right he was, but little did he realize that future rounds would be as torturous as those in 1947.[96]

The Red Scare—which meant a restriction of civil liberties—was gathering strength at the same time that civil rights concessions were under way. This contradiction can be partly explained by viewing the Red Scare as a tool to derail a leftist-influenced Black Liberation movement; this maneuver separated Left from center in the black community with civil rights concesssions designed to assuage those discomfited by the attack on former allies of the Left. The epicenter of this development was in New York City and the elected symbol for the black forces of the Left was Ben Davis.

11
Red Scare Coming, 1948

In many ways 1948 was not a very good year for Ben Davis. He was indicted. The loss of Cacchione and the failure to replace him with Si Gerson meant the weakening of the Left in the council; then Mike Quill, the combative transit union leader, began drifting from the leftist bloc. His good friend Claudia Jones was being harassed and threatened with deportation by the authorities. Worse, the overall atmosphere took on a decided chill as the Red Scare became more palpable. But all was not glum. Harlem, buoyed by a West Indian community with a culture and tradition unlike much of Afro-America, remained uniquely Davis's. As Adam Powell discovered in the 1960s, black voters in particular were not inclined to oust elected officials just because they were under attack from on high, nor were they inclined to accept what the bourgeois press said about Reds since what they said about blacks was also often misleading. New York City itself, with a large Jewish population whose progressive traditions were reinforced by anti-Semitism, remained a beacon of radicalism. The Italian-American population, led by Marcantonio, added to the progressive mix. Hope remained alive.

In July Davis set the tone by echoing a dominant view within the party at that time: "the two main issues before the American people in an overall sense are fascism at home and World War III. . . . While I would not call the Republicans and Democrats fascists, I would say there are many fascists within both parties and that both parties are heading toward fascism." Later this view was to be criticized sharply, inside and outside the party; however, it is not difficult to see why Davis would come to such a conclusion. Some have suggested that the repression was hitting only Reds and that raising the specter of fascism was misguided; this is true to an extent, although it ignores the increased repression of blacks and intimidation of liberals. Yet fascism did not arrive and Davis was wrong. However, Truman and the Democrats did turn sharply to the Right, thereby paving the way for McCarthyism.[1]

The arrests, jailings, deportations, and the shrill and hysterical political atmosphere made a deep impression on party leaders. The continued electoral success of the Left in New York City contradicted this trend and then yielded to Right-wing strength. This was noted at the time. An unsigned and undated letter to a high level government legal officer right after a late-1940s election—possibly from Fiorello La Guardia—signified what could be happening sub rosa: "There isn't anyone connected with the count, from what we can gather, who feels that the count is an honest one. Those individuals who are experienced in the game of what could be called thievery, have known how to cover up their tracks." The writer pointed specifically to one of Davis's main foes on the council: "It is curious to note that the 1's and 2's written in on large number of ballots in this section, appear to have the same characteristics. It would be interesting to have the opinion of a handwriting expert in these instances." He wailed about "this dirty business" and how it was necessary to "break up this gang." Presumably dirty tricks and electoral fraud were an obstacle for Davis and the party as well, a fact that must be considered in all post-1946 elections involving Davis. Forces larger than LaGuardia were in play, a juggernaut that could not be derailed.[2]

One problem with proportional representation was that the technology in New York, as it is now, was not appropriate for the vote count; moreover, the Tammany Tiger was a past master at fraud. As predicted, the defeat of PR also led to the council's loss of Genevieve Earle—socialite, feminist, and social worker. From the Brooklyn GOP, she was the first woman council member and the council minority leader since 1940. Stanley Isaacs, who tried hard to be fair during this period, regretted her departure: "Too bad that PR was thrown out of the window. As long as that method of election existed and those who believed in good government could act together without reference to the party leaders and party machines, you were certain of election in Brooklyn." The defeat of PR not only meant the demise of the Communist party on the council, it also meant the end of the GOP and probably the independent existence of the Liberal party. The result was a circling of the wagons and a consolidation of Democratic power that tended to foster corruption. This move toward absolute power was a partial reflection of the anti-Red Scare electoral threat.[3]

When the issue of Gerson replacing Cacchione was first bruited in 1947, the council turned a deaf ear; this attitude continued in 1948 but the struggle to overcome it became fierce and heated. Davis complained that there was no problem when Democrats sought to fill vacancies but now they wanted a "circus" because the CP was making a similar application. He was incensed at the behavior of most of his colleagues at one hearing in early 1948, which "left the threadbare arguments of the obstructionists as naked as a jay bird in whistling time." Yet Gerson was rejected 13–5; given the times, the ratio could have been worse, a fact that helps to account for the tension of the moment. The *Daily Worker* reported, "Before the final vote was taken the Council heard one of the most bitter exchanges in its record. Led by Davis the progressive minority members . . . tore into the majority report with such vehemence and polemic that it was a weary, deflated majority at the finish." A process of differentiation accelerated as the hearing "split the

Liberal Party Councilmen." Ira Palestin voted with Davis, as did Quill, Connolly, and Isaacs; the Right charged that since the party did not get fifty thousand gubernatorial votes and ballot status, it did not merit representation in the council. The result was ambivalent, however, as Gerson was not accepted or voted down, just left in procedural limbo—but he was not on the council. The Americans for Democratic Action waffled as usual, supporting Gerson but adding the protective cover that they were "vigorously opposed to Communism." Davis was indignant throughout; he charged that the hearing minutes were "doctored." His resolution on Gerson was rejected a few days later, 14–4 with one abstention; he lost Palestin and Republican Ed Rager abstained.[4]

Davis took the defeat to the streets. At a rally of two hundred people in Brooklyn he claimed, "I am proud to fight as a Negro so that a son of the Jewish people shall take his place in the Council." The events in Palestine were not just influencing the party on the National Question. In fact, Davis's electoral victories could be seen as evidence of a black-Jewish alliance. Unbowed, he introduced yet another Gerson resolution in the council. He demanded that O'Dwyer act, terming the blocking of Gerson a "city-wide scandal." It was decided that the fate of the seat would be settled at the November election. Davis signaled the importance of the election by becoming Gerson's campaign manager. But a leading indicator was Isaacs' decision to back away from his old friend and chief aide. Caution was the better part of valor.[5]

The debate in September 1948 came after Davis's indictment, after the ouster of Du Bois from the NAACP, and after the February 1948 events in Czechoslovakia. This may help explain why council member Walter Hart, who had been "harassing, intimidating and threatening witnesses" at an earlier hearing, called Davis a traitor when the Gerson issue arose again. Davis had had enough of his bullying and retorted hotly, "You're a dirty liar! I demand that you withdraw the statement." Hart was rigid: "I can state categorically that any member of the Communist party is a traitor." Davis did not back down: "I'll paste you in the face if you come over here." Two police officers stepped between them as Hart moved toward his adversary. Class struggle in New York was quickening. The *Daily Worker* called it "one of the most stormy sessions in [the council's] history" and they were right. Gerson was defeated again, this time 14–6, as Connolly, Quill, Palestin, Earle, and Isaacs joined Davis.[6]

The increased support for Gerson could have given Davis and the party false optimism; despite the skyrocketing repression, more had voted for Gerson this time than before. But whatever hope existed was rapidly dashed, for despite getting a whopping 150,369 votes in November, Gerson lost the election. "Had there been PR Gerson would have been elected twice over," Davis conceded with sadness.[7]

The tension took its toll on relationships. Davis and Quill had a "heated exchange of remarks" in a debate on transit on the council floor just after the Irish-American leader had resigned from the ALP and CIO over the Communism issue. Davis was not impressed with his excuses. "Mike is without a party," he gibed: "His own party repudiated him. He's a traitor to the working class and to the progressive movement in this country when he supports a higher subway fare. I say to Mayor O'Dwyer and to the Democratic party, you can have him, we don't [want] him." His Irish brogue sharpening, Quill replied, "I know this screwball and all the others who speak for the Communist party. They don't represent anybody." This exchange occurred in May; in September Quill stood with Davis on the Gerson vote. Was it necessary for Davis to be so sharp with a vacillating ally? An analysis by Davis and the party arguing that fascism loomed played a role in such stinging rebuttals. Nevertheless, if fascism was coming, should not Davis have been more conciliatory with potential allies?[8]

The Gerson fight was not the only tempestuous episode that gripped the council. The Red Scare meant that at least an increase in the military budget would be needed to fight Moscow and its real and assumed allies, along with an increase in the repression budget to fight real and assumed domestic Reds. Social welfare spending was tightened, homeless veterans did not go away, and voices in the council rose accordingly. Davis accused Vincent Impellitteri of violating "legislative courtesy" by refusing to give Davis time to speak at a hearing on the quickly disappearing five-cent transit fare; he had waited all day to speak. Days later the fare was hiked to ten cents over Davis's insistence that a referendum first be held, an event that led to an early confrontation with Quill. Hart had called Davis a "traitor" to the country, and in turn Davis called Quill a "traitor to the people, a betrayer of labor." Both statements contained yeast.[9]

Davis also took on O'Dwyer, denouncing his "arrogant and insulting" procedure on the higher fare. The Red Scare was hastened in New York in part because it was a convenient tool to curb the incremental dissent generated by the Cold War and its devastation of social welfare spending. Seeing this link, Davis pressed hard for everything from cheaper transit fares to cleaner streets. His patience was tested when the council voted 14–5 (Davis, Isaacs, Connolly, Palestin, and Goldberg opposing) to ask the Triboro Bridge and Tunnel Authority (in other words, his old foe Robert Moses) to build a new Madison Square Garden two-thousand-car parking garage near Columbus Circle with a $25 million bond issue. "Sharp debate" ensued, with Davis and Isaacs in the lead; Davis accused MSG of racism for not bringing in black basketball. The Garden also refused a rental for a Lenin memorial meeting. Ed Rager rose to twist this somehow into an attack on Henry Wallace, a former vice-president under FDR : " . . . I call Wallace a Communist; you're a Communist. If Davis and his crowd get into power, I and my crowd would be liquidated mercilessly, without a chance to speak at the Garden or anywhere else. And don't let Davis get away with this talk of racial discrimination. He creates more of it than anyone else." One can easily dismiss his comments on race but some analysts today in Moscow might credit his former remarks on liquidation by suggesting that Stalinist repression gave a filip to the Red Scare. Certainly the Red Scare of the post–World War I period, well before Stalin, might have been enough to convince people that the U.S. ruling class did not require that kind of justification or impetus; yet, even if U.S. Communists had distanced themselves from the USSR as other progressives did, domestic considerations still would have necessitated a Red Scare.[10]

The debate on the budget was agitated. Davis insisted that "the most glaring and significant deficiency of the budget is its failure to provide wage increases to city employees." He opposed more police, seeing them as the quintessential Praetorian Guard for repression. Central Harlem had the highest death rate from tuberculosis of any of the city's health districts; Davis called for summer vacations for children, more housing inspectors, and the training of tenants to inspect houses on a block-by-block basis. He voted stridently against the finance committee report, charging that the budget was a "[ten-cent] fare budget" and contending that it benefited real-estate interests and high-income groups and questioning the legality of the entire process. His torrid minority report wondered why more was to be spent on piers than on health and welfare. The answer? "They had in mind war preparations" and the interests of big business, Davis said. He wanted the fare hike to be rescinded, tax exemptions for small homeowners, and higher taxes on big real-estate interests. But only Connolly voted for his report.[11]

Davis continued to flay the city "war budget." He wanted more aid for Harlem, including a public market, schools, and housing. The limited power of the council particularly galled him; they could delete or reduce items but had no power to add or increase. The U.S. Supreme Court in 1989 finally agreed with his estimate of the ungainly powers of the Board of Estimate but at this point Davis's view was seen as iconoclastic at best. A clear signal was Impellitteri's "heartfelt congratulations on the glorious victory you have achieved over the destructive forces of Communism" to a visiting foreign dignitary. How could one fight Reds abroad and ignore the same *bête noire* at home?[12]

Inevitably race was not far from Davis's main concerns in the council. The council was among those seeking to conciliate blacks in order to wrest them from the Left, so when Davis introduced his traditional Negro History Week resolution, they sought to support it but only with Davis's fingerprints removed from it; his connection would at once give him the credit that they sought to deny and provide ammunition for the guilt-by-association theorists. Hugh Quinn of the council wanted Davis to withdraw his resolution in favor of another "so that the whole Council can be credited." Davis cheerfully conceded, "I'd be happy to have the whole Council sponsor it." Would it have been sectarian to act otherwise? But when Davis introduced a resolution urging the council to call on the U.S. Senate to act on antipoll tax, antilynch, and FEPC legislation, it was denied immediate consideration. To this point the Dixiecrats were too powerful and the NAACP-style strategy of moving away from the Left was not causing their resistance to crumble.[13]

Whatever relationship Davis had with Mayor O'Dwyer briskly dissolved under the strain of the Red Scare. He castigated the mayor for seeking a higher fare bill in Albany without a home rule message from the council; this was "illegal, undemocratic and in flagrant violation of the State Constitution." Then the mayor did not vigorously object when the council voted 15–3 to restrict sound trucks on city streets. Davis called it a "$5 poll tax on free speech. It was brought just to get around the Supreme Court decision in the Lockport case." Quill and Connolly joined his protest against a measure that was aimed ostensibly at a favorite Red tactic but in effect would handcuff all who sought to protest—a defining characteristic of the Red Scare. That was not enough for the mayor, who then issued an edict barring petitioners from City Hall on the premise that they were nothing but a bunch of Reds anyway. Davis was outraged, calling this "completely illegal and insulting to the elected members of the city government . . . unlawful, unwarranted, undemocratic." It applied immediately to former O'Dwyer aide Paul Ross, who had joined with Davis's allies on a particular issue. Davis saw instantly that it was "actually a smokescreen for barring any and all workers who seek to petition City Hall against the high cost of living, for better housing." But the Red Scare proved effective in squelching such dissent.[14]

But at least in the first half of 1948, it was proving difficult to gag Davis. Over his objection the council voted 13–4 to back a state bill barring use of public buildings to groups "advocating force and violence." Everyone knew who this was aimed at. Still, it should not be forgotten that this bill was linked with a slashing of social welfare programs; at one point Davis demanded that city officials resist the "red-baiting, anti-relief policy of the *World Telegram*." His voice was not heeded, nor was the council pleased when six hundred City College of New York students complained about its denunciation of Davis after he pushed for an investigation of Council member Hugh Quinn, who had alleged that students were involved in arson in a politically charged case. Davis was rebuked when the council voted to censure him for his action, and adding insult to injury, some of his colleagues heckled him about his ties to the USSR.[15]

This was the temper of the times. The November presidential election would be pivotal, so Davis utilized every opportunity to speak out. Touching a major contradiction of the epoch, he chided Truman for his soft line on lynchers while on Moscow "his militancy soars to white heat." He appealed to progressives, questioning their "gross illusions" about the Missourian; Davis considered Truman "unscrupulously and aggressively demagogic." After the Truman Democrats and the GOP ditched antipoll tax and

FEPC bills, Davis was wrathful: "while the Rome of Negro rights burns, Nero Truman is fiddling around, making profound speeches to the effect that 'dogs are essential to the country.'" He "has plenty of time to waste on the Marshall Plan, the UMT and the draft," but pleads lack of time on civil rights. The hammer of the Red Scare intimidated many blacks from speaking similarly, although they would have been found in Davis's corner a few years earlier.[16]

Davis was undeterred. He berated Truman's "revoltingly cheap and vulgar demagogy" on civil rights and called his erstwhile ally, Walter White, one of his "most pathetic apologists. . . . Truman talks like Abraham Lincoln and acts like Hitler. . . . Under capitalism the situation in our country is upside down. The officials who are doing the jailing, should be in jail." Davis was infuriated that for the "first time in our modern elections an open persecutor of the Negro people has been touted as their friend." Unfortunately for Davis, the Truman administration was paying attention. Guy Turner sent an article on one of Davis's tirades to the Oval Office with the ominous note attached, "In view of what happened at Prague why do we have to put up with such stuff as this. . . . Is this your idea of civil rights?" Turner did not have to wait long to get an answer.[17]

Davis's disdain for the president was coupled with a heightened appreciation for Henry Wallace, who was becoming increasingly estranged from the Democrats. In January Davis called Wallace's candidacy a "political bombshell." However, he realized that victory would not come easily since it was "indispensably important that Negroes be integrated into all levels of the Wallace movement—including the very top." Davis scorned Walter White's opinion that voting for Wallace was a waste: when thousands greeted the Iowan at a rally in Harlem in February, Davis was on the speaker's stand and watched as Joe Louis contributed funds to the campaign. The steady protestations of Davis et al. seemed to be reaching centrists, particularly after the stunning victory of progressive Leo Isaacson in a key Bronx congressional race. A *New York Age* editorial on 28 February 1948 was symptomatic: "We repeat this is NOT an editorial advocating the election of Henry Wallace or backing the third party movement. However, we cannot but feel that the anti-jim crow pronouncements of Henry Wallace as subscribed to by his Congressional seat-seeking protege had a [good] deal to do with the . . . victory." The *Age* was sufficiently perspicacious to see the real deal: "There are those who affirm that the only reason that Harry Truman went to Congress with a whale of a civil rights program proposal was because he feared Wallace would cut heavily into the 'balance of power Negro vote.'"

Wallace tempted the shrewd black vote but a people not yet a hundred years from slavery decided not to travel the entire course. For Communists like Davis, who knew many of the leaders and had collaborated recently with them, it was difficult to accept their opportunism, temporizing, and timidity. So he did not keep quiet about their affair with Truman; his view of White was also applied to Gordon Hancock, whom he called a "Negro misleader."

But the main tenor of his words was devoted to the presidential candidates: "It's like asking you which do you prefer—tuberculosis Truman or cancer Dewey. We don't want either. We want to be healthy and alive."[19]

Instinctively Davis did not exclude the GOP from his verbal asaults. Dewey was a frequent target but Senator Robert Taft was not exempt, either. Harold Stassen's new book, *Where I Stand*, was dismissed peremptorily as a "slightly jazzed-up version of Wall Street's program. . . . It should be 'Where I Kneel' because the man is on bended knee serving the lords of dollar imperialism." Davis's verbal wizardry did not prevent Wallace from going down to defeat in November. Some of the same voters who were sufficiently adventurous to vote for Davis for City Council were not willing to take the next step and vote for Wallace for president.[20]

While scoring his foes, Davis was busily seeking to help his friends, particularly those in the labor movement. He rushed to Paterson to address May Day participants. When Emil Rieve and leaders of the Textile Workers Union removed Communists from high posts, Davis spoke out, connecting it to the refusal to pass or even discuss routine, pro-FEPC resolutions at their convention. Rieve was allegedly reluctant since some of the southern delegates might have gotten upset. The Red Scare created an antiprogressive atmosphere that made the Right wing a chief beneficiary. Davis termed the pivotal CIO convention in Portland "a horrible nightmare . . . one could have thought that the CIO was a reincarnation of Hitler's Nazi Party rallies in the sportpalast of the Third Reich." Though the CIO convention was certainly disappointing, it is questionable if Davis's rhetorical overkill was helpful in reassuring vacillating allies.

This spirit reached the council. Over Davis's vigorous objection they voted to give city employees a day off with pay for a "loyalty day" anti-Communist parade on May Day. As ever, his words were backed with action. He fought to have fifty three city workers reinstated who had been fired with the assault on social welfare programs.[21]

The fluctuation of his supporters and the turncoat posture of others were not easy for Davis and the party to accept; they could see that the anti-Red attack would not only send them to jail but would also curb anyone who was not conservative. Whatever the case, despite their perception about the growth of fascism, they did not hesistate to engage in sharp and public polemics with others of ostensibly similar outlook. The pressure was intense, as evidenced by the mass resignations from the American Labor Party. Yet Davis called *PM*, a journal close to that party, an organ of "petty bourgeois radicalism." His criticism was true to an extent but it was not an exemplar of sound tactics.[22]

The maneuvering over the Wallace candidacy heightened these tendencies. Davis was quick to call the fight against the draft of Powell, Marcantonio, and Glen Taylor "the most magnificent struggle in Congress in modern times against the barbarous Jim Crow system in the armed force.... The irrepressible, resourceful and courageous Marcantonio bids fair to become one of the greatest legislators in all American history." But Powell was singled out for reproach because of "serious disappointments." If he "is to achieve his maximum potentialities of political independence . . . he should abandon all hesitations and doubts and resolutely identify with the Wallace-Taylor movement." Of course he was harsher toward his old foe, Randolph, who had pressured Powell for allegedly "following the Communist Party line . . . [while] the only fighting against army Jim Crow these . . . ripsnorters have engaged in has been in the newspapers." Powell remained reluctant to align with the new party; the tactical question was whether Davis response to him could have been less harsh.[23]

The continued clashing between Davis and Randolph was one of the more troubling aspects of this period; that the top black Communist and top black labor leader were continually at each other's throats did not bode well for halting the rise of the Right. The 1948 version of their dispute was over the Jim Crow U.S. Army. Davis began by scolding the White House for not issuing a simple executive order. But he was not impressed with Randolph's plan to launch civil disobedience unless desegregation commenced. Randolph, said Davis, felt "We Negroes don't care what you do with us after you get us in the army. Send us to murder Greek democrats, or to shoot down the Indonesians . . . but let us do it on an equality basis."[24] A number of progressives felt that Davis's view was overly narrow.

Davis pressed on, charging that the plan of civil disobedience spreads "division, confusion and defeatism . . . tactic of weakness and futility," and he complained that "labor and white progressives have not identified themselves with the Negro's indignation sufficiently." But the labor boss was his main target:

> Like Slick Reynolds, Mr. Randolph occasionally rises from the dead long enough to grab a headline and then goes back to sleep. He called constantly for marches on Washington that he never made or lead. In fact none of us in New York were ever able to get him to march to City Hall against jim-crow and that is only a few blocks from his office. As far as disobedience is concerned Mr. Randolph might set an example by showing that he has guts enough to disobey the jim-crowers in New York or to disobey the professional disrupter, David Dubinsky, Mr. Randolph's boss.

There was much truth in Davis's remarks but the question was not veracity but tactical soundness. Foul charge and countercharge escalated when Frank Crosswaith replied, " . . . when you are filled with waste matter, keep your mouth shut."[25]

Culpability was not all one-sided. Randolph steadfastly balked at working with the Reds on his army plans: "Of course we don't want the Communists to cooperate with us in any way, because they are a kiss of death." Davis also found it curious that the bourgeois press continued to praise Randolph despite his call for civil disobedience because he was such a firm advocate of the Marshall Plan; evidently these forces realized that Jim Crow in the army had to go and saw Randolph as a useful goad in the process. In any case, almost on signal, Randolph began to back away from his ambitious plan, similar to the way he abandoned the March on Washington years earlier; it was left to Martin Luther King—not as anti-Communist as Randolph—to implement these plans. Davis rapped Randolph as a "sheep in wolf's clothing . . . a pathological red-baiter, Soviet baiter and Wall Street bootlicker . . . constantly starting out like a lion and ending like a lamb." This was a "betrayal," Davis remarked. In any event, one result was the erosion of Randolph's mass base: "all of them put together would not fill a telephone booth."[26]

As evidenced by the above, Frank Crosswaith often substituted for Randolph in attacking Davis. As the decade wore on, his hard-nosed anti-Communism and Social Democrat ties brought him a high-level municipal post and close contacts with George Meany, William Green, Hubert Humphrey, Truman, Mary McLeod Bethune, and Norman Thomas. Their socialist pretensions were not braked since Randolph continued to address him as "Dear Comrade" and advised him paternalistically that "there are only a few Negro leaders who know enough about Communists to be able to fight them effectively." Crosswaith must have fit that category since he was chosen to broadcast over Voice of America to counter the rapidly growing notion that blacks were subjected to an atrocious racism. Crosswaith's role as designated hitman alienated Dr. C. B. Powell, no friend of Davis and publisher of the *New York Amsterdam News*, who reprimanded the labor leader for his intemperate remarks about the council member: "in all future cases you keep your letters on a higher level, as the words of this letter should never have been printed . . . there is no justification for criticism of a City Councilman in such language as exhibited in your letters."[27]

Crosswaith was enraged, terming Powell's demarche "part of an effort to appease Mr. Davis and his associates . . . [these] 'modern carpetbaggers'"; he could not understand "your alarming defense of Mr. Davis." Powell would not be swayed: "Whether I need Mr. Davis or whether I fear him is not an issue." Crosswaith commiserated with other recipients of Davis's sharp pen and tongue, telling Walter White, "to say that I envy you for being the recipient of an attack by 'Councilman' Ben Davis in yesterday's 'Sunday Worker.' Anyone fortunate enough to be spoken of in such a manner as he spoke of you, should feel proud. Did you read my letter on the 'Councilman' in the current issue of the Amsterdam News?" Yet Crosswaith's anti-Communism only served to obscure his own swing to the Right. A few years later Bruce Wright was demanding his removal from the city Housing Commission due to his naming a housing project for Stephen Foster; unaffected, Crosswaith vigorously defended the racist composer. All this was souring Davis.[28]

Davis was increasingly distressed with the drift of black and allied leadership as important civil rights bills came before Congress. He instructed black leaders especially to "get wise . . . and quit permitting themselves to be used as bait . . . [and] suckers. . . . [they] don't seem to learn or to care as long as their palms are greased, or their vanities twitted." He singled out J. Ray Jones but Walter White was rarely far from his jabs. Davis was annoyed with White's idea of the Democrats as a "lesser evil. . . . One might as well argue that because Hitler denounced Chamberlain, anti-fascist humanity should have supported Chamberlain's appeasement policies." Presumably White would have responded, "Precisely."[29]

It must be remembered that Davis's positions on these questions were primarily party positions and not just his alone. The idea of rising fascism was an aspect of this outlook. Since it was recognized that racism pushed blacks more to the Left, attacks on Randolph, White, and others could force their supporters to make them shape up or these civil rights leaders would run the risk of isolation. This was reflected in an influential book on the black vote, published in 1948, by Henry Lee Moon, NAACP publicist, who concluded, "Many of the Negro intellectuals and writers have at one time or another been influenced by Communist philosophy." Among blacks, "Communism is not regarded as the enemy. . . . [Davis was] elected neither because nor in spite of his . . . membership." Indeed, Davis was so popular that Tammany made a huge mistake by not backing him in 1945: "the smart thing would have been to work quietly for Davis without any endorsement."[30]

Other than the weakening center forces such as the NAACP, there were other disturbing ideological trends contributing to an explosive mix. There were the "white-baiters" like James Lawson who had done much to harm the alliance between Powell and Davis. Party leader Herbert Wheeldin found these people maddening: "James Lawson and his underworld followers . . . a special breed of rat . . . paid stooges. . . . They call themselves 'nationalists' . . . attempts to break up meeting . . . shouting obscene slogans against women and against Jews. . . . Rumor has it that J. Raymond Jones . . . has inspired Lawson . . . to disrupt all meetings of Ben Davis . . . because they fear the wide support which the Negro people are giving Ben and his program." Such unprincipled tactics were a precursor of 1960s behavior and made it difficult for the Reds to be models of objectivity.

Then the United Auto Workers scored Communist efforts to get blacks elected to the Executive Board of the union as "a Jim Crow proposition, just as much so as if it were a segregated room in a hotel, a seat on a train." Misguided thinking on the National Question was far from being a Communist monopoly, which illustrates that Red weaknesses are difficult to separate from an overall underdeveloped U.S. political culture.[31]

The party had its own problems, however. Though it had detected a whiff of fascism, the Communists not only blistered certain black leaders but chose this time to launch a highly visible campaign against white chauvinism within the party itself. In all fairness one should say that this campaign was utterly understandable. In the most racist nation this side of South Africa it was crucially important for the proclaimed vanguard of the working class to countenance not a hint of racism; the problem was, as the party sheepishly admitted later, that the campaign was much too internal and tended to charge the converted with blasphemy. Nonetheless, Henry Winston put his finger on a real problem. There was a "lag in registration of our Negro members in both shop and community clubs." What was at the root of this problem? Increased government repression? Winston focused on the "existence of white chauvinism . . . certain petty bourgeois contempt on the part of many cadres toward inarticulate Negro workers within the ranks of the Party organization."[32]

Unfortunately Winston had not made up a fairy tale. When the *Daily Worker* highlighted the fact that Leo Durocher, the Brooklyn Dodgers manager, had hit a black fan, a number of readers wrote to defend him, saying they wanted to hear both sides. Fred Blair, Wisconsin party leader, noted that a party club in Racine had to expel two Italo-Americans and one Bulgarian-American: "They were in business and refused to serve Negroes, claiming it would 'hurt their trade.'" Another Serbian-American comrade had threated to go to the police if his daughter's "friendship" with a black youth did not end. He was expelled. The response to a Davis column on restrictive covenants perhaps lacked sensitivity, though Davis earlier had to apologize for inadvertently implying that white attorneys played no other role than cheating and robbing. As the pressure intensified, things seemed to be becoming more confused.[33]

So the struggle against white chauvinism was launched. Isidore Begun, chair of the Bronx party, and two other leaders were removed for a while for failing "to struggle against white chauvinism and for Negro rights . . . [this] should serve as warning to our entire Party against complacency or smugness." It was charged that blacks had been removed from party posts, had been personally attacked, and were isolated; consequently, the struggle for civil rights had been reduced. The whirlwind caught up Fred Blair; he was temporarily suspended from his post because of weaknesses in "the struggle for Negro rights . . . Blair has fully recognized his weakness."[34]

The party saw the problem as "lack of knowledge of Negro life [and] history . . . failure to have Negro friends altogether . . . as at dances where white men, white women and Negro men dance but Negro women are neglected. . . . The Party member's personal life cannot be divorced from his or her political life." The "personal is political" slogan did not arise in the 1960s without roots. That is the point, for the Red Scare forced a later generation to reinvent issues without realizing that these same problems had been addressed previously. New York party leader George Blake was forthright: "white chauvinism is widespread in our Party and . . . its most deep-seated and stubborn manifestations have existed and continue to exist in the trade union sector of our Party . . . what is demanded is a more all-embracing, systematic and uncompromising struggle against white chauvinism. . . . The main danger is [not] that we have been too sharp and too critical, but that we are still too tolerant, too passive, too neglectful." The CP was obviously miles ahead of other U.S. institutions in fighting racism, particularly the internal variety. Certainly there has been a tendency in this country to avoid discussion of "white chauvinism," and again one has to ask how this atmosphere affected the party. Though it may have been overly zealous in this regard, the party's approach could only impress blacks, who were more accustomed to zeal in avoiding this fight. Yet this internal approach did chase away real and potential allies at a time when a philosophy stressing encroaching fascism should have meant attempting to attract such allies.[35]

Though Davis was warning of the growth of "American national chauvinism, with white supremacy playing a leading role," a party meeting in Harlem in March 1948 was "distinguished by its interracial character." The party was still growing. One thousand people attended a CP-held meeting at 116th Street and Lenox Avenue on the question of police brutality, and the party planned to hold a meeting every night in the street. A three-day convention of the party in July 1948 in Manhattan called for expanding the ranks from ten to thirteen thousand by Labor Day; this preceded the National Convention in August. By the end of the summer Davis and other party leaders were under indictment. Ever the historical optimist, Davis tried to put a positive spin on this disaster—"Never in the history of the Communist Party have we received such free and unlimited publicity"—but another victory like this and the party would be undone.[36]

Concomitant with the party's new thinking on race, Davis began to refine his own views: "There are, in reality, in our country two American nations—the Negro people . . . and the dominant white—or so-called Anglo-Saxon nation. . . . The Negro people are themselves moving toward recognition of their own views." He saw the erosion of the Black Belt thesis as marked by an increased stress on northern blacks as a national minority, and he also stressed the multiclass nature of Black Liberation: "Even the Negro upper classman who is not exploited as a worker, is nevertheless a second-class citizen as a Negro. . . . [U.S.] holds the entire Negro people in inferior status, irrespective of their class." This February 1948 newspaper article was the first time he had addressed the National Question formally in some time, which indicates the increased ferment on the issue. He also initiated a dialogue with the noted African-American social scientist Oliver Cox on this question, which brought a criticism of Cox from anthropologist Ruth Benedict.[37]

Then in September 1948 he summed up his thought on the matter in *Polit-*

ical Affairs. In it, he stressed that "our party has long enjoyed wide respect and admiration among the Negro people." But he regretted that there was an "inadequate grasp among large numbers of white cadre" of the Black Belt thesis and that this theory was "far too sparingly used in this field of work on the part of the national leadership, in particular on the part of the Negro Commission." He concluded with a flourish, lambasting opponents of the thesis—"these rotten elements, such as the Francis Franklins and other insects"—and concurring with the new party thrust to raise the "struggle against white chauvinism to the . . . necessary . . . fighting level." This fight, he said, was "being badly neglected," which was a reason for the "high fluctuation of Negro membership."[38]

There were changes taking place on this front. Davis was charging that the city was discriminating against the *Daily Worker*, *Morning Freiheit*, and local black papers by not designating them to carry advertising for pawnbrokers' public auctions. Interestingly a few months later the *New York Age* had taken on a more attractive format, a higher price, and a new motto ("In All Things, We Stand Together as Americans"); this, said the paper, reflected "changes in plant, changes in personnel, a change in ownership." Suddenly Schenley, the liquor monopoly with connections to high-level FBI officials, began taking out double full-page ads weekly. For a while the *Age*'s views did not change, as a November column continued the previous line, but soon their political philosophy agreed with dominant opinion.[39]

Davis persevered. In June he issued a clarion call for mass lobbying in Washington for civil rights; the response was heartening. Evidently Washington was aware of the potential for this kind of pressure, which is why integration was hastened. Davis was certainly aware of this and did not join "the worse the better" school. For example, he hailed the selection of Levi Jackson as Yale football captain as well as the ongoing struggle to garner the right to vote. But the administration had to implement integration while avoiding the taint of Communism, as happened when their Dixiecrat brethren called an "anti-poll tax" measure a "communist proposal." Pummeling the Reds into submission was one way out.[40]

Since those who ruled the United States were not willing to go all the way, the country had to wait for the King-led push of the mid-fifties. In the meantime Davis flayed as "a disgrace" the court decision upholding the Stuyvesant Town rental, though "62 per cent of the tenants polled [were] on record" against that form of discrimination. He wondered how the life sentence of Ilse Koch, a Nazi torturer, could be commuted while lynchers—"inheritors of the policies of the Third Reich"—could go free.

While the issues were swirling around, Davis was attending to business, inviting parents and children to a Christmas party at Golden Gate with "refreshments, movies, puppets and a magician show." Even though this event occurred after his indictment, Jackie Robinson and Roy Campanella showed up.[41]

Soon thereafter, however, Robinson was denouncing the Communists in Washington and Campanella would not be seen in the same room as Davis. Not unrelated was a report in the *New York Amsterdam News*: "for more than two years, a Negro special agent for the House Committee has combed Harlem and other sections of New York where Negroes live in large numbers seeking information concerning operations of the Communist underground. This special agent talked with scores of people." Then the authorities moved against Davis's closest comrade in the party, Claudia Jones; they detained and sought to deport her. After her arrest, she immediately called Davis but the arresting officers refused to wait until he could come before carting her away. A horrified Davis, with Jones at his side, held a press conference and denounced the move as "an underhanded trick to divide West Indian and American Negroes . . . clearly an attempt to intimidate the powerful Negro sentiment behind the presidential candidacy of Henry Wallace."[42]

Furious at the immigration authorities for placing their "clammy and cowardly hands" on "one of the brightest flowers of Negro American womanhood," Davis predicted that this act would signal an onslaught against the Caribbean population of New York. As usual, this was not an isolated event. Jesus Menendez, a Communist, Federation of Sugar Workers leader, and member of the Cuban House, was murdered; Gerhart Eisler, John Williamson, and Ferdinand Smith were all detained on Ellis Island and denied bail. Davis warned, "Today the victims are foreign-born leaders. Tomorrow the native-born will be snatched up." While carrying out all of his other duties, Davis felt compelled to take up this new burning question.[43]

These proposed deportations were just the beginning; the idea that socialism was being introduced by the foreign-born was the subtext of Washington's offensive, then they moved to intimidate the fellow travelers and Red allies. Prominent in that category was the Reverend Thomas Harten of Brooklyn, president of the Afro-Protective League, vice-president of the National Baptist Convention, first vice-president of the New York Baptist Convention, and one of Davis's earliest supporters when he first ran for office. Just as the indictment of the Communist leaders was emerging, he was charged with rape; charges were dropped eventually but the time and expense sent an undeniable signal to allies of the Left. More direct was the murder of Willie Milton, black Communist and tenant leader, at the hands of a Brooklyn police officer. Davis recalled that he had "just led a successful rent strike of tenants against greedy landlords." In demanding that O'Dwyer investigate, Davis raised a familiar specter, that "unprosecuted gangsterism . . . is turning the streets of New York into a Nazi Germany against striking workers, minority groups and civil liberties." Did such outrages justify Davis's view that fascism lurked around the corner, not to mention his often intemperate language?[44]

One government investigator concluded that "the Negro population of the United States is communistically inclined." This attitude meant that Reds were persecuted and black Reds were virtually flagellated. So when Davis traveled to Washington to testify about the Cole bill, which would restrict ballot access for parties allegedly advocating force and violence, he found the elements for a major flare-up. Davis charged that the two major parties "by hook or crook [plan] to prevent any new political party that challenges their bi-partisan rule." Davis's appearance was before the House Administration Election Subcommittee and "committee members were on the defensive," according to the *Daily Worker*. The unchastened Davis informed Republican Omar Burleson (Democrat-Texas), "I doubt very much that you are legally a member of Congress . . . as for force and violence, why not let Mr. Burleson try to justify the force and violence used against Negroes in Texas and other states of the South." " 'I am asking,' began Burleson. 'And what about lynching?' demanded Davis . . . 'We might as well abandon this line of questioning,' said Burleson and subsided." Why did Davis and the party tend to agree with Moscow so frequently, he was asked. " 'Marxism-Leninism is a science and its principles are applicable everywhere . . . H_2O is water in Moscow and H_2O is water in America. . . . In the Soviet Union there is no race discrimination or anti-Semitism. . . . If you want to talk about a lack of free elections . . . ' Davis laughed scornfully . . . 'let's talk about the poll tax states. There hasn't been a free election in the South since reconstruction.' "[45]

The committee was coming to realize that they were faced with a formidable opponent, so they switched tactics and asked him if he would support the bill if it were aimed at fascists. He replied, "I wouldn't support this bill even if you stood [it] on its head . . . as for substituting the word 'fascist' you know very well that Congress as it is now constituted would not be deterred by that. . . . This bill will only be used to bring the nation closer to the police state." This bravura performance was guaranteed to win Davis plaudits among blacks nationally, but the authorities were thoroughly displeased.[46]

The House Un-American Activities Committee wanted William Z. Foster to testify; the party balked and offered Davis. HUAC, aware of Davis's boisterous appearances, tried to get dirt on Davis from the FBI (who were eager to aid Richard Nixon) "as an ace in the hole as more than likely Davis when he does appear will follow the usual insulting tactics other members of the party have used . . . and they would like to have something to throw at him." At the hearing Davis vigorously denied that the party advocated the use of force and violence and insisted that they would not register as foreign agents: "We will not make a mockery of the secret ballot by publishing the names of our members. We will not wear the yellow badge of shame the American disciples of Hitler seek to place upon us." According to the *Daily*

Worker, when Davis finished, "contrary to their custom" no questions were asked. "The hearing room was packed." Speculation had it that Nixon and his colleagues were afraid to tangle with the Communist leader.[47]

HUAC's revenge was not long in coming. In mid-July 1948 Davis was at home working on a *Daily Worker* column when six FBI agents came to arrest him, on the grounds of violating the Smith Act. The time had come to put the finishing touches on the liquidation of the Left, to reduce its influence for a generation, to pave the way for a rightist upsurge to fight the Cold War and redistribute the wealth from bottom to top. Interestingly, at the arraignment many people mistook Davis for Robeson. Davis chose to stress his council record and his ethnicity in remarks to the press. When asked if the council would remove him if he were found guilty, Councilman Joseph Sharkey contradicted the view he took a year later: "Why that's silly. The people have spoken. They elected him as a Communist." Taking an apparent dig at Connolly he added, "He was honest and ran for Council as a communist—unlike some other members." Ed Rager commented, "I do not like to see him indicted. . . . Although I disagree with him, he has a right to his views." Quill called the arrest a "serious mistake" since the party consisted of only "harmless crackpots." Palestin straddled the fence.[48]

Many considered the arrest to be linked to the Progressive party convention taking place in Philadelphia and the upcoming CP convention. Stanley Isaacs sensed a frame-up and offered his assistance. Davis had not lost his talent for rhetorical embellishment in his reply: "The charges against me and my co-defendants are fantastic. In fact they are of a dime novel character." Davis also suggested tactics that the council could pursue in his defense, particularly the perceived treatment of him as a recidivist criminal. Isaacs commented, "I think you should raise the issue . . . under a plea of high personal privilege. . . . If you do, I will be glad to speak in protest."[49]

The arrest of Davis on charges of violating the Smith Act did not quash his militance: "They took my Communist Party card—my proudest possession." He continued to insist that the arrests were "examples of the way Negroes are losing their civil rights." At a press conference at his Harlem office with Patterson and Jones present he was asked if he took orders from Moscow: "[I] take orders from the membership of our party and I as a Councilman take my orders from the people who elected me." Thousands of Harlemites protested the arrests at a mass rally at 126th Street and Lenox Avenue at which Davis said, "Truman framed me, Dewey said amen, and Wallace defended me. Who do you think I'm going to vote for. . . . I'm going to be a Negro. . . . I'm going to be a Communist . . . and I'm going to fight for peace, democracy and for my people until the day I die."[50]

Dan Burley in the *New York Amsterdam News* rapped the arrest and reflected the opinion of many Harlemites: " . . . a lot of people resented seeing his picture in all the papers with a number under it like a common convict. All the man did folks say is to speak his mind and if they won't let you do that what in the hell is democracy: After all, Ben has been a champion of his people and if he gets the jail treatment, everybody had best keep real quiet as the Christian Fronters, Dixiecrats and others take over!" Burley was quite sagacious. The fact that " . . . Ben Davis has been almost synonymous with Communist" meant that he would receive special treatment.[51]

The *New York Times* chose to place his address to the party convention on the front page. Davis compared the arrests to the "Reichstag fire frame-up . . . gangsterism . . . my Communist party membership card [was taken]. In its stead, I was given a receipt. Now how can one compare a piece of paper signed by a Gestapo agent with a membership card in the Communist party?" Judge Harold Medina, who had been assigned the case, was unimpressed and confined all defendants to New York, which hit Gus Hall of Ohio particularly hard. The edict marked just the beginning of the defendants' turbulent relationship with the jurist. It also turned out that Edmund L. Cocks, foreman of the grand jury that brought forward the indictment, had been exposed earlier in the *Daily Worker* for his role in the discriminatory policies of Greenwich Savings Bank, which he served as vice-president.[52]

Defendant and war hero Robert Thompson was attacked in prison in an apparent set-up by the authorities. Davis sought to meet with O'Dwyer, and literally waved the bloody shirt, displaying Thompson's "bloodstained coat and shirt, which showed about a three inch gash." Repression had reached a new level. George Bernard Shaw was moved to intervene: "The founder of Christianity was a Communist with eleven faithful Apostles, chief of whom struck a man and his wife dead for keeping back their money from a common pool instead of sharing it. But American legislators, ostensibly Christians, don't read the Bible, much less Karl Marx. They would charge St. Peter with sedition as well as murder if he were not beyond their reach. I refrain from comment. The situation speaks for itself."[53]

And that it did. The issue was joined. Black Liberation had met the Red Scare. The rising strength of the Left, particularly among blacks, was set back—interestingly enough, just before the crucial 1948 election. Ben Davis, the symbol of militant Afro-America, was being slated for prison. He raged and raged but ultimately was marched into that dark night. The *Daily Worker* stated it curtly. "Slated for political death" in the 1949 elections were Genevieve Earle, Connolly, even Louis Goldberg of the Liberal party. The *New York Herald Tribune* of 15 December 1948 was straightforward: "High-ranking Republican leaders are seriously weighing a coalition with the Democrats to insure the defeat of the one surviving Communist member. . . . Mr. Davis has a following among Harlem Negroes which has withstood repeated raids by the major parties."[54]

12
"The Trial of the Century," 1949

It was not difficult to see why Davis and the Communist party discerned an aroma of fascism. The indictment and trial of the top party leadership was a classic frame-up based on a statute ultimately viewed as unconstitutional—the Smith Act. Then Davis was railroaded out of his council seat. It was a grueling defensive battle that took its toll in many ways. After the trial ended, Gurley Flynn commented sadly, "It is no accident that heart trouble is practically occupational with Communist leaders . . . it is evident that the past year took a far heavier toll on the health of the leaders of the Communist Party than even those of us who are their closest associates fully appreciated." Davis's premature death in 1964 can be attributed to political repression in part.

The trial of the top eleven leaders of the Communist party, the so-called CP-11 (the trial of defendant William Z. Foster was severed due to health reasons) was "probably the longest criminal trial in the history of the United States," according to the *New York Times* on 15 October 1949; there were 5 million words of testimony covering 21,157 pages at a cost of $1 million to the government. The trial lasted about nine months, with the government introducing fifteen witnesses and 332 exhibits, taking two months. The rest of the time was filled by the defense, including two months of preliminary challenges to the jury system, then the offering of thirty five witnesses and 429 exhibits. The trial cost the party ten thousand dollars per week, which is not surprising, considering that political trials are not only designed to put away defendants but also to drain and to debilitate an organization. Sensing the oncoming disaster, as early as March 1947 the party began a "Fighting Fund" that quickly raised over $140,000; they had to use every dime—and more.[2]

The official form marking the conviction of Davis was dated 21 October 1949 from the federal court of the Southern District of New York. He was convicted of "unlawfully, wilfully and knowingly conspiring to organize as the Communist Party of the U.S. of America, a society, group and assembly of persons who teach and advocate the overthrow and destruction of the Government of the U.S. by force and violence and knowingly and wilfully to advocate and teach the duty and necessity of so overthrowing and destroying the Government of the United States."³ A more maiming assault on the First Amendment is hard to imagine. Although teaching and advocating, not action, were at issue, Davis was nevertheless fined ten thousand dollars and received a five-year jail term.

The *New York Times* put it more prosaically, stating that Davis was convicted for "secretly teaching and advocating, on secret orders from Moscow, overthrow of the government."⁴ It is true that Moscow was an unindicted coconspirator, but the prosecutors were not overly bothered by the fact that they could not find any documentation showing the "hand of Moscow." David Driscoll in a letter to the *Times* published on 19 October 1949 noted cogently that basically the party was being prosecuted for ousting Browder; he asked why the trial ever had to take place, for if the CP-11 had been teaching the overthrow of the United States since April 1945, why did they wait so long to prosecute? "What clear and present danger" existed, he wondered. "A statute drawn to 'get' Communists in spite of the protections our laws throw about political parties practically guaranteed the verdict before the trial," Driscoll wrote. "The trial was a political trial. . . . I trust that the Supreme Court will be able to correct a grave error." In the end they chose not to.

Kevin John O'Brien, who has closely studied the case, argues that it was designed to derail the Progressive party "for the purpose of producing a precedent to support a preventive detention program." Harold Medina, the feisty judge in the case, had become known by defending an accused Nazi saboteur; Felix Frankfurter considered him an "insufferable egotist"; and Judge Learned Hand thought him "extremely naive." O'Brien's study found him "temperamental . . . [with] disconcerting gaps of knowledge . . . caustic . . . often seemed to be searching for reassurance . . . after seven weeks and 48 witnesses . . . Medina had been forced to make evidentiary rulings which left the distinct impression that a cover-up was at work." He agrees that placing the letter *c* by the name of potential black jurors was "at the very least suspicious" and feels that the grand jury favored "wealthy white males." On appeal, "Learned Hand, who apparently did not read the entire record before writing his opinion . . . masked his repudiation of a substantially more liberal First Amendment standard which he had articulated more than 30 years earlier in *Masses Publishing Co. v. Patten*, 244 Fed. 535, 1917." O'Brien found it simlarly distressing that the government on appeal relied heavily on the precedents in the Japanese-American internment cases.⁵

The well-connected columnist Arthur Krock, apparently after speaking to Justice Department officials, conceded that the indictment was brought to allay fears that Truman was soft on Communism; the legal shakiness of the case was recognized but the resulting hysteria proved decisive. The government prosecutors' office in the Southern District of New York was known to be riddled with organized crime influence. Attorney General Tom Clark, according to Davis, was "unfit to be dog-catcher in Podunk, and really must go."[6] The government's case relied heavily on apostates like Louis Budenz and various stool pigeons. Most of their exhibits were *Daily Worker* and *Political Affairs* articles, along with tomes from Lenin. The government wanted publicity to scare those inclined toward progressive leanings and the party wanted publicity to build a movement. Hence, newspapers galore covered the case and hundreds of telegrams denouncing the case deluged the White House.[7]

Davis was obviously the most prominent of the defendants, so an added reason for bringing the prosecution was to erode the increasing hold held by the Left on communities like Harlem. Doing this was not going to be easy. The *Oklahoma Black Dispatch*, though in the heart of the Bible Belt, expressed the sentiments of many:

> One would not have to be a Communist to admire Ben Davis . . . any Negro who parrots the will of the majority race is arbitrarily set up as a leader . . . the black man who exhibits a disposition to think for himself is immediately marked for the tommyhawk. Collusion is reached in control centers to see that every effort of this individual fails . . . we regret Ben Davis failed re-election. . . . We know the man personally. He is a great big husky fellow, with lovable eyes, who inspires you with his sincerity and genuineness. . . . of course if Ben Davis had bowed his head in resignation and submission to the prejudice and race hate he discovered all about him he would today be classified as a loyal black man.[8]

Nathaniel Thornton writing in the 17 December 1949 issue of the *Pittsburgh Courier*, had similar opinions:

> I am really disgusted at the way Negroes are being pitted against other Negroes in the fight against communism. And I want to clarify that I am not one of the fellow-travellers. However, I do think that if a Negro doesn't like communism he should keep his mouth shut and not be a stooge for the FBI. If the FBI was any good at all it would have caught those lynchers of the two Negro men and two women so brutally murdered down in Georgia. Or did it want to do so in the beginning?

Ironically, Thornton was echoing Soviet Foreign Minister Andrei Vishinsky, who accused the United States of hypocrisy for ignoring "real violations of human rights" while prosecuting Reds.[9]

Davis agreed and so did his party. As early as July 1946 the state party had argued that fascist terror had already begun—against blacks. As noted London's oppression of blacks in Africa in 1939 made it difficult for black Communists and the party to see the United Kingdom as a beacon of freedom; ten years later increased terror against blacks helped convince black communists and the party that fascism was coming. In July 1949 Davis extended the analysis.[10] As the trial wore on, hour piled on hour, Davis became exasperated:

Sitting in the Federal Court . . . day after day listening to the opium dreams, the moronic pap, the downright rubbish . . . one is provoked to bitter anger that this great and powerful country should be reduced to such idiocy . . . wasting the people's money. . . . It is too cheap and crude. It is small pickings. The strange rulings of Judge Medina, embellished with his perfectly irresistible humor.[11]

The nation's tragedy was not the trial but the layoffs, lynchings, and hunger riveting the land: "This is the main drama—these are the main issues." He found it ironic that the gravamen of the government's case was that the party was fine under Browder but a villain under Foster: "Such is the slapstick in courtroom 110," said Davis. The government's case was full of "stoolpigeons . . . this motley assortment of Van der Lubbbes and Mortimer Snerds." The obvious purpose was to "spread panic in the ranks of unions, peoples and progressive organizations-including the Party. . . . The screwball antics inherent in the heresy nature of this trial should blind no one to its grave dangers."[12]

A complicating factor in the party's fight against the Smith Act involved their earlier posture when this bill was applied to the Socialist Workers party. In 1941 Milton Howard assailed the act in the context of the prosecution of the Trotskyites, though he added, "[I] can find no objection to the destruction of the fifth column in this country . . . [we] must insist upon it." But he suggested that they be prosecuted as "agents of fascism" and not as revolutionaries, as the Smith Act intimated.[13] Party leader Carl Winter termed the act "reactionary" a few months later but hailed the conviction of the Trotskyites; after all, they had not condemned Japan's attack on the United States. Howard and Winter were not alone; the *California Eagle* called the SWP "fascists" a few months later. As the CP-11 trial began, Davis rebuked those who chided the party for not vigorously defending the SWP by asserting, "Trotsykism is not a political trend or a political party. It is gangsterism, disruption, wrecking assassination and murder. . . . The Trotskyites are a bunch of agents for fascism and they don't deserve to be considered in the same breath as us or any other decent American." Davis's vitriol simply reflected party policy but many people believed that such rhetoric ill-disposed the Communists to seek aid to fight their prosecution.[14]

The issue was highlighted when a major Bill of Rights Conference was held in New York in mid-July to rally support for Davis and his codefendants. The thirteen hundred attendees from thirty three states heard Davis speak; after he finished, Farrell Dobbs of the SWP jumped on the platform and shouted, "Davis means us when he spoke of splitters and wreckers."[15] He was booed. In 1961 Gus Hall announced that it was a "mistake" not to have fought the Smith Act prosecution of the SWP in Minnesota, but in 1949 the CP position also served to deter the necessary support of liberals and centrists.[16]

When Davis was called before a grand jury in 1939 that was investigating the party, he characterized it as "my first experience in a star chamber proceeding." Blacks were segregated in the jury room, and contributing to the slapstick aspects was the attempt to show that Davis was born in Trinidad or Jamaica and was therefore an illegal alien. Ten years later, his opinion had not changed; he felt the grand jury for the 1949 prosecution was "stacked."[17]

When the trial began there was exhaustive questioning of potential jurors who were asked about the publications they read and the organizations they had heard about; they were also asked about various columnists and politics in general. Finally a jury of eleven was picked, four of whom were African-American, with at least three of them from Harlem.

The *New York Amsterdam News* felt that there were "odd-looking people" on the jury: Judge Medina, for example, "resembles Hollywood's fabulous Adolph Menjou." They were impressed by CP-11 attorney George Crockett, an African-American who eventually was elected to Congress; "[he is] regarded as one of the most brilliant lawyers ever seen in action here." As for the prosecution, "unfortunately, from a spectator viewpoint, McGohey does not have a Negro assistant." The jury was another question: "... nobody seemed to know too much about the Harlemites ... and there was little to indicate whether they had ever participated in the community's civic and political life."[18] This jury also included a Liberal party member, American Legion members and so forth. On voir dire juror Russell Janney denied anti-Communist bias but was quoted in the *Macon Telegraph* of 22 February 1949 to the contrary. Reporter Ted Thackrey charged that he had urged a "fight to death" against Communism a week before he was chosen as a juror; even during the trial he made loud comments outside the courtroom suggesting his bias. Medina denied that this was a basis for a mistrial.[19]

Medina, a graduate of Princeton, had been on the faculty of Columbia Law School for thirty years; born in Brooklyn, his father was "Spanish-Mexican." As an attorney he assailed the blue-ribbon juries that he later upheld as a judge, calling them "prone to convict" and having an "economic bias." Before reaching the bench he was doing quite well, making a princely eighty-five thousand dollars a year even then and employing a Chinese "houseman" at his Manhattan home at 14 East 75 Street. He was annoyed about being accused of racism during the trial. Igniting the comment was a 4 October 1949 incident when Medina refused a Davis motion to permit him to sum up his case and codefendant Eugene Dennis accused the judge of "discrimination and an affront to the Negro people." To bar a Harvard Law attorney from speaking in his own behalf, however, did appear to be exalting form over content.[20]

The CP-11 trial was the first criminal case judged by Medina. He was deluged with mail. With typical understated reportage the exuberant *New*

York Times on 20 November printed, "It was suggested that he run for political office, the Presidency not excluded. . . . The majority of correspondents were certain that the Republic had been saved" by Medina. Basking in the embrace, Medina modestly conceded, "I have a far from phlegmatic disposition." Nevertheless he said that the trial had "reduced him to a state of near exhaustion."

Davis and the party objected strenuously to Judge Medina's conduct during the trial. The National Non-Partisan Committee to Defend the Rights of the twelve Communist Leaders published the widely circulated "Due Process in a Political Trial: The Record vs. the Press." It noted, "Judge Medina reserves his most [sharp] shafts for defense counsel George W. Crockett, Jr. . . . extreme contempt . . . dual standard used by the Court in applying the rules of evidence . . . protectiveness toward prosecution witnesses contrasted with badgering of defense witnesses . . . derogation of the defendants' case . . . the judge as prosecutor." And these were the milder reflections in the sixty-seven-page pamphlet put out by this committee, which was cochaired by Paul Robeson.[21]

Another study pointed to rulings to "silence and immobilize defense counsel"; Crockett was not the only attorney who served time in prison after the trial. This study too saw "discriminatory application of rules of evidence . . . badgering of defendants and defense witnesses . . . deprecation of the defendants' evidence in the presence of the jury."[22] Robeson agreed: "there I acquired a devastating contempt for court." He viewed Medina (with whom he shared connections at Princeton and Columbia) as "patronizing and insolent . . . stared rudely and antagonistically at witnesses . . . there apparently seemed to be regular traffic signals between Mr. McGohey and Judge Medina." Robeson could not understand the sustaining of objections barring Herbert Aptheker from saying if he attended Columbia.[23]

This trial by ordeal brought good friends Davis and Robeson even closer. In his biography Martin Duberman mentions that in *Othello* "Robeson himself acknowledged that a device he used to excite his nightly rage onstage was to imagine his trusted friend Ben Davis betraying him."[24] This friendship was brought directly to Robeson's attention before the House Un-American Activities Committee. At question was his praise of Davis in the 29 June 1949 *Daily Worker*: "One of my dearest friends one of the finest Americans you can imagine, born of a fine family who went to Amherst and . . . a great man."[25] Philip S. Foner refers to the idea that Robeson "the activist shows himself really significant . . . in siding not with Ralph Bunche but with the Communist Councilman Ben Davis."[26] But whatever plaudits Robeson won from some for standing by his friend led to further punishment by others.

Similarly Robeson needed the support of Davis and the party after he was quoted in Paris as allegedly calling into question the ongoing war cry against Moscow and blacks' role in it. Yet again blacks were not particularly made distraught by Robeson's words; he was expressing some of their more hidden thoughts. After his return, thousands jammed a Robeson rally at Rockland Palace sponsored by the Council on African Affairs. Davis was effusive even though his prosecutors sought to use this against him in the trial.[27]

The Rockland Palace rally was a positive jolt for Davis, the party, and Robeson. However, they were jolted again a few weeks later with the Peekskill, New York, racist, ultra-right Rally aimed at Robeson and the Civil Rights Congress. At the rally Davis was quoted by a state trooper as stating, "We are not pacifists and we are going to stand up toe to toe and slug it out . . . we will be prepared to defend ourselves." Davis, like Malcolm X, saw self-defense as intelligent.[28] In an affadavit filed during the trial Davis recalled vividly the fourth of September from five to six P.M.: "I was a passenger in an automobile . . . the car was pelted with rocks and stones . . . shattered the windshield . . . glass spattered upon me and those sitting to me . . . the car swerved again and again." The driver was bleeding. There were shouts: "Hang the Robeson niggers with a rope!" "Get the dirty Jews!" State troopers just stood by. The five passengers in the car were injured. Robeson and Irving Potash were in the car right behind Davis. Davis's worry about impending fascism was not altogether unfounded.[29]

The crafty Neil Scott maintained after the riot that it would help reelect Davis since black and fair-minded whites would be outraged: "Most of them state emphatically they are not Communist or pro-Communist. . . . They all state unqualifiedly they are tremendously dissatisfied with the way the American Negro is being treated today."[30] This was a message heard at the highest levels of U.S. society.

Paul Robeson, Jr., recalls that after the Paris uproar his father was sufficiently shaken to lend Davis his bodyguard, a "huge guy" with a "cannon of a .45 in his holster"; the guard also served as a driver; he was quite tall, "all muscle . . . bigger than Ben or Dad."[31]

In turn Davis fervently supported his friend, denouncing the "frenzied, reactionary howls against Robeson"; these barbs were designed "to intensify the already vicious war hysteria and lynch persecution against Negroes." Robeson contributed to the "cause of peace and freedom." Again Davis upbraided "the renegade and political streetwalker Max Yergan. . . . the foxy old reformist Channing Tobias and Rep. Adam Powell, with his double-talk . . . will have to answer to . . . Negroes. . . . It is precisely the great virtue of Robeson's statement that he bluntly and challengingly emphasized that the fight for peace and the fight for Negro freedom are opposite sides of the same coin, and are indivisible."[32]

Though not as heralded, Davis ignited a similar flap a few months later. He was quoted in the *New York Times* for 13 August 1950 as swearing, "[I'd] rather be a lamp-post in Moscow than President here" at a six-hundred-strong Civil Rights Congress rally in Harlem. The paper reported, "Assigned to the rally were twenty-five foot patrolmen and seven sergeants, ten mounted policemen and twenty-five detectives." This show of force was perceived as intentionally intimidating; the racism of the police combined with the disproportionately black audience also roiled the waters. The *Times* also cited Davis as remarking, "And Moscow. Ah, that wonderful place." The *New York Daily News* for the same day also had quite a time with these alleged comments. With his usual sensitivity to folklore, Davis was paraphrasing Willie "The Lion" Smith, who when asked what it meant for a musician to live in Harlem in the pre–World War II period, replied, "I'd rather be a fly on a Harlem lamp post than a millionaire anywhere else."[33] This was a comment aimed at the buckle of the Black Belt. Bojangles Robinson, a Harlem hero, allegedly once said to Newbold Morris, "'I'd rather be a lamppost in New York than a mayor anywhere else in the world!"[34] Davis's appropriation and evocation of folk culture was not appreciated by this panel of critics, though it demonstrated again that he was in tune with his constituency.

Though stuck in a courtroom for much of the time he needed to be a council member and get reelected, Davis still found time to assert himself in the mass defense. Yet the *Times* stridently raised the alarm as effectively as did anyone about effective antirepression tactics: "Congress is abundantly right in speeding legislation to outlaw the picketing of United States courts. Recent disgraceful displays in Foley Square have given ample evidence that more and stiffer legislation has been needed ... by no stretch of the imagination can the right of free speech, which we so ardently sustain, be extended to the right to make a concerted public attack on a duly authorized juror."[35] The *Times* twisted and contorted the truth to find a way to suppress the First Amendment while appearing to uphold it. The Truman administration was more direct; they simply kept lists of those opposed to the CP-11 conviction.[36]

Truman's henchmen must have been impressed with the numbers of black people who turned up on such lists. Writing in early 1949, J. Edgar Hoover told Rear Admiral Sidney W. Sowers that black party membership had jumped 32 percent, to 1,532, since 1946; New York was still the biggest district.[37] Davis's allies did not desert him during his moment of trial. "Are These Men to be Jailed Because They Fought for Ideas?" was the headline in an advertisement focusing on Davis and Winston that appeared in the *New York Age* on New Year's Day 1949; people knew that it would be a small leap to suppress ideas against Jim Crow—as the sly Dixiecrats instictively realized. Hence Davis's support among his constituency was particularly impressive. Five hundred "prominent Negro leaders" petitioned Truman and Attorney General Clark, firmly stating that the conviction would jeopardize black rights: "We take special note of the fact that two Negro leaders" were among the eleven, the petition read. Oliver Cox, Canada Lee, Earl Dickerson, and Mary Church Terrell were among the signatories. Robeson was the leader of this team.[38]

Over time Davis's support rose and crested. In March 1949 Lester Walton, former U.S. Minister to Liberia, defended Davis, holding that the prosecution was the result of "injustice and oppression." Before that Lindsay White, president of the New York-NAACP, wired the judge in Davis's trial, complaining of jury discrimination. But by October Roy Wilkins was sternly instructing his branches not to cooperate "in any movement whatsoever" in solidarity with the defendants, though he objected to the Smith Act and also racial discrimination in jury selection and operation. This was a crippling blow. The question remains: did Wilkins have a choice? Was it possible for anyone to withstand the hammer blows of repression?[39]

Langston Hughes felt he had a choice. The Harlem bard, Davis's neighbor in Harlem, compared the trial to Hitlerism since first he "locked up the Communists. The Jews were No. 2 . . . In America the Negroes are No. 2 on history's list . . . if the twelve Communists are sent to jail in a little while they will send Negroes to jail simply for being Negroes and to concentration camps just for being colored."[40] This kind of thinking was shared by the party cadre and deepened their fears of rising fascism. Apparently they misjudged the situation; fascistlike terror was aimed at blacks generally, at breaking the black-Left tie, and at breaking black Reds. And with that "threat" of black radicalism disposed of, civil rights reform was accelerated. But fascism did not arrive.

Black community leaders like Dr. Arnold Donawa (who had served in Spain), Claudia Jones, George Murphy (of the *Afro-American* newspaper chain), Theodore Ward, Revels Cayton, and Thelma Dale all felt they had a choice. They protested to the prosecution in July 1949. Davis's and Winston's defenders were busy. There was a three-quarter-page ad in the *New York Age* with a huge picture of Davis: "when they say 'outlaw the Communists' . . . It's *you* they're after! . . . Why would they like to eliminate men like Ben Davis from the City Council?"[41] The party's old ally, the Reverend Thomas Harten of Brooklyn, did not back down; he told a gathering of five hundred ministers at a Baptist Ministers Alliance meeting that he was praying for the defendants. Mother Lena Stokes, ordained minister of the Spiritualist faith, was similarly supportive.

The influential journalist and historian J. A. Rogers compared "the present furor over communism with the Negro-Catholic panic of 1741. . . . I can't see communism [as] any immediate danger to this nation. The simple truth is that the spirit of the American people incites far more to fascism than to communism. . . . The South is already largely fascistic."[42] The leading edge of fascistlike action was reaching African-Americans; although blacks were flocking to the defense of Davis and his comrades, in a racist nation that support could be dangerous.

The sterling performance of George Crockett at the trial brought admiration from African-Americans. His subsequent repeated elections in Detroit to the House by steadily increasing margins attested to his continuing popularity. His friend William Patterson of the Civil Rights Congress produced a pamphlet entitled *Censored News* in a *Time* magazine format that featured the Morehouse-trained lawyer. In it Crockett met head on the convenient bourgeois canard that the party was using blacks (naturally, elites generally ignored their own heinous record): "Every time I hear that statement I boil with resentment, that in this day and time anyone can think that Negroes are so immature, so childish, so inclined to, shall I say, be a good boy, that they can believe that any organization whether it is the Communist Party are any other organization can treat the Negroes in America as so many pawns . . . it is probably more accurate to say that Negroes have used the Communist Party. It is the one party in which they feel free to speak and to act like Americans. It is the only party that seemingly cares about the plight of Negroes in this country." This was a truth often ignored, Crockett continued. The party had used the "Negro question" as in Scottsboro "for the purpose of establishing the right of all Americans to a fair trial in a land running rough shod with prejudice." Supreme Court holdings were mute testimony to this. "You don't see a Negro lawyer at the prosecution's table and there is a very obvious reason why you don't see one. It is not the practice of the Democratic Party to employ Negroes as United States attorneys." Crockett had flagged the reason for imminent affirmative action—that is, the model set by the Left.[43]

Crockett was enthusiastic about his experience at the trial: "I have enjoyed this brief trip into the realm of freedom . . . for the first time, I have been an 'American lawyer' and not a 'Negro lawyer.' I shall continue to serve this way."[44]

Another black lawyer, Paul Robeson, tried to use his international contacts to rally support for Davis. With Ferdinand Smith he beseeched Norman Manley of Jamaica, reminding him of Davis's devotion to the West Indian cause. He wanted Manley to appear in court, provide consultations, and so forth.[45]

The progressive bar was quick to defend Davis and the defendants, both at home and abroad. The top-flight black law firm Cobb & Hayes of Washington, D.C., assisted Davis's defense, as did Dean Parker of Terrell Law School. The Harlem Lawyers Association honored four guests who were in town to observe the trial, including Ronald H. T. Whitty of the Haldane Society of Britain, M. Claude Dennery of the French progressive bar, Domingo Villamil, who had served as director-general of the Justice Department of Cuba, and Carlos Ramos of the Philippine Lawyers Guild. The latter's sister organization in the United States, the National Lawyers Guild, suffered special persecution because of their leading role in the defense. Their moves were monitored by the FBI, and to demonstrate in a legal proceeding that the NLG was Communist-dominated, the government introduced their defense of the jailed CP-11 lawyers.[46]

Certain ties between the black and white progressive bars faciliated defense of the Red leadership. Hope Stevens, West Indian patriot, founder of the National Conference of Black Lawyers and a Davis intimate, recalled at a memorial service for CP-11 counsel Harry Sacher that "He was the first man who gave me the opportunity of serving as associate counsel to a non-segregated union."[47]

The American Civil Liberties Union also was involved in the case. As usual their officials dithered and hedged. Although they backed the defendants, they supported the judge's contempt order—"we hold no brief for contemptuous conduct"—and always distanced themselves forcefully from the party in their public statements. Arthur Garfield Hays, ACLU general counsel, did not hesitate to state that the trial was not based on credible evidence and added, "I am aroused by people who believe in democracy and at the same time believe that Communists ought to be barred or placed in a separate class society."[48] On the other hand, defense of the CP-11 by I. F. Stone and various liberal forces within the Jewish People's Fraternal Order, the Civil Rights Congress, and American Labor Party was relatively strong, given the times.[49]

Many of these elements came together at the Rockland Palace at a mid-October "ball" for Davis, who of course was unable to attend. Even the *New York Post* on 16 October 1949 was impressed with the turnout: "Not since Father Divine and his cohorts gave up the place at 155 Street and 8th Avenue a couple of years ago has there been such a turnout." The police claim was that two thousand people were milling around before the ball started, even though the entry fee was $1.20 a head. There were two bands and dancing continued until three A.M. The party knew how to party.

Communists who had come out of the closet and Communists who were still there worked tirelessly in defense of their leadership. The founding meeting of the Communist Committee to Defend the 12 was held 19 February 1949 on the fifth floor of 35 East 12 Street in Manhattan. The agenda had two points: raise issues and raise funds. The Civil Rights Congress, led by Communists, was indispensable to the defense. The New York party was successful in raising $650,000 in one month and recruiting eight hundred members in a period ending in late April 1949; hundreds attended their legislative conference at 160 West 129 Street in opposition to other legislative horrow shows in Congress.[50]

Davis could have been voted Most Valuable Communist during this trial. He worked tirelessly and overtime. He was instrumental in drafting an affadavit for a mistrial, filed on 20 May 1949, on the ground, among others, that anti-Communist "propaganda" from the press and government officials was prejudicing the jury. He submitted as evidence editorials and cartoons from the New York press and singled out H. R. Knickerbocker of WOR-AM. The motion was denied.[51]

Davis did not rise to speak in court until late May, though the trial had begun in January; some saw this as a tactical error on the party's part, just as others thought it was a mistake not to rest the defense on the First Amendment. Medina threatened to jail him, anyway. He had risen to support statements by Eugene Dennis, Robert Thompson, and their attorneys concerning a court ruling barring as evidence an article written 4 July 1938 by John Gates, a party leader. The *Daily Worker* reported, "Davis uttered only one word when the judge interrupted." Davis: "It is pretty hard for the defendants to sit here like a bump on a log while a whole lot of rulings are made which are practically cutting the guts out of what our Party stands for. . . . " Judge Medina: "I consider that an extremely offensive statement. . . . " Davis: "Well, the whole trial is offensive to me and should have been thrown out a long time ago." Judge Medina: "No defendant gets very much pleasure out of a criminal trial." Davis: "Of course, and I don't see what pleasure the government should get in bringing this ridiculous and stupid trial in the first place." Judge Medina (now angry): "Now Mr. Davis do you realize that you may be forcing me to remand you during the remainder of the trial." Davis: "Well, I cannot help that. All I want to do is to say the truth. That is all. . . . And if you wanted the truth you would let our party tell what it teaches and advocates in Spain and elsewhere." Davis sat down after Medina again threatened to jail him.[52]

But Davis didn't keep quiet. He told *Daily Worker* readers that "I'm definitely charging that the Judge's behavior has no other effort than to keep me from running for council." He recalled that twelve times or more white defendants had risen to protest: "The first time a Negro defendant did so the judge threatened . . . prison. . . . This is not at all accidental." Didn't he treat Crockett the same way? "And I practiced law in Georgia, remember." He pointed out the absurdity of being placed on trial, charged with advocating the overthrow of the government, while working daily in the City Council to make the government work.[53]

Thus Davis's first day of testimony on the witness stand in July 1949 was seen as potentially flammable. The *New York Age* of 9 July felt that "Davis' first day testimony was so quietly impressive"; it even drew favorable editorial comment from the *New York Daily News*. The *Pittsburgh Courier*, also citing the *New York Daily News*, allowed J. A. Rogers to endorse Davis.[54] The bally-hooed *Daily News* editorial basically repeated the line that to better fight Communism, the country should ease repression and segregation of blacks; this philosophy was repeated like a prayer by many during the course of the Red Scare and illustrates how Communist-influenced Black Liberation set the stage for Jim Crow's demise.

If an alumnus of Amherst and Harvard Law could become a Communist and work for a paltry salary of forty dollars a week, live in an apartment renting for forty dollars month, own no stocks and bonds, drive a 1948 Dodge sedan owned by the party, own no real estate or mortgages and have no trust fund income—then what about the thousands of maltreated black workers? Would they follow Davis's lead and turn Left en masse? This was

Washington's dilemma. It was a crisis, but it was also an opportunity for the Left, as reported by the well-respected writer Joseph North in the *Daily Worker*: "Word has flown throughout the city that Councilman Davis is on the stand, and the crowds waiting in line for admission have grown. . . . standing for hours to get the chance to hear."[55]

In his memoir written from prison Davis vividly recalled the experience:

> I stayed on the witness stand less time than any other of my fellow Communist defendants who testified. . . . I would say that the main reasons for the unique handling of my appearance were two: first there was a fear of the rebound from the Negro people . . . I was pretty well known and my activities were followed with great interest not only in Harlem but all over Negro America and to some extent by darker and colonial peoples throughout the world. Secondly, my testimony had been pinpointed primarily around [Reds and black] . . . [a] brilliant record- . . . [neither] the Court nor the prosecution wished to drag that ugly skeleton out of the closet. So I had a feeling they were glad to get rid of me. In fact, all the Negro witnesses for the defense at the trial were handled in a "special way."

He recalled bitterly the attempt to portray him as "Mr. Dignity himself" while Henry Winston, the sawmill worker's son from Mississippi via Kansas City, was pictured as an "uncultured yokel."[56]

Davis was well aware of the delicacy with which the government had to handle his case . He objected strenuously during the trial and expected to have his bail revoked: "Certainly Green had been sent for much less." Then why was it not? The answer is that the Negro Question was the Achilles' heel of the trial. When Medina at one point called him a "boy," the ultimate insult for any self-respecting older black male, "I was ready to slap his well-groomed face." " . . . I had had, of course, much more experience in this type of struggle than most of the other Party leaders, having been an attorney and also having often represented the Party at congressional, senatorial and judicial hearings." This fear of the Negro Question also helps to account for the relative timidity with which the prosecution handled Davis and also reflects the damage done to the defense by Judge Medina barring him from being involved in his own defense. As for Thelma Dial, the black jury forewoman, Davis said, "I have only contempt for her." And how, he cried, could his old friend Adam Powell become "as silent as a tombstone" during the trial?[57]

Davis's testimony was filled with nuggets of information, though the judge would not let him speak of the high harassment he received in Georgia after he joined the party. At a CPA meeting in March 1945 Davis recalled questioning the party's support of Arthur Vandenberg as representative to the United Nations; it "looked as though we had begun [in] some measure to rationalize a number of things that [FDR] was doing." At the crucial 2 June 1945 CPA meeting Davis recalled saying that "on the whole we had not taken up real militant struggles against the main enemy of the Negro people, which is monopoly capitalism." Then he refined his thought: the issue was not the party failing to struggle for Negro rights but not always struggling against monopoly in doing so.[58]

Why was there so much focus at the trial on Browder and the events of 1945? The thrust of the case against Davis and his codefendants was that overthrowing Browderism was prime evidence substantiating the teaching and advocacy charge; it also suggested that the party was on trial for overthrowing a widely perceived laggard position on Black Liberation during that era.

In his testimony Davis recalled a 1945 meeting with Dennis and others: "I pointed out that the legislative front had become extremely important in recent years because fascism works in such a way that it seeks to abolish even the limited legislative rights that the people have . . . and therefore the legislative front is of much greater significance at this stage of world history because of the fact that it represents a barricade against fascist destruction" of rights. The judge and prosecution allowed him to draw an analogy between the position of blacks in the United States and Africa and Latin America. But he insisted that "talk of an American Negro Republic has no foundation in present day reality," it only existed for "education and propaganda." The Black Belt thesis was haunting the party again since it could easily be distorted into seeming as though the party supported self-segregation of blacks.[59] Davis's point that he had been questioning Browder's policies before the alleged word to denounce him came from Moscow was lost on the judge, prosecution, and jury in their haste for a conviction.[60]

Davis had to deal with yet another brushfire during the course of the trial—his canceled car insurance. Davis ferociously objected, accusing the Automobile Club of New York, but Metropolitan Life, whom Davis had harassed so intensely on the Stuyvesant Town controversy, could not have been displeased.[61]

Another brouhaha erupted when Davis sought to make his own closing statement, relieving his attorney, Harry Sacher, of the obligation. Medina said no, the request was "not made in good faith" but was a "maneuver" intended to cause "disruptive and disorderly incidents" in court. He went on to charge Davis with "contemptuous" conduct. Davis claimed he was without counsel. He had a "very narrow escape" in not being jailed for contempt like some of his codefendants.[62]

Davis was beleaguered on all fronts. When he sought to speak on WMCA, a local radio station, he was "censored" by the station: "Here I am a City Councilman, twice elected. . . . My record is public. I have made scores of speeches and written scores of articles about 18 years of public life. Could they find a single speech—or even a line of a speech in which I advocated the forceful overthrow of our government? They could not. If they could have done so, they would have quickly put that material into evidence."[63] This was obviously true but the larger agenda was to remove

Red influence from Blacks and lessen Jim Crow to improve the U.S. global image during the Cold War. So the station wanted no part of Davis's statements analogizing the 1949 trial to past events in Nazi Germany.

The trial was an ordeal for all of the defendants. Robert Thompson was assaulted in jail by hoodlums, whose convictions were then set aside by a black judge. The pressure may have led to the premature death of Davis's Amherst and Harvard Law friend Charles Houston, who was serving as attorney for defendants Winston and Irving Potash; his work on the motion concerning the excluding of blacks, workers, Jewish people and others from juries was typically brilliant and thorough, and possibly the strain of the research needed for this motion took his health. The intimidating presence of the state was ubiquitous. At the beginning of the trial in January, tempers "flared briefly but heatedly in the City Council" and "photographers crowded around [Davis]," who had called a point of personal privilege, complaining of the size and tenor of police preparations at Foley Square; this was an affront to his "dignity and status" as a council member. He was ruled out of order, appealed, and lost 16–3 with only Connolly and Walter Hart joining him.[64]

Sensitive to visual dynamics, Davis usually flanked Eugene Dennis in court, with Winston on the general secretary's other side. The party had been fairly well prepared for the not-unanticipated indictment and trial. Harry Haywood worked with Davis and Bob Thompson in preparing for depositions and in anticipating questions. Haywood was impressed with Harry Sacher, whom he characterized as "energetic and bright." Yet the fact that Dennis defended himself and Davis—an attorney, public orator, and the best-known figure—did not raises questions about certain party tactics, Medina's denial of Davis's defense set aside. Further, Dennis was well known as a wooden and uninspiring speaker, though the fact that he was the highest-ranking Red on trial carried weight in terms of his *pro se* defense. Others felt that they should have relied more explicitly on the First Amendment.[65]

Still, it is difficult to project what the party could have done differently to forestall the guilty verdict that inexorably arrived in October 1949. Though the prosecutor was contending that the overthrow of Browderism was a key element in his case, he sought to bar the indispensable testimony of William Z. Foster, who played a key role in the entire process.

Since the government seemed to be in the driver's seat tactically, the result was preordained. Just as their defense was beginning, the government trumped them by opening the so-called espionage case of Alger Hiss in the same Foley Square locale, a move seen as not coincidental by the *Daily Worker*. The defense was bested again when in the middle of the trial Judge Medina jailed Hall, Winston, and Gates. The latter was charged with contempt after he refused to name the Communists who helped him in veterans' affairs; after Hall and Winston spoke up in his defense, they too were jailed.

Later Gil Green was jailed after commenting unfavorably on a Medina ruling while he was on the stand.[66]

During the trial Davis and the party refused to shrink from hiding their solidarity with the eastern European nations, and given the hostility of the United States toward these regimes, this too could be seen as a tactical advantage held by the prosecution. At one Georgi Dimitrov memorial meeting of twenty-five hundred supporters at the Manhattan Center, Davis received a "rousing ovation. . . . A color guard carried the American and Bulgarian flags to the stage and draped a large drawing of Dimitrov as a narrator read the final speech made by Dimitrov at the Nazi Reichstag fire trial. Frequent applause greeted the narration as the inescapable parallel to the trial of the Communist leaders here hit home."[67]

These advantages, combined with rising anti-Communism, meant conviction for Davis and his colleagues. Somehow lost in the commotion was the fact that they were really jailed for overthrowing Browder and reading and teaching Marxism and Leninism. At first bail was denied. Davis's sister, visiting him in jail, was upset. Her only contact with him was through a thick steel wall with a narrow glass panel and telephone. But all the protest was not in vain, as the defendants were released on bail weeks after conviction.[68]

Davis immediately filed a motion to overturn the verdict. He pointed to the hysteria that had been whipped up and he cited newspaper articles and editorials, arguing that the minds of the jurors were poisoned against them as a result. He appealed to the court of public opinion, calling for a "renewed offensive" against the frame-up and as a tonic urged the "jailing and quarantining of this man as a political mad-dog," referring to HUAC's Parnell Thomas. It was all to no avail. The trial that had begun on 17 January 1949 at 10:43 A.M. had come to an ignominious end on 14 October at 11:25 A.M. with convictions and prison for the defendants and contempt sentences for the lawyers.[69]

The intimidating police presence, the calls for blood in the press, and the tense atmosphere still did not presage the degree of anger and violence expressed in the posttrial uprising in Harlem.[70] James Hicks, veteran black journalist, said it "was equal to the violence of the Peekskill riots. . . . I know because I was trapped in the middle of it . . . police engaged in a free-for-all with about 2,000 residents of Harlem which saw the police at times brutally club men, women and children. . . . It also saw the Harlemites retaliate by stoning policemen with bricks from the rooftops, smashing the windows of police cars and literally rushing up to policemen and burning them with flaming torches of fire." The crowd had gathered spontaneously when they heard Davis and Winston received bail, but Davis was held up until 9:00 P.M. and rumors spread that the authorities, as was their wont, had reneged. By then there was a "torchlight parade" and mounted police arrived; their horses were "frightened by the torches. . . . The horses danced around madly through the crowd and the crowd resented it . . . bedlam broke loose." Eventually Davis, Winston, and Robeson came to the Hotel Theresa, "where the largest crowd since the Joe Louis-Walcott fight gathered to hear [Davis] make a speech from the hotel balcony."[71]

A torchlight march of thousands of blacks through Harlem, followed by a rousing speech from a balcony by a Communist brought more than a frisson of apprehension to anti-Communists. It seemed all too similar to events then occurring in Madagascar, Burma, Indonesia, and South Africa, where the Left and people of color were on the march against the authorities. *Time* magazine, in the 4 November 1949 issue, was infuriated, referring to the "big, brassy Communist Ben Davis . . . smiling and cocky." "Flaming Torches and Verbal Kerosene" was their headline. Robeson was denounced for allegedly following the "party-line." Davis and Robeson, they told their readers, were happy about the violence and "looked mighty pleased with the way things were going." The *New York Times* reported that "several thousand persons went on a rampage in Harlem for two hours last night in a tumultuous outburst in celebration" of Davis's release on bail; it "looked as if [it] might develop into a riot, six policemen were injured, five slightly and six men were arrested." Seventy-five foot patrolmen, the crews of eight radio cars, and one emergency squad were gathered when "empty bottles, bricks, tin cans, pots and broomsticks were showered down on them from tenement house windows and roof tops on Lenox Avenue."[72] Unlike the *Afro-American* and the *Daily Worker*, the *Times* was not as concerned about informing their readers about injuries to Harlem blacks.

Reaction was immediate. Roy Wilkins demanded that the mayor take action against the police who committed the beatings and objected to the number of officers, 360, that had been dispatched. Davis said it was the worst assault he had seen since a similar conflict in 1935. Ted Poston of the *New York Post*, no great friend of Davis, was beaten. The "Red Squad," eager to flex its muscles, was charged with lighting the fuse. But the tenor of reaction was set when eight priests of Roman Catholic churches in Harlem blamed "an outside element" for the uprising. In December four of those arrested were given sixty days each In jail, a "savage sentence," according to their lawyer Hope Stevens.[73]

This was a perversely appropriate end to the trial: first the defendants were jailed, then their attorneys, and finally the protesters. But it was being realized in loftier circles that it was becoming more difficult to fight the Cold War and prosecute the Red Scare with millions of angry, disaffected blacks within the gates; it was particularly hard when figures respected by blacks like Ben Davis were pointing to the contradictions every day. Perhaps it was poetic justice that Blacks and their allies were as concerned with Stalinism as opponents of socialism in eastern Europe were concerned about antiblack racism. But since Davis had a following, Davis had to go. It was absolutely necessary that he be ousted from the council and imprisoned.

Benjamin J. Davis, Sr. Courtesy Benjamin J. Davis Jr. Collection, Schomburg Center for Research in Black Culture.

Joe Louis and Benjamin J. Davis, Jr. Courtesy Schomburg Center for Research in Black Culture.

Lena Horne, Ben Davis, and Cab Calloway during Davis's City Council days. Courtesy Schomburg Center for Research in Black Culture.

Thurgood Marshall and Ben Davis. Courtesy Schomburg Center for Research in Black Culture.

Smith Act victims: the defendants in the CP-11 trial. Ben Davis in the back row, third from right. Photo from *The Daily Worker*, courtesy Schomburg Center for Research in Black Culture.

13
Purged from the Council, 1949

The year 1949 brought a double defeat for Davis. As he was being prosecuted, he was also fighting for his electoral life. He was clinging to his seat in the council although powerful forces had aligned to defeat him in the November election. With the energy of a battalion, Davis fought in the council, testified in Washington, marched in picket lines, devised court strategy, and declaimed at rallies. However, the correlation of forces—as the Marxists might say—had shifted so it is hard to say that if Davis and the party had conducted themselves differently, there would have been a different result. Washington was becoming highly concerned with the Left's influence on blacks. A Faustian bargain of sorts was worked out with the black centrists: in return for breaking with the Left, civil rights concessions would be granted for which both sides would receive credit. Davis saw this instinctively and objected vociferously, though in retrospect his frenzied attacks on the centrists might have made their decision to break with the Left easier. For example, Congressman William Dawson, chair of the House Committee on Expenditures and one of the few blacks in the House, was called "window dressing" and a "party hack" by the Red council member; anyone seeking allies in an effort to avoid prison could hardly afford to publicly assail a figure like Dawson.[1]

Davis thought that the White House simply could not deliver the goods promised to the centrists. According to Steven Lawson, Davis's indictment of the White House was justified: "Although President Harry Truman had committed his administration to advancing the cause of civil rights, the Justice Department exercised restraint in prosecuting criminal cases involving racial discrimination."[2] This was coarse understatement; the black centrists did not realize that their Faustian bargain could only be implemented rhetorically in the absence of a mass movement. It would take the leftist-influenced atmosphere of the 1960s to bring White House promises to fruition.

Davis was put forward as a party representative in Washington because of his excellent skills in oratory and his legal training; HUAC and the Dixiecrats summoned him south often because he represented one of their nightmares, a black Red. Later José Ferrer was grilled by HUAC about Davis and recalled meeting Davis at Robeson's home. This was part of the continuing process of scaring celebrities away from Davis. Despite Ferrer's massive failure of memory, the committee nailed the Latino artist by producing a photograph of Robeson's birthday party with Davis "being introduced by José Ferrer, the Iago in Othello and one of Robeson's dearest friends." Exasperated, his interrogator blurted out, "It is almost unbelievable to some of us—I can only speak for myself—that it would be possible to sit on the same platform with and lend your name to [Davis] . . . and be unaware of the fact that [he] was one of the most prominent Communist members and functionaries in the Western Hemisphere."[3] This trend of hammering witnesses about their ties to Davis increased during 1949.

Davis's arrows were not all aimed at Washington. To win in November he knew he had to shore up his base, and for him that meant African-Americans and the Left. The local NAACP had a fruitful collaboration with his office, particularly on police brutality; there were special assembly-line forms to fill out for victims, which signified the level of ruthlessness of the gendarmes. It helped that Dorothy Hunton—the wife of his friend Alphaeus Hunton—was on the executive board of the Brooklyn-NAACP. But the burden of the trial and the campaign began to sour relations; it culminated when Roy Wilkins sought to bar the Left from a major civil rights mobilization, particularly the still-powerful CIO unions.[4] The vigilant Alfred Baker Lewis informed Frank Crosswaith that "the existing branch of the NAACP is now controlled by Communists and their fellow travellers and dupes." This was the prelude to the watershed purge of the Left from the NAACP at the Boston convention of 1950 that left the organization rudderless and disoriented to face the coming King-led challenge.[5]

This split came at an unfortunate moment for blacks. As ever, increased Red Scare military spending meant that less attention was paid to the pressing needs of Harlem and Bedford-Stuyvesant. Writing just after the City Council election, J. A. Rogers was amazed by the deterioration of Harlem: "In the past twenty years I have watched Harlem run more and more down at the heels. Apartments are impossible to get while nothing is done about the hundreds of condemned buildings. In congested East Harlem many live worse than pigs. Even the furnace basements are crowded. . . . Food is high and mounting higher while the government stashes it away or destroys it to keep up the price. . . . Burdensome taxes are crushing the poor." The progressive nationalist knew that "their yells for Marcantonio and Davis were in reality cries of pain for the economic pinch they are feeling. . . . A significant fact is that of the 20,008 votes Ben Davis, Communist leader, got, only 1,008 were Communist."[6] This latter figure may have been incorrect but not his overall analysis; the tragedy was that the removal of Davis from the council removed this cry of pain.

The ferocity of the siege against Davis and his allies left black New York ill-prepared to combat their problems. The uprising after Davis's trial served to validate Davis's concept that New York's "finest" were no more than "Ku Kluxers in uniform." In April Dennis Berber was shot six times by officers who expended fifteen bullets. To Davis police brutality against blacks was "the number-one public menace in New York." But this was not the sum total of Davis's mass political activity in the prelude to the election; whether barring evictions, protesting extraditions of blacks to southern peonage, or fighting for a public market in Harlem, he was black New York's tribune.[7]

As the election approached Davis was also sensitive to the changing ethnic composition of New York. His comrade Bella Dodd apparently was not as sensitive. She was expelled from the party after non–Puerto Rican tenants in a Lower East Side tenement protested her acting as counsel for a cheating landlord; then she called Puerto Ricans "lazy, dirty and immoral"; this was the kind of hurdle Davis had to overcome. Perhaps as a result, Davis paid more attention to his growing Puerto Rican constituency. In reaching out to West Indians, especially in the wake of the detention of Claudia Jones, Davis spoke out more on immigration questions; there were an estimated eighty-five thousand people from these islands in the city, and even though he was on trial he promised, "I personally will be present in my office on Saturdays from 10 A.M. to 6 P.M." to address immigration and other problems.[8]

Davis valiantly tried to attend to his council duties in the face of his cascading obligations. At first his colleagues tried to accommodate him; the council decided to meet in the spring at 5:00 P.M. instead of 1:30 P.M. But the *Daily Worker* maintained that this was "forced upon the Council by wide public pressure . . . in the past few weeks [Council] had received hundreds of protests from trade unions, Negroes and progressives." The usually anti-Communist Councilman Sharkey conceded graciously that Davis deserved his seat since "he did not sail under false colors in the election." He also said that he did not want to give Davis a basis for appeal if convicted on the ground that he was unable to attend sessions during the trial.[9]

Sharkey's solicitude may have been motivated by what the *Daily Worker* called the "verbal lacing" and the "sting of his irony and eloquence," which Davis often directed at him. In June, after one "tongue lashing," Sharkey "withdrew his motion." Unfortunately, Davis's relationship with Mike Quill was fading rapidly. Davis and Isaacs were still close but the fact that Isaacs could get enthusiastic backing from Allan Dulles, a future leader of the Central Intelligence Agency, showed the contradictions involved.[10]

As the Cold War deepened a recurring economic crisis Davis saw the focus on economic issues as a sure way to attract voters. In August he proposed a law rolling back rents to the 30 June 1947 levels. The New York Tenants Council, representing 250,000 residents, called on the City Council to back the Davis bill and oppose that of Sharkey. Davis's claim that his bill would save $50 million for Harlem tenants won applause uptown but his effort was beaten in the council, 16–2, with only Connolly voting with him.

Davis blasted the "landlord clique" that passed Sharkey's bill 14–6, yet he compromised by voting for it too, albeit with "great trepidation." The campaign to pass the Davis bill was hampered by initiatives, aimed at the Reds, to bar petitioners from City Hall and keep sound trucks off the street. The First Amendment was being sacrificed on the altar of the Red Scare. Under the guise of anti-Communism conservatives were able to snatch away the mobilization tools of Left and liberals.[11]

The budget was also subjected to Davis's scrutiny. At a hearing he tried to dispatch his aide Horace Marshall to represent him but O'Dwyer demurred: "Sit down or I'll have you put out." In his statement Davis had called for "an outlay in the budget for social services such as this city has never had before." He derided a "jim crow quota system" in "admitting delinquent children to charitable institutions." Thus he was among the five members voting against the budget. Councilman Charles Keegan of the Bronx mocked Davis's demarche: "If Ben had his way . . . the Police Department would be reduced to about two hundred members and these would be sent out to the edge of town to show people where the songbirds were found."[12]

Trying to act constructively, Davis and Connolly introduced a bill to establish a Special Committee on Unemployment and Home Relief to study the economic crisis, boost home relief, increase welfare benefits, and so on. However, having their names on the bill guaranteed it an uncertain fate at best. One overriding problem in the council was the antidemocratic Board of Estimate, which violated the one-person–one-vote rule by equating the borough presidents of populous Brooklyn and semirural Staten Island. Ultimately the Supreme Court agreed with Davis but forty years before they made up their minds Davis had introduced a bill to "break the political monopoly" of the board. He was concerned about their virtual plenary power over financial affairs and wanted to democratize the process by giving the council power to "increase, decrease or omit" appropriations. Davis also led the fight against a sales tax; Quinn and Palestin backed it in a narrow victory for the Right.[13]

Winning favorable public opinion was essential for Davis for the party to win in court and at the ballot box. This partially explains why he devoted so much time to constituent problems during the 1949 afflictions. J. A. Rogers was quite correct in portraying the crisis of everyday living gripping Harlem, and Davis set out to make this a more visible issue. For example, he went to 138 West 112 Street in Harlem to interview the Lewis family; the mother had been struck in the head by a falling ceiling after giving birth to her twelfth child. Another child had been bitten by a rat. They all lived in three basement rooms, paying sixty dollars per month. The picture in the *Daily Worker* featured a sad-looking family and Davis's comment: "I've seen bad conditions in many Harlem homes but this is the worst yet. . . . I will personally take them to the Department of Housing and Building and the Health Department and insist that the violations be removed." This was no crass exploitation of the poor, as his critics charged; the Lewises had come to his office for help. Davis immediately arranged for housing and health inspectors to visit the apartment, who promptly found violations; then Davis filed a suit for damages in the face of an attempted eviction. Davis's intervention led to the arrest of the landlord. When in April the city appropriated one hundred thousand dollars for twenty-two new building inspectors, Davis seemed to have won a victory, but he was not stirred since it amounted to a "little more than a penny per rat."[14]

Davis voted against a resolution legalizing city flophouses that passed 12–8 since he saw it as a scheme by the city to avoid finding homes for the poor and the homeless. Just as the city was voting more funds for inspectors, a raging fire gutted a Harlem tenement at 142 West 131 Street; within an hour Davis acted to secure aid for one hundred homeless and cut through red tape to get them assistance. He sought to force the Department of Welfare to withhold rent to landlords for relief clients in run-down dwellings; he called on the department to conduct surveys and urged the city's counsel to take rent dollars and place them in escrow, then defend tenants in eviction proceedings. With Ferdinand Smith and Arthur Schutzer of the American Labor Party, he tried to empower the poor by spurring the Organization of Unemployed in Harlem. Six years earlier such measures and actions would have had a good chance of getting off the ground but this was a different day.[15]

Davis's isolation in the council was compounded as Cold War issues reached the chambers. There was the question of Cardinal Mindszenty of Hungary who would end up spending years in the U.S. Embassy in Budapest because of conflicts with his government. The council voted 16–2 to back the cleric. Davis dissented. Isaacs countered: "The government did not convict him on false grounds." Davis dismissed it all as a "tempest in a teapot. . . . He has confessed he is guilty of black marketeering and conspiring with representatives of Wall Street to undermine the Hungarian government." Twisting the screw, he concluded that in any case, "fair trials are not a virtue of this country." Several thousand people picketing City Hall disagreed with him. Davis went on to expose the cardinal's anti-Semitism and opposed the effort to involve the council as a body in a pro-Mindszenty rally, but his was not a universally popular position.[16]

Then the council moved a resolution calling on the United Nations to do something about alleged religious discrimination in eastern Europe. This too passed 16–2, with Davis berating "[this] smokescreen for political reaction." Davis was called a "traitor," as was his usual partner in dissent, Connolly; Earle and Isaacs abstained. Davis's position led to threats against his life; unmoved, he wondered why the council had rejected his initiatives on police brutality if they were "so interested in tolerance and freedom." He told his fellow members, "I warn the Council that it is helping to bring about three things now tearing at the vitals of our people. They are, one, the growing and increasing danger of war, two, fascism; three, the economic chaos manifesting itself throughout the country." Anyway, he maintained, there was a "high quality of religious freedom" in eastern Europe. "Why doesn't [the Council] mention Franco Spain? Where was the Council when 6,000,000 Jews were exterminated. . . . I never heard the Council pass such a resolution. Why doesn't it mention the Negroes lynched?" By now Sharkey was blustering, "stand up and say right now whether you believe in God." Dodging the bullet, Davis suggested that Sharkey "should get down on his hands and knees before" Truman and added, "Why, if it weren't for that President where would you be now?" Someone in the gallery remarked in a stage whisper, "He wouldn't be facing jail!"[17]

But Davis was the man facing jail while simultaneously seeking reelection. Red leader Jack Stachel echoed international leftist opinion when he called this race "the most important single campaign that is being waged in our country in 1949." The CP had the opportunity to use this electoral platform in an attempt to beat back the Red Scare with one of their most attractive and well-known comrades. Even if he was jailed, the past example of Eugene Debs showed that a leftist running from behind bars could be dramatically effective. The fact that the GOP, Liberals, and Democrats backed one candidate against him demonstrated their apprehension in running against Davis; indeed, this was the only district where they put forward one candidate. They charged that Davis should not be elected since he might go to jail; Davis said he could do a better job from jail than his opponent. Such was the banter in an election during an intense Red Scare featuring the "lone Communist member of a legislative body" in the United States.[18]

Davis's district took in the West Side of Manhattan from roughly 100th to 160th streets and from the Hudson River to Eighth Avenue; excluding the area between 117th and 134th, it ran over to Madison Avenue. He had a worthy record on behalf of his constituency, but he was beaten 3–1. However, Davis was still an intriguing story. He won an absolute majority in the black areas but lost because he did not prevail in the white areas, which shows how blacks were less taken with the Red Scare than their white counterparts. The problem was that the district was at least half-white. "Even in defeat," said the *Daily Worker*, "Davis polled more Harlem votes than he did in the two previous elections."[19]

It was simple to see why the anti-Davis forces had difficulty lining up a candidate even in the middle of an anti-Communism surge. They thought it was advisable to get a black candidate since a white one would probably serve to unduly galvanize Harlem—or so they thought; but this pointed out the value of the Communist campaign since it forced the other parties to make concessions to compete. Asked first was the Reverend James Robinson of the Church of the Master in Harlem. Then Fred DeMendez, a prominent Harlem Democrat, was courted. He declined on grounds of "racial unity." So they began wooing David Capehart, undertaker and real-estate mogul. Neil Scott was pressuring Robinson to run but in early August he "suddenly" withdrew. Capehart was a nonstarter. Who was left?[20]

The answer was Earl Brown, the son of a Charlottesville Baptist minister. Like Davis, he was a Harvard graduate; most important, he was African-American. Brown majored in economics and lettered in baseball. He played with the Black Yankees, taught in the South, worked with the *New York Herald Tribune*, became managing editor of the *New York Amsterdam News*, and then went to *Life* magazine. In the *Amsterdam News* poll, he was voted a rousing "66th most popular person in Harlem" in 1949, obtaining 812 out of 200,000 votes cast.[21]

In 1940 the rival *New York Age* had criticized Brown's tenure with the *New York Amsterdam News*; they "had more libel suits on the dockets against it than any other Negro paper, and all because of the lack of knowledge of Brown." He was accused of "coloring stories of those he liked and blasting away at those he disliked." *The New York Herald Tribune*, *Life*, and *Time* magazine all viewed Brown as their "pet"; this might win him accolades below 110th Street, but uptown it was a liability.[22]

Brown was not a model of consistency. In 1945 he assessed politics as a "professional game which employs the people as pawns and dupes . . . neither the Republican nor the Democrat party desires to see first rate men capture leadership positions."[23] Two years later he uttered words that later haunted him: "It should be stated right off that it [is] poor politics for [the] major parties to gang up on a candidate."[24] He said this during an anti-Powell upsurge, when Brown was prematurely praising Henry Wallace and the ALP. "Harlem's politicians are still a putrid group of little men or men with little or no ability," he stated. These same men turned out to be his prime supporters two years later in 1949. But in 1947 Brown was humming a different tune: " . . . if we cannot combat Communism successfully in this country without employing identically the same method we accuse the Communists of employing we should be ashamed of our democratic form of government. But it may be that America's practical experience in kicking the Negro around . . . has so warped her ideals that she instinctively resorts to lynch mob methods in coping with Communism." This was quite a perceptive statement in any year but particularly so as the Red Scare was taking off; like many black intellectuals, Brown was then too smart to be fooled.[25]

But by early 1949 George Schuyler was castigating Brown for being soft on Communism—a charge that was ironic months later. The black conservative had taken umbrage at Brown's notion that " . . . if this country is so weak that it is in danger of being overthrown by a handful of Communists, it ought to be overthrown . . . the press is generally prejudiced against the [CP-11] defendants . . . nobody should be indicted and tried in court for wishful thinking or for his political beliefs." Again, Brown was quite astute.

But weeks later he had reversed field: "Mr. Davis is the kind of Councilman I do not like. He is a professional Negro and a professional Communist. One of these is bad enough but when you add either one to the other you have something or somebody simply awful to behold or to listen to." Shortly thereafter he was calling for a coalition of the anti-CP and anti-ALP forces—an alliance spearheaded by a similarly retreating wing of the black press. The *Amsterdam News* had ceased to be just a newspaper; three of their staffers—Brown, Moran Weston, and Carl Lawrence—were seeking office on a similar platform.[26]

The cunning "Harlem Fox," J. Ray Jones, had backed Davis in previous elections and what he termed his "impeccable voting record," but in 1949 Jone's career took off when in return for opposing Davis, he was offered the role of Tammany chief. Interestingly, in his memoirs he evaluates Davis positively while reproving Brown: "I knew we would have to groom Brown, write his speeches, coach him, everything . . . unable to write a political speech but also he was unable to deliver one with any elan . . . compulsive gambler . . . favored the race track, always carried the tote sheet and bet regularly on the horses . . . in debt . . . to bookies . . . an odd career." In Harlem he was known as "Look Down Brown" (because he could not or would not look people in the eye) and was the "epitome of a bossed person."[27]

Jones's estimate was shared widely. Neil Scott accused Brown of "kowtowing to the rich whites downtown and showing no interest in Harlem as such." Robeson charged that Brown was "going to do some overtime work for Henry Luce . . . he will have the dubious pleasure of splitting the Negro people . . . undermining racial unity and of furthering the interest of his masters."[28] According to the *Age* on 23 July even "some Tammany leaders" were "incensed" by the decision to choose Brown.

Brown provided an inviting target for Davis, a master of invective: "Even if I am in jail," he said, "I will be more good to you than my Uncle Tom opponent." Accusing Brown of "treachery" for running against him, he added, "They had to pick up an obscure hack to ride into public office on the discredited bugaboo of anti-communism." Later he called him a "political pipsqueak that the colored people will not even spit upon."[29] In the first draft of his bitter prison memoir Davis labeled him a "be-bop politician with a veritable juke box mind. . . . Politically he raised confusion to the level of high statesmanship. He was pitiful."[30] What may have fueled Davis's rhetoric was the widespread belief that it was gambling debts and not political principle that caused Brown to run against a man he had praised.

The presence of the Left compelled elites to grant concessions to blacks. Not only Ray Jones but Ruth Whitehead Whaley (who succeeded him as deputy commissioner of Housing), Crosswaith, and others received more attention—and benefits—with the rise of the Left. They did not seem to recognize that their aid in undermining the Left also removed one of their main trump cards and increased the strength of their main foe—the Right. Class differentiation was becoming more important among blacks but it was little recognized outside of the Left.[31]

This approach convinced the *Age*; in endorsing Davis the paper stated: "Earl Brown is a pleasant and harmless non-entity who can be relied upon to say the right thing at the right time—to the right people. [Davis] is a rootin' tootin' rip-snorting all-action fighter." Unlike other newspapers, they decided to uphold the First Amendment and not refuse ads from Davis's reelection committee.[32]

As for Davis, the roar and acclamation of the crowd was a respite from the bizarre proceedings in court. When he was introduced at one late-July Harlem rally, the crowd "applauded tumultuously and shouted, 'That's our Ben! and 'We're with you, Ben!' As the Negro Communist spoke, windows up and down the street were filled with enthusiastic listeners. Taxi drivers stopped their cabs and lined the street until the hovering cops made them move on. The crowd grew so large that it filled almost the whole block between 125th and 126th Street . . . pounding his fists, the Georgia-born Negro Councilman declared, 'It is about time they stopped the government from overthrowing the people.'"[33]

This aggressive campaigning brought Davis commendation. Du Bois headed his reelection committee. Larkin Marshall and Charles Howard flew to New York to campaign for him. Actress Fredi Washington was one of the few celebrities who did not flee from him and stood firmly by his side. Modjeska Simkins, GOP committee member of South Carolina, toured Harlem with him. The faithful Reverend Thomas Harten, "pastor of the largest Negro congregation in Brooklyn," continued to support him. Leading black journalist Claude Barnett indicated the importance of the election by seeking information for his readers. When Davis was jailed just after his conviction, journalist James Hicks expressed the sentiment that the imprisonment "is providing the most concern . . . no experienced politician is underrating the damage which he can do from within the prison walls . . . [the] twisting of his conviction as an injustice to colored people is winning sympathetic support among Harlemites." Even Roy Wilkins confided to a press conference in Los Angeles that he voted for Davis in the 1945 election.[34]

As in his past campaigns, the other pillar of Davis's electoral effort was labor. The estimated twenty-five thousand trade unionists in his district were the "chief base of support" for Davis.[35] This was certainly true for black labor—excluding of course Randolph, Crosswaith, and the Negro Labor Committee. Crosswaith cheered the routing of the Reds at the 1949 CIO convention: "the task of the responsible elements within organized labor is going to be harder, because the Communists will then concentrate on the Negro and they will move heaven and earth to exploit him . . . New York City is the one industrial area with a large Negro population where the Communists have failed to tie the Negro to their destructive wagon. The

Negro Labor Committee, supported by a mere handful of progressive unions, is responsible for their failure."[36] This was only partly true; more accurate is that Crosswaith and friends were in a position to capitalize on the anti-Communist upsurge.

Davis continued to cater to labor, especially black labor, during the 1949 campaign. During his legislative career he introduced twelve bills dealing with job protection and fair employment, twenty-five concerning black rights, and twenty-five to protect and extend civil liberties—all of which progressive labor applauded. In August he pledged "to strengthen the New York State FEPC Law so that all [railroad] crafts in the industry will be open to all men and women, regardless of race . . . to half the deliberate and growing displacement of Negro railroad workers in New York City." His platform called for a black deputy police commissioner, two black police captains for Harlem, integration of Harlem detectives, banning mounted cops from Harlem (the only residential area where they were stationed permanently), and indemnification of families of victims killed by police. This combination of race and labor politics cemented his support in a race-conscious Harlem dominated by working-class families.[37]

The Harlem Trade Union Council, under the leadership of his friends and allies Ewart Guinier, Charles Collins and Ferdinand Smith, was the locomotive for the Davis campaign. Davis's mettle was tested when a race-based labor dispute erupted in Local 968 of the International Longshore Association. In the spring of 1949 an effort arose, in Davis's words, "to eliminate Negro longshoremen from the waterfront" in this 98 percent black union. Naturally this was a right-wing, anti-Communist-led offensive. Black labor "went to Ben Davis because we knew he would fight for us." Davis went without delay to O'Dwyer: "Labor goons and hoodlum gangs connected with the reactionary, anti-Negro elements among the shipowners and union bosses" are on the march. "The very lives of these men are in constant jeopardy." Since the end of the war, membership had dropped from one thousand five hundred to seven hundred. Weeks later Davis's resolution was "still rotting in committee." The Right triumphed; blacks were purged; corruption and gangsterism increased—points conveniently neglected in the motion picture *On the Waterfront* and elsewhere. Such was the price of the Red Scare.[38]

Not just black labor backed Davis. Local 1199, drugstore workers, also supported him. Hundreds of union leaders and many locals lined up with Davis. He reciprocated when workers at Larkin Lectro went on strike for six weeks in the spring. "No candidate in New York County is more closely identified with the aims of organized labor" was the opinion of the unionists backing him. But when Max Perlow had to resign from the party in the middle of the campaign in order to comply with the Taft-Hartley Act (he was secretary-treasurer of the United Furniture Workers), the predicament facing pro-Davis unionists was clear.[39]

Despite the fact that fewer whites than African-Americans voted for him, Davis did reach out to this constituency. Annette Rubinstein, literary historian and frequent critic of the CP, backed Davis. The large ACLU-oriented sector cheered his call for a withdrawal of the ban against Howard Fast's novel *Citizen Paine*, while some of these same forces booed his demand for the removal of certain racist books from schools. Party forces influential in the film industry clubs produced a 16mm work entitled *What's Happening in Harlem* concerning the election. In mid-October crowds of three to four hundred were "common at every open-air showing." Then police began issuing summonses.[40]

With their usual understated candor the *Daily Worker* termed *What's Happening* the "finest film on Harlem ever made." It "shows a clear connection between police brutality and slum housing and high prices . . . shows how Harlem fights through Ben Davis." But the film was receiving scores of citations from the authorities. It was claimed that O'Dwyer placed four hundred "undercover men" to watch the CP in the city and be present at film showings; to that point fifty thousand had seen the film. Unsurprisingly and perhaps accurately, Davis called himself the most persecuted legislator in the country: "They have carried this persecution of me too far. They have carried it so far, many people will vote for me just because of it."[41]

When he said this Davis was reflecting the fact that the authorities took a jaundiced interest in his campaign. The FBI attended his speeches and issued criticism—a "long rambling tirade"—and were faithful readers of his *Daily Worker* columns, although their close friend Cardinal Spellman concurred with Reverend Edwin Broderick that reading CP writings like that of Davis was a "sin." At St. Catherine of Genoa Church at 506 West 158 Street—Davis country—parishioners were threatened with excommunication if they voted for Davis. Father James Kane admitted as much. Then hoodlums, reportedly from the American Legion post, attacked ALP offices at 884 Columbus and mutilated and defaced Davis posters.[42] Big Red-hunter Frederick Woltman of the *New York World-Telegram* spread the story that the party gave Tammany twenty thousand dollars when Davis got its nod in 1945, "according to an underground mimeographed publication circulated within the Communist party by members opposed to its present leadership."[43] WMCA-AM tried to interfere with the broadcast of one of Davis's speeches. The *Herald-Tribune*, though troubled by the consolidation of an all-Democrat Council, which inevitably would lead to the demise of this GOP newspaper, screamed in a 27 October 1949 editorial, "Vote Against Communist Davis . . . no one-track-minded Communist was ever more typical." Frank Crosswaith hailed the editor for this opinion.[44]

The *Times* on 31 October applauded their own foresight in endorsing a repeal of proportional representation; PR's absence certainly made Davis's task more difficult. The paper of record sniffed, "Mr. Davis has contributed more than his share to lowering of public esteem for the Council." They backed Earl Brown, the so-called fusion candidate. So did Arthur Logan, Mollie Moon, Benjamin McLaurin, C. B. Powell, and A. Philip Randolph. Herbert Bruce rounded up funds and support for Brown.[45]

The Tammany Tiger, which had wrestled with endorsing Davis in 1945, fell in line for Brown in 1949. As rules were bent to trip up Davis, doors were opened to aid Brown.[46] The *New York Amsterdam News* broke the link between the domestic and international by arguing on 29 October that Brown would win since he would "be able to help get cleaner streets and a public market for Harlem and help put a halt to police brutality" instead of the claimed "Yugoslavia and China" lines of Davis.

As mentioned earlier, the fruitful alliance of Davis with entertainers shriveled in the heat of repression. Robeson was there as usual, helping to pull together "The Gospel Train" concert for Davis at Rockland Palace; on the program were the Harmonizing Four from Richmond, Virginia; the Two Gospel Keys of Augusta, Georgia; Sister Rosa Shaw of Tampa, Florida; the Mount Lebanon Jubilee Singers, and Brownie McGhee. This was a far cry from 1945 but still formidable. The *New York Age* assessed one Davis party at the Hotel Theresa as "gay, but too many speeches" and praised the "excellent dance music."[47] Sidney Poitier also attended Davis events. The drifting away of the stars was not an act of God, however, For example, talent agencies made a concerted effort to pressure black bands to boycott Davis.

The backbone of the entire campaign was the Communist party. The party organ underlined that the campaign "has become a matter of international concern." Every section of the nation was sending funds and letters. They did so because, according to an article by Jack Stachel in the *Daily Worker*, "he is the sole communist elected official in a land whose ruling circles have made of anti-communism the instrument for . . . oppression."[48] The support Davis did receive in labor from blacks, and others was outlined by Pettis Perry:

> It is extremely important that all districts work for the sending into New York of Negro and white leaders who would speak in behalf of Comrade Davis. This would dramatize our approach to Comrade Davis' re-election and would serve as an important factor to weld the unity of the progressive forces and the Negro people.[49]

The record shows a rising drumbeat of support in 1949 for Davis from the party. The fact that it was able to obtain four thousand signatures for petitions for Davis in days indicates their aid. This activity spurred the state party's other campaigns; six thousand signatures were collected in three days, "obtained by 1,000 canvassers working in teams of two." The *Daily Worker* reported on 21 August that Davis was getting five hundred signatures a day; one canvasser noticed, "the response is better—much better—than during the Wallace campaign." Another remarked, "The voters know that Ben is on trial because he fights for Negro rights. They won't swallow this 'force and violence' stuff."[50]

And on 25 August the *Daily Worker* wrote that Davis had garnered seventeen thousand signatures.

The party was on the radio every weekday night from 20 September to election day. Davis spoke on WJZ every Tuesday night from 10:30–10:45; a party representative was on WMCA every weekday night except Wednesday from 9:05—9:15, focusing on the Davis campaign. In early November the word was that Earl Brown could lose, since Davis's "return to Harlem Thursday night was like that of a hero to his faithful followers," in part because of his fierce attacks on "police brutality."[51]

The American Labor party was also busy. Ray Tillman, a black veteran, former Dillard University student, and former member of the executive board of the Transport Workers Union ("only Negro to hold such a post") was indispensable to the party. Marcantonio, Shirley Graham, Ewart Guinier, and Charles Collins also were helpful. Davis received the ALP ballot line, they supplied him with staff, and did not hide their advocacy.[52]

On 3 June 1949 the New York City Executive Committee of the ALP designated Guinier and Davis as candidates for office on their ballot line; given the records of the other parties, this was stupendous—two African-Americans. But Connolly did not agree; he wanted the slot. Turmoil ensued and charges of racism flew.

Somehow the work continued. The ALP played a significant role in cobbling together a Non-Partisan Youth Committee to Re-elect Davis. Tillman sought to "launch an intense campaign to register the highest number of votes in the city's history" to overcome the problem of the proportional representation ban. Davis reciprocated; when the Citizens Democratic Club of Harlem gave strong support for Marcantonio, his hand was seen.[53] But the Davis-ALP tie suffered a grievous blow when Connolly bailed out, though Davis was probably too harsh in his evaluation of his erstwhile colleague: "Never a resolute fighter, he literally withered before my very eyes in the Council."[54]

In early May 1949 Joseph Goldsmith, president of the Taxpayers Union, threatened to institute a taxpayers' suit to recover appropriations for Davis's salary. As early as January moves had been afoot in the council to oust Davis and suspend his salary; the reviled Connolly blocked that resolution. But as Medina's antics became more animated, council members Hugh Quinn and Sharkey in October sought to revive this movement. "Less than an hour after the verdict," Quinn sought to remove his Red colleague. Davis's racially integrated corps of lawyers—Paul Kern, Thomas Jones, Paul Ross, and David Freedman—beat back the case in a crowded courtroom.[55]

These late-October events were part of the last act in the anti-Davis drama. In the election he was defeated soundly, though in the "solidly Negro"

Eleventh A.D., he got 42 percent of the vote (more in toto than O'Dwyer) and a significant percentage of his overall total; he lost 21,962 to 63,030 for Brown. Considering that the candidate had been jailed for three weeks in the middle of the campaign and was released only four days before the election, this was a credible effort. He was barred from voting by the state attorney general, which he considered a "cheap political maneuver." Davis campaign official Ollie Harrington has suggested that there were improper actions in the election and vote fraud; many voting booths in Harlem were not working; the election "was stolen," he believes.[56]

But an electoral defeat was not enough for Davis's fellow council members. The fact that Davis was still serving between election day and Brown's inauguration was too much for them and they sought his ejection, the first in council history. Hedging their bets, they began this maneuver in mid-October by featuring a "long and acrimonious debate" between Rager and Isaacs where the Silk-Stocking Republican was called "worse than a Communist." Connolly stood by Davis as well as Isaacs. There was scuffling outside with police as one thousand Davis fans picketed. But in late November he was expelled, 15–0, from the council, with Isaacs and Louis Goldberg (Liberal-Brooklyn) abstaining. They urged a due process hearing; Davis called it a "legislative lynching" and a "police-state procedure." Rager demanded that this "convicted traitor be removed from this room forthwith." Davis denounced the "vicious lies of this little crackpot." Naturally Davis was not allowed to vote here, either.[57]

This council session was appropriately tumultuous. Connolly resigned in protest over the ouster (though he was absent during the vote because of his brother's funeral); however, he dissented from Davis's characterization of a "Jim Crow" expulsion; he had lost in November in any case. The council sought to "forcibly remove" Davis but the Harlemite would not budge. He took his case to court immediately but lost. Stanley Isaacs balefully told Davis after the smashing defeat, "I thought your matter was handled very badly and very unjustly at the Council meeting. Moreover, I studied the Corporation Counsel's opinion and I think it quite unsound. . . . You and I see differently on many problems but I always respected you and the dignity with which you represented your community and your cause—and under miserable provocation from time to time. I do hope that the pending appeal will show the Smith Act unconstitutional, as I believe it is."[58] Meanwhile U.S. Attorney Irving Saypol, who was connected to organized crime, tried to hold up Davis's remaining semimonthly checks of $166 each. Even Earl Brown objected to that indignity.[59]

Since Davis was the only member of the council not informed by telegram of his pending ouster, he thought this would be a useful legal ground. But due process could not bear the weight of the Red Scare; although Judge Thomas Aurelio initially signed a show cause order on the matter, he ultimately retreated, reasoning that Davis had violated his oath of office.[60]

Stanley Isaacs cried out, "All I asked for was that the Council constitute itself into a meeting of the Committee, hear Mr. Davis, and then act."⁶¹ A fair trial before the hanging was asking too much.

The post mortems on this debacle for the party and democracy were as varied as the number of voices. On 12 November the *New York Amsterdam News* said that "the big mistake of the Davis campaign . . . was to concentrate on noise-making and surface canvassing . . . It was also said that too many strange workers were ordered into Harlem to campaign for Davis and that the voters are rightfully suspicious of 'Greeks bearing gifts.'" Did the party commit a tactical error here, especially by sending whites into certain black areas? Even Earl Brown was awed by the campaign of his fellow Harvard alumnus: "It is impossible for any political party to campaign as furiously and as long as the Communists at any given time and in any given place. . . . They brought in their 'troops' from near and far to campaign among the voters. And their 'troops' inveighed, shouted and spouted and marched and sang from June until election night. They visited practically every voter in Harlem two or three times."⁶²

The *New York Age* fondly recalled on 19 November that "only the ALP with its Ewart Guinier for Borough President of Manhattan considered the Negro beyond the fact that he had a vote to cast." The paper praised Davis, but then columnist Ben Richardson observed that "the election of Earl Brown did more to reinstate the Negro in the eyes of his fellow Americans than any single act [of late]"; it was "one group of phonies [defeating] another group of phonies," he inveighed.

The *Times* regretted that the council was now "composed so overwhelmingly of members of one party" (there were now twenty-four Democrats, one GOP-Liberal—Isaacs, the most principled of the lot) and the resurgence of machine and clubhouse politics. But the *Times* added, "We have the great satisfaction of seeing a complete absence of Communist and fellow traveler members . . . [Brown] is certainly an improvement over Benjamin J. Davis, Jr. . . . who would almost surely have been re-elected if PR were in effect." That was not all: "the electorate appealed to was a more diversified cross-section than fitted Mr. Davis' strategy. The number of votes that Mr. Davis was able to garner was by no means identical with Communist strength in his district, because a good many people doubtless voted for him for reasons other than his party affiliation . . . " Presumably this was some comfort. "We believe that the City Council will be able to do its business better with Mr. Davis among the absent. He was always the special pleader for a class. . . . He used the floor as a sounding board for political ideology." Davis may have blushed at these last remarks but the *Times* was able to "say good-by without regret."⁶³

The *Times* piece was too much for Robert Aeurbach, who was upset about their anti-Communism: "In our democratic form of government if the people wish to elect a Communist, a Communist should be elected." As late as the 1973 coup in Chile, the United States had refused to accept this idea. But what swayed Auerbach and thousands of others was that the post-PR council was much less diverse and democratic than its predecessor. It was also more conservative and less open to addressing deep-seated socioeconomic problems. Not only was PR killed, but then New York State passed some of the most draconian laws anywhere restricting ballot access and thereby democracy. This too was the price of the Red Scare.[64]

Ted Poston of the *New York Post* pointed out on 9 November that with Davis's loss the party "has suffered the most crushing defeat in its New York City history." However, though Davis drew masses on election night, "ironically no large crowd greeted Earl Brown . . . at his tiny storefront campaign headquarters at 2157 Seventh Avenue." Still, Brown was modest: "It was no victory of mine," the Post quoted. "It was just the defeat of the forces of Communism." The *Boston Herald* stated forthrightly that the Kremlin was not usually interested in United States elections, "but there was one contest the Russians must have kept an eye on." The *Herald* reassured their readers by alleging that the black Red "managed to get elected to the New York City Council by exploiting the race issue." They ruminated, "Russia destroys men who oppose its system with repressive laws and with bullets. We do it with votes. . . . In the marketplace, evil doctrines have never been able to stand the competition."[65] The courtroom antics, the violence, and the jammed voting machines were all forgotten in the myth-making. Meanwhile, on 19 November the *Pittsburgh Courier* called the Davis defeat "a pleasant surprise;" the party "poured . . . thousands of party henchmen and hacks drawn from all over the city and the East. Sound trucks spouting idiotic propaganda made the night and day hideous. Mile-long parades with floats and music wended their way periodically through the streets of Harlem . . . with straggling mobs of nondescript and fanatics shouting and singing."

The reaction of the *New York Herald Tribune* was curious; although an all-Democrat council basically hastened this GOP organ's demise, they saw the election and defeat of Davis as a "clear gain." The *Daily Worker* quoted an unidentified police officer at the voting booth at P.S. 81 at 215 West 119 Street, "'I guess our clubs will have to be a little heavier, now that Ben's gone . . . ' the cop smirked . . . 'Now he won't be standing on the corners yelling about beating up women and children.'" These self-indicting assertions reflect how the process had been debased.[66]

Ironically it was Lillian Gates, a future foe of Davis in party battles, who summed up the party view:

> New York City election trends embody developing political currents far more than any other single area . . . election struggles here [are] both a test of present, and a mirror of future, political trends throughout the country . . . an unholy alliance was formed to defeat [Davis], which became a national concentration point of

reaction. Democrats, Republicans, Liberals and Fusion ganged up against him and conducted a campaign of confusion, lies and distortions with the Foley Square frame-up as the center of this concentrated attack. . . . Although the defeat of [Davis] is a serious loss to the people, the vote won by him reflected a major breakthrough among the Negro people. This vote far exceeded that ever achieved among the Negro people in the Harlem area. Davis' stature as a national spokesman for the Negro people has been heightened and his influence extended. The splendid campaign for the re-election of [BD] in the 21st Senatorial District merits a special article . . . movies, open air meetings . . . elicited the grudging, admiration of practically the entire New York press . . . breakthrough . . . centered in the 11th Assembly District . . . here 46 per cent of the votes supported Davis. . . . The history of the removal of [Davis] is in itself a lesson in the high price of anti-communism.[67]

Some might argue that she was too optimistic, given the loss, but her opinion reflected similar sentiments within the party.

While Stanley Isaacs was dodging brickbats from constituents angry about his position on Davis—"I voted for you this last election. I assure you I will never vote for you again," wrote one woman—Davis was telling his ex-colleague to bear down: "The only ray of light that appeared during that infamous session of the Council when I was illegally ousted was [your] courageous and eloquent voice. . . . I look back upon six years of association with you in the Council with pleasure and pride."[68]

From this point forward, Davis's accomplishments—except for a brief period during the 1950s—were cast into a dungeon of indifference by a press that once covered his every word. Simultaneously the FBI stepped up their surveillance. Allies of a few years back crossed the street to avoid greeting him. The time of the toad had begun. The colossal opportunism of some people helps to account in part for Davis's perhaps too-impassioned denunciations of those erstwhile allies; they knew better, they knew that they knew better, and Davis knew that they knew better. But that was all over now. With the onset of war in Korea, the Red Scare reached its apogee and the black condition regressed.

14
Fighting Back, 1950–1951

The conviction and the council ouster had an immediate impact. Joseph Starobin reported bitterly from Europe, "The American in Europe is the object of derision, if not contempt. . . . Everywhere in other parts of Europe one finds a most intense interest and deep sympathy for what is happening across the Atlantic."[1] There was similar fear there about impending fascism in the United States. Mass rallies, articles, and pickets supporting Red Scare victims like Davis were common. The Civil Rights Congress was already proving that despite U.S. strength, protest abroad could not be ignored. The fact that right after the conviction Japanese authorities pondered a copycat ban of the Communist Party illustrates the international scope of the Red Scare, which mandated in turn an international campaign to confront it. But the Korean war made it more difficult for Davis and the party to reverse the harsh sentences of the Foley Square trial in 1950–51.

The *New York World-Telegram* averred on 5 October 1949 that as the "verdict [was] given, [Davis] let out an audible gasp." His reaction was understandable. There were heavy five-year sentences and ten thousand dollars fines; Judge Medina would have given them all ten years except that Congress in 1948 had reduced the sentence and he was not sure if it was meant to apply to the CP-11. According to the *New York Times* on 22 October, Davis "made an embittered statement." No longer were these deemed remarks that Davis had spoken with dignity; no, a different fate was being cast for him. On 19 October the *Times* militantly defended the trial: "The conviction . . . underlines the importance of the vital distinction between advocacy of radical or unpopular ideas and conspiring to use force to put them into effect." Fowler Harper remonstrated correctly days later, "This of course is precisely what the conviction does not underline." But the dominant opinion was reflected by the editorial writers as they re-wrote the first draft of history. The *New York Mirror* expressed the bloodlust on 5 October: "We envy those writers who will be able to comment on the outcome of the Communist trial with calm and measured detachment. Our own honest, natural and instant impulse is to yell hooray and we're going to do it. Hooray!"

Prosecutor John F. X. McGohey was promptly rewarded with a federal judgeship but on the same day William Hastie was named the first black on the Circuit Court of Appeals. The Davis speech at conviction augured the further integration of blacks into all levels of U.S. society; the Cold War mandated it, not just because of the international image but as a way to undermine leftist appeal among blacks. The pounding of the party was of crude legality; the *New York Herald Tribune* was not alone in doubting, on 21 August, if the Supreme Court would uphold the convictions; the *New York Post* concurred two days later that the "trial is a turkey ... it is difficult to believe that the Supreme Court would sustain a conviction." On 16 October, in the *New York Times*, Cabell Phillips captured the complexity of the trial and the appeal to the Supreme Court as "one of the most momentous in the recent history of that tribunal. So vast are its implications that lawyers, scholars and moralists will be arguing over it for a decade ... the inescapable fact remains that for the first time, a political party in the United States has ... been put beyond the pale of the law." As of June 1951, he said, this would include 43,000 members with 22,670 in New York State alone. "Recruitment of new members ... is bound to suffer," though "the fanatical impulses of communism are not likely to be quenched by statutes or court orders. ... The disfranchisement of a political party is not an easy price for Americans to pay for any sort of security."[2]

The *Philadelphia Tribune*, the *St. Louis American*, Hubert Delany, Earl Brown, and many others all fearlessly spoke out against the convictions. The party ignored the conventional wisdom that it was unwise to reach out directly to the high court. Aubrey Williams, publisher of the *Southern Farmer* and close to the party, wrote Justice Burton ("My dear Harold") requesting a stay.[3] Earlier Rev. Ethelred Brown, pastor of the Unitarian Church in Harlem, had reached the same justice. Burton, a former mayor of Cleveland, was not unfamiliar with progressives since the Left was a presence in his Lake Erie city. He had solicited an opinion as early as 1939 on the same issues involved in the 1949 trial.[4]

Former Harvard Law professor Justice Felix Frankfurter of the high court was also in contact with concerned citizenry about the CP-11 appeal. In a "Dear Felix" letter, Reinhold Niebuhr disagreed with his friend's siding with the majority and agreed with the dissent.[5] This desertion by some liberals disgruntled Justice Frankfurter, a former Austrian refugee. In a prickly "Dear Irving" letter, he rebuked the veteran writer Irving Dillard of the *St. Louis Post-Dispatch*, one of the few mainstream papers to oppose the verdict, " ... it always strikes me a bit odd that a man like you should be telling me privately what he does not tell his readers publicly."[6]

The party-led mobilization against the verdict was being felt. Justice Robert Jackson testified on this drive at a Senate subcommittee hearing and displayed a stack of telegrams. He derided the party's campaign in unusually harsh terms. Much went back and forth between Frankfurter and Justice Stanley Reed on the case, with Professor Frankfurter on one occasion pointing out confusion in his colleague's opinion. This confusion may have resulted from the voluminous pages and blizzard of briefs. Yet, according to Justice William O. Douglas (who with Justice Hugo Black opposed the convictions), discussion was short and brief on the case. Frankfurter was correct in suggesting that the "clear and present danger test . . . not very well understood. . . . There really was very little discussion of the whole problem." But Douglas's detractors were not satisfied by his legal points; one correspondent flatly asked him, "How in the name of God did a nut, screwball and crackpot like you get on the Bench of the Supreme Court?"[7]

Squashing Davis and the party was no academic question. Bernadette Doyle, party candidate for California's post as state superintendent of public instruction and chair of the party in San Diego, received 613,670 votes in mid-1950, just before the Korean War; this was a whopping 26 percent of the vote with one-third of it coming from San Francisco and Kern counties. The next year Henry Steinberg, legislative director of the party in Los Angeles, received 39,707 votes for the school board. So putting away Davis and his comrades was not just aimed at fellow-travelers and liberals, although this was a primary concern. This fact sheds light on U.S. Attorney Irving Saypol's attempt to bar five of the defendants from visiting their homes outside New York without an order preventing them from "teaching and advocating" revolution. But, as ever, maximum concern seemed to be reserved for black Reds. Henry Root Stern, chair of the New York State Board of Social Welfare, speaking to one hundred people at an Urban League gathering at the McAlpin Hotel, cautioned them to be wary of Davis and Robeson: "I say that all Negroes must choose between the cause of the Communist and that of the free American. They cannot have both."[8] However, this was a difficult sale to make as long as Jim Crow reigned, so Jim Crow had to go.

The Judiciary Committee of the State Senate of New York moved quickly to insure that Davis could not take advantage of any residual backing for him. After the talk of his running arose, a bill was introduced to deprive Davis of the right to run for office. It was reported out 17-1, despite the party's plea that it was an unconstitutional bill of attainder, but it was privately called the "Davis bill" by sponsors. Again, in a move that characterized his usual approach to the conviction, Davis tried to link his plight to that of his constituency: "Negroes framed by Jim Crow juries in the South as well as persons active in behalf of labor would be automatically barred from running for public office."[9]

Particularly after the onset of war, the party mobilized heavily against the convictions and for a reversal. When bail was revoked and Davis faced the prospect of a prison cell, fourteen thousand supporters rallied in midtown Manhattan. But time was running out.[10]

Davis was seeking more forthrightly to link the destiny of African-Americans with global developments, suggesting that Jim Crow was the

Achilles' heel of U.S. foreign policy. He did not spare Wilkins, White, Granger, Tobias, or Randolph in his indictment. Claire Booth Luce—"that decadent pin-up girl of the reactionary Roman Catholic hierarchy"—and her ilk were his prime target, however. Yet Davis was swimming in choppier waters. James Roark has commented that after the launching of the Red Scare and the Cold War, the black press generally "shifted its attention away from colonialism to communism. Reversing their earlier emphasis, in 1948 the five national black papers allocated four times more space to world communism than to European colonialism."[11] The newspapers were mirroring the consensus of the leadership and reflecting the pressure from on high but Davis could not resist condemning this turnabout.

After Truman launched the Marshall Plan, Davis charged, "They want to Mississippi-ize the world!" This too was his response to Korea. Speaking to a crowd of fifteen hundred at 125th and Lenox in his capacity as Harlem party chair, Davis was scalding: "If Truman, Dulles and MacArthur have ants in their pants, let them send troops into Mississippi and Georgia to fight the Ku Klux Klan." Mounted cops watched as he yelled, "to hell with white imperialists, to hell with all imperialism."[12]

It is also striking that Davis, probably more than any other party leader, raised the burning question of color. This was an issue driven by events on the Korean peninsula, where black soldiers were experiencing horrendous racism that was linked with imperialism. Worse, it was being claimed by General Mark Clark, chief of the army's field forces there, that the presence of black soldiers weakened army performance. Davis joined the Civil Rights Congress campaign on behalf of Lt. Leon Gilbert, a black soldier being court-martialed on spurious grounds.[13]

This campaign was part of a Davis offensive against the racist attack on black troops. He protested their use; Truman "can cook up a red-baiting pretext to send Negroes 10,000 miles away to die, but he can't find a single way to get the anti-lynch, anti-poll tax or FEPC bills passed." This was a telling point in Harlem. How could you fight for democracy abroad, he wondered, when it was so glaringly absent at home? Worst of all, black troops were "singled out for the hardest, dirtiest and most murderous tasks . . . southern white Ku Klux-minded officers insult and slander Negro troops under their command." He recognized immediately that "concessions" would have to be made to blacks to secure their continued cooperation. And for those not willing to go along—like Davis—there was intimidation and ultimately the prison cell.[14]

Davis was raising very sensitive questions at a time when strict national uniformity was being stressed. At a July 1950 rally in Harlem to save Willie McGee (a black Mississippian accused of raping a white woman), a *Daily Worker* reporter recalled that the "highlight of the meeting was [the] fiery hour-long speech" by Davis; "his comments were spiced by cries from the crowd of 'Amen.' . . . People leaned out of windows up and down

Lenox Avenue to hear Davis [say] . . . 'What have the Koreans done to the Negro people?'" Yet he did not stop there. Though prison stared him in the face, he did not cut his conscience to accommodate current fashion. In early 1950 he railed at yet another Truman "sell-out" of FEPC—"he talks like a saint and acts like a sinner." And he joined Marcantonio and Guinier in pressing for more black judges.[15]

Davis was gone from the council but he had not forgotten it. Earl Brown supported his appeal to the high court but Davis was still dismissive toward Brown, despite the fact that the base of support for the party was steadily shrinking. However, Davis was correct in repudiating Brown's attack on Marcantonio as this last left-winger in Congress was about to be ousted. But times had changed in the council; with Davis gone, for the first time in six years the council did not legislate Negro History Week in February 1950.[16]

Davis' base of support was not just shrinking politically. His friend and top NAACP litigator Charles Houston died in the spring of 1950; a lawyer for Winston and Irving Potash, his loss was not propitious for the CP-11 appeal. Then his other Amherst friend, Dr. Charles Drew, a pioneer in blood plasma research, also died; they were in fact "close friends," said Davis in his obituary, "where they played varsity football together." But Judge Medina refused to lift bail restrictions so that he could attend the funeral.[17]

Davis was not catering to dominant sentiment; just weeks after his conviction and council ouster he was declaring, "we should devote far more conscious effort to mastering the application of Marxism-Leninism-Stalinism to the specific conditions of our own country"; in an accompanying photograph he was autographing copies of a Stalin biography and said Communists were proud of being called "Stalinist." At a one-thousand-strong rally organized by the Harlem party at the Renaissance Casino, he urged the collection of twenty-five thousand signatures on peace petitions during the month of June alone. When the film *The Red Menace* opened in Harlem in July, Davis was on the picket line with Abner Berry, carrying a sign stating, "How About the Mississippi Menace?" Yet with all these counter hegemonic positions, in a *New York Amsterdam News* poll (reported on 7 January) to determine the "leading" Harlemites, Davis ran far ahead of Thurgood Marshall, Ralph Bunche, Hulan Jack, Frank Crosswaith, and Roy Wilkins. The fact that elites tended to display more compassion for victims of Stalinism than victims of racism made the process of winning black support problematic; there would have to be more civil rights concessions before Davis could be isolated.[18]

Davis's popularity in the face of vilification was driven by his combative stance against a long-standing Harlem scourge—police brutality and racist repression. His activism was expedited in early 1951 when Judge Henry Goddard barred Davis from leaving the jurisdiction to speak in New Haven;

stuck in New York City, he took full advantage. Davis heightened his association that year with the Civil Rights Congress, which sought to popularize the slogan "Bring our Boys back home to fight Jim Crow."[19]

Ample evidence proved that police brutality and racist violence against blacks was on the rise. The war-induced suppression of civil liberties apparently had revived the police and others, spurring on some who might otherwise restrain this bestiality. One May morning in 1951 at 2:30 A.M. Davis was to be found at one of his usual haunts—126th and Lenox Avenue; with others he was present for a vigil counting down the time until the execution of Willie McGee. The *Daily Worker* picked up the story as someone whispered in Davis's ear: "Davis stood silently for a full minute. He swallowed as though his tongue rebelled at saying what he had to say. A deep silence prevailed . . . Women screamed. Men wept and cursed." McGee had been executed. The demonstration had begun in the early afternoon with a few hundred supporters; at 7:00 P.M. there were two thousand: "the crowd changed many times during the night." Then the police moved to turn off the public address system at midnight and demanded the crowd disperse: "Langston Hughes, the poet . . . stood with his people to the end." Davis spoke twice, the first time for seventy minutes: "Drenched in perspiration he had to go home, change clothes and return to close the meeting. Davis is a down-to-earth and caustic speaker. But never before did he talk as he did last night. . . . 'My man is sure working overtime tonight,' commented a youthful listener." Davis also alleged, "a policeman is a policeman and a Negro policeman is a stooge for our oppressors. And I now call Lt. [Alfred] Eldridge the biggest Uncle Tom in New York. . . . You are no safer than the Negroes in Mississippi." This could be called overstatement, but it illustrates a continuing Davis and party problem with the concept of integration; on the one hand they questioned being co-opted by imperialism but on the other they welcomed the entry of blacks at all levels of U.S. society.[20]

Racist repression also befell W. E. B. Du Bois, who rose to Davis's defense during his trial. In February 1951 the octogenarian was indicted and put on trial for his toil on behalf of the Stockholm Peace Appeal, which sought to outlaw nuclear weapons. This, Davis marked, was a "foul and cowardly assault. . . . None of the Wall Street monopolists, or their lickspittle Trumans, are fit to tie his shoelaces." In the library of the Jefferson School of Social Science, Du Bois was honored and Davis welcomed him "into the great fraternity of the indicted. . . . But we must not go further and allow him to enter the fraternity of the sentenced."[21]

Davis was not as generous to that other stalwart of black New York, Adam Powell. Neither the war, the halting integration, nor the co-opting of certain African-Americans curbed Davis's sharp critique of this former leftist, who was now hurrying toward the center:

Until recently, Rep. Adam Powell was a militant spokesman for Negro rights. . . . Now he has adopted a new line. . . . He said, in effect, that he would give up the fight against segregation and discrimination in the armed forces "for the duration of the war" and leave the matter entirely to the tender mercies of President Truman. That, of course, is like leaving the wolf to watch the sheep . . . an abandonment of the struggle for Negro rights. . . . Whether or not he will follow this path to its logical end of complete political degeneracy and worthless- ness, depends in the first place upon him. . . . Rep. Powell's new line is a surrender to the powerful reactionary pressures exerted upon him by big business interests, with which he has strong financial, property and political ties. . . . The notorious and transparent Negro agents of imperialism . . . are exposed to do the job for their Wall Street masters. Wall Street needs a radical-sounding orator.

While there was much truth in his remarks, the real point was whether it constituted sound tactics at a moment when Davis and the party were being isolated.[22]

Even, so, this slugging of Powell, Wilkins, White, and the like apparently did not harm his influence with certain leading black musicians. Accompanied by a full complement of string instruments, Charlie Parker entertained at the "Free Ben Davis" birthday ball at the Rockland Palace; Max Roach was with him and Robeson also sang. Emerging from this session was one of Parker's most notable albums. This was not atypical. Just before this event, Miles Davis's orchestra, with J. J. Johnson and Sonny Rollins, played at the preconvention dance of the New York Labor Youth League, a fraternal organization allied with the party. Miles Davis was blunt about the group: "They're on the ball. They know what's happening." But his other comment, "This country is beginning to make me neurotic," captured the intensifying sentiments of many blacks.[23]

This support from celebrities was something for Davis to cheer about. So were the reported seventy-five thousand people marching on May Day 1951; Davis et al. were found "leading the Communist contingent." Davis's importance as a mass symbol allowed the party to relieve him from the responsibility of being part of the Hall, Winston, and John Williamson troika that constituted the secretariat after Dennis was jailed.[24]

In June 1951 the court upheld the conviction of the CP-11 defendants, with Justices Black and Douglas angrily dissenting. Prison loomed. Yet there was no political surrender after the high-court ruling. The party rallied quickly at 116th and Seventh Avenue with Davis and Rev. Mother Lena Stokes addressing the throng. This was his farewell and his voice choked with emotion as he spoke: "If I have to go to jail I'm coming back to struggle with you on the streets of Harlem again . . . whatever strength I have, I got it from my people and I'm going to use it to keep on fighting for them." He excoriated a recent article proclaiming "End of the Trail for Ben"; "This is not the end of the trail for either Ben Davis, the Communist Party or the Negro people," he said.[25]

While Davis scathingly denounced the high court, the *Daily Worker* perhaps presented a more accurate portrayal when they reported that "reaction in the top Negro leadership circles was divided with most Negro leaders agreeing with the dissent of Justice William O. Douglas." Earl Brown was speaking for many who kept their opinions private when he counseled that the decision was "as much a direct attack on our customs and constitutional rights as any Red bilge, or even sabotage . . . the court's decision cannot curb the Communists without hurting all of us . . . in effect, it beats all of us over the head."[26] The progressive intellectual Howard Meyer contrasted the U.S. posture at the United Nations, voiced by Ambassador Warren Austin, when a Soviet resolution against "Propaganda and Inciters of a New War" was moved; Austin and others, who now hailed the CP-11 loss, called this Soviet motion a restriction of free speech; was not this "Janus-faced inconsistency," Meyer complained.[27] But the magazine of the American Legion expressed governing attitudes when it accused the party of saying that Davis was a "poor Negro who had to pick cotton to live" while he actually was from an affluent background; thoughtfully, they included a picture of the Davis family home in Atlanta.[28]

In early July 1951 Judge Sylvester Ryan signed the order for the jailing of the defendants. Davis addressed the court as his own counsel. The judge interrupted and ordered him to sit down. Davis replied, "I will not be intimidated." The exchange was fierce. Davis: "I do not have the 13th, the 14th and the 15th Amendments. They are not kept in this country." Judge Ryan: "Mr. Davis, sit down and be quiet." Davis: "The enemies of the people are going to be put in jail some day, not the working class." Judge Ryan: "Sit down or I will hold you in contempt of court." Marshals then forced him to his seat.[29] The *Times* called Davis's remarks a "tirade" and added that he "kept on talking, raising his voice. The judge then called deputy marshals, who led Davis back to his seat, still talking. Finally the judge threatened to hold him in contempt if he did not sit down and keep quiet, and Davis subsided, glowering at the court." The judge belied those who saw this as a simple legal wrangle by referring to "recent world events" in deciding to jail the defendants.[30]

Just before this decision, Gurley Flynn analyzed the case and the fight against it, drawing on the lessons of the International Labor Defense, Tom Mooney, and International Red Aid: "I think it was a mistake for the defendants not to be involved much more than they were in the mass movement. . . . Defendants are always their own best defenders. . . . It was a grueling double duty for them to sit in a courtroom all day and then some go to trial and others to then take over organizational responsibilities till all hours of the night. It affected their health and limited their work in the mass movement." She must have had Davis in mind. She continued:

> There was not an adequate sustained mobilization of our party so that when we finally won review by the Supreme Court, after two years of struggle, we did [not

take] full advantage of it in a public way.... We have practically abandoned our right of assembly even in places where meetings can be held under our own or other auspices like CRC. In 1948 I spoke 144 times, in 1949 92 times; and in 1950 68 times—which is a startling example.... Comrade [Pettis] Perry tells me he spoke at only 6 mass meetings since he came East in 1948.[31]

This last generalization was true for Davis as well, although receiving fewer speaking offers is only one explanation. Others felt a First Amendment defense should have been mounted. Finally she warned against a panicky "illegalizing of ourselves."

What was the party to do? War raged in Korea with rumors about the possible use of atomic weapons and actual use of biological warfare. State repression against blacks continued, apparently unabated. The party's leadership was headed for jail and the effluvium and distinct scent of fascism wafted across the scene. Howard "Stretch" Johnson, a Harlem comrade, recalled the moment: "We decided that we should break the party down into three basic strata: one section of the party to remain legal ... the second part [in] ... deep freeze ... inactive status ... change their lives, assume new identities, live in a different way completely separating themselves from the legal communist party ... in reserve" and underground; "the 'unavailables' who had minimal contact with the legal body ... and also minimal contact with the deep freeze"; and a few were to be sent abroad. In this division of labor, Davis—the most popular defendant of the CP-11—was to go to prison and be a rallying point, illustrating the injustice of the Red Scare. Evidently Gurley Flynn's advice on "illegalizing ourselves" was to be ignored.[32]

Party patriarch William Z. Foster, who had outlined the tactics for the trial, described the posttrial approach as well:

> We must make a thoroughgoing and full-scale attack upon the capitalist system as such.... We must develop our Party's immediate program as an organic part of the whole question of the eventual establishment of socialism in this country.... Under no circumstances can we permit the prosecution, with the help of the courts, to drive a wedge between our immediate and ultimate programs, as though they had no relation to each other. This will be a real test of our ability as Marxist-Leninists.[33]

In early 1952 Foster outlined the blueprint for the next period, emphasizing making use of the exculpatory Schneiderman case, which "directly refutes the specific charges for which we are indicted.... We should stick it into their noses at every turn in the trial.... We must inject into the case the everyday activities of our Party ... we must also project, as best as we can under the present circumstances the American road to socialism.... Under no circumstances can we fail to draw upon the revolutionary experience of the workers in other lands.... We have to be on guard against tendencies towards American exceptionalism."[34]

But it was a variant of that policy of "exceptionalism"—or at least the effort to more sharply distinguish the U.S. party's policy from that of the USSR party's—which was to become the CP crisis of the mid-1950s. This was in years to come, however; for Davis, the unhappy prospect of a cold, dank prison cell in Terre Haute, Indiana, awaited. With the removal of the influence of leftists like Davis from black life through the Red Scare, the time had arrived to make concessions via *Brown v. Board of Education*—in other words, the movement toward Black Liberation.

15
Jailed for Ideas, 1951–1955

The failure of the appeal to the high court meant prison for Davis. He was incarcerated from 1951 to 1955. With Davis and other black leftists either jailed, underground, or muffled, it was now safe for more realistic elites to make modest steps toward dismantling the formidable edifice of Jim Crow. Ironically the Left, which had been in the vanguard of this process for years, would not receive any credit and would be deprived of mass influence. Moreover, the ouster of the Left and resulting strength of the Right insured that the post-Montgomery movement would not tackle the unfinished business of Reconstruction, redistributing the wealth. A major contradiction of the early fifties was that while civil rights were being expanded, civil liberties were being restricted. Hindsight suggests that the United States was swifter in dealing with its major domestic problem—racism—than Russia was in dealing with theirs—Stalinism. But Jim Crow still meant that NAACP and black Communist leaders lived cheek by jowl in Harlem's 409 Edgecombe Avenue with some degree of cross-fertilization. During this period Davis was carrying on the struggle from behind bars while the Civil Rights Congress and other forces sought to set him free.[1]

Davis was better situated than many of his comrades for prison; he had shunned marriage and having a family for some time in part because the Damoclean sword of prison had hovered above his head for years. But ironically once he entered prison, his relationship with Nina Stamler bloomed. They were married 15 April 1955, as he was being released from prison. Nina was born 1 February 1919, the daughter of a dentist of Lithuanian descent. Her father, an early socialist, started co-operative homes for working-class families. She was active in the movement, having worked closely with the Civil Rights Congress. Even though Davis had often used nationalist themes in his speeches and racists for some time had sought to stampede whites by suggesting that Communist influence meant miscegenation, and even though in the 1950s some African-Americans were not entirely comfortable with the idea of interracial marriage, Davis was not deterred. During his prison sojourn Stamler was in frequent contact with him and he came to rely on her heavily.[2]

Moving from New York to Indiana was a jarring experience for Davis.

Not surprisingly, his days in prison were not pleasant; later Gurley Flynn reported, "Ben Davis [does] not talk much about his prison experiences. But they were rough and mean, I am told by others who were there at the same time."[3] Davis's notoriety and beliefs meant that the authorities there could not ignore him. Like other blacks, he was confined to "Negro cells" and had to enter the "mess hall . . . separately"; blacks were subjected to a special persecution, and black Reds were treated worse than abject pariahs. The Terre Haute prison held twenty-five hundred inmates, 10 percent of whom were black.[4] Claudia Jones wrote that "the door to his cell remains locked during waking hours; he is denied the freedom of a recreation room where there are ping-pong tables and other facilities; access to a library; daily showers after work."[5] The perversity of Jim Crow was such that even "meritorious conduct lists" were kept segregated. These indignities bothered his sister: "I wonder how long this shall go on: It just doesn't seem possible that this can be happening to my brother."[6] Perhaps the least of his problems was the country music that blared frequently in prison.

Throughout this period, his prospective wife received racist hate mail assailing miscegenation, which she felt was "probably from the FBI."[7] At first Davis worked in the prison library, but according to Flynn, "later was put to work checking prisoners' garments. . . . Visitors are not allowed to bring written material or to make notes on their interviews unless they are scrutinized by a guard on departure. A prison guard listens to all conversations. They are allowed to discuss personal matters only. . . . Lawyers have been able to visit the prisoners irregularly . . . many difficulties have been placed in their way." That was not all: according to the *Daily Worker* of 22 May 1952,

> The imprisoned leaders are allowed to order two new books a month from publishers, at their own expense, the titles of which must be passed upon by the prison authorities. All books from Communist sources or even mildly progressive sources are barred. The new books, when they are delivered to the prisoner, must be read and turned in to the prison library before new books are ordered . . . they are allowed to subscribe to one local newspaper of the place where the prison is located, and one from out of town. They read the *N.Y. Times* and the *N.Y. Herald Tribune* and Ben Davis reads the Negro press. But they are not allowed to receive the *Daily Worker*, the *People's World*, any trade union journal, or even such liberal journals as the *N.Y. Compass*, the *Nation*.

As a result, prisoners exchanged papers so that they could be familiar with communities all over the nation.

All of the Smith Act prisoners were harassed but the black ones seemed to receive more mistreatment. Davis's visitors, according to Muriel Symington, were "under the eye and ear observation of a guard. . . . Visitors for every other Smith Act victim in federal penitentiaries are under eye observation only. Mr. Davis' only visitors are his sister and a white woman friend. . . . this gratuitous harassment springs from the fact that one visitor is white."[8] But it was bad for all of the Eleven, according to Flynn, for even lifers and murderers were allowed to receive visits from and consult with attorneys; Smith Act prisoners had to get clearance from high-level authorities, which could take weeks or months.[9]

George Crockett visited Davis just after he was jailed in 1951:

> The first thing I saw was a large prison made of red brick. If you didn't know it was a prison beforehand you'd say it was just another beautiful building in a rural area. The grounds are beautifully laid out—trees and all sorts of beautiful colored flowers . . . [one is] ushered into a room which could be taken for a reading room or library in an exclusive men's club . . . [then] I walked into another large reception room furnished with upholstered chairs and a lounge. . . . [Davis is] one of the most selfless people I ever met. . . . He said he wasn't a martyr . . . and the real martyrs are the folks back in Harlem. . . . Ben has no fear. The fear he said is for those who don't know what the future holds. He is at long last a free man. His is the freedom of the man who has been subjected to persecution and can still stand up and say, "I've taken all they can throw at me . . . I have not been conquered."[10]

One of Davis's most frequent visitors was party general counsel, John Abt. They met roughly every three or four months; the lawyer's assignment from the party was to keep him "up to date with political affairs and party affairs"; they would talk an "hour or so." The fact that he had to "make rounds" to all the prisoners allowed Abt to be their connection—or at least to the extent that prying ears and eyes allowed. He recalled a "nice big room" with wicker chairs in a "relatively new jail"; he also recalled "big arguments" with prison authorities about treatment of his clients.[11] Davis's wife recalls that a guard sat nearby whenever she visited; it was "horrible," she says.[12]

Davis played on the prison baseball team, studied Spanish, and read Einstein's theory of relativity and the autobiography of Lincoln Steffens, but his prison stay was no idyllic jaunt since he suffered significant weight loss and had to have an operation for an intestinal ailment. He had been health-conscious for years, so these problems were a real setback. Weeks after he entered prison he complained of a "painful condition in his right leg and foot, because of an old back injury."[13] This problem led to a slipped disc in his vertebrae and an end to his tennis game. The jailers' neglect of Henry Winston while imprisoned (he went blind as a result) showed that authorities could be derelict in providing health care. But the situation was worsened, according to Harry Sacher, because "various privileges are extended to white prisoners for good behavior which are denied to Negro prisoners with equally good behavior." Sacher felt that black prisoners also received inferior health care.[14]

An ever-present problem for Davis was receiving mail; since prison was designed not only to keep him off the streets of Harlem but to break him, at least spiritually perhaps politically, isolation was an essential part of this process. Thoughtfully, the *Daily Worker* published his address and urged readers to send him Christmas cards and other mail. One key project that unsettled the authorities was the writing of his lengthy memoir, which took two and a half painstaking years to complete under enormous difficulties. At first Davis was denied the freedom to write. Even after he was released, he did not get his manuscript until years later since the director of the Bureau of Prisons called his work "propaganda," and then it was returned to him only after a mass campaign and the threat of litigation.[15]

Davis's friends did not forget him when he was behind bars, particularly the always-loyal Paul Robeson. Before leaving for prison Davis told him, "everything in the apartment—and the apartment itself—are at your complete disposal. . . . I shall miss you. But as fighters for the working class and people we shall be together again."[16] Robeson was helpful in organizing the Trade Union Committee to Repeal the Smith Act and other forms of mass support. In Robeson's newspaper, *Freedom*, Davis was featured frequently. In the July 1952 issue he was compared to anticolonial leaders in Africa: "They are as proud of their leaders who behave like our Ben Davis." At the 1953 convention of the National Negro Labor Council, which he too had helped to organize, Robeson remarked, "If we concede that . . . Ben Davis belongs in a Terre Haute Jim Crow jail, then we concede McCarthy's right and Brownell's right to jail you and me and Harry Truman and to dig up Franklin Roosevelt and put him in jail too!"[17] Even before HUAC in 1956 he proclaimed that Davis was one of his dearest friends. "Nothing could make me prouder than to know him. I say he is as patriotic an American as can be."[18]

It is possible that the *Daily Worker* did not highlight the plight of their top leadership during this period, or at least as much as one would imagine. The fragmented nature of the leadership is partially responsible; some were in jail, others underground, in Mexico, and elsewhere. In addition the newspaper was having its own problems; just as Davis was entering jail, it shrank from twelve pages to eight, and the price went up. The Harlem edition disappeared, and by September 1950 the number of state editions was reduced. This latter date is critical, for it came right after the Korean War, which may have been a bigger blow to the party than the 1949 trial.[19]

At one of his last speeches in Harlem, Davis declaimed, "The sun of liberty is arising all over the world. It will rise here also." That Davis received his liberty at all is attributable in large part to a hearty band of activists who did not back down in the face of fevered Red Scare passions and who displayed their tenacity from the day he was arrested. William Patterson, Louise Jeffers, and Louise Patterson were just a few of these people. Days after Davis's jailing in 1951 the Harlem CRC launched a campaign to free him, holding a series of "mass meetings" at various times between 4:00 P.M. and 9:00 P.M. at different street corners, with "wide distribution of leaflets and literature." Abner Berry recounted that "at least two or three times a week thousands [were] attending open-air meetings . . . [to] voice their demands to 'bring back Davis to Harlem' . . . and independently a group of Harlemites [were] circulating a petition to [Truman] demanding that he use his executive powers to speed a rehearing of Davis' case."[20]

Walter White poignantly commented, "When jail doors close behind him in the not too distant future, Benjamin J. Davis, convicted Communist, will take with him into his cell a little part of you and me."[21] The words of J. Pius Barbour, editor of the *National Baptist Voice* (four million circulation), an influence on Martin Luther King and a key opinion molder, was equally eloquent in his defense of Davis.[22] Civil rights leader Willard Ransom, a top executive at the Indiana company started by Madame C. J. Walker, was similarly outspoken, but the limitations of the campaign were revealed when he had to refuse the invitation to write the black press on Davis's behalf.[23]

This Harlem-based campaign arranged for a large truck to tour the area with a huge poster reading "Free Ben Davis—Demand a Rehearing!" Volunteers released hundreds of red, blue, green, and yellow balloons with the same slogan printed on them from time to time and distributed thousands of leaflets. Their effort was so impressive that even Coast Guardsmen and Marines signed the petitions. At this time, in September 1951, the chair of the "Ben Davis Freedom Committee" was Amy Mallard—a widow of a lynch victim—and the office was at 321 West 125 Street in Harlem. Weeks later a Harlem Committee to Repeal the Smith Act was formed that included Alice Childress, Ollie Harrington, Ernest Thompson, and Charles Collins, among others. They pioneered in producing cartoon strips featuring Davis and dramatizing the case, they issued "Freedom Bonds" that facilitated contributions to the campaign, and they issued posters calling "Amnesty! Free Ben Davis." But with all that, at the end of 1951 Davis remained in prison.[24]

The year 1952 was a bleak time for the Reds; some saw the election of General Dwight Eisenhower as the arrival of the "man on a white horse" and yet another step toward a much-discussed fascism. State repression was making solidarity with Davis problematic. Party journals were still tossing garlands at him and his friends were still praising his fortitude, but a movement strong enough to free him had not materialized. Though some were suggesting that military spending was priming the economic pump, this alleged rising tide did not lift all boats in Harlem. Conditions were bleak.[25]

The *Daily Worker* columns seem to suggest that the "free Davis" campaign of 1952 did not get started until the summer; there was reason for this. The CRC was conducting struggles coast to coast and Smith Act cases were raging as well. This defense organization was akin to an overworked firefighter in a city besieged by arsonists. Yet in late July in Harlem, petitioners were finding that the 11th A.D. was still Davis country as thousands signed for amnesty in an era when some were afraid to endorse the Bill of

Rights. His defense committee then initiated a "Pledge Scroll": "We the people of Harlem are angered at your arrest and imprisonment. We recognize the injustice of your arrest. We love and respect you for the courageous fighting leadership you have consistently carried on—in and out of the City Council before your arrest over a year ago because of the unconstitutional Smith Act. We, the Negro people and those who join with us, pledge to bring you back to the community of Harlem where we need you to continue the job. We pledge not to rest until you are free!"[26] Harlem was one of the few communities where such words, aimed directly at African-Americans, could be openly circulated. An Amnesty Committee in Chicago was having similar success with protests in Washington Park.

The zenith of the "free Davis" efforts that year came with the Davis birthday gala in September featuring Charlie Parker. Tickets for this historic event were a mere $1.50 and boxes were $6.00; three thousand people appeared. At midnight Robeson lead the crowd in singing "Happy Birthday." The *Daily Worker* was ecstatic: "In one box there sat a well-known editor, in another [a] former All-American football player who is a successful businessman. And there were doctors, lawyers, labor leaders and small business people. . . . There were no anti-communist jitters."[27] The fact that they did not dare mention names of those present undermined that last bit of optimism, but the success of this event provided a reason to swagger.

The party tried to circumvent these "jitters" by running Davis for office so that Davis's supporters could express support for him in the isolation of a voting booth. Since thousands had signed Davis petitions, it was felt that he could perform credibly as candidate of the Freedom Party for the State Assembly in the 11th Assembly District, which even the *Times* had pointed to as a Davis stronghold. Jesse Gray, who eventually became one of New York's best-known tenant leaders and was also elected to the State Assembly, headed the committee to put Davis on the ballot; six hundred canvassers reported on Labor Day weekend to get enough signatures for Davis to reach the ballot; 3,128 signatures were filed, though only fifteen hundred were required. Rapturously, the *Daily Worker* reported, "In seven election districts more than one third of the registered voters signed Davis petitions." And this happened although 20,000 "peace ballots" urging a ceasefire in Korea were being collected in tandem with the Davis campaign.[28]

But rapture dissolved quickly into melancholy: " . . . the shadow of fear also falls long and heavily across Harlem's homes. Canvassers report many expressing sympathies with Davis' campaign but fearing to put their names on the petition. . . . So far the Negro press and the local big business press have blacked out the news of the Davis petition efforts . . . headquarters are open all day at 135 W. 135 St." Then the *Daily Worker* complained of a "complete press blackout on the Davis campaign [but] . . . the community 'grapevine' spread the news daily. . . . Davis was in jail, but the response of his neighbors proved that he was not isolated nor forgotten."[29] Though this was 1952, Abner Berry, Paul Robeson, Jr., Pettis Perry, and other campaigners for Davis appeared on WMCA and WLIB—which was a breakthrough, given their general exclusion from the airwaves. "Vote Ben Davis Out" was their creative slogan. Jesse Gray again turned to optimism: "There are pledges of support in the hands of Freedom Party workers right now adding up to more than half the number of voters in the district."[30]

As Truman toured Harlem in October, placards greeted him with the insignia "'Free Ben Davis.' . . . Visibly disturbed at the sight of the slogans, Truman looked away." By now Gray was blissfully euphoric, flatly predicting that Davis would get one-third of the vote. He compared the campaign to electing Kwame Nkrumah from a Ghana jail; the *Daily Worker* reported on 19 October that there were Davis committees in each of thirty-six election districts.[31] Doxey Wilkerson was well received on WLIB; he used the "good Negro soldiers / bad Negro" dichotomy of folklore and connected Davis with the latter: " . . . vote Ben Davis out of prison and send him to the State Assembly . . . [he] is a Negro leader who refuses to stay in his 'place.' He won't be an Uncle Tom for Mister Charlie . . . or even for the Devil himself. . . . Here is our chance to show the white ruling class that we Negroes will choose our own leaders." Wilkerson added, "I, too, have studied the principles of Marxism-Leninism. I teach and advocate those principles." But signifying a different climate in the black community was the fact that this kind of talk was "broadcast over this station at the same time on Tuesdays, Thursdays, and Fridays."[32] Note too Wilkerson's use of both race and class.

There was noticeable optimism as election day approached. By mid-October sixteen open-air rallies were scheduled. James Malloy was dispatched to speak for Davis at a packed capital budget hearing of the lily-white City Planning Commission at City Hall.

Malloy stressed the wretched state of Harlem. Harking back to old times, the Davis campaign led the fight to save one thousand two hundred tenants from eviction "to make way for a high rent project," the Riverton, which was ironic, given that the Metropolitan Life Insurance Company spawned this Harlem project in order to deflect attention from the all-white Stuyvesant Town. An open air meeting was held at Fifth Avenue and 133rd Street: "Mothers with infants in their arms stood for two hours in the chill air as their neighbors discussed steps to be taken . . . there were entire family groups—parents and children in the crowd." Lester Rodney, *Daily Worker* sportswriter, joined those plugging Davis, appearing on WMCA. His 1949 campaign film was shown at various open-air meetings. But with all this help Davis got only 879 votes out of twenty-five thousand cast.[33]

Yet given the political polarization, the fact that so many would vote for a jailed Communist was remarkable; propaganda from television, films, and newspapers was shrill anti-Communism. And as Fiorello La Guardia and Ollie Harrington have suggested about the 1945 and 1949 elections respectively, vote fraud or general chicanery could rarely be discounted in New York elections. Still, there was no gainsaying the shrinking number willing to identify with the Reds, in stark contrast to the recent past.

Certainly harassment was proceeding in other spheres. When HUAC brought their traveling road show to Detroit, Davis's ally the Reverend Charles Hill was grilled; activist Coleman Young was also asked about Davis. Both were accompanied by the experienced George Crockett as counsel. The committee was upset about Davis speaking at Hill's church but the pastor's response was deft:

> Are you asking me a suppositional question? If you are and want me to suppose, I will. I think that any meeting in which the first Negro councilman ever elected to the office in the state of New York were to attend would be of interest to a great number of Negroes. It would be to the credit of any party if that Negro were elected under the label of that party. . . . I would think that Negro people would be more interested in what a given candidate's program might happen to be, and what he was going to do to improve the conditions of Negro people, than any label tagged on to him by such a committee as yourselves and others. . . . Are you trying to invade the privacy of my ballot box?[34]

The committee was not impressed by his verbal facility and Hill remained a convenient target. Meanwhile, other anti-Communist investigators sought to bring Davis to New York in July 1952 but his operation for an "intestinal ailment" barred the visit. Although Davis did not win the election despite the hoopla, it did lead to a delegation, headed by the Reverend Harold Williamson of Rugged Cross Mission, seeking to visit the director of federal prisons about his jailing.[35]

The fight to free Davis quickened in 1953; part of it came from the energy and organization spawned by the November 1952 election. This was timely, for Gurley Flynn continued to report a deterioration of the conditions endured by the Smith Act prisoners: "It means a complete loss of personal freedom, a rigid confinement of body and mind, a subordination of all one's waking and sleeping hours to a monotonous routine, the effacement of individuality in work, recreation and all phases of existence. Life is suddenly slowed down, a piece is taken out of it." Davis was isolated in his age cohort; only 10 percent of federal prisoners were over forty-four and for 17,424 prisoners there were sixty-seven doctors, twenty-eight dentists, twelve nurses, and four quite busy psychologists.[36]

Patterson continued to complain that Davis "receives his visitors only under eye and supervision . . . no other Smith Act prisoners are subjected to such an indignity . . . the added indignity which Ben Davis is subjected to is because of the inter-racial factor"; here he mentioned Davis's fiancee.[34] Davis continued to be plagued by health problems, undergoing a "minor operation" in January. But in a possibly smuggled letter to his attorney he continued to plot tactics from behind bars:

> . . . today one has to try to attain the big by also hammering away on the relatively small where chances of victory are greater and which prepare the atmosphere for the conquest of the larger . . . it's simply not in the cards that one sweeping and basic democratic victory on the legal or any other front can take place at present which will correct injustices all down the line, if not reverse the trend.

He was concerned about his upcoming parole hearing: "[there is a] new Board of 7, instead of 5 . . . one being a Negro." His appearance at a Pittsburgh trial that summer was on his mind:

> There seems to have been many interesting comments, from non-partisan sources on my Pittsburgh appearance; and they're quite valuable and useful. Certain approaches I utilized there bear close examination. Incidentally, too bad I wasn't my own attorney at Foley Square with all due respect to Sacher and the other counsel.

The special discrimination visited on him continued to bother him: "Dennis, white, in '50 was permitted to serve a year's sentence there. Is it one rule for a Negro and another for a white?"

The authorities would not let him serve his contempt sentence in New York, unlike Dennis. Davis continued,

> . . . absolutely vital is the closest consultation with Foster, the foremost authority of the Party. . . . Incidentally, Foster has an uncanny grasp of the legal as well as the political, and will be of great help on the brief, if his health permits . . . anxious that you don't misconstrue my dissatisfactions . . . not directed against your personal or professional ability in any way. . . . I suggest you talk matters over with Nina.

This missive foretold the Davis- and Foster-led alliance that was to become so important in the party after 1956.[38]

The early priority for Davis was his February 1953 parole hearing. A delegation consisting of Robeson, Dolly Mason (National Committee for Defense of Negro Leadership), Kenneth Forbes, Dr. Marcus Goldman (former government geologist), Cyril Phillip, Arthur Stein, and John Abt had a two-hour meeting with the Federal Parole Board: "Judge Rogers . . . had interviewed [Davis] . . . added that Mr. Davis was probably the most intelligent prisoner whom he had ever interviewed . . . we were advised that the Board would not require Davis to recant his political beliefs as a condition for the parole. . . . However, the Board members frankly indicated that the major consideration against parole . . . was what they describe as 'community sentiment' . . . and the severe public criticism that they felt they would incur by granting parole. . . . They made it clear that the parole would be denied for this reason."[39] There was still cause for optimism, however: the recently tried CP-17 ("second-string party leaders") in New York got mostly three-year sentences and the half-hour parole meeting went four times as long as

Davis's. But at the end of the day Davis was still jailed. Moreover, the FBI was sufficiently efficient to update his Security Index Card to reflect his Indiana address, which would facilitate his being detained further in case of emergency.[40]

The tempo was intensified when Davis was called to testify as an expert on Marxism-Leninism at the trial of Steve Nelson, Ben Carreathers, and others in Pittsburgh; he was to be lodged in the county prison. This trip was bracing; it got him out of the closed confines of Indiana and on the road. It also brought his predicament to a wider audience: "Supervision over these [white] prisoners is relaxed. During waking hours the doors to their cells are unlocked. When they are not engaged in the performance of their assigned tasks they are free to repair to the reading room, where they are at liberty to engage in conversation, play ping-pong, etc. None of these privileges is extended to the Negro prisoners who meet the same proscribed standards."[41] When Davis would object, he received demerits; he was restricted in his right to see attorneys, visitors, and others.

When Davis finally arrived in the "Iron City" in late July 1953, his friends from Georgia, New York, Detroit, Chicago, and elsewhere came to greet him. The *Daily Worker* was sympathetic: "Ben Davis looked tired when friends saw him at the Allegheny County Prison. He had just finished a long car trip from Terre Haute . . . where he is serving a five-year term . . . has lost weight. His face is somewhat drawn . . . was chained hand and body on the long trip with federal marshals." He was not allowed to speak to those who had come to see him. In the court "calendars from Andy Mellon's bank hang shamelessly on the walls. There is the mahogany wainscoting and the muted lights, the big window from which you can see the brand new skyscrapers of Mellon aluminum." Five minutes into his testimony, the scene was complete when Davis was slapped with a contempt sentence.[42]

He refused to name the members of the Negro Commission of the party: "I am not turning into a stool pigeon," was his reply. The *Daily Worker* added, " . . . one felt his vitality as his voice filled this court-room, which is noted for its poor acoustics." Davis's humor was not improved when the judge suggested that blacks were involved in lynching each other, citing the tragic assassination, by racists of Florida civil rights leader Harry Moore. The paper stated, "His face was drawn by the hardships of two years in prison. His cheeks were lined. But his eyes glowed with pleasure as he saw dozens of Negro and white friends."[43]

Asked if he were still a Communist, Davis's response struck a chord within the party: "I certainly hope so. . . . I hope that they have waived the question of my dues and that I am still a member in good standing." Asked what club or party cell he was in, he replied only half-seriously that he was in prison and "There are no clubs there that I know about."[44] Ever vigilant, the FBI was placing memoranda in his file about his performance.[45]

The parole hearing and the Pittsburgh appearance were orchestrated largely by the Civil Rights Congress and William Patterson particularly. It was Patterson who led a CRC delegation to the office of Pittsburgh prosecutor Edward C. Boyle demanding the dropping of the contempt charges (Rosalee McGee, widow of Willie McGee, was at his side). The CRC in Los Angeles was instrumental in guaranteeing that the Political Prisoners' Welfare Committee adopted Davis, thereby providing him with a regular monthly allowance since he "has no family to visit him regularly."[46]

The death of McGee and the Martinsville defendants and the successful conclusion of the Du Bois trial allowed Patterson to concentrate more on his friend's case. He wrote the influential Carl Murphy of the *Afro-American* chain, "As a close and dear friend of [Davis] I want to thank you for the attention you have from time to time given to his case. . . . I noted your news account on his presence in Pittsburgh"; he was quick to correct, however: "[Davis] was not convicted of conspiring to overthrow the government by force and violence."[47] This canard was already replacing the truth. CRC friend Muriel Symington sent ten thousand copies of the effective Davis cartoon strip "'Now It's Against the Law'" to Pittsburgh during his appearance: "The National Office expects the boldest distribution of the leaflet/ . . . We expect you to visit editors of all the press, from right to left, which includes labor, the metropolitan press, the Negro press, the religious press . . . we have the ear of a much wider public than we believe . . . promote public meetings, house meetings and affairs."[48]

Already one can see how the rapid fluidity of events—the party going from the high of the pre-Red Scare era and the low of 1953—forced Davis and his comrades to catch up with reality by assuming more of an objective united front approach. But ironically the more the times required a united front, the less visible it became.

Floating on the wave of the favorable Pittsburgh appearance, Patterson contacted the influential Edward S. D'Antignac of Georgia: "I was informed by a friend of yours that you were incensed by the treatment accorded your fellow Georgian. . . . I saw [Davis] just a few short days ago in the City of Pittsburgh. . . . His face was gaunt. His figure had lost some 50 pounds in weight." He veritably sang after fruitfully meeting with him: "It was indeed a pleasure to see you again. . . . I came away from Atlanta extremely heartened. I believe that the visit to the politician will be extremely profitable . . . we have linked all other Negro prisoners who are suffering together with him."[49] Hope Stevens, a powerful St. Kitts and Harlem lawyer, was next massaged by Patterson. "Harlem bears the major responsibility" for Davis, he said; "Negro lawyers who would really fight simply for respect for human disgnity would gain immeasurably, . . . I should like to see organized . . . a group that would go to Bennett," the irascible chief of federal prisons.[50]

Days before Christmas 1952 Patterson contacted the willing Du Bois to speak for Davis.[51] CRC abetted the production of special postcards to the attorney general and special pamphlets on Jim Crow in prison (with a Davis focus); as ever, friends were urged to deluge him with holiday cards—and they did.[52]

Nineteen fifty-four was the year of *Brown v. Board of Education* and the beginning of a shift on the Negro National Question by ruling elites and the Communist party. The cooling down of the Korean War helped to ease international tensions. Patterson and the CRC took advantage of the situation by attempting to extend the united front.

Early in the year CRC organized a delegation that gave Attorney General Herbert Brownell ten thousand signatures on amnesty for Davis; they visited Senator William Langer, chair of the Senate Judiciary Committee; they also presented a draft of a bill to end segregation in federal prisons.[53]

Patterson's visit to Jim-Crow Atlanta was time well spent. The Davis name still opened doors for him. The terror of the times was reflected by his use of initials and sobriquets like "Mr. R" when communicating with Walter Aiken. Yet all was not going well, perhaps as a result of the Scare; for weeks after the successful Washington trip, Patterson conceded that he had heard nothing from the influential pair of A. T. Walden and Edward D'Antignac. Patterson wanted the effective and well-connected attorney Walden to sign on to the Davis prison desegregation suit but he refused. In turn Patterson could not resist warning of the risk of more fascistlike conditions, contending that "the Davis case will accelerate the tempo of understanding . . . may I say that all paper work and research could and would, if you desired, be done here . . . you would of course make the argument."[54] As a headline-grabbing and constitutionally important case it was alluring, but Davis remained too controversial. Moreover, *Brown* was signaling a new day for African-Americans, which made it more difficult for figures like Walden to accept that more fascistlike conditions were on the horizon.

Undaunted, Patterson persisted. Days after *Brown* he congratulated George Hays, the powerful Washington, D.C., litigator, on the victory, and in passing solicited his aid for the Davis suit. The *Afro-American* was helpful; it urged Brownell to end discrimination in federal prisons. Then the CRC sought to pull together a forum in Harlem focusing on Davis. Robeson, George Murphy, Claudia Jones, Louise Patterson, Rev. Edward McGowan, and the talented actress Beulah Richardson contributed. A coup was the assistance of Modjeska Simkins, a pioneering figure in the modern civil rights movement.[55] The forum was held at 310 Lenox Avenue: "Jamming every seat of the United Mutual Auditorium . . . several hundred Negro and white New Yorkers paid stirring tribute" to Davis, and Abt gave a "personal report about 'Ben.'"[56] He said that Davis was impatient with the pace of the amnesty campaign, not out of consideration for himself but for the rights of the people.

Davis had a right to be impatient, but compared to recent times the campaign was moving along smartly. Robert Witherspoon, a black civil rights attorney in St. Louis, agreed to join the suit. Patterson quickly visited St. Louis and spoke at the Baptist Ministerial Alliance. After *Brown* he egged his friend on. But just as the progressives were not standing still, neither were their foes; the Communist Control Act had been passed and thus the Essex County Clerk's office ruled the party's Charles Nusser off the ballot.[57]

As 1955 approached, Davis had been incarcerated since mid-1951. The campaign to free him was still active but CRC was beginning to have problems of its own. The passage of the Communist Control Act with significant liberal support signified that the tactic of excommunicating the Communists and the Left from political discourse was continuing unabated. Yet with *Brown* and its progeny, ruling elites had set in motion forces it could not totally control. Davis's suit on prison segregation, launched before the pivotal date of 17 May 1954, was bidding fair to make him the "son of *Brown*"—in other words, a brown-skinned Red would get credit for breaking down a Jim Crow barrier. The entire approach to civil rights during the Red Scare era was designed to obviate such a development.

By March 1955 Davis was ready to file another suit for the reduction of his sixty-day contempt sentence incurred during the Pittsburgh trial. The authorities were still playing hardball with him, for he had just endured three months in solitary in Terre Haute—allegedly to "protect" him. His petition argued the persistence of a "standard pattern in all Smith Act cases for the government prosecutors to try to entrap defense witnesses into contempt citations by demanding names which they knew in advance" that Davis would not give. With this filing he faced another bout of solitary confinement. A worried Davis had to be reassured by Patterson.[58]

The suits and the solitary confinement refocused attention on Davis. James Dolsen, veteran Communist, told his comrades to write Davis ("Also enclose an envelope with a special delivery stamp. . . . He has the right to send such letters out but otherwise can send only four regular letters a month")[59] Davis responded in the *Daily Worker* for 14 April 1955 with his "heartfelt appreciation" for letters that "have brought me strength, good cheer"; altruistically he expressed concern about the fates of Claudia Jones and Jacob "Pop" Mindel: the paper said, "Davis also expressed indignation over the fact that several friends to whom he has written, received envelopes containing letters from him to other persons."

The authorities in Terre Haute were unhappy with the Davis segregation suit; on paper their reflections did not correspond with their actions. The warden in late 1954 had seemed generous: "I would like to ask you at this time if you wish to apply for housing in our "C" unit quarters . . . an honor unit." He wanted Davis's "written request" after relating, "I understand you have filed an action" on segregation in prison. But weeks later, as his Smith Act term was winding down, he was transferred to the Allegheny County jail. His attorney, Hyman Schlesinger, charged that all this was in response to his desegregation suit.[60]

The authorities in Terre Haute were unhappy with the Davis segregation suit; on paper their reflections did not correspond with their actions. The warden in late 1954 had seemed generous: "I would like to ask you at this time if you wish to apply for housing in our 'C' unit quarters . . . an honor unit." He wanted Davis's "written request" after relating, "I understand you have filed an action" on segregation in prison. But weeks later, as his Smith Act term was winding down, he was transferred to the Allegheny County jail. His attorney, Hyman Schlesinger, charged that all this was in response to his desegregation suit.[60]

Davis's band of supporters was not silent. In January they had sponsored a "free Ben Davis" rally at Yugoslav Hall with the popular artists Leon Bibb, Earl Robinson, Paul Robeson, and Beulah Richardson; four hundred people attended, paying fifty cents each. The rally emphasized the effort to bar his rearrest under the membership clause of the Smith Act on top of the contempt charge he faced.[61] Schlesinger wrote P. L. Prattis of the potent *Pittsburgh Courier* about Davis's habeas corpus petition—"one of the basic constitutional issues is segregation in the Pittsburgh jail." Davis was foiling his foes by attacking segregation in whatever jail he found himself.[62] His lawsuit was accompanied in effective tandem with a mass campaign: "In New York the Ben Davis committee is canvassing door to door . . . setting up tables in crowded intersections." They sold cards for two cents each and gave away brochures; there were plans for more printings, a letter-writing campaign, and huge ads in black papers.[63]

As the time for Davis's release came closer, support for his release mushroomed. The "noted French novelist . . . Vladimir Pozner" wrote to Davis in prison near the time that *Jewish Life* expressed support for an end to the restrictions on him. Charlene Mitchell, Martha Stone, Peggy Dennis, Bill Albertson, Anton Krchmarek, Tom Nabried—hundreds of supporters wrote Davis during this time.[64] On 2 April 1955 Esther Jackson, wife of James Jackson and with Du Bois a *Freedomways* founder, told Davis, "Every day or so I run into someone who quickly pulls from his or her pocket or purse a letter from you."[65] Frances Smith wrote Davis similarly: "I can't understand why you did not get my letter. I was one of the first to write to you. Haloise was showing off with her letter and I felt pretty bad . . . so many people ask me on the street about you. We are so proud of you because of your great courage. It gives us strength to continue going under great difficulty. . . . We are doubly proud of you because you are one of us and being selfish we know you belong to us, I mean Harlem." Remember, she concluded, "It's a long alley that don't have a garbage can."[66] Prying eyes were a deterrent to discussing significant political questions in these letters. Still, when seventy-three "American intellectuals," including Ray A. Billington, John Ciardi, Du Bois, Waldo Frank, and Scott Nearing urged President Eisenhower not to prosecute further CP leaders, it was further evidence of a growing political awareness of the unconstitutionality of the

Smith Act. In October C. W. MacKay, editor of the *Afro-American*, said he was "happy to hear from" Davis: "As to the material we carried about you while you were in trouble . . . we were only too happy to do so. . . . Please let me hear from you." Davis may have been pariah in some circles but not among blacks.[67]

This tendency hastened support for his prison desegregation suit. Years later Elizabeth Gurley Flynn gave Davis substantial credit for the accomplishment of this in the United States; she saw desegregation during her jailing at Alderson and recalled that the black women incarcerated with her there knew about him. The tempo stepped up after *Brown*. The *Afro-American* was critical in publicizing the effort, and even the *New York Times* was forced to take note. Davis did say that blacks had to enter the mess hall separately and there were "separate tables in such halls"; segregation also existed in the gym and auditorium. His lawyer was an African-American and CRC veteran, Ralph Powe. It was a class-action suit that dramatized its volatile importance. The Committee to Defend Negro Leadership issued "A Plea for the Safety of Ben Davis" and warned of "possible danger of his life" due to "solitary confinement . . . 75% of white inmates there from the South . . . provovations may be made against Mr. Davis' life because of his suit against segregation." Naturally the Justice Department demurred; with the crude deftness that characterized the era, they placed Davis in solitary and then claimed that he was not subject to segregation.[68] Inspired, the progressive poet Walter Lowenfels wrote a "Sonnet" for Davis. Proudly the *Daily Worker* reprinted a supportive *Afro-American* editorial: "We hold no brief for Mr. Davis' political convictions. But we cannot help but admire his courageous outcry against this denial of elemental justice to men in federal custody."[69]

The *Afro-American* was not alone: the *Philadelphia Independent* also hailed the Davis suit. Patterson was busy as usual behind the scenes, stirring up support. "We represent the church, labor, the farm and almost every segment of the Negro people" was the opening of one of his more vital letters to Attorney General Brownell. The authorities were not accepting this lethargically. The Terre Haute warden briskly informed Nina Stamler, "We are returning under separate cover the book 'Youngblood' as it is felt it is not particularly suitable."[70] They then transferred Davis to the Allegheny County jail—and tried to duck the jurisdictional and substantive issues accordingly. Undeterred, Davis then filed in April 1955 against the jail on the same ground of illegal segregation and decided to argue his own case. In a "ruling from the bench by Hon. James R. Kirkland" on a "motion to dismiss" on 1 April 1955, the judge was quoted as saying, "There is nothing to show, on the face of this record, that the allegation of segregation was true in fact." But Davis had powerful evidence from Steve Nelson, a frequent resident of that jail: "Knowing the Allegheny jail inside out as I do I can state that Negro prisoners are kept segregated on Range 17 and at meal-times.

They are constantly humiliated, treated as second class citizens, and not infrequently ordered about by some guards as 'boys.' There are no Negro guards in this place, and of course, there [are] no Negro administrative personnel—not even one!" The case was "dismissed with prejudice," for it was "moot." Davis was about to be released; his suit had forced his jailers' hand; weeks later it was reported, "steps have been taken, it was learned, to modify segregation in the dining halls and sleeping quarters."[71]

The *Times* of 17 April 1955 described a crowd of two hundred with "Welcome Home Ben Davis" signs greeting the newly freed political prisoner at New York's Penn Station; Eugene Dennis, Robeson, and Patterson were there. He had been freed fourteen days early; a hearing had been set for 2:00 P.M., when he was to argue his case; he was freed at 1:50. The Department of Justice "was too cowardly to face the issue of segregation and discrimination," the *Daily Worker* huffed on 18 April. "On his arrival in Pennsylvania Station at 5:55 P.M. Saturday both levels of the station's concourse erupted in mass shouts of 'Welcome Ben!' 'Hi, Ben!' Friends bearing placards and a bank of flowers immediately surrounded Davis with individuals struggling to shake his hands, embrace him and kiss him . . . his face was well-smudged with lipstick." He had been released but was not free. He still faced a Smith Act indictment under the membership clause and had to post a five-thousand-dollar bond. Bessie Steinberg of Pittsburgh supplied the latter but it required a massive struggle to extirpate the former.[72]

The *New York Amsterdam News* also gave featured coverage to this story. In an exclusive interview the much-slimmer Red (he had lost thirty pounds, making him a svelte 205 pounds) pointed boldly to two hopeful signs: *Brown* and *Bandung* (the meeting in Indonesia of what came to be termed the Non-Aligned Movement) and their intimate connection. Things were looking up for the party. They did not realize that ahead were the revelations about Stalin, the intervention in Hungary, the war against Egypt (which complicated the Jewish Question in the United States), the prominence of Dr. King—and fractious, internecine conflicts within the party. Ringing in his ears was Matthew Hale's poem to him, "For Ben Davis": "Dear Ben Davis, / Give me your hand, / No cell has room for a man to stand cabined, cribbed / And confined by bars, with feet on the ground / And eyes on the stars, / If your heart is wide / As the earth is wide, / No cell can keep a man inside."[73]

Soon the party was complaining about "arbitrary restrictions" placed on Davis; they were scheduled to expire 26 December but Justice sought to extend them. Still angry about how he had out-maneuvered them, the Justice Department placed the Benjamin Davis Freedom Committee on the so-called subversives list of the attorney general, which according to the *Times* "is used by all federal agencies as a check on those seeking employment."[74] The sight and thought of once-popular Reds like Davis loose on the streets again seemed to spur the anger of the authorities. They sought to block publication of his memoir; if it were published before February 1956, "the date the subject's conditional release period ends . . . then the permission of the U.S. Board of Parole would be necessary." They crudely solved the problem by not releasing his memoir to him.[75]

Recall that this was just before COINTELPRO, the FBI's infamous so-called counter intelligence program aimed at the party but quickly extended to virtually all dissenters. But even before this sinister initiative started, Davis was receiving an increased scrutiny from J. Edgar Hoover's mafia. He had to see his probation officer "every other Tuesday," which facilitated surveillance. The FBI was upset particularly about the gumption of the desegregation suit. There were those, if one accepts certain premises, who were justifiably concerned about Communist ability to influence the developing civil rights movement and thereby interfere with the finely crafted plan to grant concessions without the Reds anywhere near the bargaining table. Davis—an elected official, a Harvard-trained attorney, an orator, writer, and organizer—had the capability of disrupting these best-laid plans. The Red Scare was useful in pushing the elite version of Black Liberation. He had moved further uptown in Harlem and his Riverside Drive apartment building was under frequent surveillance.[76]

An ostensible reason for their accelerated surveillance was put forward on 28 December 1955: "In an effort to develop information which will lead to the apprehension of Communist fugitives Gilbert Green and Henry Winston, the six top Communist leaders . . . have been selected for intensive investigative coverage." Davis was named and "imaginative Special Agents" were assigned. Davis's "Security Index Card," which would facilitate his being rounded up in case of some *soi-dissant* national emergency, was updated again, back to Harlem. One of his friends, Curt Oberg, complained in August to Davis that he had "10 or 12 different good jobs [and] on every single one sooner or later I have been fired because of my record becoming discovered so it is useless to try and keep a job for any time." He was a victim of Red-baiting. Just as the FBI was struggling to keep Davis and the party away from the civil rights bargaining table, Hoover's agents became a presence at the table where inner-party disputes were being played out.[77]

16
Party Wars, 1956–1959

COINTELPRO, or the FBI destabilization of the Communist party, was a dominant factor in exacerbating and creating contradictions within the party in the post-1956 era. The FBI played on tensions created by the disclosures about Stalin, the Soviet intervention in Hungary, the Suez Crisis, and, ironically, the burgeoning civil rights movement. Once again at the center of this troubling scenario was Ben Davis.

The anti-Communist scholar Harvey Klehr has written, "Many people assume, erroneously, that with the collapse of the New Left in the early 1970's, American radicalism disappeared."[1] He is right by a half. Though given postmortems many times by various coroners—literary and otherwise—the United States Left has been resilient. As Davis emerged from postprison restrictions in 1956, a movement was emerging in Montgomery that highlighted the glaring blot on the U.S. escutcheon—racism. As many on the Right saw it, this was a direct boon to the international Left, which was headed by Moscow. And as Richard Gid Powers reminds, the FBI began taking more serious notice of Dr. King "when it learned he had been introduced to Benjamin Davis." Hoover saw black organizations "as easy prey" for the Reds and was "concerned with civil rights organizations almost exclusively in terms of their potential as targets for Communist infiltration."[2] Given a certain point of view, Hoover was right to be concerned since the party was still one of the few national organizations with a disciplined and sophisticated core of full-time black revolutionaries that included figures with many contacts and allies still within the emerging movement. William Patterson, Doxey Wilkerson, Henry Winston, James Ford, James Jackson, Ed Strong, Louis Burnham, Ted Bassett, Harry Haywood, Hosea Hudson, Augusta Strong, Bill Taylor, Abner Berry, Claude Lightfoot, and Geraldine Lightfoot were just a few of the black comrades surrounding Davis. That they would take advantage of the moment to play a role in the movement, recruit, and help to blare headlines abroad trumpeting the fight against Jim Crow was of grave concern to the authorities.

Controversies arising in the party in 1956 were like manna from heaven for the FBI. According to Brian Glick, they seized the time by initiating

COINTELPRO (Counter-intelligence Program), which had the advantage of obstructing the party's effort to influence the newly emerging civil rights movement,

> "not by harassment from the outside, which might only serve to bring the various factions together, but by feeding and fostering from within the internal fight currently raging. . . . informant . . . will be briefed and instructed to embark on a disruptive program within their own clubs, sections, districts or even on a national level. Those informants will raise objections and doubts as to the success of any proposed plan of action by the CP leadership. They will seize every opportunity to carry out the disruptive activity not only at meetings, conventions, et cetera, but also during social and other contacts with CP members and leaders."[3]

This was one of the momentous memoranda emerging from the period: COINTELPRO not only disrupted the party, but it led to the inflaming of black-Jewish tensions, it hampered the civil rights movement, it fed paranoia, and it helped to frighten a generation away from openly leftist ties. Moreover it pushed the United States more toward the right, contributed to jingoism, and facilitated the spending of tax dollars on the military rather than human needs. The talented journalist Louis Burnham expressed the wonder of the time: " . . . where are so many of our friends: balancing political angels and devils on the heads of ideological needles. History has caught up with much good theory and there has not been time to replace it. Meanwhile we walk in a kind of limbo between the past and unknown future. At least I do."[4]

In the meantime Davis was trying to adjust to life in Harlem, this time as a married man. His wife had been a party member earlier but was no longer. The FBI took note of her job with American Communications Association, Local 40. Davis was making at most sixty-seven dollars per week and was plagued with various ailments. His widow contends that it took him a year to adjust to civilian life; he even had difficulty for a few days in crossing streets. Finally in March 1956, free from postprison restraints, Davis rushed to speak to Harlem. At his Hotel Theresa press conference, the *Daily Worker* reported, "reporters and photographers from New York dailies, Negro weeklies, the Associated Negro Press and a few foreign language newspapermen . . . he appeared trim. . . . Additional creases in his strong brown face and added furrows on his broad forehead were the only reminders of his four years in jail." He took time to comment on Eisenhower, the party, and the civil rights movement, making similar remarks at a spirited rally of one thousand at 126th and Lenox Avenue in May. But the testy inner disputes then buffeting the party limited Davis's opportunity to comment on contemporary political concerns as much as he would have liked.[5]

The report to the Soviet Communist Party Congress in the spring of 1956 that revealed the massive illegalities committed by Josef Stalin and others exploded like unstable nitroglycerin in the U.S. party. Indeed, it was not altogether coincidental that similar turmoil coursed through Communist parties in the Philippines, Brazil, Uruguay, and elsewhere. This crisis was not the first one faced by Communists in the United States. There had been the Teheran crisis and Eugene Dennis had claimed that an unhealthy situation had existed in the Political Committee between September 1939 and June 1941. Nevertheless, the Stalin revelations showed the downside of "proletarian internationalism." In other words, the U.S. party was speckled with controversy when the Soviet party exposed its dirty laundry.[6]

Dorothy Healey, the party leader from California, recalls vividly that "probably the most significant meeting that the Communist party held in twenty years was that which took place in New York starting April 28 [1956]"; there were one hundred people in the Jefferson Auditorium. Healey, like some others, was in tears about the Stalin revelations: " . . . I got up and ran out of the room. Then Davis saw me . . . and he came over to me and had the tact and comradeship to say anything to me . . . just put his arm around me and said, 'Let me take you down and find a taxi, I know New York better than you, and then you can go to your hotel.' And he did that."[7]

Davis was one of the first to try to grapple with this difficult problem. In the *Daily Worker* he wrote, "Crimes under socialism are departures" from the natural order of things while they are natural under capitalism; he conceded that "virtually all Communist movements have been more or less infected by methods of work and leadership" akin to the Soviets. But he added, "Can anyone imagine Eisenhower and Truman admitting any of these colossal crimes of their system?" He called for an "expansion of inner party democracy" and learning the "therapeutic value of self-criticism," acknowledging that "far more needs to be done" for "establishment of a collective leadership."[8] Davis's sudden candor about internal difficulties had the effect of disorienting the ranks not accustomed or primed for such.

Reaction was swift in party ranks. The response of one comrade was typical: "Ben Davis has come out with the claim that to use the Stalin 're-velations' as a basis for major reevaluation is to again place the S.U. ahead of the USA in our thinking. I am unable to make sense out of such a thought."[9] Davis was hoisted on his own petard: it was difficult to point to Moscow as a beacon and then retreat from that view when the Stalin devaluation took place. The usually staid internal party journal, *Party Voice*, was beginning to reflect the turmoil: the New York State party organizational secretary saw a "crisis" within the party, for the Stalin exposé came right after the party lost two-thirds of their members in the previous ten years. The gifted black writer and actor Julian Mayfield refuted the idea put forward by Harold Cruse that Stalin was the key to explicating these losses: "people who had been looking, wanting to leave all along, but hadn't wanted to desert the party during the McCarthy period . . . now . . . had a cause."[10] In contrast Louis Budenz and Joseph McCarthy gleefully contemplated the consequences of the turbulence gripping the party.

As if the exposure of brutality in the USSR was not sufficiently complicating, it was followed later that year—in a related development—with Soviet tanks rolling into Budapest. The patrician party leader Junius Irving Scales "happened to drop by the Party's national office at the time to see Ben Davis with whom I had a superficial but cordial relationship . . . he invited me to sit in on an important meeting about the 'Hungarian affair.' He escorted me into the meeting room with his arm about my shoulders." This may have been the last flash of tenderness before the knives came out. Scales writes, "In New York the level of bitterness between politically opposed comrades had no limits. Old friends ceased to speak to one another."[11] Again, Davis was at the center of these events. He called the first use of Soviet troops a "serious mistake" but the "second use . . . a grim and painful necessity." He linked Budapest to the Suez Crisis and suggested that that attack was launched because Israel, Britain, and other countries saw the progressives as being off-guard and off-balance. In a rare occurrence, he questioned the *Daily Worker* editorial of 5 November and the National Committee statement of that same date; he voted for the 20 November "open letter" despite what he perceived as weaknesses. At this juncture he was still conciliatory toward party leader John Gates and the forces grouped around the party organ, which were much more critical of the Soviet role and much more willing to make wholesale changes in the party.[12]

The politically rehabilitated James Ford attacked the National Committee's "open letter" on Hungary: "In the historical sense these events are going to strengthen socialism," he said in the 26 November *Daily Worker*; the committee expressed "gross errors. . . . It places the forces of imperialism in the background, the forces of peace and socialism in the forefront for condemnation." In a striking characterization, he accused the committee of "Titoism." In early November the National Committee had issued a controversial statement on Poland and Hungary: "[These] great upheavals . . . were initially and primarily mass democratic upsurges of the working class and peoples of these countries" (although right-wing influences were noted).[13] In the vote on the statement Dennis and Davis had abstained; James Jackson voted yes with qualifications; and Foster was absent. The committee's position certainly sparked polemics, and fund-raising was adversely affected.

In these "party wars," which raged intermittently until 1959, Davis is pictured as being aligned with Foster in the so-called leftist tendency. David Shannon, for example, calls Davis "one of the hardest of the party's sectarians" and of "Stalinist orthodoxy."[14] Nina Goodman calls Foster Davis's "idol" but adds that he also loved Patterson, Louis Weinstock, and Al Lannon. These conflicts wounded the party severely. After Howard "Stretch" Johnson left the party during this time he says that he "was out of commission spiritually, emotionally. . . . I actually wanted to blow my brains out, but instead of that . . . I consumed a lot of booze. . . . I've been in psychoanalysis, hypnoanalysis, group therapy and I'm just beginning to find myself."[15]

In his 1958 memoir John Gates maintained that in the post-1945 period there were two factions, one centering around Dennis and the other around Foster; only Davis and Bob Thompson supported the latter. He labels this faction "left-sectarian" but says that both groups joined in keeping the struggle behind closed doors. . . . It is also likely that Thompson and Davis, who looked upon most of us as weak, unreliable and as concealed Browderites had their eyes on the top posts but were not ready to make this known." He recounts the debates concerning the "immediacy of fascism" and the "war danger." At the April 1956 meeting Dennis gave a report criticizing past policies. Foster "stood alone, except for the half-hearted support" of Davis. He terms Davis "anathema" to those fleeing the party like himself and accuses him and Foster of destroying the party. The important point is that there did seem to be three, not two, factions: Davis-Foster, Gates, and Dennis in the middle.[16]

The post-1956 crisis is a searing event in the history of the U.S. Left, and it still generates emotion today, much like the executions of Julius and Ethel Rosenberg, for life and death were at stake. The widow of Eugene Dennis, Peggy Dennis, has viewed Davis with a lack of fondness. She recounts, presumably secondhand, the incident leading to her husband's confrontation with HUAC in the late 1940s: "Gene had suggested Ben Davis. . . . Ben insisted that Gene, as general secretary, be the one. Others sat silent, and at one point Ben challenged 'this mystery stuff that keeps Gene from taking on these kind of hearings. . . . ' Ben accused Gene of being a 'coward, afraid to go into these hostile situations.'" Then in 1956, she says, Dennis "blocked" the Foster-Davis move to oust Gates.[17] Howard Fast, a noted writer then a member of the party, recalls the following: " . . . my own belief is that the Gates faction never represented a majority of the Party. . . . It is true that numerically the Communist Party of the United States was insignificant; but it was the Communist Party of the most powerful nation on earth, and therefore it had an importance far beyond its size or effectiveness."[18]

George Charney, who clashed with Davis on the New York party structure during this time, nonetheless recalls him as "an old cherished colleague." At the April 1956 meeting, "Foster, with half-hearted backing by Ben Davis, made a furious rebuttal of the criticisms, but he was isolated. . . . [Dennis] yielded not an inch . . . to the Stalinist trend represented by Foster." After this meeting, a "special report" on Stalin was "read to us. . . . For the first time I heard charges made, first by Ben Davis, that had we had state power we would, like Stalin, have executed dissident comrades. The irony was that he was referring to himself as the imaginary victim. The whole spectacle took on an eerie cast." During the Gates fight, Charney continues,

> Ben Davis made a big point that the Negro membership overwhelmingly supported Foster and opposed the Gates wing. Up to a point this was true. In the National Committee, however, Jim Jackson and Claude Lightfoot favored Dennis, not Foster . . . [though] Harlem was united behind Davis. . . . I will never forget my meeting with the Harlem committee prior to the national convention. I was terribly alone . . . aside from some caustic remarks made by Ben, the discussion was fairly temperate. Nevertheless, it was a tense, emotional confrontation. . . . My "revisionist" position was rejected overwhelmingly . . . most vociferous supporters of Foster came from the waterfront section headed, by Al Lannon. . . . Foster's main base in New York was the garment district . . . their dedication to the party, to their Soviet Union and to their vision of communism overcame all other considerations."

The fact that Davis had Harlem and Foster had labor suggests that at least in New York the base left for Gates was mostly white intellectuals and middle strata.[19]

Dorothy Healey hesitates about Davis. " . . . I have very ambivalent feelings about Ben. On one hand, he was one of the most eloquent people in the party . . . and really far more able in analysis than others were. . . . On the other hand, he always mixed in with the questions what I considered subjective questions, personal ego and what not."[20] Since repression had removed Gil Green, Henry Winston, Gus Hall, Robert Thompson, Claudia Jones, John Williamson, and other important forces from the scene, the quality of the leadership was negatively affected. As time passed, Junius Scales—a southerner like Davis but from a Confederate family—saw a change in Davis: "At first he had seemed inclined to support Foster and crush the questioning opposition by weight of his and Foster's authority; then he shifted his position and abandoned Foster; and throughout the summer and fall I felt that he had become pathetically unsure of himself while making a loud and ominous noise—the ruin of a fine man."[21]

Paul Robeson, Jr., left the party eventually, but he speaks glowingly of Davis and remains hostile to the Gates faction: "Gates people were viewed by black, Hispanic and language cadre as your friendly left-wing bigots . . . on the issue of Black Liberation he was just hopeless." The Stalin issue, Robeson contends, was irrelevant. His father's "sympathies" were with Davis, primarily on "third world, African grounds."[22]

Steve Nelson has his own memories of Davis:

> In spite of our frequent clashes over Party policy, he had always been decent toward me and taken an interest in my work. Ben reminded me that it was he who had first nominated me for the National Committee, even before I went to Spain. More than many of the other leaders, he had made a real effort to keep in touch

with what was happening in basic industry . . . the witness who stood up for us in our Pittsburgh Smith Act trial even when it meant lengthening his own sentence with citations for contempt of court. Finally, I recalled the day he and Nina Stamler were married in our house in Pittsburgh right after his release from prison. But I still couldn't accept his point of view. And his ideas were those of the Party.

He saw this bad blood in the party as early as the post-war period: "I could always talk with Davis though—although we argued repeatedly, we maintained a mutual respect and would often go out for coffee. He'd insist that we couldn't influence these petty bourgeois organizations. . . . With Thompson and Foster, my relations were more distant." Still, "Foster, Davis and Thompson repeatedly accused us of revisionism."[23]

The general always fights the last war. Perhaps the perceptions of Foster and Davis were overly colored by the Teheran crisis. Doxey Wilkerson disagreed with many of Gates's views. He had disagreed vocally with the reiteration of the Black Belt thesis, but he and Davis did not get along and he ultimately left the party. He still believes in socialism and contends that he left more in sorrow than anger. He maintained "friendly relationships" afterwards with Winston and particularly Patterson. Retrospectively he still views the 1956 conflict as "Americanization vs. Sovietization." He accused the U.S. party of "tailing" the Soviets and for being too "bureaucratic." The party "needed major reforms . . . Americanized forms . . . changes in doctrine." In an arresting analogy he concluded, "Gorbachev's talking stuff [that] we were talking then."[24]

The U.S. party was influenced heavily by the Soviets, who had made the revolution that others had just talked about. The command-administrative procedure so popular there was reflected in the U.S. party and was heightened during the Red Scare; the exigencies of clandestine political work and repression often did not allow for full and expansive discussion before decisions were adopted. James Jackson recalls during this period that "patience and mood were shredded . . . you just come from five years in jail or underground . . . people dropping out of the party . . . confusion." His opinion is that "not everything was negative about the demand for enhancing democracy in the party . . . the underground had produced certain abuse of leadership." Foster was "unyielding" and had a low personal regard for Gates; if the patriarch won, he would still come back and ask for a revote. But "people were tired" of the heavy hand in the United States.[25] Claude Lightfoot later characterized Gates as anti-Leninist; Foster " . . . held steadfastly . . . and refused to engage in any self-criticism," while Dennis "was self-critical but refused to go over board like Gates."[26]

It is possible that prison and the tension of the times affected Davis. Days after leaving prison in 1955 he sharply and perhaps unduly rebuked the creative writer Joseph North severely for not noting in an article on Spain the role of Dr. Arnold Donawa, a former dean of the Howard University

School of Dentistry who went to Spain to be a "facial surgeon," was "often under fire," and "gave up temporarily a large practice"; he was now recovering from "hoodlum attack [that] permanently damaged his brain. . . . Why is all this, Joe? [Since] you're undoubtedly acquainted with the facts about Donowa . . . [this was] all the more unfortunate because" Donowa was black. Then he lit into North and Howard Fast for not listing Foster's books among recommended reading; this was deemed "serious."[27] Nevertheless, it would be one-sided to focus on this tendency of Davis's. For example, despite the suggestions of some, the record shows that Davis and Gurley Flynn—the top woman leader in the party—were able to maintain cordial relations, though not always agreeing on the issues and once contending for the same party post.[28]

Admittedly it was not easy to oppose Davis and Foster, a walking embodiment of the powerful black-labor alliance. Their relationship seemed to deepen under the pressure of the times. Just before Davis was jailed, he penned a tribute to Foster lauding his *Outline Political History of the Americas*. In turn Foster called Davis a "brilliant and courageous fighter."[29]

In his memoir party leader Alexander Bittleman recalls that when the Comintern favored the Jay Lovestone faction over Foster's, "[we] didn't . . . collaborate harmoniously. . . . we abided by the instructions but refused to take responsibility for majority leadership." His comments remind us that Foster had been a participant in party wars before and by the account of most comrades had been proved correct in the cold light of history. First it was Lovestone, then Browder, and now Gates; in the eyes of many comrades they embodied a triangle, or a trinity. It was like Pascal's wager on God: it was best not to bet against him.[30]

The statement of the National Committee of the party issued in the summer of 1956 was self-critical: " . . . we admit frankly that we uncritically justified many foreign and domestic policies of the Soviet Union, which are now shown to be wrong." They called themselves "an independent Marxist party. . . . " In criticizing their fraternal party in Moscow, the National Committee averred that it would be incorrect to attribute all errors to Stalin, just as it was wrong to give him credit for all "progress"; they criticized the "continuing silence" on allegations of anti-Jewish acts in the Soviet Union. The U.S. party was caught in a pre-Gorbachev wind shear from Moscow.[31]

James Ford bravely advocated that political differences among party leaders be brought into the open: "Differences do exist on very serious matters, such as, on the Middle East situation, the Negro question, questions of Poland, etc. The confusion is transparent enough to be seen in compromises and patched up statements." He recalled that even though the Negro Question was "kicked around" openly for years within the party, it did not seem to harm the issue but in fact helped it. Like a dam bursting, letters poured into the party organ urging an airing of differences among leaders. But a number of party leaders felt that the enemy could take advantage of such;

the problem was that the enemy (notably the FBI) was well aware of the differences and in certain aspects was creating and exacerbating them.[32]

Davis was in the thick of it all. He told Robeson, "I've been involved in meetings, there's been no time to see you. There's plenty to talk to you about. The meetings I've been in are of tremendous importance and I'll have to tell you about them."[33] These words were an understatement, for Davis was tossing thunderbolts repeatedly. He cited two statements on the 20th Congress of the CPSU issued "unanimously," adding, "today's differences may be tomorrow's agreement." He continued, "I believe that the biggest single overall challenge to the American party is the fight against left sectarianism." For Davis, this was a candid admission and implicit self-criticism. Yet he was disturbed by a perceived overemphasis on the "Stalin revelations" since he believed that the party was "independent" anyway. He rued the ignoring of the "objective conditions" but coupled that with the assertion that "our party, especially on the upper levels, is unfamiliar with self-criticism." "One of the most positive lessons we should learn from the Browder period," he said, "is that we should not go overboard in correcting sectarianism as we did in correcting right opportunism. . . . [Today] right opportunism is not the main danger in our Party . . . yet . . . our Party has made many massive right opportunist mistakes." Davis had put his finger on one of the major weaknesses of the party. It did tend to fight one kind of "opportunism" by instituting another kind, and his comment on self-criticism was telling, although tardy.[34]

Some correspondents did not feel that Davis had gone far enough. Davis bristled. He scored the "Browderite" views of Chick Mason, who had attacked him, and wondered why they ignored the subjective factor: "it is strange to find many leading Party members today who claim virtually that the extremely difficult objective situation of the last two years had little or nothing to do with the sectarianism which often hampered our Party's commendable and heroic activities during the last period."[35] One writer concurred that "the Smith Act and our enemies are the main cause." This was true, but the issue really was: whether the often sectarian approach toward, for example, Lester Granger, Walter White, and others was congruent with the objective conditions.[36]

Also in September 1956 the party issued the "Draft Resolution for the 16th National Convention." Everyone in the leadership voted yes, except Davis and Foster, who voted yes "with qualifications." The resolution assaulted left-sectarianism in Negro work and an inability to act on the multiclass character of that struggle; it also questioned the party's uncritical view of the CPSU. The *Times* printed extensive excerpts from this document and noted the critical decline in membership, from eighty thousand to twenty thousand. Days later Foster reconsidered and changed his vote to no. Just like in 1944, he was isolated. He felt that the resolution was overly critical of the left-sectarian trend and that the proposal for a "mass party of socialism" (or a merger with other forces) was misguided. He believed that the errors of the period were due to the support of the Progressive party, the failure to raise more sharply the idea of the parliamentary road to socialism at the Foley Square trial, and sending cadre underground. He also called the Black Belt thesis "obsolete." With evident delight the *Times* editorialized about "Communist dissension" and predicted the ouster of Foster.[37]

The authorities played a role in the turmoil by forbidding Davis to travel to Detroit to bolster allies there. The fragmenting leadership (Foster, Dennis, Davis, and Gates) put up a brave front; it urged "united support to the DW Fund Drive," despite "serious differences" on other issues. A brushfire had broken out in the largest district, New York. Though defeated 35–6 in a vote, a minority of five submitted a report calling for a "'non-Party' political Association." Other skirmishes were breaking out nationally. In "A Message to the State Conventions and Clubs of the Party," issued by the leadership on 19 December 1956, "tendencies to substitute invective for serious argument" were lamented as well as "sharp, even extreme, controversy . . . [that included] leading figures in the Party."[38] The *Times* on 24 December 1956 compared the party wars to what happened in Yugoslavia with Tito.

Then in one of his more thoughtful theoretical pieces, Davis weighed in; left sectarianism "in this new world situation will undoubtedly continue to be . . . the main danger . . . for a long period ahead." He proceeded, "In the last six or seven years our Party has come upon lean, hard days . . . extremely isolated from the main thoroughfares of mass activity. . . . The morale and fighting spirit of the Party is at an all-time low; there's a sharply critical attitude toward the leadership, which in most respects is fully justified . . . paralysis in mass activities . . . wholesale disorientation and loss of members; unnecessary tensions and strains. . . . " Although he did not agree with "a certain rigidity and with various characterizations" in Foster's above-noted article, Davis stated that "he makes a very important contribution" since the "present condition of the party is a perfect set-up for liquidation."

In his essay Davis hailed the "many positive, bold and provocative articles" generated by the controversy and concluded that comrades "cannot be turned on and off like spigots. . . . I have participated in the 'spigot' approach; but no more." It is hard to tell comrades they were boldly fighting McCarthyism, he said, then tell them they have blundered: "No wonder comrades ask themselves whether the last 10 or 15 years of their lives have been wasted." Here was a side of the much-vaunted self-criticism that was rarely noted. Dennis's April 1956 report was "correct," he said, but "in underestimating the positive role and achievements of the Party . . . it opened up a veritable Pandora's box. The search for errors by our Party almost became vulgarized into a spree, with the line between indictment of mistakes and judgment of the Party becoming very thin." Moreover, "considerable mischief" was committed in the party "by attempting to apply mechanically the lessons" of the 20th CPSU Party Congress. It was "absolutely wrong" to "dump" all of the *Daily Worker*'s "excesses" in applying these lessons on "Comrade Gates."

Major errors, he continued, were "my individual lagging on the theory of the Negro question . . . our narrow electoral policy of '48, the extreme security measures instituted, our failure to investigate the new and peculiar features of the capitalist economy in our country." The Stalin "devaluation" removed "inhibitions" that "thwarted a more basic examination . . . with national traits of our own country." He blamed Stalinism for stunting "creative development" of Marxism-Leninism.

But Davis rushed to object to the dumping of democratic centralism, Leninism, and the party itself: "how can one be so cocksure one way and then overnight be so cocksure in just the opposite direction?" He criticized Gates by name: "If that is Marxist science, I want no part of it." He questioned the narrow view of Negro "nationalism," since among blacks this trend could be progressive: "In certain areas, the situation of Negro women in the party is disgraceful." If, as the party said, black freedom was "key to unlocking the door to the further progress of the entire nation, then we should act that way"; he railed at the " . . . bitter resistance of some comrades to . . . campaign against white chauvinism." The treatment of the black cadre "is shocking"; he assailed Gates again for not putting the Negro Question "centrally"; in fact, "[he] profoundly underestimates it." The party organ, he said, was "seriously incorrect" on Hungary and the Mid-East and Gates "is one of the sources of the political disorientation among our members." His articles violated "inner party democracy" insofar as they did not reflect the views of the most recent convention. With this powerful bombshell the fight had reached a new level of intensity.[39]

His old comrade from Harlem, Herbert Wheeldin, was mocking: "His arguments possess a wonderfully fugitive quality. No matter which direction I turn, their conviction seems to escape me."[40] Davis was not repentant; he had criticized Lillian Gates and Alan Max for suggesting that "we must purge ourselves of all errors before we take any action against U.S. imperialism [and] we must purge ourselves of the errors of the Soviet Union . . . this is truly fantastic . . . how many errors of other organizations, countries and peoples are we supposed to purge ourselves of? . . . Should the Negro people, for example, purge themselves of all their weaknesses and mistakes before they demand full citizenship? Or a worker who wants a raise from the boss? How can good comrades get themselves into such a ridiculous and impotent posture. . . . Because the Soviet Marxists contributed to the tragic situation in Hungary, they should have stood by, risk letting the fascists take over power and content themselves with exclaiming 'mea culpa.' Or if one has contributed to the exposed situation of a friend, one should do nothing if a bandit threatens his life." This was, he concluded with a flourish, " . . . a hidden form of liquidation."[41]

Eugene Dennis, whose midway position was viewed subsequently by many comrades as holding probably the soundest views of the three factions (despite his untimely vacillations), was worried about this increasing hostility. In July John Williamson expressed his own unease to the general secretary: "In my humble opinion the failure to bring about a change in the social composition of the membership . . . disproportionate influences of the New York organization and the war-industrial composition, the inadequate and sometimes total failure of leading comrades to go to party branches and talk to rank and file comrades, or go and talk to factory workers or trade unionists who disagreed with us politically" were the central issues.[42] Then in early December, as chaos was breaking loose in the party, he again contacted Williamson: " . . . I have been and am under extraordinary pressure and am immersed in countless meetings . . . the recent events in Hungary have had a powerful impact here . . . many have been profoundly shaken and disoriented . . . a sizable chunk of NY and NJ is a cesspool . . . [while] . . . Midwest areas . . . [and] most of the West Coast . . . have reacted as workers and Marxists. . . . The demand that Foster and Dennis 'must go' has become more organized . . . the proposal is being openly and actively advanced in these quarters that Steve [Nelson] and Johnny [Gates] are the logical alternatives and that if their position is not upheld at the convention many will take a walk. . . . Among the Gates-NY followers, the healthiest forces are considerably influenced by L'Unita. . . . One of the big casualties of the critical and dangerous party situation [is] the lost opportunity in connection with many new developments and openings in the trade union and Negro peoples movements."[43] All the while Louis Budenz and Joe McCarthy were celebrating the fallout in the party.[44]

This battle was a precursor of sorts—as Dennis's reference to *L'Unita* suggests—of the Euro-Communism controversy of the 1970s—that is, the effort by certain European Communist parties to distance themselves from Moscow. It also was a reaction to questions of nationalism such as Zionism and white chauvinism and the stringent campaign against this latter trend within the party. The problem was that the unceasing pressure from the FBI and events themselves made it difficult for Davis and the party to assess and evaluate themselves properly. The isolation and membership losses contributed to the confusion.

So did the FBI. The CP-11 trial, as Richard Gid Powers has observed, "had its origins in [Hoover's] preparations for an emergency custodial detention program." Throughout 1956 their surveillance and harassment of the party escalated.[45]

A close watch was placed on Davis particularly. As the government was deciding what to do, an FBI agent reported, "Davis has indicated . . . that he still adheres to the Communist doctrine and the Government is mistaken if it believes he has changed his beliefs due to his past conviction." Their response was swift: "upon the expiration of Davis' probation maximum investigative efforts will be afforded this investigation and the resources of the entire underground squad of the [New York office] will be available." By April an agent was happily telling Hoover, "The fisurs of Davis have reflected that Davis no longer walks in a free, casual manner, but rather walks noticeably slow, giving the indication his back causes him some pain." Until Davis's death eight years later, the FBI maintained a ghoulish, macabre, and curious interest in his health. As tension increased in November, Davis's "activities are closely followed on a daily basis" though one of their main informants "gets Davis and another one of the main ten Communist leaders mixed up." Davis received threatening letters and was threatened with car bombs; the Cuban superintendent of his apartment building informed him immediately when FBI agents came to the building to install electronic surveillance.[46]

With revelations about Soviet anti-Semitism and the Suez Crisis, Zionism reared its head in party ranks. Davis and other black leaders were charged with anti-Semitism because they backed Egypt and condemned Israeli aggression. Neither Davis nor other party leaders reassessed their support for the creation of Israel. However, it will be interesting to see if the dissolution of the USSR will mean a second look at this momentous decision, which after all was backed avidly by the much-reviled foreign policy of Stalin. This was doubly ironic for Davis since in the pre-1948 period, few blacks—or Jews, for that matter—were as active in Jewish affairs as was he.[47]

Since the party and Moscow were so fervent in backing a Jewish state in Palestine, the entry of comrades to the party with Zionist inclinations was facilitated. It was also felt that Jews were disproportionately sympathetic to the party. Davis's electoral successes were sparked in part by substantial support from the Jewish community. Yet the events of 1956 expedited the worsening of black-Jewish relations. *Daily Worker* reporter A. B. Magil in May 1956 called on the party to raise the slogan of "Arms for Israel." The Stalin devaluation period and the resultant *glasnost* allowed such ideas to be expressed. Then Ed Strong, one of the more popular black leaders, denounced *Daily Worker* editorials on the Suez Crisis that "departed seriously from a Marxist-Leninist analysis"; it had been claimed that Egyptian and Arab provocation led Israel to launch war.[48]

Then the *New York Times* entered the picture. They reported that the American Jewish Committee had done a study of the party that concluded, "Most of the party's Negroes, the analysis said, seem to be 'behind the Foster-Dennis-Davis pro-Soviet group' . . . The Negro members, it is suggested, 'look upon racism and traditional colonialism as the prime evils to be fought' and tend to 'relative indifference about Eastern Europe.'"[49] Jews in the party were split, with workers backing Foster and intellectuals and

Yiddish-speaking activists on the other side. It was true that blacks were less susceptible to manipulation of the "Iron Curtain" issue since they had few relatives or brethren in eastern Europe and were in any case generally suspicious of initiatives that seemed to come from elites.

Davis assailed Abner Berry, objecting to his "neutralist" stand on the Mideast; in passing he noted the "strong pro-Egyptian influence among the Negro masses expressed in part . . . by the increasing growth of Moslem influence and organization in Negro communities. . . . I venture to say that Negroes are anything but neutral in this matter . . . and they're right." He downplayed the idea that this harmed black-Jewish ties, but certain Zionists were out to prove him wrong; he came under attack despite his past yeoman duty pushing issues of concern to the Jewish community.[50] The *New York Times* on 18 March 1957 charged that black Communists were "using the Jewish issue" and charging "Jewish bourgeois nationalism" in factional disputes. This infuriated Davis. He returned to the Berry piece and accused him of making an "apology for the pro-imperialist policies of the Ben-Gurion government" and condemned the "bourgeois nationalism among certain Jewish circles"; he added the obligatory "Israel has a right to a secure existence as a state" but warned that "Israel is courting national suicide" because of their "brutal aggression" against Cairo. He railed against Zionist pressure on the *Los Angeles Herald Dispatch* and other black newspapers, though he disagreed with their calling Ben Gurion "Hitler," terming it "harmful and unfortunate," but noting that the "chauvinist and far more prevalent slander is that of labelling Nasser as a 'dictator' and 'Hitler.'"[51] Aware of these contradictions, the FBI sought to capitalize on them; intentionally or inadvertently helping to inflame black-Jewish tensions.[52]

Davis was on to something. The Suez Crisis was an important milestone in the revival of Islam among blacks; Nasser was seen as in the tradition of Bandung. African-Americans, as was their wont, reacted to the flood of negative publicity directed at Nasser by flocking to his banner. But that was not the only development in this general area. Montgomery signaled that the Black Belt thesis required retooling, though "self-determination" was too potent a slogan to disappear simply because the party decided it was obsolete. These factors, along with the erosion of the Left and its heritage of militant organizing across racial lines, set the stage for the rise of Malcolm X, the Nation of Islam, and a contradictory nationalism among increasing sectors of young African-Americans. In any case, the National Question had become even more complicated.

17
When Black and White Unite, 1958–1959

The party wars had burst on the scene in 1956, but it was now 1958 and the party recognized that the internal scuffling was not helpful when a nascent African-American movement was re-emerging. One can surmise that the FBI and other authorities had distinct though not fond memories of, for example, the election of a black Red to office and growth of leftist sentiment in the not-so-distant past. COINTELPRO came into being in 1956 for certain reasons. For elites it was rather messy that Montgomery and Little Rock had occurred during the Cold War; certainly these racial hot spots were not good for public relations globally. Similarly, it was unhelpful that so many blacks could not fully understand why they should distance themselves from black Reds. The Red Scare was helpful in convincing civil rights forces to keep their distance from Communists in the Black Liberation movement. The immediate post-Brown period with the spirit of Geneva did allow Davis to gather added support, but unfortunately for Davis and the party, the situation was even more complicated for them than it was for the FBI.

This period also witnessed two important changes. Davis and the party deepened an earlier trend of softening criticism of mainstream civil rights figures like Randolph and Wilkins and acknowledging that they were incorrect in having much of their past criticism turn on disputes over foreign policy. But as time passed it seemed that the lack of criticism from the Left made these figures and their movement more susceptible to influence from the Right. Balance was needed. Second, although the Gates faction was defeated within the party, this only led to the rise of another faction, symbolized by African-American Communist Harry Haywood.

Simultaneously, it was fascinating to note how blacks seemed to stand down so disproportionately from the Gates faction. Those blacks who left the party—Haywood, Wilkerson, Berry, Johnson, and others—were not high-ranking figures like Gates, nor were all of them pro-Gates in any case. The mainstream press often tended to equate blacks with Stalinism, referring to Davis particularly since Foster was ill so often. What was the impact of this in various quarters? Why were blacks so closely identified in the popular imagination with the "Stalinists"? Was it inevitable that one of the conditions imposed by racism was resistance to tampering with perceived revolutionary doctrine? What impact did this have on the evolving civil rights movement? Were black Reds "conservative radicals"?

Political scientists Edward G. Carmines and James A. Stimson identify 1958 as a pivotal year of the African-American movement. Howard Fast had said that the party was still the Communist force in the world's most powerful nation (after all, the party was not on page one for nothing). One stoolpigeon said that despite an estimated ten-year decline from eighty thousand to twenty thousand, this still putatively important party was more dangerous in 1958 than in early 1948 since now "they [have] boiled their ranks down to the hard core." Davis was considered the hardest of the hard core, yet he still maintained contact with the Rev. Adam Clayton Powell and Dr. Martin Luther King during this pivotal year.[1]

The year began ominously with the conflict over the statement issued by Communist parties of twelve nations. Then Gates left the party with much publicity, despite the party's dwindling membership. The Red veteran from the Spanish Civil War blasted Davis, Foster—and Dennis; this and his eagerness to tell all to the mainstream press did not help his cause or his supporters left behind to fend for themselves against a determined Davis. One paper happily told its readers that the party "gave signs of nearing the end the road." Reassuring their unrealistic and headstrong compatriots in the elite, the *Times* said, "Communists have played no role at all . . . among Negroes." Concessions had to be given, the paper believed, but the past had to be avoided and the Communists should get no credit.[2]

Davis and the National Administrative Committee scolded Gates. Flynn jumped on the departed leader: "Lately in our meetings he pounded the table, denounced and attacked his long-time co-workers, and behaved in an aggressive manner. Every meeting in which he participated for many months became a stormy scene." She wondered why he was so mild on television with Mike Wallace.[3] One of Davis's closest allies, William Patterson, replaced Gates as the head of the newspaper. This was interpreted as a Paris commune-type lesson for Davis and the leadership; supervision over the party voice was deemed vital. Certainly the FBI could have celebrated the fact that the party was forced to suspend daily publication of the paper. Ferdinand Smith, a respected veteran but now deported to Jamaica where he was president of the Federation of Trade unions, told his old friend Patterson: "Gates going from the paper, and I hope all influence in the party, I think was a good thing. . . . Our mistake was that he was not taken head on at the last convention. Unity is always a most desirable thing but unity at all cost can be a mistake of the first order."[4]

Soon thereafter, A. B. Magil—a *Daily Worker* specialist on the Middle East—complained about an article published in the USSR that attacked him. After citing his recent promotions he rebutted, "If I am a revisionist, what shall be said of a Party leadership which reposed such confidence in me?"[5] With the Gates exit, the correlation of forces shifted within the party.

As of 22 February 1958 only seven of the twenty members of the National Executive Committee—which had a strong Gates influence—that had been elected the previous spring were reelected at a full sixty-member meeting of the National Committee. A resolution written by Dennis was passed attacking "right opportunism" and the "ultra-Left viewpoint." The former was represented by Gates and the latter was African-American leader Haywood. Now the National Question could no longer be ignored. Evidently left sectarianism (Davis-Foster) was no longer considered the main internal danger.[6]

The *New York Times* reported that the party was "again firmly under the control"—not of Davis and Foster—but of the CPSU. The paper added that "rightist forces suffered two major defeats at the Committee's meeting." But Davis and his allies could not be thrilled by the fact that some of the comrades allegedly more influenced by Zionism—Charney, Al Blumberg, Max Gordon, Morris Schappes, George Watt, and William Lawrence—were accusing the Foster-Davis faction of a "witch-hunt." Then Charney, Lawrence, and Watt resigned. Even if that were considered—as the baseball announcers say, "addition by subtraction"—the fact that the *Times* reported that Abner Berry and Jesus Colon and Si Gerson had signed this protest was uniquely disquieting for Davis.[7]

The situation was fluid. After Charney resigned, he identified Davis and Foster as the "pro-Soviet faction" but Davis replied by citing the departures of Gates and his camp as a "turning point." In early March the former National Executive Committee was "dissolved" and a new leadership body of fifteen was set up. But "some comrades in the minority took the position of refusing to participate in such a leadership. They declined all nominations."[8]

Just as the elites sought to win more blacks back from the Left during this period, it could be inferred that the historic identification of many Jewish people with the Left also presented a challenge. The Israel Question and the concessions that could be granted more easily to Euro-Americans allowed elites to achieve huge gains in this realm. Parallels certainly exist between the post–World War II travails of the Jewish and black communities.

The popular conception was that Foster was the titular leader of the dominant faction in the party but that real power was being wielded now by Davis and Dennis. The *New York Post* wrote, "'Anyone who challenges any decision of this group,' one dissident said, 'is immediately branded as a "white chauvinist" and automatically discredited.' Davis used this tactic on Gates in the *Daily World* fight and it is even more effective today."[9] On the other hand, blacks were playing a disproportionate role in the leadership of the party.

There was no surcease. Harry Haywood was identified closely with the "ultra-Left" faction but as Davis himself said, in New York State "certain of the most vocal spokesmen of this ultra-left are Puerto Rican and Negro comrades."[10] It could be presumed that the perceived racism of the Gates faction, as suggested by Paul Robeson, Jr., helped to convince even more some of the comrades of African descent that self-determination could not be done away with lightly. Moreover, as history clearly demonstrated, the party in New York was not just another party organization.

The FBI was active as ever. As part of COINTELPRO, the FBI said, "authority is granted the New York office to prepare the suggested leaflet attacking [Davis] . . . [it is] designed to capitalize on the current activities of the ultra-left faction of the Party. It will accuse Davis . . . of merely paying lip service in his opposition to the ultra-left faction. This leaflet should force Davis into stronger opposition to the ultra-left faction which should bring an increased animosity toward Davis from the individuals involved including many leading Negro comrades. . . . It can be claimed that Davis is reluctant to offend the group for fear he may damage his position and interfere with his ambition to become head of the CP." The FBI conjectured that Davis "has allowed [Charles] Loman to continually defy CP leadership and get away with it. Loman has always seem [sic] to be able to count on Davis as his protector. The leaflet could assert that Davis is so eager to realize his goal of becoming head of the Party he will do business with any group he feels can help him . . . such a leaflet would cause a great deal of consternation. . . . It might well force Davis to take a more active interest in checking the ultra-left group. . . . If Davis can be put on the defensive with the leaflet described above, it may damage his position as a leader of the CP."[11] The leaflet was released.

The patrons of the FBI were so audacious that they stated openly in mid-May 1958 that the FBI had ninety wiretaps on the party across the nation. Senator Kenneth Keating of New York, a liberal from the area with the densest concentration of Communists, was interviewed on television—an increasing material force in this battle—and called for increased vigilance against the party.[12] Hoover chipped in that "the most rabid group of pro-Soviets in this country are in charge of the Communist party." At a time when the USSR was being painted as the closest thing to hell on earth, this was loaded language. A wiretap on Davis by the FBI at this same moment allegedly revealed, "Again . . . Davis told his wife that 'a lot of the guys' down at CP headquarters were chauvinistic."[13]

The party was still suffering reversals. In late May Foster reported to the National Committee that his paralytic stroke the previous October had limited his work and discussion. He was sufficiently well to report that the group he termed the Right had strength in the National Committee and that delegates to the recent convention were "hostile to them." He suggested that the spirit of Geneva in 1955 pushed back sectarianism but aided what he called right opportunism: "The fact was, that the pro-Party elements carried the convention politically but were unable to win the national leadership decisively." With satisfaction Foster wrote of the "practical fusion of the

Center, identified with Comrade Dennis, and the left, identified with Comrade Davis."[14]

This unity worried the FBI. They made a leaflet charging Davis with "dereliction . . . mailed only to those Party members who are known to dislike Davis and who are seeking facts to unseat him from his current Party position." Again, the propaganda was "designed to criticize Davis for not fighting the ultra-left group as he did John Gates." Well aware of the racial and national dynamics, the FBI gloated: "[Davis] is an excellent controversial figure to cause disruption." At the same time a residual element of the trend represented by Gates was being continued in the party by Dorothy Healey, another aspect the FBI could play upon.[15]

In a sense the party wars could be seen as part of an ongoing international dichotomy between Social Democrats and Communists or various trends within Marxism or even Marxism-Leninism. In what was once the German Democratic Republic, these forces had merged into the Socialist Unity Party. In Austria, France, Spain, Sweden, Norway, Finland—most of Europe, in fact—these forces were separately organized. Because of the weakness and historic ideological poverty of the Social Democratic trend in the United States—especially their weaknesses on race and racism—there was a de facto East Germany situation in New York; that is, Social Democrats and Reds were under one roof. Hypothetically the existence of a progressive Social Democratic party would have spared the CP some of the angst of the 1950s in a number of ways, for these forces would have had their own party. Indeed, the weakness of social democracy in the United States is a major explanation for the strength of the right-wing tendency among U.S. elites, just as social democracy's difficulty in handling the question of racism helps to account for their historically small numbers, compared to the Communists.

This was the backdrop to yet another controversy, the effort to fuse these leftist forces in the state of New York. They did come together in a public forum in mid-June, but the *Times* said that "dissension began to develop . . . at [the] opening session" between Davis and the old Progressive party leader from the West Coast, Vincent Hallinan. The party was accused of acting to "split the 'unity conference' of leftists . . . by insisting that only one candidate be named for state office instead of a full slate . . . [Davis] walked out." He "resented what the [party] said was an implication that their party had played the Democrats' game" by not running "opposition candidates for certain offices." How ironic this must have seemed to Davis. The embodiment of left sectarianism, Davis was now being criticized for being a Right opportunist. This issue was nettlesome throughout the critical election year of 1958.[16]

Davis was getting it from all sides. Two linked events mirror the difficulty of the era. In one of their ubiquitous memos the FBI declared that "consideration should also be given as to the best means to break up or weaken the existing coalition" of Davis, Dennis, and Thompson "and preventing them from working harmoniously as leaders of [the party]."[17] Then Dennis confessed to John Williamson, " . . . Ben played a very disturbing role, particularly in relation to Claude [Lightfoot] and Carl [Winter]. . . . Ben is displaying some of the negative attitudes manifested in 1949–50." The FBI was such a potent force during these debates that it becomes difficult to ascertain the true origins of controversies surrounding Davis's role. Still, it could reasonably be expected that mature party leadership could handily deflect external efforts to foment discord.[18]

Problems continued to brew. In July 1958 the National Committee defeated (28–10) a resolution scoring the *Daily Worker* for backing the execution of Imre Nagy, the deposed Hungarian leader. "Sources close to the party reported that Mr. Davis had attempted at the meeting to secure the removal of Dorothy Healey . . . but was defeated. With the illness of [Foster] Mr. Davis is generally regarded as leader of the Stalinist faction."[19] When the CP celebrated its thirty-ninth anniversary in September, a "crowd of 1,300, most of them in the older age groups, half-filled Carnegie Hall."[20] The innovative and hyperactive FBI was suggesting that Flynn's "attitude toward some CP leaders [such as Davis] present an excellent opportunity for us to increase her disillusionment and add a disruptive influence in the leadership of the party." Their monitoring of her "was producing excellent information." As stated above, the problem with historical reconstruction of this period is that the FBI was involved so intimately with party wars that sorting out cause and blame becomes difficult; yet it cannot be denied that whatever the role of the FBI, some comrades' dislike of Davis was deepening.

Did the *Daily Worker* have to back the Nagy execution? Like James Jackson's earlier comment, one wonders whether—given the serious splits and adverse conditions—this kind of issue should have been pushed so forcefully; on the other hand, since the party had identified itself so closely with the fortunes of "existing socialism" in eastern Europe, and given their tendency not to duck burning issues, it would have been perceived as opportunist to act otherwise.[21]

The increased scrutiny and pressure on Davis occurred as he sought a rapprochement with the Reverend Adam Powell and other mainstream black leaders in Harlem. The village was not very large and many of their supporters knew each other well. The Red Scare made open contacts questionable. Davis's attacks on Powell during the era of left sectarianism had to be overcome. In his first postprison interview, in March 1956, Davis rose to the defense of Hulan Jack, a prominent New York black elected official. He scored the removal of the progressive Hubert Delany from his city post. But in an article in the *Daily Worker* on 23 October 1956, when internal conflict was raging, Davis showed he could avoid both left sectarianism and right opportunism in the post-Geneva era. Davis termed Powell's support for Eisenhower "a serious error of judgment which could prove costly to the Negro people and to their natural labor and liberal allies." He blamed the

Democrats in part, citing the purported deal that led to the prosecution of Powell on income-tax charges. Davis concluded, "The Negro-labor alliance is not something to be be handled casually like changing brands of cigarettes."[22]

The issue was joined when rumors emerged of Davis's old foe Earl Brown challenging Powell for Congress. The Harlem GOP was leaning to Powell "in defiance of" the party organization. But this is not what brought Harlem politics to the notice of those who traditionally had paid as much attention to this issue as they did to the Maldives.[23] Powell had obtained the "implied endorsement" of Davis. J. Ray Jones, trying to be agnostic, opined that he did not seek Red support but that Davis had the right to express his views. It was true that Davis had called for "all-out" Communist support to one of the top black leaders in the nation. Davis deplored the "scandalous assault" on Powell: "Whatever one's differences with Powell and despite his often ill-chosen and intemperate words, he stands at this historic instant as a symbol of the whole Negro liberation movement." The mellowed Davis even hailed the Liberal party for suggesting Ralph Bunche for the U.S. Senate. But he would not budge on the growing criticism of his and the party's view of the "United Socialist ticket," the so-called fusing of forces of the Left. Graciously he granted that advocates were "sincere," but in fact "they're really withdrawing from the political mainstream into militant isolation." He was particularly exercised over the role of the Socialist Workers party, a traditional target of his invective. "The most effective arena for independent political action presented by life itself is the struggle around Adam Powell in all its enormous significance and aspects," he said. In an implicit concession to Harry Haywood he added that this "[is a] national liberation issue." Davis did not accept that the party had swung, in the pattern frequently complained about, from left sectarianism to right opportunism on such questions. He did not agree that there was an insurmountable obstacle in courting centrist forces, which were under fire from the authorities; he did not agree that courting centrists like Powell while avoiding a "United Socialist" ticket comprised of other leftists presented a major problem. Others suggested that this preference for the center over the Left was just another brand of opportunism.[24]

Still, there was good reason to come rushing to the aid of Powell. The situation was too reminiscent of 1949. Those who said then that if Davis were not defended the right wing would come after Powell were right. And after Powell, they went for Dr. King. It was *déjà vu* all over again with one of the same actors, Earl Brown. He was using similar rhetoric, said Davis, accusing Powell of "class hatred" and "race hatred." Davis charged that Brown was chosen to oppose Powell since no "responsible or respectable leader" would do it. The heat was on Powell.[25] Although he rejected Communist support, interestingly enough he indicted the "red brush" anti-Communist words of Brown. But he went further to brag about his anti-

Communist credentials, including his ill-fated trip to Bandung in 1955, where he said he "stopped Communist propaganda dead in its tracks."[26]

Davis did not balk publicly at Powell's position, as he might have in the past. Instead he condemned the Liberal party for backing Brown and not Powell.[27] Why would this now anti-Communist party oppose Powell, who had broken with the Reds? "Opposition to Selective Service, the British loan, Greek-Turkish aid and the European Recovery Program back in the late forties to his advocacy of the Powell amendment that helped kill the federal school construction program bill, two years ago" was deemed reason enough to oppose the controversial cleric, according to the *Times*. Yet, opposition from influential Euro-Americans was a plus for Powell in Harlem and a kiss of death for Brown. Powell won overwhelmingly. It seemed as if the pre-1956 tactics of the party had rubbed off on the elites since they seemed to be as concerned with Powell's foreign policy views as much as any other issue. But above all, the high and mighty were concerned about the fact that Davis and Powell and Davis and Harlem might awaken the alliance of the past.[28]

Complicating matters was the contention over fusing the Left for the elections. The leading candidate of one leftist party "offers nothing," said Davis. The SWP did not offer an alternative because of its opposition to "peaceful co-existence." He lambasted their opposition to a major domestic question too, the "anti-monopoly coalition." This was "harmful and divisive," but in a move scorned by others on the Left, he argued against abstention but recommended voting for Robert Wagner for mayor on the Liberal line, despite "serious differences." John McManus of the *Guardian* was perplexed: "Mr. Davis did not attend any of the seven meetings except the last ones. . . . He therefore is in no position to talk of any group worming its way into the inner circle." He refuted the idea of SWP influence that so upset Davis. Responding, Davis apologized for seeming to suggest that they were all "dupes" of the SWP but otherwise stood by his position. Yet opposing him on this question were Du Bois, Rockwell Kent, Corliss Lamont, Hugh Mulzac, and many others. They could not be so easily dismissed. There were charges that Davis and the party had swung from left sectarianism in dealing with blacks to a combination of right and left opportunism in dealing with the Left.[29]

At the united left conference in mid-June 1958 the Communist view was defeated, 154–81; as the *Times* said, "warnings were sounded from the floor against Communist wrecking tactics." The Communists were pictured as fearful of success of the New York ticket "lest it consign the remnants of their party to oblivion."[30] The party pushed to offer only a single candidate for the U.S. Senate for the assembled forces to agree on, but the majority opted for a full slate. Almost five hundred attended. Davis and the party argued that a "full slate 'socialist' ticket" was "sectarian and . . . destined to come into a frontal clash with the labor movement." The "objective effect" of a third party "at this time" will be support for Rockefeller and the GOP. The memory of the now—unfortunately—discredited Progressive party campaign of 1948 was fresh on their minds. Others saw this Socialist effort as a Trojan horse for a resurgence of the Gates faction. Pressure from the comrades forced Hallinan to issue an "apology" for his "slanderous attack" on Davis, but Davis was unmoved, saying it did not go far enough. Others felt that Davis had missed a historic opportunity to consolidate the small U.S. Left.[31]

This issue was a cause for some anxiety. The Lower East Side club of the party publicly rebuked Davis for his "contradictory statements" on the Liberal party. Hal Koppersmith, on the other hand, found it "tragic" that the "Independent-Socialist ticket voted . . . not to cooperate" in Davis's own race for office. But Henry Abrams of the Independent Socialists refuted this attack, saying their policy was not to endorse until a candidate was on the ballot: "Since Mr. Davis is on the ballot I shall personally recommend . . . that he receive our support and, if he desires it, our official endorsement."[32]

Abrams may have spoken too soon. With the party wars easing in intensity, Davis had sought to reimmerse himself in New York politics and seek office in November. The Right wing nationally was not oblivious to these developments in New York. Veteran Red-hunter J. B. Matthews informed the apostate Louis Budenz early in 1958 that he had denounced Mayor Wagner for appointing the Reverend Dr. Gardner Taylor to the school board; the pastor upset Matthews when he allowed the funeral of the Communist Ed Strong to be held in his church; worse Davis, Patterson, and Robeson had served as pall-bearers. Davis remained composed. He still requested a meeting with the mayor to discuss concerns and appeared before the Board of Estimate, speaking for twenty minutes on taxing the rich and ending segregation. With his secretary, William Albertson, Davis demanded that the mayor and Earl Brown take a vigorous stand on Little Rock and the crushing of white terror in Davis's hometown of Dawson, Georgia.[33]

Midyear found Davis still acting like a prospective candidate. At the office of the U.S. ambassador to the United Nations, he was protesting the landing of the U.S. marines in Lebanon. And at a New York State party meeting in late July 1958 Davis set an ambitious goal of recruiting six hundred new comrades by January; certainly a campaign was a way to accomplish this goal. But showing his concern with the still-nagging conflicts, Davis pushed through a motion—passed 20–2—to set up a board to investigate and put on trial factionalism. A week later the party announced that he would run on the People's Rights party ticket for state senate from Harlem. It was like old times. Three hundred cheered Davis on at a rally at 126th and Lenox; a press conference was held at the Hotel Theresa. He opened a headquarters at 306 Lenox Avenue, and three thousand rallied at his familiar corner in late August.[34]

Similar exclamations greeted his campaign in the streets of Harlem. One woman yelled, "'Ben Davis? I thought he was dead!'" The old optimism was back. In comparing 1943 to 1958 Patterson proclaimed, "The fact is the objective situation now offers greater possibilities than were apparent at that time." Davis was granted an audience with the Greater New York Baptist Ministerial Alliance, an assemblage of four hundred churches. The ostensible issue was a new cause Davis was fighting for, the saving of Jimmie Wilson from a legal lynching in Alabama. Wilson was scheduled to die in the chair for allegedly robbing a white woman of a few dollars. Davis's old friend Rev. Harten of Trinity Baptist facilitated the visit. Harten gave Davis praise, saying that he had forsaken wealth for the movement. Later Wilson's sentence was commuted.[35]

After the party wars, this campaign was balm for Davis and may have fueled undue optimism about his prospects. With his old turn of phrase he characterized as "Uncle Tom apologists" his opponents Cora Walker and James Watson. He had to gather signatures and, as the *Worker* reported, "many canvassers not affiliated with Communists are already volunteering"; the progressive and able artist Hugo Gellert made an attractive drawing of him for his campaign literature.[36]

By early September Davis needed five thousand signatures to get on the ballot, two thousand more than necessary due to "tricks by the old party machines." Jack Stachel contenued that "the Davis campaign in Harlem has already opened up great opportunities to rebuild our Party there. . . . Already many hundreds of additional copies [of the paper] are sold each week in canvassing and at the street rallies."[37]

By the deadline 5,988 signed for Davis. Joe North graphically wrote, "The massive figure of the former councilman was etched against the Harlem sky as he stood on the loudspeaker truck and in shirtsleeves delivered a speech which electrified a crowd that inundated the two-score policeman . . . in a cheap-jack attempt to scare the listeners off . . . seldom has this writer heard a speech of this calibre." Charlotta Bass was there to endorse him, and Davis made a point himself to endorse both Powell and King: "We must fight for King. . . . You see a certain conspiracy here. If they can pick off every militant Negro, one by one . . . they will get us down where they want us."[38]

Just when a writer to the *Worker* was noting how enthusiastically Harlemites were reacting to Davis, fate intervened in the form of the authorities.[39] The *New York Amsterdam News*, read widely in Harlem, reported on 20 September, "Leading government investigative agencies were scanning the names of some 5,535 persons" who signed Davis's petitions, "including local and state and state civil service agencies," where blacks were disproportionately employed. Jesse Gray and Paul Robeson were identified as "subscribing witnesses to the petition." Then the paper dropped the other shoe: "It is highly doubtful that he would be seated if he were elected, election officials pointed out."[40]

Bets were hedged. Tammany moved to knock Davis off the ballot, but unity was growing. Two street meetings drew fifteen hundred supporters. Dorothy Healey, chair of the party in Southern California, sent one-hundred-dollars. Tammany won, however, as a court overruled Davis's attorney David Freedman and found that only 967 of the signatures were valid. The FBI had outlined the *mise-en-scène* by listing ways to oust him from the ballot. They concluded, "The political aspirations of the Communist Party USA would be considerably disrupted and injured if Davis was found ineligible to be a candidate."[41]

Not only was Davis building an entente with Powell and King, but even George Schuyler returned to compliment him. Davis, he began, "has always been my favorite Communist." He had just heard him speak on 125th Street: "I found it almost entertaining. . . . " Davis's oratorical skills were still well polished; Schuyler hoped he would get on the ballot since the race was so "dull." "I have known Ben Davis for about 30 years and what endears him to me is that he has never represented himself as anything but a Communist. . . . I like people who take a position and stick to it, no matter what the penalty may be." After all, he said, much of what he says "cannot be controverted" and was "logical." Schuyler was inclined to vote for him even though he thought Communism was "slavery." He argued for diversity: "We need in America all voices which question everything which the majority takes for granted. My experience has been that even the professed anti-Communists are very cool on civil rights." That Schuyler could be so favorable was extraordinary and signaled the possibilities—that is, if the FBI had not been so energetic.[42]

Davis appealed the Board of Elections decision to invalidate his petitions, and presaged the nationalism of the 1960s: "This Board is unfit to make such a decision. You are all white." But the elites had a no-lose proposition; at minimum Davis would be tied up in court and not in the streets. As promised, Henry Abrams of the Independent Socialists stood by his side in court as they appealed. But Davis did not leave the campaign altogether. He found time to speak to the fifteen hundred gathered at Carnegie Hall for the Communist party anniversary. James Jackson and Jesus Colon joined him for street meetings. The Court of Appeals replied by voting 6–1 to uphold the ruling against him.[43]

Party leader Arnold Johnson detailed how Davis was speaking to an average of four to five hundred fans at his rallies on Lenox Avenue. In the afternoons two thousand or more would appear in front of the Hotel Theresa, and this was at a time when the party was being hounded elsewhere. Part of the success of Davis in the party wars was the wide recognition that he had the common touch and vast personal appeal, though during this period his relations with some leading comrades were quite difficult. Johnson marveled that "no political meetings of this kind are being conducted by any other political candidate or party in any part of New York today. The only comparable event was the big huge demonstration meeting for [King]." This was a telling comparison, particularly since "when Reverend King was stabbed, Ben Davis spent the evening at the hospital."[44] Moreover, in his campaign Davis spoke on such issues as Little Rock, China, Africa, housing, and the USSR.

Against all odds, Davis tried a write-in effort after being ousted from the ballot. Five hundred filled the ballroom at the Hotel Theresa for "dancing [and] speeches." He was back on the radio on WLIB.[45] His GOP opponent was not held in high esteem by Hulan Jack, top Harlem politician. Cora Walker "had a reputation as a person who never hesitated to trample others under her feet if it served her purpose," Jack observed.[46] During the middle of the campaign, however, there was the "shocking outrage" of the attack on King. It was even more upsetting that the assailant, with her "babbling about the Communists . . . should serve as an example of what the atmosphere of red-baiting . . . can drive people to do."[47]

The campaign helped to unify the party, however, as exemplified by Healey's hundred-dollar contribution. Finally there was someone the comrades could rally around; it was a welcome respite from internal conflict. However, one writer has charged that Flynn "believed other Party members tolerated Davis' chauvinism because they had a double standard for blacks. . . . In private she also criticized him for his treatment of women and his womanizing"; this attitude, the author suggests, was not absent in 1958.[48] The sources for these bold assertions are sparse, as noted above. Certainly the record reflects that electoral campaigns showed a close and friendly alliance between them. Flynn preceded him as a People's Rights party candidate for the City Council in 1957. Davis spoke on her behalf on radio and went beyond the norms of courtesy.[49]

The mutual admiration between Flynn and Davis continued during Davis's 1958 campaign, with Flynn, a future rival for party leadership, calling him "a shining symbol . . . pioneer . . . in the vanguard, out in the front, on the firing line."[50] But with all that, Davis lost. The *Times* said he got a paltry fifty-four write-in votes. Yet Davis saw the positive: "over 150 street meetings . . . 150,000 leaflets were distributed . . . a special mailing of 20,000 pieces . . . two earlier mailings of 6,000." However, Davis was not ready for official optimism. In a private report to the party he moaned about not only being the candidate but the campaign manager, too; further, "no particular white comrade has asked to make the report but it might have been better if one had." This was part of the legacy of Gates, he said, echoing Paul Robeson, Jr. in calling his foe "that crown prince of revisionism." Yet Davis was elated about some aspects of the campaign, such as the Powell issue: "I cannot remember when A. Philip and myself as a party spokesman were on the same side." Powell was compared to Marcantonio, which was high praise indeed. The new line was paying off: "And in the course of the campaign we got 19 recruits in Manhattan. . . . We could have gotten more. . . . Seven months ago our party in Harlem . . . was practically dead." Now "it was nothing for us to speak and the Negro people would come and put dollar bills in my hand," even twenty-dollar bills. In this confidential report he noted that after the election Powell "came to me and he thanked me very profusely for making it respectful for him to go to prison." Harlem, he said, viewed Davis going to jail like Nehru and Nkrumah.[51]

It bears repeating that though subsequent historians have treated the party as an exhausted force during this period and not even worthy of examination, the FBI and other elites did not agree. They still had on their minds what has been wiped away from most others: Davis's past electoral victories and continuing support among blacks. The reconstituted line of the party simplified the chore of reviving this trend. Davis had contact with King (they had common Atlanta acquaintances) and Powell in an era when fear of Communist influence and sway was not seen as a mirage. Already Patterson was resuscitating one of the elite's worst nightmares by trying to get George Murphy to again raise, via the *Afro-American*, the Negro Question before the United Nations in the heralded, much-publicized "We Charge Genocide" campaign.[52]

Any brimming confidence of the party had to be tempered. A special internal report by the New York State party observed that "there are some fears among our Negro comrades and among many white comrades that our Party is abandoning its position that the Negro question is a national question."[53] This kind of radical change could easily be associated with the views of Gates. Moreover, this change was rising in an era of renewed citizens' councils, Little Rock crises, and the like. Pettis Perry publicly conceded that "during the past few years the Party has had serious losses among our Negro members, including some leading cadre." He argued, unlike most white former Communists, that this was not because of any revelations about Stalin, nor because of Hungary, "nor because the convention left unanswered such basic theoretical questions as that involving self-determination." Why then? The party's supposedly ill-defined outlook and program for the sprouting civil rights movement was the culprit. Although this latter point was debatable, the unease among black comrades was certainly not.[54]

Harry Haywood was an example; he symbolized the "ultra-Left" trend that robustly resisted the effort to ditch the Black Belt thesis. It is riveting to realize that Davis treated the Haywood forces more gingerly than the Gates forces. At any rate, Haywood's view was that Davis-Foster had pulled back on a "full discussion" of the issue at the 1957 convention, figuring it would split the party and open the door for Gates; so despite a consensus in the Davis-Foster faction that the position should be changed, Gates would have to be dispatched first. There was a "rumor," said Haywood, about Davis being asked why they were not dealing brusquely with the ultra-Left. Davis allegedly replied, "We've got to deal with Gates first. When we've dealt with him, then we can handle the left sectarians." After the convention, Haywood campaigned to retain the thesis but Davis, he says, blasted him: "Left to Harry here, he and me would be left alone fighting it down to the ropes. We can't afford that, we gotta get to work."[55]

The issue was not only the Black Belt but "left centers," like the Negro Labor Council, in the black community. Were these left centers sectarian, as was suggested? But with the end of the 1958 electoral efforts and the departure of many in the Gates faction, the party deemed it time to reverse the Black Belt thesis. The Stalin definition of *nation* was adopted in the draft resolution, and it was concluded that the Great Migration had undermined the "stable community" aspect of his definition. Of course, for years Davis, James Ford, James Allen, and others had denied this. But Davis was ready to concede, not least because, he argued, "many liberal and middle class forces will not be able to define" their position until the party moved. Touching on "the Haywood document," he conceded that "we have found among many of our Negro comrades resistance to changing the slogan of self-determination. These are healthy militant comrades . . . [we should not] just classify these comrades as dogmatists and sectarians." Because of the Gates faction, comrades felt that "if we made the slightest concession in the direction of change, many among our Negro comrades in particular . . . [would feel] we were giving up the whole thing . . . this question has been downgraded in the Party in the last period"; hence, resistance. He outlined three aspects of the question, "national . . . racial . . . class," and recalled that during the 1946 "re-establishment of our position . . . for the first time . . . we began to consider the racial aspect of the Negro question. Up to that time we considered it heresy for any comrade to speak of the Negro race." He urged dumping the idea that the main problem with King, Randolph, and the like was their "anti-communist attitude." The issue should be, he said, who is for and who is against "mass action."[56]

After this position was promulgated in February 1959, more than thirty years after the Black Belt thesis was first passed in the Comintern, Davis and Foster teamed up to refine it further in a joint article for *Political Affairs*. They acknowledged the oscillation between integrationist and nationalist tendencies in the black community but discarded the notion of self-determination since the black situation in the heart of imperialism made it not possible for them "to develop fully into an independent nation." Portentously they predicted that "the basic tendency of nationalism will also remain in evidence and may even last deep into socialism." Yes, the party has done some "splendid work," but "it has tended to overplay or underplay, from time to time, the various elements—race, nation and class. . . . This has served to inject some one-sidedness into its work, and has deepened and multiplied its mistakes." They stressed the importance of "democratization" of the South in expanding democratic rights generally. The line described in this article was to be the prevailing one for the party in the foreseeable future.[57]

This philosophy did not keep some people from leaving the party, including many close to Haywood. The positive side of these defections, one might think, was that at last the inner tumult had ceased; two of the major factions were gone. However, there were still other rivers to cross. Charles Loman was suspended from his post as Kings County (Brooklyn) party chair; allegedly he went abroad, apparently on party business, without proper accounting. The action was taken by Davis and William Albertson, the fifty-one-year-old Oklahoman who had replaced Charney. The Foster-Davis leadership was now under fire as "revisionist" and "Titoite"—epithets previously reserved for Gates from Haywood and Ted Allen.[58]

This report was quickly followed by a FBI directive featuring Flynn calling Davis "a demagogue who over emphasizes Negro nationalism." This should be exposed in the press, said the FBI, since it "would serve to alienate Davis . . . and have an adverse effect on Negro-white relations." One would think that after Little Rock, federal policy would have been to assuage these relations. Flynn "is expressing her dissatisfaction openly about Negro communist leader Ben Davis's refusal to allow her and other white comrades to participate in his recent ill-fated campaign in Harlem . . . charges by [Flynn] that the Negroes, under Davis are trying to capture the Party." This theory departed from the record but it did indicate that Flynn—presumably seen as isolated since she was the only woman in top leadership—was also being targeted.[59]

Mao Zedong, then in solidarity with the U.S. party, with his usual understatement told Foster in March 1959 that the party was "temporarily in a situation which is none too smooth . . . [but] Dark night has its end."[60] The FBI wanted this night to continue. In May they hatched a plan to "attempt to increase the ill feeling between [James] Jackson and Davis by sending Davis a hand-written anonymous note from Los Angeles or San Francisco advising him that Jackson used his recent trip on the west coast to gather support to unseat Davis as the dominant Negro leader in the party." They posited a lineup of Jackson, Healey, and Mickey Lima of northern California against Davis, Foster, and Dennis. But the point was that Davis and Jackson did not agree on some matters, so this directive was designed to exploit those differences.[61]

The right wing remained concerned with the party. Louis Budenz worried particularly about its influence on a slowly growing youth and student movement. The party was in the midst of another leadership transition that was causing concern, so the FBI proposed again that discord between Davis and Lightfoot be fomented to complicate matters.[62] This was in December, when one report pointed to the "high level of anti-Communist feeling" and resultant "ostracism, loss of jobs and other penalties" as major factors in the party's decline. This was a prelude to the writer's main point: "The party spokesman who disclosed that Mr. [Gus] Hall was the new leader insisted, however, that Mr. Davis and Mr. Dennis would have a relationship of 'equality' with respect to Mr. Davis. But the evidence seemed to indicate that Mr. Dennis . . . had been kicked upstairs." The story concluded that the personnel change meant the CP "appeared to be making a sharp turn to the right toward" Browder. This prognosis was not altogether inaccurate, though the replacement of Dennis by Hall was not viewed happily in all party circles.[63]

Reported further were "new strain[s] . . . new fissures . . . sharp dispute . . . intense" as Hall replaced Dennis; "giving the key factional leaders high-sounding titles while reserving actual power for Mr. Hall" was the *Times's* conclusion.[64] The FBI was blunter about these "fissures." Now they were seeking to foment a feud between Davis and his New York comrade, William Albertson: "This could be presented in such a way that half would be persuaded to support Davis and the other half to support Albertson." Stress the "personal life and idiosyncrasies" of Davis to "increase the political jealousies and ill will," was their prescription. Characteristically, they took their own advice: "bad relations between Ben Davis and other CP functionaries are not new. Davis is a very difficult man to get along with and his years in the Party have been marked by outbursts of temper, dramatic exits from meetings, fights, arguments and feuds." Just before the CP convention that led to Hall's election, the FBI wrote: "It is apparent that [Davis] is one of the most effective disruptionists inside the CP and we should be very careful before we take any steps which might change this situation. No one can work with Davis for any length of time before they become completely disillusioned with his leadership ability because of his extreme egotism and aggressive personality." They sought to pit Carl Winter against Davis. To bar Davis's further rise in the party during this convention they wanted to send out another phony letter, but feared it might lead party forces to "fight a common enemy, the FBI. This is, of course, something we must constantly guard against." They considered planting evidence that Davis was an "FBI informant" but decided not to since his "length of time" in the CP "would possibly work in [his] favor," besides "New York does not have enough handwriting samples." But such tactics were successfully used later against Albertson.[65]

What was stirring the FBI's creativity was the opening of the 17th National Convention of the party in December 1959; two hundred comrades were present, including 133 delegates. The authorities were especially upset that it convened in Harlem's Hotel Theresa—an obvious sign of alignment with the growing civil rights movement; a dozen hotels and meeting halls had been considered before the choice was made. Davis was elected national secretary and was part of a secretariat that included Dennis, Hall, Jackson, and Hy Lumer. Foster was so steadily ill that giving him an honorary post and making Dennis chairman instead seemed rational, though some felt he was being kicked upstairs. Perhaps not coincidentally, Dennis had been summoned to Washington during this period to appear before the Senate Internal Security Subcommittee, where the chief inquisitioner, J. G. Sourwine, asked him if he was aware that Davis had called him an "incompetent, a fence straddler" who must be removed. Dennis was also not in the best of health, which may have played a role in the personnel shifts, and he suffered a heart attack while in Washington—though apparently not because of Sourwine's question.[66]

Peggy Dennis, the new chairman's wife, was irate about these changes. She accused Hall of trying to undermine her husband and believed that Davis-Foster sought to "dump Gene once and for all; they would compromise on any 'title' post for him . . . [due to] sharp political differences that have existed between the three since 1945, heightened by the 1955–58 events." Davis's promotion to leadership at the national level was "further complicated by the fact that everyone wanted Ben out of N.Y. . . . because N.Y. is the last stronghold in the hands of Ben and the real leftist, sectarian policies and inactivity. . . . He has a strong group in N.Y., but there had been developing also a growing healthy element who were challenging him (Gene has cultivated that group carefully, quietly without fanfare . . .) . . . it was agreed to get Ben out of N.Y.—and 'dumped upstairs.' These people were ready to give Ben anything he wanted." She thought that Jackson and Lightfoot "did a beautiful job of challenging Ben's claim that the issue of Negro leadership rests with what is done or not done to him." Though she was close ideologically to Healey and, like her, left the party ultimately, she was not particularly pleased with her role, either. Yet she seemed to have real animus toward Davis: "The convention gave a real rebuff to Ben in that it defeated the majority of his slate from the National Committee . . . he has lost much ground and prestige; he has been 'slapped down' . . . NOW the weak sisters are becoming bold in their attitude to Ben. However, he is furious and fighting mad."[67] During this time, the FBI had proposed sparking conflict between Davis and Lightfoot, Winter, Flynn, Jackson, and others. They may not have been totally responsible for the conflicts that did erupt, but they could celebrate nonetheless.

In her memoir Peggy Dennis is no less wrathful. She accuses Davis of being angry about how Dennis "blocked" him from ousting Gates in 1956 and "stopped" a like move to oust Lightfoot, Lima, Winter, and Healey. At the convention, she charged, there was an effort to remove Dennis altogether and put Davis in as chair: "The committee members were shocked, yet immobilized by the sensitivity of the issue of promoting Negro leadership. The committee deadlocked for days . . . finally, on the twelfth day, the black comrades on the committee told Davis that the real issue in this instance was not 'Negro leadership' but Ben's leftist sectarian policies."

Pointed opinions of Peggy Dennis set aside, there is little question that the question of black leadership and the closely related question of affirmative action were difficult questions tackled by the party much earlier than other forces.[68]

Paul Robeson, Jr., who left the party in 1962 but considers himself as an ally of Davis to the end, also identifies a party "FBI faction" that was a "powerful and organized factor . . . whose influence has been ignored." The evidence suggests that Robeson is correct. Though praising Davis, he adds, "If Ben had a fault, he tended to be pretty subjective about people he didn't like"; thus when the FBI sought to frame Albertson, Davis's preexisting hostility toward him could predispose him to accept the fake evidence of the FBI faction. He feels that it was unfortunate that so many black Reds—Wilkerson, Haywood, Berry, himself, and others—were dispersed just as a new black movement was emerging: "I'll never believe that was an accident." Robeson is no doubt accurate in his belief.[69]

The recollections of James Jackson are not necessarily in accord with Peggy Dennis's. He does concede that there was an "intensity . . . and depth of [the party] crisis . . . coming from years of underground . . . apparatus had to be constructed on the run . . . it wasn't a calm, collegial library . . . some worked to exhaustion." The principal architect of the new view of the Negro Question, Jackson also acknowledges that the "prestige" of the CPSU led to "imitation" in the United States; their National Question position "didn't fit . . . but if the shoe doesn't fit, cut off the toe." The change in posture became entangled in the "factional struggle of the time," he said. Changing the line was "like taking a rattle from a baby." It was difficult, for blacks considered this Black-Belt line to be uniquely theirs. These tangled questions of the National Question and factionalism were difficult challenges to face at a time of heightened political repression.[70]

The triumph of the Cuban Revolution on the first day of January 1959 was an elixir for Davis and the party. With all the contention and strife this event was a stark reminder of why there was a party in the first place, and a revolution ninety miles from Miami showed that all things were possible. Their new line on the Negro Question seemed to be vindicated when Congressman Powell immediately called for aid to the regime of Fidel Castro and a recall of the "pro-Batista" U.S. Ambassador Earl Smith. Under Davis's direction the New York party sent a telegram to the comrades in the Popular Socialist party of Cuba (precursor of the modern Cuban Communist party), pledging solidarity, and wired Eisenhower, urging "Hands off Cuba." Throughout the year Davis repeatedly censured the "crude attempts of American imperialism to overthrow Cuba's national revolution." As part of "peace month activities" in August Davis spoke to hundreds at 116th Street and Lenox; scores of copies of *The Worker* were sold, along with "many Robeson books."[71]

Nuclear testing was also a major concern for Davis in 1959. He flayed Charles DeGaulle's refusal to end hydrogen bomb tests in Africa as "an act of barbarism . . . racist contempt." He campaigned throughout the city on the question. The position he enunciated reflected the winds of change; the party, he said, is "opposed to testing by ALL nuclear powers. . . . It could lead to the general disarmament which would relieve the people of the crushing and unnecessary burdens of the insane arms race." He sent a letter to this effect to the mayor and ridiculed the positions of Nelson Rockefeller and others, who were opposed to ending testing.[72]

Despite the party wars, Davis continued to speak out; at a CP rally in Carnegie Hall in February he declared that "school integration in New York City is the scandal of the nation." He appeared before a joint legislative session in Albany to present the Communist view on welfare, housing, and power plants. At a budget hearing in April in New York he was "forced to wait until 8 p.m. to present his statement. . . . Davis was virtually the only representative of the people's interests in the day and night-long hearings." Times had changed in more ways than one. When labor boss George Meany insulted A. Philip Randolph, a frequent recipient of Davis vitriol, the former City Council member called it "shocking and racist," though in the not-too-distant past Randolph was receiving insult from Davis himself.[73]

Davis's year-end report to the New York State party was solemn: "The low percentage of Negro members in our Party, especially of women and youth, is a danger signal for the party as a whole." His words still worried elites. But he added, "Neither the Pilgrimage to Washington, nor the two historic youth marches, could have been such big successes without the loyal and selfless participation and organizing ability of Communists." Despite horrible internal clashes, the party still had a disciplined core of full-time black revolutionaries, led by the experienced Ben Davis, who had personal contacts with both King and Powell.[74]

That was not all. Local 1199, pharmacists and health-care workers who had backed Davis when he ran for office, was leading massive hospital strikes that year. Davis termed their struggle "the cause of all humane and fairminded people." The workers were 80 to 90 percent black and Puerto Rican; it was a union that Dr. King eventually called his "favorite." Ever alert, the *New York World-Telegram* warned, "there's a similarity in the tunes played by the Commies (and by Leon Davis)," the union leader. Both stressed "race exploitation and union recognition." This was a powerful combination; and Leon Davis was known to have had ties to the party. He was forced to deny Communist influence in the union but there was little question that the opposite was the case. The times dictated that the party had to deny influence when it was present so as to advance the overall struggle; wrecking the union struggle on the shoals of anti-Communist accusations was deemed counterproductive. This episode should serve as a caution for those who blithely dismiss Communist influence in the United States in the Cold War era. Elites had to consider that despite their massive propaganda campaign, fomenting of disruption, jailings, and other activities, Davis and the party were involved in one of the most titanic labor struggles in the city in decades in helping to organize a union that was to play a critical role in the life of New York City. More severe measures had to be taken. But which ones had not been used already?[75]

18

Black Communist in the 1960s

From 1956 to 1959 the party had absorbed some of the state's heaviest blows; not only was it still standing but it was dishing out a few of its own. Nevertheless Red Scare repression exacted a heavy toll. Where once there may have been twenty thousand Reds in New York State, in 1960 there may have been two thousand; though the number of FBI agents in the ranks can be wildly overestimated, the fact is that COINTELPRO had done damage. Many people in the mass movement came to treat Communists like Davis as if they had some incurable contagious disease. The problem was that COINTELPRO was not just being tried on the Communists, it was also aimed at the mass movement. The problem for the FBI and the elites that directed them was that Davis still had some influence and a modicum of respect in this movement; and, as a few commentators predicted, driving the party underground would not necessarily squash its influence, as the organizing of hospital workers in New York City demonstrated.

It was not easy for Davis in the 1960s. By then he was in his late fifties and his health was not good. Dr. Bernard Mintz had examined him just after he left prison because of persistent and grueling back pain; he "has difficulty walking stairs" and was provided with a "Knight spinal brace." He was also in dire financial straits, now having a baby daughter to support.[1] The FBI was not above playing on his poverty: "Various department stores are pressing him for payment of bills and are threatening to take him to court." His "current precarious financial situation," they thought, along with a residual "factional dispute," might allow a prominent unnamed black personality to bring "about his defection," though they admitted "the possibility . . . appears extremely remote."[2] The extraordinary lengths to which the FBI went to prod Davis from the party were perverse evidence of his continuing importance in an era when mass protest again was proliferating.

Given the fact that they were surveilled so incessantly, it was probably a tactical mistake for Davis and Dr. Martin Luther King, Jr., to correspond. But they did. Davis had asked him to write a letter on behalf of Henry Winston, who was languishing in prison and because of the inattention of the authorities was about to lose his sight. King was incensed: "I think it is both immoral and tragic for a nation to allow any human being to face such an inhuman situation." He continued, "Your words are always encouraging, and although we do not share . . . political views I find a deeper unity of spirit with you that is after all the important thing. . . . A friend like yourself comes along with an encouraging word and this gives me renewed courage and vigor to carry on."[3] The avatar of the nascent civil-rights movement terming the top black Red "friend" was the kind of nightmare that the Red Scare and concessions to Black Liberation were designed to forestall.

Davis encouraged this approach, commiserating with King about the "resistance pursued under the concrete difficult conditions of struggle in the deep South . . . united action—among those who have many differences on manifold questions—is what the rulers of the Jim Crow system most fear." When King was stabbed in Harlem, Davis provided him with a blood transfusion. When King was coming under increasing attack from the state, Davis provided encouraging words.[4]

The White House and the FBI worried about Communist involvement when the student sit-in movement erupted in February 1960. Though Davis was not present in North Carolina, Stokeley Carmichael, the future leader of the Student Non-Violent Coordinating Committee (SNCC), had met him and was involved with the party as a youth.[5] Not coincidentally, the day after the protests began, Davis was testifying before HUAC; Jack O'Dell—a top aide to King and already under harassment for alleged leftist ties—had just stepped down. There was a harsh exchange between HUAC and Davis: " . . . you have done nothing to subpoena the lynchers of Mack Parker . . . [you are] here to try to convict people without a jury." He was asked about alleged Soviet domination of the nuclear disarmament movement but Davis would not budge: "the question is irrelevant, ridiculous garbage and I refuse to answer it."[6] An earlier witness, Albert Gaillard, had charged that Davis led the effort to capture Harlem youth for the party. With the 1960s beginning with militant student sit-ins against Jim Crow, Dixiecrats were reawakening their age-old worry that racism would compel blacks leftward.

These developments energized Davis, as his report to the National Committee meeting in Chicago in March reflected. He urged "all-out direct support to the southern Negro people's movement itself." In calling on the party to "defend Negro leadership," he reminded it that "the warnings issued by our Party upon the first Smith Act convictions that the Communists were only the first . . . were all too true." He sought to link the southern struggle with the South African effort by recommending a "boycott of all South African goods and breaking diplomatic relations with South Africa."[7]

Davis's old friend Adam Powell was under siege again, facing indictment and trial; to Davis this was "crude legal flim-flam" that he equated with his own prosecution. His feeling was that such prosecutions were designed to derail the upsurge for civil rights legislation. The bill that was introduced was "so complicated, confusing and cumbersome. . . . A Negro would have to be super-brave, wear steel-plated armor, hire a lawyer if he could find one at hand, besides being a lawyer himself—all to cast one lonely ballot." This, he said, was "putrid sham."[8]

The cease-fire in the party wars, revolution in Cuba, the student protests, and the typical spurt of activity generated by an election year seemed to bring new vigor to Davis and the party. In May he addressed an open-air meeting in front of the Hotel Theresa in "celebration of [Powell's] victory against the false income tax frame-up." He was "repeatedly interrupted with applause" as he called for support for Cuba and "the Negro people on the march" in South Africa and the United States. As the NAACP opened its fifty-first convention in St. Paul, Davis could hardly contain himself: "Never before has the convention met in such a favorable world setting. All over the globe the darker and colonial peoples, particularly in South Africa and in Cuba, backed up by the socialist countries, their staunchest allies, are throwing off the inhuman shackles of imperialist slavery . . . the white supremacy ruling class of our country has been weakened."[9]

But Davis was honest enough to lament the "internal contradictions and vacillating tendencies" of the NAACP, though gone were the heated denunciations of his preprison days. "The court arena is no longer the main area of struggle," he said, " . . . the NAACP itself has had to enter the arena of mass activity, often dragged there by many of its branches." He implored the convention to drop their anti-Communist membership ban, which "is unsound morally when it uses the same red-baiting weapon against others that the Dixiecrat class uses to persecute and even outlaw the NAACP itself." The ban was "antiquated . . . obsolete . . . as the horse and buggy or kerosene lamp in this nuclear age."[10]

For most of 1960 Davis was preoccupied with the elections. He was harsh toward the prospective Democratic nominee ("self-exposure of the innocent, boyish Senator Kennedy as a political werewolf whose claws are becoming ever more apparent"). Davis was dumbfounded by "[John] Kennedy's attempt to take unprincipled advantage of the fact that he is a Catholic." All this showed the "desperate need [for] an independent third party." He was equally dumbfounded by Jackie Robinson's support for Richard Nixon, though the difference from the old days was that he spent more time reproaching Nixon than his supporter. He conferred with George Murphy about the road ahead: "This is going to [be] a tough and complicated election campaign . . . for that reason, I want above all to talk to a number of people other than members of my own organization. Your point of view is very necessary and obligatory. What is the talk among the Negro people and liberals in Washington on Kennedy and Johnson? . . . Let me hear from you not later than next Wednesday."[11]

As the above suggests, Davis was one Communist who strived to maintain mass contacts. He attended the Republican convention that year, which apparently did not lead to FBI reports about Nixon being a Communist dupe or the Republican party being a Communist front. Through Murphy he was reaching out to "Mordecai [Johnson] . . . [E. Franklin] Frazier . . . Link Johnson, Jr." in an effort to obtain a parole hearing for Winston and insight on politics.[12] Finally, just before the election Davis announced that "the Communists support neither candidate." Why was this? "The provision of the Landrum-Griffin law invoked against the National Maritime Union, is one written by Kennedy," he said. But Davis was not going to denounce any black leaders who felt otherwise. "A most serious mistake could be made if there's a failure to differentiate between the monopoly dominated candidates of the Democratic Party" and those who support them. Gone were the lacing words of the past.[13]

This "complicated situation" was helped along by state repression that descended to extreme measures. New York sought to deny Davis a driver's license. Again, it was disturbing that such steps were not taken against his white Smith Act codefendants. He had to raise money and secure expert legal aid and go to court before he prevailed. Though the authorities lost the case, they had won in that the time spent on the case was time Davis could not spend writing King or supporting Fidel Castro.[14]

Davis was called back to appear before the Senate Internal Security Subcommittee but he was not contrite, calling Senator James Eastland "one of the worst Negro haters—and of Jewish people as well." He cited the First and Fifth amendments in refusing to answer certain questions and to others responded by demanding that they investigate lynchings and racism. This response was as provocative in 1960 as it had been in 1940. Furthermore, during the hearing, Leonard Patterson, a "former Communist . . . rose . . . and pointed out" Davis as a Red. Davis "jumped to his feet and shouted, 'Keep your filthy stool pigeons off me!' Glaring at Mr. Patterson [he] said, 'He is no credit to his race, he is a disgrace.' . . . 'You are the disgrace,' Mr. Patterson retorted." Senator Keating of New York asked Davis to step forward. He refused without a subpoena or consulting an attorney, adding, "I suggest you get the lynchers of Mack Parker up here and stop worrying about me."[15]

Behind the scenes the authorities were as concerned as ever about Davis. Eisenhower's aide Gordon Gray wrote a top military officer, General Andrew Goodpaster, worried that Davis and the Communists would stir up Communist parties in South America against his boss during Eisenhower's trip to South America.[16] At the same time the FBI was sending articles attacking Davis to party members "known to be anti-Davis." They were pondering what to do about him: "New York has been following Davis' activities with a view to counterintelligence action for some time. It has been noted that recently practically all the top leaders in the Party have clashed with him in one way or another. . . . Left to his own devices he has a considerable talent for creating dissension. . . . If, on the other hand, he leaves the Party . . . his leaving would be a terrible blow to the leadership."

Hoover replied, "the Bureau does not agree that Davis should not be a counterintelligence target because of his propensity to create confusion." Breathing new life into their old goal of turning Lightfoot against Davis was one tactic to be pursued; allegedly, "as a result of their varying viewpoints over . . . policy regarding the Negro question . . . [there is] constant friction between the two. . . . These circumstances, it is believed, hold good possibilities for counterintelligence measures to further the wedge . . . and cause additional disruption." They decided to send a letter to Foster attacking Lightfoot and hoping Davis would then be contacted by the patriarch about it, spurring an explosive chain reaction.[17]

This increased repression may have been a reflection of the fact that Davis's thrusts were increasingly drawing blood. Davis was on the scene when Fidel Castro made his trip to Harlem in 1960; the fact that tens of thousands of Harlemites warmly greeted the Cuban revolutionary was a bold political statement. The party in Harlem issued a leaflet hailing Harlem's reception of Castro at the Hotel Theresa, adding, "Speak out Now! For Congo and Independence!" Davis, "speaking on a ladder in old-time political style drew some 1,200 Harlemites." Davis defended his Cuban comrade. "Every time some one does something good you're called a Communist. So you might as well be one." The linking of Cuba and the Congo was no accident. A recurrent theme of Davis's latter years was an elevated Pan-Africanism, that linked the struggles of peoples of African descent in the diaspora with the civil rights struggle. This approach anticipated, if not reflected, the new civil rights upsurge that fomented various forms of black nationalism. Given that Africans in the diaspora were less persuaded by anti-Communism and anti-Sovietism, such a connection could have a beneficial radicalizing impact on African-Americans. In October 1960, "Negro members of the National Committee" of the party, led by Davis but including Jackson, Patterson, and others, issued a statement on the Congo and Cuba: "It is one fight, one unity—for one victory over racism and imperialist subjugation." They assailed Powell's opportunistic attack on Castro, but this statement showed that despite the jettisoning of the Black Belt thesis, the party was not unaffected by strains of nationalism.[18]

Though they did not support Kennedy, Davis and the party were not displeased with the defeat of their old adversary Richard Nixon. Going into 1961 momentum was underway with the growing protests in the South, Cuba, and the beginning of national student protests. A leading indicator was the increased number of pages of the party paper that year. The contradiction of the United States calling for human rights in every nook and cranny of the globe while jailing Reds for their beliefs and denying blacks their rights was sharpening even more. This dynamic process was aiding the party, which helps to explain why in June 1961 there was a legal cloud hanging over the party now that Davis, Hall, and Flynn had refused to register under the Smith Act.[19]

The FBI's tactics became more ugly and desperate. They accelerated their effort to break up Davis's marriage and interfere in his domestic affairs. Early in January 1961 an unnamed person was inviting Davis to be a "house guest in Atlanta, however, this would create an extremely difficult situation inasmuch as Davis' wife is of the Caucasian race and, if she should accompany him to Atlanta, it would be a departure from the normal Southern custom." This unnamed person "[will] offer Davis a financial inducement to leave the Communist Party." They sent a copy of an article on racism in the Soviet Union to Davis's home "in the expectation that Davis' wife might open the letter"; with their sexism, they pictured Davis's wife as ideologically irresolute; the article would encourage her to "attack . . . Davis for remaining in the communist movement."[20]

They did not stop there. The FBI worked overtime to stir up discord between Davis and Hall. They developed " . . . a cartoon . . . showing caricatures of Hall and Davis squaring off in a ring to fight for the prize of CP leadership clearly showing the fact that one is white and the other is Negro thus creating the impression that race is an issue . . . [to be] printed by the Bureau for anonymous mailings." They suggested using the *New York Post* or *Guardian* to carry out their plans of encouraging factionalism.[21]

Such pressure took quite a toll on party leaders and inner party democracy. It was hard to discern if a disagreement were honest or an FBI concoction or if Davis was disliked because of his personality or because of manipulation. Bewildered by the mass upsurge of the 1960s, the FBI thought that it was a party creation at the direction of Moscow, which heightened repression and increased the detrimental impact on leaders like Davis. In February 1961 Eugene Dennis died; the FBI ghoulishly seized on this death to try to provoke chaos, assuming that a power struggle would ensue. Again Davis sensed that a "dangerous pro-fascist grouping is arising in the country." Did the fact that fascism did not rise invalidate his assertion in light of the growth of the John Birch Society, Minutemen, and other groups?[22]

Then in September 1961 Foster died. Davis's closest political ally was now gone. Davis was interviewed at Foster's graveside at Waldheim Cemetery in Chicago by NBC and CBS, as dozens of photographers and reporters gathered. Also present were FBI photographers. Foster's loss made all the more important the freeing of Winston from prison; he had already gone blind. Davis complained directly to Attorney General Robert Kennedy, recalling that when "Moe Annenberg, multi-millionaire" media baron and gambler, was an inmate in federal prison and had a similar "brain tumor . . . he was released on medical parole in three days." But Winston was black—and Red—which made all the difference. Simultaneously Davis had to fight an increasing proliferation of forgeries purporting to provide party views on all manner of issues.[23]

What was worrying the government was an escalating and increasingly militant black movement that was not playing by the old rules, or in other words, that bipartisanship begins at the water's edge; this trend was a direct challenge to imperialism. The death of Patrice Lumumba in February, probably at the hands of the CIA, provoked the "most violent demonstration" in the United Nations' history. Involved in the demonstration, which had rudely disrupted the speech of Ambassador Adlai Stevenson, were black nationalists, artists—and Ben Davis. But in a precursor of times to come (one might ask to what extent the party's years of calling for self-determination had helped to prepare the path for it) blacks had "set up their own segregated picket line . . . barring white sympathizers." Later, speaking to a rally at 125th Street and 7th Avenue, Davis called for unity among the nationalist groupings; times were changing again.[24]

The objective situation was becoming more advantageous for Davis and the party; no longer were they virtually isolated in protest. Moreover, an opportunity was created for Davis and the party to influence the course of protest. Because the FBI was prone to ascribe student protest of the 1960s to party manipulation, a tendency of historians has been to ignore the party's role. In fact, the party had a major role in igniting these protests, insofar as an initial grievance of students was the effort to bar them from hearing Reds on campuses. Predictably the effort to shield the tender ears of students from the seductive words of Communists only increased youth's desire to hear and judge the controversy for themselves.

Davis always had paid attention to young people. While in the council he and Cacchione launched an investigation that proved how medical and law schools were blatantly discriminating against blacks and Jews in admissions. He pushed for revoking of tax exemptions for these institutions. On his relatively infrequent trips outside of New York he found time to speak on campuses, particularly black schools.[25]

Barring Davis from campuses did not begin in 1961; since the initiation of the Red Scare, these bastions of free thought had decided that it would be inappropriate for his words to be sampled in the marketplace of ideas. Inevitably the FBI became involved; after he had spoken at Bucknell University in 1960, it sought to widely distribute an article from the school paper on the visit since it was hostile and reflected ill on him. As the spring semester of 1961 was winding down at City College of New York—a predominantly Euro-American campus in the heart of Harlem—Davis opined that President Kennedy could end Jim Crow with the "stroke of a pen"; asked if Jim Crow could be abolished under capitalism, he said yes, but only socialism could "tear up the roots."[26]

The attempt to ban Davis from speaking at City University of New York campuses not only sparked a firestorm of protest but also directly touched and inspired Queens College student Andrew Goodman, whose murder three years later in Mississippi stirred a nation. The "Freedom Riders," the student sit-ins in the South, Dr. King, Congo, and Cuba all precipitated and prepared the path for student eruption in the fall of 1961 in New York City, three years before the Berkeley free-speech fight. In early October students protested the cancellation of an invitation to Davis to speak; the student newspaper carried a front-page editorial on it. In response City College barred speeches by Communists, pending a review of policy. The faculty then protested and students began circulating a petition to reverse the decision.[27]

Hoisted by their own petard, the *Times* editorialized that the "freedom to listen, to discuss and to make sound judgments is the essence of learning." But if the party had not registered under the Internal Security and Smith acts, that would be a different story. Signifying the distance we have come, the now-rehabilitated and respectable William F. Buckley was juxtaposed with Davis as a representative of the "radical Right." That was not the end of the drama. The ACLU objected, and then Professor Samuel Hendel, chair of the department of political science at CCNY, questioned the ban on Communist speakers. Unmoved, the administrative council of CCNY, in a seventeen-page statement, ruled that "no known member" of the party could speak on campus, an act they claimed, that was "prohibited by law." Though they presumably were not members of the party, the ban also appeared to apply to Malcolm X and William F. Buckley.[28]

The *Times*, whose editorials over the years had prepared the way for this inquisition, now had to reverse field. On 28 October they called the decision "an exercise in sophistry. It insults the intelligence of faculty and students . . . creates the image of a kindergarten rather than of a great and independent center of learning. The real issue is the student's freedom to listen and learn." Citing Malcolm and Buckley they added, "Once freedom begins to be cut down, erosion becomes uncontrollable . . . one must suspect that the council has bowed to outside political pressures possibly created by the mayoralty campaign." Students called for mass protest, and in turn, the FBI initiated a "counterintelligence operation designed to prevent [Davis] . . . from speaking before the Student Political Party of Columbia University."[29]

Like the collision of cold and warm fronts on the Great Plains that can cause a tornado, the authorities were caught between their musty rhetoric on "freedom and liberty" and the "effective" Red Scare. Columbia had to agree to allow Davis to speak, but it would be in the form of a debate on academic freedom with Mark Lane. A neighborhood paper complimented Davis as a fighter for free speech; this was a new development for a party accustomed to accusations of "Stalinist orthodoxy" and speech suppression. The student government at Barnard College condemned Queens and CCNY for barring Davis and other Communists.[30]

Protesters at CCNY were busy organizing an outdoor rally that was attended by one thousand students. Davis was ecstatic: "All the publicity I have received couldn't be bought by all the gold in Moscow. Telephones are constantly ringing at Communist party headquarters. Television and radio stations want me and I have even been invited to speak at the University of

Wisconsin."[31] Excited, the crowd screamed out for a student strike but the student government instead voted for a two-hour boycott of classes. Perceptively, the *Times* reported, "The administrators of the city colleges helped—rather than hurt—the interests of the Communist party with their [ban]."[32]

The headline in the *New York Post* of 3 November 1961 read, "Banned at City Colleges, Davis talks at Columbia"; eight hundred students appeared, though the *New York Journal-American* added that "mixed boos and cheers" greeted him. After the speech Davis wound up talking with students until 1:00 A.M. At Queens College there was a rally of four hundred, with many students wearing "Ban the Ban" buttons. The anti-Communist group Americans for Democratic Action came out against the ban. Six teachers of constitutional law at CUNY challenged the ban, and in response the CUNY chancellor invited Davis to file a brief with him. On the other hand, the president of Queens College differentiated between Soviet and local Communists; that is, it would be fine to invite the former to speak but not the latter. He analogized those "who must study atomic energy while avoiding lethal radiation." Just because society theoretically permitted all types of activities to be carried out, that did not mean that society must carry them out on campuses: "Prize fights, burlesque shows and propagandizing are not proper college activities, no matter how acceptable they may be elsewhere," he said.[33]

Leonard Machting, a member of the executive committee of the college student government, called the ban "absurd." After all, one thousand students had gathered to hear Davis on tape: "We can assume, therefore, that it is now permissible and legal to hear but not to see a 'known' Communist." One opponent of Davis was not convinced: "The average Communist speaker is highly trained in the art of deception . . . Our colleges are fertile territory for Communist propaganda. There the Communist agent finds the immature student who is gullible, inexperienced and easy prey to his ideas." They could influence foreign students too, he warned. "Reliable sources claim many agents are also registered as students and are a part of the Communist conspiracy. . . . I believe the protests against the ban by the students are Communist-inspired."[34]

By mid-November three thousand students at Queens College were on strike and boycotting class; fifteen hundred demonstrated with signs shouting "Ban the Ban!" Similar manifestations were held at CCNY and Hunter College. Editorials began to switch: " . . . [an] impressive number of faculty members at the colleges have spoken out fearlessly.. . . . The lesson to be learned is that a university . . . ought to stand firm on the courage of its convictions and ideals." Strikingly, the first crack in the ban came for Malcolm X, which suggests that Communism—with its threat to property—was seen as more of a threat than black nationalism and that the "Communist threat" helped to pave the way for nationalism. Nevertheless the students were not satisfied and took their protest to the door of the Board of Higher

Education. "Ban the Ban, Ban the Ban, We Demand the Right to Hear," they shouted. The CCNY administration did not yield. In early December Buckley, Malcolm X, and Mark Lane were allowed to appear, but not Herbert Aptheker.[35]

Finally in mid-December 1961 the ban on Communist speakers at CUNY was lifted as the administration cited a report by the Association of the Bar for the City of New York that included Bruce Wright, Louis Pollak, Robert McKay, and other leading jurists. The CCNY alumni association praised this bold stroke. Others were not so pleased. When Davis showed up to speak, The *New York Times* reported that he was "struck on the head by a sign but was not injured . . . [and was] pursued by more than 100 shoving, hissing students." Signs proclaiming "Commies go Home" were wielded. Davis termed it "hoodlumnism. . . . There could be a million of them and they wouldn't intimidate me or my party." Most of the protestors were from Ukrainian, Hellenic, and Republican groups. In a familiar event from this era, members of the "Red Squad" of the New York City Police Department took notes and names.[36]

Davis hotly denied the notion that he was "chased" as a "complete fraud." The press, he felt, was trying to turn a setback into a victory by allowing him to speak, then charging that the masses rejected him. He did acknowledge that "Birchites" were there to harass him. The *Worker* reported that "profascist students accosted" Davis at 136th and Convent streets and followed him to the subway at 127th Street and St. Nicholas, "hurling epithets" and carrying signs with the slogan "Ban the Ben, Put Ben in the Pen." But "frequent and often lengthy applause" welcomed him, and "students were even seated on the floor right up to the rostrum." Davis was not in favor of banning Buckley, though he charged him with "political cowardice" for not showing up at the Columbia forum and challenged him to a debate.[37]

The year ended on a positive note. Davis was back in the news, besieged by newspapers, radio, and television. His voice was reaching millions, although the political atmosphere remained bitterly hostile toward the Communist party. *Time* magazine for 18 May 1962 reported sadly that "the Communist lecture bureau in New York City is beside itself in gleeful culling of invitations from some 100 campuses this year, against two dozen or so last year." In the copycat manner typical of students, inviting a Red to speak was becoming fashionable and *au courant*. *Time* reported in amazement that Davis spoke to six thousand in Minnesota alone. The Communist role in helping to light the fuse that led to an explosion of the student movement is often wrongfully neglected. Nevertheless, the mainstream press remained caustically unfriendly to Davis. Ralph McGill, famed journalist from Atlanta, termed Davis "middle aged, cynical and almost certainly bored . . . [a] symbol of failure."[38]

Davis's adversaries did not retaliate just in the press. In March 1962 Davis and Gus Hall were arraigned for violating the Internal Security Act of 1950;

a thirty-year sentence now stared him in the face. The Supreme Court decision the previous fall had paved the way for arraignment; this decision kindled a twelve hundred-strong rally in protest. A two-day meeting of the National Assembly for Democratic Rights was held at the St. Nicholas Arena. Representatives of nineteen states and Washington, D.C., attended; 95 percent of those present were non-communist. In 1961–62 there was more of a recognition than in 1949 that such prosecutions were not just a threat to Reds. The higher profile in 1961–62 of the Black Liberation movement, which had been historically less anti-Communist than other sectors, helps to account for this in part.[39]

The prosecution was visible, but the FBI was also working quietly behind the scenes to destabilize Davis and the party. David Garrow reports that there were fifteen hundred FBI informants imbedded in the party in 1962. However, that was not the biggest story about the agency. Though he may not have realized it, one of J. Edgar Hoover's closest black allies was related by marriage to Davis. Archibald Carey was a power in Chicago and national politics; he was the cousin of Davis's sister's husband, Richard Carey—which was further evidence of the abject difficulty involved in isolating Davis. The Carey-Hoover relationship was unusual. Carey had been connected with the Progressive party as late as 1950 and was once associated with the Free Angelo Herndon Committee; one FBI file listed him as "a Socialist and a friend of the Communists." But it was not atypical when Carey visited Hoover in his office in 1959 and brought along his "sister-in-law . . . and his great niece." He was considered for a position on the Subversive Activities Control Board and in 1953 was appointed to the U.S. delegation to the United Nations. In reply he called Hoover one of the "ten living white persons whom I feel have done the most to help the Negro." When the FBI did a background check on Carey, Richard Carey—Davis's brother-in-law—was not even mentioned as a relative.[40]

The FBI might not have been totally ingenuous about Carey's familial ties to Davis and organizational ties to the Left, for Dr. King would stay with Carey when he visited Chicago; the pastor would confide in him and somehow these words would filter back to FBI headquarters. Simultaneously, in 1962 the bureau was becoming increasingly concerned with possible links between King and Davis. They noted particularly the pastor speaking at a testimonial to Henry Winston at the Hotel Theresa in the fall of 1961. In sum, the growth of the movement generated an increased surveillance by the bureau and utilization of unorthodox as well as more orthodox means like prosecution.[41]

The growth of the movement also generated more support from Davis. He called for release of the Freedom Riders and demanded that Kennedy send troops south. Davis, Patterson, and Lightfoot wired Attorney General Robert Kennedy, demanding action against southern terror. Davis cautioned that lawsuits to get the right to vote "are like bailing out the ocean with a thimble. . . . If the Negroes are to get their rights through the filing of suits in each individual case all over the South, this is gradualism with a vengeance." He warned that "unless the Constitution is upheld in Georgia, Mississippi, South Carolina and points South, for the Negro, it will be upheld for no one elsewhere in the country." Required now were national "demonstrations, strikes, stoppages and boycotts" in support.[42]

Davis was in solidarity with King but was concerned about the growth of black nationalism, as manifested by the rise of the Nation of Islam. He scored their "divisive opposition to Negro-white unity, its utopian black separate state objective and its tendency to withdraw its members and supporters from active struggle against the white ruling class enemy in the U.S." The party and the Muslims had "well known differences"; however, he and his party "stand shoulder to shoulder in protest against such police brutality practiced against the Negro Muslims in Los Angeles" and the HUAC "investigation." He realized that the "existence of the Black Muslim organization . . . flows out of the jim crow system."[43]

Davis also had to respond to the black middle strata in 1962. William Walker, publisher and editor of the *Cleveland Call and Post*, linked Davis, Robeson, and Du Bois, adding, "when you tie these three names together you have three remarkable men. Men with unusual talents, extraordinary abilities, exceptional degrees of leadership, courage and determination." Yet he had a "deep feeling of regret" about their chosen political path.[44] In response Davis told him, "In the first place, it is not we who are 'lost,' it is capitalism that is lost." He knew this newspaper owner "directly and indirectly through my late father" and lamented his perceived lack of insight; he suggested that he and his two close friends were in the company of Nehru, Nkrumah, and Castro, who also had been jailed and harassed by the authorities.[45]

This line espoused by Walker was symptomatic of a new trend; as Davis and his party were welcomed into campuses and halls where they had been banned, the approach to them changed accordingly. From being bludgeoned they were now being treated as sorrowful and bitter figures; to a large extent, this remains the approach to them in the 1990s. Yet for Davis this was a far sight better than the bludgeon and especially welcome, now that he had another indictment hanging over his head. In 1962 he took to the hustings, speaking nationwide on civil rights, free speech, Cuba—and on the prospect of jail awaiting him if he were to be convicted again.

The issue of his speaking on campus was just as hot in 1962 as it was in 1961. Davis railed at Queens College's policy of screening controversial speakers as a "ruse for getting around the lifting of the speaker's ban"; the college would decide if his appearance is "consonant with the educational goals of the college." The "original ban," said Davis "seems like a bone which got stuck in [the] throat" of the college president; "apparently he can't cough it up even with the help of the Administrative Council. However, I'm sure that students of Queens College, whose strikes and demonstrations contributed to lifting the ban will continue to help [the president] clear his throat."[46]

Davis was also upset with what he called the press's "one-sided" coverage of his CCNY speech; he spoke to two hundred "or more," he said, and there was "standing room only. . . . I have a tape recording of the entire proceedings which proves the fact." There was a "hoodlum demonstration [of] fifteen or twenty . . . [who] tried to settle matters with their fists . . . majority were students who came along to see that the threats of violence . . . did not go beyond threats." Bolstering Davis's point was the disciplining by the Student Council of two students for harassing Davis. His profile was heightened when the Greater New York Press Club invited Davis, a card-carrying Communist, to give an address entitled "Academic Freedom in the USA."[47]

Davis and the party were so pleased with the results of his New York college appearances that he decided to go on the road. He went to Brown University, where he was heard by five hundred. When interviewed by Providence television and asked what he would do with millionaires under socialism, Davis deadpanned, "Put them to work." When word was passed that Davis would speak at Wilmington College in Ohio, sharp criticisms emerged. WAVI radio in Dayton hit the decision to bar Davis, invited him on the air, and "broke its own records for audience response." The interview was scheduled for two hours "but the station, overwhelmed by a flood of calls, carried the program on the air for an additional and unprecedented hour." Conservatives said they would picket Davis "but the picket line failed to materialize." Davis answered "nearly 50 direct questions . . . some callers . . . reflected political . . . hostility to Davis. Others however posed the honest questions of people who have had little opportunity to hear the truth about socialism." He was also interviewed by television and radio in Dayton, Columbus, and Cincinnati. His answers were blunt; for example, Hungary 1956 was "inspired and instigated by the CIA" and it was "necessary to erect the Berlin Wall to protect the peoples of the East German Republic" from West Germany.[48]

Sarcastically, the *Newark* (N.J.) *Evening News* reported that Davis "gave a two-hour dissertation on the joys of dialectical materialism" before a crowd of four hundred at Upsala College: "The heavyset Communist leader repeatedly mopped his brow." Twenty-five sheriff's detectives in "plainclothes . . . 10 uniformed East Orange police and a smattering of FBI agents" were present. There were "no demonstrations . . . polite applause" but "jeers and laughter" when he spoke of religious freedom in the USSR and when he discussed two-way traffic out of Berlin.[49]

Davis's return to his alma mater, Harvard, was filled with nostalgia. A few years before he had been in touch with Erwin Griswold of the law school. The eminent lawyer told Davis, "You are quite wrong in saying that I do not remember you." He had followed Davis's career "with much interest and . . . with real disappointment." He was not delighted with Davis's political trajectory: "you have made two major mistakes. . . . The first of these is accepting the Marxist-Leninist analysis and philosophy." Did Davis "really think" blacks would be better off under socialism? His other error was joining the party, "an instrument of a foreign government." Yet, he insisted, he was not trying to pick a fight: "I repeat: I always thought you had great potentialities." What a shame, he wailed, that Davis had "gone down the wrong track."[50]

April 1962 found Davis at his old law school discussing "The Communist Party and Constitutional Guarantees." Times had changed. The top faculty—Griswold, Robert McCloskey, and Mark DeWolfe Howe—agreed with Davis on the unconstitutional nature of the McCarran Act, which threatened to put him behind bars for the rest of his life. Griswold, possibly feeling guilty that one of his few black law school classmates had turned Red, was regretful: "I didn't go out of my way to be friendly and made no effort to assist him . . . we failed so badly in the case of Mr. Davis." Yet it was striking that he connected Davis's turn to the Left with the racism directed at him and called for an abatement of Jim Crow to forestall the development of future Davises. Davis discussed socialism, suggesting that in the United States it would be different than in Russia since the latter did not inherit the "traditions of the Bill of Rights and therefore we . . . start on a more advanced road than they were compelled to." Ever the diplomat, Davis told the six hundred assembled faculty and students, "I really feel so proud of my alma mater." Again, he was interviewed on radio and television.[51]

After the fading actor Ronald Reagan attacked the party in a speech at Central High School in St. Paul, Minnesota, a local group sought to bring Davis to the university there. In retaliation, a cross was burned on the lawn of the president of the University of Minnesota. The school paper reported, "Some 6,200 students battled to get into the 1,200 capacity ballroom. Those left out poured into the Union cafeteria, climbed the window sills and clustered on lawns to hear Davis speak . . . [the] audience was well behaved, if somewhat hostile." The *St. Paul Pioneer Press* reported on 3 May 1962 that Davis "displayed an active sense of humor" and he was cheered when he denounced the cross-burners and fascists. Macalester College students and faculty petitioned to hear Davis after the trustees voted 18–0 to bar him.[52]

The reactionaries were furious. An "apparently spurious" statement attributed to Davis was "slipped into the (Minnesota) Daily boxes." Davis was "shocked and disgusted." The local black paper, the *Minnesota Spokesman*, welcomed Davis to counter Ronald Reagan: "having sponsored an extreme right winger we believe they had an obligation to the young people whose political education they are responsible for, to present the extremist view of the opposite numbers." The local Red, Sam Davis, proposed to Davis that he debate Reagan, but that encounter did not materialize. The *Spokesman* was taken with Davis, calling him "urbane, sophisticated, Harvard-educated Negro Communist leader"; they were not displeased that he received a "courteous hearing before an overflow crowd and got radio and TV coverage that a serious political campaigner would never dream of. . . . unprecedented radio coverage . . . [Davis was] witty, charming, well-spoken."[53] Governor Elmer Anderson challenged Davis by asking him if he would defend the United States if it were attacked. Davis challenged him to a debate, but he refused. The switchboard at the university was "tied up all day" with inquiries about Davis. A new stage in the evolution of the Red Scare had commenced, just as the Black Liberation movement was escalating.[54]

This new stage was made possible by the new political dynamics introduced by the civil rights movement. Protest was popular, marching was popular, dissenting from the status quo was popular. Davis and the party rode this wave, which ultimately dissolved the underpinnings of the Red Scare itself. Similarly, opening campuses and halls to the party set the stage for a higher level of protest and dissent. The new political dynamics particularly lubricated the path for the antiwar and civil rights demonstrations that soon were to rock campuses from coast to coast and in the process transform the nation.

This changed atmosphere helps to explain the different result that obtained when the government came after the party again with prosecutions. The anti-Communist line was changing; it was suggested that the real Red challenge was from the USSR and China, not from the United States.[55] Earlier domestic and international Communism had been linked; the civil rights movement forced an attempt at decoupling.

The hammer of the McCarran Act and the anvil of the membership clause of the Smith Act threatened to crush the party. Subpoenas were issued to Flynn, Hall, and Davis. At least Henry Winston was being released from jail but the present crisis forced Davis to curtail his triumphant tour of the campuses and concentrate on survival—a consideration that no doubt did not escape the calculations of the authorities. The party refused to register as the domestic arm of Moscow, though failure to do so carried a penalty of ten thousand dollars per day for the party and a ten thousand dollars fine and five-year jail term for each day their officers failed to register. The regulatory obligation would shift to every one of their estimated ten thousand members by December 1961. Top scientist Dr. Harold Urey of the University of California, Nobel Prize winner in chemistry, sent a letter to President Kennedy asking the government to refrain from the prosecution. Journalist Anthony Lewis observed that a successful prosecution would mean the loss of tax exemptions for Communists, their mail would be stamped with a Communist label, it would be a crime for any member to use or apply for a passport; moreover, anyone who did register could automatically be prosecuted under the Smith Act as well. The pincers of legal restraints posed serious Fifth and Eighth Amendment issues.[56]

The party was refusing to cooperate and give names. In response a federal grand jury indicted the party in March 1962. Davis was handed six counts, Hall five; each carried a maximum of five years. They were freed on five thousand dollars bail each by treasury bonds offered by Lem Harris. Then-U.S. Attorney Robert Morgenthau filed suit against the party for five hundred thousand dollars in back taxes, with Davis named specifically in the complaint. The supposition was that fighting these legal wars would tie up the party and prevent it from becoming involved in mass movements. But the party was not bereft of allies. Beijing hit the "persecution" of the party and called JFK "fascist" in a typical burst of ultraleftism. The Japanese Communist party pledged to protest Attorney General Kennedy's visit there due to oppression of the party.[57]

Davis and Hall were facing years in prison and $1.25 million in fines, though the attorney general was claiming the party was "no danger." This apparent anomaly could be explained by looking at the party's ties to the burgeoning movement. The two leaders did plead not guilty before Judge Matthew McGuire in Washington. Yet times were changing. One writer presciently called their arrest a "national disgrace. . . . Unless this dangerous pattern of persecution is reversed at once, I am fearful that extremists will use it as a precedent for further action against liberals and the entire democratic left."[58] The party itself condemned the McCarran Act and "the type of registration demanded, which would be a plea of guilty to being a foreign agent; the extraordinary penalties for non-compliance which mount up in a few days to life imprisonment; the right to invoke the Fifth Amendment; and the right of a political party to function, secure from harassment."[59]

A Hall-Davis Defense Committee was cobbled together, with Clara Colon, of Puerto Rican descent, as secretary and Flynn playing the leading role. Colon "was one of the very few who mastered the constitutional and procedural intricacies of the litigation . . . she had the ability to speak and write about our cases in simple terms that laymen could comprehend."[60] Many of their pamphlets were in Spanish. The fruits of their labor were seen when the *Afro-American* carried an exclusive interview with Davis and when twenty-five law professors—including Charles Reich, William Kunstler, Thomas Emerson, Norman Dorsen, and others— denounced the McCarran Act; this too was a change from 1949. A June 1962 rally not only featured the chief defendants but also Murray Kempton, who had been a fierce critic of the Communists, and Miriam Friedlander. Davis accurately noted that after the speaker ban was lifted at CUNY, a "healthy intellectual revolution" ensued that touched almost every campus and that would, incidentally, also guarantee his eventual freedom. Furthermore, the Black Liberation movement to which he had devoted a good deal of his life, was flowering at the proper moment and eroding the Red Scare, which was trying to propel him back to prison.[61]

The party's lawyers, John Abt and Joe Forer, filed a motion to dismiss the indictment in May 1962 but it was denied. The case went to trial in December before a judge that, according to Abt, "was about the worst judge that we could possibly have had."[62] The judge was Alexander Holtzoff, a former close colleague of J. Edgar Hoover himself. The government called only one witness—appropriately a reporter from the *Times*, Will Lissner—who told how he heard Hall say at a press conference that the party would never register. The jury was out thirty-five minutes and quickly found the party guilty. Flynn commented, "Even our own paper made a mistake and said the CP was found guilty of being a Communist action organization. The judge ruled that out very specifically. It was found guilty of only one thing—refusing to register."[63]

Davis and the party did not surrender. The defense committee kept toiling tirelessly and in early 1963 reported, "the response to our two financial appeals has been excellent." But times were changing. The Cold War–Red Scare sentiments that motivated the prosecution were not as strong as before. Moscow and Washington were coming to an agreement on nuclear testing and their relationship had improved generally; the civil rights movement had created democratic space and helped to give courage to vacillating liberals. Black Liberation was eroding the Red Scare. In June the fifteen-year-old Smith Act membership clause indictment against Davis et al was dropped. In December the Circuit Court of Appeals reversed the McCarran Act conviction.[64]

This was a joyful sixtieth birthday present for Davis; he received extensive and worldwide greetings from the Soviet Union, France, Finland, Italy, and elsewhere. Over eight hundred came to a birthday celebration for him; his young daughter, Emily, was "held aloft" by Hall. His closest comrade from the past, Claudia Jones, was now in London, where she had risen rapidly to become a top leader of the growing black community there. But she missed his counsel and their discussions. "How I'd like to be able to have [a] session with you on these questions," referring to China and the United States. "I remember our past discussions, our sharp polemics and equally our resolution of them. . . . No Damon-Pythias relationship of this nature has been repetitive on this score!"[65]

Davis took the time in 1963 to reflect on the pace and direction of the civil rights movement. He paid attention to the profitable "wage differential" that made racism attractive to the ruling class and their concomitant effort "in every possible way to use . . . chosen Negroes as a buffer to prevent the rise of the mass or even to police them."[66] Later he added, "The Negro freedom movement is an all-class movement. . . . Although the total victory sought is within the framework of the U.S. capitalism society, it will have a profound effect upon that society and will extend its shrunken frontiers of democracy . . . [Blacks] are part of the common economy of their country . . . [but] the [workers are] the most stable and consistent among the Negro people for Negro liberation."67 Speaking at CCNY in November, he noted, "While direct mass action will primarily be the offensive tactic of the Negro people's movement for some time, the Negro people should set up defense committees to protect themselves against the Klan and the kind of terror" felt in Birmingham.68

Davis was no pacifist, nor was he a narrow nationalist. But he was wrestling with the militant black nationalism that had developed in response to the ravages of racism. He seemed to fluctuate in his evaluation of the Nation of Islam. In March 1963 he appeared at a forum in Los Angeles with Terry Francois (NAACP state president), John Shabazz of the local mosque, and David Gray of the Congress for Racial Equality chapter; that Davis appeared on the same platform with these forces was evidence of the waning of anti-Communism among blacks. With almost eight hundred people in attendance, Davis called for convening every black organization to adopt a common program. He strongly defended the right of Muslims to "advocate a separate independent existence for the Negro people. Why shouldn't they stand beside us in the fight against the McCarran Act? There are many paths to freedom. We say let history decide the best course while we unite on what we agree upon instead of letting our differences keep us apart."69

But in August he concluded that blacks "have rejected the dangerous, divisive and self-defeating dogma of the Muslims . . . irrational and irresponsible drivel of Malcolm X and Elijah Muhammad . . . utterly bankrupt." Blacks have also "rejected the call for armed revolt . . . as an irresponsible and reckless playing with armed insurrection." But he knew these twists and turns were connected to racism and that the "weakest link within the broad civil rights movement is its inadequate support from white allies—in the first place from organized labor."70 Later he took a softer line on the Muslims and sought to distinguish between the leaders and rank-and-file: "there is a struggle—an internal struggle—taking place inside the Muslim organization" between progressive and narrow nationalists. This last point reflected the fact that a number of Communists were writing for the basically progressive Muslim newspaper *Muhammad Speaks*, and many had become close to Malcolm X, who was a progressive nationalist; however, he was suspended from the sect for remarks made about the murder of President Kennedy.71

The year 1963 also witnessed a recognition by blacks of Davis's unique role. The popular magazine *Jet* reported that "after 18 years of self-exile" Davis returned to Atlanta, yet "he purposely avoided rubbing shoulders with many for fear they'd be smeared with the 'Red' label after his departure . . . returned to his alma mater Morehouse." There he recalled how his father and friends gave John Hope a new Dodge and how he as Hope's chauffeur would come to the campus in "his own chauffeur-driven Pierce

Arrow, only to have to climb into Hope's car and act as chauffeur himself." Davis told old friends during the visit, "You'd better be nice to me now and I'll put in a good word for you when the revolution comes."[72] The *Atlanta Inquirer* noted on 20 April that friends "bumped into him as he walked the streets. They showed little regard for his known Communistic affiliations, rather he was extended the warmest hospitality and cordiality." The *Worker* on 2 June said he was "honored by leading Negroes of every possible political persuasion."

In Detroit he was interviewed by radio and newspapers, including Harry Golden, Jr., president of the Detroit Newspaper Guild; he was welcomed by Ed Carey, president of the City Council, and visited UAW headquarters. The Reverend Charles Hill held a reception for him where hundreds turned up and George Crockett was on hand to greet him. The militant Reverend Albert Cleague, who was to startle the nation in coming years with his Church of the Black Madonna, admitted, "I've admired Ben Davis ever since I can remember."[73] This was not the sort of isolation that J. Edgar Hoover would wish on the top black Red.

This welcome for Davis was also extended to New York, where Bayard Rustin and James Haughton of the NAACP appeared on a platform with him to discuss Birmingham. Davis was formulating a "unity program of action" that was unanimously adopted by the party, which in response to those events was calling for enforcement of Article 4, S.4 of the Constitution—that is, a republican form of government for the Deep South; enforcing the 14th Amendment, S.2—withholding federal aid to all states denying rights; setting a time limit on compliance with *Brown*; eminent domain to "deghettoize" all urban and rural communities; a permanent federal FEPC; and abolishing Jim Crow by 1 January 1964. He took this ambitious program to the NAACP convention in Chicago, where he saw a different organization: "This was not the NAACP of the '30's or '40's or even the early '50's, when the prevailing view among its leaders was that mass action, mass pressure, mass picketing and other mass peoples methods were 'Communist tactics' to be eschewed as the devil shuns holy water." No, the NAACP too was entering a new stage of militance that Davis dubbed the "spirit of Birmingham." He was overwhelmed by the resulting March on Washington, which he attended, rejecting the Red-baiting that accompanied it: "[Strom Thurmond] . . . wouldn't know a free election if it knocked him down. . . . It would be no crime if Communists were leading the Freedom Now movement. But it isn't the truth."[74] He stayed at George Murphy's home and was quite moved by their discussions.[75]

The two old friends may have been discussing Davis's frequent emphasis on Africa, as his life was coming to a close.[76] This trend was always present but as people saw how Birmingham gave the United States a black eye, the connection between the domestic and the international seemed to be taken up by an increasing number of comrades. The FBI was also trying to make hay on the international front: "At the 'Worker' banquet . . . on 10/6/63, [Gil] Green is reported to have stated 'The Chinese are our comrades—the Chinese are Marxists.' Reportedly it was necessary for Benjamin Davis to strongly and publicly refute these remarks . . . people asked 'Is this a new factional fight?' Davis said the Chinese are trying to use the race question and refuted Robert Williams' theory on the use of violence."[77]

To Davis's dying day, in 1964, the FBI was obsessed with undermining him. Their agent wrote Hoover in March 1964, "The Soviets in New York City monitor the local FBI short-wave radio transmissions. In hopes of casting suspicion upon [Davis] the New York office recently caused a message to be transmitted to an agent in a radio car, instructing him to telephone the number listed to Davis."[78] Unfortunately, just before Davis died the FBI played a similar dirty trick on his coworker William Albertson, who was then expelled "in disgrace as an informer." His wife was also "expelled from the party without a hearing." Noted civil libertarian Frank Donner has termed COINTELPRO "the most lawless [program] ever undertaken in modern history by our government."[79]

The year 1964 began nicely for Davis, however. An old friend wrote, "I was happy to learn that you are giving some time to your violin. If you will consent, I would like to present you in a violin recital in Atlanta when you come down. . . . It will be exclusive and all seats reserved. Just a simple program demonstrating that velvety tone of yours."[80] But there was not time for that. By March he was in Beth Israel Hospital with a kidney ailment. Flynn reassured Al Richmond shortly thereafter that "Ben is out of the hospital—after two weeks of tests. He had kidney stones and [the doctor] also thought it might be a growth, necessitating an operation. But apparently, that is not the case."[81] Lloyd Brown, who visited him in the hospital, found Davis "angry" at being removed from the front lines of struggle and upset at not being around to see the momentous changes that were inexorably developing. Davis had to return to the hospital. Phil Bart, who also visited him, said it was "very painful" for him; he "couldn't read the paper much at this time." For a man who lived and breathed current events, this was death before death.[82]

Two of Davis's last public acts were signing an editorial endorsing a boycott of the segregated New York public schools wherein he criticized Roy Wilkins for carping at the boycott leader, Reverend Milton Galamison. Then in August, in the wake of the Harlem uprising, he joined Patterson and Winston in a statement blasting the role of the Progressive Labor Movement which was tied to the Haywood faction.

Benjamin Davis died on 22 August 1964. In its obituary the *Times* noted that Davis "was a tall heavy-set man whose affable, open manner failed to resemble the stereotype of the left-wing political activist." He "was the third internationally known Communist to die within six weeks. The others were Maurice Thorez and Palmiro Togliatti." Although he had been hospitalized intermittently throughout the year his death was a shock. Robeson, Patterson, Hall, Hope Stevens, Jackson, and Winston spoke at his funeral.[83]

Messages of sympathy poured in. On 5 September a columnist for the *Afro-American* eulogized, " . . . in a sense [Davis] was no communist. He was a brownskinned American freedom fighter who was sick and tired of jim crow. . . . He was a handsome man . . . a man who walked with confidence, exhibiting pride in his heritage and his dark skin." Langston Hughes and Powell sent the condolences to his widow. Ralph Bunche recalled, "I had known Ben since our student days at Harvard. . . . I always respected his sincerity and courage." Ossie Davis was expansive: "One of my eternal regrets will be that when Ben let me know he was ill in Beth Israel at first I didn't go; I didn't call; I didn't write. . . . My father . . . used to tell me that his father and Ben's father were kinfolk, and seeing as how we both came from Georgia it is quite possible. I hope so . . . like every Negro in our country at least; [we] are oh so much poorer now that Ben ain't here." Charles White sent a note, even George Charney. An unfortunately not atypical note came from Elsie Levin who added, "please note I live under assumed name, not the one just signed."[84]

The Red Scare followed Davis to his grave. His funeral had been scheduled for the First Corinthian Baptist Church but dirty tricks by the police forced the ceremony to move to the Unity Funeral Home, both in New York City; they also copied the license plate numbers of those who attended and investigated them. But the evolution of Black Liberation—which he had done so much to assist—was insurance that the Red Scare would find a grave of its own.[85]

Notes

Chapter 1. Origins of a Black Revolutionary

1. *Atlanta Independent*, 25 December 1915. The siblings of Ben Davis, Sr., were Ella, Mollie, John, Mike, and George. In the unexpurgated version of his memoirs written while in prison, Ben Davis commented at length on his family: "Grandma could neither read nor write—neither could Uncle John or Uncle Mike. I used to read to them when I was about 9 or 10. . . . " During slavery his grandmother was "beaten within an inch of her life by a sadistic slave master. She had suffered many brutal whippings during slavery. . . . As a result she remained permanently crippled in her right leg. [Her husband] was defiant, constantly in trouble, a bad example for the other slaves and impudent to his owners . . . One day, she said, he was defending me from a whipping. So the master started to whip him instead of me. He must have beaten him a half a day. . . . But they couldn't break him. They almost killed him though." Davis' Uncle John died in his nineties: "he used to relate the experience of slavery and Reconstruction days to my sister and myself." He was a carpenter. (Manuscript of Ben Davis prison memoir, 6/381, 22–30. The papers of Ben Davis, collected by his family, are to be donated to the Schomburg Center for Research in Black Culture, New York, N.Y., upon publication of this book. I have followed Davis's numbering system as closely as possible.) Davis' grandmother Katherine Davis died in 1923 at the age of eighty-five (*Atlanta Independent*, 18 October 1923). Her husband had died in 1874, four weeks after his daughter Mollie was born.

2. *Atlanta Independent*, 10 September 1904. At one time residing at the Dawson residence were Davis's grandmother Katherine, along with his aunt Mollie and her two sons, Lee Davis and Thomas Reed. Davis also spoke at length in his memoir about Dawson:

. . . surrounded by big plantations owned by rich white landlords. . . . During the day in cotton picking time, one could ride through Dawson and see scores of Negroes in cotton patches with huge sacks on their backs picking cotton from sun-up to sundown—men, women and children, young and old. . . . The whole town had the atmosphere of a feudal plantation . . . railroad tracks . . . was the dividing line. . . . We lived in a big 2-story house in the center of the Negro residential district . . . a white picket fence around our house . . . a big pigpen filled with pigs and a rather ornate outhouse . . . all around us were the poorest of Negroes. . . . I often wondered how they did.

Uncles who were sharecroppers and carpenters lived nearby. Davis memoir, 1/376, 2/377, 4/379, 8/383.

3. Clarence Bacote, "The Negro in Georgia Politics, 1880–1908" (Ph.D. diss., University of Chicago, 1955), 325. Bacote blames Davis senior for African-American disfranchisement as whites allegedly took up his call that the vote should be based on property and intelligence; he also finds it curious that the right-leaning *Atlanta Constitution* frequently praised him (363).

4. *Atlanta Independent*, 10 September 1904.
5. Walter White, "Portrait of a Communist," *Negro Digest* 9 (February 1951): 84– 85.
6. Bacote, "Negro in Georgia Politics," 325.
7. John Dittmer, *Black Georgia in the Progressive Era, 1900–1920* (Urbana: University of Illinois Press, 1977), 61. Yale graduate and NAACP leader William Pickens was vitriolic in his denunciation of Davis senior on more than one occasion. See William Pickens to Editor of *Philadelphia Public Ledger*, undated [ca. 1920s], Box 7, Folders H, 19-D, and 13-S, William Pickens Papers, Schomburg Library, New York, N.Y. The Rucker sisters—Lucy Rucker Aiken, Neddie Rucker Harper, and Hazel Rucker—long time Georgians, in a 1977 interview still recalled Davis; Aiken accused him of using funds from the fraternal organization the Odd Fellows "as a backing for his paper. . . . This was the one paper in Atlanta which was fairly critical of my father . . . " (Black Women's Oral History Project, 14 and 24 April 1977, Schomburg Library, New York, N.Y. Cf. also *Atlanta Independent*, 23 July 1910).
8. Rollin Chambliss, "What Negro Newspapers of Georgia Say About Some Social Problems" (master's thesis, University of Georgia, 1933), 12.
9. John Wiley Rozier, "A History of the Negro Press in Atlanta" (master's thesis, Emory University, 1947), 39.
10. Ibid., 42.
11. Emma Lou Thornbrough, "American Negro Newspapers," *Business History Review* 41 (First Quarter 1966): 467–90, 466
12. *Atlanta Independent*, 24 December 1910.
13. Davis memoir, 90, 96.
14. *Atlanta Independent*, 23 July 1910.
15. Ibid., 12 July 1913.
16. Michael Leroy Porter, "Black Atlanta: An Interdisciplinary Study of Blacks on the East Side of Atlanta, 1890–1930" (Ph.D. diss., Emory University, 1974), 36, 53, 272–73, 278; cf. also Cliff Kuhn, *Living Atlanta: An Oral History of the City, 1914–1948* (Athens: University of Georgia Press, 1990). It is difficult to overestimate the importance of the Odd Fellows Building as a symbol for black economic progress. In his prison memoir (92) Davis concurs: "The Odd Fellows block became the center around which the entire commercial and professional life of the Atlanta Negro community was built. It remains so to this day." Frederick Detweiler (*The Negro Press in the United States* [1922; reprint. College Park, Md.: McGrath, 1968], 57–58) comments that blacks were awed by the seven-story building, which contained six stores, fifty-six offices, three lodge rooms, and a roof garden.
17. *Atlanta Independent*, 30 December 1911 and 4 August 1906; Detweiler, *Negro Press*, 57–58.
18. Dittmer, *Black Georgia*, 57, 164. Dittmer adds that at the 1912 national meeting of the Odd Fellows in Atlanta the Odd Fellows influence was felt when previously segregated parks were opened to them; *Atlanta Independent*, 12 February 1916, 17 January 1914, 23 September 1911, and 25 July 1908.
19. *Atlanta Independent*, 2 January 1915; August Meier and David Lewis, "History of the Negro Upper Class in Atlanta, Georgia, 1890–1958," *Journal of Negro Education* 2 (1959): 128–39; *Atlanta Independent*, 8 July 1927.
20. Porter, "Black Atlanta," 272–73; *Atlanta Independent*, 13 June 1914.
21. Rayford Logan and Michael R. Winston, eds., *Dictionary of American Negro Biography* (New York: Norton, 1982), 159. Evidence of the ties between the Davis family and the black political establishment of Atlanta was that the Reverend Maynard Jackson, Sr., officiated at Davis senior's funeral.
22. *Atlanta Independent*, 30 January, 19 March, and 1 July 1904. Amid the pages of this paper were ads for hair straighteners and skin lighteners. Much news was car-

ried on the Russo-Japanese War and the German-Namibia conflict (5 March and 24 June 1904). A circulation of forty-five thousand was claimed, but a week later the figure was fifty thousand, then in a few months it was one hundred thousand. Interestingly, the paper regularly used the term *Afro-American*. In his prison memoir, Davis recalled the terror of the time: "Our home was likewise a kind of underground railroad. . . . It was often that my mother would get up in the middle of the night to fix a bed for a Negro sharecropper who had escaped from some Georgia peonage farm on pain of life" (106). Testifying in 1953 at a trial in Pittsburgh, Davis recalled: " . . . I saw my own father threatened with lynching" (*Daily Worker*, 4 August 1953). Detweiler, *Negro Press*, 69, 160; U.S. Senate, *Investigation Activities of the Department of Justice*, 66th Cong., 1st sess., S. Doc. 153, 1919, 161. Cf. also *Atlanta Independent*, 27 February 1921. An editorial in the *Atlanta Independent* for 8 September 1927 calls for the release of Marcus Garvey and hails Sacco and Vanzetti. But on 20 September 1928, the paper rebuked Garvey's *Negro World* for an attack on Davis senior because of their pro-GOP stance in the face of consistent Republican assaults on Davis.

23. Benjamin J. Davis, Sr., to Booker T. Washington, 30 March 1910, Reel 314, Booker T. Washington Papers, Library of Congress, Washington, D.C. (hereafter cited as BTW Papers); Booker T. Washington to Benjamin J. Davis, Sr., 28 March 1910, Reel 314, BTW Papers, *Atlanta Independent*, 12 May 1917 (on the wealth controlled by Davis) and 25 March 1905; Benjamin J. Davis, Sr., to Emmett Scott, 26 September 1910, Reel 315, BTW Papers (also see their exchanges of 8, 13, and 17 October 1910, which included Washington).

24. Benjamin J. Davis, Sr., to Warren Logan, 6 August 1908; Booker T. Washington to Benjamin J. Davis, Sr., 30 September 1908; Booker T. Washington to Benjamin J. Davis, Sr., 29 December 1908; Benjamin J. Davis, Sr., to Booker T. Washington, 25 December 1908, all on Reel 290, BTW Papers; Louis Harlan, *Booker T. Washington: The Wizard of Tuskeegee, 1901–1915* (New York: Oxford University Press, 1983), 102, 426.

25. *Atlanta Independent*, 16 August 1913, 2 September 1905, and 18 April 1914. *Daily Worker*, 22 May 1939: said Davis junior, Washington is "unquestionably the outstanding Negro leader of the early 1900 period. . . . The [Southern Negro Youth Congress] is using his traditions."

26. *Atlanta Independent*, 28 July 1906, 28 December 1907, and 28 December 1922; Theodore Kornweibel, Jr., *No Crystal Stair: Black Life and the Messenger, 1917–1928* (Westport, Conn.: Greenwood, 1975), 239.

27. *Freedom*, December 1953 and September 1951.

28. Cf. Edward G. Carmines and James A. Stimson, *Issue Evolution: Race and the Transformation of American Politics* (Princeton: Princeton University Press, 1989).

29. *Atlanta Independent*, 1 July 1916.

30. Davis memoir, 112, 118–19: "I used to view with sardonic pleasure the little jerk water town postmaster beating a path to my father's door to get a nod of approval."

31. John Hope Franklin, *From Slavery to Freedom: A History of Negro Americans* (New York: Knopf, 1969), 524; see also Allan Lichtman, *Prejudice and the Old Politics: The Presidential Election of 1928* (Chapel Hill: University of North Carolina Press, 1979): "In their quest for equal rights, black people were confronted on the one hand by a Republican party whose friendship for their people was a tarnished memory and, on the other hand, by a Democratic party wedded to southern racism" (159), and Hanes Walton, *Black Republicans: The Politics of the Black and Tans* (Metuchen, N.J.: Scarecrow Press, 1975), 176.

32. Davis memoir, 121, 124.

33. James Street, *Look Away: A Dixie Notebook* (New York: Viking Press, 1936).

34. *Amsterdam News*, 8 July 1944; *Daily Worker*, 8 July 1944.

35. Lawrence Hogan, *A Black National News Service: The Associated Negro Press and Claude Barnett, 1919–1945* (Rutherford, N.J.: Fairleigh Dickinson University Press, 1984), 169.

36. *Atlanta Independent*, 20 September, 18 October, 4 October, and 29 November 1928; see also 21 April 1927 on Davis speaking in Savannah, Pensacola, and other places in past few weeks: "People travel for miles just to see him"; 13 October 1927 on Senator Bill Harris calling Davis "nig-r"; 1 December 1927 on Davis's organization, the "Independent Voters League," for registering voters in Fulton County; 5 July 1928, in which an editorial blames the Georgia KKK for attacks on Davis; 16 August 1928: "Augusta citizens turn out in large numbers to hear Editor B. J. Davis . . . in spite of the rain and inclement weather"; 18 October 1928, featuring a large picture of "Jim Crow 'cage'" for black Democrats at the convention in Houston; made of "chicken wire," it segregated black from white delegates.

37. Donald Lisio, *Hoover, Blacks and Lily-Whites: A Study of Southern Strategies* (Chapel Hill: University of North Carolina Press, 1985), 42, 53; *Atlanta Independent*, 12 and 19 April 1928.

38. Lisio, *Hoover, Blacks*, 67; *New York Times*, 11 July 1928.

39. Lisio, *Hoover, Blacks*, 118, 183, 265, 266.

40. *New York Times*, 10 and 28 July 1928, 18 November 1928, and 14 April 1929.

41. Kelly Miller to Herbert Hoover, 4 October 1928, Campaign & Transition, Herbert Hoover Papers, Hoover Presidential Library, West Branch, Iowa.

42. G. A. Dean to Herbert Hoover, 9 November 1928, Campaign & Transition-General Correspondence, Herbert Hoover Papers.

43. Josiah Rose to Walter Newton, 29 January and 4 February 1930, Presidential Subject: Republican National Committee, Georgia, Herbert Hoover Papers.

44. Frank Darden to Walter Newton, 4 March 1930, ibid.

45. Charles Adamson to Walter Newton, 21 April 1930, ibid.

46. Walter Akerman to Walter Newton, 25 April 1930, ibid. Cf. also E. M. Brinson to Walter Newton, 15 April 1930, ibid.: "[Davis] has been discredited in this state, and rightfully so; anytime a man that is charged with crimes from rape to less offenses and ruining and destroying the biggest corporations among his race, and getting out on some technicalities, and having been for years on the big end of this political graft, both locally and nationally, you may know that the people will not follow him in any numbers." He threatened to withdraw support for Hoover altogether unless Davis was completely removed.

47. Ben Davis, Sr., to Walter Newton, 4 August 1930, Presidential Subject: Colored Question, Correspondence, Herbert Hoover Papers.

48. Josiah Rose to Walter Newton, 30 December 1931, Presidential Subject: Republican National Committee, Georgia, Herbert Hoover Papers.

49. *Oklahoma City Black Dispatch*, 30 January 1932.

50. Josiah Rose to Lawrence Richey, 22 November 1939, Post-Presidential Indiv. Herbert Hoover Papers.

51. Ralph Bunche, *The Political Status of the Negro in the Age of FDR* (Chicago: University of Chicago Press, 1973), 487. Bunche also reported that in 1937 Davis Senior claimed that there were ten thousand black voters in Georgia: "He was a 'wet' and was sent out 'gumshoeing' in sixty-five Georgia counties to win Negro support for the beer and wine law. The law won by eight thousand votes and he claims that the 'wet' interests give Negroes credit for having won the election."

52. *Atlanta Independent*, 23 August 1928. Ibid., 15 November 1928: Davis junior writes from Chicago on the "folly of the Negro press." In the 4 August 1927 issue an article attributed to Davis junior on H. L. Mencken reflects a Booker T. Washington viewpoint; on 15 September 1927 an article by Davis junior hails John Hope. Perhaps reflecting a Davis junior influence, the paper carried a number of articles reflecting a leftist point of view. See *Atlanta Independent* for 7 December 1922: a front-page article on the Third International meeting in Moscow written by Crusader News Service (a left-leaning organization frequently used by the paper) has the headline "Communists Pledge Support to Race Equity Movement." On 21 December 1922: "Russia Negro's Hope Claude McKay Believes." Davis junior's sister, Johnnie, was apparently influenced by the times as well. See *Atlanta Independent*, 7 April 1927.

53. *Daily Worker*, 29 October 1945. At his death Davis was editor of the *National Baptist Review*. In 1959 "Davis recalled his visit to his dying father in the hospital in 1945 and how ashamed he was then as a city councilman to see cracked ceilings and other evidences of neglect" (*Worker*, 26 April 1959).

Chapter 2. The Making of a Black Revolutionary

1. *Afro-American*, 13 February 1960; J. Pius Barbour, editor of the *National Baptist Voice*, tells a different story: "One day I said to Ben Sr.: 'You have but one son and he should be named after you. Why don't you change his name to Ben Jr?' The next I heard we had a Ben Davis, Jr." (*Freedom*, September 1951).

2. Davis memoir, 17/392; W. E. B. Du Bois and Augustus Granville, eds., *The Common School and the Negro American* (Atlanta: Atlanta University Press, 1911), 61; Walter White, *A Man Called White* (New York: Viking Press, 1948), 29.

3. Mary Church Terrell, *A Colored Woman in a White World* (1940; reprint, New York: Arno, 1980).

4. Jean Carey Bond, interview with autuor, New York City, 11 May 1988.

5. Davis memoir, 17/392.

6. *Atlanta Independent*, 28 December 1917, in which Davis junior is listed as "leader of Morehouse College Orchestra." See also ibid., 8 March 1919, 15 November 1913, and 12 April 1923.

7. Davis memoir, 24/399, 25/400, 27/402.

8. Ibid., 31/406, 33/408, 34/409, 35/410.

9. Abner Berry, "All American Councilman," *New Masses* 57 (9 October 1945): 4–5; Johnnie Carey, interview with author, New York City, 2 July 1986.

10. *New York Amsterdam News*, 30 October 1943.

11. *Morehouse Maroon Tiger*, November 1949; *Atlanta Independent*, 6 December 1923; cf. also 25 December 1915.

12. Transcript and application of Benjamin J. Davis, Jr., September 1922–June 1925, Amherst College, Amherst, Mass.

13. Davis memoir, 2/433.

14. *Daily Worker*, 4 May 1945.

15. Ibid., 4 May 1945, 7 November 1937, and 18 October 1942; note from Ben Davis, Jr., 15 June 1955, Ben Davis Papers.

16. Transcript of Benjamin J. Davis, Jr., 1925–28, Harvard Law School.

17. Davis memoir, 44/613, 49/618; *New York Amsterdam News*, 20 November 1943.

18. *New York Amsterdam News*, 20 November 1943.

19. *Atlanta Independent*, 16 and 23 August 1928.
20. Ibid., 15 November 1928.
21. *New York Age*, 28 April 1945.
22. Andrew Buni, *Robert L. Vann of the "Pittsburgh Courier": Politics and Black Journalism* (Pittsburgh: University of Pittsburgh Press, 1974), 134, 236; *New York Amsterdam News*, 28 April 1945; Davis memoir, 9/440, 10/441, 12/443.
23. Michael Peplow, *George Schuyler* (Boston: Twayne, 1980), 28, 105; *Atlanta Independent*, 1 December 1928.
24. George Schuyler, Columbia University Oral History, Butler Library, New York, N.Y., 1962; *Pittsburgh Courier*, 24 January 1931: in his column Schuyler quotes a Davis letter hitting the awarding of the Spingarn Award to Richard Harrison for *Green Pastures*. Allegedly Davis suggested Abram Harris, Charles Houston, or Walter White and called "Bill Robinson . . . the best actor in the world in his line, why not give the 'honor' to him?" In another column Schuyler spoke of a "pleasant evening in Baltimore visiting with such excellent fellows as [Davis]" (*Pittsburgh Courier*, 20 December 1930). In the *Daily Worker* of 4 May 1939 Davis replied to a bitter attack by Schuyler by averring, "fortunately Schuyler is a member of a disappearing breed within the ranks of the Negro people." In his memoir Schuyler writes, "I had met the elder Davis when I visited Atlanta during my southern tour. Young Ben was as amiable as his father, and we had a good time during the month we were together. He dined at our apartment several times and listened to our latest records. Ben was not a Communist then, was not even thinking about it, but even after he became one we always got on well together. . . . I think his treatment as a young lawyer in the Atlanta courts was a contributing factor in leading him astray. Then, too, Ben had a considerable streak of opportunism and cynicism." He also had an apocryphal tale: "One reason the Communist Party always wants to select wives for their functionaries is that it is easier to keep track of their activities and opinions. This happened in the case of Ben Davis, Jr." See George Schuyler, *Black and Conservative: The Autobiography of George S. Schuyler* (New Rochelle, N.Y.: Arlington House, 1966), 167, 255. Schuyler had been assistant editor of *The Messenger*, working with A. Philip Randolph, and was a member of the Socialist party beginning in 1921. However, Ollie Harrington contends that during World War I Schuyler refused to go overseas in a black regiment. He was jailed and then bought off; at that point he began moving to the right. Harrington, a close associate of Davis, knew the black conservative well and "admired" him in part because he gave this talented cartoonist and satirist his first job. Ollie Harrington, interview with author, 1 June 1989, Berlin, Germany.
25. Walter White, *How Far the Promised Land?* (New York: Viking Press, 1955), 84.
26. *New York Amsterdam News*, 5 September 1964.
27. Jack O'Dell, interview with author, 13 November 1988, Washington, D.C.
28. *Muhammad Speaks*, 18 July 1969. Noted civil rights attorney Arthur Kinoy called Davis "a leader whose courage I had admired from afar during my student days." See Arthur Kinoy, *Rights on Trial: The Odyssey of a People's Lawyer* (Cambridge: Harvard University Press, 1983), 26. In an interview dated 18 April 1988 black novelist and intellectual Lloyd Brown told me of Davis's "intellectual honesty." Harlem resident Joseph Smallwood in 1987 spoke of Davis as "an extraordinary, good human being. I knew him as a man of principle, very much devoted to the interests of the people" (*West Side Spirit*, 21 December 1987). George Murphy of the *Afro-American* told Davis's wife, Nina, "Ben's grandfather and my paternal grandfather . . . were old friends" (George Murphy to Nina Davis, 24 August 1964, George Murphy Papers, Moorland-Spingarn Library, Howard University, Washington, D.C.) In turn Davis spoke warmly of Murphy: "I don't have to tell you how

much Ben loved and admired you, George. Just the mention of your name would bring a warm smile to his face" (Nina Davis to George Murphy, ca. 1964, George Murphy Papers). This may help to explain the favorable coverage Davis received in the *Afro-American* over the years. But despite Davis's clear historic impact, a number of writers have mentioned Davis only to dismiss him: see, for example, James O. Young, *Black Writers of the Thirties* (Baton Rouge: Louisiana State University Press, 1973), 40.

29. *Freedom*, September 1951. Curiously, in the midst of this flowing tribute, Barbour added: "I am fully aware that if the Reds get control preachers like me would go to the guillotine."

30. Paul Robeson, Jr., interview with author, 11 August 1988, New York City.

31. *Worker*, 28 April 1963.

Chapter 3. The Road to the Communist Party

1. Joseph North, "Angelo Herndon Is Back in Atlanta," *New Masses* 17 (5 November 1935): 15–16.

2. John Hammond Moore, "Communists and Fascists in a Southern City: Atlanta, 1930," *South Atlantic Quarterly* 67 (Summer 1968): 441.

3. Clarence A. Bacote, "The Negro in Atlanta Politics," *Journal of Negro History* 16, no. 4 (1955): 343. For a contemporary account of Atlanta, see Gary Orfield and Carole Ashkinaze, *The Closing Door: Conservative Policy and Black Opportunity* (Chicago: University of Chicago Press, 1991).

4. John Spivak, undated article (ca. 1932), Reel 9, Box 18, F4, International Labor Defense Papers, Schomburg Library, New York, N.Y. (hereafter cited as ILD Papers).

5. Davis memoir, 18/461, 8/451, 15/458, 22/465.

6. Dorothy Healey, "Tradition's Chains Have Bound Us," UCLA Oral History Program, 1982, 1: 200; *Herndon v. Georgia*, 174 S.E. 597 (1934). *Afro-American*, 28 January 1933; *Pittsburgh Courier*, 14 January 1933; Michael Merrill, "The Angelo Herndon Case: Free Speech in Georgia," master's thesis, Columbia University, 1972; David Entin, "Angelo Herndon," master's thesis, University of North Carolina, Chapel Hill, 1963; See also Dorothy Healey, *Dorothy Healey Remembers a life in the American Communist Party* (New York: Oxford University Press, 1990).

7. Davis memoir, 14/653.

8. William Patterson, interview, 28 February 1970, Civil Rights Documentation Project, Howard University, Washington, D.C., 14. See also William Patterson, *Ben Davis: Crusader for Negro Freedom and Socialism* (New York: New Outlook, 1967), 21. Davis's law partner, Geer (who was a native of South Carolina) left Atlanta in 1935 and died at forty-one in Louisville.

9. Roger Baldwin to George Haynes, 22 April 1933, vol. 654, American Civil Liberties Union Papers, Princeton University Library, Princeton, N.J. (hereafter cited as ACLU Papers).

10. Davis memoir, 21/505, 24/508, 33/517.

11. Angelo Herndon, *Let Me Live* (New York: Random House, 1937), 234, 237, 223, 225, 228, 231.

12. *Worker*, 13 December 1964; Davis memoirs, 21/505.

13. Davis memoir, 24/508, 33/517.

14. Ibid., 24/508, 33/517.

15. Herndon, *Let Me Live*, 223–34 and passim.

16. *New York Times*, 27 August 1933.
17. Charles Martin, *The Angelo Herndon Case and Southern Justice* (Baton Rouge: Louisiana State University Press, 1976), 59. See also *Daily Worker*, 26 December 1932, reporting on bail won for Herndon. Davis's former employer, the *Afro-American*, was impressed: "[He] took sharp issue with the prosecuting attorney and white witnesses for their use of insulting terms to designate colored people. They forced the court to rule that they must be addressed during the trial as Negroes" (*Afro-American*, 21 January 1933). Davis's objections were audacity of the highest order and left an indelible impression on African-Americans and others.
18. *Time* Magazine, 30 January 1933.
19. William Patterson interview, Civil Rights Documentation Project, Howard University, 21.
20. Davis memoir, 6/491, 84/568. See also Benjamin Jefferson Davis, *Why I Am a Communist* (New York: New Century Publications, 1947).
21. Martin, *The Herndon Case*, 197.
22. *Norris v. Alabama*, 294US587 (1935).
23. *Daily Worker*, 8 December 1932.
24. Ibid., 10 January 1933. See also *Atlanta World*, 4 January 1933, where the writer says that the swearing in of two black jurors in the criminal division of Fulton Superior Court was the "first time that Negroes have sat on juries in Georgia since 1862," giving Davis the credit. The headline writer of the *Pittsburgh Courier* of 14 January 1933 agreed: "Georgia Calls Negro Jurors to Dodge Communistic Issue."
25. *Daily Worker*, 13 May 1933.
26. Ibid., 4 February 1933.
27. According to George Schuyler in the 18 February 1933 *Pittsburgh Courier*, "It is with keen pleasure but without surprise that I read . . . of the courageous legal endeavors of the young Atlanta lawyer who sought brilliantly to free Angelo Herndon from the cruel clutches of the Georgia mobocracy. Davis is made of fine stuff. Some four years ago when we used to sit in our warm office inside the Chicago loop, looking down at the white folks scurrying along the cold, windy streets and philosophize on the plight of the downtrodden . . . I discovered that Davis was a unique Negro. In brief, he has a peculiar absence of color inferiority complex, a keen sense of humor, and necessarily a sense of proportion. . . . He is one of the few oases I find in the intellectual desert of Atlanta." The next week, on 25 February, he placed him in the pantheon with A. Philip Randolph and Walter White as "New Negroes who have not quailed nor skulked in their tents. . . . Each in his or her own way is on the firing line hewing out new paths and making fine new contributions."
28. Davis memoir, 12/581, 13/582, 14/583, 15/584.
29. *Daily Worker*, 1 February and 21 January 1933; *Washington Tribune*, 3 February 1933; Herndon, *Let Me Live*, 275. After the conviction John Howard Lawson, the ACLU, and others came to Atlanta to meet with leading officials, including the governor; Davis was present as racist insults were hurled at them. Yet even before then, the authorities were becoming concerned about Communist inroads. See U.S. Congress, House Special Committee to Investigate Communist activities in the U.S., *Investigation of Communist Propaganda, Hearings*, pt. 6, I 71st Cong., 2d sess. (Washington, D.C.: GPO, 1930).
30. Will Alexander (Commission on Interracial Cooperation) to Roger Baldwin, 24 January 1933, vol. 654, ACLU Papers; Ben Davis to Roger Baldwin, 30 April 1933, ibid., William Patterson to Roger Baldwin, 7 February 1933, ibid., Roger Baldwin to William Patterson, 24 January 1933, ibid.
31. *Daily Worker*, 14 December 1935; press release, 25 October 1935, Reel 9, Box 19, F26, ILD Papers.
32. *Daily Worker*, 26 May 1934.

33. *Daily Worker*, 30 January 1933.
34. Ibid., 13 May and 8 September 1933; 4 June 1934.
35. Ibid., 11 June 1934.
36. Ibid., 12 March 1936.
37. Harry Haywood, *Black Bolshevik: The Autobiography of an Afro-American Communist* (Chicago: Liberator Press, 1978), 404.
38. Nell Irvin Painter, *The Narrative of Hosea Hudson. His life as a Negro Communist* (Cambridge: Harvard University Press, 1979) 226, 180. Hudson was impressed with Davis, terming him a "friendly guy." He also admired his courage. When he first met him in July 1933 they drove from Atlanta to New York for "an extraordinary plenary session." There were seven in Davis's Ford; most of them were scared since there were 3 blacks and 4 whites driving through the South, in direct violation of unwritten social codes: "Ben drove every step of the way, all the way up there and all the way back. He never took a wink, night and day" (181).
39. Erskine Caldwell, "A Story That Got Lost," *New Masses* 13 (16 January 1934), 9.
40. Davis memoir, 38/522.
41. *Daily Worker*, 4 August 1933 and 20 July 1934; *Negro Liberator*, 28 July 1934; *Daily Worker*, 19 April 1934 and 14 February 1933; *Atlanta World*, 2 February 1933; *Daily Worker*, 5 June 1934.
42. Davis memoir, 35/604.
43. *New York Times*, 4 November 1934.
44. John Roper, *C. Vann Woodward, Southerner* (Athens: University of Georgia Press, 1987).
45. *Chicago Defender*, 27 October 1934.
46. *Daily Worker*, 5 June 1934.
47. Davis memoir, 1/640.
48. *Daily Worker*, 23 June 1934.
49. Davis memoir, 68/637, 69/638. See William Patterson to Roger Baldwin, 19 November 1933, vol. 654, ACLU Papers.
50. Davis memoir, 18/587; *Daily Worker*, 6 September 1933.
51. *Daily Worker*, 3 October 1933. On 21 September 1933 the *Daily Worker* reported that charges against the officer were dismissed on the grounds of "self-defense."
52. *Harlem Liberator*, 21 April and 19 May 1934; *Negro Liberator*, 15 January 1935.
53. *Harlem Liberator*, 26 May 1934; *Daily Worker*, 15 and 22 June 1934, 7 August 1934; *Negro Liberator*, 11 August 1934.
54. Davis memoir, 63.
55. *Daily Worker*, 21 June 1935.
56. Ibid., 23 June 1934; *Negro Liberator*, 18 August 1934; *Daily Worker*, 10 April and 5 July 1935; *Negro Liberator*, 8 and 29 December 1934; *Daily Worker*, 30 July and 29 May 1935.
57. *The Liberator*, 26 April 1930.
58. *Daily Worker*, 30 July 1935.
59. This criticism of Ben Davis, Sr., was not unique to the Left. In response to his actions at the recent GOP convention the *New York Age* of 20 June 1936 said that he "went back on his race . . . sunk so low . . . a marked man, shunned, hissed and branded a traitor . . . pusillanimous, knee-bending submissive Negroes of the Ben Davis ilk. . . ."
60. Press release, undated, Box 1, Crusader News Agency Papers, Schomburg Library, New York, N.Y. (hereafter cited as CNA Papers); press release, 15 March 1937, Box 1, 1937, ibid.; press release, 29 July 1940, Box 2, 1940, ibid.

61. *Daily Worker*, 12 and 13 November 1943.
62. Press release, 29 January 1940, Box 2, 1940, CNA Papers.
63. *Daily Worker*, 21 and 24 December 1935, 30 June 1934.
64. *Daily Worker*, 23 September 1936; memorandum on *Daily Worker*, undated reel 4209, Elizabeth Gurley Flynn Papers, New York University Library, New York, N.Y. *Daily Worker*, 12 February 1938, 14 November and 31 December 1936, 26 September and 21 November 1937, 26 February 1939, 1 January 1938; and 22 February 1935; *New York Times*, 2 February 1939. For a survey of Communism in the 1930s see Harvey Klehr, *The Heyday of American Communism: The Depression Decade* (New York: Basic Books, 1984).
65. Davis memoir, 59–60. See also *Narrative of Hosea Hudson*, 225. Looking back in 1964, George Murphy, in attempting to comfort Davis's widow, was of a different opinion: "Ben's father, before he died, expressed his deep understanding of Ben and his determination to take a new, a different road." George Murphy to Nina Davis, 24 August 1964, Ben Davis Papers.
66. *Negro Liberator*, 1 December 1934.
67. Ibid., 29 December 1934.
68. *Harlem Liberator*, 27 May 1933.
69. ACLU pamphlet, 1933, vol. 654, ACLU Papers: "The [ACLU] regarding this [Herndon] as a case of the utmost importance to the cause of civil liberties in the South, is aiding"; Ben Davis to Roger Baldwin, 26 June 1933, ibid.; *Daily Worker*, 16 December 1935; press release, 4 July 1937, Box 1, 1937, CNA Papers, announcing Davis's election to the new National Committee of ILD, along with Herndon. See also *Harlem Liberator*, 9 June and 6 May 1934; *Negro Liberator*, 8 and 29 September and 8 December 1934; *Liberator*, 1 August 1935. Davis's misplaced radical rhetoric should be juxtaposed against the growing radicalization of the black middle class that was spurred on by the Great Depression. Carl Murphy of the *Afro-American* said in a 1932 forum, "The Communists are going our way. For which Allah can be praised." P. B. Young of the *Norfolk Journal and Guide* praised the party for having "accepted Negroes into their ranks in both high and lowly positions." And E. Washington Rhodes of the *Philadelphia Tribune* averred, "The ideals of the Soviet Union of Russia have a fascinating appeal to American Negroes . . . it is amazing that millions of Negroes have not joined the followers of the Red flag, instead of a few thousands" (See Theodore Vincent, ed., *Voices of a Black Nation: Political Journalism in the Harlem Renaissance* [San Francisco: Ramparts Press, 1973], 203–5).
70. Davis memoir, 55/624, 58/627, 53/622: Carol King of the National Lawyers Guild played a major role in the appeal; the Georgia Supreme Court brief "was her entire handiwork" and she was described further as "a person of noble character, brilliant mind and pure heart." See also *Daily Worker*, 27 June and 30 September 1933.
71. *New York Times*, 8 October 1935; *Daily Worker*, 29 March 1935; "Guild Reporter," 1 November 1935, Reel 9, Box 18, F10, ILD Papers; *Negro Liberator*, 1 May and 1 June 1935; *Daily Worker*, 4 January 1937.
72. Herndon coverage in the Red press improved after Davis's arrival in New York: see *Daily Worker*, 19 July 1934, 9 February 1937, 10 December 1935, 21 December 1936, 8 November 1942, 25 March 1944, and 1 October 1948.
73. Carroll Van West, "Perpetuating the Myth of America: Scottsboro and Its Interpreters," *South Atlantic Quarterly* 80 (Winter 1981): 36–48; see also Hugh Murray, "The NAACP Versus the Communist Party: The Scottsboro Rape Cases, 1931–1932," *Phylon* 28 (Fall 1967): 276.
74. Schuyler, *Black and Conservative*, 187.
75. "Surveillance of Radicals in the U.S., 1917–1941," U.S. Military Intelligence

Reports, Reel 28, 0294, Major R. M. Howell Headquarters Fourth Corps Area. Office of Assistant Chief of Staff, KG-2, Fort McPherson, Atlanta, Georgia; Davis memoir, 21, 40.

76. Davis memoir, 5; Haywood Patterson and Earl Conrad, *Scottsboro Boy* (Garden City, N.Y.: Doubleday, 1950), 33, 305.

77. *Daily Worker*, 20 May and 16 November 1933, 16 May 1934; Dan T. Carter, *Scottsboro: A Tragedy of the American South* (Baton Rouge: Louisiana State University Press, 1969), 249, 313–14; *New York Times*, 17 April 1933; *Daily Worker*, 12 April, 1 December, and 5 November 1934; *Sunday Worker*, 5 April 1936.

78. *Daily Worker*, 16 February 1935.

79. U.S. Congress, House Committee on Un-American Activities, *Hearings Regarding Communist Infiltration of Minority Groups—Part 2, Testimony of Manning Johnson*. 81st Cong., 1st sess., 14 July 1949.

80. James Allen, "New Attack on the Scottsboro Defense," *New Masses*, 6 November 1934; *Daily Worker*, 18 October 1934. In the *Negro Liberator*, of 17 November 1934 Davis hit Liebowitz hard.

81. *Daily Worker*, 7 February, 9 April, 8 May, and 24 October 1934; 11 and 26 February 1935.

82. Ibid., 21 April 1933, 17 October 1934, 19 April 1933.

83. Ibid., 17 and 18 April 1933.

84. Ibid., 22 April 1933. At a meeting at the Harlem Masonic Temple the united front included A. J. Muste, a well-known Socialist and anti-Communist. Davis was elected chairman of the Scottsboro Unity Defense Committee; the fact that he had just come to Harlem indicates the esteem in which he was held.

85. Ibid., 23 and 30 October 1934, 22 and 28 November 1933, and 4 August 1937.

86. On 18 February 1935 the *Daily Worker* reported that at the Supreme Court hearings, "the doorkeeper nervously insisted that [Davis] who reported the proceedings . . . leave his brief case outside the court room. The day before, several persons . . . had walked unchallenged into the courtroom . . . with brief cases in [their] hands," most of whom were white. Davis had a spurt of activity on the case in 1937. See the *Daily Worker* for 30 July 1937. On 31 July Davis appeared in the *DW* with Mrs. Ada Wright (mother of Andy), Mrs. Viola Montgomery (mother of Olin), and Mary Alice Montgomery (sister of Olin) at a meeting on the case attended by five thousand. See also *Daily Worker*, 6 August, 4, 7, and 9 September, and 1 December 1937.

87. *Daily Worker*, 21 October 1945.

88. Ibid., 9 September 1951.

89. Press release, 15 April 1940, Box 2, 1940, CNA Papers; *Daily Worker*, 10 April 1941. Earlier he had connected the case to the larger framework: "The role of the capitalist courts is to dispense capitalist justice. . . . [Scottsboro] is a fight for the national liberation of the Negro people." Davis article, ca. 1934, Box 18, F4, Reel 9, ILD Papers.

Chapter 4. To Be a Professional Revolutionary

1. Larry Greene, "Harlem in the Great Depression, 1928–1936" (Ph.D. diss., Columbia University, 1979). See also Aaron Siskind, *Harlem Document: Photographs 1932–1940* (Providence, R.I.: Matrix, 1981); *Daily Worker*, 26 March 1934; Cheryl Lynn Greenberg, *Or Does It Explode: Black Harlem in the Great Depression* (New York: Oxford University Press, 1991).

2. Howard Johnson, interview, "Seeing Red," transcipt, Series IV, 1977, Oral History of the American Left, New York University Library, New York, N.Y.
3. Nathan Glazer, *The Social Basis of American Communism* (New York: Harcourt Brace, 1961), 180.
4. Peggy Dennis, "Short Biography of Eugene Dennis," ca. 1961, Reel 4209, Elizabeth Gurley Flynn Papers; *A Report of Proceedings and Decisions of the First International Conference of Negro Workers* (Hamburg: International Trade Union Committee of Negro Workers, 1930). Both James Ford and William Patterson were present at this gathering, which also included representatives from Africa and the Caribbean. Cf. also *The International Negro Worker's Review* 1, no. 1 (1931), followed by *The Negro Worker* 2, no. 8 (1932), both published in Hamburg.
5. Paul Lyons, *Philadelphia Communists, 1936–1956* (Philadelphia: Temple University Press, 1982), 208, n. 28.
6. *Daily Worker*, 29 August 1933.
7. "Growth of Party Membership Since Last Convention," report, New York State, Box 12, Robert Minor Papers, Columbia University Library, New York, N.Y.; *Daily Worker*, 1 July 1936. According to the *New York Times* of 19 December 1936 the party had 10,476 members in New York City, while the Socialists had 12,564. Strikingly, however, the SP had a much smaller black membership than the CP. Cf. also Mark Naison, *Communists in Harlem During the Depression* (Urbana: University of Illinois Press, 1983).
8. George Blake, "The Party in Harlem, New York," *Party Voice* 11 (June 1938): 14–20.
9. *Daily Worker*, 23 January 1936.
10. Ibid., 25 March 1936; Press release, 8 August 1938, Box 1, 1938, CNA; *Daily Worker*, 4 May 1939. It is often difficult to rely on some accounts of the party's strength. For example, the *New York Age* on 9 March 1940 reported that the Harlem party had a membership decline from five thousand in spring 1939 to 250 as of that writing and that James Ford "has been removed from power in the party councils and 'kicked upstairs' to a position of special party representative in Mexico." The membership decline is exaggerated and the report on Ford does not necessarily correspond with his being on the party ticket in the presidential race of 1940. Nathan Glazer, on the other hand, in *The Social Basis of American Communism* (p. 176) suggests that there were "only three Negroes in leading posts in the party" during this era (Davis, Ford, and Ray Hansborough) but he ignores Maude White, William Patterson, and a number of local leaders. As of mid-1937 there were five women and ten blacks among the fifty members and candidate members of the Central Committee (*Daily Worker*, 22 June 1937). The *Daily Worker* for 1 June 1940 published a financial report on the party provided by a Certified Public Accountant, Morris Greenbaum: $521,771.36 had been received during this period and $508,756.23 was paid out.
11. Irving Howe and Lewis Coser, *The American Communist Party: A Critical History* (New York: De Capo Press, 1974), 345.
12. Daniel Aaron, *Writers on the Left* (New York: Harcourt Brace, 1961).
13. *Afro-American*, 23 November 1936. Matthews's account of Davis's appearance is contradicted by numerous photographs appearing regularly in the *DW* and by accounts of his wife, James Jackson, Paul Robeson, Jr., and others, as noted below. Marvel Cooke, in an interview with the author on 6 April 1988, New York City, also does not agree with Matthews.
14. George Charney, *A Long Journey* (Chicago: Quadrangle, 1968), 149.
15. Biography titled "James Ford," undated, Box 6, William Patterson Papers, Moor land-Spingarn Library, Howard University, Washington, D.C.
16. *Daily Worker*, 24 September 1935. See also the *Daily Worker* for 23 De-

cember 1936, where Davis's query to Ford was, "'What do you think of the mass swing of the Negroes from their old-line Republican connection?'" and the *Daily Worker*, 20 September 1936. On 25 September in the same paper Ford attacked Perry Howard, black GOP leader.

17. Ibid., 19 August 1940 and 2 October 1940.

18. Ibid., 27 and 29 October 1940.

19. Ibid., 22 June 1937; press release, 28 June 1937, Box 1, 1937, CNA Papers; Marvel Cooke, interview with author, 6 April 1988, New York City.

20. *Daily Worker*, 5 August 1938; interview with Abner Berry, 2 December 1977, Series I, Tape 1, Side II, Oral History of the American Left. Symptomatic of the pressures of the period is Berry's allegation that black party leader Tim Holmes "went crazy."

21. Interview with Howard Johnson, 1977, Oral History of the American Left.

22. Interview with John Pittman, 18 November 1970, Civil Rights Documentation Project, Howard University. Pittman too was from Morehouse, class of 1926. In this interview he also stated, "Americans in general probably owe the continued existence of the United States to the fact that the Communists threw all of their weight, all of their force into the struggle against Hitler. Because it was a nip and tuck struggle." Concerning Russia's relations with other socialist countries he said, "The only time that the international movement to my knowledge, intervenes in a sense in another country is over a barrel" (referring to Czechoslovakia). Cf. also Phillip Bonosky, "The Story of Ben Carreathers," *Masses and Mainstream* 6 (July 1953): 34–44.

23. *Daily Worker*, 16 September 1940.

24. Delacy Wendell Sanford, "Congressional Investigation of Black Communism" (Ph.D. diss., State University of New York at Stony Brook, 1973), 51.

25. *Daily Worker*, 2 March 1937. Goode's glowing tribute to the Soviet Union also included a sharp attack on the Trotskyites. The *Daily Worker* for 20 June 1937 reported that Golden had been in the Soviet Union since 1932; a picture included his "chubby 3 year old daughter" Bertha. In the *Daily Worker* of 27 September 1937 Roach was called a "leading member of the Tom Mooney machine gun company" who suffered a "ghastly still-painful wound in his left shoulder." He was a member of the party. Said Davis on his death, "I knew 'Doug' Roach. I have felt his infectious enthusiasm" (*Daily Worker*, 14 July 1938).

26. *Daily Worker*, 27 March 1938. Sutton was back in the United States after almost seven years in the Soviet Union. Like Goode, he assailed the "Trotskyist wreckers." Like Davis, he was a college graduate at a time when this was not common among African-Americans. He attended Prairie View, received a bachelor's from Drake, and did graduate work at Iowa State University. He had particularly sharp words for M. Chernov, one of "21 Trotskyist-Bukharinist spies." Sutton wrote Joseph Stalin to complain about Chernov. He married in the Soviet Union in 1933 and at that writing had a three-and-a-half-year-old son, Juan. See also the *Daily Worker* for 24 January 1938, which reported how Wayland Rudd, a black actor, denied the right to vote in the South, had moved to the Soviet Union and become a citizen because, among other things, he could at least vote there.

27. Ben Davis to Paul Robeson, undated, Ben Davis Papers.

28. Paul Robeson, "Speech Delivered at the Funeral of Benjamin Davis," in *Paul Robeson Speaks: Writings, Speeches, Interviews, 1918–1974*, ed. Philip S. Foner (New York: Brunner-Mazel, 1978), 470–71, 22.

29. Lloyd Brown, interview with author, 18 April 1988, New York City.

30. Paul Robeson, Jr., interview with author, 11 August 1988, New York City. Robeson junior referred to Davis as "extraordinarily quick-footed on [the] tennis court . . . amazing . . . very quick . . . graceful . . . taught me how to play well

.... We would go to public courts in Springfield, Massachusetts ... eight miles away.... [He] belonged to the Black Tennis Club on Convent Avenue in Harlem." As for Johnson, Robeson junior refers to him as an "expert on Anglo-Saxon English [and] Chaucer" with an "extraordinary library." He shared many discussions with Robeson and was also friendly with Davis. During tense times he would provide security assistance for the actor; according to Robeson junior, Johnson took over Harlem rackets from the infamous Dutch Schulz.

31. *Daily Worker*, 27 December and 10 May 1936.

32. As quoted by Mark Naison in "Communism and Harlem Intellectuals in the Popular Front: Anti-Fascism and the Politics of Black Culture," *Journal of Ethnic Studies* 9 (Spring 1981): 1.

33. *Daily Worker*, 11 March 1939.

34. Dorothy Height, interview, February 1974–November 1976, Black Women's Oral History Project, Schomburg Center for Research on Black Culture: Height adds that she learned "tactics" from the Young Communists: "I don't whisper in meetings ... I don't like to run in and out.... I learned that you had to listen, you had to be alert, you had to watch." She observed cogently that one had to watch who is going in and out of meetings and with whom—together or minutes apart; this helped in judging the correlation of forces in the meeting.

35. Benjamin E. Mays, *Born to Rebel* (New York: Scribner, 1971), 209, 232. He states that under John Hope (head of Morehouse during Davis's tenure) "the ... student was taught never to accept the system in his own mind as being inescapable or right." He personally adds, "I have no regrets that I was accused of being a member of Communist-front organizations, for had I not been it would be prima facie evidence that in my entire career I had not been in the vanguard of those working for social justice." These admissions allowed Senator Richard Russell of Georgia and others to block Mays's appointments to the U.S. Civil Rights Commission and as ambassador to Israel during the Kennedy administration.

36. Howard Johnson interview, Oral History of the American lift. See also Lawrence H. Schwartz, *Marxism and Culture: The CPUSA and Culture* (Port Washington, N.Y.: Kennikat, 1980); Matthew Baigell and Julia Williams, eds., *Artists Against War and Fascism: Papers of the First American Artists' Congress* (New Brunswick, N.J.: Rutgers University Press, 1986).

37. Ralph Ellison, "Remembering Richard Wright," in *Speaking for You: The Vision of Ralph Ellison*, ed. Kimberly W. Benson (Washington, D.C.: Howard University Press, 1987), 189, and Marvel Cooke, interview with author, 6 April 1988. In the *Daily Worker* of 25 October 1937 Wright favorably reviews a party pamphlet that includes a prominent contribution from Davis. See also Margaret Walker, *Richard Wright, Daemonic Genius* (New York: Warner, 1988), 181, 184. Among other choice words, the author calls Wright an "opportunist.... It was hard enough being black. It was just too much being black and red." Yes, she suggests, the party was "using" Wright, but "he had used them too." Cf. Richard Wright, *American Hunger* (New York: Harper & Row, 1977).

38. *Daily Worker*, 14 April 1940; Marvel Cooke, interview with author, 6 April 1988. Marvel Cooke affirms that Wright's novel was edited substantially by herself and her mother: "'Every 't' was crossed ... in my kitchen.... He read that book to me over and over, 'chapter by chapter.'"

39. Naison, "Communism and Harlem Intellectuals," 13.

40. *Daily Worker*, 26 April 1940.

41. Ibid., 8 May and 23 June 1940. See also Sam Gon Kim, "Black Americans' Commitment to Communism: A Case Study Based on Fiction and Autobiographies by Black Americans" (Ph.D. diss., University of Kansas, 1986). The author says that the party "helped many writers such as Wright, Ellison and Himes to get jobs in gov-

ernment projects or in the Party propaganda organs. . . ." Davis, he says, "helped" Wright "move from . . . Chicago . . . when [Wright] was in trouble with Haywood"; Cf. Wilfred Samuels, *Five Afro-Caribbean Voices in American Culture, 1917–1929* (Boulder, Colo.: Belmont Books, 1977), 52: "Even conservative George Schuyler contended that it was inevitable that some blacks would identify themselves with socialist and communist movements."

42. *Daily Worker*, 9 January 1938 and 28 October 1936; *The Liberator*, 8 March 1930; *Daily Worker*, 29 December 1936 and 5 December 1937. In the *DW* for 6 April 1936 Davis wrote of "Clarence Johnstone and Jules Bledsoe, two famous American Negro artists" based in Dublin who were said to have sympathized with Mussolini's invasion of Ethiopia. See also *Daily Worker*, 24 March and 20 January 1937; Stuart Cosgrove, "The Zoot-Suit and Style Warfare," *History Workshop* 18 (Autumn 1984):77–91; Sidney Finkelstein, *Jazz: A People's Music* (New York: International, 1948); Dizzy Gillespie and Al Fraser, *To Be, or Not to Bop* (Garden City, N.Y.: Doubleday, 1979); Ira Gitler, *Swing to Bop: An Oral History of the Transition in Jazz in the 1940s* (New York: Oxford University Press, 1985). Many thanks to my colleague Douglas Henry Daniels, author of a forthcoming biography of Lester Young, for his insight on this topic.

43. *Daily Worker*, 24 June 1937; see also Alexander Joseph Young, "Joe Louis: Symbol, 1933–1949" (Ph.D. diss., University of Maryland, 1968).

44. *Daily Worker*, 30 August and 28 October 1937, 24 June and 11 November 1938, 12 September 1939.

45. Ibid., 30 August and 28 October 1937.

46. Ibid., 3 February 1937, 3 June 1939, and 2 October 1938.

47. *New York Times*, 24 December 1939.

48. *New York Post*, 22 December 1939.

49. *New York Journal American*, 22 and 24 December 1939; *New York Times*, 22 December 1939. See also John Haag, "'Gone with the Wind' in Nazi Germany," *Georgia Historical Quarterly* 83 (Summer 1989): 278–304. *Gone with the Wind* "became an immediate best seller in the Third Reich." Adolf Hitler "greatly admired the film version. . . ."

50. *Daily Worker*, 24 December 1939, 15 and 7 January 1940, 27 December 1939.

51. *New York Age*, 6 January 1940; *Daily Worker*, 3 March and 25 April 1940.

52. *Daily Worker*, 2 January 1938.

53. Loren Miller, "Harlem Without Makeup," *New Masses* 11 (13 August 1935): 11–14.

54. Greene, "Harlem in the Great Depression," 66, 57, 6, 101, 108.

55. Grover Whalen, *Mr. New York: The Autobiography of Grover Whalen* (New York: Putnam, 1955), 150, 151, 153. Whalen's credibility is also suspect when he accuses the party—without evidence—of killing and raping.

56. *New York Post*, 21 March 1935; *New York Times*, 21 March 1935; *New York World-Telegram*, 21 March 1935; Greene, "Harlem in the Great Depression," 491, 504, 508; *The Complete Report of Mayor La Guardia's Commission on the Harlem Riot of March 19, 1935* (New York: Arno Press, 1969).

57. *Daily Worker*, 19 March 1936.

58. Ibid.

59. Ibid., 1 April, 6 May, and 25 March 1936. Examples of the Harlem organizing spirit abound. See, for example, the *Daily Worker* headline for 23 October 1936: "Police club Negro Women Picketing." The women were injured at Harlem Hospital while protesting the death of thirty-nine babies; a crowd of three thousand gathered spontaneously. Other examples are: *Daily Worker*, 15 and 16 January 1937; press release, 18 January 1937, Box 1, 1937, CNA Papers (Davis and Adam Clayton Powell were successful in getting the death penalty commuted to life for three Harlem

youths); Davis interview with Judge Jane Bolin, 14 August 1939, Box 1, 1939, CNA Papers. Davis also assailed the "get the Negro" campaigns initiated in the wake of these cases and the fact that "the Harlem community has long been overstaffed by policemen who provoke disturbances by frequent brutalities" (*Daily Worker*, 2 January 1938). See also Gary Jerome Hunter, "'Don't Buy from Where You Can't Work': Black Urban Boycott Movements During the Depression, 1929–1941" (Ph.D. diss., University of Michigan, 1977). The *Daily Worker* of 30 December 1936 descibed how after a flu epidemic swept through tenements of Harlem Davis conducted a "house-to-house tour." What he found at Harlem Hospital was frightening: "The pneumonia department . . . uses a serum in the treatment of Negro pneumonia patients, in order to 'test out' its effects. . . . A needle is stuck through the chest of the patient to puncture the lung for a 'lung specimen.' The treatment is not used in any other hospital in the city."

60. *Daily Worker*, 19 January, 11 February, and 1 April 1936. But note that in a review of John Hoshor's *God in a Rolls-Royce: The Rise of Father Divine—Madman, Menace or Messiah?* (New York: Hillman-Curl, 1936), though attacking the author's "slanders against the Negro people" and generally backing Divine, Davis tends to diverge from his earlier broad approach: "The Communist Party took a firm stand with others on the United Front May Day Parade Committee last May in barring the Divine movement from the parade because of its anti-working class labor union position" (*Daily Worker*, 15 September 1936); See also Jill Watts, *God, Harlem USA; The Father Divine Story* (Berkeley and Los Angeles: University of California Press, 1992).

61. *Daily Worker*, 18 January 1937, 3 January 1936, 2 and 3 February 1938, 3 December and 5 November 1936.

62. Ibid., 19 and 27 March 1937.

63. Ibid., 17 October 1937, 7 August 1938. A frequent theme of Davis here and elsewhere was how the black struggle was essential to the overall democratization of the nation (*Daily Worker*, 22 November 1939, 24 March 1937).

64. Herbert Philbrick and James D. Bales, *Communism and Race in America* (Searcy, Ark.: Bales Bookstore, 1965), 15, copy in Louis Budenz Papers, Providence College Library, Providence, R.I.

65. Bernard and Jewel Bellush, "A Radical Response to the Roosevelt Presidency: The Communist Party (1933–1945)," *Presidential Studies Quarterly* 10 (1980): 645. See also Eric Foner, *Nothing but Freedom: Emancipation and Its Legacy* (Baton Rouge: Louisiana State University Press, 1983); Jane Degras, ed., *The Communist International, 1919–1943, Documents* (London: Frank Cass, 1971). Cf. Allison Blakely, *Russia and the Negro: Blacks in Russian History and Thought* (Washington, D.C.: Howard University Press, 1986), 160: "There is evidence that there was an especially intensive Soviet campaign in the 1920's to establish strong cultural ties between the Soviet Union and Negro America. . . . It was such efforts which convinced McKay, Robeson, Rudd and other Negro artists to visit the Soviet Union." Blacks were no doubt impressed with the militant line of the party, which contrasted sharply with their recent experience with the Dixiecrat-influenced Democrats and the lily-white Republicans. See also Earl Browder, "For National Liberation of the Negroes! War Against White Chauvinism," *Communist* 11 (April 1932): 297, 303: "It is impossible for the Communist Party to lead the struggle for Negro liberation unless it begins by burning out [of] its own ranks every manifestation and trace of the influence of white chauvinism . . . everything that touches upon the Negro question is for our Party a question of fundamental principle importance, a matter of life and death." But symptomatic of the apparent tension between self-determination and equal rights or integration is the fact that Browder carped at the idea of a "Negro Federation" within the party, mirroring some of the language federations.

66. Sam Darcy, interview, Series I, 1977, Oral History of the American Left.

67. Sam Darcy, interview by Ron Filipelli, 23 March 1971, Box 3, Folder 32, Sam Darcy Papers, New York University Library, New York, N.Y.

68. Philip S. Foner and James Allen, eds., *American Communism and Black Americans: A Documentary History, 1919–1929* (Philadelphia: Temple University Press, 1987), 180, 190; see also Haywood, *Black Bolshevik*, 218–80 and [Brooklyn] *City Sun*, 4–10 May 1988. The latter recounts contemporary struggles reflecting the notion of black self-determination. The effort in Boston to establish a town called Mandela, and attempts from the 1960s to ignite Black Power, as well as the legacy of Malcolm X, also reflect this trend.

69. Margaret Wilhemina Jackson, "Evolution of the Communist Party's Position on the American Negro Question" (master's thesis, Howard University, 1938); Sam Darcy manuscript, Box 3, Folder 34, Sam Darcy Papers; Hyman Kublin, *Asian Revolutionary: The Life of Sen Katayama* (Princeton: Princeton University Press, 1964), 319.

70. James Ford, *The Negroes in a Soviet America*, William Patterson Papers. Also indicative of the international influence is the fact that Ford cites the experience of Finland, which seceded from Soviet Russia, as an analogue. Many Communists were also struck by the experience of the Jewish Autonomous Region in the USSR; cf. also Tom Johnson's pamphlet *The Reds in Dixie: Who Are the Communists and What Do They Fight for in the South?* Reel 15, Series 6, P293, ca. 1935, Earl Browder Papers, Syracuse University Library, Syracuse, N.Y. This strongly antiracist pamphlet reflects party views of the era insofar as it stresses the class dimension of racism, or how it splits the working class and drags down wage levels. He denies the allegation that the party "demands" that blacks marry whites and vice versa, but he notes that white males sleep with black women, "nor is it unknown for white women to sleep with Negro men. It's done under cover that's all." The Black Belt thesis, he says, "does not mean we want to establish some sort of Jim Crow state." Ultimately the Black Belt should be "a federated part of the Soviet U.S." See also *The Road to Liberation for the Negro People* (New York: Workers' Library, 1937), available in the Communist Party Archives. This piece includes selections by Davis, Ford, Patterson, Herndon, Haywood, Louise Thompson, Henry Winston, and others. U.S. elites were probably not pleased with the international reach of black Communists; indeed, their impact on the gathering anticolonial struggle of their brethren in Africa is a little-explored subject. Cf. James Ford, *Imperialism Destroys the People of Africa*, pamphlet, ca. 1931, and *The Negro Worker*, ca. 1933, Box 79, National Republic Papers, Hoover Institute, Stanford University, Palo Alto, Calif. George Padmore (also known as Malcolm Nurse) of Trinidad was editor-in-chief of *The Negro Worker*, a journal; contributing editors included Ford, Cyril Briggs, Jomo Kenyatta, and Raoul Marquez of Angola. Similarly, it is ironic to note how anti-Communism in the United States also tended to have an international provenance. Cf. Joseph Goebbels, *Bolshevism in Theory and Practice* (Berlin: Müller, 1936) and, for example, *Time* magazine, 24 December 1934. Many of the items in box 79 of the National Republic Papers reflect a profound fear that aggrieved blacks will veer sharply left.

71. W. A. Domingo, interview, Box 21, Folder 3, Theodore Draper Papers, Emory University Library, Atlanta, Ga. The interviews of Draper and his emissaries did not always go well. Richard Moore was reluctant to talk, though it was 1958 and his close ties with the party had receded. The emissary refers to him as a "liar," perhaps because he did not echo the anti-Communist line. See Box 21, Folder 3. The African Blood Brotherhood had a membership of almost five thousand in the 1919–27 period. They significantly influenced Garvey's movement; for example, the national

anthem of the Universal Negro Improvement Association was written by the ABB. In 1925 the ABB forces en masse left the UNIA for the Communist party. Its influence and perhaps the West Indian backgrounds of many members is a more useful way to analyze the evolution of the Black Belt thesis than to consider only the simplistic incantation of Moscow. See the history entitled "African Blood Brotherhood," ca. 1972, Box 13, William Patterson Papers. These kinds of connections have been seen by Mark Solomon as well in a persuasive dissertation, "Red and Black: Negroes and Communism, 1929–1932" (Harvard University, 1972). See also Robert Hill, ed., *The Crusader*, 6 vols. (New York: Garland, 1987); Jeffrey Babcock Perry, "Hubert Henry Harrison, 'The Father of Harlem Radicalism': The Early Years—1883 through the Founding of the Liberty League and 'The Voice,' in 1917" (Ph.D. diss., Columbia University, 1986).

72. Abner Berry, interview, 2 December 1977, Series I, Oral History of the American Left; *Daily Worker*, 4 October 1936.

73. *The Liberator*, 1 June 1932.

74. *Daily Worker*, 30 October 1936; "Report on Negro Work," May 1938, Box 12, Robert Minor Papers; *Daily Worker*, 2 August 1938.

75. Claude Lightfoot, interview, "Seeing Red," Series IV, Oral History of the American Left.

76. Israel Amter, autobiographical Sketch, Israel Amter Papers, Tamiment Library, New York University, New York, N.Y., 93.

77. Edwin Lewinson, *Black Politics in New York City* (New York: Twayne, 1974), 60; *Negro Liberator*, 4 August 1934.

78. *Daily Worker*, 19 October 1936.

79. Frank O'Brien, "Harlem Shows the Way," *New Masses* 20 (18 August 1936): 17–18.

80. *Daily Worker*, 14 June 1940.

81. Healey, *Dorothy Healey Remembers*, 330.

82. James Robert Prickett, "Communists and the Communist Issue in the American Labor Movement, 1920–1950" (Ph.D. diss., University of California, Los Angeles, 1975), 456. Prickett makes other points that are analogous to the Red experience in the Black Liberation movement: " . . . those union leaders who were called Communists by the CIO leadership (some were Communists, but most were not) were considerably more democratic than their anti-Communist counterparts . . . the victory of the anti-Communists led to a decline in union militancy in all of the unions examined . . . " (x). He adds, " . . . there is not a one-to-one relationship between the decisions or general line of the Communist International, and the policies of the American party . . . " (28).

83. Abner Berry, interview, 5 July 1977, Series I, Oral History of the American Left.

84. *Daily Worker*, 4 July 1938, 19 August 1937.

85. *Daily Worker*, 12 and 13 February and 11 January 1938. Mark Tushnet, "The Politics of Equality in Constitutional Law: The Equal Protection Clause, Dr. Du Bois and Charles Hamilton Houston," *Journal of American History* 74 (December 1987): 895: "[Du Bois's] position can be understood as a defense of political equality coupled with a denial that integration constitutes the sole acceptable form of social equality". *Daily Worker*, 24 November 1937: here Davis wrote that James Allen's focus in his book *Reconstruction* on the black thirst for land gave "real meat to the . . . slogan for self-determination"; see also *Daily Worker*, 10 November 1940. Cf. also Gabriel Almond, *The Appeals of Communism* (Princeton: Princeton University Press, 1954).

86. *Daily Worker*, 30 June 1939. Davis described the 450 delegates as "largely

middle class and professional," but as he quoted one doctor saying, "'How can we have any practice unless Negro workers got purchasing power to pay us?'" Davis added, "The obvious weakness [here is] lack of labor representation."

87. *Daily Worker*, 16 December 1935. Adam Clayton Powell, Roy Wilkins and Charles Houston were also involved.

88. Ibid., 26 January 1936: the program of the NNC was quite advanced and included relief, jobs, aid to farmers, antilynch legislation, equality for women, and opposition to war and fascism. In the *Daily Worker* of 31 January 1936 Davis wrote that a "gavel made of [a] slave's rifle used in John Brown's uprising [was] to open session—another made of slave ship hulk to close convention." The NNC opened on Douglass's birthday (minutes of Negro Work Committee, Socialist party, 12 January 1936, New York, Box 23, Julian Steele Papers, Boston University Library, Boston, Mass.

89. William Hastie to Walter White and Charles Houston, 4 February 1936, William Hastie Papers, Harvard Law School, Cambridge, Mass.

90. "The Official Proceedings of the National Negro Congress," 14–16 February 1936, Chicago, Box 1, Folder 1/15, W. Alphaeus Hunton Papers, Schomburg Library, New York, N.Y.; *Daily Worker*, 16 February 1936.

91. Dorothy Height, interview, February 1974–November 1976, Black Women's Oral History Project. Cf. also Gunnar Myrdal, *An American Dilemma*: "as late as 1939 and 1940 . . . the local councils of the National Negro Congress were the most important Negro organization in some western cities." Cited in Herbert Shapiro, *White Violence, Black Response: From Reconstruction to Montgomery* (Amherst: University of Massachusetts Press, 1989), 260.

92. *Daily Worker*, 17 March 1936.

93. Ibid., 13 and 16 March 1936; *Nation*, 11 March 1936.

94. *Daily Worker*, 13, 21, and 22 February and 16 June 1936. See Charles V. Hamilton, *Adam Clayton Powell, Jr.: The Political Biography of an American Dilemma* (New York: Atheneum, 1991).

95. *Daily Worker*, 23 September and 21 July 1938.

96. Ibid., 12 July 1937; press release, 19 July 1937, Box 1, CNA Papers; *Daily Worker*, 5 September, 28 November, and 19 December 1937. In this last article Davis cited the current ditty, "Workers, farmers, black and white, All can vote if they unite, The registrar won't dare say no, To AF of L & CIO, Gonna Register, gonna register."

97. *Daily Worker*, 30 January 1936.

98. Ibid., 4 and 5 October 1937.

99. Ibid., 23 May 1938, 27 April 1941.

100. Press release, 25 December 1936, Box 2, CNA Papers; *Daily Worker*, 16 December 1939 and 4 June 1940.

101. John H. Seabrook, "Black and White Unite: The Career of Frank R. Crosswaith" (Ph.D. diss., Rutgers University, 1980), 269. Seabrook's work points up the hysteria in Socialist ranks about Communist incursions and successes among blacks; many of their moves in this community were simply in response to Communist initiatives. These Socialists were also argumentative; Crosswaith and Randolph feuded for a significantly long time (Correspondence, Box 1, Frank Crosswaith Papers, Schomburg Library, New York, N.Y.).

102. Julian Steele to Max Yergan, 5 January 1935, Box 23, Julian Steele Papers; *Daily Worker*, 17 December 1936; undated flyer, Box 2, Frank Crosswaith Papers; *Daily Worker*, 17 July and 29 September 1936, 8 June 1937; annual program, Second National Negro Congress, Box 1, Ernest Thompson Papers, Schomburg Library, New York, N.Y.

103. Minutes of Meeting, 29 January 1937, Reel 1, Box 2, A31, Negro Labor

Committee Papers, Schomburg Library, New York, N.Y. Ben Davis et al. to Frank Crosswaith, 1 February 1937; George Blake to Crosswaith, 11 February 1937; Davis to Crosswaith, 29 March 1937, Reel 2, Box 4, B25, ibid.; minutes of meetings, 1938–1940, Reel 4, Box 8, B83, ibid.

104. John Davis to Alfred Baker Lewis, 26 July 1937; Julian Steele to John Davis, 20 June 1936; John Davis to Julian Steele, 28 December 1936, all Julian Steele Papers. Steele was a NNC vice-president and expert fundraiser.

105. Ben Davis, *James Ford: What He Is and What He Stands For*, September 1936, Reel 1761, #1656, Radical Pamphlet Literature, Tamiment Library, New York University.

106. *Daily Worker*, 5 June 1937.

107. Ibid., 7 June 1937.

108. Lester Granger to Alfred Baker Lewis, 17 July 1936, Reel 2, Box 13, B168, Negro Labor Committee Papers.

109. Julian Steele to Marie Young, 15 July 1940, Box 23, Julian Steele Papers.

110. William H. Harris, *Keeping the Faith: A. Philip Randolph, Milton P. Webster and the Brotherhood of Sleeping Car Porters, 1925–1937* (Urbana: University of Illinois Press, 1977); Paula F. Pfeffer, *A. Philip Randolph, Pioneer of the Civil Rights Movement* (Baton Rouge: Louisiana State University Press, 1990); C. L. Dellums to A. Philip Randolph, 1941–1973, Container 6, A. Philip Randolph Papers, Library of Congress, Washington, D.C.

111. *Daily Worker*, 30 April, 2 May, 1 and 7 May 1939, 28 April 1940; *New York Times*, 28 April 1940; *Daily Worker*, 30 April 1940.

112. Speech by A. Philip Randolph, undated, Reel 15, Box 32, G30, Negro Labor Committee Papers.

113. Claude Lightfoot, interview, "Seeing Red," Series IV, Oral History of the American Left.

114. Allan Merson, *Communist Resistance in Nazi Germany* (London: Lawrence and Wishart, 1985). An editorial in the 5 July 1941 issue of the *New York Times* argued that the party's alleged flip-flop on the war was discrediting; see also Larry Ceplair, *Under the Shadow of War: Fascism, Anti-Fascism and Marxists* (New York: Columbia University Press, 1987). The impact of the trials and purges and various crimes of Stalin are still being debated by the U.S. Left. See the exchange between Paul Robeson, Jr., and Alexander Cockburn in *Nation*, 7–14 August 1989; the party was not alone in its view of the pact. See also Martin Duberman, *Paul Robeson* (New York: Knopf, 1988), 226: "Between 1936 and the 1939 signing of the Nazi-Soviet pact, criticism of the Soviet Union was rarely heard in Harlem intellectual circles."

115. *Daily Worker*, 22 June 1940.

116. Ibid., 23 June and 29 April 1940.

117. Justus D. Doenecke, "Non-Intervention of the Left: The Keep America Out of the War Congress, 1938–1941," *Journal of Contemporary History* 12 (1977): 221–36; flyer of Greater New York Committee to Keep America out of War, ca. 1938, Reel 3, Box 6, B56, Negro Labor Committee Papers; *Daily Worker*, 19 June 1940; Byron Richard Skinner, "The Double 'V': The Impact of World War II on Black America" (Ph.D. diss., University of California, Berkeley, 1978), 14–15; Gerald Robert Gill, "Afro-American Opposition to the United States' Wars of the Twentieth Century: Dissent, Discontent and Disinterest" (Ph.D. diss., Howard University, 1985).

118. *Daily Worker*, 28 November and 12 December 1936, 4 April 1938; Joseph P. Lash, *Dealers and Dreamers: A New Look at the New Deal* (New York: Doubleday, 1988), 444.

119. *Daily Worker*, 31 August, 5 and 12 September 1939; press release, 17

September 1939, Box 2, 1939, CNA Papers; *Daily Worker*, 19 September, 26 October, and 5 November 1939.

120. *Daily Worker*, 20 July 1940 and 4 February 1941.

121. Skinner, "The Double 'V,'" 89; Communist pamphlet, "Is Japan the Champion of the Colored Races?" Box 79, National Republic Papers.

122. Patrick Washburn, *A Question of Sedition: The Federal Government's Investigation of the Black Press During World War II* (New York: Oxford University Press, 1986); *Daily Worker*, 1 July 1939, 24 October 1937, 17 April 1938.

123. *Daily Worker*, 27 February 1938, 24 January 1939, 31 October 1937, 29 January 1939. William Scott, *The Sons of Sheba's Race: African-Americans and the Italo-Ethiopian War, 1935–1941* (Bloomington: Indian University Press, 1992).

124. Ibid., 18 December, 3 April, and 14 March 1938.

125. Ibid., 26 November, 20 November, and 6 September 1937; *Negro Liberator*, 2 September 1935; *Daily Worker*, 20 May 1936, 11 June and 26 February 1937.

126. *Daily Worker*, 21, 23, and 22 June 1940. Interestingly, Charles Houston was subject to praise from the Communists because of his actions at the predominantly black National Bar Association meeting in Harlem in 1939, which took place as the Stalin-Hitler pact was being negotiated. A resolution equating Communism and fascism was "sent back into committee" by a 3–1 margin, illustrating that this pact may not have caused as much controversy among an African-American community whose leading sons and daughters were Communists than in other communities. Houston declared, "I don't think Communism and fascism stand on the same basis. And I won't go on record in favor of something which I am honestly opposed to. I cannot vote for this resolution which is not at all in conformity with the truth." Also present at this gathering were Sadie Alexander, William Hastie, Sidney Redmond, and Charles Toney: *Daily Worker*, 18 August 1939.

127. *Daily Worker*, 24 June, 11 October, 27 April, and 3 September 1940.

128. Ibid., 3 April 1940, 15 January 1941; *New York Amsterdam Star News*, 20 January 1940.

129. *Daily Worker*, 5 June 1941 and 3 December 1940. In the *DW* of 8 June 1940 Davis wrote, "[a black man doesn't] intend to smother himself to death in a tank or in a submarine, to save Wall Street's anti-Negro system." In a Davis article dated 19 February 1940 (Box 2, 1940, CNA Papers) he attacked the Mississippi legislature for providing separate textbooks for black and white children. Some speak of democracy in Finland, but what of democracy in Mississippi, he charged.

130. An examination of Davis's views of FDR is revealing. In the *Daily Worker* of 30 October 1936 he hit the president hard. In the *DW* for 13 March 1938 he rejected the GOP notion that "the anti-lynching bill was killed by the New Deal Administration. . . . This is the most shameless political trickery. . . ." A few days later he was more explicit, hailing the "outstanding contribution of FDR in [the] fight against lynching." See also *Daily Worker*, 27 March and 30 July 1938. Of course, Davis's reaction to FDR fluctuated to an extent because the president himself was not consistent; however, part of this oscillation may be an early expression of "Browderism." See *Daily Worker*, 26 February, 10 and 17 April, 23 June, and 28 July 1940. On 21 October 1940 the *DW*'s slogan was "no first term for Wilkie—no third term for Roosevelt." But in the 29 October issue Davis was quoted as saying "under the great leadership of [FDR] the status of Negroes as citizens [has] been raised higher than at any time since the Civil War." See also Sheldon Bernard Avery, "Up from Washington: William Pickens and the Negro Struggle for Equality, 1900–1954" (Ph.D. diss., University of Oregon, 1970), 228, later published by the University of Delaware Press (1989).

131. *Daily Worker*, 11 May 1941, 3 November and 27 December 1940.

Chapter 5. Squeeze Play, 1940-1942

1. *Daily Worker*, 5 and 6 March 1940; *New York Times*, 6 March 1940; *Amsterdam News*, 9 March 1940; U.S. Congress, House, Committee on the Judiciary, *Hearing Before a Subcommittee on H.R. 801, an Act to Assure Persons Within the Jurisdiction of Every State Due Process of Law and Equal Protection of the Laws, and to Prevent the Crime of Lynching*, 76th Cong., 3d sess., 1940.
2. *Daily Worker*, 6 March 1940.
3. *New Jersey Herald News*, 16 March 1940.
4. Ibid.
5. *Daily Worker*, 12 April 1940 and 22 March 1940.
6. Ibid., 7 March 1940.
7. Ibid., 8 March 1940.
8. Ibid., 7 March 1940.
9. Release, 8 April 1940, Box 2, 1940, CNA Papers; *Daily Worker*, 17 and 10 March 1940.
10. Pat Toohey, "Greater Attention to the Problems of the Negro Masses!" *Communist* 19 (March 1940): 287. This was the text of a speech delivered at the meeting of the National Committee of the Communist party on 19 February 1940.
11. *Daily Worker*, 27 September 1940.
12. *New York Times*, 1 August 1940; *Daily Worker*, 18 September 1940. A number of *Daily Worker* articles show Davis's increasing involvement in the party's activities. For example, on 16 September 1941 Davis joined Ford and Robert Minor at a Harlem conference of two hundred black and white Communists. On 18 December 1941 Davis, along with Gil Green, Ford, and Abner Berry, spoke to a one-thousand-strong audience at Harlem's Renaissance Casino. Davis also was to address the 21 December 1941 Lenin Memorial Meeting at Madison Square Garden.
See *The Daily Worker* for 25-26 June 1941: in light of later charges, it is striking that Davis cited favorably the call of Roscoe Dunjee (an editor of the *Oklahoma Black Dispatch*) at the NAACP convention for continued attacks on Jim Crow despite the onset of war; see also the *Daily Worker* for 27-29 June 1941.
13. *Daily Worker*, 12 March, 20 June, 1 October, 20 November 1940; *New York Amsterdam News*, 31 May 1941; *Daily Worker*, 27 May, 21 June, and 4 July 1941.
14. *Daily Worker*, 27 July 1941.
15. Ibid., 16 September 1941.
16. Ibid., 24 October 1941; *Daily Worker*, 21 December 1941; *Daily Worker*, 28 November 1941; *Daily Worker*, 4 October 1941; *Daily Worker*, 13 December 1941.
17. Ibid., 24 October 1937.
18. Ibid., 2 November 1941; *Afro-American*, 20 December 1941; "Japanese Racial Agitation Among Negroes," 15 April 1942, G-2, Record Group 107, File 291.2, National Archives, Washington, D.C.; memorandum by Jonathan Daniels, ca. 1942, OF 4245-g, Franklin Delano Roosevelt Papers, Franklin D. Roosevelt Library, Hyde Park, New York, hereafter cited as FDR Papers; Kenneth O'Reilly, "The Roosevelt Administration and Black America: Federal Surveillance Policy and Civil Rights During the New Deal and World War II Years," *Phylon* 48 (March 1987): 20.
19. Washburn, *A Question of Sedition*, 33, 100, 175.
20. *Chicago Defender*, 18 March 1944; *Pittsburgh Courier*, 6 November 1943; *Afro-American*, 11 October 1941; cf. also John Dower, *War Without Mercy: Race and Power in the Pacific War* (New York: Pantheon, 1986), who quotes a frequently reported war anecdote with an old black sharecropper telling his white boss, "By the

way, Captain, I hear the Japs [sic] done declared war on you white folks." Concessions had to be granted to blacks, not only to spur them to fight but also to win them from the Left (176).

21. *New York World-Telegram*, 28 April 1942 and 15 and 17 November 1943.

22. *Daily Worker*, 17, 18, 21, and 31 May 1942.

23. Lee Finkle, *Forum for Protest: The Black Press During World War II* (Madison, N.J.: Fairleigh Dickinson University Press, 1975); *Daily Worker*, 14 February 1939; Detweiler, *The Negro Press in the United States*.

24. Ben Davis to Claude Barnett, 19 March 1942, Claude Barnett Papers, Chicago Historical Society, Chicago; Claude Barnett to Ben Davis, 26 March 1942, ibid.; *Daily Worker*, 6 June and 23 July 1942.

25. *New York Times*, 5 and 8 September 1942; *Daily Worker*, 1 June 1942; *New York Age*, 31 and 24 October 1942; *Daily Worker*, 31 and 23 October 1942. Of interest is George Sirgionvanni, *An Undercurrent of Suspicion: Anti-Communism in America During World War II* (New Brunswick, N.J.: Transaction, 1990).

26. *Daily Worker*, 25 August and 18 September 1942.

27. Ibid., 18 October 1942.

28. Ibid., 18, 15, and 16 October, 1942.

29. Ibid., 20 September 1942. Davis was quoted in *New Masses*, 20 October 1942: "Among the win-the-war necessities on the homefront are the breaking down of age-old injustices against the Negro people". The following *DW* citations show the breadth of Davis's Campaign: 14 and 20 September, 1, 7, 10, 13, 29, 30 October, and 2 November 1942.

30. *Daily Worker*, 3 November 1942. The *Daily Worker* for 17 October 1942 reported that Davis was to appear at five "indoor and outdoor rallies" in the Bronx in one evening.

31. Ibid., 21 and 26 October 1942.

32. Ibid., 23, 24, 28 October 1942; *New York Times*, 7 September 1942; *Daily Worker*, 4, 22, 26 September 1942.

33. J. Edgar Hoover, "General Intelligence Survey in the United States," Federal Bureau of Investigation, March 1942, OF 10B, #2076, FDR.

34. *Daily Worker*, 27, 29, and 6 September, 25 August, 30 and 21 September 1942.

35. In the *Daily Worker* of 14 October 1942 Davis stated: "There is no difference between the crimes of Berlin Hitler . . . and the crime of these Mississippi Hitlers." See also *Daily Worker*, 12, 14, 15, 16, 28 July and 8 May 1942; *New York Age*, 11 July 1942; *Daily Worker*, 20 December 1942; Ben Davis, 13 Million Negro Americans for Victory (pamphlet), 1 October 1942, Ben Davis Vertical File—Schomburg Center; *Daily Worker*, 8 July, 18 January, 13 December, and 8 February 1942. Cf. Mabel Staupers, *No Time for Prejudice: A Study of the Integration of Negroes in Nursing in the United States* (New York: Macmillan Co., 1961); Charity Adams Earley, *One Woman's Army: A Black Officer Remembers the WAC* (College Station: Texas A&M University Press, 1989); Mirjana Roth, "'If You Give Us Rights We Will Fight': Black Involvement in the Second World War," *South African Historical Journal* 15 (November 1983):85–104. There are obvious parallels between the anti-segregation concessions granted in South Africa during the war and what happened in the United States.

36. *Daily Worker*, 6, 21, 8, 9, 10, 14 October, 17 and 24 December 1942.

37. Ibid., 21 June, 25 April, 17 May, 24 and 16 June 1942.

38. Ibid., 22 February, 27 December, and 24, 25 September 1942.

39. James Egert Allen to Layle Lane, 25 September 1942, Box 1, Folder 1/5, Layle Lane Papers, Schomburg Center, New York, N.Y. Alfred Baker Lewis contri-

buted to her campaign and Oswald Garrison Villard served as honorary chairperson of the election committee. *Daily Worker*, 4 November 1942.

40. *Daily Worker*, 19, 29, 25, 31 August, 3 December, 1 September, 14 October, and 3 November 1942.

41. A. Philip Randolph to Howard O. Hunter, 28 April 1941, Box 1, Folder MG77, Gwen Bennett Papers, Schomburg Library, New York, N.Y.; Lester Granger to Howard O. Hunter, 23 April 1941, ibid. Bennett, director of the progressive George Washington Carver School, was a graduate of Columbia, a poet and painter, and studied in Paris. She had taught at Howard University. See *People's Voice*, 23 September 1944.

42. *Daily Worker*, 14, 16 June 1942; Ben Davis to A. Philip Randolph, 12 June 1942, Container 9, Brotherhood of Sleeping Car Porter Papers, Library of Congress, Washington, D.C.

43. *Daily Worker*, 18 June 1942. According to John Dower in his striking book *War Without Mercy*, "The highlight of the evening was a skit in which a black man who had just been drafted had the following lines: 'I want you to know I ain't afraid. I don't mind fighting. I'll fight Hitler, Mussolini and the Japs [sic] at the same time, but I'm telling you I'll give those crackers down South the same damn medicine.' There was, it was reported, 'bedlam' when these words were spoken, and the audience called for the actor to repeat them" (177). Given the hostility to fascism expressed in the skit, it may be that Davis's concern was sparked not so much by this particular skit but what he knew cumulatively about the war records of Randolph, the Socialists, and others.

44. Benjamin McLaurin to A. Philip Randolph, 11 May 1942, Container 7, A. Philip Randolph Papers, Library of Congress, Washington, D.C.

45. Bernard Nalty, *Strength for the Fight: A History of Black Americans in the Military* (New York: Free Press, 1986), 140.

46. Gill, "Afro-American Opposition to the United States' Wars of the Twentieth Century," 205–6; *Amsterdam News*, 4 April 1942; *Communists in the Struggle for Negro Rights*, Reel 1768, #2333, Tamiment Radical Pamphlet Series, Tamiment Library, New York University; text of Speech of A. Philip Randolph at Madison Square Garden, ca. June 1942, Reel 4, Box 7, B70, Negro Labor Committee Papers; press release, 16 September 1943, Reel 5, Box 11, B128, Negro Labor Committee Papers; Davis, *James Ford: What He Is and What He Stands For*, Tamiment Institute. Cf. also Herbert Garfinkel, *When Negroes March: MOWM in the Organizational Politics for FEPC* (Glencoe, Ill.: Free Press, 1959); Louis Ruchames, *Race, Jobs and Politics: The Story of FEPC* (New York: Columbia University Press, 1953); A. Philip Randolph to C. B. Powell, ca. 1942, Reel 10, Box 20, D29, Negro Labor Committee Papers; FBI memorandum, 16 February 1942, OF10B, #1160, FDR Papers.

Chapter 6. A Turning Point in U.S. History, 1943

1. "The Tasks of the Communist Sections Regarding Municipal Policy-Resolution of the Enlarged Presidium of the ECCI," *The Communist* 11 (February 1930):281– 88. See also V. I. Lenin, "Should Communists Participate in Bourgeois Parliaments?" *The Communist* 11 (March 1932):688–96; Richard Judd, *Socialist Cities: Municipal Politics and the Grass Roots of American Socialism* (Albany: State University of New York Press, 1989); Martin Alexander and Helen Graham, eds.,

The French and Spanish Popular Fronts: Comparative Perspectives (New York: Cambridge University Press, 1989); Helmut Gruber, *Red Vienna: Experiment in Working Class Culture, 1919–1934* (New York: Oxford University Press, 1991).

2. Pete Cacchione, Manuscript, Pete Cacchione Papers, Tamiment Institute, New York University Library, New York, N.Y. 52.

3. John Earl Haynes, "The New History of the Communist Party in State Politics: The Implications for Mainstream Political History," *Labor History* 27, no. 4 (1986):549; Joseph Starobin, *American Communism in Crisis, 1943–1957* (Cambridge: Harvard University Press, 1972), 35.

4. Si Gerson, "Electoral Coalition Problems in New York," *Political Affairs* 26 (October 1947): 894–901.

5. *Daily Worker*, 9 November 1933; Israel Amter, "Significance of the Coming Municipal Elections in New York," *The Communist* 16 (July 1937): 647–60; *Daily Worker*, 18 October, 1, 29, 30, 3 November 1937. After the opening of World War II, Alex Rose and David Dubinsky attempted to split the American Labor Party. See *Daily Worker*, 12 October 1939 and 20 May 1938.

6. Cacchione manuscript, 90, 109, 118; Literature, ca, 1943, Box 5, Reel 2, Pete Cacchione Papers; *New York Age*, 17 April 1943; *Daily Worker*, 27, 28, 30 October 1940.

7. Foner and Allen, *Communism and Black Americans*; *Daily Worker*, 22 June, 9 May, and 2 July 1936.

8. John Walter, *The Harlem Fox: J. Raymond Jones and Tammany, 1920–1970*. (Albany: State University of New York Press, 1989).

9. *Daily Worker*, 10 August 1936.

10. Ibid., 21 September 1937; see also James Ford and George Blake, "Building the People's Front in Harlem," *The Communist* 17 (February 1938):158–68.

11. Walter, *The Harlem Fox*, 74–75.

12. *Daily Worker*, 12 April and 1 June 1939; Bill Lawrence and Isidore Begun, "The New York City Elections and the Struggle Against Hitlerism," *The Communist* 20 (December 1941): 1065, 1068. Cf. also Ernest Cuneo, *Life with Fiorello: A Memoir* (New York: Macmillan Co., 1955; Arthur Mann, *La Guardia: A Fighter Against His Times, 1882–1933* (New York: Lippincott, 1959); William Manners, *Patience and Fortitude: Fiorello La Guardia* (New York: Harcourt Brace, 1976); Lawrence Elliott, *Little Flower: The Life and Times of Fiorello La Guardia* (New York: Morrow, 1983); Alan Schaffer, *Vito Marcantonio: Radical in Congress* (Syracuse: Syracuse University Press, 1966); Vito Marcantonio, *I Vote My Conscience: Debates, Speeches, and Writings, 1935–1950* (New York: Vito Marcantonio Memorial, 1956); Gerald Meyer, "Vito Marcantonio: A Successful New York City Radical Politician," Ph.D. diss., City University of New York, 1983; Terry Ruderman, "Stanley M. Isaacs: The Conscience of New York," Ph.D. diss., City University of New York, 1977; Julian Jaffe, *Crusade Against Radicalism: New York During the Red Scare, 1914–1924* (Port Washington, N.Y.: Kennikat, 1972: five Socialists were expelled from the New York State Legislature in 1920; Houston Irvine Flournoy, "The Liberal Party in New York State," Ph.D. diss., Princeton University, 1956; Robert Frederick Carter, "Pressure from the Left: The American Labor Party, 1936–1954," Ph.D. diss., Syracuse University, 1965; John Haynes, ed., *Communism and Anti-Communism in the U.S.* (New York: Garland, 1987).

13. *Daily Worker*, 5 November 1942; Paul Robeson, Jr., interview with author, 11 August 1988, New York City. Robeson also concluded that Davis was in the wrong post as a party leader but should have sought to be a "mass leader."

14. *Daily Worker*, 29 April 1936; Ben Davis, Jr., "The Negro People in the Elections," *The Communist* 15 (October 1936): 975–87.

15. *Daily Worker*, 18, 22 September and 31 December 1936; 28, 1, 23, 29 October 1937.

16. Ibid., 25 March, 9 October 1938, 5 July 1939, 20 July 1940; "Minutes of Meeting to Organize Sub-Committee to Work Among the Negro People in Connection with the Election Campaign," 15 July 1940, Box 12, Robert Minor Papers.

17. Dennis M. Anderson, "Proportional Representation Elections of Toledo City Councils, 1934–1949," *Northwest Ohio Quarterly* 59 (Autumn 1987): 153–77. See also Maurice Isserman, *Which Side Were You On?* (Middletown, Conn.: Wesleyan University Press, 1983). George H. Hallett, Jr., in "Brooklyn's Stake in the PR Ballot" (Box 1, Genevieve Earle Papers, Municipal Archives, New York, N.Y.) writes that under PR, the voter put *1* by one's first choice for the office, *2* by second choice, and so on. Yonkers also had PR; see Literature, Box 7, Reel 3, Pete Cacchione Papers, for much on PR. Cf. also Enid Laberman, "The Case for Proportional Representation," in *Choosing an Electoral System: Issues and Alternatives* ed. Arend Lijphart and Bernard Grofman (New York: Praeger, 1984): 41–51.

18. Frederick Shaw, *The History of the New York City Legislature* (New York: AMS Press, 1968), 238.

19. *Hamilton v. Brennan*, 203 Misc. 536, 119 NYS 2d 8 (Sup. Ct. 1953); *Daily Worker*, 10 November 1952, 12 November 1953.

20. Davis memoir, 26.

21. Report by Pete Cacchione on upcoming 1943 elections, ca. 1943, Reel 2, Box 5, Pete Cacchione Papers. Cacchione received positive publicity in the black press, which preordained that the same would hold true for Davis: see *New York Age*, 26 June 1943. see also Howard Fast, "Ben Davis Walks on Freedom Road," ca. 1943, Box 5, Robert Minor Papers.

22. Report by Pete Cacchione on upcoming 1943 elections.

23. *Daily Worker*, 7 February, 28 June, 4 July, 1 April 1943; "How Ben Davis Helped Save a Doomed Negro Soldier," ca. 1943, Ben Davis Vertical File—Schomburg Center; *Daily Worker*, 14 March 1943.

24. Ben Davis, *The Negro People and the Communist Party* (pamphlet), ca. 1943, Communist Party Archives.

25. *People's Voice*, 3 July 1943; *Daily Worker*, 8, 3, 5, 11 August 1943.

26. *New York Times*, 28 March 1943; *Daily Worker*, 23, 26, 29, 30 August and 16 September 1942, 28 March and 2 April 1943; *People's Voice*, 3 April 1943; *Daily Worker*, 11, 18, 25 April, 18 June, 29 April, 16 March, 21 April, 26 June, 1 November, and 24 January 1943.

27. *Daily Worker*, 4, 22, 1 February, 17, 26 March, 23 June, and 17 July 1943.

28. Ibid., 18 March 1942; Franklin D. Roosevelt to Michael Kennedy, 1 January 1943, Box 2, Reel 4203, Elizabeth Gurley Flynn Papers, New York University Library, New York; memorandum, 25 February 1943, Box 2, MG77, Gwen Bennett Papers; *Daily Worker*, 6 January, 21 February, and 20 April 1943.

29. *New York Age*, 4 September 1943; pamphlet on Carl Brodsky, ca. 1943, Box 4, Robert Minor Papers; *Daily Worker*, 4 September 1943.

30. Adam Clayton Powell to Herbert Bruce, 21 August 1943, Box 2, Herbert Bruce Papers, Schomburg Library, New York, N.Y.; Davis memoir, 9/699.

31. Quoted in *Daily Worker*, 13 September 1943.

32. Marvel Cooke, interview with author, 6 April 1988.

33. *Daily Worker*, 30 October 1941; *People's Voice*, 31 October 1942.

34. Davis memoir, 31.

35. Adam Clayton Powell, *Adam by Adam: The Autobiography of Adam Clayton Powell* (New York: Dial, 1971), 67. Powell cites proudly his 1956 Veterans of Foreign Wars award granted because of his staunch fight against Communism.

36. Claude Lewis, *Adam Clayton Powell* (Greenwich, Conn.: Fawcett, 1963), 52; Neil Hickey and Ed Edwin, *Adam Clayton Powell and the Politics of Race* (New York: Fleet, 1965), 53, 108–9.

37. "Character of Case—Internal Security-C, Custodial Detention," 26 February 1943, 100–22864, Federal Bureau of Investigation, New York.

38. *Daily Worker*, 20 March 1938, 3 and 31 October 1943.

39. *New York Amsterdam News*, 30 and 16 October 1943; *Daily Worker*, 9 October 1943.

40. *Daily Worker*, 3 October 1943.

41. *Daily Worker*, 9 and 14 October 1943.

42. Ibid., 20 October 1943.

43. Davis memoir, 24/714.

44. *New York Amsterdam News*, 16 October 1943; Davis memoir, 24/714.

45. "Beaver-Ramapo Democrat," 25 July 1943, Box 2, Herbert Bruce Papers; Walter, *The Harlem Fox*, 162.

46. *Daily Worker*, 23 and 21 October 1943; see also ibid., 8 January, 27 and 28 October 1943; text of WQXR speech, 1 October 1942; article, 26 October 1942; "Call to Action," published by Lincoln-Douglas Club of the Communist Party, 30 October 1943, all in Ben Davis Vertical File—Schomburg Center; there was also something of a nationalist appeal by Davis's campaign. One flyer suggested, "Register to Elect a Negro to the City Council" (undated flyer, Ben Davis Vertical File). Cf. also Davis's comment in another flyer, "The Story of Ben Davis, Jr.," ca. 1943, Communist Party Archives; *Daily Worker*, 30 October 1943.

47. *Daily Worker*, 25 September 1943; campaign stationery, 1943, Ben Davis Vertical File—Schomburg Center; clipping, ca. 1943, Reel 15, Box 31, G13, Negro Labor Committee Papers; *Daily Worker*, 7 October 1943.

48. *Daily Worker*, 12 October 1943; *New York Age*, 30 October 1943.

49. Marvel Cooke, interview with author, 6 April 1988; *Daily Worker*, 19 October and 29 September 1943.

50. Flyer, 23 October 1943, Reel 2, Box 5, Pete Cacchione Papers; *Daily Worker*, 25, 26, 29 September 1943; Davis memoir, 26/716.

51. *Daily Worker*, 25 October 1943.

52. Frances Smith to Ben Davis, ca. 1955, Ben Davis Papers. In an interview on 9 August 1988, Audley Moore, his campaign manager, stated that a week before the election Davis had doubts about his ability to win. He wanted her to lower the price of the rally to twenty-five cents (Oral History of the American Left, Series I). The *New York Amsterdam News* for 30 October 1943 had a headline reading, "Double Victory Rally Backs Ben Davis, Jr.," but their editorial backed not Davis but John Ross.

53. Pamphlet on 1943 Campaign, ca. 1943, Ben Davis Vertical File—Schomburg Center; *Daily Worker*, 5 October 1943; *People's Voice*, 30 October 1943.

54. Ian Hall, interviewed on WLIB-AM—New York City, 23 March 1988. Phil Schaap, in a 5 June 1988 interview with the author placed the Parker concert on 26 September 1952 at Rockland Palace. (Schaap is a noted New York authority on jazz.) He pointed to Teddy Wilson as an influence on a number of musicians. In another interview with the author, on 2 March 1988, Howard "Stretch" Johnson went further and referred to Wilson as the "Marxist Mozart." He recalled Cy Oliver and Al Haig as also being sympathetic to the Left and Dizzy Gillespie as being "quite revolutionary" in outlook. See also W. C. Handy to Ben Davis, 1 February 1956, Ben Davis Papers; flyer, 2 January 1959, Ben Davis Papers; *Daily Worker*, 1 May 1941; *People's Voice*, 9 and 30 October 1943; *Daily Worker*, 22 November, 7 December, and 28 October 1943.

55. *Daily Worker*, 5 March 1941; *People's Voice*, 21 March 1942; program, 11

June 1943, Box 1, Folder 1/3, Wilhemina Adams Papers, Schomburg Center for Research in Black Culture, New York, N.Y.

Davis was quite critical of Frazier's work on the black family, claiming that it "falls short of reaching tenable scientific conclusions . . . does not go to the decisive economic roots. . . . The class structure within the Negro people is recognized but placed upon an incorrect and superficial color basis. The mulattos, contend the author, represents the upper class, the middle class . . . brown complexion, and the proletariat is black." *Daily Worker*, 23 November 1941.

56. Walker, *Richard Wright*, 155; Lloyd Brown, interview with author, 18 April 1988; Addison Gayle, *Richard Wright: Ordeal of a Native Son* (Garden City, N.Y.: Doubleday, 1980), 89:

Wright had been assigned to 'New Challenge' by the affable astute Benjamin J. Davis, one of the black titans of the Party. Davis was impressive. Standing well over six feet, he dwarfed most of his contemporaries in intellectual stature as well as height. He was less doctrinaire than the almost intractable Harry Haywood, more confident and assured than James Ford. "A party hack with a law degree," Wilson Record called him, but the descriptions nowhere befits the man. . . . His background as a journalist made him more charitable toward the young writer than other Communist leaders had been. The struggle against racism and oppression, he knew, was one requiring the unanimity of all, writers and workers alike. He had put his journalistic skills at the service of the Party. An intellectual, Davis had no disdain for intellectuals . . . he offered the young man a position as staff writer for the "Daily Worker." Wright at once felt a certain sense of ease with Davis that he had not experienced with other party bosses, black or white. Davis' solicitation of him as a writer was flattering. . . . "Go back to your writing," Davis ordered him . . . "and leave politics to the Party." . . . In his review of "Native Son" Davis chided the author for his mysticism, for not identifying clearly enough for the reader the negative forces acting against Bigger and the positive forces acting in his behalf. . . . Davis was different. He was an intellectual; he had lived in both worlds, that of the bourgeois blacks and that of the urban proletariat. He walked the streets of Harlem daily, was well known and respected among workers and bourgeois alike.

Gayle claims that after Davis ordered Wright to join the Office of War Information, the latter refused and quit the party (144, 120). Yet what is striking about this description by Gayle, an African-American writer, is how favorable it is to Davis and how it contrasts sharply with more negative assessments penned by Euro-American writers. *Daily Worker*, 8 December 1942.

57. Gayle, *Richard Wright*, 162–63; *Daily Worker*, 6 August 1944; *New York Herald Tribune*, 28 July 1944; *New York Journal American*, 28 July 1944.

58. C. L. R. James to Constance Webb, ca. September 1944, Box 1, C. L. R. James Papers, Schomburg Center for Research in Black Culture, New York, N.Y.; *Daily Worker*, 1 April 1945. Davis called *Black Boy* "a furious and terrifying story of the impact of the Jim Crow system. . . . The book is intensely subjective. In fact it is limited by its subjectiveness. But people are not born subjective . . . a young Negro . . . has subjectiveness forced into his marrow. This heavy pressure pushes him to view the world . . . entirely through glasses colored by his own personal suffering. . . . It is important, however, that this subjectiveness be overcome. . . . *Black Boy* says some wholly unacceptable things about the Negro's capacity for genuine emotion. . . . The point is: Will Wright himself be able to overcome this limitation of subjectivity?. . . . There is no doubt that Wright wields a brilliant and stormy pen. . . . It is vitally important that the artist who reflects and the artist who sees the way out should be one and the same person. . . . Jim Crow is here, yet Jim Crow is also being driven defeated from the scene. Life is not static. . . . Wright does not see the positive, constructive side and therefore the mirror of his pen does not give a complete picture." See also Jabari Onaje Simama, "Black Writers Experience Communism: An Interdisciplinary Study of Imaginative Writers, Their Critics, and the

CPUSA" (Ph.D. diss., Emory University, 1978), 208: "[*The Outsider*] spoke to his opportunism and his conscious or unconscious desire to place his craft at the service of reactionary forces"; and Kenneth Kinnamon, *The Emergence of Richard Wright: A Study in Literature and Society* (Urbana: University of Illinois Press, 1972). Walker, *Richard Wright*, 111; *Daily Worker*, 1 July 1956. Abner Berry was forthright: "Under present circumstances I am not prepared to say that he did not have unpleasant experiences in the party . . . [still] Wright possessed a snobbery which he could not hide when in the company of those less literate than himself. . . . Remember we praised him once when we should have been sharply critical of him as a close friend; let us not damn him now that he has moved a step or two in the direction of humanity."

In an article, ca. 1975 (Box 6, William Patterson Papers), Ollie Harrington says that Wright told him that he would never allow the book published under the title *American Hunger* to be published. He also states that Wright became "obsessed" with the Central Intelligence Agency. J. Edgar Hoover complained about Wright's *12 Million Voices*; see J. Edgar Hoover to SAC-NY, 9 December 1942, 100-157464-1, Federal Bureau of Investigation, Washington, D.C., and the FBI's report on Richard Wright, 8 July 1944, 100-41674, 15 January 1944: he was rejected by the armed forces for "'psychoneurosis, severe, psychiatric rejection; referred to Local Board for further psychiatric and social investigation . . . his interest in the problem of the Negro has become almost an obsession." Moreover, "confidential informants" monitored Wright; see SAC-NY to J. Edgar Hoover, 8 August 1944, 100-41674, FBI. It was "urgent" news when Wright criticized the Reds as "intolerant," but this did not allow the bureau to withdraw Wright's "Security Index card," which marked him for detention (J. Edgar Hoover to SAC-NY, 7 May 1945, 100-41674, FBI). The FBI also claimed that when Wright applied for a passport in 1958, he provided information on the Red ties of others (report, 3 April 1958, 100-157464, FBI).

59. *Daily Worker*, 8 May 1943; Langston Hughes to "Dear Pat," 10 August 1964, Box 2, William Patterson Papers; "Sonnet for Ben Davis," by Walter Lowenfels, undated, Reel 23, Fox 39, J-10, Civil Rights Congress Papers, Schomburg Center for Research in Black Culture, New York (hereafter cited as CRC Papers); Walter Lowenfels, *My Many Lives: The Autobiography of Walter Lowenfels. Volume 2: The Poetry of My Politics* (Homestead, Fla.: Olivant Press, 1968). The *Daily Worker*, of 12 June 1949 printed Harold Cruse's "first published story." Yglesias wrote film and book reviews for the party organ; see *Daily Worker*, 22 October 1956. On the faculty of the School for Democracy, closely affiliated with the Left in New York City, were Alain Locke and W. C. Handy (Literature, undated, Box 1, Folder MG77-1/10, Gwen Bennett Papers).

60. *Daily Worker*, 15 September 1940. Davis was sensitive to the fact that at many of the massive Harlem rallies featuring these celebrities, African-Americans were not always present in representative numbers: "People from all walks of life were present . . . overwhelming predominance of [whites]. . . . It is unfortunate that wider attendance of the Negro people was not in evidence. . . . partially explained by the extremely high admission." See also *Daily Worker*, 18 October 1942, 22, 23, 30 October 1943; James Haskins, *Lena Horne* (New York: Coward-McCann, 1983); Helen Arstein and Carlton Moss, *In Person: Lena Horne* (New York: Greenberg, 1950), 184–87; *Daily Worker*, 1 October 1943.

61. Pete Cacchione to Branch Rickey, 7 June 1943, Box 4, Reel 2, Pete Cacchione Papers; *Daily Worker*, 5 December 1943; *New Masses*, 21 September 1943; Ben Davis to Paul Robeson, 26 October 1943, Paul Robeson Papers, Schomburg Library, New York, N.Y.

62. Merle Miller, *The Judges and the Judged* (Garden City, N.Y.: Doubleday, 1952), 54–55.

63. *Daily Worker*, 24 September 1950; Gail Lumet Buckley, *The Hornes: An American Family* (New York: Knopf, 1986), 208; Canada Lee to Ed Sullivan, 15 November 1949, Box 1, Canada Lee Papers, Schomburg Center for Research in Black Culture, New York, N.Y.; Louis Budenz, *The Cry Is Peace* (Chicago: Regnery, 1952), 23; Memorandum, 2 April 1964, 100-3-116, FBI.

64. *Daily Worker*, 2 October 1949.

65. Louis Sass, "On Some Problems of the Harlem Section," *Party Organizer* 7 (March 1934): 19–21.

66. Israel Amter, "The Elections in New York," *The Communist* 15 (December 1936): 1141–53. At this point sixteen thousand Communists were in the state, with ten thousand in the unions. In the *Daily Worker* for 9 June 1936 Davis stated, "Negro Communists capable of leading the 12,000,000 American Negroes will henceforth be the goal of the Communist Party in developing and training its Negro members."

67. *Daily Worker*, 9 and 17 March 1943; Elizabeth Barker, "Building a Mass Party in Harlem," *Party Organizer* 1, no. 1 (1943): 9–12.

68. Doxey Wilkerson, "The Negro in the War," *New Masses* 49 (14 December 1943): 18–19; *Daily Worker*, 6 September 1943.

69. Ben Davis to Essie Robeson, 27 April 1943, Paul Robeson Papers.

70. *Daily Worker*, 19 September and 28 October 1943.

71. *Daily Worker*, 30 October and 1 November 1943.

72. Charles Lomax, "Harlem Plays a Winner," *Party Organizer* 1 (December 1943): 11–15; Patrick Washburn in *Question of Sedition*, 181, details Red ties with the black press; *Daily Worker*, 8 October 1943.

73. Audley Moore, interview, Oral History of the American Left, Series I. Moore expresses resentment at white women dating black men in the party and complains about blacks not being allowed to meet separately. But her veracity can be challenged directly when she claims, "Ben didn't know two people in Harlem when he ran." She adds that the party "wanted to take me out of the campaign before election . . . they didn't want Ben to win." She also complains about her absence from his memoir. The Scottsboro slogan "death to the lynchers" and the party's "nation in a nation" thesis were what first inspired and attracted her. She says she "trained" Richard Moore. Inferentially she indicates why she joined the party despite the fact she "never mastered" Marxism-Leninism and at best understood only a "smattering." The "nationalists," she says, "weren't so much about organizing as talking from street-corners . . . [they] didn't organize mass struggles." Her hope then was for a Marxist-Leninist party of blacks led by Robeson. *Daily Worker*, 20 November 1943, 8 June 1941, 27 October and 3 June 1943, and 2 March 1951. At the funeral of Jenkins Davis recalled, "She never forgot the West Indian people from which she sprang."

74. Ben Davis to Elizabeth Gurley Flynn, 4 October 1943, and Pete Cacchione to Elizabeth Gurley Flynn, 8 December 1943, Reel 4206, Elizabeth Gurley Flynn Papers: "The success of the campaign to a great measure can be attributed to comrades like you and Mother Bloor, as well as other members of our National Committee." *Daily Worker*, 24, 27, 26 October 1943; the quotation is from ibid., 11 November 1943.

75. *Daily Worker*, 29 November 1943. The FBI maintained a consistent interest in any NAACP friendliness to the party during this period, despite the not-infrequent clashes between the party and association (Main File no. 62-78270, 100-136-34, FBI).

76. *Daily Worker*, 30 December and 30 November 1943.

77. Harvard Sitkoff, "American Blacks in World War II: Rethinking the Militancy-Watershed Hypothesis," in *The Home Front and War in the Twentieth Century*, ed. James Titus (Washington, D.C.: GPO, 1982), 153.

78. *Daily Worker*, 31 January and 18 July 1943, 14 September 1941; "Communists in the Struggle for Negro Rights," ca. 1943, Communist Party Archives.

79. *Daily Worker*, 23 May and 8 June 1943. Despite Davis's souring relationship with Randolph the labor leader, his overall ties with labor soared during this period. See *Daily Worker*, 26 October 1943 and 10 January 1943. In his memoir he recalled Harry Bridges and San Francisco workers generally with awe and affection (Davis memoir, 9/42), but in the *Daily Worker* for 10 October 1942 he blasted the Boilermakers Union for their color bar.

80. *Daily Worker*, 29 and 30 November 1943.

81. Gil Green, "The New York City Elections," *The Communist* 22 (December 1943): 1103.

82. Ibid.

83. *Daily Worker*, 10 and 12 November 1943.

84. Dominic Capeci, Jr., *The Harlem Riot of 1943* (Philadelphia: Temple University Press, 1977), 161.

85. *Daily Worker*, 12 December 1943.

86. *New York Amsterdam News*, 13 November 1943. John Ross, black GOP candidate, got 20,000 of his 23,390 votes "from the white folks downtown." This suggests that blacks were much more willing to vote for Communists than whites. The *New York Amsterdam News* for 20 November wrote that the Davis election "proves conclusively that white voters will vote for qualified Negroes for political offices."

87. *Daily Worker*, 12 November and 4 December 1943.

88. *New York World-Telegram*, 16 November 1943.

89. *New York Times*, 10 November 1943. Councilman James Phillips of Queens snarled, "It is my earnest hope that the PR method . . . be relegated to the ash heap as soon as possible." The *Times* added, "The drive to repeal PR is expected to recruit strength from the greater representation that left-wing viewpoints will have in the new Council." Their headline read, "Negro Communist Chosen to Council."

90. Robert Moses to President, Bronx Chamber of Commerce, 12 November 1943, Box 18, Robert Moses Papers, New York Public Library, N.Y.

91. Jane Garland Gleerup to Thomas Dewey, 11 November 1943, Thomas Dewey Papers, University of Rochester Library, Rochester, N.Y.

92. Davis memoir, 31/721, 15/705.

93. *Daily Worker*, 14 November 1943.

94. Ibid., 11 November 1943; Davis memoir, 1/277. But with all his notoriety, Davis recalls in his memoir how he was still constantly mistaken for the other Ben Davis, the West Point military man.

Chapter 7. "Browderism," 1944

1. *Daily Worker*, 22 December and 4, 5, 19 November 1943; *New Masses*, 8 August 1944.

2. George Mand to Frank V. Kelly, 27 June 1944, Robert Moses to George Mand, 9 December 1943, and George Mand letter, 15 November 1943, all Box 23, Robert Moses Papers; *New York Amsterdam News*, 22 January 1944.

3. *Daily Worker*, 23 April and 11 September 1944; "New World a-Coming," Box 2, Canada Lee Papers; *Daily Worker*, 10 September and 22 October 1944.

4. *Daily Worker*, 8 May, 25 April, and 12 July 1944.

5. Ibid., 11 January, 13 February, 3 and 24 March, and 21 August 1944. On the general context of the Left and politics during this era, see Kenneth Waltzer, "The

American Labor Party: Third Party Politics in New Deal-Cold War New York, 1936-1954 "(Ph.D. diss., Harvard University, 1977); Josh Freeman, *In Transit: The Transport Workers Union and New York City* (New York: Oxford University Press, 1992); and Steven Fraser, *Labor Will Rule: Sidney Hillman and the Rise of American Labor* (New York: Macmillan Co., 1991). Though useful on the question of class, these works are not helpful in explicating the major theme of this work, which concerns the left and "race."

6. Ibid., 20 May, 17 September, 29 February, 21 and 26 September 1944; Arnold Johnson, "The Ohio Membership Campaign," *The Communist* 23 (April 1944): 319–26; Pete Cacchione to Philadelphia Board of Elections, 13 September 1944, Box 5, Reel 2, Pete Cacchione Papers.

7. *Daily Worker*, 21, 23, 25, 28 June, 7, 29 September 1944.

8. Ibid., 23 July 1944.

9. Ibid., 26 November 1944; Ben Davis to Roy Wilkins, 15 April 1944, and Roy Wilkins to Ben Davis, 24 April 1944, NAACP Papers, Library of Congress, Washington, D.C.

10. *Daily Worker*, 15 September and 24 November 1943; *People's Voice*, 18 December 1943, 19 February 1944; *Daily Worker*, 13 February and 5 January 1944.

11. *Daily Worker*, 18 March, 28 May, 11 June, 27 and 29 July, 13 August, and 18 December 1944.

12. *New York Amsterdam News*, 3 June, 1 January, and 13 May 1944.

13. *People's Voice*, 25 November 1944.

14. Ibid., 11 November 1944; *Daily Worker*, 22 June 1944; *New York Amsterdam News*, 1 January and 1 April 1944.

15. *Daily Worker*, 22 July, 17 September, 19 November, and 7 October 1944. Davis called for "piling up a majority for Roosevelt such as no President has ever received in the history of the country," though he advocated voting for him not on the Democratic line but the American Labor Party line, since it "counts more than a vote on any other line" (*Daily Worker*, 5 November 1944). This was part of party maneuvering. Gil Green, according to FBI documents, allegedly suggested that "all the leading Communists except [Davis and Cacchione] should enroll as ALP members for the coming election. He stated the reason for the exception . . . was that in the event in next elections, if these two were not endorsed by the ALP, they would have to run for political office as independents, and they should, therefore enroll as independents for the 1944 elections" (memorandum, 24 September 1944, NY-100-13472, p. 32, FBI, in box 5, Gil Green Papers, New York University Library, New York).

16. *Daily Worker*, 20 August, 1 and 29 October, 2 July, 8, 9, 15 October, and 7 May 1944; *People's Voice*, 15 October 1944; *Daily Worker*, 16 April 1944.

17. Lewinson, *Black Politics*, 78.

18. Si Gerson, *Pete: The Story of Peter V. Cacchione, New York's First Communist Councilman* (New York: International Publications, 1976), 17.

19. Ibid.

20. *Daily Worker*, 1 January 1944; resolutions, various dates, Reel 3, Box 7, Pete Cacchione Papers; Davis memoir, 15/679; "Minority Office Account," Reel 3, Box 7, Pete Cacchione Papers; *Daily Worker*, 13 October 1944.

21. File card, ca. 1944, Ben Davis Vertical File-Schomburg Center; *Daily Worker*, 11 June 1944. Cf. also *Proceedings of the Council for the City of New York, Volume I, 15 January 1944 to 20 June 1944*. Davis introduced bills and resolutions on such issues as Negro History Week, soldiers' voting, dismissal of an anti-Semitic police officer, Jewish emigration to Palestine, overcharging by pawnbrokers, poll tax repeal, a permanent FEPC, referendum on raising the transit fare, opposing the Equal Rights Amendment for women (which he felt would erode protective legislation),

and so forth. All the while Davis was maintaining a high profile as a party leader and involved in the top councils of the Communists: see *Daily Worker*, 23 March 1944. For further background on Davis's opposition to the ERA, which was a consistent party position for decades, see Resolution No. 18, 25 January 1944, Ben Davis Vertical File. See also *Daily Worker*, 17 April 1944: in reply to Davis, black women were invited to become applicants in Miss Subway contests, a suggestion that Davis endorsed.

22. Edith Isaacs, *Love Affair with a City: The Story of Stanley Isaacs* (New York: Random House, 1967), 47; Resolution No. 35, 15 February 1944, Ben Davis Vertical File-Schomburg Center; Stanley Isaacs to Joseph Cadden, 15 January 1948, Box 15, Stanley Isaacs Papers, New York Public Library; New York, N.Y. Isaacs contributed funds to the Communist-led Civil Rights Congress. See Ben Davis to "Dear Mr. Isaacs," 8 August 1944, Box 10, Stanley Isaacs Papers; Audley Moore to Stanley Isaacs, 20 October 1943, Box 9, Stanley Isaacs Papers; file on Stanley Isaacs, Box 183, National Republic Papers.

23. *Daily Worker*, 10 March 1952.

24. *Daily Worker*, 4 October, 13 May, 20 June, and 26 January 1944; Resolution No. 19, 25 January 1944, Ben Davis Vertical File-Schomburg Center.

25. *Daily Worker*, 21 December and 16 February 1944; Resolution No. 65, 31 March 1944, Ben Davis Vertical File-Schomburg Center; *Daily Worker*, 22 June 1944; *New York Amsterdam News*, 8 July 1944; *New York Times*, 2 April 1944; Rev. Harten to Charles Collins, 7 March 1944, Reel 2, Box 4, Pete Cacchione Papers; *Daily Worker*, 4 and 8 January 1944; *Proceedings of the Council of the City of New York, Volume II, 11 July 1944–27 December 1944*; *The Chief*, 15 December 1944; *Daily Worker*, 8 December 1944.

26. *People's Voice*, 23 September 1944; Intro. no. 76, 15 May 1944, Ben Davis Vertical File-Schomburg Center; *Daily Worker*, 16 September, 13, 17, 31 December, 27 August, and 28 March 1944; *People's Voice*, 19 February 1944; *Daily Worker*, 12 March, 18 June, 21 December, and 28 November 1944.

27. Literature and memoranda, ca. 1944, Reel 3, Box 6, Pete Cacchione Papers; Intro. no. 40, 8 February 1944, Ben Davis Vertical File-Schomburg Center; *Daily Worker*, 15 November 1944.

28. Resolution, 5 January 1944, and Intro. no. 68, 18 April 1944, Ben Davis Vertical File-Schomburg Center; *Daily Worker*, 1 March and 21 May 1944; Pete Cacchione and Ben Davis to "Dear Friends and Fellow Citizens," 24 May 1944, Reel 2, Box 4, Pete Cacchione Papers. The two council members urged their constituents to "take definite steps against this budget cut" and sought to mobilize them by calling for "special meeting [s] . . . letters and post cards"; *Daily Worker*, 21 June 1944.

29. *New York Times*, 21 June 1944: the session on taxes involved a "clamorous three hours in wrangling." *Daily Worker*, 28 December 1944. The other errors viewed ruefully in hindsight by Davis and Cacchione were their vote "to extend the term of City Council members from two to four years" and "to vote for an antidiscrimination housing bill that did not specifically ban discrimination in Stuyvesant Town." Apparently Vito Marcantonio called Browder, "who put the squeeze on Pete and Ben via a phone message" (Gerson, *Pete*, 166, 168).

30. Dominic Capeci, Jr., "Fiorello H. La Guardia and the Stuyvesant Town Controversy of 1943," *New York Historical Society Quarterly* 32 (October 1978): 292, 299, 307, 310. See also Edward Lewis to Stanley Isaacs, 1 June 1943, Box 10, Stanley Isaacs Papers. Marquis James, in *The Metropolitan Life: A Study in Business Growth* (New York: Viking Press, 1947), 385–86, writes, "In Stuyvesant Town the buildings were to cover about one-quarter of the land. There were to be thirty-five of them, thirteen stories high, grouped about a three-acre central park . . . made possible by

the Redevelopment Companies Law of [New York State] . . . the city condemned the land. Because of the extra expense of slum clearance, [New York City] froze for twenty-five years the assessed valuation."

31. *New York Times*, 5 June 1943; *New York Herald Tribune*, 5 June 1943; C. R. Wilmer to Stanley Isaacs, 20 May 1943, Box 9, Stanley Isaacs Papers.

32. Robert Moses to F. H. Ecker, 24 July 1943, Box 19, and ibid., 23 August 1943, Box 18, Robert Moses Papers. Moses carefully read the *People's Voice* and kept a file on this journal; he forwarded to Ecker their bitter and harsh 12 June 1943 editorial denouncing Met Life.

33. *Daily Worker*, 5, 12, 13, 19 June, 16 July, and 29 and 21 October 1943.

34. *People's Voice*, 15 January 1944; *Daily Worker*, 6 and 23 January 1944; *New York Times*, 16 February 1944; *Daily Worker*, 16 February 1944.

35. *Daily Worker*, 12, 18, 30 April and 2 May 1944.

36. Ibid., 3, 16, 27 May and 9 June 1944; *People's Voice*, 15 July 1944.

37. *Daily Worker*, 20 September 1944; Robert Moses to F. H. Ecker, 12 July 1944, Box 21, Robert Moses Papers; Daily Worker, 11 and 29 March 1945; *People's Voice*, 16 December 1944.

38. *Daily Worker*, 24 June 1946, 9, 10, 11, 15 July 1947; *New York Times*, 20 August 1947; *Daily Worker*, 29 September 1948.

39. Stanley Isaacs to Ben Davis, 29 December 1948, Box 16, Stanley Isaacs Papers.

40. *Daily Worker*, 6 January, 11 April, 12 August, 19 June 1949. Ray Tillman, Davis's campaign manager announced that Harlem Labor Party activists would picket City Hall to protest the mayor's support of Met Life in the *Daily Worker* of 18 August 1949; see also *Daily Worker*, 16 February 1951. It should not be forgotten that Davis was also a major supporter of rent control in New York City: see Ben Davis letter, 18 September 1944, Ben Davis Vertical File-Schomburg Center.

41. *Daily Worker*, 11 March 1943; José Arizala, ed., "Latin America: Democracy Must Be Won, Not Waited For," *World Marxist Review* 31 (July 1988): 100 (Communists participated in the governments of Cuba in 1943–44, Ecuador 1944–46, and Chile 1946–47); Kevin Shillington, *History of Southern Africa* (Essex, England: Longman, 1987), 157; in the *Daily Worker* for 9 July 1939 Blas Roca, general secretary of the party in Cuba, speaks of the "New Deal" in Cuba; see also Trevor Munroe, *The Marxist Left in Jamaica* (Mona, Jamaica: ISER, 1977); Resolution on Liquidation of the Communist Party of Puerto Rico, 21 May 1944, Hunter College, CUNY Library, New York; Dimitris Sarlis, "Lessons of the Greek Resistance in Today's Struggle," *World Marxist Review* 29 (June 1986): 61–66; Eugene Varga, "Against Reformist Tendencies in Works on Imperialism," *Political Affairs* 28 (December 1949): 74–86.

42. *Daily Worker*, 30 July 1942, 25 April 1943, 25 March and 7 January 1945.

43. Ibid., 2 July and 15 March 1939. Note that the Communist-led International Labor Defense backed a wiretapping measure introduced by Congressman Emmanuel Celler that would eventually victimize them as well (*Daily Worker*, 6 May 1942). See also *Daily Worker*, 4 February 1943 and 23 April 1939.

44. Roger Elliot Rosenberg, "Guardian of the Fortress: A Biography of Earl Russell Browder, U.S. Communist Party General Secretary from 1930–1944" (Ph.D. diss., University of California-Santa Barbara, 1982); William Winch Bilderback, "The American Communist Party and World War II" (Ph.D. diss., University of Washington, 1974); Robert L. Cleath, "Earl Russell Browder: American Spokesman for Communism, 1930–1945" (Ph.D. diss., University of Washington, 1963). In the *Daily Worker* for 18 October 1942 Browder was reported as having met Under Secretary of State Sumner Welles and retracting an attack on China policy, and the

People's Voice for 8 July 1944 carried a two-page ad on Browder's book. See also Earl Browder, "Why an Open Letter to Our Party Membership," *The Communist* 12 (August 1933): 761.

45. *Daily Worker*, 7 October 1940, 20 February, 28 May, 1 March, 28 September, and 1 and 12 December 1941.

46. *Daily Worker*, 9 February 1942. See also Ben Davis, Jr., "The Communists, the Negro People and the War," *The Communist* 21 (August 1942): 633–39, in which Davis calls Browder a "great statesman and leader." *Daily Worker*, 5 October 1942; Ben Davis to Earl Browder, 9 November 1942, Reel 1, 1–2, Earl Browder Papers; *Daily Worker*, 13 January 1943.

47. *Daily Worker*, 19 October 1943; Ben Davis to Earl Browder, 12 December 1943, Reel 1, 1–22, Earl Browder Papers: in this letter Davis commented that the president of Amherst "showed his class prejudice by snubbing me [and] a couple of Negro students when I returned there in the midst of the Herndon and Scottsboro cases back in 1936. Meikeljohn was a much better type of fellow."

48. Ben Davis to Earl Browder, 4 March and 7 April 1944, Reel 1, 1–22, Earl Browder Papers.

49. Ibid., 15 June 1944, Reel 1, 1–22, Earl Browder Papers: "I am ready to write that book mentioned to you many weeks ago . . . to give an approach to the solution of fundamental problems in the specific field of Negro rights, in the light of the postwar period. . . . The overall objective should be to influence election developments among the Negro communities. . . . Your own ideas will be invaluable to me and to the work. . . . I conceive of the book as a kind of unofficial expression of the policy of the CPA. Perhaps this could be done at your home when we could have some music too." Davis is referring to the fact that Teheran also meant the junking of the Black Belt thesis; ironically this could have been appropriate since the war inspired the migration that was undermining this thesis. However, junking of the thesis acquired the taint of Teheran, and after Browder's ouster the party reclaimed the thesis with a clinging vengeance, though it did not conform—arguably—to the objective conditions in the nation. In the *Daily Worker* for 18 June 1944 Davis wrote, "Earl Browder's new book, *Teheran—Our Path in War and Peace*, contains the clearest and most unanswerable indictment of racial discrimination in the armed forces yet to appear." See also *Daily Worker*, 13 May and 25 June 1944.

50. Max Weiss, "Toward a New Anti-Fascist Youth Organization," *The Communist* 22 (September 1943): 792–805; Hans Berger, "Concerning a Charge of Betrayal," *The Communist* 23 (May 1944): 431–39.

51. David Goldway, "On the Study of Browder's Report," *The Communist* 23 (March 1944): 237.

52. Doxey Wilkerson, "The Maryland-District of Columbia Enlightenment Campaign," *The Communist* 23 (May 1944): 441, 449.

53. *Daily Worker*, 21 January 1945.

54. Claudia Jones, *Lift Every Voice for Victory* (New York: New Age, 1942), 9.

55. Eugene Braddock, "For Victory—Win Negro Rights," *Clarity* 3 (Summer 1942): 40.

56. Washburn, *A Question of Sedition*, 132. "Stretch" Johnson alleges that he did not accept the view expressed by Jones and Braddock about the Double V, saying that it did lead to conflict with other Reds, as, for example, Abner Berry. Howard "Stretch" Johnson, interview, Series I, Oral History of the American Left.

57. *New York Age*, 6 and 27 June, 11 and 18 July 1942.

58. Ibid., 3 January 1948. This charge of Red inaction on black rights became popular after the war. Davis also had to respond to Horace Cayton making a similar charge and it was an issue during his 1945 reelection race. Nevertheless, a late 1944

poll showed that 70 per cent of the blacks queried did not feel that Reds had abandoned the struggle for equality (*Daily Worker*, 17 December 1944).

59. "Survey of Racial Conditions in the United States," 24 September 1943, by J. Edgar Hoover, 10b, Box 21, #2420, FBI, 126, 418, 624, 151, FDR Papers. The paranoia of the FBI is suggested by their worry over Japanese nationals marrying "Negresses" and creating a "fifth column."

60. Ben Davis letter, 15 February 1944, Ben Davis Vertical File-Schomburg Center. Davis charged that his old foe Frank Crosswaith was working with the bourgeoisie, "pointing out the so-called Reds in various progressive Negro people's organizations in New York"; see "Inflammatory Propaganda," undated, Record Group 107, File 291.2, U.S. Army; Division of Press Intelligence to G-1, 13 December 1941, Record Group 165, File 15640-129; and Grogan to G-1, 11 February 1942, Record Group, File 15640-136, National Archives, Washington, D.C. See also *New Masses*, 15 February and 28 March 1944.

61. Christopher Johnson, *Maurice Sugar: Law, Labor and the Left in Detroit, 1912–1950* (Detroit: Wayne State University Press, 1988), 281, 152, 243. He also sheds light on the role of Moscow in bringing the "Popular Front" to the United States, observing that there was a Popular Front before the Popular Front—i.e., before the Seventh World Congress of the Comintern. The front can thus be seen as a reaction and ratification of what was already going on in countries like the United States and France rather than a *diktat* from on high. Similarly, he makes the point that the Nazi-Soviet pact was not overly disruptive to Communist organizing in Detroit. See also works by Steven Fraser and Josh Freeman cited above (n. 4, chap. 8, for Fraser; n. 10, chap. 13, for Freeman); Carmen Anthony Notaro, "Franklin D. Roosevelt and the American Communist, Peacetime Relations, 1932–1941" (Ph.D. diss., State University of New York-Buffalo, 1969); *People's Voice*, 31 July 1943; *Daily Worker*, 12 August 1942; *People's Voice*, 1 July 1944. The problem of the party is suggested by the twenty-one-thousand-strong "Negro Freedom Rally" at Madison Square Garden: "Every mention of FDR's name brought repeated cheers . . . " (*New York Amsterdam News*, 1 July 1944).

62. *Daily Worker*, 30 July 1944; *New Masses*, 19 September 1944; *Daily Worker*, 31 October 1944.

63. *Daily Worker*, 3 December 1944.

64. Ibid., 24 December 1944.

65. Ibid., 20 January and 28 February 1943; Ben Davis to "Dear Friend," 18 September 1944, NAACP Papers; *Daily Worker*, 7 March 1944; Ben Davis comment, ca. 1946, Reel 4, Box 8, Pete Cacchione Papers; *Daily Worker*, 6 and 17 December, 4 June, 28 May, 2 December, 25 August, and 4 February 1944; *People's Voice*, 25 November and 16 December 1944.

66. *Daily Worker*, 16 April, 4 June, and 22 October 1944.

67. James Ford, "Teheran and the Negro People," *The Communist* 23 (March 1944): 263.

68. *Daily Worker*, 20 August, 17 November, and 13 December 1944.

69. National Committee of Communist Party meeting, 8 February 1944, Box 8, Folder 11, Theodore Draper Papers. At the bottom of this document is scribbled, "Note: This is meeting which FBI men took down in adjoining room. . . ."

70. Earl Browder, "Teheran—History's Greatest Turning Point," *The Communist* 23 (January 1944): 7.

71. William Z. Foster, *In Defense of the Communist Party and the Indicted Leaders* (New York: New Century, 1949), 12. See also Philip J. Jaffe, *The Rise and Fall of American Communism* (New York: Horizon, 1975), 60.

72. Sam Darcy, interview, Series I, Oral History of the American Left; Sam

Darcy manuscript, Box 3, Folder 34, Sam Darcy Papers; *Daily Worker*, 13 April 1944.

73. *Daily Worker*, 27 March 1944; "Decisions of the National Committee of the Communist Party," *The Communist* 23 (February 1944): 107–8; *Daily Worker*, 21, 23, 27 May 1944.

74. Remarks of Ben Davis, 8 February 1944, Box 8, Folder 11, Theodore Draper Papers.

Chapter 8. Unity and Struggle, 1945

1. Ben Davis to Essie Robeson, 30 March 1945, Paul Robeson Papers; Ollie Harrington, interview with author, 1 June 1989, Berlin, Germany.

2. Raoul Damiens, "Duclos: Worker-Statesman," *New Masses* 20 (8 September 1936): 15–17; *Daily Worker*, 27 December 1939.

3. William Z. Foster, "Browder Again Tries to Destroy the Communist Party," *Political Affairs* 39 (June 1960): 43.

4. *Daily Worker*, 24–27 May 1945; *Italy Today*, Box 5, Folder 29, Theodore Draper Papers (this publication published the Duclos letter and commented favorably). See also *The* New York Herald Tribune's *23 Questions about the Communist Party Answered by William Z. Foster*, January 1948 (in possession of author). After his ouster Browder was received with "honor in Moscow"; apparently there was a little-noticed conflict between the American and Russian parties over this. Asked if he or "officers or members" of the U.S. party had "direct or indirect consultation" with the CPSU, Soviet government, or Comintern about this, Foster gave a curt no. He added, "This question is misdirected—you might inquire in Moscow." The overemphasis on the party being a "hand of Moscow" has obscured examination of tensions that arose from time to time between the CPUSA and CPSU. The impact of the dissolution of the Comintern on the U.S. party's desire to dissolve should also be considered. See also Gabriel Kolko, *The Politics of War: The World and U.S. Foreign Policy, 1943–1945* (New York: Random House, 1978). Kolko denies that the Duclos letter indicated a more aggressive Soviet foreign policy, as was often suggested; certainly the above comments of party patriarch Foster point in that direction. Arthur Krock in the 30 May 1944 *New York Times* suggests that the liquidation of the U.S. party was "made . . . simpler" by the initiation of Sidney Hillman's political machine (Hillman was the influential labor leader considered to be close to FDR), which was seen as at least the beginning of a third party or a Democratic party takeover; presumably the CP would have been present at the creation of this momentous development. Cf. Steven Fraser, *Labor Will Rule: Sidney Hillman and the Rise of American Labor* (New York: Macmillan Co., 1991).

5. Communist Party National Committee Meeting, 22 May 1945, Reel 2, Series 2.3, Theodore Draper Papers. Unless otherwise noted, the subsequent transcriptions or notes on this series of meetings can be found in the Draper Collection.

6. Ibid., 18 June 1945.
7. Ibid.
8. Ibid.
9. Ibid.
10. Ibid.
11. Ibid., 22 May and 2 June 1945, Box 5, Folder 29.
12. Ibid., 20 June 1945, Reel 2, Series 2.3.

13. Ibid.
14. Ibid., 19 June 1945, Box 36, Folder 4D, Series VII, Philip Jaffe Papers, Emory Univerisity Library, Atlanta, Ca.
15. Telephone conversation, 3 June 1945, 100-12304, FBI. An unidentified person in this dialogue is quoted as saying: " . . . sometimes we can have a correct line and fight for it in such a manner as not to carry everybody with us. . . . You can fight for that correct line in such a god damn manner that instead of promoting unity you'll have the opposite effect." This was a problem faced by the party in 1945 and again in 1956; at times in fighting what they termed "right opportunism," there was a drift to "left opportunism" or sectarianism.
16. *Daily Worker*, 6 January, 14 and 18 February, 8 April 1945.
17. Ibid., 28 January and 24 October 1945. An editorial advises against universal military training, thus signaling a reversal by the party.
18. Ben Davis, "The Army Tackles Jim Crow," *New Masses* 55 (3 April 1945): 15–16; *Daily Worker*, 4 March 1945; *New Masses*, 10 July 1945.
19. *Daily Worker*, 11 and 18 March 1945; *People's Voice*, 24 March 1945.
20. *Daily Worker*, 22 July 1945.
21. *Daily Worker*, 4 April 1947, 25 April 1950.
22. Communist Party, "The Present Situation and the New Tasks," 26–29 July 1945 (in possession of author); *PM*, 30 July 1945; *Daily Worker*, 4 June 1945.
23. William Z. Foster, "The Struggle Against Revisionism," *Political Affairs* 24 (September 1945): 782–99.
24. Claudia Jones, "Discussion Article," *Political Affairs* 24 (August 1945): 717, 718.
25. A. B. Magil, "Discussion Article," *Political Affairs* 24 (August 1945): 721–25.
26. *Daily Worker*, 14 July 1945; Jacob Mindel, "Discussion Article," *Political Affairs* 24 (August 1945): 726–30; *Daily Worker*, 5 April 1959.
27. *People's Voice*, 23 June 1945.
28. Jesus Colon, "To the National Commission of the CPA," ca. 1945, Jesus Colon Papers. He added that Browder had backed Albizu Campos, "whose influence . . . was, and at present, continues to be . . . to a great extent reactionary." In addition to Darcy, Ford, and Minor, Ray Hansborough also took some of the heaviest blows among the leadership in the wake of Teheran.
29. Sam Darcy to Bill Dunne, 7 July 1945, Box 1, Folder 22, Sam Darcy Papers. He was harsh toward Foster; cf. Sam Darcy to William Z. Foster, 29 June 1945, Box 1, Folder 23, ibid., and Saul Wellman [acting secretary, National Review Commission of Communist Party] to Sam Darcy, 2 November 1945, Box 1, Folder 11, ibid.
30. William Z. Foster, *History of the Communist Party of the United States* (Westport: Greenwood, 1968), 434.
31. *Daily Worker*, 4 December 1946, 10 June 1945.
32. Earl Browder, "On the Negroes and the Right to Self-Determination," *The Communist* 23 (January 1944): 83–85. This statement captured what a number of comrades were thinking at the time. See, e.g., Eugene Braddock, "Negro Youth Fights in the American Tradition," *Clarity* 3 (Spring 1942): 40–52: " . . . the struggle for Negro liberation today is a struggle to integrate fully the Negro people on a basis of equality into all phases of the program to win the war."
33. Roi Ottley, *"New World a-Coming": Inside Black America* (Boston: Houghton-Mifflin, 1943), 243, 244.
34. St. Clair Drake and Horace Cayton, *Black Metropolis* (New York: Harper & Row, 1962), 740.
35. *New York Times*, 24 and 25 July 1945.
36. *Pittsburgh Courier*, 11 August 1945.

37. Ibid., 4 August 1945.
38. Ibid., 18 August 1945; Julius Adams to Walter White, 24 July 1945, NAACP Papers.
39. *Pittsburgh Courier*, 13 and 20 October 1945.
40. *People's Voice*, 27 October 1945; *Daily Worker*, 6 November 1945. Ironically, Doxey Wilkerson, who opposed the thesis, took on Davis's detractors: see *People's Voice*, 4 and 11 August 1945; *Daily Worker*, 13 August 1945.
41. *Daily Worker*, 10 February 1945.
42. Ibid., 7 May 1945; *New York Age*, 12 May 1945.
43. *People's Voice*, 10 May 1945; *New York Amsterdam News*, 19 May 1945.
44. *New York Age*, 23 June 1945; *Daily Worker*, 25 June and 21 July 1945.
45. *New York Herald Tribune*, 21 and 22 July 1945.
46. Ibid., 25 and 26 July 1945.
47. *New York Times*, 24 and 25 July 1945; Edward J. Flynn, *You're the Boss* (New York: Viking, 1947), 175, 192. This Tammany leader admits to being charged with corruption and ties to organized crime and Japanese militarists; Nevertheless—or perhaps necessarily—there are not-unfavorable references to Russia during a postwar trip there.
48. *Daily Worker*, 24 July 1945.
49. *New York Amsterdam News*, 28 July, 4 and 18 August 1945; *New York Age*, 28 July 1945; *New York Times*, 29 July 1945; *Daily Worker*, 2 August 1945; *New York Herald Tribune*, 3 August 1945; *People's Voice*, 4 August 1945.
50. *New York Amsterdam News*, 4 August 1945.
51. CP National Committee, 18 June 1945, Reel 2, Series 2.3, Theodore Draper Papers; see also Fraser, *Labor Will Rule*.
52. CP National Committee, 19 June 1945, Reel 2, Series 2.3, Theodore Draper Papers.
53. Ibid., 20 June 1945.
54. *People's Voice*, 16 June, 7 and 28 July and 4 August 1945.
55. *New York World-Telegram*, 18 July 1945; *Daily Worker*, 15 and 18 July 1945.
56. *PM*, 24–26 July 1945.
57. Eugene Dennis, *America at the Crossroads: Postwar Problems and Communist Policy* (pamphlet) (New York: New Century, 1945) (in possession of author); *PM*, 24–26 July 1945.

Chapter 9. Victory, 1945

1. *People's Voice*, 20 October 1945; *New York Age*, 27 October 1945; *Daily Worker*, 30 September and 17 October 1945; *Afro-American*, 27 October 1945.
2. *Daily Worker*, 28 April 1945; *New York Times*, 2 May 1945.
3. *Daily Worker*, 2, 5, 30 May, 6 June, 30 July, and 30 September 1945.
4. Ibid., 2 October and 17 August 1945.
5. Ibid., 18 April 1944, 25 April and 17 June 1945.
6. Ibid., 20 and 22 October 1945; *People's Voice*, 27 October and 3 November 1945.
7. *Daily Worker*, 26 October and 10 August 1945; Ben Davis to Thurgood Marshall, 3 July 1945, NAACP Papers: "Dear Thurgood: I appreciate very much your offer to assist in the passage of the bill to establish an interracial and group unity committee in the Mayor's office." See also Thurgood Marshall's letter to Ben Davis, 28 June 1945, NAACP Papers.

8. *Daily Worker*, 17 September 1945.
9. *New York Age*, 13 October 1945; "Proposed Budget for Councilman Cacchione's Office," 3 December 1945, Reel 2, Box 4, Pete Cacchione Papers (Cacchione received $70 per week); *Daily Worker*, 7 October 1945; *Proceedings of the Council of the City of New York, Volume I, January 3, 1945–June 28, 1945* (the detailed listing reflected in this source suggests that Davis used the council as a bully pulpit to raise important issues to his constituencies, whether or not they fell neatly within the jurisdiction of the council); *Daily Worker*, 28 February 1945.
10. *People's Voice*, 20 January 1945; *Daily Worker*, 22 May, 21 and 25 June, and 17 January 1945; *New York Times*, 18 April 1945; handbill, ca. 1945 (Davis bill to "set up a committee on interracial and group unity" in Mayor's office), Box 5, Robert Minor Papers.
11. *Daily Worker*, 18, 20, 22, 29 September, 17 October, 1 November, and 3, 8, 20 December 1945; *Peoples Voice*, 15 December 1945.
12. *Daily Worker*, 31 January, 16 April, and 11 June 1945; *New York Amsterdam News*, 29 September 1945; *People's Voice*, 9 June 1945; *Daily Worker*, 21 November 1945.
13. Adam Clayton Powell, *Marching Blacks: An Interpretive History of the Rise of the Black Common Man* (New York: Dial, 1945), 199, 158, 95, 69.
14. *People's Voice*, 13 May 1944.
15. *Daily Worker*, 1 January 1945.
16. Memo by James Lawson, undated, Box 2, Herbert Bruce Papers; *New York Post*, 10 April 1944; memo on Adam Powell, 31 October 1944, 100-51230, FBI.
17. *People's Voice*, 3 November 1945; *Daily Worker*, 29 December 1945; Davis memoir, 10/262: "One day late in '45 I sought an interview [with Powell]. . . . We had a long and fruitful discussion [concerning collaboration]."
18. *New York Times*, 24 March 1989; circular, undated, "McLaurin campaign," container 130, Brotherhood of Sleeping Car Porter Papers.
19. *New York Times*, 28 July 1945; *People's Voice*, 4 August 1945.
20. *People's Voice*, 15 September 1945. (The Women's Committee to Re-Elect Ben Davis, one of the most important components of his campaign, was composed primarily of African-American women in their thirtys and fortys.) "People's Avenger," no. 1, 1945, Ben Davis Vertical File-Schomburg Center.
21. Press release, 20 October 1945, "McLaurin Campaign," Container 130, Brotherhood of Sleeping Car Porters Papers.
22. Quoted in *New York Amsterdam News*, 27 October 1945.
23. Press release, 29 October 1945, "McLaurin Campaign," container 130, Brotherhood of Sleeping Car Porter Papers.
24. Unsigned letter to William O'Dwyer, 31 October 1945, and press release, 3 November 1945, "McLaurin Campaign," container 130, Brotherhood of Sleeping Car Porters Papers.
25. Press release, 3 November 1945, and handbill, 29 October 1945, "McLaurin Campaign," Container 130, Brotherhood of Sleeping Car Porter Papers.
26. Frank Crosswaith to McLaurin Campaign Committee, 24 October 1945, Reel 15, Box 31, Negro Labor Committee Papers; Article by Frank Crosswaith, 10 October 1945, Box 1, Frank Crosswaith Papers; *New York Amsterdam News*, 16 June 1945.
27. Frank Crosswaith to unidentified person, 3 October 1953, Reel 5, Box 9, and Frank Crosswaith to Walter Reuther, 15 October 1953, Reel 1, Box 1, Negro Labor Committee Papers.
28. *Daily Worker*, 1 July 1945.
29. *New York Times*, 6 and 25 October and 29 August 1945; Davis memoir, 9/42; *Daily Worker*, 15 and 30 October 1945; *New York Age*, 3 November 1945. Showing

that Davis had his thumb on the pulse of Harlem was the fact that the ad for his reelection in the *New York Age* highlighted his submission of a bill to the council "against overcharges by pawnbrokers." The ad also pointed out, "You are entitled under the law to two hours off from work to vote."

30. *Daily Worker*, 11 October and 23 April 1945: after Davis addressed a meeting of the Fur Floor and Shipping Clerks Union on Bretton Woods, Dumbarton Oaks, and San Francisco, the union endorsed his reelection; *Daily Worker*, 24 June 1945: Local 19 of CIO-United Office and Professional Workers Union called for Davis to get all three party nods; *Daily Worker*, 26 June 1945: Supporters of Davis included Local 830, Retail and Wholesale Employees Union staff, Morris Muster (president of United Furniture Workers), and Samuel Lewis (business agent for United Retail and Wholesale Department Store Employees Union, Local 3; *Daily Worker*, 3 July 1945: The District Board of the United Electrical Workers urged ALP to nominate Davis; leaders of CIO-United Retail and Wholesale Workers Union backed Davis; Fur Workers Joint Board calls on ALP to back Davis; *New York Times*, 20 July 1945: Greater New York-CIO Council endorses Davis and Mike Quill for reelection.

31. *Daily Worker*, 20 November and 9 December 1945.

32. Ibid., 14 October 1945; *New York Amsterdam News*, 20 October 1945.

33. "Conference to Protest Police Brutality," 8 December 1945, Box 4, Reel 2, Pete Cacchione Papers. The Brewer incident was just one of many police/crime cases that roiled the waters of Harlem during this election year.

34. *Daily Worker*, 29 April, 13 May, 3 and 26 June, 4 July, 15 October, and 25 and 28 December 1945.

35. Ibid., 1 June 1945.

36. Circular, ca. October 1945, Box 5, Robert Minor Papers; flyer, ca. October 1945, and pamphlet, ca. October 1945, Ben Davis Vertical File-Schomburg Center; *Afro-American*, 27 October 1945.

37. Davis memoir, 20/917, 5/929, 7/931.

38. *People's Voice*, 13 October and 3 November 1945; Davis memoir, 13/937; *New York Age*, 22 September 1945; *Daily Worker*, 13 October 1945; *New York Amsterdam News*, 27 October 1945.

39. *Daily Worker*, 1 and 9 September, 25 August 1945; *Chicago Defender*, 18 August 1945.

40. *New York Age*, 7 April 1945. The *New York Amsterdam News* was not part of the Davis fan club.

41. *People's Voice*, 27 October and 17 November 1945; *Daily Worker*, 9 October 1945; *People's Voice*, 20 October and 28 April 1945.

42. *Daily Worker*, 9 October 1945; *New York Age*, 20 October 1945; *Daily Worker*, 22 October 1945; *People's Voice*, 20 October and 17 February 1945.

43. *People's Voice*, 22 December and 3 November 1945; *Daily Worker*, 29 July and 15 February 1945; *People's Voice*, 20 January 1945; *Daily Worker*, 19 June 1945; *People's Voice*, 3 February 1945.

44. *Daily Worker*, 17 May 1945; Howard Fast pamphlet, ca. 1945, 4/48–20, Fiorello La Guardia Papers, Municipal Archives, New York, N.Y.; *Daily Worker*, 17 and 31 October and 21 January 1945; memorandum, ca. 1945, Box 97, Vincent Impelliteri Papers.

45. *Daily Worker*, 22 March 1944, 9 February, 20 May, 1 and 29 July, 3 August 1945; *New York Times*, 13 August 1945; *Daily Worker*, 19 August 1945.

46. *Daily Worker*, 29 October, 2 and 16 November 1945. There were still internecine party battles during the campaign. One unnamed author suggested that the party was not pushing black rights during the latter stages of the Browder period for fear of harming coalitions or upsetting whites: "this is a capitulation to white chauvinism," was his considered opinion (memo on Negro work, 28 July 1945, Robert Minor

Papers). At the CPA convention Davis averred that dissolving the party in the South showed "the enormous crime of the old line." But even here Ray Thompson of California said that blacks "want integration in the national line, not self-determination" (*Daily Worker*, 27 July, 23 and 20 September, 16 June, 5 August, and 19 September 1945).

47. *Daily Worker*, 23, 25–27 September 1945; *New York Times*, 24 and 27 September 1945; *Daily Worker*, 28 September 1945.

48. *New York Times*, 5 October 1945 (quoting the *Chicago Defender* and the *Oklahoma Black Dispatch*); *New York Amsterdam News*, 6 October 1945. See also *Daily Worker*, 6 October 1945; *New York Times*, 7 October 1945; *Daily Worker*, 8 October and 2 November 1945.

49. Davis memoir, J-82.

50. *New York Times*, 9 November 1945.

51. *Daily Worker*, 7 November and 6 May 1945; *New York Times*, 11 and 18 November 1945; *Daily Worker*, 14–18 November 1945; *Afro-American*, 17 November 1945; *Daily Worker*, 20 November and 23 December 1945.

52. Max Gordon, "Labor Moves Forward in the New York Elections," *Political Affairs* 24 (December 1945): 1079–87. Gordon also found it remarkable that Davis's victory was achieved "in the face of a vicious campaign of slander" by McLaurin et al.

53. *New York Times*, 22 and 21 November 1945.

54. Matthew P. Cronin to Fiorello La Guardia, 16 November 1945, 4/48-16, Fiorello La Guardia Papers.

Chapter 10. Cold War Coming, 1946–1947

1. *Daily Worker*, 10 and 6 January 1946; *Proceedings of the Council of the City of New York, Volume I, 9 January–25 June 1946*. During this period Davis introduced bills or resolutions on subway fare and contruction, building a municipal power plant, building a state medical and dental school in light of discrimination by private schools against blacks and Jews, appointing a black to the local Board of Education, organizing a state FEPC, appointing a special prosecutor in a police brutality case in Freeport, and numerous bills concerning veterans.

2. *Daily Worker*, 29 January and 30 March 1946; *New York Times*, 10 April 1946. The progressive bloc—Davis, Cacchione, Quill, and Connolly—called for the state legislature to hold a special session to increase state aid to the city; *Daily Worker*, 13 and 30 May 1946. Joining the four in the 17–6 vote were Liberals Louis Goldberg and Ira Palestin; *New York Times*, 12 July 1946; *Daily Worker*, 23 January, 10 April, and 27 November 1946.

3. *New York Times*, 6 March 1946; *Daily Worker*, 6 March 1946; *People's Voice*, 6 March 1946; John Cooney, *American Pope: The Life and Times of Francis Cardinal Spellman* (New York: Times Books, 1984).

4. John J. Sheahan to Vincent Impelliteri, 9 March 1946, Vincent Impelliteri Papers; *New York Times*, 13 and 16 March 1946; *Daily Worker*, 13 and 15 March 1946.

5. *New York Times*, 26 June 1946; *Daily Worker*, 7 July, 26 June, 3 March, and 10 April 1946. Detente had not disappeared totally in the council, however, for they honored Dr. Juan Marinello, vicechair of the Cuban Senate and leader of the Communist party, during his New York visit.

6. See, e.g., Gerald Horne, *Black and Red: W.E.B. Du Bois and the Afro-American Response to the Cold War, 1944–1963* (Albany: State University of New York Press, 1985); Gerald Horne, *Communist Front? The Civil Rights Congress, 1946–1956* (Rutherford, N.J.: Fairleigh Dickinson University Press, 1987).

7. Minutes of meeting of Minority City Council Members, ca. January 1946, Box 4, Reel 2, Pete Cacchione Papers.

8. *Daily Worker*, 30 January, 6 April, 18 September, and 14 May 1946. Over two-hundred thousand pieces of literature were distributed in support of the Davis FEPC bill.

9. *Peoples' Voice*, 26 January 1946; *Daily Worker*, 7 February and 12 May 1946; Eric Walrond to "Mr. Watkins," 22 May 1946, 1/3, Box 1, Folder MG77, Gwen Bennett Papers; People's Voice, 11 May 1946; *Daily Worker*, 9 July and 6 December 1946.

10. *Daily Worker*, 5 and 17 February 1946.

11. Memo, 14 February 1946, Box 12, Robert Minor Papers.

12. *Daily Worker*, 18 February 1946.

13. Flyer, "Jim Crow Must Go," 8 May 1946, Reel 4207, Elizabeth Gurley Flynn Papers.

14. *Daily Worker*, 6, 8, 27, 19, 20 January 1946.

15. *Daily Worker*, 27 and 23 January 1946.

16. *Daily Worker*, 8, 10, 23, 24 February 1946. Adam Clayton Powell was sarcastic about Randolph's March on Washington Movement, "an organization with a name it does not live up to, an announced program that it does not stick to and a philosophy contrary to the mood of the times cannot live" (Powell, *Marching Blacks*, 159).

17. *Daily Worker*, 16 and 23 June, 24 November 1946.

18. *Daily Worker*, 23 February, 30 June, 29 July 1946. For background on Black veterans and violence in the postwar era see Florence Murray, ed., *The Negro Handbook, 1946–1947* (New York: Wyn, 1947), 347–56.

19. Davis memoir, 22/207, 16/268, 17/269; *Daily Worker*, 22 September and 31 December 1946.

20. *Washington Star*, 29 March 1946, "William Hastie" file, Box 240, National Republic Papers.

21. *Daily Worker*, 2 February 1946; *People's Voice*, 16 March 1946; *Daily Worker*, 31 March, 21 and 25 April, 30 June 1946. Davis and Houston were old friends from Amherst. Cf. Genna Rae McNeil, *Groundwork: Charles Hamilton Houston and the Struggle for Civil Rights* (Philadelphia: University of Pennsylvania Press, 1983), 104.

22. *Daily Worker*, 7 and 19 June, 21 July and 13 November 1946.

23. *Daily Worker*, 2 June and 20 September 1946; *New York Times*, 4 December 1946.

24. *Daily Worker*, 11 January, 8 and 24 March 1946; *People's Voice*, 27 April 1946; *Daily Worker*, 26 May, 7 June, and 15 July 1946.

25. *Daily Worker*, 18 August 1946; *New York Times*, 8 August 1946; *Daily Worker*, 19 August and 8 September 1946.

26. Gerald Goodman to "Dear Comrade Pete," 26 October 1946, and Pete Cacchione to Gerald Goodman, 4 November 1946, Reel 2, Box 4, Pete Cacchione Papers.

27. *Daily Worker*, 29 July and 10, 12, 13 September 1946; *New York Times*, 20 September 1946; *People's Voice*, 28 September 1946.

28. *Daily Worker*, 28 September and 1, 7, 10 October 1946.

29. Ibid., 17 July, 14–16, 18, 20 October 1946.

30. *People's Voice*, 19 October 1946; *Daily Worker*, 21, 23, 5 October 1946.

31. *Daily Worker*, 27 October 1946; *New York Age*, 2 November 1946; *People's Voice*, 2 November 1946; *Daily Worker*, 4 November 1946.
32. *New York Times*, 6 and 7 November and 13 December 1946.
33. *Daily Worker*, 6, 7, 19 November and 2 December 1946.
34. Ibid., 3 February and 28 April 1946; *New York Age*, 15 April 1946.
35. *New York Amsterdam News*, 16 February 1946; Benjamin J. Davis, "Crusading Congressman," *New Masses* 60 (2 July 1946): 10–12.
36. *People's Voice*, 2 February 1946; *Daily Worker*, 11 December 1946; *New York Age*, 26 October 1946.
37. Ben Davis, *No Jim Crow Army! No Jim Crow War For Wall Street!* (pamphlet), Tamiment Library, New York University; Alfred Baker Lewis to Frank Crosswaith, 9 November 1946, Reel 15, Box 31, G23, Negro Labor Committee Papers.
38. *Daily Worker*, 14 April, 16 December, and 7 April 1946.
39. "Souvenir Program . . . Salute to Ben Davis . . . Mass Rally for Peace and Democracy . . . The Chicago Coliseum, 15th and Wabash," 13 January 1946, Reel 4206, Elizabeth Gurley Flynn Papers. *The Daily Worker* of 6 May 1946 describes a rally at Golden Gate, attended by five-thousand and preceded by a six-block-long parade supporting the CIO's "Operation Dixie" organizing drive. Davis, Powell, and Marcantonio spoke. The "followers" of Father Divine "turned out en masse." *Daily Worker*, 30 October 1946; file, "Campaign Violence," 1946 Campaign, Box 44, Vito Marcantonio Papers, New York Public Library, New York, N.Y.
40. George Lipsitz, "A Rainbow at Midnight: Strategies of Independence in the Post-War Working Class" (Ph.D. diss., University of Wisconsin, 1979); *Daily Worker*, 19 October, 28 December, and 25 July 1947.
41. *Daily Worker*, 23 November 1947; Ben Davis to Essie Robeson, 5 November 1947, Paul Robeson Papers.
42. *Daily Worker*, 13 and 6 January, 9 August, and 18 May 1947.
43. *Daily Worker*, 24 and 26 May, 2 June, 28 May, 8 June, and 30 November 1947; Davis memoir, 3/47, 4/189, 14/199, 24/209; Ben Davis to Essie Robeson, 7 August 1947, Paul Robeson Papers.
44. Malcolm X, *The Autobiography of Malcolm X* (New York: Grove Press, 1965), 77.
45. *Daily Worker*, 16 July 1944, 8 March and 13 January 1946.
46. Robert Minor, *Tell the People How Ben Davis Was Elected* (pamphlet), April 1946, Tamiment Library, New York University.
47. *Daily Worker*, 25 June 1947; Ben Davis, "Build the Negro People's Movement," *Political Affairs* 26 (November 1947): 996–1005; Davis, *Why I Am a Communist*.
48. *Daily Worker*, 22 June, 5 May, and 30 April 1946.
49. Tinsley E. Yarbrough, *A Passion for Justice: J. Waties Waring and Civil Rights* (New York: Oxford University Press, 1987).
50. James Ford, "Mobilize Negro Manpower for Victory," *The Communist* 22 (January 1943): 40–41.
51. Clippings, various dates, Box 29; report by Robert Thompson, 6 September 1945, Box 45; discussion on Negro Work Report, 14 February 1946, Box 12; undated article, Box 12; all in Robert Minor Papers.
52. Claudia Jones, "On the Right To Self-Determination for the Negro People in the Black Belt," *Political Affairs* 25 (January 1946): 67, 76. For more on Jones, see Buzz Johnson, *"I Think of My Mother": Notes on the Life and Times of Claudia Jones* (London: Karia Press, 1985).
53. William Z. Foster, "On Self-Determination for the Negro People," *Political Affairs* 25 (June 1946): 549.

54. Francis Franklin, "The Status of the Negro People in the Black Belt and How to Fight for the Right of Self-Determination," *Political Affairs* 25 (May 1946): 438, 443.

55. Doxey Wilkerson, "The Negro and the American Nation," *Political Affairs* 25 (July 1946): 657.

56. James Allen, "The Negro Question," *Political Affairs* 25 (November 1946): 1046–56. Davis and Wilkerson clashed repeatedly on the theory of the National Question. Wilkerson avers that many black Reds welcomed the Browder line, though Harry Haywood particularly resented abandoning the thesis. "We were not friends," is Wilkerson's terse description of his relationship with Davis, terming him "authoritarian" and "dominating," though he was an "able man" who "defended his positions effectively." Wilkerson says that Davis "went along with the line whatever it was and when the line changed, he went along with that whatever it was"; however, this attitude was part of Communist culture and not just a Davis trait. Doxey Wilkerson, interview with author, 6 May 1988, Norwalk, Conn.

57. "Draft Resolution of the Negro Commission of the Communist Party of the United States on the Negro Question," 10 July 1946, Box 4, Reel 2, Pete Cacchione Papers.

58. [Communist Party], *The Communist Position on the Negro Question* (New York: New Century, 1947).

59. Ben Davis, *The Path of Negro Liberation* (pamphlet) (New York: New Century, 1947), Communist Party Archives; Idem, *Why I Am a Communist*.

60. *Daily Worker*, 5 June 1947.

61. Memorandum, 18 September 1946, 100-149163, FBI; National Negro Congress file, 61-6728, H.Q., FBI; *Daily Worker*, 16 February 1946 and 3 May 1947: Granger did not like Davis's position on Browder but "that's Party business . . . what I respect about Ben is the fact that as a young practicing attorney . . . he gave up his law career and the security it implied to defend Angelo Herndon at at time when all of the other 'legal brethren' were discreetly hiding in the coat closets, [and] Ben Davis supported human freedom at a time when glib professors of democracy were taking the easy way out. For this reason I like and respect Ben Davis." In the *Daily Worker* for 7 December 1947, in addition to flailing Granger, Davis also hit Charles Johnson, Truman Gibson, and Francis Rivers for backing the Marshall Plan. "Report on Campaign of Layle Lane, Socialist for State Senate, 1947," Box 1, Folder 16, Layle Lane Papers.

62. *Daily Worker*, 21 December 1947; *New York Age*, 19 July 1947; *Daily Worker*, 13 July 1947; *New York Age*, 22 March 1947.

63. *New York Amsterdam News*, 17 and 31 May 1947.

64. Washburn, *A Question of Sedition*, chap. 5, n. 50; *New York Times*, 22 December 1954; "Memorandum on Negro Newspapers," undated, Box 29, Robert Minor Papers; *Daily Worker*, 20 April 1947; *New York Amsterdam News*, 20 December 1947.

65. *People's Voice*, 25 December 1943, 19 December 1942, 20 November 1941, 19 January and 20 April 1946.

66. *People's Voice*, 22 November and 27 December 1947, 17 January and 17 April 1948, *Daily Worker*, 19 December 1947.

67. Doxey Wilkerson, interview with author, 6 May 1988; Marvel Cooke, interview with author, 6 April 1988.

68. Duberman, *Paul Robeson*, 670. The ever-watchful Duberman calls Sommers Davis's "lover." Davis suggests that Yergan was quite close to Browder and was disoriented by his removal (Davis memoir, 11/423, 19/431); *Daily Worker*, 22 December 1948.

69. *Daily Worker*, 5 March 1947; memorandum, ca. 1950, Box 2, Herbert Bruce Papers: "The Reds supplied the sinews to elect Powell"; *Daily Worker*, 25 October 1950; press release, 4 May 1949, Claude Barnett Papers, Chicago Historical Society, Chicago: "Of late this alliance has cooled but at one time it was said that Mr. Davis would follow Powell into Congress, when and if the Congressman decided to retire."
70. *Daily Worker*, 9 and 11 March 1947.
71. Ibid., 26 May 1947.
72. Ibid., 2 and 19 June 1947.
73. *Proceedings of the Council of the City of New York, Volumes 1 and 2: 8 January 1947–24 June 1947 and 2 July 1947–23 December 1947*. The record shows that Davis introduced bills or resolutions on such disparate issues as Negro History Week, farm subsidies, firefighting in Harlem, the banning of a Howard Fast novel, racist school textbooks, pay raises for teachers, Jackie Robinson, rent hikes at Riverton and Stuyvesant Town, Jewish emigration to Palestine, antilynching, FEPC, and so on; "Full Record of Councilman Benjamin J. Davis in the City Council," ca. 1949, in possession of Doxey Wilkerson; *Daily Worker*, 15 January 1947.
74. Statement by Ben Davis and Pete Cacchione on budget of Board of Education at 110 Livingston Street, 17 January 1947, Box 5, Reel 12, Pete Cacchione Papers. In the *Daily Worker* for 5 February 1947 Davis demanded that the mayor "hold the fare hearings in 'one of the city's large armories'" rather than in a conference room at the Board of Estimate; *Daily Worker*, 22 December 1947; *New York Times*, 24 December 1947; *Daily Worker*, 24 December 1947.
75. *Daily Worker*, 18 February 1947.
76. Pete Cacchione to Ben Davis, 17 February 1947, Box 4, Reel 2, Pete Cacchione Papers; *Daily Worker*, 17 June and 12 October 1947, 19 May 1946.
77. *Daily Worker*, 26, 29, 30 September 1947; Cesar Andreu Iglesias, ed., *Memoirs of Bernardo Vega: A Contribution to the History of the Puerto Rican Community in New York* (New York: Monthly Review Press, 1984), 230–31.
78. *People's Voice*, 7 June 1947; *Daily Worker*, 4 January, 11 and 13 September, 13 January, and 18 June 1947; *New York Amsterdam News*, 21 June 1947; *Daily Worker*, 3 March 1946.
79. *Daily Worker*, 11 and 19 June 1947.
80. Ibid., 11 December, 24 October, and 14 November 1947.
81. Ibid., 5 March, 23 April, and 11, 14, 15 June 1947. *New York Times*, 15 June 1947.
82. Ibid., 7 May, 25 June, 5 and 8 February 1947; *New York Times*, 30 March 1947.
83. *Daily Worker*, 16 September and 16 November 1947; Davis memoir 16.
84. *New York Times*, 16, 19, 4 December 1947.
85. Stanley Isaacs to Ben Davis, 2 May 1947, Box 15, Stanley Isaacs Papers. Interestingly, Isaacs addressed Davis as "Dear Ben," while Davis invariably replied "Dear Mr. Isaacs"; *Daily Worker*, 27 May 1947: Davis urges that a black such as Bertram Baker be appointed to the council seat vacated by Anthony DiGiovanna.
86. *Daily Worker*, 24 October 1947; Charles Garrett, *The La Guardia Years: Machine and Reform Politics in New York City* (New Brunswick, N.J.: Rutgers University Press, 1961), 234, 235, 242.
87. Belle Zeller and Hugh A. Bone, "American Government and Politics: The Repeal of PR in New York City—Ten Years in Retrospect," *American Political Science Review* 42 (December 1948): 1131, 1133, 1136, 1137, 1144. Leading political figures for some time had kept a wary eye on CP strength: see Communist Party, 1938–1940, Reel 20, Governorship Microfilm, Herbert Lehman Papers, Columbia University Library, New York, N.Y. In 1965 the issue arose again. J. Raymond

Jones favored it, as did John V. Lindsay and Franklin D. Roosevelt, Jr. Isaacs, Jacob Javits, and Robert F. Kennedy also endorsed it (New York Times, 16 June 1965). Cambridge, Mass., still has PR. "Cambridge residents now laugh about the theorists who predicted an end to democracy and say the system has worked the way it is supposed to" said the *New York Times* on 14 November 1987. Particularly they like the diversity it brings, despite the complexity. In the same story, Arend Lijphart, professor at the University of California, San Diego, echoes the contemporary view: "In New York City, it was abolished because it worked the way it was supposed to work and some Communists were elected." Nevertheless, PR proponents in the 1947 election did not effectively confront the complaint expressed in 1937 about PR by the *New York Age* on 4 December 1937. With the Board of Aldermen system, despite the corruption, there were blacks elected from the nineteenth and twenty-first districts in Harlem. They opposed PR, calling it "pretty rotten." There were also contradictions in the party posture. The self-determination line would appear to favor the kind of district elections that the *Age* favored but, as noted, some party theorists tried to dispute the notion that Davis was elected by Harlem; the fact that the party was tending to view northern blacks as a national minority should not be forgotten, though it does not necessarily vitiate the point.

88. *New York Times*, 13, 14, 17, 18 November 1943.
89. Ibid., 21 and 29 November 1945.
90. Robert Moses to Col. Charles Keegan, 24 September 1947, and press release, 4 October 1947, Box 30, Robert Moses Papers; Moses sought to export his viewpoint, traveling to Boston to speak. J. Joseph Connors, secretary to Boston's mayor, unctuously told him, "Boston may some day need your powerful arguments" (J. Joseph Connors to Robert Moses, 6 November 1947, Box 30, Robert Moses Papers). The idea of PR leading to fascism was quiet common, as Isaacs indicated to Gerson: "I had to debate the problem with Walter Hart the other night and he asserted quite soberly that if it had not been for PR World War II would never have started. He regards it as responsible for the success of both Hitler and Mussolini" (Stanley Isaacs to Si Gerson, 9 October 1947, Box 14, Stanley Isaacs Papers). By conflating Communism and fascism this argument fed into the burgeoning concept of "totalitarianism" and the substitution of fighting the USSR instead of Germany as a rationale for the Cold War, Red Scare, and increased spending on military contracts.
91. *New York Times*, 1 and 3 November 1947; *Daily Worker*, 3 April 1947; *New York World-Telegram*, 19 November 1945; *New York Times*, 15 November 1947; *Daily Worker*, 4 and 6 September 1947.
92. *New York Amsterdam News*, 16 August and 25 October 1947; *Daily Worker*, 27 October 1947; *New York Amsterdam News*, 1 November 1947; *New York Age*, 1 November 1947.
93. *Daily Worker*, 4 October 1947.
94. Ibid., 7, 26, 29 October 1947; flyer, 29 October 1947, Ben Davis Vertical File-Schomburg Center. *Daily Worker*, 9 October 1947: "Get a Sub for Ben! Recruit for Ben!" was the cry at the testimonial. *Daily Worder*, 11 October 1947: for Davis's birthday the county CP gave him a car, the clothing workers gave him a suit, the fur and leather workers gave him a wallet, the shoeworkers gave him shoes, and the bakers gave him a cake. *Daily Worker*, 20 October, 2 November, and 30 October 1947; flyer, ca. 1947, Ben Davis Vertical File-Schomburg Center; flyer, ca. 1947, in possession of Doxey Wilkerson.
95. *Daily Worker*, 5, 7, 9 November 1947. Cacchione's funeral came right after the PR loss. Davis was the major speaker and twelve thousand attended this funeral cum mass demonstration (*Daily Worker*, 9 November 1947).
96. *New York Age*, 15 November 1947; Ben Davis to Essie Robeson, 5 November 1947, Paul Robeson Papers.

Chapter 11. Red Scare Coming, 1948

1. Ben Davis to Essie Robeson, 5 July 1948, Paul Robeson Papers.
2. Unsigned letter to Attorney General Nathan Goldstein, ca. 1945, 4148-16, Fiorello La Guardia Papers.
3. Stanley Isaacs to Genevieve Earle, 19 July 1949, Box 1, Genevieve Earle Papers.
4. *Daily Worker*, 17, 22, 25 February, 20 January, and 1 February 1948.
5. Ibid., 1 and 2 March 1948. *New York Times*, 15 September 1948: council votes down resolution calling for boycott of UK goods because of Israel; the vote is 18-1 on a resolution introduced by Connolly. *Daily Worker*, 13 April 1948; Stanley Isaacs to Dorothy Chase, 13 September 1948, Box 16, Stanley Isaacs Papers.
6. *New York Times*, 22 September 1948; *Daily Worker*, 22 September 1948.
7. *Daily Worker*, 4 November and 29 September 1948.
8. *New York Times*, 21 May 1948; *Daily Worker*, 25 January, 28 April, and 21 May 1948.
9. *Daily Worker*, 13 and 19 April 1948; *Proceedings of the Council of the City of New York, volume I, 7 January–22 June 1948. Proceedings of the Council of the City of New York, 6 July–21 December 1948, Volume II*. Davis was involved in resolutions or bills such as those calling for a black on the Board of Education, establishing a free state university, assailing the draft, establishing a municipal milk plant, ending discrimination against Puerto Ricans in housing, and condemning Arabs during the fighting over the new state of Israel. Like many on the Left, Davis's view of this controversy was one-sided, in part due to Moscow's influence. Cf. also *Annual Report of the Board of Elections in New York City: 1943, 1945, 1949*.
10. *Daily Worker*, 12 March 1948; *New York Times*, 2 March 1948; *Daily Worker*, 24 February 1948. It has been argued that what has been designated as Stalinism did help to make the post–World War II Red Scare worse; however, if one compares the coverage received by Bolshevism after World War I in the so-called mainstream press with Stalinism, the similarities tend to overshadow the differences.
11. *Daily Worker*, 23 June 1948; *Proceedings of the Council of the City of New York, Volume II, 6 July–21 December 1948*.
12. *Daily Worker*, 22 December 1948; Vincent Impelliteri to Italian Prime Minister Alcide deGasperi, 23 April 1948, Vincent Impelliteri Papers.
13. *Daily Worker*, 28 January and 9 June 1948.
14. Ibid., 7 March and 22 and 13 September 1948.
15. Ibid., 9 March, 14 April, and 18 May 1948.
16. Ibid., 14 and 21 March and 23 and 30 May 1948.
17. Ibid., 30 July, 1 August, and 19 September 1948; Guy Turner to Harry S. Truman, 29 February 1948, O.F. 144A, Harry S. Truman Papers, Truman Presidential Library, Independence, Mo.
18. *Daily Worker*, 16 February and 4 January 1948.
19. Ibid., 3, 15, 26 October 1948.
20. *New Masses*, 6 January 1948; *Daily Worker*, 8 November and 18 April 1948.
21. *Daily Worker*, 25 April, 16 May, 26 December, 3 May, and 22 September 1948.
22. File, ALP Campaign, Box 44, Proceedings, State Executive Committee—ALP, 7 January 1948, Vito Marcantonio Papers; *Daily Worker*, 11 January 1948.
23. *Daily Worker*, 27 June and 26 July 1948.
24. Ibid., 15 February and 11 April 1948.
25. *New York Amsterdam News*, 17 April 1948.

26. A. P. Randolph to Howard Coles, 28 July 1948, Container 16, A. Philip Randolph Papers; *Daily Worker*, 8 and 29 August 1948.

27. Letters to Frank Crosswaith, Reel 9, Box 18, D5; A. P. Randolph to Frank Crosswaith, 10 March 1954, Reel 9, Box 18, D8; Frank Crosswaith to N.Y. newspaper editors, 19 April 1948, Reel 11, Box 24, E15; C. B. Powell to Frank Crosswaith, 6 May 1948, Reel 11, Box 24, E15, all in Negro Labor Committee Papers.

28. Frank Crosswaith to C. B. Powell, 10 May 1948, Reel 11, Box 24, E15, and Frank Crosswaith to Walter White, 26 April 1948, Reel 4, Box 7, B74, Negro Labor Committee Papers; Pittsburgh Courier, 17 July 1954.

29. *Daily Worker*, 4 April and 25 and 15 August 1948. Ibid., 15 December 1949: said Davis, "Big Business will rely principally upon its first assistant, social Democracy, the worst enemy of a militant united struggle for Negro rights—upon right wing Negro reformists and corrupt lieutenants of Wall Street and upon the Trotskyites and 'Socialist' splitters."

30. Henry Lee Moon, *Balance of Power: The Negro Vote* (Garden City, N.Y.: Doubleday, 1948), 120, 121, 171; Harry Raymond, *The Ingrams Shall not Die!*, Reel 1808, #6668, Tamiment Radical Pamphlet Series, New York University. Said Davis, "The Ingram case presents the immediate danger of the extension of the special pro-fascist persecution of the Negro people in the South. . . . Neither Truman nor any of the Republican presidential aspirants have taken one step even to denounce this conspiracy."

31. *Daily Worker*, 2 October 1949; *Pittsburgh Courier*, 16 April 1949.

32. Henry Winston, "Some Aspects of Party Work," *Political Affairs* 27 March 1948): 238–50.

33. *Daily Worker*, 15 May 1949, 21 and 20 June 1948, 5 September 1948.

34. Ibid., 25 May and 10 July 1949.

35. "The Struggle Against White Chauvinism," ca. 1949, CP Education Department, Leon Kramer Papers, University of Wisconsin, Madison, Wisc.; George Blake, "The Ideological Struggle Against White Chauvinism," Report given at CP's Industrial Conference on Struggle for Negro Rights and Against White Chauvinism, 8 October 1949, Reel 1750, 579, Tamiment Radical Pamphlet Series, New York University.

36. *Daily Worker*, 22 March, 18 May, 12 July, and 17 October 1948; Schedule for Program for CP—14th National Convention, Reel 4207, 2 August 1948, Elizabeth Gurley Flynn Papers.

37. *Daily Worker*, 8 February 1948; Oliver Cox to Ben Davis, 12 September 1948, and Ruth Benedict to Ben Davis, 30 March 1948, Ben Davis Papers.

38. Ben Davis, "The Negro People's Liberation Movement," *Political Affairs* 27 (September 1948): 880–98.

39. *Daily Worker*, 29 April 1948; *New York Age*, 21 September 1948; *New York Age*, 24 November 1948; *Daily Worker*, 24 October 1948.

40. *Daily Worker*, 13 June and 12 December 1948; *New York Age*, 3 April 1948; *Daily Worker*, 12 September 1948.

41. *Daily Worker*, 22 December, 21 September, and 24 and 28 December 1948.

42. *New York Amsterdam News*, 25 December 1948; *Daily Worker*, 25 March, 7 February, and 3 August 1948.

43. *Daily Worker*, 7 February, 3 August, 20 February 1948; *New York Times*, 1 March 1948.

44. *Daily Worker*, 11 July 1948; *People's Voice*, 18 January 1947; *Daily Worker*, 18 and 20 July 1948.

45. *New York Age*, 23 July 1949; *Daily Worker*, 18 January 1948.

46. *New York Amsterdam News*, 24 January 1948; *Daily Worker*, 25 January 1948; *New York Age*, 31 January 1948; *Daily Worker*, 11, 12, 14 May 1948.

47. L. B. Nichols to Clyde Tolson, 18 February 1948, 100-149163-69, FBI; *New York Times*, 21 February 1948; *Daily Worker*, 22 February 1948.
48. *Daily Worker*, 21 November 1948; *New York Age*, 24 July 1948; *Daily Worker*, 21 and 22 July 1948; *New York Times*, 21 July 1948.
49. Stanley Isaacs to Ben Davis, 21 July 1948, and Ben Davis to Stanley Isaacs, 24 July 1948, Box 15; see also Stanley Isaacs to Ben Davis, 30 July 1948, Box 16, all Stanley Isaacs Papers.
50. *New York Star*, 22 July 1948; *Daily Worker*, 15 August 1948; *Daily Worker*, 23 July 1948.
51. *New York Amsterdam News*, 31 and 24 July 1948.
52. *New York Times*, 3 August 1948; *Daily Worker*, 15, 22 and 29 August 1948.
53. *Daily Worker*, 23, 29, 24 September 1948; *New York Times*, 21 October 1948.
54. *Daily Worker*, 31 October, 21 November 1948; 17 October 1948; 13 December 1948.

Chapter 12. The Trial of the Century, 1949

1. *Daily Worker*, 5 March 1950.
2. Ibid., 1 February 1949, 27 March 1947; *New York Times*, 15 October 1949. The eleven defendants were: Engene Dennis, Henry Winston, John Williamson, Jacob Stachel, Robert G. Thompson, Ben Davis, John Gates, Irving Potash, Gil Green, Carl Winter, and Gus Hall.
3. Legal Document, No. C128187, 21 October 1949, Ben Davis Papers.
4. *New York Times*, 15 October 1949; Jacob Spolansky, *The Communist Trial in America* (New York: Macmillan Co., 1951).
5. Kevin John O'Brien, "*Dennis v. U.S.*: The Cold War, the Communist Conspiracy and the FBI" (Ph.D. diss., Cornell University, 1979). He adds that the CP "had obviously been forewarned because copies of a statement denouncing the arrests . . . were being distributed even as the group left the building." During the trial there were "omnipresent pickets on the Foley Square traffic island. They changed 'jump, jump' to Medina after . . . [Defense Secretary James] Forrestal had taken his own life . . . or . . . 'How do you spell Medina? R-A-T' or '2, 4, 6, 8, we don't want a fascist state." The American Bar Association and other organizations called for a ban on picketing at the court house as a result. O'Brien cites *ACA, CIO v. Douds*, 339 US 382 (1950), as a key to understanding the CP-11 case.
6. *New York Times*, 14 June 1949. *New York Times*, 3 April 1988: Prosecutor Irving Saypol received a job through the intervention of organized crime. See also Sidney Zion, *The Autobiography of Roy Cohn* (New York: Lyle Stuart, 1988), which confirms that organized crime traditionally determined the appointment of the U.S. Attorney; *Daily Worker*, 14 Devember 1947.
7. File on Angela Calomiris, 25 January 1949, 65-9944 2050 & 65 9944 2164, FBI; File on CP-11 case, ca. 1949, Reel 20, Box 32–33, G10; trial exhibits, CP-11 case, ca. 1949, Reel 21, Box 35, G33; press clippings on CP-11 trial, ca. 1949, Reel 64, Box 117, X80; all in CRC Papers; see also editorials from New York newspapers denouncing the CP-11, ca. 1949, Box 5, Robert Minor Papers; File: Communist Leaders, Box 478, General File, and file on CP, 263A, Box 882, Harry S. Truman Papers; Smith Act Case File, Box 1, Matt McGohey Papers, Truman Presidential Library, Independence, Mo.
8. *Oklahoma Black Dispatch*, ca. 1949, Box 3, Folder 3/3, Paul Robeson Papers.
9. *New York Times*, 22 October 1949.

10. *Daily Worker*, 30 July 1946.
11. Ibid., 23 January 1949; *Daily Worker*, 22 May 1949.
12. Ibid., 8 August 1949. At a rally of three thousand Harlem residents, Davis added, "the enemy of the Negro people is not in Moscow, Czechoslovakia, Hungary or Romania—our enemy is in Mississippi, Georgia and among those in this country who force us to sit behind curtains in trains as though we were lepers . . . Harlem landlords who overcharge us for rat-infested firetraps . . . [and the] bourbon landlord lynchers of the South."
13. Ibid., 16 August 1941. Howard called the Smith Act the "modern edition of the 'sedition' law . . . obviously antagonistic to the Constitution . . . and to most of the state constitutions. The workers do not support such laws."
14. Ibid., 19 December 1941, 12 May 1942, 13 February and 15 June 1949.
15. *New York Times*, 17 July 1949. At the conference Davis viewed the trial as a smokescreen by "the men of Wall Street, the imperialists, who wish to conquer the world, to drown all peoples in blood, to suck the world dry for their own profits."
16. *Daily Worker*, 18 July 1949; *New York Post*, 8 June 1961.
17. Davis memoir, 6/282; *Nation*, 26 February 1949; *Daily Worker*, 30 January 1949; jury challenges, ca. 1949, Reel 63, Box 112, X51, and Reel 20, Box 34, G29, CRC Papers.
18. *New York Amsterdam News*, 12 and 19 March 1949.
19. *Daily Worker*, 20 March 1949; *Daily Compass*, 23 August 1949; *Daily Worker*, 24 August 1949. *Daily Worker*, 16 February 1949.
20. *Daily Compass*, 16 October 1949; *New York Daily News*, 15 October 1949.
21. National Non-Partisan Committee to Defend the Rights of the 12 Communist Leaders, "Due Process in a Political Trial; The Record vs. the Press," 1949, Reel 4, Eugene Dennis Papers, State Historical Society, Madison, Wisc.
22. "Study" of CP-11 Transcript, ca. 1949, Reel 63, Box 114, X84, CRC.
23. Paul Robeson, "The Trial of Judge Medina," 26 August 1949, Box 2, Folder 2/9, Paul Robeson Papers. Davis memoir, unnumbered page.
24. Duberman, *Paul Robeson*, 264.
25. House Committee on Un-American Activities, *Investigation of the Unauthorized Use of Passports*, 84th Cong. 2ed sess., 24–25 May 1956. Of interent is Charles Payne's dissertation, "Paul Robeson: A Psychobiographical Study of the Emotional Development of a Controversial Protest Leader" (Northwestern University, 1987, p. 136): unlike Duberman, Payne points to significant turning points in Robeson's life such as the burning of the Reichstag and the rise of fascism. Robeson did benefits for Jewish refugees in 1933 and began to see the parallel between the Jewish in Germany and African-Americans in the United States; moreover, he was outraged when in 1931 London passed a statute that benefited "white" members of the Commonwealth like Canada, Australia, New Zealand, and South Africa but excluded India.
26. Foner, *Paul Robeson Speaks*, 7.
27. *Daily Worker*, 5 June 1949. Duberman, *Robeson*, 345: "Indeed, the popular reaction in the black community to his alleged remarks in Paris did not fully coincide with the black leadership's presentation of it. . . . Even after the cold war climate deepened, Harlemites could not be stampeded into an automatic anti-Soviet response. . . . few black members left the party after the Stalin revelations."
28. *Daily Worker*, 20 and 26 June 1949; R. Davis of Troop 'K' to Troop Commander, 31 August 1949, Thomas Dewey Papers.
29. Davis affadavit after Peekskill, 1949, CP-11 trial, vol. 17, CRC Papers (Schomburg, supplementary); *Daily Worker*, 9 and 11 September 1949.
30. *Daily Worker*, 15 and 21 September 1949; *New York Times*, 6 September 1949; *Daily Worker*, 11 September 1949.

31. Paul Robeson, Jr., interview with author, 11 August 1988. Robeson junior also recalls a dispute as to whether his father should be asked to testify in the trial.

32. *Daily Worker*, 8 May 1949.

33. *New York Times*, 28 February 1988.

34. Newbold O. Morris, *Let the Chips Fall: My Battles Against Corruption* (New York: Appleton-Century-Crofts, 1955), 152. Morris also recalls that the Davis-led battle over Stuyvesant Town "kept me awake at night" (283).

35. *New York Times*, 28 August 1949.

36. "Medina Trial," ca. 1949, 263-A, Box 883, Harry S. Truman Papers.

37. J. Edgar Hoover to Rear Admiral Sidney W. Sowers, 15 February 1949, Box 167, President's Secretary Files, Harry S. Truman Papers.

38. Text of advertisement, ca. 1949, Reel 14, Box 23, B17, CRC Papers; *Daily Worker*, 29 August 1948.

39. *Daily Worker*, 10 March 1949; *New York Age*, 5 February 1949; Roy Wilkins to branches, 18 October 1949, Group II, A206, NAACP Papers.

40. Undated clipping of Langston Hughes, Reel 20, Box 34, G26, CRC Papers.

41. *Daily Worker*, 10 July 1949; *New York Age*, 12 April 1947; *Daily Worker*, 25 March and 4 December 1949.

42. *Pittsburgh Courier*, 24 September 1949.

43. *Censored News*, pamphlet, ca. 1949, Copy in author's possession.

44. Crockett summation at CP-11 trial, 14 October 1949, Reel 20, G14, Box 33, CRC Papers; *Daily Compass*, 16 October 1949.

45. Paul Robeson and Ferdinand Smith to Norman Manley, 2 July 1951, Box 1, folder 1/4, Paul Robeson Papers.

46. *New York Age*, 12 March 1949; Assistant Attorney General A. M. Campbell, Criminal Division, to FBI Director, 10 March 1949, HQ-1007321 140, FBI; memorandum, 12 Febuary 1953, HQ-1007321-888-10010769, FBI.

47. Ann Fagan Ginger and Eugene M. Tobin, eds., *The National Lawyers Guild: From Roosevelt through Reagan* (Philadelphia: Temple University Press, 1988), 193.

48. Herbert Levy to Editor, *New York World-Telegram*, 14 June 1949, vol. 49, ACLU Papers; *New York Times*, 21 June 1949 and 14 December 1961.

49. *Daily Compass*, 14 October 1949; *Daily World*, 1 May 1949.

50. "Minutes of Founding Meeting of Communist Committee to Defend the 12," 19 February 1949, Reel 4215, Elizabeth Gurley Flynn Papers. Absent were James Jackson, Robert Minor, Ed Strong, Fred Fine, Nemmy Sparks, Pettis Perry, William Schneiderman; present were Anton Krchmarek, Anne Burlak of Boston, Gurley Flynn, Claude Lightfoot of Chicago, Mother Bloor, Herbert Wheeldin, Israel Amter, and William Albertson. (It is striking that so many of the key black comrades missed this meeting.) *Daily Worker*, 4 March, 29 April, and 4 and 10 January 1949.

51. Davis affadavit, 20 May 1949, Reel 20, Box 33, G15, CRC.

52. *Daily Worker*, 27 May 1949. The *New York Times* put a different spin on the story: " . . . in one of the most abusive and disorderly of the almost daily attacks on the judge in the nineteen-week trial . . . Mr. Davis, who is a graduate of Amherst College and Harvard Law School and whose conduct hitherto had been the most dignified of any of the defendants. . . ." The *Times* mentioned Medina's boredom with the trial and contempt for the defendants and their "double talk, pseudo-scientific jargon and Communist slogans." See Kinoy, *Rights on Trial*, 80: Davis spoke with the Distinguished Professor of Law at Rutgers about a "political counteroffensive within the courtroom itself" during the trial. But Kinoy feels the attorneys "completely overshadowed" the defendants, a major error. After the verdict, he writes, "the Cold War instrument was fashioned and ready for use from one end of the country to the other."

53. *Daily Worker*, 30 May 1949; Davis added, "He has singled out Crockett for abuse even when all the other attorneys protested just as vigorously." *New York Age*, 11 June 1949.

54. *Pittsburgh Courier*, 23 July 1949; *New York Daily News*, 9 July 1949: "Instead of raising a rumpus and insulting the judge, he made what we think was a dignified and persuasive presentation of the reasons why he he became a Communist . . . [but] Mr. Davis was played for a sucker . . . as long as discrimination against minorities exist here, the Reds will have a talking point, and there will be suckers to fall for their lying promise of better treatment under the Red Flag. The faster we can wipe out the remaining injustices of this type, the better for all of us except the Communists." The *New York Times* of 8 July 1949 reported that Davis was "courteous on the stand" and had "dignity," quoting him as saying, "The fact that I had been luckier than most people in education and income did not shield me from what all Negroes suffered." *New York Times*, 9 July 1949: Davis denied teaching force and violence; "[he] maintained a dignified and respectful manner toward the court in contrast to" Gates and Gil Green. *New York Times*, 12 July 1949: Davis denies that the party advocates segregation of blacks in a separate nation; "Sitting in the witness chair, Davis frequently thumped the table in front of him with his hand to emphasize points in his testimony." Then Medina asked Davis to "be a good boy . . . 'I don't want to be a good boy,' replied Davis curtly." *New York Times*, 13 July 1949: The Davis story for that day concerned Davis admitting making false statements in admission to the Georgia bar, registering to vote, and to drive in New York; "Under cross examination, like previous defense witnesses [Davis] proved evasive and forgetful." Davis alleged that he did not include insulting references to him in preparing the record for the Herndon appeal: "That was my first trial case. I made many mistakes." The *Daily Worker* coverage inevitably had a different slant. 10 July 1949: After Davis was threatened with jail, the paper related, "Judge Medina, his voice bristling with anger, warned Davis to eliminate from his testimony matters of jim crow and race discrimination ruled out before." Medina would not allow into evidence his first bill, concerning racism, which he put forth in the City Council in January 1944; Davis vigorously took the oath when sworn in. The *DW* underscored his testimony that he was arrested with Heywood Broun and fined ten dollars in 1935 for picketing the *Amsterdam News* during the strike. 8 July 1949: A first-page banner headline reports Davis taking the stand, third after Gates and Green. 11 July 1949: Stories mentioned schools attended, relatives born in slavery, attending a "small tumbledown rural school." At Amherst he was listed as an "unclassified student" where he played football, starred on the debating team, played in the orchestra and sang in the choir. He termed the Herndon case the "turning point in my life." Reading the classics of Marxism-Leninism, "I began to think what I could do to fight Jim Crow and lynching. So I joined the Communist Party." 12 July 1949: Medina again threatens Davis with jail "but the calm scholarly persistence of Davis, coupled with a vigorous courtroom argument by . . . Eugene Dennis . . . caused [Medina] to relent slightly." Davis "spoke in a soft, clear and dignified tone."

55. Davis testimony, 29 June 1950, 100-23825, FBI; *Daily Worker*, 1 July 1949. Membership card of Communist Party, 1946, and copy of 1948 Constitution, Reel 21, Box 35, G44, G53, CRC Papers: For an income over $60 a week, the dues were two dollars; for $25 to $60, one dollar; under $25, thirty five cents; unemployed, ten cents.

56. Davis memoir, 10/953.

57. Ibid., 10/952, 7/949, 17/959, 3/963, 5/965, 11/976, 20/1006.

58. Transcript, direct examination of Ben Davis, 11: 8333ff., CRC Papers (Schomburg supplementary materials). Davis hit the continuation of the no-strike pledge that emerged from this meeting.

59. Transcript, 11: 8426, 8488, CRC Papers; testimony of Ben Davis in Foley Square case, Box 11, Folder 23, Theodore Draper Papers.
60. Summary of CP Trial by Max Gordon, 10 July 1949, Reel 20, Box 33, G19, CRC Papers.
61. *Daily Worker*, 9 August and 21 September 1949.
62. Opinion of Judge Harold Medina on Davis application to be his own attorney, 1949, Reel 63, Box 114, X83, CRC Papers. See also *Censored News*, 1949, in possession of author: Medina had told Crockett at one point, "Now you be a good boy" and "I will hear not any more about lynching—I'm sick and tired of it."
63. *Daily Worker*, 6 October 1949; Ben Davis speech, 5 October 1949, WMCA, Reel 63, Box 114, X83, CRC Papers.
64. *Daily Worker*, 7 and 19 January 1949; *New York Times*, 19 January 1949.
65. *New York Times*, 15 October 1949; *Daily Worker*, 13 February and 18 March 1949.
66. *Daily Worker*, 4 April, 2 and 23 May, 5, 21, 12 June 1949.
67. Ibid., 25 July and 2 August 1949.
68. Ibid., 16, 23 and 30 October and 4 November 1949.
69. Ibid., 10 November 1948; "Memo re: Petition for Re-hearing" for Ben Davis, 1949, Reel 4, Box 5, A80, CRC Papers. Cited was evidence introduced at trial concerning his anti-Jim Crow acts, which was treated as "'window dressing'" or "'Aesopian'" by the judge; thus, it was argued, when antiracism can be dismissed so cavalierly, all antiracist efforts are in peril; Transcript of CP-11 trial, U.S. Court of Appeals for 2nd Circuit, CRC Papers (Schomburg supplementary materials).
70. *Daily Worker*, 22, 23, 25 November and 5 December 1949.
71. *Afro-American*, 12 November 1949.
72. *New York Times*, 4 November 1949. *Daily Worker*, 4 November 1949: their reporter said the crowd was five-thousand strong, a "great throng", and awaited Davis at 126th and Lenox while another crowd awaited at 110th and Lenox; the torchlight parade began traversing Lenox when the police beat the protesters at 114th Street.
73. *Daily Worker*, 6 November 1949; *New York Times*, 6 November 1949; *Daily Worker*, 1 December 1949.

Chapter 13. Purged from the Council, 1949

1. U.S. Congress, House Committee on Un-American Activities, *Hearings Regarding Communist Infiltration of Minority Groups—Part I*, 81st Cong., 1st sess, 13, 14, and 18 July 1949; *Communist Influence Among Negroes—Fact or Illusion*, National Urban League pamphlet, ca. 1949, Ben Davis Vertical File-Schomburg Library; *Daily Worker*, 6 February 1949. For further on the "Faustian bargain," see previously cited works by the author.
2. *Daily Worker*, 7 and 13 March 1949; Steven Lawson et al., "Groveland: Florida's Little Scottsboro," *Florida Historical Quarterly* 65 (July 1986): 14. The Groveland Massacre, typical of the times, involved a black G.I., Sam Shepherd, who returned home not wanting to work for whites; after the alleged rape of a white woman, his home and property were destroyed. In a gesture typical of historians, the authors credit the NAACP and the Workers' Defense League but not the crucial role of the CRC in exposing this outrage. See Horne, *Communist Front*, 192–95.
3. *Daily Worker*, 13 May 1949; House. Committee on Un-American Activities, *Hearings on Communist Infiltration of Hollywood Motion Picture Industry*, 82d

Cong., 1st sess., March–April 1951, 548, 550, 554, 663, 665 Will Geer was queried about his affiliation with an artists' group that backed Davis for City Council; he took the Fifth Amendment. By the time of the 1949 trial and electoral campaign, most of the "stars" who had flocked to Davis in those different days of the 1945 campaign had disappeared. See Eric Bentley, ed., *Thirty Years of Treason: Excerpts from Hearings Before the House Committee on Un-American Activities, 1938–1968* (New York: Viking, 1971), 305, where the author tells how Lena Horne was scorned for giving "free entertainment" in an affair "honoring the commie election of Ben J. Davis . . ." (*Hollywood Life*, 13 July 1951).

4. John Powers and Samuel Korb to Ben Davis, 9 February 1949, Ben Davis Papers; Daily Worker, 8 January 1950.

5. Alfred Baker Lewis to Frank Crosswaith, 16 February 1950, Reel 15, Box 31, Negro Labor Committee Papers.

6. *Pittsburgh Courier*, 19 November 1949.

7. *Daily Worker*, 31 July, 24 April, and 15 June 1949.

8. Ibid., 19 June, 18 September, 28 August, and 20 March 1949. Despite the trial and the repression, a Harlem edition of the *DW* was begun in February 1949. This was a response to the demise of the *People's Voice*. Said Davis, "The paper will not be a rival of the Negro press. It will desire to cooperate with [them] and will be glad to sponsor and cooperate in any project for the general welfare of the community."

9. Ibid., 9 March 1949; when council member Walter McGahan introduced a resolution to excuse Davis from council due to the trial, Davis saw a subterfuge and protested: see *New York Times* and *Daily Worker* for 25 January 1949. The *Proceedings of the Council of the City of New York, Volumes I & II*, 5 January–23 June 23 1949 & 7 July–28 December 1949 show that despite being on trial and handling other responsibilities, Davis remained active in the council. During this period he introduced bills or resolutions on issues such as Stuyvesant Town, Negro History Week, jury reform, state aid to cities, repeal of the Taft-Hartley Act, traffic safety near schools, unemployment, West Indian immigration, attacks on "Negro longshoremen," rent strikes, rent control, no use of New York Police Department in strikes, reduction in force of NYPD, etc.

10. *Daily Worker*, 2 January, 1 February, and 15 June 1949. Ben Davis to Stanley Isaacs, 12 February 1949, Box 16, Stanley Isaacs Papers: "The courage which you demonstrated in the City Council last Tuesday will long be remembered by me personally. . . . While we disagree on many questions, you have my profound respect and admiration." Allan Dulles to Stanley Isaacs, 1 September 1949, Box 17, Stanley Isaacs Papers: "I am delighted with our local city ticket." See also Freeman, *In Transit*.

11. *New York Times*, 18 August 1949; *Daily Worker*, 18, 23, 31 August 1949; *New York Times*, 31 August 1949; *Daily worker*, 21 September 1949.

12. *Daily Worker*, 10 April 1949; *New York Times*, 18 May 1949.

13. *Daily Worker*, 2 March, 25 May and 12 June 1949.

14. Ibid., 10, 17, 20, 27 March and 3 April 1949.

15. Ibid., 20 March and 5, 6, 29, 17 April 1949.

16. Ibid., 9, 10, 11, 15, 16 February 1949.

17. Ibid., 25 February 1949.

18. Ibid., 14 September 1949; *New York Times*, 27 April 1949.

19. *New York Times*, 27 April 1949; *Daily Worker*, 1 May 1949; *New York Times*, 9 November 1949; *Daily Worker*, 12 October 1952, 1 and 13 November 1949; "A Tribute to Councilman Benjamin J. Davis," 1949, Ben Davis Papers.

20. *Daily Worker*, 12 June, 13 July 1949; *New York Amsterdam News*, 6 August 1949.

21. In an article Robert Vann attacked Brown for his criticisms of Joe Louis, Earl

Brown Vertical File-Schomburg Library; *Christian Science Monitor*, 25 October 1949. Ollie Harrington, interview, with author, 1 June 1989: Harrington, who served as campaign manager for Davis, claims that Brown was saved from a very difficult situation by Harvard and allies of Henry Luce, making him unduly obligated to them. See also *New York Times*, 5 November 1949; *New York Amsterdam News*, 12 February 1949.

22. *New York Age*, 20 July 1940.
23. *New York Amsterdam News*, 11 August 1945.
24. Ibid., 22 November 1947.
25. Ibid., 13 December, 13 September, and 6 December 1947. As late as May 1949 Brown was denouncing the Harlem district leaders who weeks later were backing him against Davis (*New York Amsterdam News*, 28 May 1949).
26. Ibid., 12 February, 29 January, 7 May, 4 June, and 28 May 1949.
27. Walter, *The Harlem Fox*, 164, 203.
28. *Daily Worker*, 16 October, 29 and 31 July, 2 August, 24 July 1949.
29. Ibid., 12 September 1949; *New York Times*, 16 September 1949; *Daily Worker*, 19 September 1949; *Afro-American*, 29 October 1949.
30. Davis memoir, 995, 1008–9.
31. *New York Amsterdam News*, 14 August 1948; *New York Age*, 8 October 1949.
32. *New York Age*, 15 October 1949.
33. *Daily Worker*, 31 July 1949.
34. Ibid., 1 May 1949; *Afro-American*, 5 November 1949; "A Message" from Davis on 1949 re-election, in possession of Doxey Wilkerson; statement to Harlem from Du Bois on reelection, 29 July 1949, in possession of Doxey Wilkerson; *Daily Worker*, 2, 3 November and 9 October 1949; Si Gerson to Claude Barnett, 20 July 1949, Claude Barnett Papers; *Daily Worker*, 4 September 1949; *Afro-American*, 29 October 1949; *Daily Worker*, 15 July 1949.
35. *Daily Worker*, 23 September 1949.
36. Frank Crosswaith to "Noah," 1 November 1949, Reel 4, Box 7, B76, Negro Labor Committee Papers.
37. *Daily Worker*, 1 May, 2 August, and 10 July 1949.
38. Ibid., 10 and 24 April, 16 October, 23 and 27 March, and 29 May 1949.
39. *New York Age*, 22 October 1949; *Daily Worker*, 25, 28, 10 July, 23 October, and 29 April 1949; flyer on labor support, ca. 1949, Box 13, Robert Minor Papers; *Daily Worker*, 7 June 1949.
40. *Daily Worker*, 15 May 1949: Annette Rubenstein on Davis: "he has fought for all poor people of the city . . . he has proved himself an honest and independent champion of the people." *Daily Worker*, 29 September 1949: the racist books were *How to Create Cartoons* and *Lanterns on the Levee*. *Daily Worker*, 20 October 1949: the film was available from Contemporary Films (80 Fifth Avenue). *Daily Worker*, 25 October 1949.
41. *Daily Worker*, 30 October 1949: "The only ones who do not seem to care for [the film] are the cops, who in the past week have issued a score of summonses to the movie operators"; *Daily Worker*, 2 and 7 November 1949: after his release from jail just after the trial, Davis held two mass rallies, a reception, a dozen meetings, a press conference, a radio broadcast, and an open-air rally. Ted Thackrey of the *Daily Compass* endorsed Davis and opposed the council effort to oust him as a member (*Daily Compass*, 24 October 1949).
42. Report on Davis speech, 18 January 1950, New York, 100-23825, FBI; *New York Daily News*, 25 July 1949; *Daily Worker*, 9 November and 22 July 1949.
43. *New York World-Telegram*, 5 October 1949; *Daily Worker*, 7 October 1949.
44. Frank Crosswaith to editor, ca. 1949, Reel 11, Box 24, E15, *Negro Labor Committee Papers*.

45. Earl Brown to "Dear Herb," 14 December 1949, Box 1, Herbert Bruce Papers.

46. *New York Times*, 4 August 1949.

47. *Daily Worker*, 1 November 1949; *New York Age*, 3 September 1949; *Daily Worker*, 7 June and 2 October 1949.

48. *Daily Worker*, 14 September 1949: The Stachel article continued, "The reelection of Ben Davis under these conditions would be one of the biggest blows to this attempt to outlaw the Communist Party." *Daily Worker*, 9 October and 4 August 1949.

49. Pettis Perry, "Next Stage in the Struggle for Negro Rights." *Political Affairs* 28 (October 1949): 41.

50. *Daily Worker*, 22 May, 3, 9, 14, 25 August 1949. *Daily Worker*, 28 August 1949: leading lights on the Davis reelection also included Ollie Harrington, Hope Stevens, Mary Lou Williams, Frederick O'Neal (who later became a leading Social Democrat among actors and the AFL-CIO), Nettie Washington (granddaughter of Booker T. Washington), Hugh Mulzac, and George Murphy. At Davis's reception J. A. Rogers dropped by, as did Frank Fields (a composer for the film *Body and Soul*); see also *Daily Worker*, 26 August 1949.

51. Ibid., 21 September 1949; text of Si Gerson radio speech, 22 September 1949, Reel 20, Box 34, G30, CRC Papers; *Daily Worker*, 12 October, 8 November, and 9 October 1949.

52. *Daily Worker*, 7 August and 27 March 1949. Ibid., 8 May 1949: Graham served as secretary of the Citizens Committee of One Thousand to Re-Elect Davis (Du Bois was co-chair). See also Shirley Quill, *Mike Quill—Himself: A Memoir* (Greenwich, Conn.: Devin Adair, 1985), 194, 199: "From the union's earliest days he had had serious ideological disagreements with the Communist activists." She too stresses the party-Quill confrontation over raising the transit fare as catalyzing the deterioration of their relationship.

53. Fact Sheet on American Labor Party, 3 June 1949, Series I, Ac. 2245, BE, "Ne-Nu," American Labor Party Papers; Rutgers University Library, New Brunswick, N.J. (hereafter cited as ALP Papers); *New York Times*, 6 September 1946; Alan Wolfe, "The Withering Away of the American Labor Party," *Journal of Rutgers University Library* 31 (June 1968): 46–57; Report on Vito Marcantonio, 25 November 1950, 100-28126-52, 100-53054, 100-28126-66, FBI; Ben Tiedman (Secretary-Treasurer, Local 1, Baker and Confectionery Workers International Union) to Doug McMahon, 25 June 1949, Series I, Ac. 2245, "F-N," ALP Papers; *Daily Worker*, 14 August 1949; *New York Times*, 17 September 1949; *Daily Worker*, 18 September and 1 November 1949.

54. Davis memoir, 963–64, 990–91, 995, 1008– 9.

55. *New York Times*, 11 May 1949; *Daily Worker*, 14 and 16 February and 25 and 26 January 1949; Stanley Isaacs to Genevieve Earle, 19 July 1949, Box 17, Stanley Isaacs Papers; *Daily Worker*, 16 and 19 October 1949; *New York Times*, 15 October 1949; Charles C. Haney to Stanley Isaacs, 20 October 1949, Box 17, Stanley Isaacs Papers; *New York Age*, 22, 24, 26–29 October 1949; Davis memoir, 26/1013, 28/1015, 18/1034, 53/238.

56. *Daily Worker*, 9, 10, 15 November 1949; *New York Times*, 8 November 1949; *Daily Worker*, 6 November 1949; Ollie Harrington, interview with author 1 June 1989.

57. *New York Times*, 19, 22, 27, 29 October and 29 November 1949.

58. Ibid., 8 December 1949; *Daily Worker*, 8 December 1949; *New York Times*, 29 November 1949; *Daily Worker*, 29 November 1949; *Davis v. Impelliteri*, 197 Misc. 162 2d 159 (Sup. Ct. 1950); Stanley Isaacs to Ben Davis, 12 December 1949, Box 16, Stanley Isaacs Papers.

59. *Daily Worker*, 29 and 11 November 1949.
60. Ibid., 4 and 6 December 1949; 15 January 1950.
61. Stanley Isaacs to Martin J. Gavin, 1 December 1949, Box 17, Stanley Isaacs Papers; *Daily Worker*, 20 November 1949; *New York Times*, 14 January 1950.
62. *New York Amsterdam News*, 26 November 1949.
63. *New York Times*, 10 and 9 November 1949.
64. Ibid., 16 November 1949.
65. *Boston Herald*, 10 and 13 November 1949.
66. *New York Herald Tribune*, 11 November 1949; *Daily Worker*, 13 November 1949.
67. Lillian Gates, "New York's 1949 Elections," *Political Affairs* 28 (December 1949): 46, 47.
68. Jean Bovey to Stanley Isaacs, 5 December 1949, Box 17, and Ben Davis to Stanley Isaacs, 9 December 1949, Box 16, Stanley Isaacs Papers.

Chapter 14. Fighting Back, 1950–1951

1. Joseph Starobin, "Europe Judges the Smith Act," *Masses and Mainstream* 4 (October 1951): 1, 6; *New York Times*, 16 October 1949; Alonzo Hamby, *Liberalism and Its Challengers: FDR to Reagan* (New York: Oxford University Press, 1985), 87: Hamby concludes that the Smith Act prosecution was "questionable. . . . In effect, the administration decided to jail the Communists for the crime of having planned to engage in verbal denunciation of the government, not for acts of violence or espionage."
2. *New York Times*, 10 June 1951.
3. CRC press release, 11 June 1951, Reel 20, Box 34, G28, CRC Papers; Aubrey Williams to Harold Burton, Box 75, 13 June 1951, Harold Burton Papers, Library of Congress, Washington, D.C.
4. Harold Burton to Ethelred Brown, 24 June 1950, Box 1, Ethelred Brown Papers, Schomburg Center for Research in Black Culture, New York, N.Y.; Robert Shoup to Harold Burton, 28 November 1939, Box 374, Harold Burton Papers: "Some time ago you requested information concerning the history, the principles and more particularly the position of the Communist Party" on overthrowing of the government; "such information to be used as a guide in determining the right of Communists to freedom of speech in the City of Cleveland"; he attached various Communist International material, U.S. party information, and other matter, adding, "After studying all the above material, it is quite difficult to readily determine whether the Communists are entitled to freedom of speech. However, I have arrived at a conclusion which I feel justifies the right of the Communists to this inalienable privilege."
5. Reinhold Niebuhr to Felix Frankfurter, 20 June 1951, Box 34, F-14, Felix Frankfurter Papers, Harvard University Law Library, Cambridge, Mass.
6. Felix Frankfurter to Irving Dillard, 8 June 1951, Box 34, Felix Frankfurter Papers; *St. Louis Post-Dispatch*, 5 June 1951.
7. Felix Frankfurter to Stanley Reed, 17 February 1951, 14 March 1951, Boxes 40–43, Felix Frankfurter Papers; *New York Times*, 22 June 1951; "Transcriptions of Conversations Between Justice William O. Douglas and Prof. Walter F. Murphy, Tape Recorded During 1961–63, Princeton University Library, 1981, 259; Ellen Schrecker, "Archival Sources for the Study of McCarthyism," *Journal of American History* 75 (June 1988): 202 (Douglas "reported that the justices did not bother to

discuss the issues"); undated clipping, Box 205, William O. Douglas Papers, Library of Congress, Washington, D.C.

8. *Daily Worker*, 12 June, 11 and 18 July 1950, and 10 April 1951; *New York Times*, 5 November 1949 and 2 April 1950.

9. *Daily Worker*, 8, 9, 13, 19 February 1950.

10. Ibid., 14 and 22 August 1950. Ibid., 17 October 1949: after the verdict, five thousand rallied at Rockland Palace with thousands more outside.

11. Ibid., 23 March 1950; Ben Davis, "The Negro People in the Fight for Peace and Freedom," *Political Affairs* 29 (June 1950): 101–13; James Roark, "American Black Leaders: The Response to Colonialism and the Cold War, 1943–1953," *African Historical Studies* 4, no. 2 (1971): 265.

12. *Daily Worker*, 2 July 1950. On 3 July The *DW* reported that Robeson, Davis, and Hugh Mulzac joined in a "Hands-Off Korea" rally at 125th and Lenox.

13. Ibid., 23 July 1950; Samuel Banks, "The Korean Conflict," *Negro History Bulletin* 36, no. 6 (1973): 131–32; *U.S. News & World Report*, 11 May 1956; *Daily Worker*, 22 November 1950.

14. *Daily Worker*, 3 September 1950; Ben Davis, "On the Use of Negro Troops in Wall Street's Aggression Against the Korean People," *Political Affairs* 29 (October 1950): 50, 51; Robert Griffith, "The Chilling Effect," *Wilson Quarterly* no. 2 (1978): 135–36; Ronald W. Johnson, "The Korean Red Scare in Missouri," *Red River Valley Historical Review* 4, no.2 (1979): 72–86: after the war started, many anti-Communist ordinances and organizations sprang up; Ronald J. Caridi, *The Korean War and American Politics: The Republican Party as a Case Study* (Philadelphia: University of Pennsylvania Press, 1968).

15. *Daily Worker*, 27 January and 24 July 1950.

16. Ibid., 14 May, 4 June, 26 October, and 5 November 1950.

17. Ibid., 27 April 1950, 31 March 1944, 6 April 1950.

18. Ibid., 1 January 1950: Davis to speak on "Stalin and the Struggle for Negro Liberation" at the United Mutual Auditorium, 310 Lenox Avenue. Ibid., 3 January 1950. Ibid., 9 January 1950: two hundred and fifty people attend the forum as Davis hailed continued integration but warned against the promotion of individuals as a substitute for full equality; Ibid., 16 May, 11 and 16 July 1950.

19. *New York Times*, 26 January 1951; *Daily Worker*, 16 May 1951; *New York Times*, 2 February 1951; *Daily Worker*, 14 March 1951.

20. *Daily Worker*, 15, 9, 8 May 1949.

21. Ibid., 12 February 1951. Ibid., 14 February 1951: Davis admitted that Du Bois "has certainly influenced me" and compared "the culture of Truman the letter writer" with the "culture of Dr. Du Bois whose writings and books have influenced generations of white and Negro youth." He continued, "If we had fought harder against the incarceration within the United States of Paul Robeson, if we had brought more workers into the fight to save the Martinsville Seven—and if we had won—then we would not have had this indictment of Dr. Du Bois." George Murphy and Doxey Wilkerson also spoke.

22. Ibid., 15 March 1951. Interestingly, a recent biography of Adam Powell barely mentions Davis or the Communists, despite their important relationship in the 1940s. See Hamilton, *Adam Clayton Powell, Jr*.

23. Flyer, ca. 1952, Reel 14, Box 23, B2, CRC Papers; Gary Giddins, *Celebrating Bird: The Triumph of Charlie Parker* (New York: Morrow, 1987), 112. Giddins says that as Robeson sang "Water Boy," Parker ran on stage with a glass of water. *Daily Worker*, 6 May 1951. Ibid., 10 May 1951: concerning Willie McGee, Miles Davis was irate: "How can they sentence a man to die like that. I sent a telegram about the Martinsville Seven."

24. *Daily Worker*, 2 May 1951. See also Ben Davis, "On the Colonial Liberation

Movements (On the Occasion of the 71st Birthday, on December 21, 1950, of Joseph Stalin, Leader and Teacher of the World Working Class and All Toiling Humanity)," *Political Affairs* 29 (December 1950): 37–49.

25. *Daily Worker*, 5, 15 June 1951. In his farewell speech Davis also said that blacks need "more leadership from the workers. We need railroad workers, domestic workers, steelworkers, and all other kinds of workers, to put some fighting strength into the liberation battles." (*Daily Worker*, 19 June 1951).

26. Ibid., 10 and 11 June 1951.

27. *New York Times*, 1 July 1951.

28. Magazine of American Legion, April 1951, Ben Davis Vertical File-Schomburg Center.

29. *Daily Worker*, 3 and 8 July 1951; press release, 3 July 1951, Reel 20, Box 34, G28, CRC Papers.

30. *New York Times*, 3 July 1951.

31. Elizabeth Gurley Flynn, "Politial Significance of Defense Work. Memo to All Districts from Defense Committee," Fall 1950, Reel 4209, Elizabeth Gurley Flynn Papers.

32. Howard Johnson, interview, ca. 1977, Series IV, Oral History of the American Left.

33. William Z. Foster, "Confidential Outline of Party Policy in the Trials," undated, Reel 4210, Elizabeth Gurley Flynn Papers.

34. Ibid., Communist policy on the trials, 15 January 1952, Reel 4210, Elizabeth Gurley Flynn Papers.

Chapter 15. Jailed for Ideas, 1951–1955

1. Marvel Cooke, interview with author, 6 April 1988.

2. Memorandum on Ben Davis, NY 100-23825, 100149163-FBI; *Afro-American*, 4 June 1955: Davis marries "his secretary . . . blonde daughter of a prominent Bronx dentist"; *New York Amsterdam News*, 28 May 1995: "A middle-aged white secretary whose love for [Davis] did not dim during his almost four years in jail" marries him in the Bronx. Davis's sister, the bride's parents, and "a couple of close friends" are present. As noted, Martin Duberman claims a close relationship between Davis and Diane Sommers a secretary at the Council on African Affairs; as an articulate, well-dressed, intelligent—and single—activist, Davis was quite popular socially. Cf. *Daily Worker*, 8 September 1944: "with lovely Miss Ethel Rainford, ex-chairman, Communist Political Association" of the 11th A.D. "at farewell party . . .[Davis was] guest of honor at the affair for which hundreds showed up, many more than could be accommodated." See also the interview with Louise Patterson, 16 November 1981, Series I, Oral History of the American Left. This leading activist intellectual and wife of William Patterson comments, "I think that a leader married to a black woman can be much more effective in the community. . . . When Patt and I married, there was a real celebration on the part of many black women to see that one of the leaders of the Communist Party had married a black woman." On the question of effectiveness, Patterson's point was probably more true in the post-1960s era of heightened racial awareness than at the time of Davis's marriage; Davis's widow recalls no hostility from black women as a result of the marriage. His close friend Claudia Jones kept her informed and close to Davis during his jailing. Nina Goodman, interview with author, 22 June 1986.

3. *Daily Worker*, 31 August 1958.
4. CRC press release, 3 July 1951, Ben Davis Papers: All New York papers feature Davis's address to the court on sentencing; *Petition of Ben Davis v. Herbert Brownell* (U.S. District Court-Washington, D.C.), ca. 1955, Reel 4, Box 5, A79, CRC Papers.
5. Article by Claudia Jones, June 1954, Box 3, Folder 3/11, Paul Robeson Papers. See also Claudia Jones, "Ben Davis and Amnesty: From Terre Haute to Harlem," June 1954, Ben Davis Vertical File-Schomburg Century, and Claudia Jones, "From Terre Haute to Harlem," *Masses and Mainstream* 7 (June 1954): 27–29.
6. Johnnie Carey to Ben Davis, 7 April 1955, Ben Davis Papers. See also Gil Green, *Cold War Fugitive: A Personal Story of the McCarthy Years* (New York: International Publishers, 1984), 238–42. Green provides a useful description of segregation in the Terre Haute federal prison.
7. Nina Davis Goodman, interview with author, 28 June 1986.
8. Muriel Symington to James Bennett [director, Federal Bureau of Prisons], 14 August 1953, Reel 4, Box 5, A78, CRC Papers.
9. *Daily Worker*, 28 May and 21 August 1953.
10. Ibid., 23 and 19 September 1951.
11. John Abt, interview with author, 15 April 1988. Abt found Davis "very sharp intellectually . . . very warm as a human being."
12. Nina Davis Goodman interview, 28 June 1986. She smuggled at least 1 letter out to Abt.
13. *Daily Worker*, 9 December 1951; *People's Voice*, 29 July 1944: "[Davis] is going in for tennis these days and is dieting also . . . he only eats four meals a day now."
14. The *Daily Worker* for 10 January 1954 quotes Claudia Jones: "Did you know that both Gus Hall and Ben Davis were advocates of non-heavy smoking and in fact did not smoke for long periods of time?"; *ibid.*, 11 October, 16 December, and 19 October 1951. Despite his myriad of problems, Davis was concerned about Claudia Jones's "continued imprisonment . . . [which] passes beyond monstrous brutality" (undated letter from Ben Davis, Ben Davis Papers); Harry Sacher to Howard McGrath, 16 October 1951, Reel 4, Box 5, A80, CRC Papers: "His request for permission to correspond with the most intimate of his friends has been denied . . . and the only persons with whom he is permitted to correspond are his sister and myself."
15. *Daily Worker*, 4 April 1954 and 23 December 1951. *New York Times Book Review* for 14 August 1960 printed a number of letters agreeing with Davis that his manuscript should be released to him. Margaret Reynolds wrote: "Not until today did I realize that the Federal Government exercised such powers of censorship inside prison walls. Call me hopelessly naive but I thought the First Amendment protected all of us alike." *New York Times*, 24 July 1960; Corliss Lamont to Milton Friedman, 6 December 1956, and Milton Friedman to Corliss Lamont, 13 December 1956, Box 3, Bill of Rights Fund Papers, Columbia University Library, New York, N.Y. Davis's attorney sought $2000 for the "cost of the litigation" to get the manuscript back. William Patterson was highly critical of the unexpurgated version of this manuscript. He felt that it "deals at too great length with inner-Party differences" (probably the Teheran period). He also objected to the "subjective treatment of Powell," the reference to Tito as a "Yugoslav Quisling," and wrote: "Ben's treatment of a number of vital questions leaves much to be desired from a Marxist point of view. . . . Much should not be written now because of the present historical situation and the demands upon us as an American political party." He questioned the omissions of Ford and Gates and cautioned that publication "must be handled with the greatest care that can be exercised" (William Patterson analysis of manuscript,

ca. 1960, Ben Davis Papers). In the manuscript Davis conceded that prison "can cause one to become lopsided in his opinions" (Davis memoir, 4).

16. Ben Davis to Paul Robeson, undated, Paul Robeson Papers; Credentials Committee Report, Trade Union Committee to Repeal the Smith Act Act, 21 June 1952, Box 1, Pettis Perry Papers, Schomburg Center for Research in Black Culture, New York, N.Y. At this point, scores of AFL and CIO unions were represented.

17. Speech by Paul Robeson, NNLC Convention, 4–6 December 1953, Box 2, Folder 2/3, Paul Robeson Papers.

18. *Afro-American*, 23 June 1956,

19. *Daily Worker*, 11 February 1950, 1 July 1951. On 16 April 1950: the paper was printing 68,513 copies and aiming for 100,000 by the end of the year; 23 April 1950: printing 72,000 copies; 7 May 1950: printing 156,932 copies (a May Day edition); 21 May 1950: printing 82,173.

20. Ibid., 25 July 1948: despite a "heavy rainstorm" twenty-five hundred attend four street rallies in Harlem in defense of Davis; *Daily Worker*, 2 February 1951: at this all-night vigil for the Martinsville 7, "A cheer rose from the crowd that packed every foot of the sidewalk when former City Councilman Benjamin J. Davis climbed to the speakers' platform atop the truck at 126 Street and Lenox Avenue.... 'It is raining now but I don't care if it snows or storms or sleets, this struggle must go on.'" *Daily Worker*, 27 June and 10 and 19 August 1951.

21. *Progressive*, November 1950.

22. *Daily Worker*, 15 August 1951.

23. Ibid., William Patterson to Willard Ransom, 16 May 1954 and 2 April 1954, Willard Ransom to William Patterson, 25 March 1954, Reel 4, Box 5, A78, CRC Papers.

24. *Daily Worker*, 19 August, 10 and 23 September, and 6 November 1951; undated Davis cartoon strip, Reel 4, Box 5, A80, CRC Papers; undated "Freedom Bond," Ben Davis Papers; undated posters, Reel 52, Box 92, V1, V7; petition for Davis freedom, ca. 1951, Reel 4, Box 5, A80; anmesty for Smith Act petition victims, ca11 1951, Reel 21, Box 39, J., all in CRC Papers; undated flyer, Ben Davis Vertical File-Schomburg Center.

25. John W. Preston, "Developments in Negro People's Movement," *Political Affairs* 31 (February 1952): 32–42. *Daily Worker*, 12 March 1952: three thousand at Carnegie Hall rally on the Smith Act, Feinberg Law, and other repressive laws to hear Mrs. Andrew Simkins, South Carolina NAACP Secretary: "Harry T. Moore was sent to his death by a bomb and Benjamin J. Davis was sent to prison for the same reason. But the American people can recall Ben Davis." *Daily Worker*, 7 July 1952 "Three Nazi war criminals have just been anmestied and let out of jail in West Germany" while Davis resides in a prison cell. *Freedom* for March 1952 quotes Eslanda Robeson: "I know a real-life Communist . . . a personal family friend of long standing . . . a wonderful guy. His name is [Ben Davis] . . . our little family calls him Benjy . . . I am not afraid of Communists. They are not bothering me. (In fact it is the Klansmen . . .) So am I going to stand by my friend Benjy. I would have no respect for myself as a person if I did less. What kind of security have you got, if you have no respect for yourself." In the same issue Paul Robeson writes: "I thought of my great and good friend Ben Davis—it's about time a major fight was launched to free Ben. People in Harlem continuously ask, 'How is Ben? We need him.'"

26. *Daily Worker*, 23 July, 3, 8, 10, 13, 17, 19 and 16 September 1952.

27. Ibid., 26 and 29 September 1952.

28. Ibid., 28 July, 3 August, 3, 8, 14 September, 16 October, and 4 August 1952.

29. Ibid., 31 August 1952. *New York Times*, 6 September 1952: 2,610 signatures on Freedom Party petition for State Assembly seat; *Daily Worker*, 7 and 8 Septem-

ber 1952; undated flyer, ca. 1952, Reel 2409, Elizabeth Gurley Flynn Papers; *Daily Worker*, 14 February 1952.

30. *Daily Worker*, 2 October 1952: Abner Berry on WLIB on behalf of Davis's electoral campaign at 10:15 A.M; ibid., 9 and 10 October 1952.

31. Ibid., 13 October 1952; *New York Times*, 12 October 1952; *Daily Worker*, 15 and 16 October 1952. The campaign was to collect twenty thousand ceasefire ballots in an effort to link Davis directly with the increasingly antipopular Korean War.

32. Address by Doxey Wilkerson, 16 October 1952, WLIB-AM, 10:15–0:25 A.M., in possession of Doxey Wilkerson.

33. *Daily Worker*, 17, 19, 23, 27, 29 October and 6 November 1952.

34. U.S. Congress, House Committee on Un-American Activities, *Communism in the Detroit Area*, 82d Cong., 2d sess., February 1952, 2825.

35. *Daily Worker*, 6 July, 29 June, and 12 November 1952.

36. Ibid., 2 June 1953.

37. Ibid., 21 August and 1 January 1953.

38. Benjamin Davis letter, 13 September 1953, Ben Davis Papers.

39. Report of Hearing Before the Federal Parole Board re: Ben Davis application for parole, 10 February 1953, Reel 4209, Elizabeth Gurley Flynn Papers; press release, February 1953, Claude Barnett Papers.

40. Davis Security Index Card, 10 June 1953, 100-149163-149, FBI; *New York Times*, 11 and 14 February 1953; *Daily Worker*, 11 February 1953; see also report on Davis, 29 June 1950, 100-149163-100, FBI.

41. *Daily Worker*, 18 and 21 May 1953.

42. Ibid., 31 July and 2–5, 9 August 1953.

43. Memorandum and Order by Judge R. F. Marsh, 3 August 1953, Western District Court of Pennsylvania, Reel 4, Box 5, A79, CRC Papers; *Daily Worker*, 4 August 1953.

44. *Daily Worker*, 5, 9, 11 August 1953.

45. Memoranda, 9 and 23 September 1953, 69-665-1, FBI.

46. *Freedom*, July 1953; *Daily Worker*, 6 and 18 August 1953.

47. William Patterson to Carl Murphy, 22 September 1953, Reel 4, Box 5, A5, CRC Papers; ibid., 4 March 1954.

48. Muriel Symington to CRC-Pa., 2 June 1953, Reel 4, Box 5, A78, CRC Papers.

49. William Patterson to Edward S. D'Antignac, 9 September and 4 February 1954, Reel 4, Box 5, A78, CRC Papers.

50. William Patterson to Hope Stevens, 10 September 1953, Reel 4, Box 5, A78, CRC Papers.

51. Speech Delivered by W. E. B. Du Bois on Anmesty for Smith Act victims, 17 December 1953, Reel 4, Box 5, A80, CRC Papers.

52. Printed postcard, petition, and pamphlet, Ben Davis Papers; *Daily Worker*, 20 December 1953.

53. Memorandum, 18 February 1954, Ben Davis Papers; *Daily Worker*, 12 February 1954; press release, 18 February 1954, Reel 4, Box 5, A80, CRC Papers; Memorandum from SAC, WFO, 100-1664, 10 March 1954, 100-149163, FBI. The delegation also included James Ford, Louise Jeffers, Marta Correa, Pauline Milores, and Saul Gross. Note the ethnic and gender balance and the deployment of the underutilized asset James Ford; *Daily Worker*, 12 and 23 February 1954.

54. William Patterson to Walter Aiken, 5 February and 11 March 1954, Reel 4, Box 5, A78, CRC Papers; William Patterson to A. T. Walden, 11 and 19 March 1954, Reel 4, Box 5, A78, CRC Papers.

55. William Patterson to George Hays, 21 May 1954, Reel 4, Box A78, CRC; *Daily Worker*, 19 March and 21 June 1954; tribute to Ben Davis, 29 June 1954, Box 2, William Patterson Papers; Louise Patterson et al. to "Dear Friend," ca. June

1954, Ben Davis Papers; William Patterson to Modjeska Simkins, 30 June 1954, Reel 4, Box 5, A78, CRC Papers; press release, 17 June 1954, Reel 4, Box 5, A80, CRC Papers.

56. *Daily Worker*, 1 July 1954.

57. William Patterson to R. L. Witherspoon, 19 April 1954, Reel 4, Box 5, A78; R. L. Witherspoon to William Patterson, 21 April 1954; and William Patterson to R. L. Witherspoon, 7 and 21 May 1954; all Reel 4, Box 5, A78, CRC Papers; *Daily Worker*, 27 June 1954. As a attorney Davis maintained special ties and solidarity with his profession. *Daily Worker*, 17 February 1954; W. E. B. Du Bois, February 1954, "This Man I Know," Ben Davis Vertical File-Schomburg Library: the octogenarian, like many others, emphasized Davis's "sincerity"; *Daily Worker*, 1 and 24 October 1954. The New Jersey Supreme Court upheld the decision to bar Nusser from the ballot.

On the other hand, relations between the Left and centrists could still exist. The Harlem centrist Wilhemina Adams wrote to "Mrs. Vito Marcantonio," calling Marc "my friend . . . one of the finest men ever lived . . . a great man and humanitarian, which are so few." Adams was a Democratic party and Urban League activist in Harlem. Bella Bodd called her "Willie," telling her in 1945, "Rest assured that all my flower business will go through your shops and that I will tell my friends." This also suggests how in an era of Jim Crow, black business could find white friends more easily in the Left. Adams was also in touch with Henry Luce, Nelson Rockefeller, Herbert Lehman, Robert Wagner, Edith Sampson, Adam Clayton Powell, J. Raymond Jones, and others, and was a force in the national and local Democratic parties (she was Democratic leader in the 17th A.D.). The Red Scare in the black community was designed in part to win over centrists like her from the Left. Certainly non-Left whites were forced to pay more attention to Adams after the Red Scare was launched. Wilhemina Adams, 9 August 1954, Box 3, Folder 3/3, and Bella Dodd to Wilhemina Adams, 10 May 1945, Box 1, Folder 1/2, Wilhemina Adams Papers. Davis's future wife, Nina Stamler, was still having trouble getting through to him. See P. J. Madigan (warden) to Nina Stamler, 20 July 1954, Ben Davis Papers.

58. Press release, 11 March 1955, Ben Davis Papers; *Daily Worker*, 3 and 10 March 1955; William Patterson to Ben Davis, 10 March 1955, Box 2, William Patterson Papers.

59. *Daily Worker*, 29 March 1955.

60. P. J. Madigan to Ben Davis (No. 8454-TH), 15 December 1954, Ben Davis Papers; *Daily Worker*, 15 December 1954, 25 February and 3 March 1955.

61. *Daily Worker*, 17 and 28 January and 16 February 1955; U.S. District Court for Western District of Pennsylvania, Petition for Writ of Habeas Corpus, *Benjamin J. Davis v. John Sloan et al.*, 1955, Ben Davis Papers.

62. Hyman Schlesinger to P. L. Prattis, 5 April 1955, Ben Davis Papers.

63. Card and brochure, ca. 1955, and Regina Frankfeld to "Dear Friend," 17 January 1955, Reel 4, Box 5, A80, CRC Papers.

64. *Daily Worker*, 8 April 1955; *Jewish Life*, April 1955, Ben Davis Vertical File-Schomburg Center.

65. Esther Jackson to Ben Davis, 2 April 1955, file of 1955 letters, Ben Davis Papers.

66. Frances Smith to Ben Davis, ca. 1955, Ben Davis Papers.

67. C. W. MacKay to Ben Davis, 4 October 1955, Ben Davis Papers.

68. *Daily Worker*, 31 August 1958; *Afro-American*, 25 December 1954 and 16 April 1955; *New York Times*, 14 December 1954; *Ben Davis v. Herbert Brownell*, U.S. District Court for Washington, D.C., 1955, Ben Davis Papers; *Daily Worker*, 15 December 1954 and 7 March 1955; "A Plea for the Safety of Ben Davis," 27 January 1955, Ben Davis Papers.

69. *Jewish Life*, March 1954, Ben Davis Vertical File-Schomburg Center; *Daily Worker*, 19 March 1954.
70. *Philadelphia Independent*, 25 December 1954; *Afro-American*, 17 July 1954; clippings, 1954, Reel 4, Box 5, A80, and William Patterson to Leon Ransom, 1955, Reel 4, Box 5, A78, CRC Papers; Ben Davis to Herbert Brownell, 1954, and P. J. Madigan to Nina Stamler, 5 January 1955, Ben Davis Papers.
71. *Daily Worker*, 11 and 14 April 1955; Davis suit, 6 April 1955, Ben Davis Papers; press release, 28 March 1955, Reel 4, Box 5, A79, CRC Papers; "Ruling from the Bench," 1 April 1955, Ben Davis Papers; *Daily Worker*, 4, 10, 15 April 1955; Claudia Jones, *Ben Davis: Fighter for Freedom* (New York: National Committee to Defend Negro Leadership, 1954), copy owned by author. Essie Robeson wrote in her introduction, "[Davis] is an old valued friend of mine and of my family. . . .We love the man."
72. *New York Times*, 17 April 1955; Memorandum, 1 June 1955, 100-149163, FBI. Davis apparently claimed that after prison he would seek employment with Freedom Associates.
73. *New York Amsterdam News*, 23 April 1955; *Daily Worker*, 13 July 1954.
74. *Daily Worker*, 15 August 1955; *New York Times*, 12 April 1955.
75. Memorandum, 29 June 1955, 100-149163, FBI.
76. Tyrus Fain et al., eds., *The Intelligence Community: History, Organization and Issues* (New York: R. R. Bowker, 1977), 412: of the 3,247 COINTELPRO proposals, 1850 were aimed at the CP and 540 at the black movement. Of the 2,370 implemented, 1,388 were committed against the CP; memoranda, 15 April and 11 October 1955, 3 January 1956, 100-149163, 100-149163-203, FBI; memorandum, 19 April 1955, 100-149163-184, FBI; memorandum, 5 April 1955, 100-149163-183, FBI.
77. Memorandum, 28 December 1955, 100-149163, FBI; director of FBI to SAC-NY, 9 March 1955, 100-149163, FBI; Curt Oberg to Ben Davis, 20 August 1955, Ben Davis Papers.

Chapter 16. Party Wars, 1956–1959

1. Harvey Klehr, *Far Left of Center: The American Radical Left Today* (New Brunswick, N.J.: Transaction, 1988), xi.
2. Richard Gid Powers, *Secrecy and Power: The Life of J. Edgar Hoover* (New York: Free Press, 1987), 368, 324; Kenneth O'Reilly, *Racial Matters: The FBI's Secret War Against Black America, 1960–1972* (New York: Free Press, 1989).
3. Brian Glick, *War at Home: Covert Action Against U.S. Activists and What We Can Do About It* (Boston: South End Press, 1989), 74; Ward Churchill and Jim Vander Wall, *COINTELPRO Papers* (Boston: South End Press, 1989). The fact that COINTELPRO is still plaguing the United States suggests the importance and potency of this demarche.
4. Louis Burnham to George Murphy, 29 September 1957, George Murphy Papers, Moorland-Spingarn Library, Howard University, Washington, D.C. Cf. also O'Reilly, *Racial Matters*, 266: "Recruitment of black informants to cover the Communist party had always been a priority, in part because the CPUSA's lingering obsession with white chauvinism protected black members from suspicion. White communists who accused Negro comrades of working for the FBI often found themselves accused of racism and drummed out of the party. As a result, the Bureau recruited a disproportionately high number of black informants. In some local communist units during the early 1960's, all of the FBI informants were black."

5. Nina Davis Goodman, interview with author, 22 June 1986; memorandum, 24 April 1956, 100-23825, FBI; *Daily Worker*, 7 March 1956; *Daily Worker*, 15 April 1956: "Public Reception for Mr. and Mrs. Benjamin Davis" on 20 April at 8:30 P.M. at the Hotel Theresa; *Daily Worker*, 16 and 23 May 1956. Davis was in parlous financial straits on leaving prison; fortunately friends like Paul Robeson and Lloyd Brown were able to lend a hand. Lloyd Brown, interview with author, 18 April 1988; Lloyd Brown, *Iron City* (New York: Masses and Mainstream, 1952). His already strong relationship with Robeson seemed to deepen after prison. Just before leaving Allegheny County jail he wrote his friend, ". . . I've lost none of my old starry-eyed admiration for you. Prison experience, however, should enable me to being [sic] something more our more than a quarter of a century of personal friendship. . . . There are legendary stories of you in every prison in America. . . . I've lost some weight which didn't hurt . . . you could lose a bit yourself." Ben Davis to Paul Robeson, 20 March 1955, Paul Robeson Papers. Davis was also close to Paul junior. Earlier Davis had said about Robeson, " . . . his image is always with me. Fully 80 per cent of Paul's and my time together is spent adoring him from afar." Ben Davis to Essie Robeson, 7 August 1947, Paul Robeson Papers. Similarly, during this time Essie Robeson rose to Davis's defense after he was attacked in *Ebony*. Eslanda Robeson to *Ebony*, 16 September 1957, Paul Robeson Archives, Berlin, Germany.

6. José Lava, "Twenty Years In Prison," *World Marxist Review* 30 (June 1987): 58: "after the 20th Congress of the CPSU which denounced the personality cult period and its abuses, an intelligence officer brought me a copy of 'U.S. News and World Report' with anti-communist coverage of the Congress." Saloma Malina, "Renovating the Party," *World Marxist Review* 31 (January 1988): 40: the Brazilian Communist Party "found itself in grave crisis . . . latter half of the 1950's." Rodney Arismendi, "We Live in a New Changed World," *World Marxist Review* 31 (January 1988): 25: "In 1955 the Communist Party of Uruguay went through a profound crisis which led to a change of its leadership"; Meeting of National Board of Communist Party, 22 May 1945, Box 5, Folder 29, Theodore Draper Papers. The emphasis on *glasnost* in the former Soviet Union caused a number of articles to be printed about past disputes in the international Communist movements. Similarly, as Fidel Castro reportedly complained after being chided by the United States for not instituting *glasnost*, "first they call us Soviet puppets, now they criticize us for not being Soviet puppets." Again, what has been involved in the international Communist movement is not so much the "hand of Moscow," not so much dictation as emulation. Cf. Yuri Girenko, "The Background to a Split," *World Marxist Review* 32 (February 1989): 91–93 (the author blames Moscow for the split with Yugoslavia); interview with Ignacio Gallego and Francisco Palero, *World Marxist Review* 32 (April 1989): 54–57. While shedding light on their mid-1970s split, these Spanish Communists also revealed the culture of the international Communist movement. Gallego: "we in the PCE [party] did not use all the means at our disposal including discussion, to find a way out the crisis . . . lack of proper polemics." Palero: "Comrade Gallego is right in saying that our critique of the socialist states then was often too acerbic and categorical, and usually incorrect. But then such intolerance was in varying degrees characteristic of much of the international communist movement." Natalia Smirnova et al., eds., "History of the Communist Movement: Facts, People, Ideas; What Kind of Man Was Sandino?" *World Marxist Review* 32 (April 1989): 88–93. In dealing with this patriot, says the writer, the Comintern sought to push him and his followers "into a Procrustean bed of theoretical schemes by which the governing bodies of the Comintern were then held captives." On North America see Norman Penner, *Canadian Communism: The Stalin Years and Beyond* (Toronto: Methuen, 1988); Lionel Lewis, *Cold War on Campus: A Study of the Politics of Organizational Control* (New Brunswick, N.J.: Transaction, 1988); Elaine Tyler May, *Homeward Bound: Amer-*

ican Families in the Cold War (New York: Basic Books, 1988); Gerry Horovitz, "Ben Davis and the Communist Party: A Study in Race and Politics," *UCLA Historical Journal* 4 (1983): 92–107; Sethard Fisher, "Marxist Prescriptions for Black American Equality," *Phylon* 45, no. 1 (1984): 52–66.

7. *Dorothy Healey Remembers*, Healey, 430; interview with Dorothy Healey, Series IV, Oral History of the American Left.

8. *Daily Worker*, 9 April 1956. Ben Davis to director of FBI, ca. 1956, COINTELPRO, 100-3-104, Sec. 1, FBI: Davis allegedly reports his concern about the style of work of the leadership, saying that it is not directly connected with the masses. At the 29 April 1956 meeting of the National Committee of the party, many termed party policy over the past decade as Left sectarian, but not Davis. On the point of retaining the term *Marxism-Leninism* in the preamble to the constitution of the party, Foster was alone in voting yes, Davis abstained.

9. E. S., "Toward a Socialist Democracy," *Party Voice* (New York Communist Party), October 1956, Jesus Colon Papers; Excerpts from report by state organizational secretary of New York State CP, *Party Voice*, July 1956, Jesus Colon Papers.

10. Julian Mayfield, interview, 13 May 1970, Civil Rights Documentation Project, Howard University; Louis Budenz to Joe McCarthy, 25 April 1956, Louis Budenz Papers.

11. Junius Irving Scales and Richard Nickson, *Cause at Heart: A Former Communist Remembers* (Athens: University of Georgia Press, 1987), 313, 293. General Telford Taylor, Columbia Law School professor and prosecutor at Nuremberg, provides a devastating critique of the Smith Act in his foreword.

12. *Daily Worker*, 28 November 1956; Gyula Thurmer, who served as as aide to the Hungarian party's leader, raises striking points about the events of 1956 in the Moscow-based *New Times* for 12 June 1989. Note that when Janos Kadar (the Hungarian leader who emerged after the tumult of 1956) died, according to the *New York Times* of 14 July 1989, "tens of thousands of Hungarians of all ages and from all over this country filed past the coffin . . . in a surprising and spontaneous outpouring of mourning for a leader."

13. *Daily Worker*, 5, 6, 18 November 1956. In the *New Times* for 12 June 1989 a writer has interesting comments about Hungary 1956; National Committee, "On the Events in Hungary," *Political Affairs* 35 (December 1956): 1–5. Ben Dobbs, a former party leader in California who became a Social Democrat, still distinguishes and differentiates the 1956 Soviet intervention (which he supported then and now) and the 1968 intervention in Prague (which he still opposes). Ben Dobbs, interview with author, 6 July 1990.

14. David Shannon, *The Decline of American Communism: A History of the Communist Party of the U.S. Since 1945* (New York: Harcourt Brace, 1959), 265, 329. Shannon says that after the Duclos letter, Davis was the "party's most important Negro leader"; he also gives him credit for reviving the Black Belt thesis and starting the antiwhite chauvinism campaign. When Davis ran for attorney general in 1946, votes came from "all the neighborhoods with a significant Communist vote were low- or lower-middle income areas with a high proportion of Negro or immigrant inhabitants."

15. Nina Davis Goodman, interview with author, 28 June 1986; Howard Johnson, "Seeing Red," Series IV, Oral History of the American Left. See also Aileen S. Kraditor, *"Jimmy Higgins": The Mental World of the American Rank-and-File Communist, 1930–1958* (Westport, Conn.: Greenwood, 1988); *Daily Worker*, 31 July 1952.

16. John Gates, *The Story of an American Communist* (New York: Nelson, 1958), 104, 107, 110, 133, 164, 181, 183, 188, 189; *Daily Worker*, 31 July 1952 (photo of Davis and Gates). In her dissertation Helen Camp points out that Dennis in January 1956 at Carnegie Hall called for a new direction for the CP, well before the Stalin

devaluation speech in Moscow. Helen Collier Camp, "Gurley: A Biography of Elizabeth Gurley Flynn, 1890–1964" (Columbia University, 1980), 547.

17. Peggy Dennis, *The Autobiography of an American Communist* (Westport, Conn.: Lawrence Hill, 1977), 170.

18. Howard Fast, *The Naked God: The Writer and the Communist Party* (New York: Praeger, 1957), 60.

19. Charney, *Long Journey*, 193, 266, 269, 289. Charney was an advocate of liquidating the party in favor of a "political association."

20. Healey, *Dorothy, Healey Remembers*, 538.

21. Scales, *Cause at Heart*, 381.

22. Paul Robeson, Jr., interview with author, 6 August 1988.

23. Steve Nelson, James R. Barrett, and Rob Ruck, *Steve Nelson: American Radical* (Pittsburgh: University of Pittsburgh Press, 1981), 400, 287, 288.

24. Doxey Wilkerson, interview with author, 6 May 1988.

25. James Jackson, interview with author, 6 April 1988.

26. Claude Lightfoot, *Chicago Slums to World Politics: Autobiography of Claude Lightfoot* (New York: New Outlook, 1986), 120. Party lawyer John Abt finds it ironic that Gates was one of the CP leaders who predicted imminent fascism and then assailed the tactics subsequently deployed to combat that vision. Abt also casts serious doubt on the credibility of Jack Childs, who some thought was the party liaison with the USSR relaying orders from Moscow. See "Oral History of John Abt," ca. 1987, Reference Center for Marxist Studies, New York, N.Y., 78, 102, 105. Cf. David Garrow, *The FBI and Martin Luther King, Jr.: From "Solo" to Memphis* (New York: Norton, 1981).

27. Ben Davis to Joe North, 31 May and 9 December 1955, Joe North Papers, Boston University Library, Boston, Mass. On the other hand, writer John Howard Lawson contacted Davis to examine his work. John Howard Lawson to Ben Davis, 30 May 1955, Ben Davis Papers.

28. Rosalyn Baxandall in *Words on Fire: The Life and Writings of Elizabeth Gurley Flynn* (New Brunswick, N.J.: Rutgers University Press, 1987), with the use of selective evidence puts forward a Davis-Flynn antagonism. (See also Helen Collier Camp, "Gurley.") The following citations refute that hypothesis: *Daily Worker*, 21 October 1943: Flynn calls Davis "one of the finest men I know"; *Daily Worker*, 4 November 1945: Flynn on Davis: "He is pleasant, sunny-dispositioned, friendly, has a wonderful sense of humor, is modest and unassuming"; cf. also introduction of Ben Davis by Elizabeth Gurley Flynn over WMCA-AM, 29 October 1947, Reel 4206, Elizabeth Gurley Flynn Papers: "a tireless, eloquent, devoted champion of the rights of the plain people"; Nina and Ben Davis to Elizabeth Gurley Flynn, 4 May 1956, Reel 4210, Elizabeth Gurley Flynn Papers: "Heartfelt greetings to our Elizabeth, a great leader . . . "; Ben Davis to Elizabeth Gurley Flynn, ca. 1958, Reel 4220, Elizabeth Gurley Flynn Papers: "with love and admiration." Nina Davis Goodman disagreed sharply with the notion of some sort of antagonism between Davis and Flynn. Some people, she said, may be mistaking the fact that Davis was a "loner [who] didn't socialize except with Robeson" for antagonism. Nina Davis Goodman, interview with author, 2 June 1988. John Gates also had fond words for Flynn at one point: John Gates to Elizabeth Gurley Flynn, 6 October 1947, Reel 4209, Elizabeth Gurley Flynn Papers. The FBI cites Davis as being positively inclined toward Gil Green: FBI Report, 10–12 August 1945, New York State Convention of CP, NY-100-13472, Box 5, Gil Green Papers. In discussing Green Davis limned his "tremendous contributions . . . if he leaves it will not be because of any weaknesses in his work here . . . the District has grown under his leadership." Veteran Harlem leader Ted Bassett, in his late eighties as this book was being written, calls Davis "one of the most beloved leaders of the Afro-American people . . . worked tirelessly to build

coalitions of the party with other institutions." Ted Bassett, interview with author, 6 April 1988.

29. Ben Davis, "Foster's Contributions to the Cause of National and Colonial Liberation," *Political Affairs* 30 (March 1951): 36–50; *Daily Worker*, 15 March 1951, 21 October 1952, 25 January and 14 March 1955; Ben Davis, "Foster: Fighter for Correct Theory," *Political Affairs* 35 (April 1956): 40–48; *Daily Worker*, 18 April 1956; Chick Mason, "Sources of Our Dilemma: A Rejection of the 'Right Opportunist-Left Sectarian' Explanation by Our Leadership," July 1956, Tamiment Library, New York University.

30. Alexander Bittleman, Autobiography, Box 1, Folder 15, Alexander Bittleman Papers, New York University Library, New York, N.Y.

31. "Statement of the National Committee, CPUSA," *Political Affairs* 35 (July 1956): 34–36. The statement was opposed by Foster.

32. *Daily Worker*, 6 August 1956.

33. Ben Davis to Paul Robeson, 24 June 1956, Ben Davis Papers.

34. *Daily Worker*, 2 September 1956. Davis also regretted how the party "rejected the double-V campaign of the Pittsburgh Courier. . . . That was one of the gems of Browder's leadership."

35. Ibid., 1 October and 5 August 1956.

36. Nat Yamish, *Pursuit and Survival: A Left Immigrant in America* (San Francisco: Apex, 1981), 84; *Daily Worker*, 14 October and 18 September 1956.

37. "Draft Resolution for the 16th National Convention of the CPUSA," 13 September 1956 (in possession of author); *New York Times*, 23 September 1956; *Daily Worker*, 27 September 1956; William Z. Foster, "On the Situation in the Communist Party," *Political Affairs* 35 (October 1956): 15–45; *New York Times*, 4 October 1956.

38. *Daily Worker*, 7 and 13 November 1956; Statement of New York State Communist Party, 8 December 1956, Reference Center for Marxist Studies; "A Message to the State Conventions and Clubs of the Party," 19 December 1956, Tamiment Library, New York University.

39. Ben Davis, "The Challenge of the New Era," *Political Affairs* 35 (December 1956): 14–40.

40. *Daily Worker*, 7 December 1956.

41. Ibid., 17 December 1956; see also ibid., 5 December 1956.

42. John Williamson to Eugene Dennis, 6 July 1956, Reel 6, Eugene Dennis Papers.

43. Eugene Dennis to John Williamson, 2 December 1956, Reel 6, Eugene Dennis Papers; Eugene Dennis, *Letters from Prison* (New York: International Publishers, 1956).

44. Louis Budenz to Joe McCarthy, 13 October 1956, Louis Budenz Papers. Browderism weighed heavily on Williamson in his memoir. Cf. John Williamson, *Dangerous Scot: The Life and Work of an American "Undesirable"* (New York: International Publishers, 1969), 147.

45. Powers, *Secrecy and Power*, 292; *New York Amsterdam News*, 7 January 1956; *Daily Worker*, 1, 13, 16, 17, 20, 26 January, 27 February, and 5 March 1956.

46. *Daily Worker*, 11 March 1956: Interviewed by Augusta Strong, Davis is seen as in "apparently good health." Memorandum, 17 January 1956, NY-10023825, 199-149163, FBI: "Investigation further reflects he will possibly share an apartment with singer Paul Robeson and family"; memorandum, undated, 100-23825, 100-149163, FBI: On 7 February 1956 Davis "had requested permission to travel outside the limits of the Southern District of New York. He stated Davis requested permission to visit the residence of John Steuben . . . Flemington, New Jersey, over the forthcoming weekend . . . left-wing friend who has been ill with heart disease for 2 or 3

years and is now bedridden"; memorandum, 28 February 1956, NY-100-23825, 100-149163, FBI; memorandum, undated, 100-149163, FBI; report, undated, 100-23825, 149163, FBI: Davis had "scars and marks, two moles on left temple, mole on left cheek . . . dapper in dress, very relaxed mannerisms"; report to J. Edgar Hoover, 17 April 1956, 100-149163, FBI; report, 8 November 1956, 100-149163, FBI. Nina Davis Goodman, interviews with author, 22 June 1986 and 28 July 1988. On 28 June she said that despite the harassment, Davis had no trouble falling asleep; right after the 11:00 P.M. news he was "out."

47. *Daily Worker*, 3 April 1938: Davis attacks "plight of the Jewish people in Germany, Austria, Poland . . . makes all mankind shudder . . . show me an anti-Semite and I will show you a Negro-hater." In this article he assailed a *Pittsburgh Courier*, 26 March 1938, editorial that was not as sympathetic as his viewpoint. *Daily Worker*, 20 April 1938: Davis laments that three University of Delaware students were hazed due to their Jewishness, one had a swastika put on his face; he also mentions that anti-Jewish attacks on FDR, etc., are "part of the present drive of Big Business and its allies against labor." *Daily Worker*, 22 April 1938: Davis hits Henry Ford's anti-Semitism, ". . . the most arrogant open shop, anti-social tyrant in America. . . . Fordism is Hitlerism . . . number one Jew-baiter of American history." *Daily Worker*, 25 April 1938: Davis says here that "Jews constitute a comparatively small percentage of the Party's total membership." *Daily Worker*, 18 October 1943: Rabbi Max Felshin backs Davis for election. *Daily Worker*, 27 October 1943: Davis and Eugene Connolly at an election rally at Irving Plaza sponsored by Jewish-American Fraternal Committee to Elect win-the-war Candidates. *Daily Worker*, 9 February 1944: Davis says fire James Drew, pro-fascist cop, and joins unanimous council vote in favor of open door to Jewish immigration into Palestine. *Daily Worker*, 3 March 1944: Stanley Isaacs and Davis join East Side rally against anti-Semitism with Jewish war veterans. *Daily Worker*, 24 September 1944: Davis says that "Roosevelt haters . . . anti-Semitism and anti-Negroism go together." *Daily Worker*, 7 April 1945: Davis to speak at meeting memorializing Warsaw ghetto; Mary Lou Williams will play. *Daily Worker*, 24 September 1945: Davis et al. to introduce resolution calling for probe of anti-Jewish outbreaks in Bronx and Brooklyn. *New Masses*, 23 October 1945: Davis speaks to Lower East Side gathering shortly before Succoth and receives an overwhelming response. *Daily Worker*, 26 October 1945: Davis hails suspension of fascist Brooklyn teacher May Quinn. Flyer, ca. 1945, Box 5, Robert Minor Papers: Davis issues bilingual leaflet in Hebrew and English: "As regards Palestine, I have demanded the immediate abrogation of the British White Paper and the opening of the door of Palestine to those victims of Nazi terror who wish to live there. I support the building of a Jewish National Home in a free and democratic Palestine on the basis of Arab-Jewish collaboration." *People's Voice*, 22 January 1946: Davis and Rubin Saltzman of the Jewish IWO shake hands as both are honored at dinner of the International Workers Order for having done most for interracial harmony. *Daily Worker*, 8 June 1946: Davis censures the city administration for honoring General Tadeusz Bor, "Polish Traitor," cited by the American Slav Congress as anti-Semitic. *Daily Worker*, 15 June 1946: Davis criticizes the refusal to reverse field on May Quinn, who is upheld by the state. Davis: " . . . a shameful victory for anti-Semitism and fascism." *Daily Worker*, 26 May 1947: Davis calls for United Nations mandate over Palestine and open-door policy in United States and Palestine for displaced European Jews. He admonishes the United Kingdom and calls for the United States to "guarantee the national rights" of both Arabs and Jews to "bring about a transfer of the mandate over Palestine from the British government to the end that it may establish in Palestine a free, democratic and sovereign state." *Daily Worker*, 9 March 1948: Davis votes for resolution, which was unanimously passed, calling for Palestine partition though he criticizes it for hailing the State

Department's "courageous activities." *Daily Worker*, 12 March 1948: Davis calls Palestine policy of United States part of the Marshall Plan. *Daily Worker*, 28 November 1948: Davis blasts the "Machiavellian role" of Ralph Bunche, which seeks to "undermine, betray and pervert the new Jewish state into an imperialist war base" and the "hostile and callous attitude" of Bunche toward Israel. Davis points to "reactionary Arabs" as problem, not Israel, though he issued a mild criticism of "certain forces within the Israel government." Along with Hastie, Bunche "is one of several imperialist-minded Negroes." It is striking that while many of the *Daily Worker*'s views hold up over the years, those on Israel have not had such a good record. Unfortunately, Stalinism, which is ritualistically blamed for party errors elsewhere, generally is not noted when this issue is mentioned. Cf. *Daily Worker*, 31 October 1948.

48. Arthur Liebman, "The Ties That Bind: The Jewish Support for the Left in the U.S.," *American Jewish Historical Quarterly* 66 (December 1976): 1–25; *Daily Worker*, 30 and 31 May, 23 July, 22 November, 31 October, 1 and 2 November 1956.

49. *New York Times*, 27 January 1957. The press played more than just a reporting role during this period; they were conscious representatives of anti-Communism. Cf. James Aronson, *The Press and the Cold War* (Boston: Beacon, 1973).

50. *Daily Worker*, 8 and 13 March 1957.

51. Ibid., 28 March 1957; *New York Times*, 28 March 1957; *Daily Worker*, 7 May 1957. Sub-committee of National Committee-CPUSA, "An Evaluation of the "*Daily Worker*," *Political Affairs* 36 (September 1957): 26–33: On the Mideast the party organ "showed great sensitivity to the feelings of the Jewish people, though . . . not the same awareness of the need to keep in mind the feelings and sentiments of the Negro people."

52. J. Edgar Hoover to Gordon Gray, 23 July 1958, FBI Series, Box 2, FBI L-N(2), OSANSA, Staff Files, Dwight D. Eisenhower Papers, Eisenhower Presidential Library, Abilene, Kans.

Chapter 17. When Black and White Unite, 1958–1959

1. Carmines and Stimson, *Issue Evolution*; "Questions by Kirby," undated, Ben Davis Papers. Garrow, *The FBI and Martin Luther King, Jr.*, 23: the NY-FBI opened a file on King when Davis "approached King outside of a New York church. . . . King and black singer Harry Belafonte had met with [Davis] . . . detailed the assistance that a number of supposed leftists had provided during the Montgomery bus boycott." See also Michael Belknap, "Review Essay: Above the Law and Beyond Its Reach: O'Reilly and Theoharis on FBI Intelligence Operations," *American Bar Foundation Research Journal* (Winter 1985): 201–15.

2. *New York Times*, 1, 11, 12 January 1958.

3. *Daily Worker*, 13 and 26 January 1958.

4. Ferdinand Smith to William Patterson, 26 January 1958, Box 2, William Patterson Papers.

5. A. B. Magil to National Committee-CPUSA, 13 February 1958, Box 1, Folder 14, Hosea Hudson Papers, Schomburg Center for Research in Black Culture, New York, N.Y.

6. *New York Times*, 22 February 1958.

7. Ibid., 25 February 1958.

8. Ibid., 8 March 1958; *Worker*, 9 March 1958.

9. *New York Post*, 16 April 1958.

10. Ben Davis, "A Reply to Opposition Views," CP-NYS, *Party Voice*, April 1958, Box 2, Folder 5, Hosea Hudson Papers.
11. SAC, New York, 100-129802, 11 April 1958, Director, FBI, 100-3-104-565, COINTELPRO, FBI.
12. *New York Times*, 19 May 1958.
13. SAC, New York, 100-129802, 21 May 1958, Director FBI, 100-3-104, COINTELPRO, FBI.
14. William Z. Foster, "To the National Committee," 26 May 1958, Box 1, Folder 5, Hosea Hudson Papers.
15. SAC, New York, 100-129802, 5 June 1958, Director, FBI, 100-3-104, Sec. 15, FBI; Dorothy R. Healey, "On the Status of the Party," *Political Affairs* 37 (March 1958): 40–48.
16. *New York Times*, 14 and 15 June 1958.
17. SAC, New York, 100-129802, 25 March 1958, Director FBI, 100-3-104, COINTELPRO, FBI.
18. Eugene Dennis to John Williamson, 5 July 1958, Reel 6, Eugene Dennis Papers.
19. *New York Times*, 12 July 1958.
20. Ibid., 27 September 1958.
21. SAC, New York, 100-129802, 24 December 1958, Director FBI, 100-3-104, COINTELPRO, FBI; Ben Davis, "A Reply to Opposition Views," *Party Voice*, August 1958, Jesus Colon Papers; *People's World*, 18 January 1958: Foster's stroke was serious.
22. *Daily Worker*, 15 March 1951, 2 March, 23 October, and 5 December 1956: Davis called "outrageous" the effort of House Democrats to deny Powell committee rank and patronage; Powell was "an outstanding leader." This was an "insult to the Negro people and to all democratic Americans. . . . It smells of the slaveowner's attitude." Here Davis is reviving one of his favorite phrases of the past: "the stench of the slave market." Davis's new restraint was on display since he was quoted not long after Powell's horrendous neocolonialist performance at the watershed Bandung meeting of the budding nonaligned movement. In the past this would have weighed much more heavily on Davis.
23. *New York Times*, 28 and 31 May 1958.
24. *Worker*, 1 June 1958. (The *Daily Worker* became a weekly in 1958, also changing its name.)
25. Ibid.
26. *New York Times*, 5 August 1958.
27. *Worker*, 24 August 1958.
28. *New York Times*, 29 October 1958.
29. *Daily Worker*, 3 November 1957; *Worker*, 8 June 1958; *Daily Worker*, 15 June 1958.
30. *New York Times*, 16 June 1958.
31. *Worker*, 22 and 27 June 1958.
32. Ibid., 6 July, 14 and 28 September 1958.
33. Memo from J. B. Matthews to Louis Budenz, 25 March 1958, Louis Budenz Papers; *Worker*, 30 March, 4 May, and 29 June 1958.
34. *Worker*, 27 July 1958: During the picket line at the U.N., "a drizzling rain fell" as Davis and the protesters were "accompanied by a battery of cameramen, some reporters and several cops." Davis's sign read, "Defend Negro Children's Rights in Little Rock—Mr. President, Stop the Use of Armed Forces Against Arab Freedom!" *Worker*, 3, 10, 17, 24 August 1958.
35. Ibid., 24 and 31 August, 5 October 1958.
36. *Worker*, 31 August 1958.

37. Ibid., 31 August 1958.
38. Ibid., 14 September 1958.
39. *Worker*, 14 September 1958.
40. *New York Amsterdam News*, 20 September 1958.
41. Ibid., 21 September 1958; *New York Times*, 23 September 1958; *Ben Davis v. Board of Elections*, Petitioner's Memo of Law, 1958, Ben Davis Papers; SAC, New York, 100-129802, 26 September 1958, FBI Director, 100-3-104, Sec. 18, COINTELPRO, FBI.
42. *Pittsburgh Courier*, 27 September 1958.
43. *Worker*, 5 and 19 October, 28 September, 26 October 1958.
44. *Worker*, 12 October 1958.
45. *Worker*, 28 October and 2 November 1958.
46. Hulan Jack, *Fifty Years a Democrat: The Autobiography of Hulan E. Jack* (New York: New Benjamin Franklin House, 1982), 172. Jack, a former Manhattan borough president who was ultimately hounded by the authorities, ultimately aligned himself with Lyndon LaRouche.
47. *Worker*, 28 September 1958.
48. Baxandall, *Words on Fire*, 219-20; *Daily Worker*, 18 October 1957; Speech by Ben Davis, 29 October 1957, Reel 4207, Elizabeth Gurley Flynn Papers.
49. Elizabeth Gurley Flynn to Ben Davis, 10 December 1957, Ben Davis Papers. Flynn received 710 votes in the City Council election in the first council race for the party since Davis was ousted in 1949 (*New York Times*, 7 November 1957).
50. Elizabeth Gurley Flynn article on Davis, 31 August 1958, Reel 4220, Elizabeth Gurley Flynn Papers.
51. Ben Davis speech, 3 November 1958, Ben Davis Papers; *New York Times*, 3 December 1958; *Worker*, 16 November 1958; report by Ben Davis to the New York Communist party, [1958], Ben Davis Papers. At the New York State party convention in 1959, William Albertson echoed Davis's analysis: "The Davis campaign was a stimulus to the unity around Powell's candidacy; it added serious political and ideological content to the election campaign as such. . . . It was an example of election campaigning through struggle . . . it re-established the Party in the Harlem community . . . an example of the merging of mass work and public Party action. . . . Mainly through the person of Comrade Davis, our Party . . . has appeared at almost all open legislative and budget hearings."
52. William Patterson to George Murphy, 7 March 1957, George Murphy Papers.
53. "The Negro People and the Economic Crisis," Excerpts from Report to Conference on Negro work, 26–27 April 1958, "Party Voice," Box 2, Folder 2/5, Hosea Hudson Papers.
54. Pettis Perry, "The Party and the Negro People," *Political Affairs* 37 (February 1958): 24.
55. Haywood, *Black Bolshevik*, 600; SAC, Buffalo, 100-4379-104, Sec. 58, COINTELPRO, FBI, 100-3-104, FBI. Davis travels upstate to look into a dispute within the party there.
56. National Committee-CPUSA, "Theoretical Aspects of the Negro Question" (Draft Resolution), *Political Affairs* 37 (January 1959): 42–46; supplement to *Party Affairs*, issued by National Committee-CPUSA, "Theoretical Aspects of the Negro Question in the United States," February 1959 (in possession of author).
57. William Z. Foster and Ben Davis, "Notes on the Negro Question," *Political Affairs* 38 (April 1959): 33–43.
58. *New York Times*, 9 January and 27 February 1959. *Worker*, 8 November 1959: Davis and Albertson issue a statement on Charles Loman and the reaction of the bourgeois press. They deny Gates's charge that embezzlement was involved.

59. A. M. Belmont to F. J. Baumgardner, 10 February 1959, Sec. 22, 100-3-104, FBI.
60. Mao Zedong, "Reply" to Foster, *Political Affairs* 38 (March 1959): 31.
61. SAC, New York, 14 May 1959, Director FBI, Sec. 26, 100-3-104, COINTELPRO, FBI.
62. "The Reds—What Now?" 13 July 1959, Louis Budenz Papers; F. J. Baumgardner to A. H. Belmont, 8 December 1959, Sec. 31, 100-3-104, COINTELPRO, FBI.
63. *New York Times*, 13–15 December 1959.
64. Ibid., 15 December 1959.
65. SAC, New York, 29 October, 13 and 23 November 1959, Director FBI, Sec. 30, 100-3-104, FBI; SAC, New York to FBI Director, 24 December 1959, Box 1, Gil Green Papers; SAC, New York, 24 December 1959, Sec. 31, COINTELPRO, 100-3-104, FBI.
66. *Worker*, 20 December 1959; *New York Times*, 8 and 12 December 1959.
67. Peggy Dennis to unknown person, 27 December 1959, Reel 6, Eugene Dennis Papers.
68. Dennis, *Autobiography*, 237.
69. Paul Robeson, Jr., interview with author, 11 August 1988.
70. James Jackson, interview with author, 6 April 1988, 17 October 1986. Jackson adds that though many blacks did not feel altogether comfortable with the Black Belt thesis, there was "no other organization" with the militant thrust of the CP; thus, some felt like "ingrates" to challenge party views. "Some of us had reservations on one or another aspect" of the party program "but we took the whole package." Because of his "experience of work in the South . . . I . . . did a two-year study" with Gunnar Myrdal in the south and "travelled extensively . . . talked with everybody . . . had a chance to probe the question . . . to assess what are the feasible factors." Ironically, in the underground Jackson had "leisure . . . I did some basic studies . . . had discussions." There was a "conference on a farm" during that time with Winston, Gil Green, and others where they studied the "census." Lenin had done it in 1910 but, says Jackson, they had not. He acknowledges his differences with Davis. "I was junior to Ben . . . but juniors grow up. . . . I had a big responsibility underground . . . I was not particularly shy." He also agrees that "not everything was negative about the demand for enhancing democracy in the party . . . the underground had produced a certain abuse of leadership." Jackson also did not support Davis for the post of chairman after Dennis and Foster died; he backed Flynn on the premise that Davis was too connected to the difficult battles of the recent past and his rise might exacerbate party tensions. See his James Jackson, *Revolutionary Tracings* (New York: International Publications, 1974).
71. *Worker*, 11 January, 15 February, 26 July, and 2 August 1959.
72. Ibid., 2 August and 12 July 1959; *New York Times*, 12 December 1959.
73. *New York Times*, 26 February 1959; *Worker*, 1 March, 26 April, 28 June, 13 September, and 4 October 1959.
74. Ben Davis, "The Party's Program for Peace and Social Progress in New York State," Report to New York State Convention of the Communist Party, 26–28 November 1959, Communist Party Archives.
75. *Worker*, 31 May and 14 June 1959; *New York World-Telegram*, 2 June 1959. Local 1199 has been one of the most important forces in New York City since this strike. Their strikes and militant support for Dr. King once brought to their platform figures as diverse as Malcolm X and Roy Wilkins. Thus they served as a unifying force when the party had to stay in the background, which is not to suggest that they were some sort of Communist front. It should be noted that this writer served as special counsel for Local 1199 from 1985–88. See also Leon Fink and Brian Greenberg,

Upheaval in the Quiet Zone: A History of Hospital Workers' Union, Local 1199 (Urbana: University of Illinois Press, 1989).

Chapter 18. Black Communist in the 1960s

1. Dr. Bernard Mintz, 24 June 1959, Ben Davis Papers; Lloyd Brown, interview with author, 2 May 1988.

2. SAC New York, 100-129802, 29 November 1960, Sec. 44, FBI Director, 100-3-104, COINTELPRO, FBI. The unnamed black personality referred to "had known Davis for many years . . . and considered him to be a very intelligent individual . . .[he] volunteered to assist in any manner to get Davis to renounce the CP and become a useful citizen. . . . Davis' departure would create a huge void in the Party, a void it might never be able to fill . . . being well-respected by Davis, may provide the ideal individual to ultimately persuade Davis to renounce his affiliation with the CP. . . . should be furnished with some idea as to the present character of Davis" The agent proceeded to give a personality profile of Davis and then continued, "Present salary is $90 per week . . . [he and Nina] have had any number of quarrels, some of which have bordered on the violent side, over the complete lack of finances. . . . [Davis] has a tremendous amount of pride." With the party "decline . . . [Davis] has shown evidence of becoming more and more disenchanted with the Party. He has criticized virtually everyone in its leadership calling them 'meatballs,' 'eggheads,' and 'idiots' . . . Davis' comrades look upon him as a 'careerist.'" It is said that Davis had spoken to Congressman Powell about his plight, who wanted him to renounce the party; it is unclear if Powell is the prominent black personality picked to seduce Davis. In any case, the FBI wanted a "well known, successful and highly respected individual such as [deleted] Roy Wilkins . . . [to] not attempt to point out the errors in [Davis's] ways [but] would . . . be in the position to make him a firm, definite offer." The elements would be money, prominence, and "some title." This prominent personality may have been from Atlanta: "He further stated that he is going to attempt through other Negro leaders of means to see if a position of Negro leadership could be offered to Davis . . . he would [also] like to make contact with Davis' sister." It should be emphasized that FBI memoranda have to be read very carefully; like other U.S. intelligence agencies they seemed to be devotees of the self-fulfilling prophecy. Also like other subordinates, agents were not above inflating the truth to make an impression on their superiors. Hoover wanted to hear much of the above. For example, the report states that Davis told his wife that he would leave the party "if he had something else to turn to." Questions can be raised about such allegations. Unfortunately certain historians have treated sentences from FBI reports as if they were carved on a tablet and brought down from the mountain. The report is reproduced here at length not for the asserted truth of the matter but to indicate the state of mind of the FBI. See also SAC, New York, 100-23825, 29 August 1960, Sec. 39, FBI Director, 100-3-104, COINTELPRO, FBI; ibid., 7 October 1960, Sec. 41.

3. Martin Luther King to Ben Davis, 23 April 1960, Ben Davis Papers.

4. Ben Davis to Martin Luther King, 19 June 1960, and ca. 1960, Martin Luther King Papers, Boston University Library, Boston, Mass.

5. J. Edgar Hoover to Gordon Gray, 1 March 1960, FBI Series, Box 1, OSANSA, FBI, Dwight Eisenhower Papers; Clayborne Carson, *In Struggle: SNCC and the Black Awakening of the 1960s* (Cambridge: Harvard University Press, 1981), 162.

6. U.S. Congress, House Committee on Un-American Affairs, *Communist Training Operations, Part 2*, 86th Cong., 2d sess. 2–3 February 1960.
7. Ben Davis, *Upsurge in the South: The Negro People Fight for Freedom*, March 1960, Ben Davis Vertical File-Schomburg Center.
8. *Worker*, 26 April 1959, 10 and 17 April 1960.
9. Ibid., 1 May 1960; George Crockett to Ben Davis, undated, Ben Davis Papers; *Worker*, 19 June 1960.
10. *Worker*, 19 June 1960.
11. Ibid., 3 July 1960; Ben Davis to George Murphy, 16 July 1960, George Murphy Papers.
12. Ben Davis to George Murphy, 21 July 1960, George Murphy Papers.
13. Worker, 16 October 1960.
14. Ibid., 25 October 1959: Davis is represented by Sandy Katz of the firm of Frank Donner, Arthur Kinoy and Marshall Perlin. *New York Law Journal*, 7 July 1960; Frank Donner to Corliss Lamont, 26 October 1960, and Ben Davis to Corliss Lamont, 9 December 1960; both Box 3, Bill of Rights Fund Papers: the Morgan heir provided $250 for the defense; *New York Times*, 7 July 1960; *Worker*, 6 September and 25 October 1959; *New York Times*, 9 August 1960; *Worker*, 14 August and 17 July 1960.
15. *New York Post*, 3 February 1960; *New York Times*, 3 and 4 February 1960.
16. Gordon Gray to General Andrew Goodpaster, 17 February 1960, FBI Series, Box 1, FBI (10), OSANSA, Staff Files, Dwight Eisenhower Papers.
17. SAC New York, 2 March 1960, Sec. 34, FBI Director, 100-3-104, COINTELPRO, FBI; SAC New York, 29 April 1960, Sec. 36, FBI Director, 100-3-104, COINTELPRO, FBI; FBI Director, 100-3-104, 11 May 1960, Sec. 36, SAC New York, COINTELPRO, *FBI*; SAC Chicago, 100-32864, 28 October 1960, Sec. 42, FBI Director, 100-3-104, COINTELPRO, FBI. Walter Goodman, *The Committee: The Extraordinary Career of HUAC* (New York: Farrar, Straus and Giroux, 1968), 423: HUAC questions Davis, Robeson, and Jesse Gray about the Vienna Youth Festival. A major act of repression against Davis was the effort of the Bureau of Prisons to keep and not release the lengthy memoir he drafted in prison. As noted, this act stirred sufficient outrage to make the pages of the *New York Times Book Review*. The American Civil Liberties Union was not moving as eagerly on this issue as some might have hoped. Their associate director assured Davis, "We are working hard on the problem but do not plan to press for legislation." Alan Reitman to Ben Davis, 26 May 1961, Ben Davis Papers.
18. *Worker*, 24 April, 1 May, and 2 October 1960.
19. *New York Post*, 8 June 1961; *New York Times*, 9 June 1961; pamphlets on Davis-Hall Defense Committee, ca. 1961, Jesus Colon Papers. *I. F. Stone's Weekly*, 12 June 1961: The iconoclastic journalist charged that the Supreme Court's ruling on the Internal Security Act "betrays the U.S. to its real enemies."
20. SAC Atlanta, 30 January 1961, 100-2727, Sec. 46, FBI Director, 100-3-104, COINTELPRO, FBI: SAC New York, 100-129802, undated, FBI Director, 100-3-104, Sec. 43, COINTELPRO, FBI.
21. F. J. Baumgardner to A. H. Belmont, 20 March 1961, Sec. 48, 100-3-104, COINTELPRO, FBI; "Baumgardner to Sullivan," Ca. Spring 1961, Sec. 53, 100-3-104, COINTELPRO, FBI; SAC New York, 100-129802, 1 September 1961, Sec. 55, FBI Director, 100-3-104, FBI.
22. *Worker*, 12 February and 16 April 1961.
23. Ibid., 24 and 24 September, 22 October 1961; Ben Davis to Robert Kennedy, 22 June 1961, Ben Davis Papers. *New York Times*, 25 November 1961: Davis hits new "Labor-Negro Vanguard Party" organized by Clarence Coggins, calling it a "de-

magogic provocation." *Worker*, 3 September 1961: Davis and Mildred McAdory, chair of the Harlem party, brand as a "provocation and forgery" a leaflet purporting to give the party's view on the election. The FBI was after Powell again also. See Adam Clayton Powell to Ben Davis, 13 September 1961, Ben Davis Papers. Memorandum, 31 May 1961, 100-51230-218, FBI, and J. Walter Yeagley to J. Edgar Hoover, "Confidential," 1 September 1961, 100-51230-224, FBI. The FBI suspected Powell of being a secret party member: "The file fails to reflect information that would establish Party membership. In the circumstances . . . it is our opinion that the existing facts are insufficient to establish under the provisions of Title 18, USC Section 1001 that he falsified the form in denying present and past membership in the Communist Party" (Memorandum to W. C. Sullivan, 7 September 1961, 100-51230-225, FBI).

24. *New York Times*, 16 February 1961 (a photo shows Davis being pushed by a police officer); flyer—CP rally at Carnegie Hall, 3 March 1961, Ben Davis Papers. *Worker*, 12 March 1961: Davis, speaking at *Worker* anniversary and Foster birthday celebration, hails U.N. Lumumba demonstrations.

25. "Report of the Special Investigating Committee of the Council of the City of New York," 1946, Box 4, Reel 2, Pete Cacchione Papers; *Daily Worker*, 19 October 1945: eight hundred are present at Hunter College as Davis condemns negative "racial" quotas; *Daily Worker*, 24 December 1946: particularly culpable in perpetrating this antiblack and anti-Jewish discrimination were New York University, Columbia University, and Cornell Medical School; Davis sought to make this offense a crime. See also *New York Times*, 21 May 1946, and *Daily Worker*, 2 February 1941: Davis speaks on Rapp-Coudert hearings, designed to eliminate Communist and leftist teachers from the city campuses. *Daily Worker*, 10 October 1940: Davis and James Ford at Shaw University in Raleigh, North Carolina, where they participate in a two-hour forum with 450 students from Shaw and the University of North Carolina; *Daily Worker*, 12 November 1940.

26. *New York Times*, 1 October 1958: Davis denied right to speak at CCNY, where he had been invited to speak to the Marxist Discussion Club. But he would not be denied. He "addressed students . . . from a sound truck just one block from the campus" on the issue of "Peace and Integration." *New York Times*, 17 October 1958; *Worker*, 26 October 1958; SAC Philadelphia, 100-42492, 30 March 1960, Sec. 35, FBI Director, 100-3-104, COINTELPRO, FBI; *Worker*, 14 May 1961.

27. *New York Times*, 12, 11, 19 October 1961; *Worker*, 15 and 17 October 1961.

28. *New York Times*, 18 October 1961; *New York Post*, 9 and 11 October 1961; *New York Times*, 11 October 1961; *Worker*, 15 October 1961; *New York Times*, 21 and 27 October 1961.

29. F. J. Baumgardner to William Sullivan, 30 October 1961, 100-3-104, Sec. 58, COINTELPRO, FBI. Apparently the FBI had bugged a CP leadership meeting: "Ben Davis was of the opinion that President Kennedy's meeting with Republican leaders are meetings of a sinister character and are designed to lay the basis and create conditions for military intervention in Cuba. . . . Davis commented that there is a weakness in the peace movement because it was unable to stop the invasion of Cuba. He said that it was stupid to call [JFK] a murderer, the invaders were murderers. He felt that the Party should strike a very heavy blow at the CIA and hold [JFK] responsible." There was alleged discussion of Davis's role and his proposal "that he go to Harlem to re-establish the Party's relationship with the Negro people." Memorandum, 27 April 1961, Sec. 51, 100-3-104, COINTELPRO, FBI: FBI alleges that the leadership was "particularly annoyed" with Davis. SAC New York, 100-129802, Sec. 51, 5 May 1961, FBI Director, 100-3-104, COINTELPRO, FBI: discussion of how to use against Davis and others a proposed New York State bill to take the drivers' licenses of those convicted by the Smith Act; SAC New York, 100-

129802, Sec. 51, 17 May 1961, FBI Director, 100-3-104, COINTELPRO, FBI: FBI intends to float a rumor on the party ousting Davis "through its contacts in the mass media. . . . It is felt that Davis has been suspected of causing leaks in the past and is known that the CP leadership knows it cannot control Davis. . . . Such an item appearing just before the meeting will do much to convince the CP leadership that Davis is truly a 'troublemaker' and possibly push Davis over "the brink"; FBI Director to SAC New York, 19 May 1961, COINTELPRO, FBI: the director of the FBI believes that if a leak occurs it will unite the party against outside forces; Davis would be criticized at an upcoming meeting anyway, so there was no need for additional distractions.

30. *New York Times*, 31 October 1961; *Morningsider*, 2 November 1961; *New York Times*, 1 November 1961.
31. *New York Times*, 3 November 1961.
32. Ibid., 4 November 1961.
33. Ibid., 13 November 1961; *New York Post*, 3 November 1961; *New York Journal-American*, 3 November 1961; *Worker*, 24 November 1961; *New York Times*, 14 and 15 November 1961; *Worker*, 5, 7, 10, 21 November 1961.
34. *New York Times*, 16 November 1961.
35. Ibid., 17 and 23 November, 1 December, 18, 3, 8 November, and 8 December 1961.
36. Ibid., 17–19, 22 December 1961; First Report, B.S.S., #607-M, 22 December 1961, New York City Police Department.
37. *Worker*, 31 and 19 December 1961.
38. *New York Herald Tribune*, 8 April 1962.
39. Ibid., 31 March 1962; *New York Times*, 24 September 1961.
40. David Garrow, "FBI Political Harassment and FBI Historiography: Analyzing Informants and Measuring the Effects," *Public Historian* 10 (Fall 1988): 5–18; Beresford S. B. Trottman, ed., *Who's Who in Harlem* (New York: Magazine & Periodical Printing & Publishing Co., 1950). Richard Carey was born in Macon, Georgia, 16 June 1905 and graduated from the University of Iowa Medical School. Memorandum, 22 March 1949, 100-16830, FBI; M. A. Jones to Carter DeLoach, 23 June 1959, 7759135, FBI; Memorandum from J. Edgar Hoover, 23 May 1962, David Garrow Papers, Schomburg Center for Research in Black Culture, New York, N.Y.; memorandum from Archibald Carey, 3 March 1964, ibid.; "Special Inquiry," 12 August 1953, 77-59135, FBI. Archibald Carey also had ties to Patterson, Robeson, the National Negro Congress, and other prominent black activists. There was particular concern on the part of the FBI about his ties to Patterson, with the investigation reaching into the White House. See J. Edgar Hoover to Sherman Adams, 12 August 1953, 77-59135, FBI. Robert Nemiroff, interview with author, 14 September 1988. Arch Carey performed the wedding ceremony when Nemiroff and Lorraine Hansberry were married. Her mother attended Carey's church. Jean Carey Bond, Davis's niece and daughter of Richard Carey, maintains that her father was "not estranged" from Arch Carey, though there was "not that much contact." Jean Carey Bond, interview with author, 29 August 1988; *People's Voice*, 16 October 1943: pictures of Davis, Jean Carey Bond, and Davis's sister.
41. Carter DeLoach to Mr. Mohr, 19 May 1965, Box 30, David Garrow Papers; memorandum, 11 October 1962, 100-438794, FBI; memorandum, 21 September 1962, 10279-83, FBI: concern is expressed here about party ties to the NAACP.
42. *Worker*, 11 June and 24 December 1961; 19 August and 2 September 1962.
43. Ibid., 28 August 1962.
44. Ibid., 11 February 1962; *Cleveland Call and Post*, 16 December 1961.
45. *Worker*, 11 February 1962.
46. *New York Times*, 8 January 1962; *Worker*, 9 January 1962.

47. *New York Times*, 13 January 1962; *Worker*, 21 and 23 January 1962.
48. *Worker*, 24 February 1963; *Brown University Herald*, 14 February 1963; *Worker*, 11, 25, 18 February and 8 April 1962; *Wilmington (College) Monitor*, 9 April 1962.
49. *Newark (N.J.) Evening News*, 10 April 1962.
50. Erwin Griswold to Ben Davis, 26 February 1957 and 17 February 1958, Ben Davis Papers.
51. *Worker*, 24 April 1962.
52. Ibid., 15 April 1962; *New York Times*, 1 May 1962; Minnesota Daily (Minneapolis), 3 and I May 1962.
53. *Minnesota Daily*, 8 May 1962; *St. Paul Pioneer Press*, 31 March 1962; *St. Paul Dispatch*, 2 April 1962; *Minnesota Spokesman* (Minneapolis), 4 and 11 May 1962.
54. *St. Paul Pioneer Press*, 18 April and 30 March 1962; *Fargo Forum*, 3 May 1962; *Minnesota Daily*, 2 May 1962; Sam Davis to Ben Davis, 30 March 1962, Communist Party Archives. *New York Times*, 2 May 1962: When Davis attempted to address the League of Women Voters convention in Minneapolis, he was "rebuffed." He then asked to debate George Romney. *University of Washington Daily*, 31 October 1962: controversy on Davis speaking, Gus Hall barred from speaking earlier. *Worker*, 12 June 62: after the lifting of the speaker ban at Queens College, the dean of students tells the Marxist Discussion Club that if they did not disinvite Davis he would take "appropriate action."
55. *New York Times*, 9 and 7 June 1961. *Worker*, 18 June 1961: two dozen reporters, photographers, and television journalists present at press conference. *New York Times*, 11 June 1961: the high court upholds the Smith Act membership clause, along with the McCarran Act. *New York Times*, 22 and 5 June 1961. Ibid., 16 July 1961: 150 picket the *Times* to protest acceptance of a paid ad from the party protesting the Supreme Court decision.
56. *Worker*, 10 November and 9 July 1961; *New York Times*, 19, 20, and 26 November 1961.
57. *New York Times*, 1 and 2 December 1961; 17 January and 3 February 1962; Communist Party, "On the Arrest of Gus Hall and Benjamin Davis," *Political Affairs* 41 (April 1962): 1–4; *New York Times*, 16, 17, and 20 March 1962.
58. *Worker*, 20, 25, 27 March, 3 and 8 April 1962; *New York Times*, 31 March and 4 April 1962.
59. Elizabeth Gurley Flynn to "Dear Friend," 12 April 1962, Reel 4220, Elizabeth Gurley Flynn Papers.
60. Undated memo on Clara Colon, Jesus Colon Papers.
61. *Afro-American*, 3 April 1962; *New York Times*, 15 June 1962; *Worker*, 17 June and 1 July 1962.
62. *Worker*, 6 May 1962; "Oral History of John Abt," ca. 1987, *Reference Center for Marxist Studies*.
63. *Worker*, 16 and 18 December 1962; *New York Times*, 18 December 1962; *New York Amsterdam News*, 22 December 1962; *Worker*, 13 January 1963.
64. *Worker*, 21 April and 4 June 1963; *New York Times*, 30 August 1963; *Worker*, 22 December and 3 February 1963; *New York Times*, 19 November 1961.
65. *Worker*, 22 and 29 September and 13 October 1963; Claudia Jones to Ben Davis, 13 August 1963, Ben Davis Papers; *Worker*, 8 September 1963.
66. Ben Davis, "Tokenism and Gradualism in the Struggle for Negro Rights," *Political Affairs* 42 (February 1963): 16.
67. *Worker*, 4 August 1963.
68. Ibid., 10 November 1963.
69. Ibid., 10 March 1963.

70. Ben Davis, "New Stage of Negro Freedom Movement," *Political Affairs* 42 (August 1963): 19–32.
71. Davis report, 1 October 1963, Ben Davis Papers.
72. *Jet*, 16 May 1963.
73. *Worker*, 12 May 1963; *Detroit Free Press*, 13 May 1963. Davis said in the interview that his mother died of a stroke after the KKK stoned their home. He added, "I am discriminated against by virtue of being a black man and I am a Communist by virtue of the fact that I want to fight against that discrimination." On current events, he warned that President Kennedy "will run the risk of world war by telling Russian ships to get out of the Atlantic, but he can't find the money, will or courage to put [Ross] Barnett in jail or prosecute Gen. Edwin Walker."
74. *Worker*, 11 and 23 June, 28 and 30 July, and 25 August 1963.
75. Ben Davis to George Murphy, 30 August 1963, George Murphy Papers.
76. N. Numade, *The African Revolution: Three Essays*, introduction by Ben Davis (New York: New Century, 1963); copy owned by Tamiment Institute; Herbert Aptheker to Jesus Colon, 17 May 1960, Jesus Colon Papers (there is much correspondence in these files from the Cuban Communist Party, especially Blas Roca); William Patterson to George Murphy, 21 February 1963, George Murphy Papers: they are aiding Cheddi Jagan in establishing a university in Georgetown.
77. SAC Chicago, 100-3952, to FBI Director, 100-35868, 22 October 1963, Box 3, Gil Green Papers.
78. SAC New York, 100-129802, 16 March 1964, FBI Director, 100-3-104, COINTELPRO, FBI.
79. H. T. Lovin, "The Lyndon Johnson Administration and the Federal War on Subversion in the 1960s," *Presidential Studies Quarterly* 17 (Summer 1987): 559–72; Frank Donner, "Let Him Wear a Wolf's Head: What the FBI Did to William Albertson," *Civil Liberties Review* 3 (April–May 1976): 18.
80. "Val" to Ben Davis, 24 January 1964, Ben Davis Papers.
81. Elizabeth Gurley Flynn to Al Richmond, 16 March 1964, Reel 4220, Elizabeth Gurley Flynn Papers.
82. Lloyd Brown, interview with author, 2 May 1988; Phil Bart, interview with author, 2 May 1988.
83. *New York Times*, 24 August 1964; *Worker*, 25 and 30 August 1964.
84. Langston Hughes to Nina Davis, undated, Ben Davis Papers. Other letters to Nina Davis were from Adam Powell, undated; Ralph Bunche, 25 August 1964; Ossie Davis, undated; Charles White, 25 August 1964; George Charney, 19 August 1964; Elsie Levin, 28 August 1964. George Murphy's letter dated 24 August 1964 said, ". . . books will yet be written to tell future generations of the day-to-day contributions he made to help usher in America, of, by, and for the people. . . . Ben was the first editor of the *Afro-American's* weekly magazine. Ben's grandfather and my paternal grandfather Murphy, were old friends. . . . Ben's father, before he died, expressed his deep understanding of Ben and his determination to take a new, a different road."
85. Commanding Officer, Bureau of Special Services, 27 August 1964, BSS, 432-M, New York City Police Department. The "Red Squad" minutely scrutinized Davis throughout his stay in New York.

Selected Bibliography

Books and Articles

Aaron, Daniel. *Writers on the Left*. New York: Harcourt Brace, 1961.

Alexander, Martin, and Helen Graham, eds. *The French and Spanish Popular Fronts: Comparative Perspectives*. New York: Cambridge University Press, 1989.

Allen, James. "The Negro Question." *Political Affairs* 25 (November 1946): 1046–56.

Almond, Gabriel. *The Appeals of Communism*. Princeton: Princeton University Press, 1954.

Amter, Israel. "The Elections in New York." *The Communist* 15 (December 1936): 1141–53.

———."Significance of the Coming Municipal Elections in New York." *The Communist* 16 (July 1937): 647–60.

Anderson, Dennis. "Proportional Representation Elections of Toledo City Councils, 1934–1949." *Northwest Ohio Quarterly* 59 (Autumn 1987): 153–77.

Arismendi, Rodney. "We Live in a New Changed World." *World Marxist Review* 31 (January 1988): 20–27.

Arizala, José, ed. "Latin America: Democracy Must Be Won, Not Waited For." *World Marxist Review* 31 (July 1988): 88–100.

Aronson, James. *The Press and the Cold War*. Boston: Beacon, 1973.

Arstein, Helen, and Carlton Moss. *In Person: Lena Horne*. New York: Greenberg, 1950.

Avery, Sheldon B. *Up from Washington: William Pickens and the Negro Struggle for Equality, 1900–1954*. Newark: University of Delaware Press, 1989.

Bacote, Clarence A. "The Negro in Atlanta Politics." *Journal of Negro History* 16, no. 4 (1955): 333–50.

Baigell, Matthew, and Julia Williams, eds. *Artists Against War and Fascism: Papers of the First American Artists' Congress*. New Brunswick, N.J.: Rutgers University Press, 1986.

Banks, Samuel. "The Korean Conflict." *Negro History Bulletin* 36, no. 6 (1973): 1311–32.

Barker, Elizabeth. "Building a Mass Party in Harlem." *Party Organizer* 1, no. 1 (1943): 9–12.

Baxandall, Rosalyn. *Words on Fire: The Life and Writings of Elizabeth Gurley Flynn*. New Brunswick, N.J.: Rutgers University Press, 1987.

Békés, Csaba. "New Findings on the 1956 Hungarian Revolution. *Cold War International History Project Project Bulletin* 1, no. 2 (Fall 1992): 1–3.

Belknap, Michael. "Review Essay: Above the Law and Beyond Its Reach: O'Reilly and Theoharis on FBI Intelligence Operations." *American Bar Foundation Research Journal* (Winter 1985): 201–15.

Bellush, Bernard, and Jewel Bellush. "A Radical Response to the Roosevelt Presidency: The Communist Party (1933–1945)." *Presidential Studies Quarterly* 10 (1980): 645–61.

Bentley, Eric, ed. *Thirty Years of Treason: Excerpts from Hearings Before the House Committee on Un-American Activities, 1938–1968.* New York: Viking, 1971.

Berger, Hans. "Concerning a Charge of Betrayal." *The Communist* 23 (May 1944): 431–39.

Blake, George. "The Party in Harlem, New York." *Party Voice* 11 (June 1938): 14–20.

Blakely, Allison. *Russia and the Negro: Blacks in Russian History and Thought.* Washington, D.C.: Howard University Press, 1986.

Bonosky, Philip. "The Story of Ben Carreathers." *Masses and Mainstream* 6 (July 1953): 34–44.

Braddock, Eugene. "For Victory—Win Negro Rights." *Clarity* 3 (Summer 1942): 32–42.

———. "Negro Youth Fights in the American Tradition." *Clarity* 3 (Spring 1942): 40–52.

Browder, Earl. "For National Liberation of the Negroes! War Against White Chauvinism." *Communist* 11 (April 1932): 295–309.

———. "On the Negroes and the Right to Self-Determination." *The Communist* 23 (January 1944): 83–85.

———. "Teheran—History's Greatest Turning Point." *The Communist* 23 (January 1944): 3–8.

———. "Why an Open Letter to Our Party Membership." *The Communist* 12 (August 1933): 707–69.

Brown, Lloyd. *Iron City.* New York: Masses and Mainstream, 1952.

Buckley, Gail Lumet. *The Hornes: An American Family.* New York: Knopf, 1986.

Budenz, Louis. *The Cry Is Peace.* Chicago: Regnery, 1952.

Bunche, Ralph. *The Political Status of the Negro in the Age of FDR.* Chicago: University of Chicago Press, 1973.

Buni, Andrew. *Robert L. Vann of the "Pittsburgh Courier": Politics and Black Journalism.* Pittsburgh: University of Pittsburgh Press, 1974.

Capeci, Dominic, Jr. "Fiorello H. La Guardia and the Stuyvesant Town Controversy of 1943." *New York Historical Society Quarterly* 32 (October 1978): 289–310.

———. *The Harlem Riot of 1943.* Philadelphia: Temple University Press, 1977.

Caridi, Ronald J. *The Korean War and American Politics: The Republican Party as a Case Study.* Philadelphia: University of Pennsylvania Press, 1968.

Carmines, Edward G., and James A. Stimson. *Issue Evolution: Race and the Transformation of American Politics.* Princeton: Princeton University Press, 1989.

Carter, Dan T. *Scottsboro: A Tragedy of the American South.* Baton Rouge: Louisiana State University Press, 1969.

Ceplair, Larry. *Under the Shadow of War: Fascism, Anti-Fascism, and Marxists.* New York: Columbia University Press, 1987.

Charney, George. *A Long Journey.* Chicago: Quadrangle, 1968.

Churchill, Ward, and Jim Vander Wall. *COINTELPRO Papers*. Boston: South End Press, 1989.
[Communist Party.] *The Communist Position on the Negro Question*. New York: New Century, 1947.
———. "Decisions of the National Committee of the Communist Party." *The Communist* 23 (February 1944): 107–8.
———. "On the Arrest of Gus Hall and Benjamin Davis." *Political Affairs* 41 (April 1962): 1–4.
———. "Statement of the National Committee, CPUSA." *Political Affairs* 35 (July 1956): 34–36.
———. "The Tasks of the Communist Sections Regarding Municipal Policy-Resolution of the Enlarged Presidium of the ECCI." *The Communist* 9 (February 1930): 281–88.
[Communist Party, U. S. National Committee.] "Theoretical Aspects of the Negro Question" (draft resolution). *Political Affairs* 37 (January 1959): 42–46.
Complete Report of Mayor La Guardia's Commission on the Harlem Riot of March 19, 1935. New York: Arno Press, 1969.
Cooney, John. *American Pope: The Life and Times of Francis Cardinal Spellman*. New York: Times Books, 1984.
Cosgrove, Stuart. "The Zoot-Suit and Style Warfare." *History Workshop* 18 (Autumn 1984): 77–91.
Cripps, Thomas. "The Dark Spot in the Kaleidoscope: Black Images in American Film." In *The Kaleidoscopic Lens: How Hollywood Views Ethnic Groups*, edited by Randall Miller, 15–35. Englewood, N.J.: Ozer, 1980.
Cruse, Harold. *The Crisis of the Negro Intellectual*. New York: Morrow, 1967.
Cuneo, Ernest. *Life with Fiorello: A Memoir*. New York: Macmillan Co., 1955.
Davis, Benjamin J. "Build the Negro People's Movement." *Political Affairs* 26 (November 1947): 996–1005.
———. "The Challenge of the New Era." *Political Affairs* 35 (December 1956): 14–40.
———. "The Communists, the Negro People and the War." *The Communist* 21 (August 1942): 633–39.
———. "Foster: Fighter for Correct Theory." *Political Affairs* 35 (April 1956): 40–48.
———. "Foster's Contributions to the Cause of National and Colonial Liberation." *Political Affairs* 30 (March 1951): 36–50.
———. "The Negro People in the Elections." *The Communist* 15 (October 1936): 975–87.
———. "The Negro People in the Fight for Peace and Freedom." *Political Affairs* 29 (June 1050): 101–13.
———. "The Negro People's Liberation Movement." *Political Affairs* 27 (September 1948): 880–98.
———. "New Stage of Negro Freedom Movement." *Political Affairs* 42 (August 1963): 19–32.
———. "On the Colonial Liberation Movements (On the Occasion of the 71st Birthday, on December 21, 1950, of Joseph Stalin, Leader and Teacher of the World Working Class and All Toiling Humanity)." *Political Affairs* 29 (December 1950): 37–49.

———. "On the Use of Negro Troops in Wall Street's Aggression Against the Korean People." *Political Affairs* 29 (October 1950): 47–56.

———. "Tokenism and Gradualism in the Struggle for Negro Rights." *Political Affairs* 42 (February 1963): 14–26.

Degras, Jane, ed. *The Communism International, 1919–1943, Documents.* London: Frank Cass, 1971.

Dennis, Eugene. *Letters from Prison.* New York: International Publishers, 1956.

Dennis, Peggy. *The Autobiography of an American Communist.* Westport, Conn.: Lawrence Hill, 1977.

Detweiler, Frederick. *The Negro Press in the United States.* 1922. Reprint. College Park, Md.: McGrath, 1968.

Dittmer, John. *Black Georgia in the Progressive Era 1900–1920.* Urbana: University of Illinois Press, 1977.

Doenecke, Justus D. "Non-Intervention of the Left: The Keep America Out of the War Congress, 1938–1941." *Journal of Contemporary History* 12 (1977): 221–36.

Donner, Frank. "Let Him Wear a Wolf's Head: What the FBI Did to William Albertson." *Civil Liberties Review* 3 (April–May 1976): 12–22.

Dower, John. *War Without Mercy: Race and Power in the Pacific War.* New York: Pantheon, 1986.

Drake, St. Clair, and Horace Cayton. *Black Metropolis.* New York: Harper & Row, 1962.

Duberman, Martin. *Paul Robeson.* New York: Knopf, 1988.

DuBois, W. E. B., and Augustus Granville, eds. *The Common School and the Negro American.* Atlanta: Atlanta University Press, 1911.

Earley, Charity Adams. *One Woman's Army: A Black Officer Remembers the WAC.* College Station: Texas A&M University Press, 1989.

Elliott, Lawrence. *Little Flower: The Life and Times of Fiorella La Guardia.* New York: Morrow, 1983.

Ellison, Ralph. "Remembering Richard Wright." In *Speaking for You: The Vision of Ralph Ellison*, edited by Kimberly W. Benson, 187–98. Washington, D.C.: Howard University Press, 1987.

Fain, Tyrus, et al., eds. *The Intelligence Community: History, Organization, and Issues.* New York: R. R. Bowker, 1977.

Fast, Howard. *The Naked God: The Writer and the Communist Party.* New York: Praeger, 1957.

Fink, Leon, and Brian Greenberg. *Upheaval In the Quiet Zone: A History of Hospital Workers' Union, Local 1199.* Urbana: University of Illinois Press, 1989.

Finkelstein, Sidney. *Jazz: A People's Music.* New York: International Publishers, 1948.

Finkle, Lee. *Forum for Protest: The Black Press During World War II.* Rutherford, N.J.: Fairleigh Dickinson University Press, 1975.

Fisher, Sethard. "Marxist Prescriptions for Black American Equality." *Phylon* 45, no. 1 (1984): 52–66.

Flynn, Edward J. *You're the Boss.* New York: Viking, 1947.

Foner, Eric. *Nothing but Freedom: Emancipation and Its Legacy.* Baton Rouge: Louisiana State University Press, 1983.

Foner, Philip S., and James Allen, eds. *American Communism and Black Amer-*

icans: A Documentary History, 1919–1929. Philadelphia: Temple University Press, 1987.
Ford, James. "Mobilize Negro Manpower for Victory." *The Communist* 22 (January 1943): 38–46.
Ford, James. "Teheran and the Negro People." *The Communist* 23 (March 1944): 260–66.
Ford, James, and George Blake. "Building the People's Front in Harlem." *The Communist* 17 (February 1938): 158–68.
Foster, William Z. "Browder Again Tries to Destroy the Communist Party." *Political Affairs* 39 (June 1960): 43–48.
———. *History of the Communist Party of the United States*. Westport, Conn.: Greenwood, 1968.
———. *In Defense of the Communist Party and the Indicted Leaders*. New York: New Century, 1949.
———. "On Self-Determination for the Negro People." *Political Affairs* 25 (June 1946): 549–54.
———. "On the Situation in the Communist Party." *Political Affairs* 35 (October 1956): 15–45.
———. "The Struggle Against Revisionism." *Political Affairs* 24 (September 1945): 782–99.
Foster, William Z., and Benjamin J. Davis, Jr. "Notes on the Negro Question." *Political Affairs* 38 (April 1959): 33–43.
Franklin, Francis. "The Status of the Negro People in the Black Belt and How to Fight for the Right of Self-Determination." *Political Affairs* 25 (May 1946): 438–56.
Franklin, John Hope. *From Slavery to Freedom: A History of Negro Americans*. New York: Knopf, 1969.
Fraser, Steve. *Labor Will Rule: Sidney Hillman and the Rise of American Labor*. New York: Free Press, 1991.
Fraser, Steve, and Gary Gerstle, eds. *The Rise and Fall of the New Deal Order, 1930–1980*. Princeton: Princeton University Press, 1989.
Freeman, Josh. *In Transit: The Transport Workers Union and New York City*. New York: Oxford University Press, 1992.
Gallego, Ignacio, and Francisco Palero. Interview. *World Marxist Review* 32 (April 1989): 54–57.
Garfinkel, Herbert. *When Negroes March: MOWM in the Organizational Politics for FEPC*. Glencoe, Ill.: Free Press, 1959.
Garrett, Charles. *The La Guardia Years: Machine and Reform Politics in New York City*. New Brunswick, N.J.: Rutgers University Press, 1961.
Garrow, David. *The FBI and Martin Luther King, Jr.: From "Solo" to Memphis*. New York: Norton, 1981.
———. "FBI Political Harassment and FBI Historiography: Analyzing Informants and Measuring the Effects." *Public Historian* 10 (Fall 1988): 5–18.
Gates, John. *The Story of an American Communist*. New York: Nelson, 1958.
Gates, Lillian. "New York's 1949 Elections." *Political Affairs* 28 (December 1949): 46–59.
Gayle, Addison. *Richard Wright: Ordeal of a Native Son*. Garden City, N.Y.: Doubleday, 1980.

Gerson, Si. "Electoral Coalition Problems in New York." *Political Affairs* 26 (October 1947): 894–901.

———. *Pete: The Story of Peter V. Cacchione, New York's First Communist Councilman.* New York: International Publishers, 1976.

Giddins, Gary. *Celebrating Bird: The Triumph of Charlie Parker.* New York: Morrow, 1987.

Gillespie, Dizzy, and Al Fraser. *To Be, or Not to Bop.* Garden City, N.Y.: Doubleday, 1979.

Ginger, Ann Fagan, and Eugene M. Tobin, eds. *The National Lawyers Guild: From Roosevelt through Reagan.* Philadelphia: Temple University Press, 1988.

Girenko, Yuri. "The Background to a Split." *World Marxist Review* 32 (February 1989): 91–93.

Gitler, Ira. *Swing to Bop: An Oral History of the Transition in Jazz in the 1940s.* New York: Oxford University Press, 1985.

Glazer, Nathan. *The Social Basis of American Communism.* New York: Harcourt Brace, 1961.

Glick, Brian. *War at Home: Covert Action Against U.S. Activists and What We Can Do About It.* Boston: South End Press, 1989.

Goebbels, Joseph. *Bolshevism in Theory and Practice.* Berlin: Muller, 1936.

Goldway, David. "On the Study of Browder's Report." *The Communist* 23 (March 1944): 232–40.

Goodman, Walter. *The Committee: The Extraordinary Career of HUAC.* New York: Farrar, Straus and Giroux, 1968.

Gordon, Max. "Labor Moves Forward in the New York Elections." *Political Affairs* 24 (December 1945): 1079–87.

Green, Gil. *Cold War Fugitive: A Personal Story of the McCarthy Years.* New York: International Publishers, 1984.

———. "The New York City Elections." *The Communist* 22 (December 1943): 1103–10.

Greenberg, Cheryl Lynn. *Or Does It Explode: Black Harlem in the Great Depression.* New York: Oxford University Press, 1991.

Griffith, Robert. "The Chilling Effect." *Wilson Quarterly*, no. 2 (1978): 135–36.

Gruber, Helmet. *Red Vienna: Experiment in Working Class Culture, 1919–1934.* New York: Oxford University Press, 1991.

Haag, John. "'Gone With the Wind' in Nazi Germany." *Georgia Historical Quarterly* 83 (Summer 1989): 278–304.

Hamby, Alonzo. *Liberalism and Its Challengers: FDR To Reagan.* New York: Oxford University Press, 1985.

Hamilton, Charles V. *Adam Clayton Powell, Jr.: The Political Biography of an American Dilemma.* New York: Atheneum, 1991.

Harlan, Louis. *Booker T. Washington: The Wizard of Tuskeegee. 1901–1915.* New York: Oxford University Press, 1983.

Harris, William H. *Keeping the Faith: A. Philip Randolph, Milton P. Webster and the Brotherhood of Sleeping Car Porters, 1925–1937.* Urbana: University of Illinois Press, 1977.

Haskins, James. *Lena Horne.* New York: Coward-McCann, 1983.

Haynes, John, ed. *Communism and Anti-Communism in the U.S.* New York: Garland, 1987.

Haywood, Harry. *Black Bolshevik: The Autobiography of an Afro-American Communist.* Chicago: Liberator Press, 1978.

Healey, Dorothy. *Dorothy Healey Remembers a Life In the American Communist Party.* New York: Oxford University Press, 1990.

———. "On the Status of the Party." *Political Affairs* 37 (March 1958): 40–48.

Herndon, Angelo. *Let Me Live.* New York: Random House, 1937.

Hickey, Neil, and Ed Edwin. *Adam Clayton Powell and the Politics of Race.* New York: Fleet, 1965.

Hill, Robert, ed. *The Crusader.* 6 vols. New York: Garland, 1987.

Hogan, Lawrence. *A Black National News Service: The Associated Negro Press and Claude Barnett, 1919–1945.* Rutherford, N.J.: Fairleigh Dickinson University Press, 1984.

Horne, Gerald. *Black and Red: W.E.B. Du Bois and the Afro-American Response to the Cold War, 1944–1963.* Albany: State University of New York Press, 1985.

———. *Communist Front? The Civil Rights Congress, 1946–1956.* Rutherford, N.J.: Fairleigh Dickinson University Press, 1987.

Horovitz, Gerry. "Ben Davis and the Communist Party: A Study in Race and Politics." *UCLA Historical Journal* 4 (1983): 92–107.

Hoshor, John. *God in a Rolls-Royce: The Rise of Father Divine—Madman, Menace or Messiah?* New York: Hillman-Curl, 1936.

Howe, Irving, and Lewis Coser. *The American Communist Party: A Critical History.* New York: De Capo Press, 1974.

Inglesias, Cesar Andreu, ed. *Memoirs of Bernardo Vega: A Contribution to the History of the Puerto Rican Community in New York.* New York: Monthly Review Press, 1984.

Isaacs, Edith. *Love Affair with a City: The Story of Stanley Isaacs.* New York: Random House, 1967.

Isserman, Maurice. *Which Side Were You On?* Middleton, Conn.: Wesleyan University Press, 1983.

Jack, Hulan. *Fifty Years a Democrat: The Autobiography of Hulan E. Jack.* New York: New Benjamin Franklin House, 1982.

Jackson, James. *Revolutionary Tracings.* New York: International Publishers, 1974.

Jaffe, Julian. *Crusade Against Radicalism: New York During the Red Scare, 1914–1924.* Port Washington, N.Y.: Kennikat, 1972.

Jaffe, Philip J. *The Rise and Fall of American Communism.* New York: Horizon, 1975.

James, Marquis. *The Metropolitan Life: A Study in Business Growth.* New York: Viking Press, 1947.

Johnson, Arnold. "The Ohio Membership Campaign." *The Communist* 23 (April 1944): 319–26.

Johnson, Buzz. *"I Think of My Mother": Notes on the Life and Times of Claudia Jones.* London: Karia Press, 1985.

Johnson, Christopher. *Maurice Sugar: Law, Labor and the Left in Detroit, 1912–1950.* Detroit: Wayne State University Press, 1988.

Johnson, Ronald W. "The Korean Red Scare in Missouri." *Red River Valley Historical Review* 4, no. 2 (1979): 72–86.

Jones, Claudia. *Ben Davis: Fighter for Freedom.* New York: National Committee to Defend Negro Leadership, 1954.

———. "Discussion Article." *Political Affairs* 24 (August 1945): 717–20.
———. "From Terre Haute to Harlem." *Masses and Mainstream* 7 (June 1954): 27–29.
———. *Lift Every Voice for Victory*. New York: New Age, 1942.
———. "On the Right to Self-Determination for the Negro People in the Black Belt." *Political Affairs* 25 (January 1946): 67–77.
Judd, Richard. *Socialist Cities: Municipal Politics and the Grass Roots of American Socialism*. Albany: State University of New York Press, 1989.
Kelley, Robin D. G. *Hammer and Hoe: Alabama Communists During the Great Depression*. Chapel Hill: University of North Carolina Press, 1990.
Kinnamon, Kenneth. *The Emergence of Richard Wright: A Study In Literature and Society*. Urbana: University of Illinois Press, 1972.
Kinoy, Arthur. *Rights on Trial: The Odyssey of a People's Lawyer*. Cambridge: Harvard University Press, 1983.
Klehr, Harvey. *Far Left of Center: The American Radical Left Today*. New Brunswick, N.J.: Transaction, 1988.
———. *The Heyday of American Communism: The Depression Decade*. New York: Basic Books, 1984.
Klehr, Harvey, and John Haynes. "'Moscow Gold': Confirmed at Last?" *Labor History* 33 (Spring 1992): 279–93.
Kolko, Gabriel. *The Politics of War: The World and U.S. Foreign Policy, 1943–1945*. New York: Random House, 1978.
Kornweibel, Theodore, Jr. *No Crystal Stair: Black Life and the Messenger 1917–1928*. Westport, Conn.: Greenwood Press, 1975.
Kraditor, Aileen S. *"Jimmy Higgins": The Mental World of the American Rank-and-File Communist, 1930–1958*. Westport, Conn.: Greenwood Press, 1988.
Kublin, Hyman. *Asian Revolutionary: The Life of Sen Katayama*. Princeton: Princeton University Press, 1964.
Kuhn, Cliff. *Living Atlanta: An Oral History of the City, 1914–1948*. Athens: University of Georgia Press, 1990.
Laberman, Enid. "The Case for Proportional Representation." In *Choosing an Electoral System: Issues and Alternatives*, edited by Arend Lijphart and Bernard Grofman, 41–51. New York: Praeger, 1984.
Lash, Joseph P. *Dealers and Dreamers: A New Look at the New Deal*. New York: Doubleday, 1988.
Lava, José. "Twenty Years in Prison." *World Marxist Review* 30 (June 1987): 56–61.
Lawrence, Bill, and Isidore Begun. "The New York City Elections and the Struggle Against Hitlerism." *The Communist* 20 (December 1941): 1055–71.
Lawson, Steven, et al. "Groveland: Florida's Little Scottsboro." *Florida Historical Quarterly* 65 (July 1986): 1–26.
Lenin, V. I. "Should Communists Participate in Bourgeois Parliaments?" *The Communist* 11 (March 1932): 688–96.
Lewinson, Edwin. *Black Politics in New York City*. New York: Twayne, 1974.
Lewis, Claude. *Adam Clayton Powell*. Greenwich, Conn.: Fawcett, 1963.
Lewis, Lionel. *Cold War on Campus: A Study of the Politics of Organizational Control*. New Brunswick, N.J.: Transaction, 1988.
Lichtman, Allan. *Prejudice and the Old Politics: The Presidential Election of 1928*. Chapel Hill: University of North Carolina Press, 1979.

Liebman, Arthur. "The Ties That Bind: The Jewish Support for the Left in the U.S." *American Jewish Historical Quarterly* 66 (December 1976): 1–25.

Lightfoot, Claude. *Chicago Slums to World Politics: Autobiography of Claude Lightfoot.* New York: New Outlook, 1986.

Lisio, Donald. *Hoover, Blacks and Lily-Whites: A Study of Southern Strategies.* Chapel Hill: University of North Carolina Press, 1985.

Logan, Rayford, and Michael R. Winston, eds. *Dictionary of American Negro Biography.* New York: Norton, 1982.

Lomax, Charles. "Harlem Plays a Winner." *Party Organizer* 1 (December 1943): 11–15.

Lovin, Hugh T. "The Lyndon Johnson Administration and the Federal War on Subversion in the 1960s." *Presidential Studies Quarterly* 17 (Summer 1987): 559–72.

Lowenfels, Walter. *My Many Lives: The Autobiography of Walter Lowenfels. Vol. 2: The Poetry of My Politics.* Homestead, Fla.: Olivant Press, 1968.

Lyons, Paul. *Philadelphia Communists, 1936–1956.* Philadelphia: Temple University Press, 1982.

Magil, A. B. "Discussion Article." *Political Affairs* 24 (August 1945): 721–25.

Malcolm X. *The Autobiography of Malcolm X.* New York: Grove Press, 1965.

Malina, Soloma. "Renovating the Party." *World Marxist Review* 31 (January 1988): 40–47.

Mann, Arthur. *La Guardia: A Fighter Against His Times, 1882–1933.* New York: Lippincott, 1959.

Manners, William. *Patience and Fortitude: Fiorella La Guardia.* New York: Harcourt Brace, 1976.

Marcantonio, Vito. *I Vote My Conscience: Debates, Speeches, and Writings 1935–1950.* New York: Vito Marcantonio Memorial, 1956.

Martin, Charles. *The Angelo Herndon Case and Southern Justice.* Baton Rouge: Louisiana State University Press, 1976.

May, Elaine Tyler. *Homeward Bound: American Families in the Cold War.* New York: Basic Books, 1988.

Mays, Benjamin E. *Born to Rebel.* New York: Scribner, 1971.

McNeil, Genna Rae. *Groundwork: Charles Hamilton Houston and the Struggle for Civil Rights.* Philadelphia: University of Pennsylvania Press, 1983.

Meier, August, and David Lewis. "History of the Negro Upper Class in Atlanta, Georgia, 1890–1958." *Journal of Negro Education* 2 (1959): 128–39.

Merson, Allan. *Communist Resistance in Nazi Germany* London: Lawrence and Wishart, 1985.

Meyer, Gerald. *Vito Marcantonio: Radical Politician, 1902–1954.* Albany: State University of New York Press, 1989.

Miller, Merle. *The Judges and the Judged.* Garden City, N.Y.: Doubleday, 1952.

Miller, Randall, ed. *The Kaleidoscopic Lens: How Hollywood Views Ethnic Groups.* Englewood, N.J.: Ozer, 1980.

Mindel, Jacob. "Discussion Article." *Political Affairs* 24 (August 1945): 726–30.

Moon, Henry Lee. *Balance of Power: The Negro Vote.* Garden City, N.Y.: Doubleday, 1948.

Moore, John Hammond. "Communists and Fascists in a Southern City: Atlanta, 1930." *South Atlantic Quarterly* 67 (Summer 1968): 441.

Morris, Newbold O. *Let the Chips Fall: My Battles Against Corruption*. New York: Appleton-Century-Crofts, 1955.
Munroe, Trevor. *The Marxist Left in Jamaica*. Mona, Jamaica: ISER, 1977.
Murray, Florence, ed. *The Negro Handbook, 1946–1947*. New York: Wyn, 1947.
Murray, Hugh. "The NAACP Versus the Communist Party: The Scottsboro Rape Cases, 1931–1932." *Phylon* 28 (Fall 1967): 276.
Naison, Mark. "Communism and Harlem Intellectuals in the Popular Front: Anti-Fascism and the Politics of Black Culture." *Journal of Ethnic Studies* 9 (Spring 1981): 1–26.
Naison, Mark. *Communists in Harlem During the Depression*. Urbana: University of Illinois Press, 1983.
Nalty, Bernard. *Strength for the Fight: A History of Black Americans in the Military*. New York: Free Press, 1986.
Nelson, Steve, James R. Barrett, and Rob Ruck. *Steve Nelson: American Radical*. Pittsburgh: University of Pittsburgh Press, 1981.
Numade, N. *The African Revolution: Three Essays*. Introduction by Benjamin Davis. New York: New Century, 1963.
O'Reilly, Kenneth. *Racial Matters: The FBI's Secret War Against Black America, 1960–1972*. New York: Free Press, 1989.
———. "The Roosevelt Administration and Black America: Federal Surveillance Policy and Civil Rights During the New Deal and World War II Years." *Phylon* 48 (March 1987): 12–25.
Orfield, Cary, and Carole Ashkinaze. *The Closing Door: Conservative Policy and Black Opportunity*. Chicago: University of Chicago Press, 1991.
Ottley, Roi. *"New World a-Coming": Inside Black America*. Boston: Houghton Mifflin, 1943.
Painter, Nell Irvin. *The Narrative of Hosea Hudson: His Life as a Negro Communist in the South*. Cambridge: Harvard University Press, 1979.
Patterson, Haywood, and Earl Conrad. *Scottsboro Boy*. Garden City, N.Y.: Doubleday, 1950.
Patterson, William. *Ben Davis: Crusader for Negro Freedom and Socialism*. New York: New Outlook, 1967.
Penner, Norman. *Canadian Communism: The Stalin Years and Beyond*. Toronto: Methuen, 1988.
Peplow, Michael. *George Schuyler*. Boston: Twayne, 1980.
Perry, Pettis. "Next Stage in the Struggle for Negro Rights." *Political Affairs* 28 (October 1949): 33–46.
———. "The Party and the Negro People." *Political Affairs* 37 (February 1958): 20–25.
Pfeffer, Paula F. *A. Philip Randolph, Pioneer of the Civil Rights Movement*. Baton Rouge: Louisiana State University Press, 1990.
Philbrick, Herbert, and James D. Bales, *Communism and Race in America*. Searcy, Ark.: Bales Bookstore, 1965.
Powell, Adam Clayton. *Adam by Adam: The Autobiography of Adam Clayton Powell*. New York: Dial, 1971.
———. *Marching Blacks: An Interpretive History of the Rise of the Black Common Man*. New York: Dial, 1945.

Powers, Richard Gid. *Secrecy and Power: The Life of J. Edgar Hoover.* New York: Free Press, 1987.
Preston, John W. "Developments in Negro People's Movement." *Political Affairs* 31 (February 1952): 32–42.
Quill, Shirley. *Mike Quill—Himself: A Memoir.* Greenwich: Devin Adair, 1985.
Roark, James. "American Black Leaders: The Response to Colonialism and the Cold War, 1943–1953." *African Historical Studies* 4, no. 2 (1971): 253–370.
Robeson, Paul. "Speech Delivered at the Funeral of Benjamin Davis." In *Paul Robeson Speaks: Writings Speeches, Interviews. 1918–1974*, edited by Philip S. Foner, 470–71. New York: Brunner-Mazel, 1978.
Roper, John. *C. Vann Woodward Southerner.* Athens: University of Georgia Press, 1987.
Roth, Mirjana. "'If You Give Us Rights We Will Fight': Black Involvement in the Second World War." *South African Historical Journal* 15 (November 1983): 85–104.
Ruchames, Louis. *Race, Jobs and Politics: The Story of FEPC.* New York: Columbia University Press, 1953.
Rustin, Bayard. *Down the Line: The Collected Writings of Bayard Rustin.* Chicago: Quadrangle, 1971.
Samuels, Wilfred. *Five Afro-Caribbean Voices in American Culture, 1917–1929.* Boulder, Colo.: Belmont Books, 1977.
Sarlis, Dimitris. "Lessons of the Greek Resistance in Today's Struggle." *World Marxist Review* 29 (June 1986): 61–66.
Sass, Louis. "On Some Problems of the Harlem Section." *Party Organizer* 7 (March 1934): 19–21.
Scales, Junius Irving, and Richard Nickson. *Cause at Heart: A Former Communist Remembers.* Athens: University of Georgia Press, 1987.
Schaffer, Alan. *Vito Marcantonio: Radical in Congress.* Syracuse, N.Y.: Syracuse University Press, 1966.
Schrecker, Ellen. "Archival Sources for the Study of McCarthyism." *Journal of American History* 75 (June 1988): 197–208.
Schuyler, George. *Black and Conservative: The Autobiography of George S. Schuyler.* New Rochelle, N.Y.: Arlington House, 1966.
Schwartz, Lawrence H. *Marxism and Culture: The CPUSA and Culture.* Port Washington, N.Y.: Kennikat, 1980.
Scott, William. *The Sons of Sheba's Race: African-Americans and the Italo-Ethiopian War, 1935–1941.* Bloomington: Indiana University Press, 1992.
Shannon, David. *The Decline of American Communism: A History of the Communist Party of the U.S. since 1945.* New York: Harcourt Brace, 1959.
Shapiro, Herbert. *White Violence, Black Response: From Reconstruction to Montgomery.* Amherst: University of Massachusetts Press, 1989.
Shaw, Frederick. *The History of the New York City Legislature.* New York: AMS Press, 1968.
Shillington, Kevin. *History of Southern Africa.* Essex, England: Longman, 1987.
Sirgionvanni, George. *An Undercurrent of Suspicion: Anti-Communism in America During World War II.* New Brunswick, N.J.: Transaction, 1990.
Siskind, Aaron. *Harlem Document: Photographs 1932–1940.* Providence, R.I.: Matrix, 1981.

Sitkoff, Harvard. "American Blacks in World War II: Rethinking the Militancy-Watershed Hypothesis." In *The Home Front and War in the Twentieth Century*, edited by James Titus. Washington, D.C.: GPO, 1982.

Smirnova, Natalie, et al., eds. "History of the Communist Movement: Facts, People, Ideas; What Kind of Man Was Sandino?" *World Marxist Review* 32 (April 1989): 88–93.

Spolansky, Jacob. *The Communist Trial in America*. New York: Macmillan Co., 1951.

Starobin, Joseph. *American Communism in Crisis, 1943–1957*. Cambridge: Harvard University Press, 1972.

———. "Europe Judges the Smith Act." *Masses and Mainstream* 4 (October 1951): 1–7.

Staupers, Mabel. *No Time for Prejudice: A Study of the Integration of Negroes in Nursing in the United States*. New York: Macmillan Co., 1961.

Street, James. *Look Away: A Dixie Notebook*. New York: Viking Press, 1936.

Terrell, Mary Church. *A Colored Woman in a White World*. 1940. Reprint. New York: Arno, 1980.

Thornbrough, Emma Lou. "American Negro Newspapers." *Business History Review* 41 (First Quarter 1966): 466–90.

Toohey, Pat. "Greater Attention to the Problems of the Negro Masses!" *Communist* 19 (March 1940): 278–88.

Trottman, Beresford S. B., ed. *Who's Who in Harlem*. New York: Magazine and Periodical Printing and Publishing Co., 1950.

Tushnet, Mark. "The Politics of Equality in Constitutional Law: The Equal Protection Clause, Dr. Du Bois, and Charles Hamilton Houston." *Journal of American History* 74 (December 1987): 884–903.

Tyler, Bruce. *From Harlem to Hollywood: The Struggle for Racial and Cultural Democracy, 1920–1943*. New York: Garland, 1992.

Van West, Carroll. "Perpetuating the Myth of America: Scottsboro and Its Interpreters." *South Atlantic Quarterly* 80 (Winter 1981): 36–48.

Varga, Eugene. "Against Reformist Tendencies in Works on Imperialism." *Political Affairs* 28 (December 1949): 74–86.

Vincent, Theodore, ed. *Voices of a Black Nation: Political Journalism in the Harlem Renaissance*. San Francisco: Ramparts Press, 1973.

Walker, Margaret. *Richard Wright, Daemonic Genius*. New York: Warner, 1988.

Walter, John. *The Harlem Fox: J. Raymond Jones and Tammany, 1920–1970*. Albany: State University of New York Press, 1989.

Walton, Hanes. *Black Republicans: The Politics of the Black and Tans*. Metuchen, N.J.: Scarecrow Press, 1975.

Washburn, Patrick. *A Question of Sedition: The Federal Government's Investigation of the Black Press During World War II*. New York: Oxford University Press, 1986.

Watts, Jill. *God Harlem USA: The Father Divine Story*. Berkeley and Los Angeles: University of California Press, 1992.

Weiss, Max. "Toward a New Anti-Fascist Youth Organization." *The Communist* 22 (September 1943): 792–805.

Whalen, Grover. *Mr. New York: The Autobiography of Grover Whalen*. New York: Putnam, 1955.

White, Walter. *How Far the Promised Land?* New York: Viking Press, 1955.
———. *A Man Called White.* New York: Viking Press, 1948.
———. "Portrait of a Communist." *Negro Digest* 9 (February 1951): 84–85.
Wilkerson, Doxey. "The Maryland-District of Columbia Enlightenment Campaign." *The Communist* 23 (May 1944): 440–49.
———. "The Negro and the American Nation." *Political Affairs* 25 (July 1946): 652–68.
Williamson, John. *Dangerous Scot: The Life and Work of an American "Undesirable."* New York: International Publishers, 1969.
Winston, Henry. "Some Aspects of Party Work." *Political Affairs* 27 (March 1948): 238–50.
Wolfe, Alan. "The Withering Away of the American Labor Party." *Journal of Rutgers University Library* 31 (June 1968): 46–57.
Wright, Richard. *American Hunger.* New York: Harper & Row, 1977.
Yamish, Nat. *Pursuit and Survival: A Left Immigrant in America.* San Francisco: Apex, 1981.
Yarbrough, Tinsley E. *A Passion for Justice: J. Waties Waring and Civil Rights.* New York: Oxford University Press, 1987.
Young, James O. *Black Writers of the Thirties.* Baton Rouge: Louisiana State University Press, 1973.
Zedong, Mao. "Reply" [to Foster]. *Political Affairs* 38 (March 1959): 31.
Zeller, Belle, and Hugh A. Bone. "American Government and Politics: The Repeal of PR in New York City—Ten Years in Retrospect." *American Political Science Review* 42 (December 1948): 1127–48.
Zion, Sidney. *The Autobiography of Roy Cohn.* New York: Lyle Stuart, 1988.

Dissertations and Theses

Avery, Sheldon Bernard. "Up from Washington: William Pickens and the Negro Struggle for Equality, 1900–1954." Ph.D. diss., University of Oregon, 1970.
Bacote, Clarence. "The Negro in Georgia Politics, 1880–1908," Ph.D. diss., University of Chicago, 1955.
Bilderback, William Winch. "The American Communist Party and World War II." Ph.D. diss., University of Washington, 1974.
Bolster, Paul Douglas. "Civil Rights Movements in Twentieth-Century Georgia," Ph.D. diss., University of Georgia, 1972.
Camp, Helen Collier. "Gurley: A Biography of Elizabeth Gurley Flynn, 1890–1964." Ph.D. diss., Columbia University, 1980.
Carter, Robert Frederick. "Pressure from the Left: The American Labor Party, 1936–1954." Ph.D. diss., Syracuse University, 1965.
Chambliss, Rollin, "What Negro Newspapers of Georgia Say About Some Social Problems," Master's thesis, University of Georgia, 1933.
Cleanth, Robert L. "Earl Russell Browder: American Spokesman for Communism, 1930–1945." Ph.D. diss., University of Washington, 1963.

Entin, David. "Angelo Herndon." Master's thesis, University of North Carolina, Chapel Hill, 1963.
Flournoy, Houston Irvine. "The Liberal Party in New York State." Ph.D. diss., Princeton University, 1956.
Gill, Gerald Robert. "Afro-American Opposition to the United States' Wars of the Twentieth Century: Dissent, Discontent and Disinterest." Ph.D. diss., Howard University, 1985.
Greene, Larry. "Harlem in the Great Depression, 1928–1936." Ph.D. diss., Columbia University, 1979.
Hunter, Gary Jerome. "'Don't Buy from Where You Can't Work': Black Urban Boycott Movements During the Depression, 1929–1941." Ph.D. diss., University of Michigan, 1977.
Jackson, Margaret Wilhemina. "Evolution of the Communist Party's Position on the American Negro Question." Master's thesis, Howard University, 1938.
Lipsitz, George. "A Rainbow at Midnight: Strategies of Independence in the Post-War Working Class." Ph.D. diss., University of Wisconsin, 1979.
Maclean, Nancy. "Behind the Mask of Chivalry: Gender, Race, and Class in the Making of the Ku Klux Klan of the 1920s in Georgia." Ph.D. diss., University of Georgia, 1989.
Manners, George Emanuel, "History of Life Insurance Company of Georgia, 1891–1955," Ph.D. diss., Emory University, 1959.
Matthews, Carl S., "After Booker T. Washington: The Search for a New Negro Leadership, 1915–1925," Ph.D. diss., University of Virginia, 1971.
Merrill, Michael. "The Angelo Herndon Case: Free Speech in Georgia." Master's thesis, Columbia University, 1972.
Meyer, Gerald. "Vito Marcantonio: A Successful New York City Radical Politician." Ph.D. diss., City University of New York, 1983.
Notaro, Carmen Anthony. "Franklin D. Roosevelt and the American Communist, Peacetime Relations, 1932–1941." Ph.D. diss., State Universitry of New York, Buffalo, 1969.
O'Brien, Kevin John. "Dennis v. U.S.: The Cold War, the Communist Conspiracy and the FBI." Ph.D. diss., Cornell University, 1979.
Payne, Charles. "Paul Robeson: A Psychobiographical Study of the Emotional Development of a Controversial Protest Leader." Ph.D. diss., Northwestern University, 1987.
Perry, Jeffffrey Babcock. "Hubert Henry Harrison, 'The Father of Harlem Radicalism': The Early Years—1883 through the Founding of the Liberty League and 'The Voice,' in 1917." Ph.D. diss., Columbia University, 1986.
Porter, Michael Leroy, "Black Atlanta: An Interdisciplinary Study of Blacks on the East Side of Atlanta, 1890–1930," Ph.D. diss., Emory University, 1974.
Prickett, James Robert. "Communists and the Communist Issue in the American Labor Movement, 1920–1950." Ph.D. diss., University of California, Los Angeles, 1975.
Rosenberg, Roger Elliot. "Guardian of the Fortress: A Biography of Earl Russell Browder, U.S. Communist Party General Secretary from 1930–1944." Ph.D. diss., University of California, Santa Barbara, 1982.
Rozier, John Wiley, "A History of the Negro Press in Atlanta." Master's thesis, Emory University, 1947.

Ruderman, Terry. "Stanley M. Isaacs: The Conscience of New York." Ph.D. diss., City University of New York, 1977.
Sanford, Delacy Wendell. "Congressional Investigation of Black Communism." Ph.D. diss., State University of New York, Stony Brook, 1973.
Seabrook, John H. "Black and White Unite: The Career of Frank R. Crosswaith." Ph.D. diss., Rutgers University, 1980.
Simana, Jabari Onaje. "Black Writers Experience Communism: An Interdisciplinary Study of Imaginative Writers, Their Critics, and the CPUSA." Ph.D. diss., Emory University, 1978.
Skinner, Byron Richard. "The Double 'V': The Impact of World War II on Black America." Ph.D. diss., University of California, Berkeley, 1978.
Solomon, Mark. "Red and Black: Negroes and Communism, 1929–1932." Ph.D. diss., Harvard University, 1972.
Waltzer, Kenneth. "The American Labor Party: Third Party Politics in New Deal-Cold War New York, 1936–1954." Ph.D. diss., Harvard University, 1977.
Young, Alexander Joseph. "Joe Louis: Symbol, 1933–1949." Ph.D. diss., University of Maryland, 1968.

Interviews Conducted by Author

Phil Bart, 2 May 1988, New York, N.Y.
Ted Bassett, 6 April 1988, New York, N.Y.
Jean Carey Bond, 11 May and 29 August 1988, New York, N.Y.
Lloyd Brown, 18 April 1988, New York, N.Y.
Johnnie Carey, 2 July 1986, New York, N.Y.
Marvel Cooke, 6 April 1988, New York, N.Y.
Nina Stamler Davis Goodman, 2, 22, and 28 June 1986, Yonkers, N.Y.
Ollie Harrington, 1 June 1989, Berlin, East Germany
James Jackson, 17 October 1986 and 6 April 1988, New York, N.Y.
Jack O'Dell, 13 November 1988, Washington, D.C.
Paul Robeson, Jr., 6 and 11 August 1988, New York, N.Y.
Phil Schaap, 5 June 1988, New York, N.Y.
Doxie Wilkerson, 6 May 1988, Norwalk, Conn.

Manuscript Collections

Boston University Library, Boston, Mass.
Allan Knight Chalmers Papers, 1916–65
Martin Luther King Papers
Joseph North Papers
Julian Steele Papers
Chicago Historical Society Manuscript Collection, Chicago. Ill.
Claude A. Barnett Papers, 1919–67
Columbia University Library, New York, N.Y.

Bill of Rights Fund Papers
Genevieve Beavers Earle Papers, 1935–50
Herbert Lehman Papers
Robert Minor Papers
Communist Party Archives, Communist Party-USA, 235 West Twenty-third Street, New York, N.Y.
Reference Center for Marxist Studies
Emory University Library, Atlanta, Ga.
Theodore Draper Papers, 1919–70
Philip J. Jaffe Papers, 1920–80
Harvard Law School Library Cambridge, Mass.
Felix Frankfurter Papers, 1914–65
William Henry Hastie Papers, 1916–76
Hoover Institute, Stanford University, Palo Alto, Calif.
National Republic Papers
Hunter College Library, City University of New York, New York, N.Y.
Jesus Colon Papers
Library of Congress, Manuscripts Division, Washington, D.C.
Brotherhood of Sleeping Car Porters Papers
Harold Hitz Burton Papers, 1953–67
William O. Douglas Papers
National Association for the Advancement of Colored People Papers
A. Philip Randolph Papers
Booker T. Washington Papers
Moorland-Spingarn Library, Howard University, Washington D.C.
Civil Rights Documentation Project
George Murphy Papers
William Patterson Papers
Municipal Archives, New York N.Y.
Genevieve Earle Papers
Fiorello La Guardia Papers
New York Public Library, New York, N.Y.
Stanley Myer Isaacs Papers, 1889–1962
Vito Marcantonio Papers
Robert Moses Papers
New York Public Library, Schomburg Center for Research in Black Culture, New York, N.Y.
Wilhemina F. Adams Papers
Gwendolyn Bennett Papers
Earl Brown Vertical File
Ethelred Brown Papers
Herbert Bruce Papers
Civil Rights Congress Papers
Crusader News Agency Papers
Frank R. Crosswaith Papers (Negro Labor Committee Records)
David Garrow Papers
Hosea Hudson Papers
W. Alphaeus Hunton Papers
International Labor Defense Records
C. L. R. James Papers
Layle Lane Papers

Canada Lee Papers
Negro Committee Records, 1925–69
Pettis Perry Papers
William Pickens Papers, 1905–54
Paul Robeson Papers
Ernest Thompson Papers

New York University, Tamiment Library, New York, N.Y.
Israel Amter Papers
Alexander Bittleman Papers
Peter Cacchione Papers
Sam Darcy Papers
Elizabeth Gurley Flynn Papers
Gil Green Papers
Robert Moses Papers

Presidential Libraries
Dwight D. Eisenhower Papers, 1916–52, Dwight D. Eisenhower Library, Abilene, Kans.
Herbert Clark Hoover Papers, Hoover Presidential Library, West Branch, Iowa
Franklin Delano Roosevelt Papers, Franklin D. Roosevelt Library, Hyde Park, N.Y.
Harry S. Truman Papers, Truman Presidential Library, Independence, Mo. (Includes Matt McGohey Papers.)

Princeton University Library, Princeton, N.J.
American Civil Liberties Union Papers

Providence College Library, Providence, R.I.
Louis Francis Budenz Papers, 1953–67

Syracuse University Library, Syracuse, N.Y.
Earl Russell Browder Papers, 1891–1967

University of Rochester Library Rochester, N.Y.
Thomas E. Dewey Papers

Rutgers University Library, New Brunswick, N.J.
American Labor Party Papers

Wisconsin State Historical Society, Madison, Wis.
Eugene Dennis Papers
Elizabeth Gurley Flynn Papers, 1917–23

University of Wisconsin Library, Green Bay, Wis.
Leon Kramer Papers

Frequently Cited Newspapers

Afro-American (Baltimore), 1933, 1936, 1941, 1945, 1949, 1960, 1964
Atlanta Independent, 1904–28
Atlanta World, 1933
Chicago Defender, 1933–34, 1939, 1944–46
Harlem Liberator, 1933–34
Liberator (New York), 1930, 1932, 1935
Negro Liberator (New York), 1934–35
New Masses, 1934–36, 1942–46, 1948
New York Age, 1934, 1936–37, 1940–49

New York Amsterdam News, 1940–48, 1950, 1963–64
New York Daily Worker, 1932–63
New York Herald Tribune, 1943–45, 1949, 1962
New York Journal American, 1939, 1944, 1961
New York Post, 1935, 1939, 1944, 1949, 1961
New York Star, 1948
New York Times, 1928–29, 1933–64
New York World-Telegram, 1935, 1942–43, 1945, 1949, 1959
People's Voice (New York), 1941–48
Pittsburgh Courier, 1926, 1930–33, 1940, 1943, 1945, 1949, 1954, 1958
PM (New York), 1945
Washington (D.C.) Star, 1946

Oral Histories

Black Women's Oral History Project, New York Public Library, Schomburg Center for Research in Black Culture, New York, N.Y.

Columbia University Oral History Program, Butler Library, New York, N.Y.

Oral History of the American Left, Tamiment Library, New York University, New York, N.Y.

University of California Oral History Program, Library, Los Angeles, Calif.

Index

Aaron, Daniel, 55
Abramowitz, Tessie, 163
Abrams, Henry, 293, 295
Abt, John, 256, 262, 265, 321
Abyssinian Church, 91, 134, 182
Acheson, Dean, 171
ACLU. *See* American Civil Liberties Union
Adams, Julius, 147
Adamson, Charles, 25
Aeurbach, Robert, 241–42
AFL. *See* American Federation of Labor
Africa, 11, 14, 79, 81, 168, 212, 323. *See also* South Africa
African Blood Brotherhood, 69
African Nationalist Movement, 182
Afro-American, 27, 55, 79, 87, 88, 107, 120; Davis eulogized by, 325; Davis interviewed by (1962), 320; on Davis's NYC Council campaign of 1945, 154, 155; on Harlem march after CP-11 trial, 226; on Louis's support of Davis, 154; Murphy of, 218, 297; National Question and, 297; on prison discrimination, 265, 267, 268, 269
Afro-Protective League, 206
Aiken, Walter, 265
Akerman, Walter, 25
Albertson, William, 267, 293, 299, 300, 302, 324
Alexander, Raymond Pace, 109, 172
Alexander, Will, 40
Algeria, 119
Algren, Nelson, 61
Allen, James (communist), 44, 51, 68
Allen, James Egert (NAACP), 75, 93, 149, 162, 180, 298
Allen, Lewis, 106
Allen, Ted, 299
"All Peoples Party," 99
ALP. *See* American Labor party
American Bar Association, 66

American Civil Liberties Union (ACLU), 36, 40, 52, 65, 220, 237, 312
American Communications Association, Local 40, 272
American Crusade to End Lynching, 171, 177
American Federation of Labor (AFL), 74, 76, 85, 98, 158, 172
"Americanism" policy of Communist party, 63, 71
American Jewish Committee, 283
American Labor party, 13, 98, 100, 121, 123, 174; Brown's praise for (1947), 233; CP-11 support from, 220; Davis's nominations by, 151–53, 239; Davis's NYC Council campaign of 1949 supported by, 239; Harlem leaders push Davis nomination by, 148; *New York Age* on, 241; on New York City Council budget (1946), 167; New York City Executive Committee of, 239; New York Council banning of testimony from, 187; *New York Times* on, 149; Organization of the Unemployed and, 231; Quill and, 168, 195; resignations from (1948), 195, 199; state senator elected by, 175; vote similarity between CP and (1943), 188; vote totals of (1945), 165
American Legion, 50, 91, 190, 237, 251
Americans for Democratic Action, 188, 194, 313
Amherst College, 29–30, 33, 48, 59, 104
Amnesty Committee, 259
Amsterdam News. See *New York Amsterdam News*
Amter, Israel, 44, 70, 89, 91, 93, 98, 112–13, 114, 152, 175
Anderson, Dennis, 100
Anderson, Elmer, 319
Anderson, Marian, 62
Andrews, William T., 103, 161

425

Annenberg, Moe, 310
Anti-lynching legislation, 83–86, 89, 169, 171, 177, 197–98, 247
"Anti-monopoly coalition," 292
Anti-Semitism, 90, 278, 283
Aptheker, Herbert, 215, 314
Armed forces. See Military
Armstrong, Henry, 62
Armstrong, Louis, 110
Artists, 60, 62, 108, 110, 119–20, 155. See also Celebrities; specific artists by name
Associated Press, 32
Association of the Bar for the City of New York, 314
Association of Trade and Commerce, Harlem, 146
Atlanta Board of Trade, 20
Atlanta Constitution, 42
Atlanta Independent, 18–19, 21, 23, 28, 31, 88
Atlanta Inquirer, 323
Atlanta Six case, 43
Atlanta University, 20, 28
Atlanta World, 39, 40
Atlantic Charter, 106, 137
AT&T, 74
Aurelio, Thomas, 240
Auschwitz, 81
Austin, Warren, 83, 251
Australian Communist party, 138
Austria, 289
Automobile Club of New York, 223

"Back to Africa." See Garvey, Marcus; Garveyism
Bacote, Clarence, 18, 20, 35
Baker, Elizabeth, 111
Baldwin, Roger, 36, 40, 47
Ballot access issues, 48, 98–99, 174, 242, 266, 295
Baltimore Afro-American, 32
Bandung, Indonesia, 269, 284, 292
Baptist Laymen's League of Georgia, 20
Baptist Ministers Alliance, 218, 266
Barbour, J. Pius, 21, 33, 258
Barbusse, Henri, 44
Barclay, Edwin, 109
Barnard College, 312
Barnett, Claude, 88, 235
Barry, Edward, 148–49
Bart, Phil, 324

Bartow County (GA) GOP committee, 25
Baseball, 62, 63, 154–55, 182
Basie, Count, 108, 110, 120, 121, 155
Basketball, 63
Bass, Charlotta, 294
Bassett, Ted, 44, 66, 92, 173, 271
Batista y Zaldivar, Fulgencio, 302
Bayne, S. F., 124
Begun, Isidore, 203
Bellush, Bernard, 67
Bellush, Jewel, 67
Bender, Ed, 113
Benedict, Ruth, 204
Ben-Gurion, David, 284
Benjamin Davis Freedom Committee, 258, 269
Bennett (chief of federal prisons), 264
Bennett, Gwen, 93–94, 113
Berber, Dennis, 229
Berkeley free-speech fight, 312
Berle, A. A., 79
Berlin Wall, 317
Bernstein, Leonard, 155
Berry, Abner, 29, 30, 58, 69, 71, 75, 109, 248, 258, 260, 271, 284, 285, 287, 302
Bethel AME church, 91
Bethune, Mary McLeod, 94, 169, 172, 201
Bibb, Leon, 267
"Big Six," 28
Bilbo, Theodore, 147, 150, 158, 159, 171, 172, 177
Billington, Ray A., 267
Bill of Rights, 318
Bill of Rights Conference, 213
Bill of Rights for Negroes, 52
Bittleman, Alexander, 139, 278
Black, Hugo, 66, 246, 250
Black Belt South, 11, 67–72
Black Belt thesis, 70, 73, 136, 150, 158, 159–60, 160, 178, 309; Browderism and, 138; Communist party and repudiation of, 152, 153; controversy surrounding, 137; Davis on liquidation of, 143; Davis's support of, 71, 145, 151, 204, 205; Davis's thoughts on in 1949, 223; description of, 11, 67–72; Ford on, 179, 298; Foster on, 280; Haywood on, 297, 298; history of, 67–72; as issue in Davis's 1945 campaign, 145, 151; Jones on, 179; McLaurin's

criticism of, 160; Montgomery on, 284; *New York Amsterdam News* on, 146, 147; Patterson's support of, 138; *Pittsburgh Courier* on, 147; White on, 146, 147; Wilkerson on, 140, 277
Black Boy, 109
Black-Jewish relationships, 194, 283, 285
Blacklisting of communist supporters, 110
Black marketeers in World War II, 156
Black nationalism, 14, 281, 309, 313, 316, 322
Black press, 88–89, 115, 122, 133, 162–63, 178, 247. *See also* specific newspapers
Black Republic. *See* Black Belt thesis
Black secession, 67–72. *See also* Black Belt thesis
Black Star Line, 112
Black Yankees, 233
Blair, Fred, 203
Blake, George, 55, 75, 204
Bloch, Emmanuel, 91
Blood bank segregation, 102, 138, 140
Bloor, Mother, 108
Blumberg, Al, 287
Bolshevik Revolution (1917), 10
Bond, Jean Carey, 28
Bone, Hugh A., 188
Boston Chronicle, 88, 104, 107, 122
Boston Herald, 242
Boston NAACP, 107
Bourke-White, Margaret, 46
Bourne, St. Claire, 132
Boyle, Bernadette, 246
Boyle, Edward C., 264
Braddock, Eugene, 131–32
Braddock, James, 62
Brantley, Henry, 91
Braxton, Gene, 48. *See also* Herndon, Angelo
Brażil, 67, 273
Brewer, Guy, 146, 148, 150, 161, 162
Brice, Carol, 160
Bridges, Harry, 182
Briggs, Cyril, 44, 45, 69
Broderick, Edwin, 237
Brodsky, Carl, 99, 104
Brodsky, Joseph, 49
Bronx Chamber of Commerce, 116
Brooklyn Dodgers, 203
Brooklyn-NAACP, 228

Brotherhood of Sleeping Car Porters, 40, 72, 74, 75, 77, 83, 95, 114, 158
Browder, Earl, 44, 56, 68, 71, 81, 91, 93, 97, 128, 135, 179, 211, 213, 278, 279; on Black Belt thesis, 138; Citizens Committee to Free, 109; Communist party resolution against, 181; CP-11 trial and, 223, 225; as *Daily Word* editor-in-chief, 131; Davis's support of, 130, 131, 136; debate over fate of, 137–46, 151; facing prison in 1941, 130; Franklin on, 180; ouster of, 137–46, 148, 149, 150, 153. *See also* Browderism
Browderism, 12, 71, 74, 86, 89, 97, 103, 118, 119–36, 152, 154, 158, 160, 179, 273, 277, 300; abandonment of, 137–46; Black Belt thesis and, 138; CP-11 trial and, 223, 224; *Daily Worker* on, 144; defined, 119, 128; Dennis on, 273; essence of, 128; Foster on, 138, 143; Gates on, 275; Metropolitan Life Insurance Company discrimination and, 126–28; National Question and, 139, 145, 179, 180; *New York Times* on, 279; Roosevelt and, 133; sales tax and, 125; Stuyvesant Town housing complex and, 125–28; taxes and, 125. *See also* Factionalism in CPUSA
"Browder Radio Fund," 65
Brown, Earl, 150, 292, 293; background of, 233, 234; on Communist party in Harlem, 151; on CP-11 convictions, 245, 251; on Davis's appeal, 248; Davis's loss to in 1949, 239, 240; on Davis's NYC Council campaign of 1949, 241; on Davis Sr., 22–23; *New York Age* on, 234, 235; *New York Post* on, 242; *New York Times* on, 241; on Powell, 291; supporters of, 238, 292
Brown, Edgar, 122
Brown, Ethelred, 105, 245
Brown, John, 72
Brown, Lloyd, 59, 109, 324
Brown, Sterling, 169
Brownell, Herbert, 257, 265, 268
Brown University, 317
Brown v. Board of Education, 13, 253, 265, 266, 268, 269, 285, 323
Bruce, Herbert, 106, 148, 149, 150, 157, 238
Buchanan, Charles, 103, 183

Buckley, William F., 312, 314
Bucknell University, 311
Budenz, Louis, 110, 212, 273, 293, 299
Bukharin, Nikolai, 67
Bunche, Ralph, 26, 215, 248, 291, 325
Burleson, Omar, 207
Burley, Dan, 208–9
Burma, 226
Burnham, Louis, 271, 272
Burns, Kay, 29
Burton, Harold, 91, 245
Byrnes, Jimmy, 172

Cacchione, Pete, 97–98, 101, 102, 107, 111–12, 114, 148, 165, 192, 193, 311; Browderism and, 120; budget proposals of, 125; death of, 187; effectiveness of, 122–28; failing eyesight of, 123; integration and, 173; on Madison Square Garden, 185; ouster attempts against, 187; petition signatures for, 163; on police brutality, 161; as role model for communists, 122–28; on sales tax, 167; on Spellman greeting, 168; on transit fare, 185; vote totals of, 120, 164–65; on Western Union strike, 172
Caldwell, Erskine, 41, 46
California Eagle, 213
Calloway, Cab, 108
Campanella, Roy, 205–6
Campbell, Bob, 173
Campus movement. *See* Student movement
Canada, 67, 129, 180
Cannon, George, 107, 121, 162
Capeci, Dominic, 115, 126
Capehart, David, 233
Capetown City Council, 119
Carey, Archibald, 315
Carey, Ed, 323
Carey, Richard, 59, 163, 315
Caribbean Union, 79
Carib News, 99
Carlyle, Una Mae, 160
Carmichael, Stokely, 306
Carmines, Edward G., 286
Carreathers, Ben, 263
Carroll, William, 161
Carter, C. Gibbs, 80
Carter, Jimmy, 88
Carver, George Washington, 59, 127
Castro, Fidel, 302, 308, 309, 316

Cayton, Horace, 147
Cayton, Revels, 218
CBS, 310
CCNY, *See* City College of New York
Cedartown Cotton and Export Company, 25
Celebrities, 12, 61–62, 108–10, 120, 160, 238. *See also* specific celebrities by name
Censored News, 219
Central Intelligence Agency (CIA), 229, 311, 317
Chamberlain, Neville, 202
Chambers of Commerce, 116, 124, 156
Chandler, Albert "Happy," 154
Charney, George, 56, 275, 276, 287, 299, 325
Chiang Kai-Shek, 134
Chicago Defender, 42, 88, 121, 162–63, 164
Childress, Alice, 258
Childs, Morris, 134
China, 76, 80, 87, 130, 134, 319, 320, 321, 324
Christian Fronters, 209
Church, Robert, 23, 28
Church of the Black Madonna, 323
Churchill, Winston, 81, 167, 168, 172, 174, 175
Church of the Master, 232
CIA. *See* Central Intelligence Agency
Ciardi, John, 267
Cigarette taxes, 125
CIO. *See* Congress of Industrial Organization
Citizen Paine, 237
Citizens Committee to Free Earl Browder, 109
Citizens Democratic Club of Harlem, 239
Citizens Non-Partisan Committee to Elect Benjamin J. Davis, 107
Citizens Union, 163
Citron, Alice, 124
City College of New York (CCNY), 311, 312, 313, 314, 322
City University of New York (CUNY), 313, 314
"City Wide Action Conference," 121
Civil liberties, 9, 249, 254. *See also* specific types
Civil rights, 9, 11, 88, 176, 178, 179, 254, 295. *See also* Civil rights movement

INDEX 429

Civil Rights Congress (CRC), 49, 50, 51, 52, 78, 173, 177, 182, 216, 219, 220, 244, 249, 268; anti-communist sentiment effects on, 266; Davis's freedom sought by, 254, 258, 264, 265, 266; Gilbert defended by, 247; rally against, 216
Civil rights movement, 11, 14, 60, 136, 271, 285, 319, 321–22, 323. *See also* Civil rights; specific organizations
Civil War, 97
Clark, Conrad, 186
Clark, Mark, 247
Clark, Tom, 211–12, 217
Cleague, Albert, 323
Clemente, Gary, 187
Cleveland, 119
Cleveland Board of Education election, 119
Cleveland Call and Post, 316
Clurman, Harold, 46
Cobb, Montague, 33
Cobb & Hayes law firm, 219
Cocks, Edmund L., 209
COINTELPRO, 13, 14, 269, 271–72, 285, 288, 305, 324. *See also* Federal Bureau of Investigation (FBI)
Colahan, Thomas, 149
Cole Bill, 207
Colgate College, 104
College campuses, 311, 312, 313, 314, 316–19. *See also* specific schools; Student movement
Collins, Charles, 106, 158, 174, 236, 239, 258
Collins, Rip, 63
Colon, Clara, 320
Colon, Jesus, 287, 295
Color and Democracy, 142
Colored Citizens Organization of Fairfield County, Connecticut, 107
Colombian Communist party, 138
Columbia, Tennessee pogrom, 12, 171, 172
Columbia University, 312, 313
Comic strips on Davis, 258, 264
Comintern. *See* Communist International
Commerce and Industry Association of New York, 189
Commission on Human Rights, 156
Committee of Artists for Davis, 155

Committee on the Improvement of Race Relations, 124
Committee to Aid the Fighting South, 177
Committee to Defend Negro Leadership, 268
Communist, The (later *Political Affairs*), 131, 145
"Communist Attitude Toward Writers," 137–38
Communist Committee to Defend the 12, 220
Communist Control Act, 266
Communist International, 9, 50, 54, 67, 68, 69, 76, 97, 134, 293
Communist party of Australia, 138
Communist party of Brazil, 273
Communist party of Canada, 67, 129
Communist party of Colombia, 138
Communist party of Cuba, 129, 138, 302
Communist party of France, 137–38
Communist party of Harlem, 53, 54, 55, 58, 62, 64–66, 68, 92, 93, 99, 111, 120, 190, 248
Communist party of India, 133
Communist party of Japan, 68, 244
Communist party of Mexico, 68, 120
Communist party of New York, 98, 140, 204, 273, 302, 303
Communist party of New York County, 93
Communist party of South Africa, 54, 68, 138
Communist party of the Philippines, 273
Communist party of the Soviet Union, 128–29, 134–35, 142, 196, 208, 211, 279, 287, 319; Africa and, 172; black press on, 88, 178; centralism in, 140; CPUSA relationship with, 9, 10, 67–69, 87, 128–29, 134–35; influence of, 134–35, 142, 196; National Question and, 302; NYC Council election of 1949 and, 242; racism and, 176. *See also* Soviet Union
Communist party of Uruguay, 273
Communist party of Wisconsin, 203
Communist party USA, 12, 40, 41, 146, 167, 208, 212, 252, 277, 287, 296, 304; in 1930s, 83; in 1938, 55; in 1940s, 83; in 1951, 245; "Americanism" policy of, 63, 71; antiracism of, 107; artists' support for, 60, 108, 110, 119–20; in Atlanta, 42–43; attempt to bar from

Communist party USA (*cont'd*)
ballot (1946), 174; black leaders criticized by, 72; blacks in, 58, 59, 60, 77, 111, 112, 301, 302; black-white unity in, 84, 157, 173–74; black women in, 58, 111, 112; Browderism and, *see* Browderism; celebrity support for, 12, 61–62, 108–10, 120; college barring of, 311, 312, 313, 314, 316; on college campuses, 312, 313; Committee on Constitution of, 135; Convention of 1959 of, 300; Coordinating Committee for Employment and, 74; Cuban revolution and, 307; Darcy's expulsion from, 135; Davis's joining of, 43; Davis as national board member of, 143; Davis as national secretary of, 300; Davis support from, 238–39; democratic centralism and, 68; deportations of members of, 206; "Double V" and, 131, 132; "Election Platform Demands" of, 69–70; electoral successes of, 11, 97–98 (*see also* New York City Council election of 1943); electoral "threat" by, 13; factionalism in, *see* Factionalism in CPUSA; FBI and, 13, 132–33, 182, 263, 270, 279, 282, 290, 299–300, 301, 302, 305, 310, 315, 323–24; "Fighting Fund" of, 210; founding of, 68; on Georgia ballot, 48; German-Soviet Non-aggression Pact and, 75, 78; Great Depression and, 55; growth of in 1938, 55; Herndon case and, 38, 39, 40, 52; heyday of activism in, 83, 107, 115; Hoover on, 92; hospital workers in New York City organized by, 305; on integration, 184; international ties of, 50; isolationism and, 79; Lower East Side club of, 293; Muslims and, 316; NAACP and, 10, 11, 47, 49, 50, 51, 171, 254; name of changed to Communist Political Association, 128, 135, 139; National Administrative Committee of, 286; National Board of, 173; National Committee of, 86, 130, 135–36, 140, 142, 151–52, 173, 274, 276, 278, 301, 306, 309; National Executive Committee of, 287; National Negro Department of, 138; National Question and, 265, 287; Negro Commission of, 205, 263; Nominations Committee of, 93; Political Committee of, 93, 273; Powell on, 105; Powell's split with, 182, 184; racism in members of, 181, 203–5; rally of 1939 of, 79; Randolph criticized by, 202, 285; recruitment of Davis by, 38; right to exist questioned in 1941, 109; on Roosevelt, 133, 138; Scottsboro case and, *see* Scottsboro Nine case; Social Democrats and, 289; Socialist party and, 75, 77; Soviet party relationship to, 9, 10, 67–69, 87, 128–29, 134–35; speakers class of, 102; in student movement of 1960s, 306, 307, 311, 314; vote totals of 1945 for, 165; on World War II, 86–96; writers' support for, 109–10

Communist Political Association, 128, 135, 138, 139, 142

"Conference to Protest Police Brutality" at Harlem YMCA, 161–62

Congo, 309, 311

Congress of Fraternal and Benevolent Organizations, 90

Congress of Industrial Organization (CIO), 74, 76, 77, 98, 145, 158, 164, 170, 174, 176, 182, 195, 199, 228, 235

Connolly, Eugene, 149, 152

Connolly, Tom, 83, 85, 187, 194, 195, 196, 197, 208, 209, 224, 229, 230, 231, 239, 240

Conrad, Earl, 155–56

Conscription, 78, 141, 198, 199–200

Consolidated Edison, 74

Cooke, Marvel, 58, 61, 104–5, 107, 183

Coolidge, Calvin, 23

Cooper, Esther, 182–83

Coordinating Committee for Employment, 74, 90

Coser, Lewis, 55

Cosmopolitan Tennis Club, 30

Costello, Frank, 113

Council on African Affairs, 172, 216

Court picketing, 217

Cowley, Malcolm, 46

Cox, Oliver, 204, 217

CP-11 trial, 210–26, 233, 244, 248, 252, 256, 282; Harlem uprising after, 225–26, 228–29; responses to convictions at, 244–53; sentencing at, 244; Supreme Court upholding of convictions of, 250–51; treatment of prisoners after, 255, 256, 257, 261, 262, 263, 264, 265, 266, 267, 268, 305–6, 310

CP-17, 262–63

CPUSA. *See* Communist Party USA
CRC. *See* Civil Rights Congress
Crisis, The, 73
Crockett, George, 215, 218–19, 221, 256, 261, 323
Cronin, Matthew, 165
Crosswaith, Frank, 151, 161, 176, 182, 200, 202, 228, 248; anti-communist sentiment of, 75, 76, 234, 235, 236, 237; columnist job lost by, 96; Davis's criticism of, 47, 201; on March on Washington, 95; National Negro Congress and, 72; National Shoe strike and, 74
"Crusade Against Lynching," 171, 177
Crusader News Agency, 45–46
Cruse, Harold, 110, 273
Cuba, 129, 138, 206, 219, 302, 307, 309, 311, 316
Cuban Communist party, 129, 138, 302
Cuban Revolution, 14
Cullen, Countee, 44, 107, 109
CUNY. *See* City University of New York
Curson, Ted, 108
Czechoslovakia, 194, 198

Daily Worker, 31, 38, 39–40, 41, 43, 44, 51, 122, 168, 201, 257, 263, 281, 302, 324; in 1944, 115; on anti-labor bills, 186–87; Armstrong's praise of, 62; on blacks in major parties, 173; Browder as editor-in-chief of, 131; on Browderism, 144; on Columbia, Tennessee pogrom, 171; on Communist party growth in 1943, 111; on Cox, 209; on CP-11 trial, 212, 221, 222, 224; daily publication suspended by, 286; Davis at, 45, 46, 50, 60, 66, 86, 93; on Davis's Atlanta trip (1963), 323; Davis attacks Red baiting in (1945), 149; on Davis's attorney general campaign, 174; Davis charges New York City discrimination against, 205; Davis criticises Powell in, 290; on Davis's Harlem speech, 1956, 272; on Davis's HUAC appearance, 207–8; on Davis's HUAC subpoena, 164; on Davis's NYC Council campaign of 1945, 149, 152, 158; on Davis's NYC Council campaign of 1949, 232, 238, 239, 242; Davis's praise for, 266; on Davis's release from prison, 269; on Davis's speaking ability, 184; on Davis's speech at CCNY, 314; on Davis's speech on Willie McGee, 247–48, 249; on Davis's state assembly campaign from prison, 259, 260; Dickerson and, 78; Duclos's writings for, 137; on Durocher's hitting baseball fan, 203; FBI agents as readers of, 237; Ford's petition on baseball in, 63; on "free Davis" efforts, 258, 259; on free speech, 314; fund drives and, 140; on Gerson as prospect for City Council, 193–94; Granger's praise of, 75; on Great Depression, 53; Harlem Bureau of, 61, 62, 63; on Harlem fundraising, 99; on Harlem march after CP-11 trial, 226; on Harlem poverty, 230–31; on Hitler, 132; on Israel, 283; on Andrew Jackson, 129; Jones speaks on Davis to, 149; Lewis on, 176; Malcolm X on, 177; on Marshall Plan endorsement by NYC Council, 186; McGill of, 286; on Metropolitan Life Insurance segregation, 126; on Nagy execution, 290; National Negro Congress and, 72; on NYC Council election of 1943, 104, 105, 106, 107, 108, 112, 113; on NYC Council hours, 229; on NYC Council Marshall Plan endorsement, 186; on NYC Council unity, 123; on parade in support of Davis for Congress, 90–91; Patterson as head of, 286; Pegler on, 88; on petition drive in state senate race, 294; on price gouging, 103; on prison conditions, 255; on prison segregation, 268; on proportional representation, 187, 188, 189; on Randolph and NNC, 77; on Randolph rally planned for Madison Square Gardens, 94; "Red Indian Dance" ad in, 129; Robeson's praise of Davis in, 215; on Roosevelt, 133; on Schmeling defeat, 62; on Senate Judiciary Committee hearing, 84, 85; on Soviet invasion of Hungary, 274; on Stalin, 273; subs for during 1943 campaign, 101–2; on Supreme Court upholding of CP-11 conviction, 250–51; on Tojo, 132; on Truman, 1945, 138; U.S. neutrality criticized by, 79; on Wallace, 138; World War II and, 80; on Wright, 109
Daily World, 287
Dale, Thelma, 218

Dana, Peter, 89
Daniels, Jonathan, 176
D'Antignac, Edward S., 264, 265
Darcy, Sam, 67, 69, 135–36, 144
Darden, Frank, 25
David T. Howard High School, 27
Davis, Aaron, 17
Davis, Ben (Rev.), 17
Davis, Ben (Rev.'s son), 17
Davis, Ben, Jr.: 1940–1942, 83–96; 1943, 97–118; 1944, 119–36; 1945, 137–53, 154–66; 1946–1947, 167–91; 1948, 192–209; 1949, 210–226, 227–43; 1950–1951, 244–53; 1951–1955, 254–70; 1956–1959, 271–304; 1960s, 305–25; on Africa, 323; as American Labor party candidate, 239; arrest of, 208–9; athletic ability of, 30; as *Atlanta Independent* staff member, 19, 28, 31–32; background of, 17; bail revoked, 246; barred from involvement in own defense, 214, 222; birthday party for (1944), 120; birthday party for (1951), 250; birthday party for (1952), 259; birth of, 17, 27; Black Belt thesis and, *see* Black Belt thesis; on black nationalism, 316; black press criticized by, 31–32; Browder and, *see* Browder, Earl; Browderism and, *see* Browderism; Bucknell University speech of (1960), 311; Carey's relationship with, 315; car insurance cancelled, 223; CCNY speech of (1961), 311; celebrities and, 108, 160, 238 (*see also* specific celebrities by name); Charney description of, 56; civil rights figures and, 285 (*see also* specific people by name); on civil rights movement, 321–22, 323; college barring of, 311, 312, 313, 314, 316; Communist party factionalism found disturbing by, 141; as Communist party national board member, 143; as Communist party national secretary, 300; as Communist Political Association vice president, 68; congressional campaign of, 86, 89–93; conviction of, 210–11; at *Daily Worker*, 45, 46, 50, 60, 66, 93; death of, 27, 324–25; departure of from Georgia, 41; Dewey criticized by, 122; driver's license denied for by New York, 308; on Duclos letter, 138; early views of whites, 28; education of, 27, 28–31; effectiveness of in office, 122–28; efforts for release of from prison, 254, 257, 258–69; facing prison while seeking re-election, 232; father compared to, 20, 26, 85; father's relationship with, 46–48; FBI and, 207, 263, 270, 282–83, 288, 299–300, 310, 315, 323–24; financial condition of, 305; Flynn's relationship with, 278, 296; Foster praised by, 278; Foster's relationship with, 144–45, 148, 262, 298–99; funeral of, 325; Garvey criticized by, 71; Gates's relationship with, 274; *Gone with the Wind* attacked by, 63; on Green's pamphlet, 55; harassment of in Georgia, 222; Harlem beauticians supported by, 163; Harlem nurses supported by, 163; Harlem public schools and, 66; Harlem uprising after trial of, 225–26, 228–29; health of, in 1960s, 305; Herndon case and, *see* Herndon, Angelo case; HUAC appearance of, 164, 207, 306; on Hungary, 274; illegal alien charges against, 214; immigration questions answered by, 229; indictment of, 194, 204, 320; on integration concept, 249; Internal Security Act of 1950 and, 314–15; Isaacs praised by, 243; Isaacs's relationship with, 123–24, 187, 208, 229, 243; joining of Communist party by, 43; Claudia Jones's relationship with, 58, 321; King correspondence with, 305; King endorsed by, 294; King's relationship with, 286, 295, 303, 305, 315, 316; on Korean War, 247; labor support for, 235–37; law school days of, 30–31; as "leading Harlemite," 248; in League of Struggle for Negro Rights, 57; as *Liberator* editor, 43–44; lifestyle of as communist leader, 221; Loughlin's praise of, 148; marriage of, 27, 254, 255, 262, 268, 272, 277, 310; on Marshall Plan, 247; Matthews's description of, 56; militance of, 29–30; musical ability of, 28, 29; Muslims and, 322; NAACP and, *see* National Association for the Advancement of Colored People; naming of, 27; New York attorney general campaign of, 174–75; on nuclear testing, 303; NY Board of Elections appeal by, 295;

NYC Council campaign of 1943 of, see New York City Council election of 1943; NYC Council campaign of 1945 of, see New York City Council election of 1945; NYC Council campaign of 1949 of, 207, 209, 227–43; on NYC Council Finance Committee, 167, 185; NYC Council issues of, 194–97; on NYC Council Parks Committee, 185; NYC Council purging of, 210, 227–43; on NYC Council Rules Committee, 167, 185; on NYC Council State Legislation Committee, 185; NY state assembly campaign of from prison, 259, 260; NY state senate campaign of 1958 of, 293, 294–95, 296; obituary of, 324; occupations of, 20; parole hearing of, 262; petitioning by, 238–39, 294; on police brutality, 239; Powell criticized by, 249–50, 290; Powell endorsed by, 294; Powell's relationship with, 73, 158, 175, 202, 286, 290, 295, 296–97, 297, 303; in prison, 254–70; prison memoirs of, 222, 234, 257; prison segregation suit of, 266–70; on racial slander, 124; racial views refined by, 204–5; Randolph criticized by, see under Randolph, A. Philip; refusal of to register under Smith Act, 309; release of from prison, 268, 269; reminiscence about roots, 17; on Republican party, 26; Republican party convention of 1960 attended by, 307; Republican party's courting of, 36; return of to Atlanta in 1963, 322; return of to Harvard University, 317–18; reversal of Internal Security Act conviction of, 321; Robeson defended by, 216; Robeson's relationship with, 59–60, 110, 215 (see also Robeson, Paul, Sr.); on Roosevelt, 82, 89, 90, 100, 103, 114, 122, 133; on sales tax, 125; "Security Index Card" of FBI for, 263, 270; Senate Internal Security Subcommittee appearance of, 308; Senate Judiciary Committee appearance of, 83–86, 89; sentencing of, 244; Smith Act and, see Smith Act; in solitary confinement, 266, 268; speaking method of, 184–85; speeches on college campuses by, 312, 313, 314, 316–19; Stuyvesant Town housing complex and, 125–28; on subway fares, 125; trial of, see CP-11 trial; as Uptown Chamber of Commerce vice chair, 156; on U.S. military in Lebanon, 293; U.S. senatorial nomination of (1946), 174; voting rights taken away from, 240; wife of, 27, 254, 255, 262, 268, 272, 277, 310; Wilkins criticized by, 324; Wilkins's endorsement of, 163; Women's Committee to Re-elect, 158; on World War II, 86–96; Wright's relationship with, 61, 107, 109; write-in effort of, NY state senate race, 296

Davis, Ben, Sr., 9, 18, 21, 28, 44, 45, 155, 325; birth of, 17; Citizens Committee to Free Earl Browder and, 109; death of, 26, 156; description of, 18; Dittmer's description of, 18; education of, 20; fraternal organizations belonged to, 20; KKK attacks on, 22; naming of Ben Jr. by, 27; New Deal and, 26; newspaper of, see *Atlanta Independent*; in NYC Council election of 1943, 106; occupations of, 20; patronage investigation of, 22; in Republican party, 17, 18, 19, 21, 22, 23, 24, 85, 106, 173; Republican party ouster of, 24, 25; son compared to, 20, 26, 85; son's relationship with, 46–48; son supported by, 26; White's description of, 18

Davis, Elizabeth, 17
Davis, Emily, 321
Davis, George, 17
Davis, Glover, 43
Davis, Jefferson, 17
Davis, John, 76
Davis, Johnnie, 28
Davis, Katherine (Mrs. Mike Haynes), 17
Davis, Leon, 303
Davis, Miles, 250
Davis, Nina Stamler (Davis's wife), 254, 255, 262, 268, 272, 277, 310
Davis, Ossie, 325
Davis, Sam, 318–19
Davis, Sylvia, 17
Davis, "Willa" Porter, 17
Davis-Isaacs bill against discrimination, 126–27
Dawes, William, 75
Dawson, Georgia, 293
Dawson, William, 227
Debs, Eugene, 232

DeGaulle, Charles, 303
Delany, Hubert, 245, 290
DeMendez, Fred, 232–33
Democratic centralism, 68
Democratic Farmer Labor Party, 98
Democratic party, 22, 35, 70, 79, 156, 162, 232, 243, 291, 308; in 1943, 115; Brown's criticism of (1945), 233; coalition with (1946), 174; Columbia, Tennessee pogrom and, 171; Communist party success effects on, 155–56; Crockett's criticism of, 219; Davis's criticism of, 171; Davis's criticism of at Senate Judiciary Committee hearing, 83; Davis registers as member of, 152; Davis's relationship with, 121, 122; Davis supported by, 1945, 148, 163; fascism and, 192; on FEPC, 197–98; Jim Crow laws and, 116; Metropolitan Life's discrimination and, 127; movement of to right (1948), 192; National Committee of, 149; in New York City, See Tammany Hall; on NYC Council after Davis's ouster, 190, 237, 241, 242; in NYC Council election of 1943, 107; platform of 1944 of, 133; on poll tax, 197–98; proportional representation and, 119, 188, 189, 193; Republican party coalitions with, 209, 232; on welfare, 190; White on, 202
"Democratization" of the South, 299
Dennery, M. Claude, 219
Dennis, Eugene, 54, 152–53, 173, 300; on Browderism, 273; centralist views of, 289; as Communist party chair, 301; Communist party factionalism and, 273, 274, 275, 280, 282, 287; at CP-11 trial, 221, 223, 224; Davis criticized by, 290; death of, 310; FBI and, 289, 299, 300; Gates's criticism of, 286; Hall's replacement of, 300; heart attack of, 301; HUAC and, 275; on Hungary, 274; on National Question, 140; on Poland, 274; in prison, 250, 262; release of from prison, 269; Senate Internal Security Subcommittee appearance of, 301
Dennis, Peggy, 267, 275, 301, 302
Deportations of communists, 206
Desegregation. See Integration
Detroit Newspaper Guild, 323
Detweiler, Frederick, 19
Dewey, John, 160

Dewey, Thomas E., 89, 116, 117, 122, 156, 174, 175, 199, 208
Dexter Avenue Baptist Church, Montgomery, 50
Dial, Thelma, 222
Dickens, Fred, 149
Dickens, Lloyd, 146, 150
Dickerson, Earl, 78, 217
DiFalco, Samuel, 115
Dillard, Irving, 245
Dimitrov, Georgi, 68, 225
Discrimination: in jury selection, 218; in labor unions, 129; in military, 95, 102, 133, 140, 144, 176, 181, 200–201, 247; in New York Police Department, 229; in prisons, 265; WACs strike in protest of, 141. See also Racism; Segregation
Dittmer, John, 18, 19, 20
Dixiecrats, 85, 92, 147, 164, 170, 171, 205, 209, 217, 227, 306, 307
Dixon, Dean, 169
Dobbs, Farrell, 213
Dodd, Bella, 139, 229
Dodgers, 203
Dolsen, James, 266
Donawa, Arnold, 59, 218, 277–78
Donner, Frank, 324
Dorsen, Norman, 320
"Double V," 131, 132
Douglas, Aaron, 59
Douglas, William O., 246, 250, 251
Douglass, Frederick, 72, 73, 87, 156
Draft, 78, 141, 198, 199–200
Drew, Charles, 30, 169, 248
Driscoll, David, 211
Driver's license denial by New York, 308
Duberman, Martin, 215
Dubinsky, David, 75, 161, 162, 182, 200
Du Bois, W. E. B., 14, 20, 21, 27, 66, 172, 176, 183, 235, 264, 267, 292, 316; *Color and Democracy* by, 142; controversial positions of, 72; departure of from NAACP, 72; indictment of, 249; NAACP and, 194; on Stockholm Peace Appeal, 249; trial of, 249, 264; on World War II, 87
Duclos, Jacques, 137–38, 141
"Due Process in a Political Trial: The Record vs. the Press," 215
Duke and Duchess of Windsor, 62
Dulles, Allan, 229
Dulles, John Foster, 247

INDEX

Dun & Bradstreet, 172
Dunham, Katherine, 155
Dunjee, Roscoe, 88
Durocher, Leo, 203
DW Fund Drive, 280

Earle, Genevieve, 188, 190, 193, 209, 231
Eastland, James, 158, 160, 308
Ebenezer Baptist Church, 19
Ecker, F. H. (Fred), 126, 127, 128
Edwards, Thyra, 75
Edward Waters College, 158
Egypt, 269, 283, 284
Ehrenberg, Ilya, 169
Eisenhower, Dwight, 84, 258, 267, 272, 273, 290, 302, 308
Eisler, Gerhart, 67–68, 69, 206
Eldridge, Alfred, 249
Eldridge, Roy, 155
"Election Platform Demands of the CP," 69–70
"Electoral district captains," 101–2
Elks, 20
Ellender, Allen (senator), 171
Ellington, Duke, 12, 61, 102, 108, 116, 121, 155
Ellison, Ralph, 60, 61
Emancipation Proclamation, 92
Emerson, Thomas, 320
Emory University, 42
Engels, Friedrich, 156
Equal Employment Opportunity Commission, 170
Ernst, Morris, 40, 160
Ethiopian invasion by Italy, 80, 81
Euro-Communism controversy, 282
Europe, 9, 176, 244. *See also* specific countries
European military integration, 129
Evens, William, 174

Factionalism in CPUSA, 269, 271–84, 287, 288, 289, 293, 300, 310, Davis disturbed by, 141; Dennis and, 273, 274, 275, 280, 282, 287; FBI and, 279, 290, 299–300, 301, 310; Ford and, 278; Foster and, 275, 276, 277, 278, 279, 280, 282, 287; Gates and, 274, 275, 281, 282, 285, 287, 288, 289, 293; *New York Post* on, 287; *New York Times* on, 284, 300. *See also* Browderism

Fair Employment Practices Commission (FEPC), 136; Communist party support of, 173; Davis's support of, 124, 134, 141, 156, 158, 170, 236, 323; Democratic party's ditching of, 197–98; Hoover on, 92; Isaacs's introduction of bill for, 169; Claudia Jones on, 170–71; National Council for, 170; Powell on, 158, 170; Republican party's ditching of, 197–98; Roosevelt's support of, 133; Textile Workers Union and, 199; Truman and, 170, 247, 248
Farmer, James, 160
Farr, Tommy, 62
Farrell, James, 46
Fascism, 12, 59, 76, 80, 82, 132
Fast, Howard, 163, 237, 275, 278, 286
Father Divine, 65, 105, 176, 220
Fauset, Arthur Huff, 59
FBI. *See* Federal Bureau of Investigation
Federal Bureau of Investigation (FBI), 9, 13, 67, 79, 88, 110, 269, 289–90, 297, 307, 308–9; Albertson framed by, 302; black-Jewish tensions and, 284; black press and, 133; Communist party and, 13, 132–33, 182, 263, 270, 279, 282, 290, 299–300, 301, 302, 305, 310, 315, 323–24; Counter-intelligence Program of (COINTELPRO), 13, 14, 269, 271–72, 285, 288, 305, 324; *Daily Worker* and, 237, 286; Davis and, 207, 243, 263, 270, 282–83, 288, 295, 299–300, 310, 315, 323–24; Davis's ballot access and, 295; at Davis's Upsala College speech, 317; Davis's wife's suspicions about, 255; Dennis harassment by, 289, 299; Flynn and, 290, 299, 301; Foster harassment by, 309; at Foster's funeral, 310; Harlem activities of, 81–82; inflation of Red threat by, 133; King surveillance by, 271; letters to anti-Davis party members from, 308; Louis surveillance by, 182; National Lawyers Guild monitored by, 219; *New York Age* and, 205; *People's Voice* criticized by, 157–58; "Security Index Card" of, 263, 270; student movement and, 306, 311, 312; Thornton's criticism of, 212; Winston surveillance by, 270; wiretapping by, 141, 288; in World War II, 96

Federal Communications Commission, 187
Federal Council of Churches, 36
Federation of Sugar Workers, 206
Federation of Trade Unions, 286
FEPC. *See* Fair Employment Practices Commission
Ferrer, Jose, 110, 155, 227–28
Field, Fred, 162
Finland, 289, 321
First Amendment, 183, 187, 211, 217, 221, 224, 230, 235. *See also* Free speech
Fisk University, 29, 57
Fitzgerald, Ella, 62, 108
Flynn, Edward J., 149
Flynn, Elizabeth Gurley, 91, 93, 99, 108, 112, 113, 139, 140, 170, 210, 321, 324; as Communist Political Association vice president, 135; on CP-11 case, 251–52; on Davis's prison experience, 255; Davis's relationship with, 278, 296; FBI and, 290, 299, 301; Gates criticized by, 286; as Hall-Davis defense committee leader, 320; on prison conditions, 255, 261; on prison integration suit, 267–68; Smith Act registration refused by, 309; subpoena issued to, 319
Foner, Eric, 67
Foner, Philip, 68, 215
"For Ben Davis," (poem by Matthew Hale), 269
Forbes, Kenneth, 262
Ford, Henry, 10
Ford, James, 60, 68, 77, 81, 86, 138, 144, 271; background of, 57; baseball and, 63; on Black Belt thesis, 179, 298; on black migration from South to North, 179; on black participation in Communist party, 54; Browderism and, 134; Charney on, 56; Communist party demotion of, 143; on Communist party factionalism, 278; on Communist party influence in Harlem, 40; as Communist Political Association vice president, 68; Edwards praised by, 75; on Hungary, 274; as *Liberator* contributor, 44; on National Question, 143, 278; *Negroes in a Soviet America* pamphlet by, 68–69; in NYC Council election of 1943, 108, 117; Socialist party criticized by, 76; Trade Union Non-Partisan Committee and, 99; vice-presidential candidacy of (1932), 69; on Wright, 61
Ford, Joseph, 148, 150
Foreman, Clark, 177
Forer, Joe, 321
Formosa, 87
Forsch, James W. *See* Ford, James
Fort-Whiteman, Lovett, 99
Foster, James, 278
Foster, Stephen, 129, 201, 202
Foster, William Z., 46, 68, 134, 139, 140, 173, 213, 274, 297; on Browderism, 138, 143, 144; Communist party factionalism and, 275, 276, 277, 278, 279, 280, 282, 287; on Communist party unity, 288–89; CP-11 trial testimony of, 224; Davis's criticism of, 135–36; Davis's relationship with, 144–45, 148, 262, 298–99; death of, 310; on Duclos letter, 137–38; FBI at funeral of, 310; FBI harassment of, 309; funeral of, 310; Gates's criticism of, 286; HUAC and, 207; illness of, 210, 288, 290, 301; on National Question, 180, 298–99; *Outline Political History of the Americas* by, 278; on post–CP-11 trial tactics, 252; presidential candidacy of (1932), 69; Robeson on, 141; on Taft-Hartley Act, 187; trial dropped for, 210; WOR radio refuses to broadcast talk of, 187
Four Freedoms of Roosevelt, 92, 137
"Fourteen Points" of Woodrow Wilson, 69
France, 130, 137–38, 289, 321
Franco, Francisco, 232
Francois, Terry, 322
Frank, Waldo, 46, 267
Frankfurter, Felix, 211, 245
Franklin, Francis, 180, 205
Franklin, John Hope, 22
Frazier, E. Franklin, 109
Free Angelo Herndon Committee, 315
"Free Ben Davis" efforts, 254, 257, 258–69
Freedman, David, 239, 295
Freedom, 257
Freedom House, 142
Freedom Now movement, 323
Freedom party, 259, 260
Freedom Riders, 311, 315
Freedom Road Club, 184

Freedomways, 182, 183, 267
Freeport, New York slayings, 171, 172
Free speech, 312, 313, 314. *See also* First Amendment
French Communist party, 137–38
Friedlander, Miriam, 320
Friendship Baptist Church, 29

Gaillard, Albert, 306
Galamison, Milton, 324
Gale, Moe, 110
Garner, John, 83, 84
Garret, Charles, 188
Garvey, Marcus, 11, 21, 32, 69, 70, 71, 112, 179
Garveyism, 147, 179
Gates, John, 221, 278, 280, 301; on Black Liberation, 276; Charney on, 276; Communist party factionalism and, 274, 275, 281, 282, 285, 287, 288, 289, 293; contempt charges against, 224; Davis's criticism of, 281, 296, 298; Davis's relationship with, 274; Dennis on, 282, 287; Flynn's criticism of, 286; memoir of, 275; National Committee influenced by, 287; on National Question, 281, 297; racism and, 288; Wilkerson's criticism of, 277
Gates, Lillian, 242–43, 281
Gaulden, Rose, 111, 112, 128, 173, 190
Gayle, Addison, 109
Geer, John, 35, 37, 39, 51
Geer, Will, 120
Gellert, Hugo, 46, 294
"General Intelligence Survey" of Hoover, 92
Geneva, 176, 285, 288
George, Walter, 22
George Washington Carver School, 113
Georgia Supreme Court, 47
German Democratic Republic, 289
German invasion of Soviet Union, 78, 79, 82, 86, 87
German-Soviet Non-Aggression Pact of 1939, 11, 75, 78, 79, 83, 134
Germany, 137, 317
Gerson, Si, 98, 100, 111–12, 113, 123, 124, 165–66, 187, 192, 193, 194, 195, 287
Ghana, 260
Gibson, Josh, 63
Gilbert, Leon, 247
Glaser, Joe, 110

Glazer, Nathan, 54
Goddard, Henry, 248
God That Failed, The, 109
Goebbels, Paul Joseph, 173
Gold, Ben, 81, 107, 134, 184
Goldberg, Louis, 187, 195, 209
Golden, Harry, Jr., 323
Golden, O. J., 59
Goldman, Marcus, 262
Goldsmith, Joseph, 239
Goldway, David, 131
Gomes, Albert, 169
Gone with the Wind, 63
Goode, John, 59
Goodman, Andrew, 311
Goodman, Bennie, 110
Goodman, Gerald, 173
Goodman, Nina, 274
Goodpaster, Andrew, 308
GOP. *See* Republican party
Gorbachev, Mikhail, 277, 278
Gordon, Eugene, 115, 132
Gordon, Max, 165, 287
Gorky, Maxim, 61
Graham, Shirley, 27, 239
Grand United Order of Odd Fellows, 19, 21, 27, 35, 39, 41
Granger, Lester, 40, 53, 60, 66, 72, 74, 75, 77, 80, 94, 99, 114, 146, 160, 182, 279
Graves, Bibb, 50
Gray, David, 322
Gray, Gordon, 308
Gray, Jesse, 259, 260, 294
Great Britain, 11, 212, 274, 321
Great Depression, 46, 51, 53, 55, 59, 100
Great Eastern News Corporation boycott of *People's Voice*, 175
Greater New York Baptist Ministerial Alliance, 294
Greater New York Committee to Keep America Out of War, 79
Greater New York Press Club, 317
Great Migration, 298
Greece, 129
Green, Gilbert, 55, 113, 114–15, 117, 134, 135, 140, 152, 222, 225, 270, 276, 324
Green, William, 201
Greene, Larry, 64, 65
Griswold, Erwin, 317–18
Gropper, William, 46
Guardian, 292, 310

438 INDEX

Guinier, Ewart, 236, 239, 241, 248

Haldane Society of Britain, 219
Hale, Matthew, 269
Hall, Gus, 134, 209, 213, 224, 250, 276, 300, 301, 310, 319, 321, 325; indictment of, 320; Internal Security Act of 1950 and, 314–15; refusal to register under Smith Act, 309
Hall, Ian, 108
Hall, Otto, 39, 68
Hall-Davis Defense Committee, 320
Hallinan, Vincent, 289, 293
Hamid, Sufi Abdul, 70
Hammond, John, 62
Hampton, Lionel, 108, 121, 169
Hampton Institute, 17
Hancock, Gordon, 57, 199
Hand, Learned, 211
Handy, W. C., 108
Hansberry, Lorraine, 14
Harlem, 12–13, 30, 33, 45, 51, 53, 55, 56, 57, 72, 81, 92, 96, 102, 127, 230–31; "All Peoples Party" in, 99; Association of Trade and Commerce in, 146; Castro's trip to (1960), 309; Citizens Democratic Club of, 239; Communist party of, *see* Communist party of Harlem; Davis's first report to after election of 1943, 119–20; Davis's move to, 58; government agents in, 206; in Great Depression, 100; Left and, 212; NAACP in, 53; National Negro Congress and, 73; *New York Amsterdam News* poll of leading people in, 248; in NYC Council election of 1943, 106, 107; Organization of Unemployed, 231; "political maturity" of, 121; problems of in 1930s, 64–65; public schools in, 66, 92; Republican party in, 291; revolutionary literature sold in, 51, 66; Riverton house project in, 127, 260; Rockland Palace of, 40; Schmeling defeat and, 62; Scottsboro-Herndon conference in, 52; Scottsboro Nine trial and, 51; Unitarian Church in, 245; uprising in after CP-11 trial, 225–26, 228–29; West Indian community in, 81; World War II and, 81
"Harlem Charter," 106
Harlem Civil Rights Congress, 257–58
Harlem Committee to Repeal the Smith Act, 258
Harlem Community Art Centre, 93
"Harlem Fox." *See* Jones, J. Raymond
Harlem Hospital, 185
Harlem Labor Center, 74
Harlem Lawyers Association, 66, 91, 219
Harlem Liberator. See *Liberator*
"Harlem Non-Partisan Committee for Supreme Court Reform," 66
Harlem People's Book Shop, 66
Harlem Peoples School for Negro Liberation, Democracy, and Peace, 65–66
"Harlem Renaissance," 12
Harlem Riot of 1935, 64–65
Harlem Trade Union Council, 236
Harlem West Indian Defense Conference, 81
Harlem Young Communist League, 58
Harmonizing Four, 238
Harper, Fowler, 244
Harrington, Ollie, 61, 137, 240, 258, 260
Harris, Lem, 320
Harrison, William, 88, 104, 107
Hart, Walter, 186, 194, 224
Harten, Thomas, 90, 103, 206, 218, 235, 294
Harvard Alumni Bulletin, 81
Harvard Law School, 30–31, 48
Harvard University, 317–18
Hastie, William, 48, 73, 88, 171, 178, 245
Hathaway, Clarence, 46, 81
Haughton, James, 323
Hawkins, Coleman, 108
Hawkins, Erskine, 62, 110
Haynes, George, 36
Haynes, Mike, 17
Hays, Arthur Garfield, 40, 91, 160, 220
Hays, George, 265
Haywood, Harry, 41, 68, 224, 271, 285, 287, 291, 297, 298, 299, 302, 324
Healey, Dorothy, 36, 71, 273, 276, 289, 290, 295, 296, 299, 301
Hearst press, 116. *See also* specific newspapers
Height, Dorothy, 60, 73, 99
Hendel, Samuel, 312
Herbst, Josephine, 46, 61
Herndon, Angelo case, 31, 32, 35–43, 47, 48, 49, 50, 51, 52, 54
Herndon family, 28
Hertzog, J. B. M., 80
Hicks, Granville, 46

Hicks, James, 225, 235
Hill, Arnold, 72
Hill, Charles, 177, 261, 323
Hill, Jack, 30
Hillman, Sidney, 151, 152
Hiss, Alger, 224
Hitler, Adolf, 79, 81, 82, 90, 95, 102, 114, 131, 137, 141, 159; CIO compared to, 199; *Daily Worker* on, 132; front against, 87; HUAC compared to, 207; Metropolitan Life's policies compared to policies of, 126; *Oklahoma Black Dispatch* and, 164; racism of, 168; Truman compared to, 198
Holiday, Billie, 58, 108, 110, 120, 155
Hollywood reaction to Davis's 1943 election, 119
Holocaust, 155, 232
Holtzoff, Alexánder, 321
Holy Trinity Baptist Church, Brooklyn, 90
Homelessness, 156
"Honor Roll of Race Relations," 121
Hood, Otis, 165
Hook, Sidney, 40
Hoover, Herbert, 22, 24, 25, 36
Hoover, J. Edgar, 13, 92, 217, 269, 271, 282, 283, 288, 309, 315, 321, 323, 324
Hope, John, 28, 322–23
Horne, Lena, 12, 58, 108, 110, 116, 155, 183
Horten, Thomas, 91
Horton, Asadata Dafora, 62
Hospital workers union, 303–05
House Administration Election Subcommitee, 207
House Un-American Activities Committee (HUAC), 50, 155, 164, 207, 208, 215, 225, 227–28, 257, 261, 306, 316. See also. McCarthy; McCarthyism
Houston, Charles, 29, 40, 47, 48, 65, 73, 109, 172, 224, 248
Hoving, Walter, 157
Howard, Charles, 235
Howard, Milton, 213
Howard, Perry, 22, 73
Howard University, 24
Howe, Irving, 55
Howe, Mark DeWolfe, 318
HUAC. *See* House Un-American Activities Committee
Huber, John, 157
Hudson, Hosea, 41, 271

Hudson, John, 37, 40
Hughes, Langston, 44, 45, 46, 58, 60, 102, 103, 110, 155, 218, 249, 325
Human Rights Commission, 156
Human rights violations in Europe and Soviet Union, 9, 13
Humphrey, Hubert, 201
Hungary, 231, 269, 271, 274, 281, 282, 317
Hunter, Oscar, 59
Hunter College, 313
Hunton, Alphaeus, 228
Hunton, Dorothy, 228

ILD. *See* International Labor Defense
Impelliteri, Vincent, 195, 196
Independent. See Atlanta Independent
Independent Citizens' Committee, 152
Independent Socialists, 293, 295
India, 46
India Communist party, 133
Indonesia, 172, 226
Ingram, Rex, 61, 110
Integration, 136, 145, 173, 184, 205; of baseball, 62, 63, 154–55, 182; Black Belt thesis vs., 136; Davis on concept of, 249; of European military, 129; of New York City schools, 303; of NYC fire department, 124; of prisons, 265–70
Internal Security (McCarran) Act of 1950, 312, 314–15, 318, 319, 320, 321, 322
"Internationale," 40
International Labor Defense (ILD), 36, 37, 40, 41, 50, 51, 52, 70, 251
International Ladies Garment Workers Union, 75, 188
International Longshore Association, 236
International Publishers, 138
International Red Aid, 251
International Trade Union Committee of Negro Workers, 54
International Workers' Order, 45, 163
"Iron Curtain" speech of Churchill, 167, 168, 172, 174, 175
Isaacs, Stanley, 98, 100, 195; career of, 124; on Davis's arrest, 208; on Davis's expulsion from the City Council, 240, 241; Davis's relationship with, 123–24, 187, 208, 229, 243; Dulles's support for, 229; FEPC bill introduced by,

440 INDEX

Isaacs, Stanley (cont'd)
  169; on Gerson, 194; Metropolitan Life's discrimination and, 126–27, 128; on Mindszenty, 231; proportional representation and, 188, 190, 193; vote totals of (1945), 164–65
Isaacson, Leo, 198
Islam, 284
Israel, 274, 283, 284
Israel African Methodist Episcopal Church, 174
Israel Question, 287
Isserman, Abraham, 91
Italian invasion of Ethiopia, 80, 81
Italy, 321
Ives-Quinn law, 154

Jack, Hulan, 102, 248, 290, 296
Jackson, Andrew, 129
Jackson, Esther, 267
Jackson, James, 57, 183, 267, 271, 274, 276, 277, 290, 295, 299, 300, 301, 302, 309, 325
Jackson, Jesse, 33, 57, 59, 177
Jackson, Levi, 205
Jackson, Margaret Whilhemina, 68
Jackson, Robert, 245
Jamaica, 46, 129, 286
James, C. L. R., 109
Japan, 11, 68, 76, 80, 82, 87, 92, 93, 244
Japanese-American internment, 12, 119, 129, 211
Japanese Communist party, 320
Jeffers, Louise, 257
Jefferson, Thomas, 42, 71
Jefferson School of Social Science, 157, 249
Jenkins, Dorothy, 112
Jerome, V. J., 61
Jet, 322
Jewish-black relationships, 194, 283, 285
Jewish-Left relationship, 287
Jewish Life, 267
Jewish People's Fraternal Order, 220
Jewish Question, 269
Jewish state in Palestine, 283
Jewish support for Davis, 117
John Birch Society, 32, 310, 314
Johnson, Arnold, 119, 165, 295–96
Johnson, Ellsworth "Bumpy," 60
Johnson, Henry Lincoln, 21
Johnson, Howard "Stretch," 53–54, 58, 60, 128, 252, 274

Johnson, J. J., 250
Johnson, James Weldon, 47
Johnson, John, 60
Johnson, Link, Jr., 308
Johnson, Lyndon, 307
Johnson, Manning, 50, 51, 75
Johnson, Mordecai, 308
Johnson, Oakley, 80
Jones, Claudia, 14, 208, 265, 266, 276; on Black Belt thesis, 179; on Browderism, 144; on CP-11 trial, 218; Davis's relationship with, 58, 81, 321; deportation of threatened by authorities, 192, 206; detention of, 206, 229; on "Double V," 131, 132; on FEPC bill, 170–71; Herndon's refusal to testify against, 48; in London, 321; on prison conditions, 255; on World War II, 131, 132
Jones, J. Raymond, 99, 106, 147–48, 149, 150, 151, 190, 202, 234, 291
Jones, Thomas, 239
Jordan, Vernon, 35
Josephson, Barney, 62
Josephson, Matthew, 46
Joshi, P. C., 133
Jury selection discrimination, 218
Justice, Robert, 100
Justice Department, 227, 268, 269
Justice Department of Cuba, 219

Kane, James, 237
Katayama, Sen, 68
Keating, Kenneth, 288, 308
Kee, Salaria, 59
Keegan, Charles, 230
Kempton, Murray, 320
Kennedy, John Fitzgerald, 307, 309, 311, 315, 319, 320, 322
Kennedy, Robert, 310, 315, 320
Kent, Rockwell, 292
Kerensky, Aleksandr, 37
Kern, Paul, 239
King, Martin Luther, Jr., 13, 19, 21, 28, 32, 33, 175, 201, 205, 228, 258, 269, 291, 308; Davis's endorsement of, 294; Davis's relationship with, 286, 295, 303, 305, 315, 316; Davis's support of, 298; FBI surveillance of, 271; letter to Davis from, 305–6; May's influence on, 60; E. D. Nixon and, 77; stabbing of, 296, 306; student movement in New York City and, 311; on Winston's

INDEX

imprisonment, 305–6, 315; Winston testimonial speech by, 315
Kirkland, James R., 268
KKK. *See* Ku Klux Klan
Klehr, Harvey, 271
Knickerbocker, H. R., 220
Knights of Pythias, 20
Koch, Ilse, 205
Koppersmith, Hal, 293
Korea, 87, 259
Korean War, 243, 244, 246, 247, 249, 252, 257, 265
Kornweibel, Theodore, 21
Krchmarek, Anton, 267
Kremlin. *See* Communist party of the Soviet Union
Krock, Arthur, 211
Krumbein, Charles, 98
Ku Klux Klan, 20, 22, 24, 37, 41, 49, 66, 85, 247, 322
Kunstler, William, 320
Kusinen, Otto, 68

Labor unions, 31, 53, 74, 77, 166, 172, 176, 213, 322; "All Peoples Party" and, 99; Davis supported by, 235–37; discrimination in, 129; hospital, 303–5; Metropolitan Life's discrimination and, 128; in NYC Council election of 1943, 106; postal workers', 57; Smith Act and, 257; strikes and, 58, 74, 141, 172, 236. *See also* specific unions
La Guardia, Fiorello, 98, 99, 109, 126, 150, 151, 165, 193, 260
Lamont, Corliss, 46, 292
Lamont, Thomas, 81
Lampell, Millard, 177
Lancaster, J. W., Jr., 107
Landrum-Griffin law, 308
Lane, Layle, 93, 107, 182
Lane, Mark, 312, 314
Langer, William, 265
Lanier, R. O'Hara, 169
Lannon, Al, 274, 276
Larkin Lectro strike, 236
Law, Oliver, 59
Lawrence, Carl, 234
Lawrence, Jacob, 169
Lawrence, William, 287
Lawson, Elizabeth, 45
Lawson, James, 157, 182, 186, 202
Lawson, Steven, 227
"Leadbelly" (Huddie Ledbetter), 169

"Leading Harlemites" poll of *New York Amsterdam News*, 248
League of Struggle for Negro Rights, 43, 51–52, 60
Lebanon, 293
Lee, Canada, 103, 110, 120, 169, 171, 217
Lee, Euel case, 39
Lehman, Herbert, 89, 116
Lehman-Dewey governor's race, 116
Leigh, Vivian, 63
Lenin, V. I., 29, 37, 79, 134, 156, 178, 195, 212
Leninism, 281
Le Seuer, Meridel, 46, 140
Lessing, Doris, 110
Levin, Elsie, 325
Lewinson, Edwin, 122–23
Lewis, Alfred Baker, 76, 77, 176, 228
Lewis, Anthony, 319–20
Lewis, Claude, 105
Lewis, Edward, 149
Lewis, Ira, 110
Lewis, John L., 77, 79, 93
Lewis family of Harlem, 230–31
Lewisohn Stadium, 185
Liberal party, 148, 151, 158, 165, 168, 187, 193, 194, 209, 232, 241, 243, 291, 292, 293
Liberator, 43–44, 45, 46, 47, 51, 62
Liberia, 28, 109, 218
Liebowitz, Samuel, 50, 51
Life magazine, 233
"Lift Every Voice" (column), 46
Lightfoot, Claude, 70, 78, 271, 276, 277, 290, 299, 301, 309, 315
Lightfoot, Geraldine, 271
Lima, Mickey, 299, 301
Lincoln, Abraham, 72
Lipsitz, George, 176
Lisio, Donald, 23, 24
Lissner, Will, 321
Little Rock, Arkansas, 285, 293, 297, 299
Local 1199, hospital workers union, 303–5
Locke, Alain, 110, 169
Logan, Arthur, 238
Logan, Rayford, 20
Loman, Charles, 113, 288, 299
Long, Avon, 160
Lord & Taylor Department Store, 157
Los Angeles Herald Dispatch, 284

Loughlin, Edward, 148, 149, 150
Louis, Joe, 12, 58, 62, 110, 154, 176, 182, 198
Lovestone, Jay, 68, 278
Lowenfels, Walter, 110, 268
Loyless, Tom W., 18
Luce, Claire Booth, 247
Luce, Henry, 145, 234
Lumer, Hy, 301
Lumumba, Patrice, 311
Lunceford, Jimmie, 108
L'Unita, 282
Lynching, 172, 207, 212, 232, 263. *See also* Anti-lynching legislation
Lynn, Winfred, 95
Lyons, Paul, 54

Macalester College, 318
MacArthur, Douglas, 247
Machting, Leonard, 313
MacKay, C. W., 267
Macy's, 103
Madagascar, 226
Madison, Arthur, 91
Magil, A. B., 144, 283, 286
Malcolm X, 175, 177–78, 216, 284, 312, 313, 314, 322
Malin, Julius, 70
Mallard, Amy, 258
Malloy, James, 260
Maltz, Albert, 46
Manhattan Medical Association, 107
Manley, Norman, 219
Manufacturers Hanover, 156
Mao Zedong, 299
Marcantonio, Vito, 98, 151, 152, 154, 172, 174, 175, 176, 192, 199–200, 228, 239, 248
Marches on Washington, 22, 78, 94, 95, 113, 114, 170, 201, 303, 323
Marching Blacks, 175
Marines in Lebanon, 293
Marshall, Horace, 230
Marshall, Larkin, 235
Marshall, Thurgood, 40, 47, 48, 58, 107, 171, 248
Marshall Plan, 186, 189, 198, 201, 247
Martin, Joe, 170
Martin, Louis, 88
Martin, Rev., 41
Martinsville defendants, 264
Marx, Karl, 209
Marxism, 163, 289

Marxism-Leninism, 207, 281, 289
Mason, Chick, 279
Mason, Dolly, 262
Masons, 20
Masses Publishing Co. v. Patten, 211
Matthews, J. B., 293
Matthews, Ralph, 56
Max, Alan, 281
Mayfield, Julian, 273
Mays, Benjamin, 60
McCarran Act. *See* Internal Security Act of 1950
McCarthy, Joseph, 32, 257, 273, 282. *See also* House Un-American Activities Committee (HUAC); McCarthyism
McCarthyism, 45, 101, 150, 192, 273, 280. *See also* House Un-American Activities Committee (HUAC); McCarthy, Joseph
McCloskey, Robert, 318
McGee, Rosalee, 264
McGee, Willie, 52, 247–48, 249, 264
McGhee, Brownie, 238
McGill, Ralph, 314
McGohey, John F. X., 215, 244–45
McGowan, Edward, 265
McGuire, Matthew, 320
McKay, Robert, 314
McLaurin, Benjamin, 72, 74, 75, 80, 95, 147, 151, 158, 159, 160, 161, 162, 163, 165, 238
McManus, John, 292
McPhail, Larry, 154–55
Meany, George, 201, 303
Medina, Harold, 209, 211, 213, 214, 215, 220, 222, 223, 224, 225, 239, 244, 248
Mellon, Andrew, 263
Menendez, Jesus, 206
"Message to the State Conventions and Clubs of the Party, A," 280
Messenger, 21
Metropolitan Life Insurance Company discrimination, 64, 126–28, 223, 260
Mexican Communist party, 68, 120
Meyer, Howard, 251
Michigan Chronicle, 88, 182
Middle East, 281. *See also* specific countries
Miley, Thomas Jefferson, 189
Military, 49, 133; black press and, 182; integration of in Europe, 129; in Lebanon, 293; racism in, 247; segregation

of, 95, 102, 133, 140, 144, 176, 181, 200–201, 241
Miller, James, 174
Miller, Kelly, 24, 73
Miller, Loren, 46, 64
Miller, Merle, 110
Mills, Saul, 164
Milton, Willie, 206
Mincey, S. S., 25
Mindel, Jacob "Pop," 144, 266
Mindszenty, Cardinal, 231
Minerbrook, Gwendolyn, 127
Ministers' Committee to Elect Davis, 105
Minnesota Daily, 318
Minnesota Spokesman, 318, 319
Minor, Robert, 44, 54, 69, 93, 98, 99, 134, 143, 169, 178, 182
Mintz, Bernard, 305
Minutemen, 310
Mississippi elections, 172
Mitchell, Congressman, 84
Mitchell, Charlene, 267
Montgomery, Alabama, 284, 285
Montgomery, Olin, 52
Moon, Henry Lee, 202
Moon, Mollie, 238
Mooney, Tom, 251
Moore, Audley, 92, 105–6, 107, 111, 112, 140
Moore, Fred, 88
Moore, Harry, 263
Moore, John Hammond, 35
Moore, Richard, 45, 99
Morehouse College, 28–29, 30, 322–23
Morehouse Maroon Tiger, 29
Morgenthau, Robert, 320
Morning Freiheit, 205
Morris, Newbold, 125, 159, 217
Morrison, A. W., 41
Morrow, E. Frederic, 84, 85
Moscow. *See* Communist party of the Soviet Union; Soviet Union
Moscow, Warren, 184
Moses, Robert, 119, 125, 126, 127, 163, 182, 189, 195
Moton, R. R., 47
Mount Lebanon Jubilee Singers, 238
Mount Olivet Baptist Church, 120
MOWM. *See* March on Washington Movement
Muhammad, Elijah, 322
Muhammad Speaks, 33, 322

Mulzac, Hugh, 292
Murphy, George, 107, 110, 218, 265, 297, 307, 308, 323
Murphy, Robert, 110
Murray, William, 174
Muslims, 316, 322
Mussolini, 71

NAACP. *See* National Association for the Advancement of Colored People
Nabried, Tom, 267
Nagy, Imre, 290
Naison, Mark, 61
Nakamura, Kaju, 80
Nalty, Bernard, 95
Nasser, Gamal Abdel, 284
Nation, The, 73, 255
National Assembly for Democratic Rights, 315
National Association for the Advancement of Colored People (NAACP), 18, 32, 33, 42, 48, 66, 83, 121, 142, 149, 162, 177, 194, 202, 248, 322, 323; in Boston, 107; in Brooklyn, 228; Columbia, Tennessee pogrom and, 171; Communist party and, 10, 11, 47, 49, 50, 51, 171, 254; conscription and, 78; conventions of, 72, 78, 79, 80, 81, 86, 87, 129, 307, 323; Coordinating Committee for Employment and, 74; Davis's attendance at conventions of, 72; Davis's congressional campaign endorsement by, 90; on Davis's NYC Council campaign of 1945, 155; Du Bois's departure from, 72; Edwards praised by, 75; in Harlem, 53; human rights petition to United Nations by, 176; legislative program of, 1945, 141; on Lynn's stand against segregated military, 95; Metropolitan Life's discrimination and, 128; National Negro Congress and, 73; in New York, 218; on NYC Council election of 1943, 116; on police brutality, 228; on proportional representation, 188, 190; purge of Left from, 228; Scottsboro Nine trial and, 49, 50, 51, 52; Spingarn Award of, 86; World War II and, 82
National Association of Manufacturers, 130
National Baptist Convention, 206
National Baptist Voice, 258

National Committee for Defense of Negro Leadership, 262
National Conference of Black Lawyers, 11, 220
National Council for FEPC, 170
National Council of Negro Women, 162
National Dental Association, 179
Nationalism, 14, 281, 309, 313, 316, 322
National Lawyers Guild, 11, 219
National Maritime Union, 161, 308
National Negro Commission, 179
National Negro Congress (NNC), 46, 72, 73, 74, 75, 76, 77, 78, 90, 140, 172, 173, 182
National Negro Labor Council, 257
National Negro Tennis Championships, 30
National Non-Partisan Committee to Defend the Rights of the Twelve Communist Leaders, 215
National Question, 11, 32, 51, 53, 76, 77, 78, 79, 177, 222; *Afro-American* and, 297; in Brazil, 67; Browderism and, 139, 145, 179–81; in Canada, 67; Communist party and, 265, 287; complications of (1957), 284; Davis refines position on, 204–5; Dennis and, 140; description of, 66–72; FBI and, 309; Ford and, 143, 278; Foster and, 180, 298–99; Gates and, 281, 297; Lightfoot and, 309; Palestine and, 194; Patterson and, 297; Soviet Union Communist party and, 302; UAW and, 202. *See also* specific proposed solutions
National Shoe strike, 74
Nation of Islam, 33, 284, 316, 322
Native Son, 61, 87, 109
Nazis, 62, 80, 86, 87
NBC, 77, 310
Nearing, Scott, 267
Negro-Catholic panic of 1741, 218
Negro Convention Movement, 72
"Negroes Against War Committee," 79
Negroes in a Soviet America, 68–69
Negro Freedom rallies of 1940s, 114, 182, 186
Negro History Week, 123, 156, 169, 196, 248
Negro Labor Committee (NLC), 75, 76, 235, 236
Negro Labor Council, 298

Negro Labor Victory Committee, 90, 96, 106, 147, 158
Negro Liberator. See *Liberator*
Negro Nation thesis. See Black Belt thesis
Negro Newspaper Publisher Associations, 88
Negro People and the Communist party, The, 102
Negro People's Committee to Aid Spanish Democracy, 80
Negro Playwrights Company, 110
Negro Question. *See* National Question
Negro Resolution of Socialist party, 76
"Negro Work Committee" of Socialist party, 72
Nehru, Jawaharlal, 297, 316
Nelson, Steve, 263, 268, 276–77, 282
Newark Evening News, 317
New Deal, 26, 66, 145
New Economic Policy of Lenin, 134
New Jersey Herald News, 85
New Masses, 29, 41, 70, 119, 169
New Redeemer Church, 120
Newton, Walter, 24, 25
New York Age, 32, 63, 84, 86, 88, 89, 132, 178; ad supporting Davis and Winston in, 217, 218; on Brown, 233, 234, 235; changes in (1948), 205; on CP-11 trial, 221; Davis's attorney general campaign ad in, 174; Davis criticized by, 132; on Davis's NYC Council campaign of 1943, 104, 107, 115; on Davis's NYC Council campaign of 1945, 148, 151, 155–56, 163; on Davis's NYC Council campaign of 1949, 235, 238, 241; FBI and, 205; on March on Washington Movement, 114; on proportional representation, 190; on Republican nomination of Davis, 148; on Riddick's running against Davis, 148; Schenley ads in, 205; on Tammany Hall endorsement of Davis (1945), 148; on Wallace, 198
New York Amsterdam News, 22, 29, 31, 39, 45, 51, 58, 81, 95, 201; on Black Belt thesis, 146, 147; on Brown, 238; Brown with, 233; on CP-11 trial, 214; on Davis's arrest, 208–9; Davis's criticism of, 122; on Davis's HUAC appearance, 164; on Davis's NYC Council campaign of 1945, 146, 147,

150, 151, 157, 163; on Davis's NYC Council campaign of 1949, 241; on Davis-Powell relationship, 175; on Davis's release from prison, 269; on government intimidation of petition drive, 294; on HUAC agents in Harlem, 1948, 206; "leading Harlemites" poll of, 248; on Leftist influence in Harlem, 189–90; on March on Washington Movement, 22; on NYC Council election of 1943, 104, 105, 111, 115–16; on petition drive in state senate race, 294–95; on Powell, 121; Randolph's accusations against, 96; Randolph's criticism of Davis quoted in, 160; staff members of run for office, 234; strike at (1935), 58
New York Baptist Convention, 206
New York Board of Elections, 295
New York Board of Higher Education, 313–14
New York City, 12–13, 54, 106
New York City Board of Education, 185
New York City Board of Elections, 165
New York City Board of Estimates, 126, 185, 196, 238, 293
New York City Corporation Counsel, 185
New York City Council, 186; Cold War issues and, 231; Davis purged from, 227–43; Democratic party after Davis's ouster from, 237, 241, 242; Finance Committee of, 167, 185; labor support for Davis's re-election to, 235–37; Liberal party on, 241; Parks Committee of, 185; Rules Committee of, 167, 185; Special Committee on Unemployment and Home Relief, 230; State Legislation Committee of, 185. *See also* specific elections
New York City Council election of 1941, 97
New York City Council election of 1943, 11, 12–13, 83, 89, 93, 96, 97–118, 145; anti-Communist reaction to, 117; artists' support in, 108, 110; campaign literature in, 112; celebrity support in, 108–10; Davis, Sr. in, 106; Davis's behavior after, 122–28; Davis's reaction to, 117; effects of, 115, 118, 119–21; "electoral district captains" in, 101–2; Jewish support in, 117; labor unions in, 106; leaders of campaign in, 113; opposition to Davis in, 106; proportional representation and, 100–101; response to, 115; vote fraud in, 112, 113, 115, 116; vote totals for Davis in, 114, 120
New York City Council election of 1945, 137, 145–46, 148–49, 150–53, 154–66; Black Belt thesis as issue in, 145, 151; *Daily Worker* on, 149, 152, 158; NAACP and, 155; *New York Age* on, 148, 151, 155–56, 163; *New York Amsterdam News* on, 146, 147, 150, 151, 157, 163; *New York Times* on, 148, 149, 150, 164; *People's Voice* on, 151, 152, 155, 163; *Pittsburgh Courier* on, 163–64; Powell and, 148, 158, 162; Robeson and, 155
New York City Council election of 1949, 207, 209, 227–43
New York City Department of Housing and Building, 230
New York City Department of Welfare, 231
New York City Fire department integration, 124
New York City Health Department, 231
New York City Housing Authority, 161, 182
New York City Housing Commission, 201–2
New York City Planning Commission, 260
New York City Police, 12, 161–62, 228, 229, 239
New York City Police "Red Squad," 314
New York City school integration, 303
New York City Sponsoring Committee for a NNC, 72
New York City student eruption of 1961, 311–14
New York Compass, 255
New York County Communist party, 93
New York Court of Appeals, 295
New York Daily News, 93, 122, 124, 217, 221
New York Herald Tribune, 116, 126, 148, 149, 150, 188, 209, 233, 237, 242, 245, 255
New York Journal-American, 63, 313
New York Labor Youth League, 250

New York Mirror, 244
New York NAACP, 218
New York police brutality, 12, 161–62, 228, 229, 239
New York Police Department, 229
New York Post, 46, 188, 220, 226, 242, 245, 287, 310, 313
New York state attorney general campaign of Davis, 174–75
New York State Board of Social Welfare, 246
New York State Communist party, 98, 273, 303
New York State Senate campaign of Davis (1958), 293, 294–95, 296
New York State Senate Judiciary Committee, 246
New York Tenants Council, 229
New York Times, 23, 24, 42, 48, 54, 63, 91, 113, 116, 280, 289, 314, 321; on American Jewish Committee study of Communist party, 283; on baseball segregation, 154; on black communists, 284, 286; on Browderism, 279; on Browder ouster, 146; Brown endorsed by, 238; on Communist party (1947), 187; on Communist party factionalism, 284, 300; on Communist party membership (1956), 279; on CP-11 trial, 210, 211, 214–15, 216–17, 244, 245, 251; on Davis's arrest, 209; on Davis's attorney general campaign results, 175; on Davis's NYC Council campaign of 1945, 148, 149, 150, 164; on Davis's NYC Council campaign of 1949, 241; on Davis's NY state senate campaign, 296; Davis's obituary in, 324; on Davis's release from prison, 268; on Davis's speech at CCNY, 314; on free speech, 312, 313, 314; on Harlem march, 226; on Herndon case, 37–38; on Marshall Plan endorsement by NYC Council, 186; on May Day celebration (1947), 184; on Metropolitan Life's discrimination, 126; on NYC Council Marshall Plan endorsement, 186; on picketing courts, 217; Powell opposed by, 292; prison availability of, 255; on prison segregation, 268; on proportional representation, 165, 188, 189, 237; on sales tax proposal, 125; on Soviet Union Communist party, 287; on Tammany Hall endorsement of Davis, 148, 149; on united left conference (1958), 292; on Western Union strike, 172
New York World-Telegram, 116, 122, 124, 146, 152, 189, 197, 237, 244, 303
Niagara Movement, 21
Niebuhr, Reinhold, 160, 245
Niles, David, 170
Nixon, E. D., 77
Nixon, Richard, 207, 307, 309
Nkrumah, Kwame, 260, 297, 316
NLC. *See* Negro Labor Committee
NNC. *See* National Negro Congress
Non-Aligned Movement, 269
Non-Partisan Youth Committee to Re-elect Davis, 239
Norris, Ida, 52
Norris v. Alabama. See Scottsboro Nine case
North, Joseph, 35, 222, 277, 278, 294
North Carolina Mutual Insurance Company, 86
Norway, 289
"Now It's Against the Law" comic strip, 264
Nuclear testing, 303
Nuremberg laws, 82, 126
Nusser, Charles, 101, 266

Oberg, Curt, 270
O'Brien, Kevin John, 211
O'Connor, Harvey, 46
Odd Fellows, 19, 21, 27, 35, 39, 41
O'Dell, Jack, 13, 33, 306
Odets, Clifford, 46
O'Dwyer, William, 149, 150, 154, 159, 189, 194, 195, 197, 206, 209, 230, 236, 237, 240
Office of Price Administration, 103, 156
Oklahoma Black Dispatch, 25, 88, 164, 212
"Oklahoma" cast, 108
Omega Psi Phi, 57
O'Neal, Frederick, 155
On the Waterfront, 236
"Order of the Bandanna," 47
O'Reilly, Kenneth, 88
Organization of Unemployed, 231
Othello, 228
Ottley, Roi, 146
Outline Political History of the Americas, 278

Paderewski, Ignace, 29
Palestin, Ira, 194, 195, 208, 230
Palestine, 283
Pan-Africanism, 309
Parent Teachers Association, 156
Parker, Charles "Yardbird," 108, 250, 259
Parker, Dean, 219
Parker, Mack, 306, 308
Party Organizer, 111, 112
Party Voice, 273
Party wars. *See* Factionalism in CPUSA
Pascal, Blaise, 278
Patterson, Haywood, 49, 50
Patterson, Leonard, 308
Patterson, Louise, 44, 257, 265
Patterson, William, 9, 14, 27, 57, 208, 271, 274, 277; birthday celebration for, 1951, 52; on Black Belt thesis, 138; on Browderism, 138, 144; "Censored News" pamphlet by, 219; Civil Rights Congress and, 49; on Congo, 309; congressional campaign of, 86; on Cuba, 309; as *Daily Worker* head, 286; on Davis's anti-lynching testimony, 85; at Davis's funeral, 325; Davis greeted by, on release from prison, 269; on Davis's NY state senate campaign of 1958, 294; on Davis's prison conditions, 261; Davis's prison release efforts of, 257, 264, 265, 266; Herndon and, 36, 38, 40; Kennedy telegram sent by, 315; in League of Struggle for Negro Rights, 57; on National Question, 297; on prison conditions, 261; prison segration suits and, 268; on Progressive Labor movement, 324; Soviet foreign policy and, 79; "We Charge Genocide" campaign and, 297; wife of, 58
"Peaceful co-existence," 292
Peale, Norman Vincent, 165
Pearl Harbor, 87
Pegler, Westbrook, 88, 93
Pemberton, James, 150
"People's Institute for Harlem," 103
People's Rights party, 174, 293, 296
People's Voice, 103, 108, 120, 132, 186; boycott of, 175; campaign endorsements (1946), 174; on Communist party barring from ballot, 174; on Davis's attorney general campaign, 174; on Davis's NYC Council campaign of 1945, 151, 152, 155, 163; Davis's praise of, 122; demise of, 182, 183; FBI criticism of, 157–58; Great Eastern News Corporation boycott of, 175; on McLaurin campaign, 158, 160; Powell and, 174, 182, 183; on proportional representation, 189; Richardson's praise of Davis in, 168
People's World, 255
Perlow, Max, 236
Permanent Committee for Better Schools, 66, 92
Perry, Pettis, 152, 252, 260, 297
Peters, Paul, 60
Peterson, L. F., 23
Petitioning, 294–95
Philadelphia Independent, 268
Philadelphia Tribune, 245
Philbrick, Herbert, 67
Philippine Communist party, 273
Philippine Lawyers Guild, 219
Phillip, Cyril, 133, 173, 262
Phillips, Alfred J., 168
Phillips, Cabell, 245
Phillips, James, 168
Phillips, Wendell, 162
Pickens, William, 47, 80, 81, 87
Picketing of courts, 217
Pinckney, Joseph, 148
Pittman, John, 58
Pittsburgh Courier, 39, 48, 74, 79, 84, 88, 110, 132, 182, 267; on Black Belt thesis, 147; on CP-11 trial, 212, 221; on Davis's NYC Council campaign of 1945, 163–64; on Davis's NYC Council campaign of 1949, 242
Pittsburgh Smith Act trial, 277
"Plea for the Safety of Ben Davis, A," 268
"Pledge Scroll," 259
PM, 87, 152, 188, 199
Poitier, Sidney, 110, 238
Poland, 79, 172, 274
Police brutality, 12, 103, 161–62, 228, 229, 239
Political Affairs (formerly *The Communist*), 131, 165, 204–5, 212, 298
Political Prisoners' Welfare Committee, 264
Pollak, Louis, 314
Pollitt, Harry, 135

Poll taxes, 89, 92, 122, 129, 145, 172, 179, 197–98, 205, 207, 247
Popular front. *See* United front
Popular Socialist party of Cuba, 302
Porter, Michael Leroy, 19, 20
Porter, "Willa" (Mrs. Ben Davis, Sr.), 17
Postal workers' union, 57
Poston, Ted, 46, 226, 242
Potash, Irving, 134, 216, 224, 248
Pound, Roscoe, 31
Powe, Ralph, 268
Powell, Adam Clayton, 13, 53, 156, 192, 233; Browderism and, 120; Bruce's opposition to, 106; on Castro, 302, 309; "City Wide Action Conference" of, 121; on Communist party, 105, 157; Communist party split with, 182, 184; congressional campaign of, 174, 291; Coordinating Committee for Employment and, 74, 90; at Council on African Affairs' rally, 172; CP-11 trial and, 222; Davis's appeal to about "riots" of 1943, 103; Davis's congressional campaign supported by (1942), 91; Davis's criticism of, 184, 200, 216, 222, 249–50, 290; Davis's death and, 325; Davis's endorsement of, 294; Davis's NYC Council campaign of 1945 supported by, 148, 158, 162; Davis's relationship with, 73, 158, 175, 202, 286, 290, 295, 296–97, 297, 303; Davis's support of, 121, 292; Davis supported by, 104, 108; Eisenhower supported by, 290; FEPC supported by, 158, 170; income tax evasion charges against, 291, 307; indictment of, 306; La Guardia opposed by, 105; Lawson and, 186, 202; *Marching Blacks*, 175; Metropolitan Life's discrimination and, 127, 128; "Negroes Against War Committee" addressed by, 79; at Negro Freedom Rally (1943), 114; NNC and, 73; NYC Council departure of, 104; in NYC Council election of 1943, 108; *People's Voice* and, 174, 182, 183; on police beating of Brewer, 161; Progressive party and, 199–200; Randolph's criticism of, 200; at Randolph's Madison Square Gardens rally, 94; on Roosevelt's "court-packing" proposal, 66; seamen's strike and, 74; split with communists, 182; Trade Union Non-Partisan Committee and, 99; trial of, 306; Truman's exclusion of from White House invitation, 184; Wallace and, 200
Powell, C. B., 96, 201, 238
Powers, Richard Gid, 271, 282
PR. *See* Proportional representation
Prattis, P. L., 88, 267
Prickett, James, 71
Primus, Pearl, 108, 120, 155, 169
Princeton-Amherst football game, 1924, 30
Prison: *Afro-American* on discrimination in, 265, 267, 268, 269; Browder facing in 1941, 130; conditions in, 255, 261; Davis in, 254–70; Davis's campaign from, 259, 260; Davis's release from, 268, 269; Davis's suit against segregation of, 266–70; Dennis in, 250, 262; Dennis's release from, 269; discrimination in, 265, 267, 268, 269; efforts toward release of Davis from, 254, 257, 258–69; harassment in, 255; integration of, 265–70; *New York Times* available in, 255; Pittsburgh, 267; racism in, 254–70; segregation in, 255, 265–70; suit against segregation of, 266–70; Winston in, 256, 305–6, 310
Progressive Labor Movement, 324–25
Progressive party, 208, 211, 280, 289, 293, 315
Proportional representation, 112, 119, 152, 237, 239, 241, 242; campaign to repeal, 119, 187–88, 189, 190–91; consequences of ending of, 190–91, 193; *Daily Worker* on, 187, 188, 189; Democratic party and, 119, 188, 189, 193; ending of, 101, 116, 123, 190–91, 193; explanation of, 100–101; impact of, 101, 194; Isaacs and, 188, 190, 193; NAACP and, 188, 190; *New York Age* on, 190; *New York Times* on, 165, 188, 189, 237; Peale on, 165; *People's Voice* on, 189; Tammany Hall and, 119, 188, 189, 193
"Provisional Committee for the Defense of Civil Rights in Harlem," 65
Puerto Rican Communists, 144
Puerto Rico, 129, 172

Quebec, Canada, 67
Queens College, 312, 313

Quill, Mike, 120, 123, 125, 163, 164, 168, 172, 186, 187, 192, 194, 195, 197, 208, 229
Quinn, Hugh, 196, 197, 230, 239

Race Relations Institute, 182
Racism, 11, 13, 168, 203, 271; in Communist party members, 203–5; Communist party of the Soviet Union and, 176; in early-twentieth-century Atlanta, 20, 22; effects of on Davis, Jr., 34; in military during Korean War, 247; in New York Police Department, 229; in prison, 254–70; in Soviet Union, 176, 310. *See also* Discrimination
Radcliffe College, 28
Rager, Ed, 123, 194, 195–96, 208, 240
Ramos, Carlos, 219
Randolph, A. Philip, 53, 102, 235, 296; Bennett supported by, 94; Brotherhood of Porters and, 75, 77; Brown supported by, 238; civil rights groups attacked by, 96; Committee on the Improvement of Race Relations and, 124; Communist party and, 72, 202, 285; Coordinating Committee for Employment and, 74; Davis's criticism of, 86, 132, 162, 170, 176, 177, 182, 200, 202, 247, 285, 298; Davis criticized by, 93, 94; Davis's praise of, 73; Davis's relationship with, 53, 121; march on Washington initiated by, 78; McLaurin and, 95, 158, 159, 160; Meany's criticism of, 303; NNC and, 77; on NYC Council election of 1943, 113; Soviet Union criticized by, 77; on World War II, 79, 82
Rankin, John, 150, 160, 164, 165, 169
Ransom, Willard, 258
Raymond, Harry, 171
Reagan, Ronald, 318, 319
Reconstruction, 72
Red Cross blood segregation, 102, 138, 140
Red Menace, The, 248
"Red Squad" of New York City Police Department, 314
Reed, Stanley, 245
Reich, Charles, 320
Religious freedom in Soviet Union, 317
Rent control in NYC, 103
"Report on Negro Work," 69
Republican Club of Savannah, 25

Republican party, 21, 79, 82, 108, 123, 124, 130, 148, 168, 189, 190, 193, 240, 241, 243, 293, 296; of Bartow County, GA, 25; blacks ousted from, 22–26, 35, 71, 100; blacks rejected by, 35; Brown's criticism of, 233; coalition against (1946), 174; Columbia, Tennessee pogrom and, 171; Communist party success effects on, 155–56; convention of 1944 of, 173; convention of 1960 of, 307–8; Davis Jr. at convention of 1960 of, 307–8; Davis Jr. courted by, 36; Davis Jr. supported by, 163; Davis Jr.'s criticism of, 26, 83, 100, 122, 199; Davis Sr. in, 17, 18, 19, 21, 22, 23, 24, 85, 106, 173; Davis Sr. ousted from, 24, 25; Democratic party coalitions with, 209, 232; fascism and, 192; on FEPC, 197–98; Garvey's support of Democrats against blacks in, 70; in Harlem, 291; Jim Crow laws and, 116; in Lehman-Dewey governor's race, 116; Liberal party coalition with, 232; McLaurin nomination by, 158; Moore in, 112; *New York Age* and, 89; *New York Herald Tribune* and, 237, 242; on NYC Council budget, 167; in NYC Council election of 1943, 107; on poll tax, 197–98; Tobias and, 104
Republican State Central Committee of Georgia, 21, 25
Reynolds, Slick, 200
Richardson, Ben, 105, 168, 175, 241
Richardson, Beulah, 265, 267
Richmond, Al, 324
Rickey, Branch, 110
Riddick, Vernon, 148
Rieve, Emil, 199
Rising Wind, A, 141–42
Rivers, Francis, 121
Riverton housing project, 127, 260
Roach, Doug, 59
Roach, Max, 250
Roark, James, 247
Robbins, Jerome, 155
Roberts, Lucky, 108
Robeson, Essie, 111, 137, 176, 190–91
Robeson, Paul, Jr., 33, 59, 99, 216, 260, 276, 296, 302
Robeson, Paul, Sr., 9, 14, 27, 56, 57, 59, 208, 217, 228, 279, 288, 302; American Crusade to End Lynching and, 177;

Robeson, Paul (cont'd)
  anti-lynching bills and, 177; on baseball integration, 154, 182; biography of, 215; black artists and, 110; on Browder, 141; *Cleveland Call and Post* on, 316; at Council on African Affairs rally, 172, 216; CP-11 trial and, 215, 219, 226; at Davis birthday party (1951), 250; at Davis birthday party (1952), 259; at Davis's funeral, 325; Davis greeted by on release from prison, 269; Davis interview with on U.S. neutrality, 80; in Davis's NYC Council campaign of 1943, 108; in Davis's NYC Council campaign of 1945, 155; in Davis's NYC Council campaign of 1949, 238; at Davis's parole hearing, 262; Davis's petition drive and, 294; Davis praised by, 215; Davis's prison release efforts of, 257; Davis's relationship with, 59–60, 110, 215; at Davis's victory celebration (1943), 117; as football mentor for Davis, 30; at "free Davis" forum (1954), 265; at "free Davis" rally (1955), 267; at Harlem uprising following CP-11 trial, 226; HUAC appearance of, 257; as *Liberator* financial supporter, 44; National Non-Partisan Committee to Defend the Rights of the Twelve Communist Leaders and, 215; at Negro Freedom Rally (1943), 110; *People's Voice*'s dropping of column by, 183; rally against, 216; Stern's criticism of, 246; Trade Union Committee to Repeal the Smith Act and, 257; on U.S. neutrality, 80
Robinson, Bill "Bojangles," 217
Robinson, Earl, 267
Robinson, Jackie, 58, 155, 205–6, 307
Robinson, James, 105, 130, 232, 233
Rockefeller, John D., 10
Rockefeller, Nelson, 293, 303
Rockland Palace, Harlem, 40
Rodney, Lester, 260
Rogers, J. A., 79, 147, 218, 221, 228, 230
Rolfe, Red, 63
Rolland, Roman, 46
Rollins, Sonny, 250
Roosevelt, Eleanor, 122, 149, 154, 176
Roosevelt, Franklin D., 51, 66, 77, 81, 82, 85, 92, 143, 144, 148, 170, 195, 222, 257; Browderism and, 133; Communist party view of, 138; Communist view of, 95; Davis on, 82, 89, 90, 100, 103, 114, 122, 133; Four Freedoms of, 92, 137
Roosevelt, Theodore, 21, 124
Rose, Charles, 115
Rose, Josiah, 24, 25, 26
Rosenberg, Ethel, 275
Rosenberg, Julius, 275
Rosenwald housing project, Chicago, 127
Ross, John, 107
Ross, Paul, 197, 239
Roumain, Jacques, 45
Royal Theater, 40
Rubinstein, Annette, 237
Rushmore, Howard, 63
Russell, Richard, 48
Rustin, Bayard, 323
Ryan, Sylvester, 251

Sacco and Vanzetti case, 31
Sacher, Harry, 220, 223, 224, 256, 262
Sales tax, 125, 167
Sanders of the River, 60
Savoy Ballroom closing, 103
Saypol, Irving, 240, 246
Scales, Junius Irving, 274, 276
Schappes, Morris, 287
Schlesinger, Hyman, 266
Schmeling, Max, 62
Schneiderman, William, 134, 252
Schomburg Library "Honor Roll of Race Relations," 121
School integration in New York City, 303
Schutzer, Arthur, 231
Schuyler, George, 32, 33, 39, 47, 49, 79, 80, 84, 147, 158, 162, 182, 233, 295
Scott, Emmett J., 20
Scott, Hazel, 108, 110
Scott, Neil, 186, 216, 233, 234
Scott, W. A., 40
Scottsboro Action Committee, 51
Scottsboro Defense Committee, 52
Scottsboro Nine case (*Norris v. Alabama*), 35, 38, 47, 48, 49–52, 54, 62, 112, 158, 159, 162, 178, 219
Seabury, Samuel, 189
Seamen's strike, 74
Secession. *See* Black Belt thesis
Second front, 89, 93, 102, 114

"Security Index Card" for Davis, FBI, 263, 270
Segregation, 224; as Achilles' heel of U.S. foreign policy, *See also* Discrimination 246–47; beginning of end of, 137; at blood banks, 102, 138, 140; of military, 95, 102, 133, 140, 144, 176, 181, 200–201, 241; in Pittsburgh prison, 267; in prisons, 255, 265–70. *See also* Discrimination
Self-determination. *See* Black Belt thesis
Senate Internal Security Subcommittee, 301, 308
Senate Judiciary Committee, 83–86, 89, 265
Separate Negro state. *See* Black Belt thesis
Shabazz, John, 322
Shannon, David, 274
Sharkey, Joseph, 208, 229, 230, 232, 239
Shaw, Frederick, 101
Shaw, George Bernard, 209
Shaw, Rosa, 238
Shaw University, 57
Sheahan, John J., 168
Sherman Anti-Trust Act, 74
Simkins, Modjeska, 235, 265
Simpson, Louise, 158
Sinclair, Upton, 61
Sissle, Noble, 62
Sitkoff, Harvard, 113
Smith, Cotton Ed, 160
Smith, Earl, 302
Smith, Elwood, 160
Smith, Ferdinand, 107, 183, 206, 219, 231, 236, 286
Smith, Frances, 267
Smith, Wendell, 182
Smith, Willie "The Lion," 217
Smith Act, 258, 259, 279, 308, 312; CP-11 prosecutions under, *see* CP-11 trial; Davis's arrest under, 208; Davis's speech to National Committee on, 306; Douglas's opposition to convictions under, 246; Eisenhower urged to end prosecutions under, 267; entrapment and, 266; Harlem Committee to Repeal the, 258; Isaacs's view of, 240; membership clause of, 267, 269, 319–20, 321; Pittsburgh trial under, 277; refusals to register under, 309, 320; sentences and fines, 244; Socialist Workers party and, 213; Trade Union Committee to Repeal, 257; unconstitutionality of, 267
Social democracy, 10, 289
Socialist Call, 94
Socialist party, 40, 72, 74, 75, 76, 77, 94, 95, 96, 111, 151
Socialist Unity party, 289
Socialist Workers party, 213, 291, 292
Sommers, Diane, 183
"Sonnet" for Davis by Walter Lowenfels, 268
Sourwine, J. G., 301
South, Eddie, 160
South Africa, 11, 54, 68, 80, 81, 129, 138, 203, 226, 306, 307. *See also* Africa
South America, 308
Southern Farmer, 245
Southern Negro Youth Congress, 72, 77, 177
Southern Worker, 46
Soviet-German Non-aggression Pact of 1939. *See* German-Soviet Non-aggression Pact of 1939
"Soviet Negro Republic." *See* Black Belt thesis
Soviet Union, 59, 142, 145, 196, 288; Africa and, 172; anti-Semitism and, 207, 278, 283; birthday greetings to Davis from, 321; black press on, 88, 178; Communist party of, *see* Communist party of the Soviet Union; dissolution of, 283; German invasion of, 78, 79, 82, 86, 87; German Non-Aggression Pact with, *see* German Non-Aggression Pact of 1939; Golden on, 59; Goode on, 59; government of, *see* Communist party of the Soviet Union; Hoover on, 288; human rights violations and, 13; intervention of in Hungary, 271, 274; racial equality in, 87; racism in, 176, 310; Randolph's criticism of, 77; reforms of 1956 in, 13; religious freedom in, 317; socialism in, 79; Sutton on, 59; U.S. alliance with in World War II, 97, 105; in World War II, 88, 93, 97, 105
Sowers, Rear Admiral Sidney W., 217
Spain, 59, 232, 289
Spanish Civil War, 80, 277, 286
Spanish fascism, 59

Sparks, Nemmy, 139
Speaks, Sara Pelham, 121
Special Committee on Unemployment and Home Relief, 230
Spellman, Francis, 168, 237
Spelman College, 29
Spingarm Award, 86
St. Catherine of Genoa Church, 237
St. Louis American, 245
St. Louis Argus, 39
St. Louis Post-Dispatch, 245
St. Luke's Hall, 51
St. Mark's Church, 51
St. Patrick's Day Parade Arrangements Committee, 168
St. Paul Pioneer Press, 318
Stachel, Jack, 232, 238, 294
Stalin, Joseph, 10, 13, 37, 67, 68, 79, 109, 128, 134, 156, 269, 297, 298; *Daily Worker* on, 273; disclosures about, 271, 271–76, 278–80, 281, 282; FBI and disclosures about, 271; Israel and, 283; *Oklahoma Black Dispatch* and, 164; U.S. military training and, 141
Stalinism, 226, 281
Stamler, Nina. *See* Davis, Nina Stamler (Davis's wife)
Starobin, Joseph, 98, 244
Stassen, Harold, 199
State assembly campaign of Davis from prison, 259, 260
State Department, 171
Steele, Julian D., 75, 77, 107
Steffens, Lincoln, 46, 256
Stein, Arthur, 262
Steinberg, Bessie, 269
Steinberg, Henry, 246
Stern, Henry Root, 246
Stevedore, 61
Stevens, Hope, 59, 183, 220, 226, 264, 325
Stevenson, Adlai, 311
Stimson, Henry, 95
Stimson, James A., 286
Stockholm Peace Appeal, 249
Stokes, Mother Lena, 218, 250
Stone, Harlan, 50
Stone, I. F., 220
Stone, Martha, 267
Strikes, 58, 74, 141, 172, 236. *See also* specific strikes
Strong, Augusta, 271
Strong, Ed, 72, 271, 283, 293

Student eruption in New York City (1961), 311–14
Student movement, 14, 306, 311, 312, 313, 314, 319. *See also* College campuses
Student Non-Violent Coordinating Committee (SNCC), 306
Student Political Party of Columbia University, 312
Stuyvesant Town housing project, 125–28, 147, 161, 190, 205, 223, 260
Subversive Activities Control Board, 315
Subway fares, 125
Suez Crisis, 271, 274, 283, 284
Summer Hill School, 27
Supreme Court, 48, 50, 52, 66, 196, 211, 219, 230, 245, 250–51
Sutton, John, 59
Sutton, Percy, 59
Sweden, 289
"Sweet Auburn" district of Atlanta, 19
SWP. *See* Socialist Workers party
Symington, Muriel, 255, 264

Taft, Robert, 199
Taft-Hartley Act, 186, 187, 236
Talmadge, Eugene, 42
Tammany Hall, 121, 154, 158, 159, 190, 202, 237; Brown endorsed by, 238; Bruce and, 106; Communist Party ballot status and, 98–99; Davis's ballot status and, 295; Davis endorsement by, 145, 146, 148, 149, 150; Davis's opponents endorsed by, 151; Garvey and, 70; Jones made chief of, 234; proportional representation and, 119, 188, 189, 193. *See also* Democratic party
Tatum, Art, 108
Taxes: Browderism and, 125; cigarette, 125; poll, 89, 92, 122, 129, 145, 172, 179, 197–98, 205, 207, 247; sales, 125, 167; utility, 125
Taxpayers Union, 239
Taylor, Bill, 271
Taylor, Gardner, 293
Taylor, Glen, 200
Taylor, Recy, 141
Teheran Line. *See* Browderism
Terrell, Mary Church, 28, 217
Terrell Law School, 219
Terry, John, 51
Textile Workers Union, 199

Thomas, Norman, 40, 74, 75, 93, 94, 95, 170, 201
Thomas, Parnell, 225
Thompson, Bob, 275
Thompson, Ernest, 258
Thompson, Katie, 120
Thompson, Louise, 51, 58
Thompson, Robert, 175, 179, 209, 221, 224, 276, 277
Thompson, William F., 31, 140, 289
Thorez, Maurice, 324
Thornbrough, Emma Lou, 19
Thornton, Nathaniel, 212
Thurmond, Strom, 323
Tillman, Ray, 239
Time magazine, 38, 226, 314
Tito, Josip Broz, 280
Tobias, Channing, 102, 104, 114, 115, 149, 216, 247
Togliatti, Palmiro, 324
Tojo, Hideki, 132
Toohey, Pat, 83, 84, 85, 86, 134
Toronto Communists, 129
To Secure these Rights: The Report of the President's Committee on Civil Rights, 176, 178, 179
Totten, Ashley, 40
Townsend, Willard, 182
Trade Union Committee to Repeal the Smith Act, 257
Trade Union Non-Partisan Committee for the Selection of a Negro to the NYC Council, 99
Trade unions. *See* Labor unions
Trade Union Unity League, 62
Transport Workers Union, 239
Triboro Bridge and Tunnel Authority, 195
Trinidad, 46, 81
Trotsky, Leon, 37, 109, 170
Trotskyism, 10, 61, 75, 76, 170, 213
"Trotskyist-Bukharin Clique," 79
Truman, Harry, 148, 192, 201, 211, 232, 250, 257, 273; civil rights and, 176–77, 178, 179, 181, 227; CP-11 opponents list kept by, 217; Crosswaith's defense of, 161; Davis's criticism of, 161, 170, 172, 197, 198, 199, 208, 247, 248; FEPC and, 170, 197, 247, 248; "free Ben Davis" slogans disturbing to, 260; Harlem tour of, 260; Hastie appointment sought by, 178; Marshall Plan and, 247; petitions for Davis re-

hearing sent to, 1951, 258; Powell excluded from White House invitation from, 184; *To Secure these Rights: The Report of the President's Committee on Civil Rights*, 176, 178, 179; strikes of 1946 and, 172; unions and, 172; United Nations plan of, 138
Truman Doctrine, 186
Turner, Francis, 178
Turner, Guy, 198
Turner, Henry, 21
Tuskeegee Institute, 17, 20, 21, 59
Twelve Million Black Voices, 109
27 Club, Atlanta, 39
Two Gospel Keys, 238

UAW. *See* United Auto Workers
Ulbricht, Walter, 135
Un-American Activities Committee, 50
UNIA. *See* Universal Negro Improvement Association
Union for Democratic Action, 169
Unions. *See* Labor unions
Unitarian Church in Harlem, 245
United African Nationalist Movement, 157
United Auto Workers (UAW), 202
United front, 10, 11, 40, 52, 66, 72, 74–75, 78, 96, 137–38, 150, 292–93; Communist International and, 97; NAACP and, 83; Randolph and, 77; World War II and, 76, 80, 82, 88
United Furniture Workers, 236
United Nations, 231, 293, 297, 311
United Negro Allied Veterans of America, 186
United Negro Bus Strike Committee, 74
United Negro College Fund, 145, 157
United Socialist ticket, 291
Universal Negro Improvement Association (UNIA), 70
University of California–Berkeley, 312
University of Chicago, 57
University of Minnesota, 318
University of Wisconsin, 312–13
Upsala College, 317
Uptown Chamber of Commerce, 124, 156
Urban League, 40, 42, 53, 60, 72, 77, 149, 174, 182, 246
Urey, Harold, 319
Uruguay Communist party, 273

U.S. attorney general's subversives list, 269
U.S. Board of Parole, 269
U.S. congressional campaign of Davis, 86, 89–93
U.S. senatorial nomination of Davis (1946), 174
USSR. *See* Soviet Union
Utility taxes, 125

Vandenberg, Arthur, 222
Van West, Carroll, 49
Vanzetti, Bartoloneo, 31
Veterans Committee for Davis, 154
Villimil, Domingo, 219
Vishinsky, Andrei (Soviet foreign minister), 212
Voice of America, 201
Vorhees Institute, 112
Vote fraud in NYC, 112, 113, 115, 116, 165–66, 175, 193, 240, 261

Wagner, Robert, 292, 293
Wagner Labor Act, 129, 133
Waiting for Lefty, 58
Walden, A. T., 35, 36, 265
Waldheim Cemetary, Chicago, 310
Walker, Cora, 294, 296
Walker, Madame C. J., 258
Walker, Margaret, 109
Walker, William, 316
Wallace, Henry, 138, 139, 145, 177, 195, 198, 199, 200, 206, 208, 233, 238
Wallace, Mike, 286
Walton, Lester, 218
Ward, Theodore, 170, 218
Waring, J. Waties, 179
Washburn, Patrick, 88, 132
Washington, Booker T., 20, 21, 127
Washington, Fredi, 108, 185, 235
Washington marches. *See* Marches on Washington
Watkins, Dave, 155, 163
Watson, James, 294
Watt, George, 287
Watts riots, 14
WAVI Radio, Dayton, 317
Weaver, George, 182
Webb, Chick, 62
Webster, James, 85
"We Charge Genocide" campaign, 297
Weinstock, Louis, 274
Weinstone, William, 98

Welsh, Edward, 99
Werner, Ludlow, 132, 163
West, Carroll Van, 49
West, Don, 42, 177
Western Union strike, 172
West Indian Defense Conference, Harlem, 81
West Indies, 11, 79, 81
Weston, Moran, 105, 147–48, 163, 234
West Virginia, 181
Whalen, Grover, 64
Whaley, Ruth, 151, 158, 162, 163, 165, 234
What's Happening in Harlem, 237
Wheeldin, Herbert, 202, 281
Where I Stand, 199
Whipper, Leigh, 61
White, Charles, 169, 325
White, Josh, 102, 108, 120
White, Lindsay, 218
White, Maude, 43, 45, 58, 173
White, Walter, 53, 73, 113, 116, 125, 199; on Black Belt thesis, 146, 147; on black schools, 27; Communist Party attacked by, 121; Crosswaith on, 201; Davis praised by, 33; Davis's criticism of, 48, 72, 86, 121, 133, 175, 182, 202, 247, 250; on Davis's imprisonment, 258; Davis's review of book by, 141–42; on Davis Sr., 18, 27; Democratic party and, 202; Democratic party platform criticized by, 133; on foreign policy, 175; Herndon case and, 47, 48; Scottsboro Nine case and, 51; Truman and, 181, 198; World War II and, 81, 82, 86
Whitty, Ronald H. T., 219
Wilkerson, Doxey, 111, 113, 131, 139, 140, 141, 180, 181, 183, 260, 271, 277, 285, 302
Wilkie Memorial Fund, 142
Wilkins, Roy, 53, 58, 73, 95, 103, 116, 121, 163, 218, 226, 228, 235, 247, 248, 250, 285, 324
Willebrandt, Mabel Walker, 23
William Morris Agency, 110
Williams, Aubrey, 245
Williams, Kenneth, 185–86
Williams, Mary Lou, 108, 120
Williams, Robert, 324
Williamson, Harold, 261
Williamson, John, 131, 206, 250, 276, 282, 290

Wilmington College, 317
Wilson, Jimmie, 294
Wilson, Teddy, 12, 108, 120
Wilson, Woodrow, 69, 147
Winston, Henry, 60, 248, 250, 271, 276; bail posted for, 225, 226; blindness of, 256, 305–6; contempt charges against, 224; at CP-11 trial, 222, 224, 225; Davis's attempt at parole hearing for, 308; at Davis's funeral, 325; FBI surveillance of, 270; freed from prison, 310; King on, 305–6, 315; neglect of in prison, 256, 305–6; Paris committee for freedom of, 109; in prison, 256, 305–6, 310; on Progressive Labor Movement, 324; promotion of in Communist party, 173; release of from prison, 319; on white chauvinism in Communist party, 203; Wilkerson's relationship with, 277
Winston, Michael, 20
Winston-Salem City Council, 186
Winter, Carl, 213, 290, 300, 301
Wise, Stephen, 47
Witherspoon, Robert, 265–66
WJZ Radio, 239
WLIB Radio, 260, 296
WMCA Radio, 190, 223, 237, 239, 260
Woltman, Frederick, 146, 237
Women's Army Corps (WACs) strike, 141
Women's Committee to Re-elect Davis, 158
Woodward, C. Vann, 42
"Worker Brigade," 107
Workers Defense League, 93
World-Telegram, 116
World War I, 10, 11, 78, 79, 82

World War II, 12, 53, 63, 78, 79–80, 82, 86–96; black marketeers in, 156; black press in, 88; civil rights and, 11, 88; Davis on NYC Council during, 123, 124; Davis's position on, 86–96; "Double V" and, 131, 132; lack of black support for, 11, 88, 90; price gouging during, 103; riots of 1943 during, 102–3; Soviet Union in, 88, 93, 97, 105; U.S. alliance with Soviet Union in, 97, 105; U.S. neutrality in, 11, 78–80, 81, 82, 83, 86–87
WOR Radio, 187, 220
WQXR Radio, New York, 90
Wright, Ada, 52
Wright, Bruce, 201, 314
Wright, Richard, 45, 46, 60, 61, 62, 76, 86, 107, 109
Writers on the Left, 55
Writers' support for Communist party, 109–10. *See also* Celebrities
Wyatt, Lee, 37

Yagol, Nathan, 42
YCL. *See* Young Communist League
Yergan, Max, 73, 99, 110, 177, 183, 216
Yglesia, Jose, 110
Young, Charles, 125
Young, Coleman, 261
Youngblood, 268
Young Communist League (YCL), 55, 62, 131
Young Men's Republican Club of Georgia, 21
Youth Council resolution, NAACP, 78
Yugoslavia, 130, 172, 280

Zeller, Belle, 188
Ziff, W. B., 32
Zionism, 282, 283, 284, 287

www.ingramcontent.com/pod-product-compliance
Lightning Source LLC
Chambersburg PA
CBHW030212170426
43201CB00006B/64